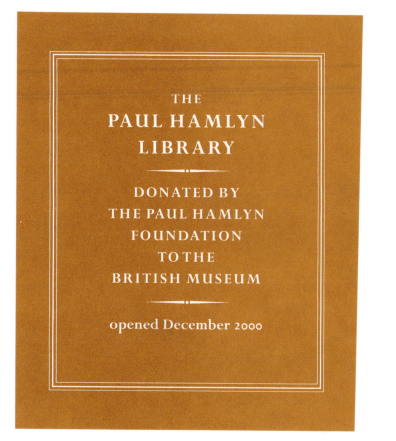

Mesopotamia
Before History

Mesopotamia Before History

Petr Charvát

London and New York

First published as *Ancient Mesopotamia – Humankind's Long Journey into Civilization*
by the Oriental Institute, Prague, 1993

This revised and updated edition published 2002
by Routledge
11 New Fetter Lane, London EC4P 4EE

Simultaneously published in the USA and Canada
by Routledge
29 West 35th Street, New York, NY 10001

Routledge is an imprint of the Taylor & Francis Group

© 2002 Petr Charvát

Typeset in Garamond by
M Rules
Printed and bound in Great Britain by
TJ International Limited, Padstow, Cornwall

British Library Cataloguing in Publication Data
A catalogue record for this book is available from the British Library

Library of Congress Cataloging in Publication Data
 Charvát, Petr.
  Mesopotamia before history / Petr Charvát.–Rev. and updated ed.
   p. cm.
  Rev. ed. of: Ancient Mesopotamia. c1993.
  Includes bibliographical references and index
  1. Iraq–Civilization–To 634. 2. Iraq–Antiquities. 3. Excavations (Archaeology)–Iraq.
  I. Charvát, Petr. Ancient Mesopotamia. II. Title

  DS70.7 .C47 2002
  935–dc21   2001058964

ISBN 0–415–25104–4

Contents

List of figures   vii
Introduction   xi

1 The Palaeolithic   **1**

Pilot sites   1
     Shanidar 1
     Palegawra 2
Interpretation   2
     The origin of man as a biological species 2
     The Palaeolithic of ancient Mesopotamia 3
         Economy 4
         Society 4
         Metaphysics 5

2 The Mesolithic or Epipalaeolithic   **6**

Pilot sites   6
     Shanidar B1 6
     Zawi Chemi Shanidar 6
     Karim Shahir 7
Interpretation   8
     Economy, technology 8
     Society 9
     Metaphysics 10

3 The Neolithic   **13**

Pilot sites   13
     Jarmo, or Qalaat Jarmo 13
     Umm Dabaghiyah 14
     Tell Hassuna 16
     Yarimtepe I 18
     Choga Mami 21
     Tell es-Sawwan 22
Interpretation   25

Economy   25
Society   35
Metaphysics   37

4   The Chalcolithic   **42**

Pilot sites   42
Tell Arpachiyah   42
Yarimtepe II   45
Eridu   46
Tepe Gawra   49
Tell Awayli   53
Tell Madhhur   55
Interpretation   57
Economy   57
Society   74
Metaphysics   90
Conclusions   95

5   The Uruk culture: A civilization is born   **98**

Pilot sites   98
Uruk   98
Khafajeh - Sin 'temple'   106
Grai Resh   108
Tepe Gawra   109
Interpretation   116
Economy   116
Society   131
Metaphysics   150
Conclusions   158

6   When kingship descended upon the earth:
the Jemdet Nasr and Early Dynastic periods   **160**

Pilot sites   160
Uruk   160
Jemdet Nasr   162
Abu Salabikh   165
Fara   166
Kiš   167
Ur   170
Sakheri Sughir   173
Tepe Gawra VI   174
Interpretation   176
Economy   176
Society   196
Metaphysics   222

7   Conclusions   **234**

Bibliography   240
Index   271

Figures

0.1   The Mesopotamian alluvial plain   xii

1.1   A pre-pottery Neolithic skull from a Palestinian site   3

2.1   Masonry of cigar-shaped sun-dried mud bricks, aceramic Neolithic site of Nemrik   7

2.2   Two of the phases of the aceramic Neolithic house at Qermez Dere   10

2.3   The border between irrigated land and the clayey steppe in southern Mesopotamia   12

3.1   A Neolithic 'husking tray'   14

3.2   One of the tells in the clayey steppe of southern Mesopotamia   16

3.3   Painted and appliqué designs on Hassuna culture Neolithic pottery from Yarimtepe I   19

3.4   Forms of Neolithic pottery of the Hassuna culture from Yarimtepe I   19

3.5   An irrigated field in southern Mesopotamia   22

3.6   Forms of Hassuna culture Neolithic pottery from Yarimtepe I   23

3.7   The sun setting over the alluvial plain of southern Mesopotamia   24

3.8   Forms of Hassuna culture Neolithic pottery from Yarimtepe I   25

3.9   The river Euphrates, a scene familiar to the ancient Mesopotamians   28

3.10   A Neolithic painted bowl of the Samarra culture   29

3.11   Reconstruction of the use of a Neolithic chipped-flint borer   31

3.12   Head of a Neolithic Samarra culture female statuette from Tell Songor A   32

3.13   The river Euphrates leaves the Taurus mountain ranges and flows into the Syrian plains   34

3.14   A Neolithic Samarra culture female statuette from Tell Songor A   37

3.15   Neolithic chipped stone industry of the Hassuna culture from Yarimtepe I   38

3.16   Examples of Neolithic ground stone industry and chipped stone items of the Hassuna culture   39

3.17   Close to the Euphrates and Tigris rivers the clayey steppe gives way to lush greenery   40

4.1   Examples of Neolithic ground stone ornaments from the aceramic Neolithic site of Tell Maghzaliya   44

4.2   Examples of Neolithic ground stone industry from the aceramic Neolithic site of Tell Maghzaliya   46

4.3   Neolithic ground stone bracelets from Tell Maghzaliya   47

4.4   A valley in the Taurus mountain range   48

4.5   Neolithic beads of stone and obsidian from Tell Maghzaliya   51

4.6	Neolithic beads of stone, obsidian and shell from Tell Maghzaliya	52
4.7	Summits and slopes of the Taurus mountain ranges	53
4.8	A Neolithic ground stone hoe. Hassuna culture, Yarimtepe I	55
4.9	Reconstruction of a Neolithic house. Hassuna culture, the site of Hajji Firuz	56
4.10	The estuary of the Nahr el-Kelb river on the outskirts of the modern city of Beirut	58
4.11	Chalcolithic sickles of burnt clay. Ubaid to Uruk age	59
4.12	A Chalcolithic painted bowl. Halaf culture, the site of Tell Brak	61
4.13	A Chalcolithic painted bowl. Halaf culture, the site of Tell Halaf	62
4.14	A Chalcolithic painted bowl. Halaf culture, the site of Tell Arpachiyah	63
4.15	A Chalcolithic painted bowl. Halaf culture, the site of Tepe Gawra	64
4.16	A Chalcolithic painted bowl. Halaf culture, the site of Tell Arpachiyah	65
4.17	A Chalcolithic painted bowl. Halaf culture, the site of Tell Arpachiyah	66
4.18	A Chalcolithic painted bowl. Halaf culture, the site of Chagar Bazar	66
4.19	A Chalcolithic painted bowl. Halaf culture, the site of Chagar Bazar	67
4.20	Ubaid culture sickles of baked clay point to the high level of Ubaid pyrotechnology and know-how	68
4.21	A Chalcolithic painted cup. Halaf culture, the site of Chagar Bazar	69
4.22	A Chalcolithic painted jar. Halaf culture, the site of Tell Arpachiyah	69
4.23	A Chalcolithic painted jar. Halaf culture, the site of Tell Arpachiyah	70
4.24	A Chalcolithic painted jar. Halaf culture, the site of Tell Arpachiyah	70
4.25	The Mediterranean port of Byblos	71
4.26	A Chalcolithic model of a seagoing ship. Late Ubaid culture, the site of Eridu	72
4.27	A Chalcolithic painted jar. Final phase of the Halaf culture, the site of Tepe Gawra	73
4.28	A Chalcolithic painted bowl. Early Ubaid culture, the site of Eridu	74
4.29	A Chalcolithic painted bowl. Early Ubaid culture, the site of Eridu	75
4.30	A Chalcolithic painted bowl. Early Ubaid culture, the site of Eridu	76
4.31	Typical local houses built of clay or stone with ceilings of timber	77
4.32	Chalcolithic painted cups. Late Ubaid culture, the site of Eridu	78
4.33	A Chalcolithic spouted bottle and spouted painted jugs. Late Ubaid culture, the site of Eridu	79
4.34	Modern houses with domed roofs of clay in Harran, south-east Turkey	80
4.35	A Chalcolithic female statuette. Halaf culture, the site of Yarimtepe III	82
4.36	Chalcolithic animal figurines. Halaf culture, the site of Yarimtepe III	82
4.37	A Chalcolithic female statuette. Late Ubaid culture, the site of Tell Awayli	83
4.38	A Chalcolithic sealing from the west Iranian site of Susa	84
4.39	Pendant seals of stone of the Chalcolithic age. Halaf culture, the site of Yarimtepe II	86
4.40	A necklace of cowrie shells used among groups of small beads for a Chalcolithic sealing of a jar with a lid	88
4.41	Ubaid culture beakers available to wide circles of Chalcolithic consumers	89
4.42	A series of Chalcolithic round buildings (tholoi) on stone foundations. Halaf culture, the site of Tell Arpachiyah	93
5.1	Pottery vessels of the Uruk culture	98
5.2	A Late Uruk sealing showing a man ascending a ladder with a sack of grain	99
5.3	A bevelled-rim bowl of the Late Uruk age	100
5.4	Ubaid or Uruk age spindle whorls from Uruk	102
5.5	Late Uruk fishing hooks of copper from Habuba Kabira	105
5.6	Amulets and pendants worn in the Late Uruk age	107

5.7	Reconstructed view of the Late Uruk fortified site at Hassek Höyük	117
5.8	Late Uruk age tools	123
5.9	A Late Uruk lock	127
5.10	Reconstruction of a Late Uruk 'temple' on a terrace	130
5.11	Scenes carved on the Late Uruk alabaster vase from Uruk	140
5.12	A Late Uruk grave from Jemdet Nasr	144
5.13	Brick masonry of the 'great residence' at Jemdet Nasr	148
5.14	Large round kilns in one of the annexes of the Jemdet Nasr 'great residence'	151
5.15	A proto-cuneiform text from Uruk	152
5.16	A spindle whorl from Jemdet Nasr with a sign of proto-cuneiform writing	154
5.17	A fragment of a protective bitumen coating bearing an impression of a reed mat	156
5.18	Two spindle whorls from Jemdet Nasr on which images of women and men 'danced'	157
5.19	Fresco painting of a leopard dating to the Late Uruk age from Tel Uqair	158
6.1	A brick from Jemdet Nasr preserves the impression of the mat on which it was laid to dry	160
6.2	Fragments of painted pottery from Jemdet Nasr	163
6.3	A spindle whorl from Jemdet Nasr	170
6.4	A sealing on clay from Jemdet Nasr	173
6.5	A sealing on clay bearing an image of a temple façade with a central doorway	177
6.6	The reverse side of the preceding sealing showing clear impressions of a reed mat	178
6.7	An Early Dynastic depiction of milking cows on a temple frieze	180
6.8	A solid-footed goblet of the Early Dynastic age	185
6.9	A copper/bronze bowl from the grave of King Meskalamdu at Ur	186
6.10	An impression of a cylinder seal on clay from Jemdet Nasr	189
6.11	The reverse side of the preceding seal impression showing the folds and wrinkles of a leather bag	189
6.12	Statuette of a pink stone bull from Jemdet Nasr	191
6.13	The corner of a monumental brick building from the earlier part of the Early Dynastic age at Jemdet Nasr	194
6.14	The present state of the later Early Dynastic 'Abu temple' at Tell Asmar on the Diyala river	201
6.15	Two solid-footed goblets of the earlier part of the Early Dynastic age	203
6.16	Large jars of water were frequently provided at the courts of temples of the third pre-Christian millennium	209
6.17	The once spacious residences of the Near Eastern élites of the third pre-Christian millennium	212
6.18	A Sumerian warrior of the Early Dynastic age on a mother-of-pearl inlay from Mari	213
6.19	A silver vase of Enmetena or Entemena, ensi of Lagash	216
6.20	Reconstruction of an Early Dynastic Sumerian temple. The Bagara of Ningirsu at Lagash	220
6.21	A copper/bronze jar from the grave of King Meskalamdu at Ur	224
6.22	A contemporary burial excavated at the Early Dynastic building at Jemdet Nasr	225
6.23	A spouted flagon of copper/bronze from the grave of King Meskalamdu at Ur	226
6.24	Two libation vessels(?) of gold and silver from the grave of King Meskalamdu at Ur	228
6.25	Fragment of a sculptured plaque of the later Early Dynastic age from Lagash	232

Introduction

This book was written in 1991–1992 but incorporates elements of research that I carried out much earlier, in fact, since the beginning of the 1970s. It is an account of my work over a period of time when I was labouring *ad maiorem Orientis antiquissimi gloriam* only in my spare time, having had, principally for existential reasons, quite different official commitments. A further impulse towards the writing of this text has been constituted by my lectures on the archaeology of ancient Mesopotamia at the Faculty of Philosophy of Charles University, Prague, in 1982–1983 and then in 1990–1991. Things have changed considerably since 1993 and now courses on ancient Oriental archaeology have been included in the curricula of two other universities in the Czech Republic. I greatly appreciate the interest in my book expressed by colleagues both at home and abroad, as well as the decision by Routledge to launch a new edition of this treatise, on which I worked for most of the years 2000–2001.

As to the spatiotemporal dimension of this book, 'Mesopotamia' is to be understood in terms of the present territory of the Republic of Iraq. Sites outside this are cited for parallels but not systematically investigated. 'Ancient' means from the earliest human occupation of Mesopotamia down to 2334 BC when a fully fledged territorial state emerged in the territory in question.

In all my subsequent considerations, I view archaeology as the study of material traces of human behaviour in the past. I fear that all definitions concerning only the utilitarian aspects of past human activities are, for one thing, too narrow, and, for another, too much biased by the modern point of view. I believe that there is no a priori division of ancient, and especially preliterate, human activities into 'utilitarian' and those which we have perceived until recently, in coarsest pseudo-Marxist terms, as 'determined by the economic base'. If we fall prey to putting forward questions determined by our own vision of the past, we clearly run the risk of finding in our materials only answers to precisely this kind of interrogation which, in such a case, will be a loss well merited on our part. For myself, I can only confess that I have never felt conceited enough to prescribe to the ancients what they should and what they should not have done. My chief concern and fascination has always been best expressed by the famous maxim of Vere Gordon Childe, namely 'what happened in history'. This orientation, in its essence rather palaeo-historic than purely archaeological and incorporating data yielded by written sources as soon as they appear, leads me to rely especially on two categories of evidence: those singular sources that comprise the greatest possible amount of information about human behaviour in the past, and then whole sets of data compared among one another, either on various sites in a single time segment or on a single site throughout subsequent periods of time. In this vision, a single corn of grain gives evidence on the behaviour of whole generations of ancient agriculturalists and is to be preferred to whatever ingenious spiritual constructs may be put forward by modern specialists to classify such evidence as pottery rims, architectural plans or art motifs. Of course, I hasten to add

Figure 0.1 The Mesopotamian alluvial plain. Unlike many other lands of the world, southern Mesopotamia displays only one single precise, definable and certain landscape feature: the line of the horizon, a frontier between two indefinites – the borderless clayey plain and the vast expanses of the sky.

that this statement involves in no way any depreciatory attitude to such pursuits. All I wish to point out is that such procedures, having immense value in terms of individual subhistorical disciplines like archaeology, art history, philology (in relation to written evidence) and the like belong properly to the heuristic phase of historical research while their relevance to the synthetical phases of the historian's work is mediated by the amount of historical information they carry.

This essentially comparative manner of viewing the past opens the way to classifications of phenomena which we may not understand presently but which, by their repeated occurrence in well-defined spatiotemporal contexts, supply information relevant to the historical processes. What I have in mind here is a kind of 'archaeological syntax' of the individual components of material culture. I fear that up to now, archaeological research has in many instances tended to result in 'archaeological lexicography', wherein individual pieces of information are disengaged from their original contexts and re-arranged into intellectual constructions that may have little in common with their original environment. A case in point is the current practice of publication of major sites in the form of treatments of individual find categories (pottery, stone or metal artifacts, ecofacts and the like), in which the reconstitution of the original find contexts represents a highly laborious and time-consuming procedure. Even if we do not know what the ancient clay figurines were used for, for instance, their transfer from settlement rubbish to the proximity of graves or even to their interiors clearly gives palaeohistorical evidence worth registering. It is thus on such highly eloquent sources, broad comparisons and notices of presence or absence that my reasoning is based. I shall be pleased to hear any constructive criticism and, of course, I do humbly confess the authorship of all the errors and inconsistencies. Yet, I do claim the legitimacy of my approach, attempting to integrate all indications of the sphere of material evidence and later of written texts into a coherent pattern of understanding and explanation of the historical course of events. (On modern archaeological method and theory see Kosso 1991.)

The reader may perhaps be surprised to find Neolithic artifacts illustrated in sections on the

Chalcolithic. The reason behind this is my desire to provide as many illustrations as possible of the common, 'ordinary' artifacts that turn up so frequently in excavations of prehistoric but also later sites. In this manner, the later chapters, dedicated to the emergence and rise of literate society and the state, can feature highly accomplished examples of material culture. In their turn, these will then provide meaningful insights into the dynamics of historical movements of later times.

In the time which has elapsed since the publication of the first version of this book in 1993, a number of excellent studies on the same subject have seen the light of day. Highly inspiring examples of these are Bernbeck 1994; Breniquet 1996; Forest 1996; Frangipane 1996; Maisels 1993; Myers 1997; Pollock 1999; Postgate 1994; and Sasson *et al.* 1995. It is a considerable honour and pleasure for me to join this modest attempt to the fruit of efforts applied by such distinguished authors. If and when I diverge from their lines of reasoning, I certainly do not do so because of disregard for their conclusions. I rather feel convinced that the many paths we pursue lead to one goal common to all of us – more light on the history of ancient Mesopotamia, one of the pristine civilizations of humankind, to the inhabitants of which we are all so much obliged to this day.

I acknowledge with pleasure my indebtedness to those who have helped me along. My work was carried out in two institutes of the then Czechoslovak Academy of Sciences, Archaeological and Oriental. I must begin with thanking cordially Dr Jana Pečírková, Vice-Director of the Oriental Institute in 1993, who initiated a series of events that led ultimately to my finding employment in the latter institute whereby my sixteen-year banishment from ancient Oriental studies ended. In both institutes, I have greatly profited from discussions with, and the suggestions of, a number of learned friends and colleagues. In the Institute of Archaeology, I feel especially obliged to Slavomil Vencl, Natalie Venclová, Zdeněk Smetánka, Jan Klápště and Jan Frolík. In the Oriental Institute, my thanks go to Blahoslav Hruška and Jiří Prosecký, who has been my patient tutor in matters of computer use. A number of questions were clarified as a consequence of my studies in the library of the Seminar für Vorderasiatische Altertumskunde der Freien Universität Berlin, for the kind permission of access to which, as well as for help in a number of interconnected questions, I am obliged to Prof. Dr Johannes Renger of the same university. I have always greatly profited from discussions with, and the suggestions of, Prof. Dr Hans J. Nissen of the Freie Universität Berlin. Roger J. Matthews, Director of the British Archaeological Expedition to Iraq, not only invited me to participate in the 1989 Jemdet Nasr campaign but made accessible to me the rich funds of the Baghdad library of the BAE, wherefore I thank him most cordially. I am obliged for most interesting discussions and hints to Susan Pollock of the State University of New York at Binghamton, NY. For manifold help, a host of interesting suggestions and assistance in practical matters I am indebted to Jean-Louis Huot of the French Archaeological Institutes in the Near East (Damascus, Amman, Beirut), Annie Caubet of the Louvre Museum in Paris as well as to Jesús Gil Fuensanta, Head of the Spanish Archaeological Mission to Turkey, of which I am now a member. I greatly appreciate the move of Gwendolyn Leick who first suggested that Routledge take up the new edition of this book, and thank the anonymous assessor who found such kind words for it.

My wife, Kateřina Charvátová, and both my sons, Jan and Ondřej, had to live with the ancient Mesopotamians for more than a decade. I acknowledge my debt of gratitude to them for all they have done to help me.

This book is dedicated to the memory of Zdeněk Charvát, my father, and Lubor Matouš, my professor and tutor who led my first steps into ancient Oriental history.

Petr Charvát
Prague, 23 June 2001

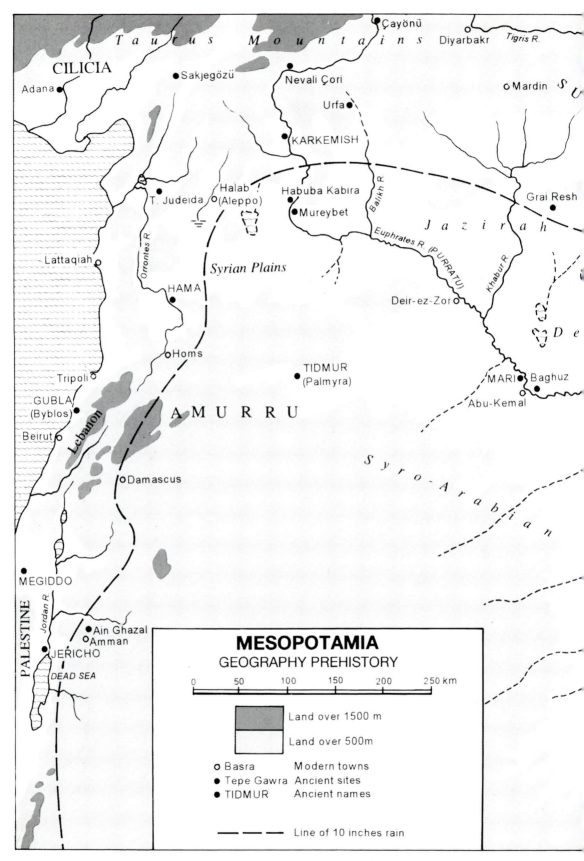

Taurus Mountains

CILICIA

Diyarbakr

Tigris R.

Çayönü

Adana

Sakjegözü

Nevali Çori

Mardin

Urfa

KARKEMISH

T. Judeida

Halab
(Aleppo)

Habuba Kabıra

Mureybet

Balikh R.

Grai Resh

Euphrates R. (PURRATU)

Jazirah

Lattaqiah

Syrian Plains

Orrontes R.

HAMA

Khabur R.

Deir-ez-Zor

De

Homs

TIDMUR
(Palmyra)

MARI

Baghuz

Abu-Kemal

Tripoli

GUBLA
(Byblos)

Beirut

Lebanon

AMURRU

Syro-Arabian

Damascus

MEGIDDO

PALESTINE

Jordan R.

Ain Ghazal
Amman

JERICHO

DEAD SEA

MESOPOTAMIA
GEOGRAPHY PREHISTORY

| 0 | 50 | 100 | 150 | 200 | 250 km |

Land over 1500 m

Land over 500m

○ Basra   Modern towns

● Tepe Gawra   Ancient sites

● TIDMUR   Ancient names

— — —   Line of 10 inches rain

Source: Based on Georges Roux (1966) *Ancient Iraq*. Harmondsworth: Penguin, pp. 458–459.

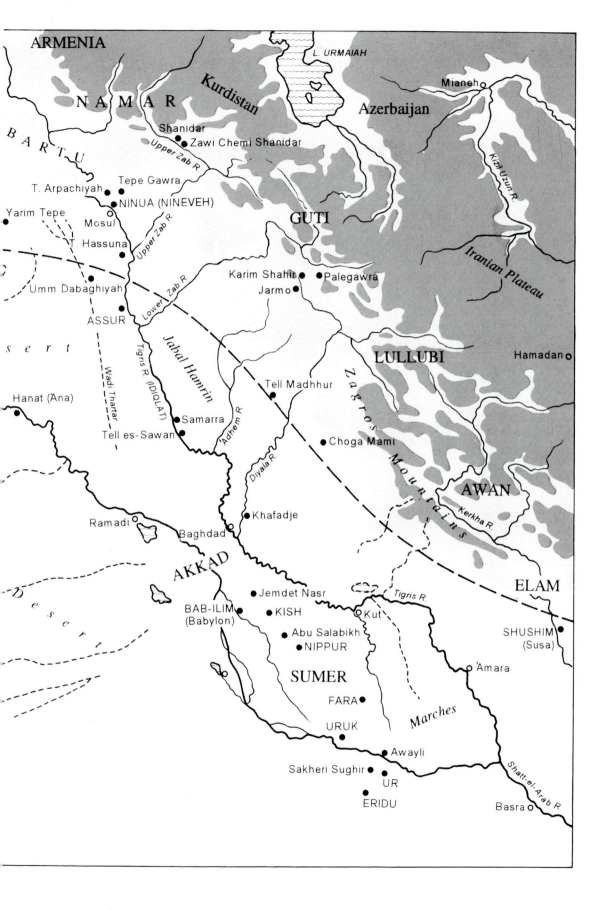

Chapter One

The Palaeolithic

Pilot sites

Shanidar

A cave at an altitude of 750 m above sea level in the lower part of a mountain valley, 35 km west of Rawanduz. A US excavation of 1951, 1953, 1956–1957 and 1960 directed by R. S. Solecki. The four stratigraphical horizons of the cave are marked from above (A, B, C and D). The deepest D layer has yielded settlement evidence belonging to the Mousterian (Middle Palaeolithic). A C-14 date from the upper part of this layer is 48,300 + / – 3000 BC but the Mousterian settlement obviously ends at a time around 40,000 BC. The Neanderthal settlers of Shanidar lived by hunting wild goats, sheep, cattle and boar, deer, bear, fox and other animals as well as by collecting turtles, molluscs, snails and doubtlessly other edible substances as well. Excepting the organic materials for which no evidence has survived, they made stone tools, chipping off flakes from small globular or disc-shaped cores and shaping these into points, blades and burins. This may be the first instance in history in which obsidian, imported in other periods of Mesopotamian history from the territory of present-day Turkey, has been treated by human hand (on obsidian in general see Hurcombe 1992). The deposits of horizon D have yielded remains of nine human individuals (2 infants, 3 young adults and 4 older adults) either buried or left in the empty cave. The remains of one of these individuals bear traces of multiple wounds and illness, as a consequence of which this man, who died at an age around 40 years, was almost immobile and could hardly pursue any activities beyond the closest proximity of the campsite, much like another individual the remains of whom were found here. In the course of investigation of another burial of this horizon the existence of a layer consisting of flowers has been indicated by pollen analysis. The grave bottom(?) might thus have been covered with flowers. An elderly man whose remains were left at the site might have died as a consequence of a stab wound between his eighth and ninth rib on the left side of his chest (the earliest trace of intra-species human violence?). On the site see Solecki 1954; Braidwood and Howe 1960, esp. pp. 60, 147, 149, 152–153, 156, 165–166; Hrouda 1971, 28–29; Kozlowski and Sliwa 1977, 48–49 and 78; Trinkaus 1983; Solecki 1997.

Layer C, radiocarbon-dated approximately between 35,000 and 25,000 BC, has yielded evidence for an Upper Palaeolithic blade industry called Baradostian, of rather mediocre quality (burins, scrapers, points, blades, notched blades, flakes, perforators and fabricators: Braidwood and Howe 1960, 147 and 154). Pollen analysis indicates a colder and more humid climate than that of the present time for the period when the cave was not inhabited, i.e. 25,000–12,000 BC.

Horizon B has been divided by the excavator into two stages, B2 and B1. Of these, only the

B2 stage, which has yielded evidence of the Upper Palaeolithic Zarzian culture and a C-14 date of 10,050 +/–400 BC, belongs to the Palaeolithic. In the vicinity of the site, pollen analysis bears out the presence of plant cover including cypress, pinia and chestnut, of a rather savannah-like character. The local climate is likely to have been colder and more humid than today but drier than in the preceding phase. The local community hunted again wild goat, sheep, cattle and boar, bear, fox and beaver (an innovation) and collected, among others, turtles and molluscs, in greater numbers than in the earlier period. The chipped industry is dominated by denticulated and notched blades and features scrapers, burins and borers. Some 10 per cent of these products are made up of microliths (bladelets, triangles, lunates, etc.). Obsidian, possibly of east Turkish origin, is prominently represented here but no evidence for coarse ground or chipped industry has been retrieved (Braidwood and Howe 1960, 60, 155–156, 170; Solecki and Solecki 1983, 126–129; Hole 1987a, esp. pp. 355ff.; Annex 732; Solecki 1997).

Palegawra

A shallow rock shelter at an altitude of *c*.1,080 m in a mountain slope overlooking a valley 20 km west-north-west of Sulaimaniyah. A US excavation of 1951 and 1955 directed by R. J. Braidwood. Six C-14 dates reaching from 12,530 to 9640 BC (Annex 727). Of the two layers represented at the site, the upper one belongs to the fourth–third pre-Christian millennium and to later times, perhaps as far as the Islamic period. A base of this layer at a depth of *c*.60 cm has yielded a group of artifacts which may date into the Mesolithic (microliths, obsidian tools, crushing stones, pebble grinders, fragment of a chipped and ground heavy axe or hoe, fragments of ground and polished marble bracelets). It is only with the lower layer that we arrive at the Upper Palaeolithic. Palaeobotanical evidence attests to the woodland character of the ancient landscape (principally oak, also tamarisk, poplar and an unidentified coniferous tree). The local community procured their subsistence by hunting onager(?), wild goat and sheep and less so gazelle, wild cattle, deer, wild boar, wolf, fox, lynx(?), small rodents, small birds, unidentified fish and sweetwater crab. They also collected hedgehog, turtle, frog, sweetwater molluscs and snails. This site has yielded the most ancient possible evidence available up to now for the domesticated dog (Clutton-Brock 1980, 39; van Loon 1991a, 300; Cauvin 1994, 35). Abundant finds attest to the utilization of chipped stone industry items such as blades, scrapers, burins, borers, fabricators, cores and geometrical microliths and, to a lesser extent, of bone implements and pendants. Imported obsidian is present at the site. A newly introduced artifact category represents the coarse chipped and ground industry of stone such as a stone with a groove, perhaps for straightening arrow or other shafts, a big axe or hoe and a grinding stone. (See Braidwood and Howe 1960, 28, 57–59 and 180; Hrouda 1971, 29; Solecki and Solecki 1983, 126–127; Hole 1987a, esp. p. 357.)

INTERPRETATION

The origin of man as a biological species

Taxonomically, the family of Hominidae includes all living and extinct forms of man. This family is presently divided into two genera: *Australopithecus*, totally extinct today, and *Homo*, covering both living and extinct representatives.

On present evidence, the very first truly human creatures – erect Australopithecinae moving on two legs – appeared on the present-day territories of Tanzania and Ethiopia some 3,800,000–3,500,000 years ago. Living in south and east Africa for some three million years, they disappeared approximately one million years ago.

Some time between 2,200,000 and 1,800,000 years ago, the same region has yielded evidence for different hominids with greater volume of brain space. In this case it remains to be decided whether these belong to the highest form of Australopithecus or to representatives of a quite different species and genus, *Homo habilis*. The most recent Homo habilis remains date back to 1,300,000 years ago.

For a certain period of time, both above-mentioned hominids obviously lived contemporaneously, and sometimes even on the same territory (north-east Africa) with another form of extinct predecessor of man, named *Homo erectus*. The most ancient representatives of this last-named species roamed the earth some 1,900,000 years ago and it is possible that their external appearance fell into the variation range of the documented forms

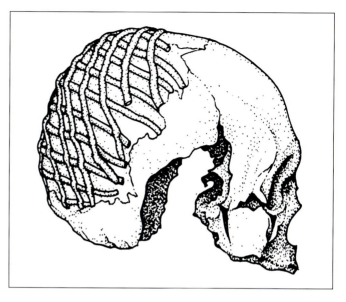

Figure 1.1 This pre-pottery Neolithic skull from a Palestinian site has received a most peculiar surface treatment by modelling (after Schmandt-Besserat 1998b, 9, Fig. 10). May we see in it a depiction of the fashion of hair styles in prehistoric times?

of modern man. Homo erectus might have survived as late as *c.*400,000 years ago and, in addition to Africa, appears to have settled both Asia and possibly Europe.

Homo erectus seems to constitute the development substrate for the archaic forms of both the present *Homo sapiens* known from the Old World *c.*600,000–500,000 years ago and the classical Neanderthal man, *Homo sapiens neanderthalensis*, documented in Europe and south-west Asia since about 130,000–90,000 years ago.

Development in the direction of the presently existing human species, *Homo sapiens sapiens*, seems to have taken place in Africa, perhaps from as early as 100,000 years ago. From that continent our ancestors crossed first to south-west Asia (Qafzeh, present-day Israel, 90,000 years ago?, Cauvin 1994, 29) and then continued to Europe (35,000 years ago?). On their way they might have integrated and completely assimilated the communities of classical Neanderthals (Bruce Dickson 1990, 31–37; Trinkaus and Shipman 1993; Tattersall and Schwartz 2000).

The Palaeolithic of ancient Mesopotamia

The most ancient human remains known presently from the ancient Near East might have been excavated at the Ubaidiya site in the valley of Jordan (Kozlowski and Sliwa 1977, 35–37; Noy and Brimer 1987; Negev 1990, 389; Bar-Yosef 1997a). Supposed to belong to an individual of the Homo erectus species, they date from about one million years ago. Nevertheless, the earliest traces of physical presence of man in Mesopotamia come from the Shanidar cave of a much later time period and I shall therefore commence with them.

Economy

In spite of the prevalence of rather adverse climatic conditions in the Middle Palaeolithic age, human beings of that time occupied a much wider range of geographical and ecological zones than before, displaying an amazing versatility in finding a variety of approaches to the problem of food procurement. There is nevertheless a possibility that the Mesopotamian environment was less harsh than other parts of the earth's surface and that the local conditions did not differ much from the present-day climate (Braidwood and Howe 1960, 166–167). A major component of the diet of these early communities must have been meat of large and medium-size mammals, ambushed or hunted collectively. Climatic conditions probably helped to preserve the considerable volume of meat procured in this way. Although the collection of plant food is likely to have played an important role, no information is available on this subject.

The face of the earth changed in Upper Palaeolithic times (*c.*15,000–10,000 years ago). The maximum of the cold and dry phase datable around 18,000 BC was followed by a gradual rise in the average temperature which led to the expansion of woodland, woodland-steppe or steppe vegetation over most of the Mesopotamian territory. The ensuing proliferation of all forms of wildlife wrought a profound effect on the subsistence strategies of the early hunters who no longer felt the necessity to amass large meat volumes as reserves, choosing at large among all sorts of game and complementing their diet with birds, fish or aquatic animals in which they had not been interested before (on the Mesolithic diet of inhabitants of the Syrian site of Abu Hurayra see Molleson and Jones 1991, esp. p. 538). This must also have been the age of considerable development of plant food collection (on its role in ethnographic societies see most instructively Sahlins 1972). That large quantities of wild ancestors of modern cereals, growing in mountain valleys of the ancient Near East, may be collected without any particular effort has been clearly demonstrated by Jack Harlan's experiments (see Cauvin 1978, 72; Hruška 1986, 216–217; Harlan 1994). An additional factor which might have contributed to the welfare of communities of this age is the trend, observed in recent nomadic and hunter-gatherer societies and doubtlessly valid for the Upper Palaeolithic as well, of seasonal movement of the communities in a calendrical cycle determined by the availability of resources in accordance with the properties of various ecological niches. For our region we may envisage winter gatherings of people in the riverine plains where they could hunt animals in great numbers and perhaps catch a crop after the winter rains. In the hot weather, such communities would (disperse? and) seek subsistence in the mountains, with their fresh supplies of wild animals and well-watered valley bottoms offering all kinds of edible plants. A summary of information on this mode of Palaeolithic subsistence may be found in Peoples and Bailey 1988, 138–139, as well as in Bruce Dickson 1990, 188–189. European specialists now propose seasonal movements of this kind over distances up to 200 km but some particularly valuable commodities might have involved travel much farther (up to 900 km, see Weniger 1991, esp. pp. 92–93 and 98–101).

Society

Though the range of information on social life of the Neanderthal communities is understandably very limited, blood kinship and the nuclear family seem to have played a major role together with group solidarity. Child burials show that minors did enjoy full membership in human groups and remains of individuals who lived fairly long in spite of health problems like lowered mobility (Shanidar) or loss of teeth indicate the amount of help that members of individual communities extended to one another. Nonetheless, it was in this age that man, in the first documented instance, raised a violent hand against one of his or her own kind. This is shown by the wound sustained by one of the individuals buried(?) at Shanidar.

The complexity of social life of Upper Palaeolithic groupings ostensibly grew. In that age, the significance of kinship surpassed blood ties and became a principle on which even wider social bodies were structured. We may imagine an overall diffusion of reciprocal gifts and services as well as the increasing significance of the wider group ('band'), especially as holder of corporate rights to the use of subsistence sources such as hunting grounds or springs of potable water. Cooperation and pooling of labour may not have been a rarity, especially in larger communal undertakings such as hunting. This brought forth food surplus which even the Upper Palaeolithic hunter-gatherers might have employed, especially in the process of (ceremonial) exchanges, as a cementing agent of new alliances and a means for the construction of bigger social units (e.g. Weniger 1991, 97–98). In spite of the extraordinary measure of mobility of such nomadic groups, specialists have become aware that in situations when human communities open up abundant and geographically well circumscribed resources, fully sedentarized communities of hunter-gatherers may well exist (on all these questions see Sahlins 1972). Nevertheless, most of the ancient communities probably adopted the nomadic lifestyle with the cyclical transfers in search of fresh resources which, in fact, supplied constant abundance (see Bray 1976 on the related problems) but which also inhibited the growth of human population groups beyond a certain 'safety range' by the practical obstacles it presented to the rearing of children (see Vencl 1991, 225).

Metaphysics

The very dim light that modern research has been able to shed in the mental sphere of the Neanderthals outlines hardly more than the first signs of appreciation of the aesthetic appeal of the outer world (first evidence for ornament) and the only 'rite de passage' evidenced for a very long period to come, that of burial of the dead. Children were most frequently laid to rest in graves, followed by men and by very rare interments of women (Freeman 1980, 85; Bruce Dickson 1990, 48–52 and 90; Bar-Yosef 1997b, esp. p. 425). The dead sometimes received tools or joints of meat and were thus presumably believed to continue their existence in some other world. Behaviour addressing the symbolic sphere may be envisaged behind the possible presence of flowers in the grave of one of the Shanidar Neanderthals. This may allude to colour symbolism, uniting, in a number of human communities, in the assignation of such values as vigour, life and sex to the colour red, purity and fertility to white and mourning, death and putrefaction to black (Bruce Dickson 1990, 206).

In the reconstruction of the spiritual world of the Upper Palaeolithic hunter-gatherers of Mesopotamia it may be legitimate to resort to an analogy with their counterparts living in the Mediterranean. People of that age probably viewed the world as essentially determined by sets of binary oppositions making up an unstable but recurrent equilibrium. They perhaps believed in the determination of movement of both the world and human society by the periodicity of cyclically repeated acts linked to one another and setting all the poles of the binary structures into their respective trajectories, perhaps in the manner of the Chinese Yin–Yang symbolics. Among these sets of binary oppositions sexuality, and especially female sexuality, played a particular role. This is likely to be reflected not only by the well-known 'Venus' figures of Europe but changes in the social position of women probably lay at the root of the fact that more women received burial than before and that they now went to the nether world with their grave goods much as men. The Mediterranean area has brought forth the first examples of what may have been shrines or sacred spaces of this age. A fixed place in contemporary communities belonged to the first specialists in spiritual affairs, the shamans, who ventured into the non-material world and undertook operations involving manipulations of the supernatural order to achieve practical results. None of these are known from ancient Mesopotamia.

Chapter Two

The Mesolithic or Epipalaeolithic

PILOT SITES

Shanidar B1

This phase probably belongs to the ninth pre-Christian millennium (a C-14 date: 8650 +/–300 BC, Annex 732). In this age, colder and more humid than today but drier than the preceding period, as the pollen analysis shows (for all citations see pp. 1–2), a human community made use especially of the front part and portal of the cave. The proportion of pollen of wild grasses of the type of predecessors of modern cereals is suspected to have risen. The hunters of the community brought in wild goats (mainly) and wild sheep, constituting together 90 per cent of all the bones, killing especially young (male?) animals. Unlike their fellows of the nearby and contemporary Zawi Chemi Shanidar site they did not bring deer to the site, if they caught it. Food collection is evidenced by the occurrence of snails and of grinding stones, presumably for plant victuals. They used stone for the production of chipped industry (denticulated and notched blades, scrapers, borers, burins, up to 25 per cent of microliths, most frequently of bladelets and lunates) and ground and polished items (grinding-stone sets, whetstones?, bored stone spheres). Other substances treated include organic materials (basketry) and small quantities of raw copper and imported obsidian. The site showed pits and pavements in some areas. A certain time after the desertion of the local settlement one of the nearby groups employed the spacious cave portal as a site for the deposition of their dead (32 persons in 27 graves, mostly children). Among these, a few descended to the nether world without any equipment while others were given ornaments, especially pendants (1,500 items in one grave). Another individual carried a stone knife hafted into its bone handle by bitumen. In one grave a woman was laid to rest accompanied by a necklace, a grinding stone and red ochre pigment. Some of the skulls of this cemetery bear traces of trepanation.

Zawi Chemi Shanidar

A site 4 km downstream from the Shanidar cave on a river terrace in a montane valley 35 km north-west of Rawanduz. A US excavation of 1956–1957 and 1960 directed by Ms R. L. Solecki. The site occupies an approximately oval area, the axes of which amount to 275 and 215 m with the cultural layer attaining the thickness of 1.45 m. It dates into the ninth millennium BC (a C-14 date of 8920 +/–300 BC [Annex 736] or 9217 +/–300 BC [Jawad 1974]). Pollen analyses show the predominance of a colder and more humid climate than today but drier in comparison with the preceding period. There are again indications of an increase in the proportion of wild grasses of the type of predecessors of modern cereals, which is less marked than at the Shanidar cave in the B1 horizon. The local population hunted wild goat, wild sheep and deer; wild sheep gradually prevail among the hunted species much in the same manner as wild goat at the cave. A corresponding decrease in the representation of wild goat and deer at Zawi Chemi is observable, as well as a concentration on young animals. A phenomenon *sui generis* is the cutting away of wings of large birds of prey such as eagles or vultures. Food collecting is represented only by snails and grinding stones. The site has yielded the most ancient architectural remains of Mesopotamia known to date (see p.10 on Qermez Dere) in the form of foundations of round walls built of stone. The local population used stone implements in the forms of chipped industry (choppers, chisels, knives, etc., including the microlithic component; sickle blades are missing here) and ground and polished industry (grinding-stone sets, whetstones, grooved stones, bored stone spheres, axes or hoes). In addition to these, they processed a number of other materials including bone (awls, spatulae, knife handles), horn, antler, ivory and less frequently raw copper, obsidian and bitumen, a source of which is 160 km from here.

Karim Shahir

A site on a high cliff in an intermontane plain 13 km east of Chemchemal. A US mission of 1951 directed by B. Howe. The site's extent amounts to *c.*60 by 70 m with the thickness of the cultural layer *c.*30 cm. It probably belongs to the ninth or early eighth millennium. Analysis of charcoal and snails found here indicates that the settlement bordered an area covered by Mediterranean slope vegetation in the form of an open grassland with bush islets and individual trees. The local community hunted wild sheep and less intensely deer and wild boar, as well as some wild cattle, gazelle, red deer, wolf and fox. They collected turtles, molluscs and plant food which they treated on grinding stones. The settlement area, covered by a regular cultural layer, displayed stone concentrations (pavements?) and heaps of animal bones as well as pits, some of which contained rock fragments, and hearths both in pits and on the surface. No other remains of any possible constructions turned up. Implements and other articles were made of stone chipped on the spot (mostly notched blades and flakes and cores, much rarer blades, some from sickles, flakes, scrapers, burins, and borers, some 4 per cent of microlithic bladelets) or ground and polished (axes or hoes, grinding-stone sets, crushing stones, stone vessels, rings, bracelets and pendants), of imported obsidian (rare), bone or shell (awls, pendants) and, for the very first time, of burnt clay. Two clay statuettes, one of which was lying in a pit by the centre of a round stain of red ochre colour, belong to the last-named products. The site may have served as a production plant for chipped industry, exploiting local sources of the raw material (up to a distance of 15 km). Nevertheless, the quality of the local stonework decreased visibly in comparison with Palaeolithic sites such as Palegawra.

On all three sites see Braidwood and Howe 1960, esp. pp. 28, 52–54, 153, 157 and 170; Clark 1967, 121; Solecki and Solecki 1983, 126–129; Gebel 1984 in the register and esp. pp. 272–276; Hole 1987a, esp. pp. 361ff.; and Solecki 1997.

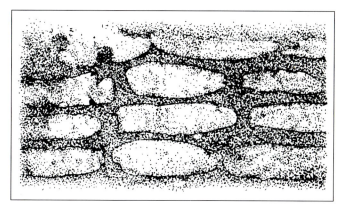

Figure 2.1 Masonry of cigar-shaped sun-dried mud bricks. House 1A, middle phase (eighth millennium BC) of the aceramic Neolithic site of Nemrik (after Kozlowski and Kempisty 1990, 355, Pl. 1).

INTERPRETATION

Economy, technology

In spite of the relatively short duration of this historical epoch it is of enormous importance since it was then that the first indications of processes which ultimately led to far-reaching transformations of both material and spiritual life of early human communities and which affect mankind to this very day appeared on the horizon. I have decided to drop the current usage of calling this period Epipalaeolithic since this alludes too much to ties with the preceding period. In fact, I believe that the Mesolithic epoch possesses a distinct character which differentiates it both from the earlier and from the later periods of time.

The twin areas of early human subsistence strategy, hunting and food-gathering, both show visible changes. The general character of the environment kept improving as the temperature rise continued from the preceding period and both woodland and steppes grew in extent. In fact, the Mesolithic period may well constitute a climatic and vegetational optimum that offered the richest subsistence sources to ancient man (see in general Moore 1983, esp. pp. 92–93 and Fig. 2 on p. 105; on the 'user-friendly' Mesolithic, as against the Neolithic diet in Syria, see Molleson and Jones 1991, esp. p. 538). The Mesolithic communities seem to have responded with a selection of subsistence procedures with an eye to the particular food sources likely to have promised the most substantial advantages. Hunters visibly abandoned the earlier practice of indiscriminate killing of a variety of animals in favour of concentration on a few species, first and foremost wild sheep and goats. Long-term contacts with such animals must have rendered them familiar to the hunters and it is hardly accidental that these two species constituted the first domesticated animals of the world (Clutton-Brock 1980, 39–40; Bökönyi 1994). Concentration on a particular species, however, was carried even farther by a narrower selection of young animals as meat sources. Regardless of whether this pertains to young males, as has been surmised earlier in connection with the obvious advantages that such a hunting strategy would have brought for the breeding of animals, or to young animals in general, the hunters were clearly very particular about what they brought down, applying such procedures constantly even to various animal species (wild goats at Shanidar B1, wild sheep at Zawi Chemi; on the problem in general see Maisels 1990, 63–64). Of course, these statements relate to trends rather than to omnipresent conditions: for instance, the inhabitants of Qermez Dere hunted gazelle, sheep and goat, but also fox, hare and various birds and small mammals (Watkins 1992, 179).

A similar degree of specialization and rationalization may be observed in the sphere of food-gathering. From now on, ancient Mesopotamian sites exhibit three artifact categories that facilitated the daily chores of the local housewives: harvesting tools, that is, knives or sickles with stone blades exhibiting the typical sheen that emerges from repeated and long-term contact of the cutting edges with organic acids oozing from the cut stalks; digging implements such as axes or hoes and bored stone spheres, perhaps weights for digging sticks; and sets of grinding stones for the treatment of the more consistent components of plant food. The production of this new heavy industry even necessitated the introduction of a new technology of stone-working employing polishing and grinding of particular kinds of stone. Indications of the increased presence of pollen of wild grasses of the type of ancestors of modern cereals both at Shanidar B1 (more) and at Zawi Chemi do not exclude the possibility of cultivation of such plants at this early age or even of their deliberate sowing. This phenomenon is better elucidated by findings from contemporary Syrian sites where these grasses turn up in the Euphrates valley, clearly outside their natural biotope of well-watered valleys by the borders of mountain ranges (Sherratt 1980b, 104; van Zeist and Bakker-Heeres 1984; Cauvin 1978 and 1994). It is thus not excluded that in addition to regular collection of plant food, the ancients may have intentionally diffused edible plants into areas where they had not grown previously. The motives behind all these activities are hardly immediately apparent but likely to be sought in a multitude of features of early social life. For a most interesting alternative explanation, viewing as a primary impetus towards domestication of both plants and animals the need for social-status legitimation involving sumptuous food-giving and thus necessitating on-the-spot production of larger volumes of comestibles, see Hayden 1990. A sample of plant material has come forth from Qermez Dere (Matthews and Wilkinson 1991, 180), where lentils, various pulses and wild cereals constituted components of the human diet (Watkins 1992, 179).

Taking into account all these new features we must nevertheless clearly realize that such practices still fell short of the anthropogenic manipulation of genetic structures of both plants and animals apparent in materials dating to the Neolithic. Mesolithic men and women made use of the opportunities offered to them by the prodigal environment, opening a great range of reserves to gather experiences on which their successors elaborated. Abundance spurred curiosity, new resources were opened (a variety of stones, raw copper, bitumen) and new technologies such as grinding and polishing stones and even the ABC of chemical production, visible in the lime plasters of Qermez Dere (Watkins 1990, 339–341), were introduced. The traditional pattern of a calendrically determined nomadic cycle following the availability of subsistence resources in space and time clearly survived but that various communities could follow various trajectories is clearly demonstrated by differences in the composition of game even on neighbouring sites (goats against sheep at Shanidar and Zawi Chemi). Such transfers in space may be attested to by the occurrence of imported obsidian which the ancients may have procured in the course of their sojourns in the montane valleys of what is now eastern Turkey. Specialization and rationalization does not leave aside even the production sphere; witness the site of Karim Shahir, clearly concentrating on the exploitation of the local sources of stone for the production of chipped industry.

The Mesolithic economy thus shows, embedded in the traditional lifestyle, early human capacities for the observation of regularities in nature, for the recognition of their mechanisms and of their significance for the human world, as well as for putting these observations to practical use in subsistence activities, including regional specialization and obvious sharing of the results of labour of various communities.

Society

In this area the developments assumed rather inconspicuous forms, resulting in situations different from the preceding age only by shades and hues but sometimes eloquent enough. First and foremost, men and women of that age invented fashion: not content with ornaments from perishable matter which must have been frequently worn from time immemorial, they now decided to apply both their skill and their energy to the shaping of even the hardest materials available such as stone (but also bone) into pendants, bracelets and rings. Why they did this is not clear and we can only suggest that as a part of their vision of the world, they now perceived more clearly, or rather ascribed greater significance to, particular features of the individual community members both within their respective groupings and vis-à-vis the external world. In this aspect we may recall the most pertinent observations of Lewis Mumford in the sense that 'the first attack of primitive men and women on their "environment" signified most probably an "attack" on their own bodies' and that such phenomena be best explained as a human effort to

> dictate their terms to nature, however clumsily defined. All this, of course, points in a most
> prominent manner to deliberate attempts at mastering one's own self, at the assertion of one's

own self and, regardless of the perverse and irrational manner in which this happens, at the perfection of one's own self.

(Bruce Dickson 1990, 44)

This tendency to classify fellow human beings together with the rest of the world may well have led to the formulation of the first principles governing typically male and typically female behaviour, documented by an ingenious analysis of the Neolithic Catal Hüyük materials by Ian Hodder (1987). Unfortunately, these attempts at formulation of the essentials of public relations are very likely to have led also to the confrontation of both human individuals and communities and to interactions ranging from affectionate friendliness to violent conflicts (Kozlowski and Kempisty 1990, 349; Watkins 1990, 344; Vencl 1991). The fact that even in this period of plenty, human beings could not refrain from applying the ingenuity with which they procured their subsistence to plotting against their brothers and sisters does not sound particularly encouraging. Nevertheless, it is a fact.

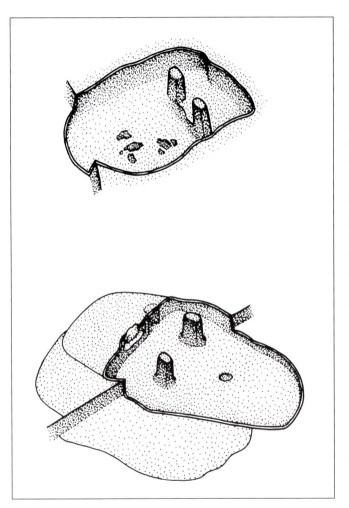

Metaphysics

Far from having at our disposal knowledge of the same character as that of the preceding period, we shall have to be content with the observation of differences. The first feature to strike the eye is without doubt the ritual character of settlement sites, mirrored clearly by archaeological evidence. The site of Qermez Dere in north Iraq (Wilkinson and Matthews 1989; Watkins 1990 and 1996) included sunk features, the interiors of which were carefully coated with clay and provided with good-quality lime plaster. In their central parts their builders erected free-standing pillars of clay on stone cores, which bore moulded decoration and a coating of red clay and white lime plaster and laid down pits and hearths (Figure 2.2). Unlike the ordinary settlement features, these buildings were kept scrupulously clean throughout their existence and after the extinction of their functions they underwent

Figure 2.2 Two of the phases of the aceramic Neolithic house at Qermez Dere (ninth–eighth millennium BC). The walls and floor were plastered with mud covered by a fine white layer. The two pillars modelled from clay would be present throughout the entire 'life period' of the house. In a later phase (below), a stone which had once stood between the two pillars was erected independently in a plastered and red-coloured niche in one of the building's walls (after Watkins 1996, 83, Fig. 2 and 84, Fig. 5).

deliberate demolition and levelling with clean clay. The lower parts of the levelled ruins served as repositories for some rather unusual objects such as bones of large animals in the case of the earlier house or stone pendants and six human skulls in the later one. These 'houses of life' (see p. 5 for the colour symbolism) may well have embodied a 'codification' of the proper relationships among the inhabitants of the site and their environment, both visible and invisible, by means of ritual procedures which did not yet assume an institutional character but nevertheless reflect an increasing interest in (and therefore presumably a growing sense of responsibility for) legitimate relationships between people, animate and inanimate nature and the supernatural world. Of course, this 'higher' component of metaphysical thought constantly saturated common everyday practices likely to have had a magical significance. At this historical moment, we find the very first entry of such a ubiquitous category of archaeological finds from Mesopotamia as the anthropo- and zoomorphic statuettes of clay (mostly of women and cattle, on which see in general Hamilton et al. 1996). The quantity of materials at our disposal does not suffice for an assessment of the measure to which the Palaeolithic character of female statuettes, portraying mature women of all age categories and likely to have served in common everyday rituals accompanying brides, wives, mothers and household managers all through their lives (Bruce Dickson 1990, 211–214) underwent transformation in the Mesolithic. Certain parallels with the burial rite, such as the occurrence of a female statuette deposited in a pit with red pigment at Karim Shahir compared with a body of a woman buried with red pigment at Shanidar B1, suggest the possibility of substitution rituals but this is just one of the interpretation possibilities. Another feature to be noted here is the foundation of the most ancient cemeteries of Mesopotamia (Shanidar B1). Of course, these constitute little more than a sample of the original population (children in this instance). What was the postmortal treatment of the rest of the population we may only guess, the only hint at partial burials being supplied by the Qermez Dere human skulls. All this points to a more deeply nuanced vision of human society expressed in the particular treatment of various groups of deceased community members and in the grave goods with which they travelled to the nether world. Let us note that necklace pendants, the most usual equipment items given to the children buried in front of the Shanidar cave, were also ceremonially 'interred' at the latest 'house of life' of Qermez Dere. (On various questions concerning social inferences from burial practices the results of Lewis Binford are most pertinent; see King 1978; Wright 1978; on ancestor cults see McCall 1995). There is thus a possibility of fairly differentiated ideas about the postmortal lives of human beings and of the necessity to 'send them off' by various itineraries to the nether world, perhaps in accordance with the roles they had played in the course of their lives. This emphasizes further the variability and richness of the reflection of both the human and the non-human world and attempts at a lawful and just ordering of human affairs in accordance with generally shared ideas of the structures directing all processes within the universe.

In summary, we may put forward the following characterization of the Mesolithic age:

a) In the sphere of economy and technology an increasing interest in the natural processes and resources, and experiments with new raw materials, including preparation of artificial materials (lime plasters) and the introduction of new technologies as well as so far only extensive manipulation of subsistence sources (without genetic mutations) but also regional economic specialization (Karim Shahir);

b) In the social sphere the focus on particular characteristics of both individual personalities and whole groups and, in the context of persistent egalitarianism in which the prestige of every individual was defined by his or her age, sex and personal achievement, attempts at socially codified behaviour norms which would reflect such inherent differences;

Figure 2.3 The border between irrigated land and the clayey steppe in southern Mesopotamia. In arid environments such division lines can be quite sharp and well-defined.

c) In the spiritual sphere a definition and creation of material incarnations of a balanced, harmonious and generally acknowledged structure of relationships among people and their visible and invisible environment, periodical renewal of this balance and practical application of such principles and ideas in the form of everyday-life rituals which may have employed the stratagem of substituting images for either initiators or targets of such rituals.

In the area of mental development of the human race, we perceive today the inhabitants of Mesolithic Mesopotamia – together with other contemporary populations of the Near East – as those who laid the foundations upon which all subsequent developments within this civilizational context rest. They clearly indulged in the essential activities of any civilized human group, so pertinently described by Claude Lévi-Strauss: the evidence, gathered through the experience of any human community, is classified and ordered into a systematic explanation of the structure of the world and of the situation of the human race within it. This system then defines practical attitudes towards the world and is expressed by various symbol structures, among which the system of audio-oral symbols, or human speech, and of visual symbols, namely all forms of representative arts, occupy the most important positions. The essential characteristics of all human communities up to recent time – economic specialization, social differentiation and complex spiritual reflection of the visible world – may be documented in this period of time. The difference between this and later epochs of human history does not seem to lie in the absence of certain human traits – our Mesolithic ancestors were presumably just as 'civilized' as we are – but rather in the context, or 'lifestyle', in which these traits were embedded and which constituted the set of coordinates and the frame of reference defining the sense of application of the human intellect.

Chapter Three

The Neolithic

Pilot sites

Jarmo, or Qalaat Jarmo

A tell in an extensive montane valley 12 km east of Chemchemal. A US excavation of 1948, 1950–1951 and 1954–1955 directed by R. J. Braidwood. The current size of the tell (axe lengths) amounts to *c*.90 by 140 m with the thickness of the cultural layer reaching up to 7 m. A series of nineteen C-14 dates indicates dating between 9290 BC and 4545–3395 cal. BC (Annex 716–717). The analysis of charcoal pieces shows that the site was once surrounded by an open woodland-steppe landscape featuring oak, tamarisk and the *Prosopis* shrub, while the animal remains suggest that the site's inhabitants moved about in savannah landscapes but also in open stony plains, as well as in woods and mountain forests. The local community procured their subsistence by a series of approaches. They clearly experimented with the cultivation of emmer wheat (*Triticum dicoccum*) and einkorn wheat (*Triticum monococcum*) but did not advance as far as the full domestication of these cultigens. Of course, they far from neglected the gathering of wild plant food such as wild barley, wild peas, wild lentils, wild beans and other pulses, among which some clearly approached the threshold of domestication, pistachios and acorns. Fully domesticated animals of Jarmo include dog, goat and, in later strata, pig; the local hunters brought in onager(?), gazelle, wild sheep and wild goat, wild cattle, wild pig, deer, hare, wolf, fox, bear and various kinds of birds and fish. A sample of collected food includes snails, turtles, molluscs and crabs. The architecture present at the site could be articulated into sixteen phases most of which belong to the pre-pottery age. Only the five uppermost strata have yielded pottery finds. The locals built their houses of pounded earth on stone foundations. Clay floors sometimes received reed-mat substructures and doors may have turned on stone pivots set both into the thresholds and the architraves. The windows were hardly more than loophole-shaped apertures so the house interiors must have been very dark and their inhabitants probably performed their daily activities in rectangular court areas (crushing of plant food, cooking on hearths situated both on the surface and in pits, heating of furnaces situated in house interiors). Individual households were dispersed over the site without any apparent and systematic layout. The local community employed a series of materials. The most usual resource of ancient Mesopotamia, clay, was used for building but, in the final stages of the site, also for the production of pottery (large storage jars, pots, bowls, cylinder-shaped goblets, all of light and burnished ware sometimes decorated by splashes of red colour), for the shaping of pendants and for clay statuettes of women and animals of which some 5,000 were found (a proportion among them bearing the red paint). The local population shaped various kinds of stones into chipped industry (mainly blades, in a number of instances from sickles and sometimes bearing traces of the bitumen hafting, less numerous scrapers, borers, notched blades and microliths, the quantity of which amounts to almost 40 per cent of all chipped industry) and worked with imported obsidian. By grinding and polishing rock pieces they manufactured axes or hoes, bored stone discs (digging-stick weights?), grinding-stone sets, stone vessels, of which fragments of at least 350 items were found here, and, to a more limited extent, spoons, whetstones or pendants. The site has also yielded remains of at least 225 polished stone bracelets and what may be carved images of circumcised penises. The local specialists seem to have mastered the technique of rotation boring of stone items with the addition of an abrading agent (Larsen 1991, 139). Bone was used for turning out awls, rings and pendants. Of metals, the Jarmo community knew lead (Moorey 1985, 122). Quite definitely they worked with organic materials but only traces of matting and basketry, impressions of fine textiles and bitumen products survived. On the site see Braidwood and Howe 1960, 26–27, 38–40, 42–48, 64–65 and 172; Hrouda 1971, 30; Jawad 1974, 13; Gebel 1984, 274–275 and in the register on p. 319; Watson 1997.

Umm Dabaghiyah

A tell 80 km south-west of Mosul. A British excavation of 1971–1974, directed by D. Kirkbride. This site is situated in a steppe-plain landscape with gypsum and salt outcrops in a limit zone of dry farming. Four strata of Neolithic settlement of Hassuna and pre-Hassuna culture (*c.*6000 BC). The local archaeological evidence indicates a series of subsistence practices carried out at the site

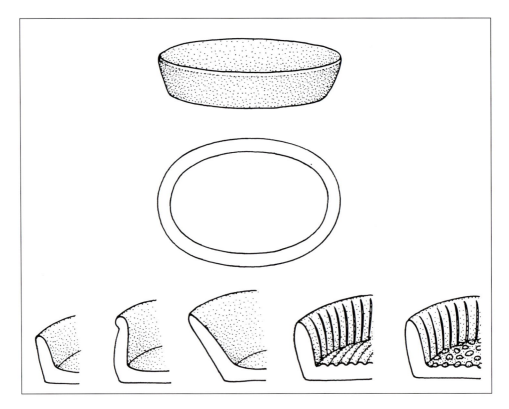

Figure 3.1 A Neolithic 'husking tray' of pottery for cleaning cereal grain of impurities. Hassuna culture (seventh–sixth millennium BC), from Yarimtepe I (after Munchaev and Merpert 1981, 97, Fig. 22).

and both in its close and farther vicinity. The limited extent of local agricultural production is indicated by scanty finds of barley, emmer and einkorn wheat. On the other hand, the presence of cultivated peas and lentils and of a single grain of the six-row bread wheat (*Triticum aestivum*) points to the possibility of contacts with agriculturally more favourable areas. Of the collected plant food, wild barley and wild grasses left their traces on the site. The same inconspicuous position is occupied by animal husbandry: some 9 per cent sheep and goat remains and less than 2 per cent cattle, pig and dog remains. The record of the subsistence activities is dominated by hunting gazelle (16 per cent) but especially onager (66–70 per cent). Hunting activities in the immediate vicinity of the site probably resulted in the deposition of the remains of fox, hare, rat, wild boar and various birds, while larger pieces of game such as aurochs or badger had to be carried from the piedmont area of Jebel Sinjar over a distance equal to about a three-day march. Materials turning up at the site suggest a similarly wide exploitation area. In addition to game, Jebel Sinjar is likely to have provided the site's inhabitants with plate silex and tree trunks which they used for building construction. Long-distance exchange is represented by obsidian and by dentalium shells from the Arabo-Persian Gulf or the Mediterranean Sea. Grinding stones were made of material obtained from a source some 34 km from the site and average-quality chipped industry from silex turning up *c.*16 km away. The site is thus apparently characterized by a 'broad-spectrum economy', integrating agricultural, animal-husbandry, hunting and gathering subsistence approaches. The four architectural phases of the site are preceded by the earliest, fifth layer which left in the subsoil circular or oval gypsum-revetted basins and ashy refuse strata with evidence for the production of chipped industry, as well as traces of painting of interiors of both geometrical and figural character and of using the colour red. From layer IV upwards (the layers being numbered from the uppermost one) the site always consists of a large complex of rectangular chamber building and a group of average-level living houses. The chamber complex consists of rows of rectangular chambers with floors of trampled earth (in most cases) and without doors, separated by walls some 50 cm thick of clay strongly tempered with chopped straw but without clay plaster. The chamber fillings have yielded outrageously few finds: hardly more than sherds, in one case some 2,400 smaller and *c.*100 larger balls of fired clay, possibly slingshot, a few items of chipped and ground stone industry and pieces of red pigment. Storage jars were sunk into floors in two cases. Large masonry pens and evidence for the butchering of hunted animals in the courtyards of the chamber complex point to a connection with treatment of food (a storage complex?). In contrast, the living houses accompanying the chamber complex display 2–3 rooms with trampled-earth floors, each enclosed by thinner walls of sandy untempered clay, sometimes plastered with gypsum, with narrow loophole-shaped windows. Rooms had hearths and further facilities for processing food (basin-shaped storage spaces?) as well as other 'furniture' such as gypsum-stone shelves, wall niches and cellars(?) in floors. In some instances the visitors to such houses could admire fresco paintings of both geometrical patterns and figural scenes (an onager frieze, a hunting scene?). Interior hearths could have been connected with kilns with chimneys adhering to the exterior house walls. The rooms were roofed with the aid of tree trunks and the accessibility of roofs is borne out by remains of staircases. As early as the ancient layer IV some of the living houses had to give way before the enlargement of the chamber complex. Layer III virtually duplicated the plan of layer IV; in the final phase of this settlement the site was evacuated and the house entrances immured. Phase II structures must have been deserted when the site was in full bloom, as is indicated by the quantity of remaining household articles such as pottery, and they displayed evidence for caved-in roofs. At that time, a part of the work was probably carried out in the open (the occurrence of paved areas). The inhabitants employed a variety of materials. They used clay for the building of houses and for the production of mobile items like pottery (decorated with moulded blobs in the forms of onagers or people, with painting and incisions, burnished and fired at low temperatures; see Bernbeck 1994,

116–119), slingshot, ornaments or figurines. The local sources supplied materials for chipped industry (arrowheads, blades, scrapers, borers, burins, microliths) while the imported flint and obsidian came in in the form of ready-made, mostly blade tools. The ground and polished industry featured axes used obviously for the butchering of game, grinding-stone sets, bored stone spheres, beautiful vessels of marble and alabaster as well as some ornaments such as bracelets. Bone served for the production of various awls, scrapers and spatulae. Other work carried out at the site included the production of textiles and the burning of lime. A cemetery in which the bodies were laid to rest in a crouched position but had no grave goods, situated on the slope of the site, may belong to the local Neolithic community. On the site see Munchaev and Merpert 1981, passim, see the register p. 317; Kirkbride 1982; Mortensen 1983; Gebel 1984, 277 and in the register on p. 321; Bernbeck 1994, 116–119.

Tell Hassuna

A site 30 km south-east of Mosul. A British–Iraqi excavation of 1943–1944 directed by S. Lloyd and F. Safar. C-14 dates: layer Ia: 1690–820 cal. BC (erroneous?), layer V: 6435–5420 cal. BC (Annex 714) or 5301 BC (uncalibrated; Bernbeck 1994, 346). The series of fifteen settlement layers excavated in this tell may be divided into several units: layers Ia, Ib–VI and VI–XV. The layers denoted as Ia obviously represent remains of seasonal campsites (at least three). Evidence for the subsistence procurement from here is very limited. Goat bones imply animal husbandry while massive stone axes or hoes indicate substantial interference with the environment (felling of trees?). Sickle blades are missing but clay spheres and ovals (slingshot?) do point to the

Figure 3.2 One of the tells in the clayey steppe of southern Mesopotamia. To this day, the local landscape is studded with thousands of such sites, perpetuating the memory of generations of people who gave the land their best efforts and ultimately found their last resting place in it.

exploitation of uncultivated landscape. Thick ashy strata supply an eloquent testimony both of the role of fire in this community and of the very simple manner of rubbish disposal. No traces of architecture have survived and only hearths, some of which were paved with pebbles and sherds set occasionally into 'primitive mortar', around which the artifacts clustered, could be excavated. Again, the site hosted experts in work with various materials. Clay served for the production of both coarse and large storage jars and fine burnished pottery vessels (see Bernbeck 1994, 126–127). Stone was chipped (scrapers, blades, fewer borers and burins), ground and polished (axes or hoes with traces of bitumen hafting), procured from both near and far (obsidian). Awls of bone represent another artifact category while the metals procured by these food-gatherers were antimony and malachite. Treatment of organic materials is represented by traces of woven mats and spindle whorls for spinning thread. The local settlers left behind not only blocks of red pigment but also a child burial in a storage jar and, in another case, a body of a deceased adult close to which a storage jar and an axe/hoe of stone were found.

Layers Ib, Ic, II, III, IV, V and VI are characterized by the first occurrence of clay-brick architecture and by a change in the cultural character of the site. From now on, the subsistence procedures adopted by the local inhabitants included agriculture (two-row barley?) or rather consumption of plant food attested to by the frequent occurrence of sickle blades and grinding stones and by storage spaces in houses but also animal husbandry (sheep, goat, cattle) and hunting. The character of treatment of natural resources is sufficiently elucidated by the excavation of room 17 in layer II. In addition to pottery and storage jars, this room contained a workshop for the production of chipped industry, especially of sickle blades (cores, blades, flakes, a finished sickle with a cutting edge composed of blades hafted into the wooden handle by bitumen), as well as five bone awls, a goat's or ram's horn (raw material?), clay spheres and ovals (slingshot?) and blocks of red pigment. Overland contacts are borne out by the occurrence of obsidian and probably Iranian turquoise (see Crawford 1972; Ismail and Tosi 1976, esp. pp. 106–107). From the Ib layer the local inhabitants built houses with trampled-earth floors from clay blocks. Among their interior furnishings the grain silos coated with bitumen outside, sunk into floors and sometimes gypsum-plastered inside, attracted the greatest amount of archaeological attention. Kilns and furnaces, originally represented by pottery vessels in secondary use, were increasingly built of raw clay. The buildings made up loose clusters around courtyards, one of which, belonging to layer V, was drained by means of a conduit piercing the enclosure wall and lined with stones. Layer Ic has yielded a plan of a round structure used, according to the accompanying finds, for habitation. Of the natural resources treated on the site, clay undoubtedly merits most of our attention. It served both for building purposes and for pottery-making. In layers Ib, Ic and II, the 'Archaic' (polished and painted with geometrical patterns) and 'Standard' (incised in layers II–V, incised and painted later on) wares turn up. Conspicuous Samarran wares with painted concentric ornaments accompany the domestic pottery from layer III up to the beginning of layer VI (Bernbeck 1994, 126–127 and 142–152). In addition to pottery building, the local population used clay for the fashioning of 'slingshot', spindle whorls as well as for figurines, including a large female statuette with a body of red clay and head of green clay, displaying an elaborate hairdo, originally perhaps with horns on the head. The inhabitants of the site trimmed stone into chipped industry (especially scrapers, blades, including sickle components, fewer borers and burins), sometimes on the spot (room 17 of layer II) and turned out ground and polished items. These include heavy stone hoes, axes, disc-shaped objects or grinding-stone sets and also bracelets, pendants and vessels of stone. The first seal of stone appeared in layer II (von Wickede 1990, 81–82, Table 43). Awls and spatulae, at least some of which were hafted into their handles by bitumen, were made of bone. Local craftsmen and craftswomen experimented with metals, as is proved by the presence of raw antimony and malachite (copper ore); red pigment turned up as well. A number of child burials

in pots (twins in one case) were interred below the house floors and some rooms or their furnishings even provided the last refuge for deceased community members (two bodies, one of
them headless, in a layer III silo). The excavators found an isolated human skull in a layer IV pit.

Layers VI–XV belong to subsequent periods of time. Halaf culture predominates in strata
VI–XI, with walls in layers VII (a round structure) and X. Layers XI–XII are characterized by
Ubaid culture pottery while strata XIII–XV have yielded mixed Halaf, Ubaid and later Assyrian
materials (Lloyd and Safar 1945; de Contenson 1971; Munchaev and Merpert 1981, passim, see
the register on pp. 317–318; Bernbeck 1994, 126–127 and 142–152; Danti 1997).

Yarimtepe I

A tell above a watercourse 7 km south-west of Tell Afar, a USSR excavation of 1969–1976
directed by R. M. Munchaev. C-14 dates: layer VII – *c.*5300–5000 BC, 6470–5525 BC (Annex
735). The life of this site may be roughly divided into three major segments: features preceding
layer XII and layer XII itself, layers XII–VII and layers VII–I. All these strata belong to the
Hassuna and Samarra cultures. The subsistence activities of the local population are treated in a
summary fashion by the final publication and it is thus difficult to submit a detailed historical
sequence. Agriculture is present from layer XII (two-row and six-row wheats, *Triticum dicoccum*
and *T. durum Desf.*, *T. aestivum*, *T. spelta*; cultivated barleys, *Hordeum distichum* and *H. vulgare
nudum*, but also a transitional form between wild and cultivated barley, *H. lagunculiforme Bacht*;
peas and other *Leguminosae*) but evidence of collection of wild grasses (*Gramineae*) appears as
well. In the same manner, animal husbandry (sheep, goat, cattle, pig, dog) is accompanied by a
wide range of game hunted with the aid of dogs and including wild boar, mouflon, gazelle,
onager, wild goat, roe deer, leopard and jackal. Hunting activities are also borne out by analyses
of working traces on chipped industry (Munchaev and Merpert 1981, 122 – cutting of meat and
cleaning of hides). Treatment of natural resources will be discussed below. Overland contacts are
elucidated by the occurrence of imported obsidian, the quantity of which gradually decreases.
Turquoise, probably of Iranian origin, turns up first in layer X and its volume grows in layers IX
and VIII.

Much as at Hassuna, the most ancient settlement remains of Yarimtepe I (features preceding
layer XII and layer XII itself) differ from the rest of the finds. Most of the pre-layer XII evidence
comes from pits which may have been left after excavation of building materials and filled in by
clayey and ashy refuse strata. The local inhabitants left behind a remarkable architectural creation,
a massive square platform of which one side measures 3 m, revetted by clay walls and composed
of blocks of red and black clay. There may be a connection with some of the extraordinary architectures of the East Anatolian site of Çayönü Tepesi on the upper Tigris (Schirmer 1990). On the
other hand, rectangular and round buildings of layer XII display so many irregularities that the
authors of the final publication hesitate to assign habitation functions to them. For instance, a
round building or tholos 333 contained dispersed bones of adult humans, though this layer contains most frequently baby burials, but also a pot with sheep bones. In addition to pottery
sherds, such objects as a fragment of a marble vessel, a goat jaw, obsidian fragments, numerous
ochre stains as well as an exquisite necklace of sixty-eight colourful beads (grey, grey-yellow, grey-
green, green, red, yellow, white, blue – chalcedony, shell, carnelian, mother-of-pearl, rock crystal,
lazurite?) turned up here. In addition to this exceedingly rich array of decorative stones, material culture of this most ancient Yarimtepe phase features a higher frequency of stone arrowheads,
suggesting the significance of hunting. Hassuna 'Archaic' ware with painted geometrical patterns
occurs from layer XII (Figure 3.3).

Houses of layers XI–VIII are built of clay blocks on artificially levelled areas on foundation

Figure 3.3 Painted and appliqué designs on Hassuna culture Neolithic pottery from Yarimtepe I (after Munchaev and Merpert 1981, 94, Fig. 19 and 96, Fig. 21)

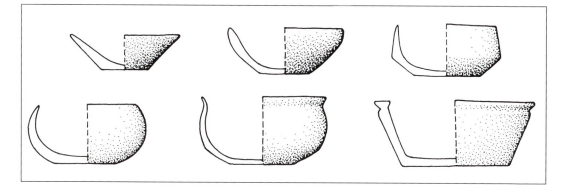

Figure 3.4 Forms of Neolithic pottery of the Hassuna culture from Yarimtepe I (after Munchaev and Merpert 1981, 95, Fig. 20)

layers of reed matting. Clay tempered with cut straw or gypsum served for floors. Doors could revolve on pivot stones and the interiors were heated by means of hearths or clay-built kilns. Layer X yielded a fragment of a kiln plaque with apertures attesting to the presence of two-compartment vertical-updraught kilns on the site. Housewives used storage jars and perhaps also the features attested to by elevated platforms enclosed by post-holes with grinding stones nearby. The evidence gathered by S. A. Jasim (1989, 86) on the much later Ubaid culture site of Tell Abada may suggest that these be interpreted as remains of intramural granaries. House walls usually bear clay plaster, and roofing was done by means of timber baulks covered by matting and insulating layers of clay or gypsum. Some structures of layers X and IX display foundations consisting of complex systems of parallel screen walls, clearly comparable with those of Çayönü Tepesi (Schirmer 1990, 365, Fig. 1; 368, Fig. 3; 371, Fig. 5; 377, Fig. 10). In layer VIII, this architectural type does not occur any more, having been replaced by buildings consisting of a series of rectangular chambers leaning on one another, quite like the above-mentioned East Anatolian site in its later phases.

Among the natural resources treated at the site, clay occupies a primary position in the archae-ological perspective, both as a building material and for pottery making (Figure 3.4). Hassuna 'Archaic Painted' and coarse wares predominate from layer XII to layer VII (for a detailed analy-sis of the local pottery see Bernbeck 1994, 100–115). Clay was also used to fashion spindle whorls and 'slingshot'. Rather surprisingly, clay statuettes are missing though they do turn up from layer V of the site upwards (Munchaev and Merpert 1981, 265). The local masters trimmed both local quartz stone and imported obsidian into chipped tools. Quartz refuse indicates that tools of this material took shape on the spot while most of the obsidian tools were brought in ready-made. The proportion of obsidian tools decreases in layers IX and VIII. Among the shapes, blades including sickle components (the number of which grows steadily) predominate, followed by scrapers and borers. It has already been mentioned that layer X saw the first ornaments of turquoise and that the volume of this material grows throughout layers IX and VIII. Heavier ground and polished stone items include axes, perforated discs (digging-stick weights?), hollowed-out stone receptacles, perhaps used for crushing softer substances, grinding-stone sets, a whetstone, stone vessels and grinding plates or palettes; hoes are conspicuously absent. The quantity of coarse stone industry increases in layer VIII where stone spindle whorls turn up for the first time and where the first traces of 'tool cults' are discernible (a miniature greenstone axe, a perforated stone disc of exquisite marble). Layers IX, VIII and VI have yielded finds of stone seals with incised net patterns and suspension loops on their rear sides. As usual, bone served for the manufacture of awls and spatulae. Malachite (copper ore) turned up in layers XII–V while copper products, pendants of cold-hammered metal, occurred in layers XI, X and VII. A lead bracelet was found in layer XII. Handling of organic matter is attested to by finds of reed mat-ting. The universal and mixed character of local production activities is eloquently illustrated by the contents of the rectangular space 234 of layer VIII, well comparable to room 17 of Hassuna layer II. This features pottery sherds, a mortar of stone, quartz (produced on the spot) and obsidian chipped industry, a number of marble and limestone palettes, grinding stones and ochre stains.

Among the deceased inhabitants of the site, babies and children were usually laid to rest in pots and interred below the floors of living quarters or, in some cases, in rooms of which some may have been erected as tombs, sometimes provided with wall and floor gypsum plasterings. Treatment of dead adults included the exposure of a dismembered(?) body in a living room (Munchaev and Merpert 1981, 49, grave 134, layer XI), deposition of dispersed remains in a sep-arate closed chamber (ibid., room 282, layer XI) or in a burial pit (ibid., grave 126, layer XI). It is worth noting that animals sometimes received the same postmortal treatment as humans (pieces of carcasses below the floor of room 363, ibid. 51). Deceased children received grave goods for the first time: a baby of grave 129, layer X, pottery sherds and a spindle whorl (ibid. 82), and another one of grave 144, layer IX, quartz and obsidian flakes (ibid. 83). A find of a large storage jar containing a part of a marble palette, a grinding stone (mano) and fragments of other storage jars below the enclosure wall of the courtyard of homestead XXXIII of layer X (ibid. 52) may represent a building sacrifice or ritual deposit. More light on the spiritual life of the site's inhabitants is shed by finds of bones with a series of short vertical strokes, obviously counting devices of a sort (seven examples, 9–28 strokes, from layer X upwards; Munchaev and Merpert 1981, 130, with ref.), and by a change in the character of later necklaces. The chequered collier of layer XII is succeeded by ornaments composed of a single kind of stone in layers X (ten disc-shaped carnelian beads found among the walls of a 'grille-plan' structure, Munchaev and Merpert 1981, 138) and IX (nine cylindrical pendants and five tripartite 'spacer beads' of turquoise found by a kiln orifice, ibid.). The site is supposed to have yielded a small clay whistle or ocarina (Rashid 1996, 20).

Layers VII–I in the central part of the site did not yield any architectural remains. Hassuna 'Standard' ware predominates in them. The excavators' trench may have probed an ancient space free of buildings. Layers VII and VIII have yielded two uncalibrated C-14 dates of 5200 and 5090 BC (Bernbeck 1994, 346; on the site Munchaev and Merpert 1981; Yoffee and Clark 1993, 73–114; Bernbeck 1994, 100–115).

Choga Mami

A tell 125 km north-east of Baghdad by the town of Mandali at a point where a minor watercourse flows out of a hilly range into a plain. A British excavation of 1967–1968 directed by J. Oates. Available C-14 dates for the Transitional phase (i.e. transition of the Samarra and Hajji Muhammad = Ubaid 1 cultures): 6200–5325 cal. BC (Annex 708) and 4896 BC, (uncalibrated Bernbeck 1994, 346). Of the five layers of the local settlement four belong to the classic and late Samarra culture while the uppermost one constitutes the above-mentioned Transitional phase with some later revivals (an Ubaid culture well). Among the subsistence activities attested to by the site, agriculture is amply documented. The local farmers grew especially emmer and einkorn, as well as bread wheat, naked barley, both two-row and six-row, and large-grained oats; the samples contain admixtures of rye-grass as well as wild grass seeds. Other cultivated plants include clover, pea, lentil, blue vetchling and linseed. Wild flax and oats were not cultivated in the ancient Near East but occur as weeds, especially in winter cereal fields (Oates 1969, 143). The size of the flax seeds as well as the presence of a number of plants demanding water converge to indicate artificial irrigation of the local fields, which is borne out by the archaeological documentation of a water conduit channel, one of a series by which the local inhabitants conveyed water flowing down the conical deposit of materials eroded by the upper part of the watercourse and deposited at its entrance into the plain to their fields (Figure 3.5). The site has yielded wild plants exhibiting seed sizes indicating that at least some of these must also have grown on irrigated land. All the seeds but especially the naked barley ones display evidence for the diminishing of their size, indicating certain agrotechnical problems which may perhaps have been caused by salinization of the local arable soil. On the other hand, the growing quantity of sickle blades indicates that the ancient population did not lack the vegetable component of their diet but was rather harvesting wild plants. That the locals were able to procure these over considerable distances is borne out by the presence of pistachio nuts which had to be brought from highland woods. The dovetailing of agriculture and food-gathering on the site is matched by evidence for cooperation among the local shepherds and hunters. Of the usual sequence of Neolithic domestic animals – sheep, goat, cattle, pig and dog – the last one confirms the presence of hunting strategies which brought to the site such game as deer, fox, gazelle, wild boar, wild sheep and goat, wolf and onager. The increasing number of gazelle remains may have resulted from complications in the local agricultural production (salinization?). The local settlement consisted of free-standing house clusters of the usual Neolithic character built of large elongated clay blocks and including small rectangular spaces (granaries?). Treatment of natural resources at Choga Mami fits in with evidence offered by other Neolithic sites. Clay served both for building and for pottery making and within the local Samarra wares a particularly interesting position is occupied by the creations of the last, Transitional phase. This is now assumed to display connections both with Halaf culture and with the earliest phases of Ubaid culture (Tell Awayli, see Bernbeck 1994, 228–233). Among other clay products the female statuettes and a quantity of pendants of varying shapes, some bearing painted decoration, are striking. Stone-trimming provided the local users with such chipped industry items as blades, especially sickle blades, the quantity of which gradually grows but ultimately falls, but also scrapers, borers and microliths; a number of these were apparently

Figure 3.5 An irrigated field in southern Mesopotamia. Water is conveyed by means of the central conduit branching off into series of parallel corollary channels running perpendicular to it and taking the irrigation water among the furrows directly to the individual plant beds. The Sumerian sign GÁNA depicts exactly one half of such a field, pointing to the antiquity of this kind of arrangement.

made on the spot. The overwhelming majority of chipped stone tools (97.1 per cent) were manufactured from local raw quartz. Imported obsidian accounted for a very limited quantity of implements (2.9 per cent) which kept constantly diminishing (from 5.7 per cent in the lowermost layer via the 2.6 per cent of the last Samarra culture stratum up to the 0.9 per cent in the Ubaid well). The usual types of ground and polished stone industry include the markedly traditional stone bracelets and the group of bone industry contains a less frequent needle with an eyelet (Helbaek 1972; Hijara et al. 1980, 151, 154; Meadow 1971, 140f.; Mortensen 1973; Munchaev and Merpert 1981, passim, see the register on p. 318; Oates 1969, 1972 and 1982; Oates and Oates 1976).

Tell es-Sawwan

A tell 100 km north of Baghdad and 10 km south of the modern town of Samarra, presently on the Tigris. An Iraqi excavation of 1964–1984 directed successively by B. A. as-Soof, F. Wailly, Kh. al-Adhami, Gh. Wahida, W. Y. al-Tikriti and D. G. Youkhana, followed by a French campaign of 1988–1989 directed by C. Breniquet. C-14 dates: nine, from levels I, II and III, from 6345–5490 cal. BC to 5349 BC (Annex 731, see also Bernbeck 1994, 346). The site consists of five settlement layers, the lower two of the Hassuna and the upper three of the Samarra cultures, as well as a cemetery underlying the lowest architectural layer. The cemetery entombed remains of children, adolescents and adults in crouched positions with heads to the south but frequently with faces to the west, occasionally wrapped in matting which may have been coated with bitumen, accompanied by stone ornaments (pendants and beads sown on clothing), alabaster vessels (bowls, pedestalled bowls) and figurines of females and animals as well as objects which have been interpreted as representing penises. A dominant feature of the local grave goods is the presence of semi-precious stones such as carnelian or turquoise (pendants), the latter probably of Iranian origin (Crawford 1972; Ismail and Tosi 1976, 106–107). In layers X–VIII of Yarimtepe I, the proportion of turquoise grows as that of obsidian diminishes. One of the graves has also yielded copper pendants. The new excavation has shown that beads could have decorated clothing items such as belts. C. Breniquet (1991b, 83) believes that the interments were sunk from the house floors belonging to the two earliest architectural layers (I and II). These are dated by the presence of painted and incised Hassuna 'Standard' wares and by a C-14 date of 5506 +/–73 BC. Evidence for the subsistence activities offered by the site falls again into the binary sets of agriculture-cum-gathering and shepherding-cum-hunting. Cultigens present on the site include the predominant emmer wheat, perhaps einkorn and a small quantity of bread wheat; the barley group is characterized by the prevalence of the two- and six-row hulled variety with the six-row naked ranking second. The biggest flax seeds from here again imply artificial irrigation. Collected plant food is represented by fruit of the *Caper* and *Prosopis* shrubs. The local flocks were composed of sheep, goat and perhaps cattle, and guarded by dogs which also helped to hunt gazelle, onager, wild boar, roe deer and maybe wild cat. Fish and freshwater mussels complemented the diet. Treatment of natural resources is compatible with Neolithic usages: bone for awls and spatulae, clay for building and making pottery (Bernbeck 1994, 163–178) and various minor objects, metal for ornaments from graves below layer I; organic matters represented by matting and baskets, sometimes coated with bitumen, and stone for the chipped (blades), ground and polished industry, vessels and ornaments. Some interest has been aroused by the presence of clay female statuettes similar to the Jarmo examples and historians of technology and art alike admire a plaster cast of a seal impression bearing the image of two stylized human figures sitting back to back with contracted legs and raised hands found in layer II (von Wickede 1990, 84–85, Table 53). This find of unique artistic quality outlines a possible connection with the Neolithic cultures of the middle Euphrates region in present-day Syria (Tell Buqras, Tell al-Kaum).

Pottery finds date layers IIIA, IIIB, IV and V into the Samarra (C-14 date: 5349 +/–86 BC) and Halaf cultures (layer V: Breniquet 1991b, 81, 88). It is questionable whether the earliest fortification ditch present on the site dates to layer I (when it could have enclosed a more limited area,

Figure 3.6 Forms of Hassuna culture Neolithic pottery from Yarimtepe I (after Munchaev and Merpert 1981, 94, Fig. 19 and 96, Fig. 21)

Figure 3.7 The sun setting over the alluvial plain of southern Mesopotamia

see Breniquet 1991b, plan on Fig. 3 p. 80) or IIIA, but in any case, its depth reached 3 m and its width 2.5 m and having been sunk into the living rock, it enclosed the settlement together with a rampart with buttresses (on this see Bernbeck 1994, 243–246). Within the area delimited by the fortification stood at least seven large houses numbering 10–12 rooms each together with other rectangular constructions (granaries?). In the IIIB phase, the granaries(?) seem to represent a transformation of earlier buildings (Breniquet 1991b, 75–81, 87–88). The houses were built of clay bricks, sometimes formed in moulds, and their floors bore an occasional coating of bitumen or gypsum. Some of the village streets were paved. The defensive ditch seems to have gone out of function by the time of layer IV as one of the structures thus dated rests directly on the surface of its fillings (Breniquet 1991b, 75–81). The material culture of the site makes the common Neolithic impression. While the chipped industry of layer IV is characterized by a limited number of blades, scrapers and points, layer V ushers in some changes. The microlithic component of the industry (borers, points, backed bladelets, very few sickle blades) acquires more prominence while normal-size tools are represented by scrapers and cutting implements. This may also point to the increasing importance of hunting activities towards the end of the site's life period. Layer III has yielded both seals and two round to oval plaster discs (diameters 8 and 21 cm), perhaps pot lids, bearing repeated impressions of a seal of the same pattern but of varying dimensions. These discs turned up in the context of buildings interpreted as granaries. Let us finally note that the last, fifth layer displays remains of a sizeable round structure of the Halaf culture period on stone foundations (Breniquet 1991b, 75–81, 88). On the site see Flannery and Wheeler 1967; Meadow 1971 132–134; Crawford 1972; Helbaek 1972, 44; Ismail and Tosi 1976 106–107; Munchaev and Merpert 1981, passim, see the register on p. 317; von Wickede 1990, 82–85; Breniquet 1991a and 1991b; Bernbeck 1994, 163–178.

INTERPRETATION

Economy

Inhabitants of Neolithic Mesopotamia availed themselves of the experience and know-how gathered by preceding generations to introduce fundamental changes in the subsistence sphere. Intimate knowledge of the biology of plants and animals helped them to create completely new economic sources, the nourishing qualities of which were improved by deliberate efforts resulting in genetic manipulation of the natural organisms. Nevertheless, even from this point of view the Neolithic period represents an 'experimental laboratory', in which the most talented members of communities living together in the traditional style only verified their theoretical conclusions and tested the range of possibilities of procuring better and more plentiful food sources for their fellow humans. Systematic exploitation of all the Neolithic discoveries, the full impact of which on human society would ultimately change the face of the earth, did not occur until later.

Let us at first take up the question of cultivation of domesticated plants (see Sherratt 1980b; Hopf 1988; Zohary and Hopf 1988; Maisels 1990, 65–67; Harlan 1994; Harris 1996; van Zeist and Bottema 1999). Their wild ancestors were not far away: montane valleys in the fringe areas of both the Zagros and the Taurus ranges, to which the early settlers could ascend up the streams of local watercourses, belong to the original biotopes of the predecessors of modern cultivated barleys and wheats. The same regions saw the emergence of the earliest cereal cultigens. Describing this process, we will do well to realize that cereals (i.e. annual grasses), cultivated by mankind for food, may be cytogenetically divided according to the number of chromosome groups in the cell cores of the plants into two-row, four-row and six-row types. Two-row wild cereals include a number of species related to wheats. According to the currently held opinion, one of these wild grasses (*Triticum aegilopoides, Aegylops squarrosa*, most probably *Triticum boeoticum*) was transformed by cultivation into the two-row *Triticum monococcum*, or einkorn wheat. The ancestor of the recently cultivated barley (*Hordeum vulgare var. hexastichum*) is now sought in the two-row wild barley *Hordeum spontaneum*. Neolithic peasants brought about the change of the four-row wild grass *Triticum dicoccoides* into the domesticated *Triticum dicoccum*, or emmer wheat. In this connection, a particular importance must be ascribed to the occurrence of six-row cultigens, namely wheats of the *Triticum aestivum* type with variants *T. a. vulgare, T. a. sphaerococcum, T. a. compactum* and *T. a. spelta* and barley of the modern *Hordeum vulgare var. hexastichum* variety. Not having any wild ancestors, these species clearly represent artificial

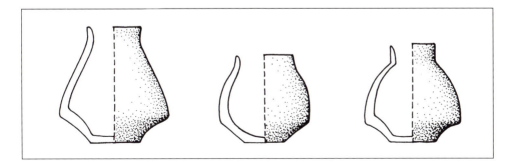

Figure 3.8 Forms of Hassuna culture Neolithic pottery from Yarimtepe I (after Munchaev and Merpert 1981, 94, Fig. 19)

creations of prehistoric experimentators, most probably by cross-breeding *T. dicoccum* (emmer wheat) with one of the two-row wild grasses, for instance, the above-mentioned *Aegylops squarrosa* (see Tosi 1976, 174; Zohary and Hopf 1988, 17–18, Table 4 on p. 26; Maisels 1990, 65–67). Finds of six-row cultigens, of which the earliest example known to date comes from Umm Dabaghiyah, thus bear out beyond all doubts not only profound knowledge of natural processes on behalf of Neolithic cultivators but even their practical interference with plant genetic structures, serving thus as an example of the epoch-making discoveries of this period providing the base for human subsistence to this very day. Practical measures adopted by Neolithic peasants seem to have been simple but efficient. We may envisage protection of plants, sowing them in specially conditioned plots of land, selection of sturdier and especially non-shattering individuals (because of the losses of shattering varieties releasing the grains easily in the cutting process) and, ultimately, cross-breeding (see Maisels 1990, 66). The most ancient evidence for artificial irrigation dating to this period (Choga Mami, see also Sherratt 1980c, esp. pp. 322ff.) points to the fact that not even this sophisticated agrotechnology remained hidden from our Neolithic ancestors. At Choga Mami, the local topography indicates that irrigated fields are likely to have been situated close to the village. Such layouts could have occurred more frequently as it has been observed that Samarra culture sites tend to be situated some 1.5–3 km apart. This leaves the radii of 750 to 1500 m for distances between the village centres and the farthest points of their fields (Oates 1980).

Is it possible to estimate the proportion of the general food procurement provided for by intensive agriculture? In this instance we shall draw on the results of US research carried out on sites of the Deh Luran plain, the environment of which approximates that of the Mesopotamian plains (Hole and Flannery 1967; Hole, Flannery and Neely 1969). In the earliest Bus Mordeh phase (7500–6750 BC) of the Ali Koš period (*c.*7500–5500 BC), results of intensive agriculture made up less than 10 per cent of all the plant remains there (Hole and Flannery 1967, 169f.; Hole, Flannery and Neely 1969, 343f.). In the middle Ali Koš phase (*c.*6750–6000) this proportion increased to 40 per cent but in the final Mohammad Jaffar phase (*c.*6000–5600) it fell again to a mere 4 per cent (Hole and Flannery 1967, 175–177; Hole, Flannery and Neely 1969, 347–354). The plant component of the Neolithic diet thus included a sizeable portion of wild collected food, uncultivated cereals, other grasses and other comestibles such as pistachio nuts, as the occasion may have offered (on the cereal component of Neolithic diet and the ways and means of its treatment see Ruf 1993, albeit on European prehistoric materials). The Deh Luran plain sites do show, however, that the proportion of wild plant food ultimately decreased (Hole and Flannery 1967, 169–177; Hole, Flannery and Neely 1969, 343–354) though this process need not have necessarily been universal or unilineal. The Choga Mami evidence points to the conclusion that in spite of the diminishing seed size indicating problems in intensive agriculture, the significance of plant food grew, as is represented by the increasing quantities of sickle blades. The most logical interpretation of this situation would envisage harvesting of wild plants. In the case of Choga Mami, H. Helbaek (1972, 39) believes that the quite unusual quantity of rye-grasses must have been caused by their growing on irrigated land and thus this sophisticated agrotechnology need not have been confined to cultivated plants only. The relation between systematic cultivation of plant food and its collection was clearly far from rigidly fixed and could vary in time and place. One of the aspects involved in this situation may be elucidated by authors of the Deh Luran plain excavations who noticed the absence of unequivocally summer products (Hole, Flannery and Neely 1969, 343ff.), understanding this feature as a testimony for seasonal occupation of their sites. The relatively low output of intensive agriculture is also indicated by pollen spectra from the Neolithic of adjacent regions such as Syria which show the major disturbances of natural vegetation brought about by man to date as late as *c.*4000 BC (van Zeist and Woldring 1980, 120; Bottema 1993; van Zeist and Bottema 1999). The same situation is likely to have characterized the vicinity of Neolithic Catal Hüyük which can hardly be considered an exclusively agricultural site (Bottema and Woldring 1984, 148, agriculture in pollen spectra only from *c.*3000 BC). We may note in this connection that a number of pre-industrial communities practise the simplest slash-and-burn agriculture because it places the lowest demand on labour input and hardly any impulse towards the intensification of this component of subsistence activities is visible (Maisels 1990, 34–35). On the other hand, the cultivation of quite new plant food species must have also resulted in major adjustments of the spiritual life of early humans, including not only new conceptualizations of the universe and of the situation of men and women in it (Hodder 1987; Felten 1993) but even repercussions for cult and ritual. Some of these new features might have even provided ritual sanctions to protect plants in particularly sensitive periods of their life cycle, perhaps in the manner documented for yam growing in Oceania (see Coursey 1972, esp. pp. 223ff.).

Let us notice the fact that the latest investigations point to the conclusion that most of the early cultigens of the prehistoric Near East were domesticated over a relatively short period of time and within a rather limited geographical area (Cauvin 1994, 183). Another aspect of Neolithic life brought forth by recent investigations is the decrease in comfort and greater stress under which humans lived, in comparison with the preceding Mesolithic times. For example, the Neolithic diet wore down the teeth of contemporary inhabitants of Syrian Abu Hureyra to a considerably greater extent than did the Mesolithic diet (Molleson and Jones 1991). Other human remains found at the same site yielded evidence for physically demanding work, including collapse of neck vertebrae due to carrying heavy loads on the head (Kiple 1996, 21). The food-producing economy was no fun: remember that the waggon would not be invented until the Chalcolithic.

Much in the same vein, animal husbandry and hunting represented two poles linked by a continuum of particular modes of subsistence. For the first time in history, Neolithic breeders put at the disposal of their communities herds of economically important animals differing from their wild ancestors (see Bökönyi 1994; Becker 1999). The fact that early hunters had been accompanied by tame dogs since the Palaeolithic (Palegawra) has already been noted. The Neolithic multiplied the host of domesticated animals with the addition of sheep and goats, bred out of their wild ancestors, *Capra aegagrus* (goat) and *Ovis orientalis* (sheep), perhaps in this very region (see also Croft 1995, 165). The transformation of the wild *Bos primigenius* into domestic cattle took place sometime during the sixth pre-Christian millennium in the east Mediterranean. Up to now, the most limited number of remains bear out the domestication of the pig from its wild ancestor *Sus scrofa* (Clutton-Brock 1980, esp. pp. 39–40; Flannery 1983). Nevertheless, most of the domesticated animals of the Neolithic displayed a high degree of variability and low type stability (Hole, Flannery and Neely 1969, 263f.). Authors of the Deh Luran plain excavations point to the conclusion drawn during the analysis of palaeozoological material that the local herds must have been in contact with other domestic animals (ibid. 350). This implies the mobility of shepherd groups. The emergence of specialized animal husbandry went hand in hand with changes in hunting practices. At the beginning of this period the Deh Luran hunters persisted in the traditional killing of wild goats (Hole and Flannery 1967, 169ff.) but for the rest of the Neolithic their counterparts concentrated mainly on gazelle and onager, quadrupeds living in the open plains (ibid. 169–178). The hunting of such animals represents a fairly complex affair (see the complete failure of Alexander the Great's cavalry in this aspect: Adams and Wright 1989, 446), requiring careful organization and cooperation of groups of experienced hunters. The catching of onagers in provisional pens by directing the animals through a system of net barriers, driven by the sight of hunters and by sounds emitted by them, is documented by the early medieval paintings from the Jordanian site of Quseir Amra (Blazquez 1981, 192–194, Figs 4–6; Blazquez 1983). The introduction of specialized animal husbandry was thus paralleled by changes in hunting strategy which by the Neolithic required the cooperation of relatively numerous human groups as well as efficient organization of the whole enterprise. This conclusion is borne out by evidence from the Tepe Guran site where the Neolithic population hunted more gazelle than their predecessors who relied heavily on domestic goats (Mortensen 1972). The Neolithic inhabitants of the Deh Luran plain sites also consumed more aquatic animals (fish, mussels, turtles, crabs) and migratory water birds than before (Hole and Flannery 1967, 175f.; Hole, Flannery and Neely 1969, 265f.). This may have been caused by the improvement of climate, supposed to have been warm and humid by then (Moore 1983, 93 and Fig. 2 on p. 105) and favourable to the vegetation that might have covered large areas of presently arid landscapes. Hunting activities could have varied even along the chronological axis: the intensification of gazelle hunting, observed at Choga Mami, could well be connected to the local decrease in cereal seed size. The conclusion that the local population, confronted with an agrarian crisis, responded with an increase in the exploitation of wild edible plants and by the intensification of hunting activities seems thus to lie at hand (a similar argument is pursued by Miller 1996, 524).

It need not be particularly stressed that much as in other spheres of human enterprise, animal husbandry was hardly ever a purely economic affair. Social and symbolical issues undoubtedly played their role (Keswani 1994).

The agricultural production of the Neolithic period may thus have consisted of a range of diverse activities of which intensive agriculture, gathering of wild edible plants, animal husbandry and hunting-cum-food-collection constituted border lines or rather points. In between these, the particular and concrete subsistence activities chosen by each community oscillated according to

Figure 3.9 The twin rivers of Mesopotamia have since time immemorial played a major role as the main communication arteries. Navigating the Euphrates upstream as far as the present Syro-Turkish border area, the ancient Mesopotamians could well have seen scenery similar to this.

what factors seemed most opportune at the given moment. There are no clear preferences and obviously hardly any fixed strategies: movements which would seem to us 'progressive' are accompanied by such 'regressions' as, for instance, increased insistence on food-gathering and hunting following the impact of an agrarian crisis(?) at Choga Mami. The commonly accepted and acknowledged 'lifestyle' stubbornly refused to bow to the mechanistic ideas of twentieth-century materialist-minded historians.

The sphere of technology has been given undue prominence in archaeological attention ever since the beginnings of Near Eastern field excavations. While it must be admitted that the technological level of processing the natural resources of the society in question provides an important indicator of its position on the temporal and civilizational scale and that some products have gradually acquired an additional significance which the ancients could hardly have foreseen (e.g. the importance of pottery for dating and classification of archaeological sites), it is by no means a sole index of 'progressivity' of the ancient community in question. It has repeatedly been emphasized that the significance of technological procedures and of the material culture in general must always be assessed against the background of a whole set of patterns of economic, social, political and spiritual life of the given society (on this see Oates 1980, 306; Pfaffenberger 1988). Modern research tends to prefer the mental reflection of the world to subsistence pressures as the vehicle of social changes (Cauvin 1978, 139–142). Recent research has confirmed the assumption that for a truly historical perspective of the context of every studied human population, investigation of the energy flow, more particularly of the amount of energy harnessed per capita and of the manner in which this energy is handled, distributed and invested is to be preferred to purely technological considerations. Essentially, the changes in Neolithic technology are few in number and far below the significance of the genetic manipulations of subsistence sources which, by the Neolithic period, resulted in the appearance of visibly new cultigens and domestic animals.

Neolithic craftsmen and craftswomen did not forget the art of turning out artificial, chemically transformed materials (lime burning at Umm Dabaghiyah). They employed bitumen for its impregnating and hafting qualities and bone for the traditional production of awls and spatulae. As to clay, in addition to being used as building material and for the production of such minor items as spindle whorls, ornaments and figurines, clay was now employed for the production of pottery decorated by such procedures as burnishing, painting and incisions (see most extensively Munchaev and Merpert 1981, 87–114; on contemporary painted pottery Bernbeck 1994, 129–141; McAdam 1995) (Figure 3.10). Technologically, these early pots are hardly particularly eloquent; having

Figure 3.10 A Neolithic painted bowl of the Samarra culture (sixth millennium BC) from Samarra (after Bernbeck 1994, Pl. IV)

been built by hand, they obviously received firing at temperatures obtainable by combustion in open hearths, though fragments of a massive clay plaque with numerous apertures in the Xth layer of Yarimtepe I (Munchaev and Merpert 1981, 75) do indicate the presence of more sophisticated pyrotechnological facilities. It seems that as early as this age, the potters were quick enough to discover an optimum composition of clay paste for making vessels to be used for the millennia to come, even resorting to mixing various types of available raw materials if the desired pottery paste could not be found in a raw state (Makovicky and Thuesen 1990, esp. pp. 32–37, as well as Blackham 1996). The firing temperature of early Near Eastern pottery, varying between 850 and 1100 degrees centigrade down to the Uruk period, was clearly maintained right from the beginnings of local pottery production (Makovicky and Thuesen 1990, 40). At least some of the designs on Samarra-style painted pottery have been interpreted as potters' marks (Bernbeck 1994, 268–275).

The exploration of natural resources and their distinctive properties led the Neolithic prospectors to more profound knowledge of particular qualities of metals and to their processing. Their employment as ornaments shows that they were treated just like other coloured stones worn in necklaces (copper pendants from Yarimtepe I). Another aspect of the early metallurgy is shown by finds of lead from Jarmo and Yarimtepe I (a bracelet). Unfortunately the state of preservation of these products does not allow us to determine if the copper was hammered or cast, but its distinctive 'plasticity' was certainly known. Copper-smelting could have been discovered accidentally in the course of firing pottery painted with colours prepared from copper- and iron-containing minerals (Moorey 1982b, 18 and 1985, 22f.). Neolithic people were presumably perfectly acquainted with work employing organic matter, summarily used but hardly surviving. They worked with wood, wove mats of reeds and rushes, produced textiles and probably turned out a great many more things from perishable matter of which we will hardly ever learn (on flax cultivation see van Zeist and de Roller 1991/1992, 81–82, and van Zeist and Bottema 1999, 32). As to the production of stone items, it is interesting to note that while the early settlers of the plain were quick to identify and open local resources of flint which they used for common everyday tools (at Umm Dabaghiyah, such a source of raw material was some 16 km from the site), the exotic obsidian products arrived in most cases in the form of finished tools and very little production of them took place on the plain sites. This bears out craft specialization and parallels from both archaeology and ethnography allow the assumption of specialized highland producer communities mining the stone and turning out large amounts of half-finished products and tools which they subsequently exchanged with the lowland settlers for their surplus products, though such phenomena are by no means a Neolithic innovation (see p. 7 on the site of Karim Shahir). A visible index of changes is represented by the clear impoverishment of the type range of chipped industry, narrowing to the predominant blades, especially sickle components, followed by scrapers and borers. This gives very few clues as to their true use because most of the everyday service tool kit was represented by simple untrimmed flakes. The practical employment of every tool category should, where possible, be investigated for the identification of traces left by the working procedures. Thus it could be demonstrated that some of the Yarimtepe I arrowheads served as borers (Munchaev and Merpert 1981, 120). Stones suitable for the production of ground and polished implements were also extracted (at Umm Dabaghiyah at a distance of *c.*34 km from the site) and traditional products fashioned out of them, sometimes with considerable mastery (the Tell es-Sawwan alabaster vessels). It is worth mentioning that the bead-makers of Jarmo might have used borers with flat points, the efficiency of which was increased by the addition of an abrading agent (Larsen 1991, 139). In short, the first Neolithic revolution was accomplished with tools and material equipment that differed but little from those employed by the preceding Mesolithic populations. This, of course, did not prevent the Neolithic inventors from making brilliant discoveries, testing them in practice and enriching through them the lives of their communities. The modest material garb disguises the resplendent achievements of the Neolithic mind.

A wide range of possibilities for assessment of external contacts of the Neolithic communities is opened by excavations results. The most conspicuous evidence for overland contacts is, of course, constituted by the presence of exotic materials such as obsidian, Iranian(?) turquoise, marine shells (Arabo-Persian Gulf or the Mediterranean?) or, in the Deh Luran plain, hematite from Fars (Hole, Flannery and Neely 1969, 350–357). Naturally, this is only the most conspicuous component of the volume of exchanged goods which must have included a variety of commodities. There exists now unequivocal evidence for the exchange of agricultural products (cultivated pea, lentils and six-row wheat brought to Umm Dabaghiyah), wild and gathered comestibles (pistachio nuts at Choga Mami), for contacts of cattle herds belonging to various communities (Ali Koš in the Deh Luran plain: Hole, Flannery and Neely 1969, 350)

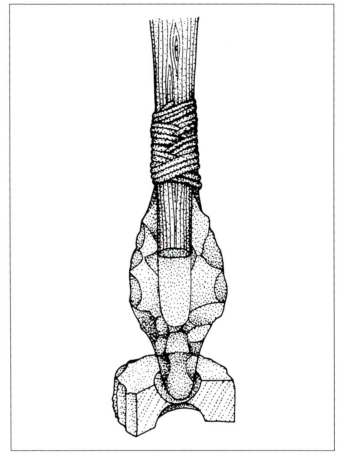

Figure 3.11 Reconstruction of the use of a Neolithic chipped-flint borer (after Ferchland and Wartke 1990, leaf 2)

and for transport of (sections of?) hunted game (animals, presumably from Jebel Sinjar, at Umm Dabaghiyah) as well as for exploitation of natural resources situated quite definitely outside the activity zones delimited by the radii of 5 and 10 km from the site, assumed to cover the subsistence areas of agriculturalists and hunters (Dennel 1980, 41; on the 5 km agricultural radius in Chalcolithic India see Pappu-Shinde 1990, esp. pp. 326–330). A case in point is naturally the Umm Dabaghiyah site with its well-developed exploitation pattern of local resources of stone (silex source 16 km away and grinding-stone source 34 km away) and wood (tree trunks from Jebel Sinjar). Something similar has now been proposed for Mesolithic and Neolithic Jericho where a number of ecozones, from riverine forests to mountain slopes, supplied the local inhabitants with their harvests (Röhrer-Ertl 1996). Up to now, this evidence has been interpreted in terms of a complex pattern of inter-regional trade (see, for instance, the discussion in Mortensen 1983 or Munchaev and Merpert 1981, 116–121). This, of course, is one of the likely forms in which exotic commodities available at only a limited number of sources circulated throughout the network of consumer commodities, but it is not necessarily the only one. In order to provide for goods exchanged with others, the plain dwellers would have had to accumulate some specific surplus, most probably consisting of agricultural products (given the environment in which

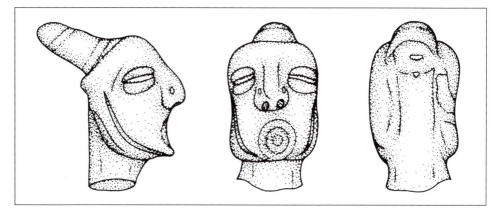

Figure 3.12 Head of a Neolithic Samarra culture female statuette from Tell Songor A (after Forest 1996, 37, Fig. 23)

they were settled). Now this is precisely what they did not do. As we have seen above, theirs was a 'broad-spectrum economy', applying to a varying degree agricultural, food-collecting, cattle-keeping and hunting activities without any visible bias to a particular kind of this enterprise which would have brought them the necessary surplus (with a possible exception of Umm Dabaghiyah, a hunting site). Moreover, it would seem strange that they would have tended to procure essentially the same commodities which were the fruits of their labour (foodstuffs, for instance). But what if it were not the goods but the people who moved around, as has been suggested most pertinently for the earliest Neolithic of the Indian subcontinent (Fairservis 1991, 110)? In fact, the possibility of seasonal transhumance between highland and lowland sites was hinted at by the authors of the Deh Luran plain excavations who noticed the absence of summer products in their sites, interpreting them as winter camps (Hole, Flannery and Neely 1969, 343ff.). A number of other features of the archaeological record seem to point in this direction. These include the marked similarity between the sites of Çayönü Tepesi (eastern Anatolia, Schirmer 1990) and Yarimtepe I, the homogeneity of artistic creation embodied in contemporary seals of Mesopotamia and Syro-Cilicia (von Wickede 1990, 81, 85 and 92) or, alternatively, the presence of wild flax and oats, possible winter weeds, at Choga Mami. Reinhard Bernbeck (1994, 194–195) has provided indications that may point in our direction as well. If the classical Samarra-style pottery turns up in northern Mesopotamia up to about the latitude of Assur, and only from there 'dissolves', or rather 'trickles off' into the mixed Hassuna-Samarra assemblages, this again may mean that ostentatious consumption, involving the use of exquisite pottery, tended to be topographically bound to the Tigris-bank riverine encampments. The existence of the Samarra-style pottery complex Sawwan–Samarra–Baghouz, finding little reflection in sites farther north and west, may actually be interpreted in this direction as well – activities performed along the banks of the Tigris might have mirrored different aspects of Neolithic social life than those of the submontane sites. All this, in turn, may find confirmation in the variance of subsistence activities (Bernbeck 1994, graph in Fig. 36 on p. 277). Submontane sites tend to depend on cattle-keeping and possibly hunting (ibid. – Dabaghiyah, Choga Mami, Yarimtepe I); of the riverside abodes, at least Sawwan displays an animal-husbandry sector leaning on livestock and fishing complemented by hunted game. The Neolithic lowland sites (or at least their initial stages) could represent winter encampments in which extensive hunting of the plain-living game (gazelle, onager) would have been accompanied by sowing of winter cereals. An analogy is provided by the Zagros site of Tepe Guran (Mortensen 1972), originally such a winter camp, which gradually grew into an all-year(?) village where the agriculturalists supplemented their diet by hunting and food-gathering. Let us also note that at the (admittedly much later) Uruk culture site of Tepe Shaffarabad in the Deh Luran plain, gazelle hunting was a winter pursuit (Wright, Miller and Redding 1980, 276, Table V). Some time around the winter–summer transition, in spring (in subrecent times, this happened in April), the lowland groups would have (split? and) moved into the highlands where they could graze their herds on fresh pastures, gather newly grown plant food and cultivate summer crops on the well-watered valley bottoms; the possibility of an alternative set of 'congregation sites' where people gathered to tap the natural riches available at large such as the biotopes of wild cereal grasses is to be reckoned with. In fact, a remarkable parallel exists, though from a different spatiotemporal context which is nevertheless at the other end of the Mediterranean – Spain and southernmost France at least since the Middle Ages (Le Roy Ladurie 1975, esp. pp. 156–169). Here the sheep transhumance involved a calendrically fixed sequence of herd movements, the pivot stages of which were the months of May (ascent to the upland pastures) and end of September or early October (descent to the lowland winter quarters). Lambs are born around Christmas (for confirmation by the Near Eastern data see Wright, Miller and Redding 1980, 271; Wright, Redding and Pollock 1989, 108–109; Hruška 1995, esp. pp. 82–83) and in May they are usually grown enough to walk even over heavy ground and to be weaned so that sheep can be milked from that time on. In May the shepherds with their herds usually ascend the summer pastures whereupon the sheep are sheared and new wool employed to settle all accounts, debts and obligations that the shepherds or their masters might have incurred before, the season of cheesemaking following in the months of June and July. These May and October thresholds fit so well the winter–summer and summer–winter transitions in the Near East that I cannot resist the temptation to quote the whole sequence in this connection, just for the sake of comparison. At any rate, arguments in favour of such a hypothesis include the importance of sheep for the animal husbandry of Neolithic Mesopotamia and the non-stationary character of settlement of this period, indicated both by the scanty representation of such non-nomadic domesticates as pig (Hole 1983, 183; Meadow 1992, 263–264) and by the very limited number of cemeteries, implying a low degree of territorialization of contemporary human groups (see pp. 36, 81–83 and 91). Moreover, let us notice that the plains of the Taurus submontane zone do have sufficient rainfall for the winter crops but do not support cultivation of summer crops (Weiss 1983, 40). Such a model of winter–summer transhumance (suggested also by Maisels 1990, 119, Fig. 4.4; on modern ethnographic parallels from the Near East see Hall 1930, 151–152; Marx 1978, esp. p. 46; Köhler-Rollefson 1992, 14–15; Levy 1992, esp. p. 70) may offer explanations for all the deviations from the expected state of affairs such as the limited degree of specialization of the plain dwellers and of identical general character of the local and imported goods at lowland sites. Furthermore, we may perceive the plain settlements as congregation sites in which large numbers of people could have lived together temporarily. This is suggested by two facts. First, all such localities have yielded evidence for hunting gazelle and onager, a fairly complex business requiring a number of participants and efficient organization. Let us not forget that such sites as Umm Dabaghiyah bear out the long-term and systematic character of hunting activities leaving their imprint in a number of aspects of the site (the storage complex, the chipped industry, local works of art). Other sites like this now famous congregation point may be discovered with time (for a possible parallel to the Dabaghiyah storage complex at Kharabeh Shattani see Baird 1995, 6–8). Second, it has been noticed that Samarra culture sites tend to be bigger than those of the Halaf culture (Oates 1980, 309; for a similar situation around contemporary Tepe Yahya in southern Iran see Damerow, Englund and Lamberg-Karlovsky 1989, viii). In short, it has been fittingly remarked that 'the sites were permanent but the people in them were not' (Harris, Gosden and Charles 1996, 440).

The resulting idea is thus one of winter congregations of more numerous communities in the lowlands practising large-scale hunting, animal husbandry and cultivation of winter crops. Such gatherings would provide occasion for more elaborate patterns of social life including some collective ritual practices which might have left behind such evidence as clay statuettes or mural paintings (for Palaeolithic but also later evidence see Peoples and Bailey 1988, 138–139, and Bruce Dickson 1990, 200–202; in addition to the above-mentioned sites, see also the murals and terrazzo pavements of Tepe Guran, Mortensen 1972). Having thus survived winter, such congregations would (split into smaller groups? and) ascend to the mountains for the hot season where they could cultivate and gather summer crops, hunt and collect fresh food and graze their animals on the mountain slopes, perhaps streaming together at parallel convergence sites where a multitude of summer resources could have been tapped. After all, movements of the same community between lowland and upland sites have existed up to very recently (Allan 1972, 221). The above cited Indian example shows that this pattern may have ultimately led to permanent occupations of both highlands and lowlands and to the emergence of settlement clusters characterized by identical geographical situations, forming local sodalities (Fairservis 1991, 110). Such a model would also provide a handy explanation for the growing independence of Mesopotamian plain sites from the highland sources, reflected most conspicuously by the decreasing proportion of obsidian tools in the chipped industry (Deh Luran sites, Yarimtepe I, Choga Mami, see Munchaev and Merpert 1981, 116–118). This process may well be illustrated by the situation of Choga Mami where the number of sickle blades and the significance of gazelle hunting grow with

Figure 3.13 At this point the river Euphrates leaves the Taurus mountain ranges and flows into the Syrian plains. From prehistoric times, resources of the highlands – stone, metal and high quality wood – were shipped into the plains through this area.

time, accompanied by the diminishing of seed size (consequence of salinization?) and by decreasing quantities of obsidian. Did this occur in response to the problems brought about by application of the transhumance model as a better adaptation to the local environment, leaning on the exploitation of uncultivated landscape? Of course, the local community could also have been exposed to a prolonged famine period (Miller 1982, 31). Ultimately, such transhumance features with a matching timetable of summer–winter movements do not only constitute the base of modern Bedouin life in the northern regions of the Arabian peninsula but may be traced there as far back as the pre-Islamic era (Macdonald 1992, esp. pp. 9–10). The model does not seem to be confined to the Old World (Mexico: Macneish 1972, 71–73).

In conclusion, then, I believe that the Neolithic economy may be characterized as a 'broad-spectrum' enterprise weaving a wide range of subsistence activities, some of them of fairly complex nature (intensive agriculture with genetic manipulation of plants and artificial irrigation, food-gathering, animal husbandry, hunting), into a pattern of seasonal spatiotemporal movements of the population groups which, upon investigation of the economic potential of a given landscape or set of landscapes, chose the subsistence strategy that seemed most appropriate at the given moment. The initially high degree of mobility and well-developed trend towards the exploitation of different landscapes, most conspicuously highlands and lowlands, underwent changes, the consequence of which might have been more or less permanent occupation of both the mountain ranges and the plains (a case in point being the site of Jarmo). This induced the communities in question to seek better adaptation to the local conditions as well as to try their best to arrive at some form of 'modus vivendi' with neighbouring population groups in the same geographical setting.

Society

The Neolithic period is commonly assumed to have represented the golden age of egalitarian, kinship-based society (on this see Boehm 1993; marriage in such communities: Reynolds and Kellett 1991; kinship terminology: Peoples and Bailey 1988, 231–232; an ethnological model for Mesopotamian prehistory: Forest 1996, 21–22). Diagnostic features of the contemporary burial practices clearly point towards undifferentiated human communities in which all members ultimately rose to positions of importance according to their age, sex and personal achievements. This is revealed by the separate burials of children (under house floors) and adults (mostly outside the settlement) and by possible differentiation between male and female grave goods, although the evidence from Yarimtepe I (graves 129 and 144) is very meagre. Such conclusions have been convincingly argued for by Lewis Binford and tested, *inter alia*, in the Near East (for instance Wright 1978, 212–213). In such societies, kinship constitutes the integrative principle enabling cooperation and energy pooling as well as sharing the output of variously oriented production groups by means of reciprocity (on which see Racine 1986). In extreme cases, it may even take over the role of 'social insurance', buffering the impact of unexpected disasters of any kind (for Africa see, for instance, Miller 1982, 31). Typical features of communities of this historical phase have been subsumed as a) hereditary right to the membership in the given community of all individuals born in it; b) hereditary right of the same individuals to receive support of various kinds from their community; c) the obligation of the same individuals to offer similar support to the other community members in their turn (Maisels 1987, 333–334). The fact that most Neolithic habitation houses were small could indicate the prevalence of patriarchal usages in that period (McNett 1979, 63). A factor worth considering is the lack of clearly differentiated cemeteries; the only possible exception, Samarra, was excavated so long ago that no certainty as to the possible overlying structures may now be obtained. It has been observed that clearly delimited cemetery areas and, in general, the interconnected ancestor cult practices tend to indicate claims to well-defined economic resources such as, for instance, agricultural land (Whalen 1983, 35–36). The lack of such phenomena in Neolithic Mesopotamia may attest to less well-developed links with communal territories and constitute another argument in favour of the transhumance model sketched above. Another conspicuous feature is the larger size of Tell es-Sawwan houses (10–12 rooms) as against the earlier sites (2–3 rooms at Umm Dabaghiyah). How far this may indicate the growth of family size, or even emergence of larger social units (extended families?) remains unclear though such arguments as the visibly greater amount of work invested in the site (communal pavements or defence measures such as the Phase III ditch) do not contradict it. How far the Mesopotamian Neolithic knew extended families remains a mystery. One example, con-sisting of two married couples, of which one had one child, and three single adults who probably inhabited one single homestead, is attested by a house model from the Neolithic site of Platia Magula Zarkou in Greece (Alram-Stern 1996, 164).

Evidence for larger-scale communal activities is turning up: at Khirbet Garsour a well of this period has been excavated (Wilkinson and Matthews 1989, 263) and other examples are known from contemporary Palestine (Athlit 2: Monteil 1995, 134–137, esp. pp. 135–136). The egali-tarian character of Neolithic society notwithstanding, prestige certainly did play a role (on prestige goods at Nemrik 9 and Qermez Dere see Ambos 1996). A most interesting hint in this direction has been supplied recently by Reinhard Bernbeck (1994, graph in Fig. 21 on p. 111). He has shown that at one of the best-studied Neolithic sites of Mesopotamia, Yarimtepe I, the morphological composition of Hassuna-age pottery varies only little but that the variety of dec-orative patterns ornating the same utensils grows as time goes by. This enables us to perceive the growth of such an important characteristic of the Neolithic society of Mesopotamia as ostenta-tious commensality. The surfaces of a more or less identical range of vessel forms, once quite plain and without decoration, put on a richer and more varied ornament as time passed – an indica-tion of a growing aesthetic, and therefore presumably also 'public' and socially relevant functions of pottery-vessel use. A social innovation of cardinal importance ought to be seen in the emer-gence of seals, or rather of matrices with suspension loops interpreted as seals. So far, impressions of any kind are known only at Tell es-Sawwan (II and III) where they might have travelled from the middle Euphrates regions of present-day Syria. None of the earliest seals turned up in graves and they may not have been too closely and intimately tied to individuals. Some aspects of their forms which seem to point to the sphere of virility and (male) sexuality may allude to symbolism connected with the sphere of progeny, fertility and proliferation of the human race (a seal in the form of a bull's leg from Ras Shamra VC: von Wickede 1990, Table 1; a seal depicting a wild he-goat: ibid. Table 7 and p. 43; seals depicting human faces: ibid. Table 10 and p. 48, Table 28 and pp. 76–77; a seal depicting a human foot: ibid. Table 26; a seal in the form of a circumcised penis[?]: ibid. Table 4 and p. 43). Pierre Amiet has published a most interesting, though later (Late Uruk?) seal from Susa, in the form of an embracing couple. The sealing surface, represent-ing the lower side of the seal on which the couple lie, shows a depiction of a small human figure wrapped, from the waist down, in some kind of skirt, just like a baby in diapers (Amiet 1972, pp. 47 and 62, No. 414, SB 5539 and Pl. 58). Here the act of producing a seal impression is directly assimilated to human sexual intercourse producing offspring. The necessity to identify individ-uals by seal impressions may suggest the emergence of more extensive kin-based units (extended families? lineages?), maintaining their coherence by some form of cultivated tradition. As I have noted above, the stylistic unity of the Mesopotamian and Syro-Cilician seals (von Wickede 1990, 81, 84–85) represents the general permeability of the whole area, likely to constitute an argument in favour of the above sketched transhumance hypothesis, but also the spiritual coher-ence of the lowland communities which may have formed regional sodalities assumed in contemporary Indian developments (see Fairservis 1991, 110).

In short, then, the society of Neolithic Mesopotamia may be characterized as egalitarian, kin-based, probably patrilocal and possibly patrilinear. In some instances the impact of a trend towards the aggregation of larger kinship units (extended families? lineages?) could be guessed.

Metaphysics

It can hardly be overstressed that an attempt at the assessment of changes in the Neolithic spiritual world as against its Mesolithic predecessor is an extremely precarious affair with more than a fair chance at failure. Hardly any shrines or cultic establishments may be expected at this period of time when no conditions for the maintenance of specialized cultic personnel and structures existed, and the Catal Hüyük evidence has been re-interpreted convincingly by I. Hodder (1987). There are, nevertheless, some indications of extraordinary furnishings of at least some settlement structures. A room at Choga Mami containing in each corner a pedestal with a hearth (Oates 1978, 117) may be seen as continuation of practices observed at the Mesolithic site of Qermez Dere (see pp. 10–11). Such structures are of extraordinary importance as they may help us to pinpoint the sites of peculiar cultic activities which, given the fact that under conditions of widely dispersed populations the desired coherence and integration of the expanding groups is usually maintained by means of elaborate ritual procedures such as ancestor cults, may indicate sites enjoying particular esteem and, perhaps, playing the role of 'departure points' for subsequent settlement filiations. Aperception of the world, of mankind's position within it, of proper relationships within human society as well as the ensuing practical attitudes may well have been expressed and conditioned by some form of myth (on myths in general see *Le Mythe* 1988).

A material incarnation of ritual or magical rather than religious practices is represented by female (perhaps also animal) figurines of clay and stone, found so frequently at various Neolithic sites (Figure 3.14) (on female statuettes see Oates 1978, 121–122, in general Hamilton *et al.* 1996). They are conspicuously absent from some sites while in other localities they may appear in a belated fashion (Yarimtepe I – missing in pre-XII to VI but present in V–I, see pp. 18–21). At the Jordanian Neolithic site of Ain Ghazzal, worshippers may have approached a stone statuette of this type, located under the open sky on the outskirts of the village, along a stone-paved pathway

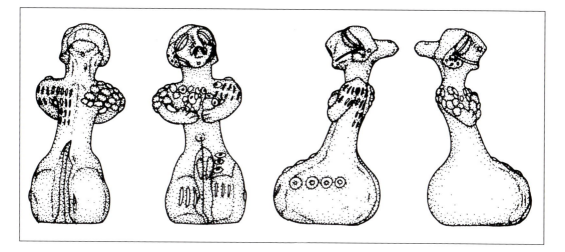

Figure 3.14 A Neolithic Samarra culture female statuette from Tell Songor A (after Forest 1996, 37, Fig. 23)

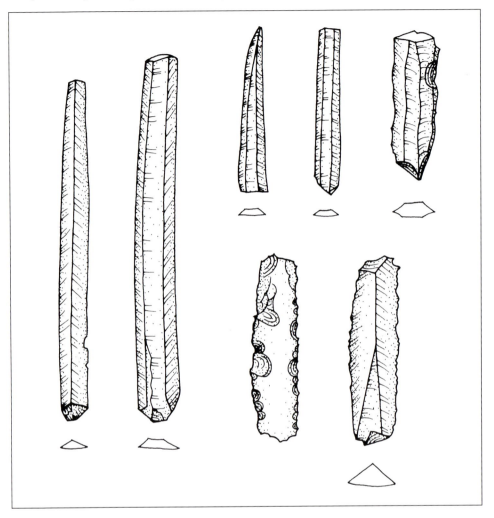

Figure 3.15 Neolithic chipped stone industry of the Hassuna culture from Yarimtepe I (after Munchaev and Merpert 1981, 116, Fig. 34)

(Schmandt-Besserat 1998a). Their association with the colour red (Jarmo, Hassuna) and practices observed at Mesolithic sites may imply that they were in some way associated with life energy and they may have constituted specific invocations of the female procreative force, not related only to progeny but to all the contributions that housewives brought in. Indeed, the Neolithic life may well be envisaged as composed of the male and female activity spheres with males procuring comestibles outside the settlement sites (hunting and animal husbandry) and females applying their skills close to these sites or within them (agriculture and/or gardening). Grain and other plant food brought in by the mistresses of Neolithic houses may thus have been connected with the female procreative force, and abundant harvests, in addition to the birth of sons and daughters, might have been 'secured' by rituals involving the female (and animal?) statuettes. The connection of these figurines (attested since the Mesolithic – see Karim Shahir) with the origins of agriculture may well prove worth investigating. The association of the colour red with life, vigour and procreative force may even be pursued as far as the decoration painted on Hassuna and Samarra culture pottery in this hue. The fact that in agricultural societies domestic pottery is usually made by housewives moves this assumption a shade closer to probability. In this connection the white colour of the limestone female statuettes accompanying the Tell es-Sawwan dead may be of relevance. The colour white is frequently associated with purity but also with fertility (Bruce Dickson 1990, 206), and at Tell es-Sawwan this seems to be confirmed by the presence of stone penises in the graves. At any rate, these statuettes accompanying deceased community members probably have a different background from the ordinary examples of clay. The sphere of colours seems to be indicative of changes in attitudes towards the external world. The necklace of sixty-eight beads abounding in colours of most diverse materials found at Yarimtepe I layer XII (Munchaev and Merpert 1981, 138) may well reflect the Mesolithic ostentatious display of whatever exquisite materials were at hand. As against this, necklaces found in the upper layers of the same site (ten carnelian beads in layer X and fourteen turquoise pendants in layer X, both perhaps complete sets – Munchaev and Merpert 1981, 138) are usually limited to one single mineral or one single colour (the two might well have been identical in the Neolithic vision) and may thus imply the first crystallization of an image of a universe structured by sets of stable relationships between human beings and the rest of the world. An illustrative case might be an individual's lucky stones, cards, numbers and weekdays as identified by modern horoscopes. It would have been logical if the considerable mastery of Neolithic men and women over the physical and chemical properties of natural objects led them to envisage the universe as an ordered and coherent structure harmonizing all the seemingly disparate and discontinuous manifestations of natural powers and processes.

There is, in fact, evidence to the effect that the Neolithic population saw the world as a unified whole but the identification of particular settings and consequences of this perception cannot be disengaged from material evidence at the time being. Neolithic seals and seal impressions (von Wickede 1990, 38–49, 72–87, 90–92, Tables 1–53) offer four kinds of diverse structures: a) net- and lattice-shaped patterns; b) patterns consisting of rectangles or triangles gradually diminishing and set into one another; c) spiraliform or oval patterns; and d) depictions of human and animal figures. Among these categories a), c) and d) occur in the territory of ancient Mesopotamia. Leaving the figural motifs aside for the moment, let us concentrate on the nets/lattices and spirals. Parallel lines crossing one another at various angles represent indeed the

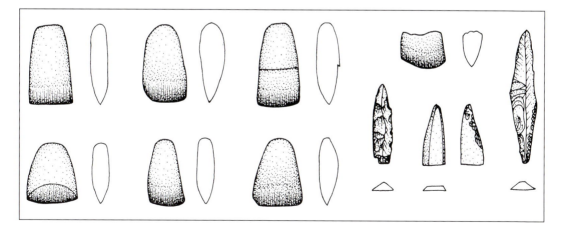

Figure 3.16 Examples of Neolithic ground stone industry (axes) and chipped stone items (arrowheads) of the Hassuna culture (after Munchaev and Merpert 1981, 121, Fig. 35)

simplest decorative devices conceivable but their individual traits merit attention. The first and most remarkable feature is undoubtedly their extremely large diffusion sphere, comprising most of the uppermost segment of the 'Fertile Crescent' (Zagros and Taurus piedmont areas as far as Ras Shamra), where they turn up in more or less identical forms visibly different from those of adjacent regions such as, for instance, the interlace and guilloche patterns of Çatal Hüyük (von Wickede 1990, 60, Fig. 24). Second, the nets/lattices ornate not only Hassuna culture pottery (Munchaev and Merpert 1981, 94–102, Figs. 19–29, passim) but also a pendant from Jarmo (von Wickede 1990, 50, Fig. 21:2) which may well have played an amuletic function. As to the ovals and spirals (von Wickede 1990, 40, Fig. 20:1 – a stamp from Jarmo), there seems to be a relation to the rotating patterns borne by Samarra culture pottery (von Wickede 1986, 32). Unfortunately, both ornament types remain at the most abstract level so that no convincing interpretation can be put forward. A connection with apperception of the universe as a single, unified and patterned structure may be only suspected. The lattice patterns with horizontal and perpendicular lines, and nets with a series of obliquely crossing lines may have been understood as distinct entities. A seal from Tell Judeidah with a 'Union Jack' ornament may, then, constitute a combination of a lattice and net scheme. Is this an 'alliance' or 'union' seal of two sodalities in the Indian sense (Fairservis 1991, 112)?

Let us now summarize in brief. Much in the vein of the explorative, enterprising and challenging spirit of their Mesolithic predecessors and making full use of the favourable natural conditions when, in consequence of a warmer and more humid climatic phase, considerable areas were covered by wood, open woodland or at least steppe vegetation, Neolithic communities circulated over the territory of ancient Mesopotamia in regular, calendrically determined sequences of transhumance between the plains and highlands, making full use of improvements of the subsistence

Figure 3.17 Only in the closest proximity to the Euphrates and Tigris rivers do the greys and browns of the clayey steppe give way to the lush greenery of reeds and herbaceous vegetation cover.

strategies they had introduced and obtaining their daily bread by means of a 'broad-spectrum economy' (intensive agriculture, gathering of wild comestibles, animal husbandry, hunting). These seasonal cycles might have involved winter gatherings of large but temporary human congregations indulging, among others, in large-scale hunting but possibly also in elaborate social and ritual procedures, followed by summer dispersals into smaller groups retiring into shaded mountain valleys for the hot season or, alternatively, by concentrations in montane areas exploiting the untapped local resources. Possessing the full range of technological know-how of their ancestors upon which they kept elaborating (pottery, cold-worked metals), Neolithic groups tended to resort to subsistence patterns which seemed the most opportune at the given moment, including historically 'backward' sequences such as that of Choga Mami where the local community responded to problems with intensive agriculture (diminishing seed size as a consequence of soil salinization?) by greater reliance on the harvesting of wild plants and hunting gazelle. These complex strategies undoubtedly resulted in the gathering of a considerable amount of experience and expertise by the population groups, but the society retained its egalitarian, kinship-based, patrilocal(?) and possibly patrilinear character, pooling the efforts of all its members and sharing out the fruits of their labours. The size of basic residential units might have grown and life in longer-settled communities probably resulted in sanitary and defence measures usually expected from much later communities such as the paved lanes or ditch and rampart fortifications of Tell es-Sawwan. Neolithic highland and lowland settlers might well have begun to perceive a 'world order', a single structure beyond all the particular manifestations of life, integrating visible and invisible natural phenomena by complex interconnections and patterning and assigning to each individual his or her place within the universe together with other classes of both animate and inanimate beings. Such convictions could have been expressed by elaborate symbolism involving, for instance, colours and might have supplied a base for 'practical operations' of magical but perhaps ultimately pragmatic character, leaving such material traces as human and animal statuettes.

Chapter Four

The Chalcolithic

PILOT SITES

Tell Arpachiyah

A tell 20 km east of Mosul excavated by a British mission of 1933 directed by M. Mallowan and J. Cruikshank Rose and an Iraqi excavation of 1976 directed by I. Hijara. C-14 dates: Hijara 2\3 = Mallowan pre-TT 10: 6170–5425 cal. BC; TT 8: 6320–5455 cal. BC; TT 6: 6114 BC (Annex 697–698). Of the sixteen settlement layers documented, the lowermost twelve, i.e. Mallowan's TT 6–10 and Hijara's layers VI–XI are Halafian. Mallowan's TT 5 layer consists of mixed Halaf and Ubaid materials and the uppermost layers (TT 4–1) belong to the Ubaid culture. Five layers of Halaf culture buildings with kilns, tholoi and paved roads as well as an Ubaid culture cemetery were excavated at the foot of the tell. The lower two of these layers (depths 3 and 5 m) precede TT 10 and are thus contemporary with Hijara VI–XI while the upper three (depths 0–2.5 m) run parallel to TT 6–10. The richest evidence on the subsistence of the local population has been collected by I. Hijara. Among the cereals present, emmer, hulled and naked six-row barley as well as two-row hulled barley predominate while einkorn, a hexaploid wheat (*T. compactum*?) and lentils turn up. The mixed TT 5 layer yielded grains of naked unhusked emmer and barley while barley was absolutely predominant in the filling of a well levelled in TT 4. Wild-growing plants are represented by pieces of tamarisk charcoal and by spring grasses like *Aegilops crassa* or *Adonis annua* in the Hijara layers. Both the 'burnt house' of TT 6 and the well filling of TT 4 have yielded evidence of undetermined wood. Local inhabitants kept cattle, pigs, sheep and goats and occasional arrivals on the site include gazelle, larger canids, onager, fish and frogs (the last perhaps not ancient). Hijara's evidence documents a marked increase in the representation of pigs somewhere in his layers XI or X while more cattle were present since his layer VII. This phenomenon was accompanied by a quantitative decrease in sheep and goat remains outside the area enclosed by the rampart wall. Sheep outnumbered pigs by about 3–4 to 1. Slaughter ages indicate that pigs were most probably kept for food (slaughter age below 1 year) and cattle for milk (slaughter age over 3 years).

The lowermost four layers excavated by I. Hijara (XI–VIII) document an average settlement site with shelters, heating installations, a well and rubbish layers. In the subsequent phases (VII–VI) the top of the site was enclosed by a rampart within which the first tholos architecture with two ante-rooms, finding a parallel at Yarimtepe II, appeared. At this level the first graves known at the site received remains of the local inhabitants including a crouched body lying on the right side and skulls deposited in a very unusual painted vase (von Wickede 1986, 22, Fig. 26) and in bowls. The rampart protecting the site was retained in the following stratum (Hijara VI), when tholoi and buildings with gypsum-covered floors and walls with traces of paintings stood within it. No 'civilian settlement' outside the fortification existed at that time but the custom of burying human heads in pots and bowls continued. Upon their desertion, these buildings were filled in with clean earth to provide foundations for subsequent buildings. The precinct of Hijara V (= TT 10) consisted of two tholoi without ante-rooms, built now for the first time on stone foundations, and a well, the filling of which yielded a quantity of obsidian tools, again surrounded by a tauf fortification wall. Another tholos stood at this time by the foot of the hill. The architectural layout of TT 9 included again a tholos without ante-room at the hilltop, this time without its rampart, and two such features at the foot of the hill. This changed in TT 8 when a tholos with ante-room appeared at the top of the hill with another one of its kind at the foot. This latter tholos, built of clay only and partly sunk below the ancient surface, was after cessation of its functions filled in with pisé; a female statuette and sherds of painted pottery were found in its ruins. The hilltop tholos was accompanied by an obviously two-compartment pottery kiln of which only the heating chamber with its central pillar survived. The last tholos architecture may be dated to TT 7 when two tholoi with ante-rooms were situated with their longer axes at right angles on the hilltop, accompanied by two graves with outstanding examples of painted pottery, one of them having a flagon and a bowl lying within a dish. This time there was no tholos below the hill but that area contained, for the first time, trampled roads lying on foundations of pottery sherds and paved with river pebbles, the maximum width of which amounted to 1.2 m.

The entire layout of the site was transformed in TT 6. A large rectangular house built of pisé with clay-plastered walls and ceilings consisting of matting, timber baulks and clay now occupied the centre of the tell area. The inner furnishings of this house might have included wooden shelves leaning on the walls on which individual objects could have been deposited. The house contained a considerable quantity of objects of both everyday use and of a higher aesthetic appeal, presumably used in non-average activities. Implements included chipped stone industry employing both flint and obsidian together with flint cores and flakes and obsidian cores (and flakes?). Of a whole series of ground stone celts found here one still retained a shade of its curved wooden handle. Metal finds feature a piece of lead and two pin fragments of copper. Vessels found in this house were made of stone (both local stones and obsidian and chlorite; one of the obsidian vases bears traces of boring with a tubular drill) in normal and miniature sizes, of white frit and of painted pottery, the latter represented by some of the most exquisite creations of prehistoric Near Eastern potters.

In addition to the production of stone tools the inhabitants of this house obviously engaged in colour-grinding and painting activities, possibly in the course of production of painted pottery. Grinding palettes for these materials were made out of grey, pink and white stones and pigment blocks matched these colours (black, red, yellow in place of white). A large group of seal impressions on clay was lying on the floor of this house (for some see Charvát 1994, 10). Items of personal adornment found here include geometrical and zoomorphic pendants as well as those shaped like parts of the human body and like a gabled house, and necklace beads of geometrical shapes. A complete necklace consisted of lozenge-shaped obsidian beads alternating with cowrie shells with cut-away upper parts in which the interior fillings of red pigment were visible. Works of art, and possibly even cultic paraphernalia, are represented by a remarkable couple of a large female and a smaller male statuette, coarse outlines of human heads and busts carved of limestone as well as animal-shaped vessels (dove, hedgehog?). Ancient music comes alive with a series of bone tubes with a trumpet-like mouthpiece of grey limestone (see Rashid 1996, 20). A most peculiar category of objects unearthed here consists of a human finger-bone found together with the couple of statuettes (one female, one male) of stone and with the stone busts, accompanied by stone imitations of the same kind of relic. The exceptional social significance of this house obviously necessitated the building of another series of roads at the foot of the hill laid down in the same manner as those described in the preceding layer TT 7.

The TT 6 house perished in a fire and after the mixed TT 5 layer the Ubaid culture sets in in strata TT 4–1. These have yielded remains of buildings of bricks, clay blocks or pisé with trampled-clay floors and roofs of reeds and matting. Some of the door frames contained pivot stones. The local population group used domed bread ovens. These houses, of which some yielded contemporary seal impressions, were bordered by an Ubaid period cemetery. Most of the bodies reposed in simple pits, only two in stone cists, being oriented east–west with heads towards both these cardinal points. The deceased were lying on both sides with slightly flexed knees. Pottery, pendants, celts and animal bones (sheep, goat) accompanied the dead. An anthropological assessment of human remains from this cemetery indicates the preponderance of strong young men with good nutrition and diet (Mallowan and Linford 1969).

Throughout the site's existence the inhabitants of Arpachiyah worked with a quantity of materials. Artificial products are represented by the above-mentioned frit vessels. Bone items include points, some hafted in their handles by bitumen, spatulae and palettes. Combs depicted on pottery may have been made of wood as no traces of them have survived (Mallowan and Rose 1935, 166, Fig. 78: 28). Clay was used for a variety of products, first and foremost for the manufacture of both the ordinary and the marvellous painted pottery. Shapes include dishes, bowls, vases, flagons, pedestalled and plain cups and miniatures. The painted decoration gradually developed into stylized geometrical patterns (most recently see von Wickede 1986). Halaf- and Ubaid-style pottery from Arpachiyah were made from different clay sources (Davidson and McKerrel 1980). Other clay products include female and animal statuettes, spindle whorls, tokens (reel-shaped, biconical, conical, spherical as well as those in the shapes of human hands and feet), jar stoppers and 'slingshot'. The modest metal finds feature, in addition to the TT 6 items, a chisel cast in an open mould from the 'upper layers' (Ubaid?). As well as the organic substances mentioned above the sealing evidence bears out cord- and rope-making. The site hosted expert workers in stone. In addition to the above cited evidence for the chipped industry, it is worth noting that Messrs Munchaev and Merpert who saw a part of the Arpachiyah collection in London have observed the preponderance of finished obsidian tools over those of flint and the prevalence of blades among the obsidian tools (Munchaev and Merpert 1981, 218). C. Renfrew (1964, 76) has determined the Arpachiyah obsidian as coming from several sources in eastern

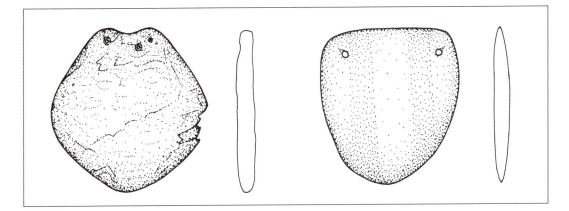

Figure 4.1 Examples of Neolithic ground stone ornaments from the aceramic Neolithic site of Tell Maghzaliya (eighth–seventh millennium BC) (after Yoffee and Clark 1993, 36, Fig. 2: 25: 1–30)

Anatolia. Ground stone items consist of celts or small axes, grinding-stone sets, perforated tools and pivot stones. Stone vessels (bowls, pedestalled bowls, jugs), pendants and beads, referred to above, complete the picture (Mallowan and Rose 1935; Hijara *et al.* 1980; von Wickede 1991).

Yarimtepe II

A tell 7 km south-west of Tell Afar, a USSR excavation of 1970–1976 directed by R. M. Munchaev and N. Ya. Merpert. C-14 dates: nine, levels III, VI, VII and VIII, from 6600–5485 cal. BC to 5290–4765 cal. BC (Annex 736, and Bernbeck 1994, 346). Among the local tells this one yielded evidence of nine layers of a Halaf culture settlement of which the lowermost one is published. The local population subsisted on mixed farming, herding and exploitation of uncultivated landscape. Among the cereal remains, barley, especially of the hulled variety (*H. vulgare, H. lagunculiforme,* possibly also *H. distichum*) with admixtures of wheat (*T. dicoccum, T. aestivum, T. spelta*), is present. As to the animals, the local inhabitants kept sheep and goats, the remains of which constitute 68.7 per cent of all bones present (counting the individuals); sheep predominate over goats. These might have served as sources of milk and hair as most of them were apparently killed at adult ages while pigs and cattle, most of which were slaughtered at tender ages, probably constituted a source of food. The overall number of domestic animals, among which the excavators refer, in addition to those mentioned above, to donkey and dog, amounts to 83 per cent of all bone, the remaining 17 per cent made up by such hunted animals as gazelle (59.3 per cent), wild sheep (18.5 per cent), wild goat (11 per cent), onager, jackal, tiger, porcupine and wild goose. The ecological niches inhabited by the hunted animals and representing the environment in which the local population was procuring food include steppes together with marginal desert regions, submontane landscapes and intermontane plains.

The architecture of Yarimtepe II's earliest phase is characterized by tholoi, clearly used for living, and by systems of linear alignments of single and multiple rectangular chambers, presently interpreted as granary basements. Buildings were erected of oval-shaped clay blocks, true bricks being extremely rare; their interiors bore clay plasterings and floors were simply trampled. Heating installations are represented by various types of kilns, including a rather sophisticated vertical two-compartment pottery kiln with a combustion chamber and firing room separated by a clay plaque perforated repeatedly for the circulation of heat, renewed at least once on the same site.

The settlement has yielded a number of sub-floor burials both of adults and of children. Some of the bodies underwent cremation while in other cases only parts of corpses were buried (lone skulls). The filling of one of the graves contained a stylized female statuette. In some instances the locals dug small pits in which painted pottery, including anthropomorphic and zoomorphic vessels, stone receptacles and, in one case, unique trapezoidal microlithic implements, all of which had gone through fire, were buried under tholos LXVII. An instance of ritual(?) cremation of an animal in a hearth filled in subsequently with stones has been recorded.

As to treatment of natural materials on the site, bone was used to manufacture the usual points and spatulae. Clay served for the production of exquisite painted pottery, spindle whorls, 'sling-shot' (the filling of one of the tholoi contained over 1000 pieces) and stylized female statuettes, most of which ended up in settlement layers. All in all, thirteen pieces of copper ore or of indistinct copper artifacts were found on the site, including a unique copper seal from the filling of tholos LXVII. One of the beads may have been hammered out of pure copper and the local population might have tapped the same ore deposit as the Hassuna culture community of Yarimtepe I. Stone supplied material for chipped and ground industry. The presence of production waste indicates on-the-spot production of the industry of local quartz (nuclei and mostly blades, also

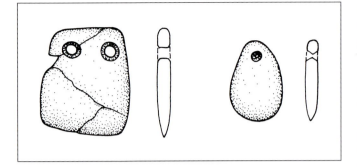

Figure 4.2 Examples of Neolithic ground stone industry. Pendants from the aceramic Neolithic site of Tell Maghzaliya (after Yoffee and Clark 1993, 36, Fig. 2: 25: 1–30)

points, scrapers and borers). In the case of obsidian, ready-made tools prevail. The microliths have all but vanished save for the 'building deposit' below tholos LXVIII (a painted pot and three trapezoidal microliths of obsidian). Stone was ground into grinding implements, perforated spheres and spindle whorls. Flat wedge-shaped celts, absent from the earliest layers, turned up in upper strata. The local population used stone vessels and adorned themselves with stone beads and pendants including pendant seals. A deposit from grave 11/58 contained 328 beads of soft white stone, 234 shell beads and 10 beads of carnelian (Munchaev and Merpert 1981; Yoffee and Clark 1993, 129–162; Munchaev 1997).

Eridu

A tell 40 km south-west of Nasiriyah excavated by British expeditions in 1854 (J. E. Taylor) and 1918–1919 (R. C. Thompson and H. R. Hall) and by an Iraqi mission, directed by F. Safar, M. A. Mustafa and S. Lloyd in 1946–1949. Of the site's prehistoric features a sequence of 'temple' buildings (layers XVII–VI), an Ubaid period multi-phase settlement ('Hut Sounding') and a cemetery of the same culture have been excavated. The site has offered an extremely limited amount of palaeoecological evidence. The 'Hut Sounding' has yielded bones of cattle with limited quantities of sheep and goat remains. Of the wild animals onager and then gazelle, wild boar and otter have been identified (Flannery and Wright 1966). The deepest layers of the 'temple sequence' (XIX and XVIII) belong to the Eridu culture (= Ubaid 1). The four parallel walls some 0.5 m apart in layer XVIII may represent vestiges of architecture better known at Tell Awayli and Tell es-Sawwan (Huot 1989, 30, Figs 3, 4 and 5). Layers XVII to XIV are characterized by pottery decoration in the Hajji Muhammad style (= Ubaid 2). The rectangular 'apsidal' annexes to buildings of layers XVII and XVI contain internal brick blocks ('altars') accompanied, in the latter case, by another such block in the centre of the interior. The surface of this block bears traces of fire and it is surrounded by ashy layers. From this moment on, twin blocks of this kind represent a constant feature of the furnishings of Eridu 'temple' interiors. Both of the above-mentioned structures could have borne roofs of timbers. Among the small finds a female statuette from layer XVI merits attention. In layers XVII and XVI kilns were situated close to the exterior walls of the structures in consideration and this seems to have been also the case of the layer XV structure, perhaps a 'pigeon-hole granary' of the Tell Awayli type (Huot 1989, 32). Phase XIV is represented by a platform which originated by filling in and levelling ruins of the Phase XV structure with the distinctive bricks used throughout phases XV–XIV. The platform might have borne some architecture of which, however, all traces have vanished. Pottery finds permit the assignment of layers XIII–VI to the Ubaid culture proper (= Ubaid 3 and 4). Layers XIII–XII showed no architectural evidence but yielded a number of small finds including mixed Hajji Muhammad- and Ubaid-style pottery, 'tortoise jars', a female statuette and the first clay muller (slender cone with a nail-like head and shaft bent at the point) to turn up on the site (layer XII). In layer XII, earlier ruins were enclosed by brick walls, the intervening space filled in by sandy material and levelled by a capping horizontal layer and a 'temple' with protruding 'bastions' at the corners erected on the top of the terrace thus formed. The terrace was subsequently expanded by an addition of a zone of cellular constructions levelled by dumped-in materials. Of the accompanying finds, let us notice beads of frit and obsidian and the first baked-clay sickle found at the site. This form of terrace building was repeated in layers X and IX when the preceding ruins were levelled and new buildings erected on the platforms laid down in this manner. Such Phase IX finds as spindle whorls, ground and chipped stone celts and hoes (even a dog skeleton is present) and also a seal with a geometrical pattern indicate the domestic character of at least some of the activities once performed on the site. The structure of layer VIII was the first one to have assumed the form of a building with a central nave flanked on both sides by linear alignments of rectangular rooms. Although small finds denote at least some of the building's functions as domestic (chipped flint and obsidian tools, ground and chipped celts, a bone point with traces of bitumen hafting), this phase may not have been entirely devoid of cult features. In addition to a 'tortoise jar' with fish bones immured in one of the building's niches, the enigmatic curving coils of clay some 30–40 cm long and hidden below the pavement at the west 'altar', perhaps representations of snakes, may indicate some ritual usages (chthonic cults?). The overall characteristics of this building were reiterated by the next layer VII with another central-hall building on the pavement of which rested a debris layer some 40 cm thick and covered by another paved surface. Together with the presence of domestic rubbish (fish bones) inside the building, this points to its profane nature, but non-average finds such as part of an obsidian vessel, a seal depicting an insect(?) and a snake sculpture of painted clay imply either the presence of élite individuals or some extraordinary activities. Such a mixed character of the intramural finds persists also in the following layer VI. At that time the old building was pulled down to a wall height of some 120 cm, the remaining space filled in with bricks and another central-hall building erected on the substantially enlarged terrace. Walls of the lateral chambers of this house bore a whitewash but domestic refuse was left to accumulate on the pavement until it reached the thickness of some 20 cm when it received another pavement layer. The refuse consisted of well-developed ashy layers (one of the side chambers was even entirely filled in with ash), bones of fish and small animals and pottery sherds but it also included a group of beads of carnelian, bluish frit and white marble as well as a pendant in the shape of a sitting human figure and sherds of painted pots with excised triangular openings ('braziers') and a bowl with appliqué snakes. Upon extinction of the building's function it was again backfilled with bricks to provide a platform for the next stage. 'Temples' I–V are represented by successive revetments added to the walls of the terrace on which Temple VI was standing.

Traces of an Ubaid culture settlement were uneathed in the 'Hut Sounding'. This passed through fourteen prehistoric settlement layers clearly falling into two distinct periods (layers XIV–X and VIII–I), separated by a sterile stratum IX. There is evidence of mudbrick architecture and of reed constructions plastered from both sides with clay. In addition to such clay products

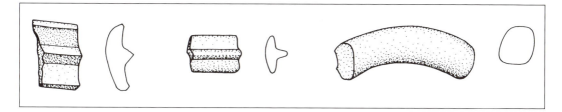

Figure 4.3 Neolithic ground stone bracelets from Tell Maghzaliya (after Yoffee and Clark 1993, 36, Fig. 2: 25: 1–30)

as pottery, mullers and a clay bead, the baked-clay sickles turned up in strata of the later segment (VIII–I). The local inhabitants made use of ground stone for celts, grinding stones and net sinkers. Chronologically the 'Hut Sounding' layers most probably fall within the Temple XII–VI period. The Ubaid cemetery correlates with the local layers IV–VII (Wright and Pollock 1986, 326).

Another settlement site of Ubaid 2 (= Hajji Muhammad) with finds of female statuettes has been cut into by the extensive cemetery which might have once entombed the remains of 800–1,000 deceased but of which 193 graves were excavated. Chronologically it runs parallel to Temple VI and 'Hut Sounding' IV–VII. The bodies were interred either in simple pits or in brick cists without paved bottoms, covered over with single brick courses after deposition of the deceased. They were lying supine with hands along their sides or in the pelvis. In the frequent cases of repeated burials older bones were simply pushed aside and fresh bodies installed. In some instances children accompanied adults but most frequently they occupied their own graves. Pottery, usually deposited at the grave corner by the deceased's right foot, tended to include the set of a jar, bowl and cup. Articles of personal attire consisted of 'earrings', i.e. short elongated pieces of obsidian and pink stone, bored at one end and found at both sides of two skulls, beads worn on the neck, on wrists, in the waist area and also excavated across the lower leg bones, originally perhaps sewn on a garment hem. Two instances of white shell beads at the waist and black obsidian beads on the hem have been recorded. In addition to this a few stone vessels and a single macehead of stone turned up in the graves. A very few graves contained additional human skulls (twelve in grave 97), animal bones or whole skeletons (a dog with an animal bone at its jaws). A

Figure 4.4 One of the valleys in the Taurus mountain range. The bottoms of such valleys were the natural homeland of many of the wild grasses that have been cultivated into present-day cereals.

number of finds came to light among the graves or under the cemetery surface. These include animal bones (some of which even turned up on the brick covers of the burial cists), the renowned boat model, stone vessels, a macehead, female statuettes and a unique clay figurine of a man. Anthropological assessment of the skeletal remains points to the rather heterogeneous character of the population as well as to the extremely worn state of their teeth, frequently abraded to gum level. The implications of this fact for the reconstruction of the diet and life conditions of the Ubaidian population of Eridu remain to be evaluated. Similar situations have elsewhere been interpreted as so-called bruxism, a consequence of socio-economic stress in isolated endogamous societies (Feffer and Périn 1987, 147).

Later Uruk period remains are represented by three architectural complexes on the site. The building in Square H5 has a regular central-hall plan with layers of settlement rubbish and a kiln in one of the subsidiary rooms. 'Temple I' boasts a façade of a wavy outline, built of small stones plastered over with gypsum. Levelling layers leaning on this façade have produced mosaic cones of grey stone and white gypsum, the heads of the latter being covered with sheet copper, as well as Uruk period pottery. The 'Portico Building' had originally been founded in four naves and rebuilt later on as a central-hall structure, again with settlement refuse (fish bones). One of the buildings excavated in the last century by W. Taylor, conceivably of Uruk date, bore a mural painting of a man carrying a bird on his wrist and accompanied by a smaller male figure. An Uruk period(?) deposit at an unspecified part of the site yielded palaeobotanical evidence: hulled six-row barley and possibly *T. sphaerococcum* wheat, date stones (*Phoenix dactylifera*) and a textile fragment, perhaps of flax (Safar, Mustafa and Lloyd 1981; Danti and Zettler 1997).

Tepe Gawra

A tell 25 km north-east of Mosul, excavated by a US mission, directed by E. A. Speiser and Ch. Bache, in 1927 and 1931–1938. C-14 dates: XIX: 6285–5485 cal. BC (Annex 711); XVIII–XVII: 4875–3670 cal. BC (ibid.); XVIII: 5605–5190 cal. BC (ibid.); XVII: 5210–4730 cal. BC (ibid.); XII: 4920–4450 cal. BC (ibid.). The twenty settlement layers documented here begin in the mature Halaf period and end somewhere in the second pre-Christian millennium. Layers XX–XII may date into the Halaf and Ubaid culture periods. Palaeoecological evidence has not been systematically collected by the excavators. The most ancient settlement traces have been unearthed in the Gawra foothill area and belong to the Halaf culture. A well which had once supplied water to the prehistoric community was, after cessation of its function, used on at least four successive occasions to receive more or less ceremonially deposited bodies of juvenile and adult persons. The deepest layer of the tell numbered XX did not yield any more extensive and intelligible architectural remains beyond those of a round tholos. The following strata XIX, XVIII and XVI (Halaf culture) seem to represent rebuildings of an average settlement compound comparable with situations observed, for instance, at Yarimtepe II and Tell Awayli and including circular tholos structures built of clay. Burials turned up frequently under house floors. A cemetery of layer XVII sheltered 19 adult bodies, 7 children and 5 babies, most of whom rested on their right sides in simple pits. Adults tended to descend to the nether world provided with pottery while children wore beads.

In the three following phases, datable to the early Ubaid culture (XVI, XVA, XV), the compound, the successive phases of which have been documented, consisted of two segments separated by a shallow gully. The east segment acquired gradually more prominent residential functions while the west segment obviously retained economic and storage facilities indicated by a series of parallel walls (granary foundations?) and kilns. The most accomplished version of the residential segment in layer XVI assumed the form of a central hall flanked by two alignments of rectangular rooms. The north wall of the central hall bore a mural painting of alternating rows of red and black lozenges on a whitewashed background. Entrances from the central hall to the subsidiary rooms were situated in the hall's longer sides by the corners in pairs facing each other and at identical distances from the corners. This seems to be the nascent period of the pronounced binarity reflected by the entrances and interior furnishings of 'temples' in layers XIII–XII which display symmetrical paired elements in their structuring. Burial customs of layer XV were characterized by two features which became dominant on the site from this time on. First, child burials prevailed numerically over those of adults. Second, the uniformity of body deposition in layer XVII now collapsed and the deceased were interred lying both on their right and left sides.

Fundamental changes took place in layers XIV–XII (late Ubaid). In Gawra XIV the whole area of the site was occupied by a single building representing a version of the central-hall structure flanked on the longer sides by irregularly doubled alignments of subsidiary rectangular rooms, erected on rubble foundations. In layer XIII this was replaced by a central-square layout enclosed on three sides by buildings planned on the same structural principle as the central hall flanked by subsidiary rooms (the eastern, northern and central 'shrines'). All the entrances from outside were doubled and the front wall of the central hall of the northern 'shrine' was articulated by two niches. The walls of the central hall and entrance rooms of the central 'shrine' (9–12) bore a coating of red paint. The three 'shrines' did not constitute a single preconceived unit. The chronological priority apparently belongs to the eastern 'shrine' the users of which may have drawn their water from a well in the area of the future northern 'shrine'. The northern 'shrine' followed suit, having been erected after the well had fallen into disuse and had been levelled by settlement rubbish including pottery sherds, a numerous group of seal impressions and a skull of a saluki dog. The finishing touch was put in by the insertion of the central 'shrine', the last component of the architectural group of layer XIII. This proliferation of the central-hall buildings continued in the next layers XIIA and XII when the site received a more or less coherent building layout consisting of such buildings, among which the excavators singled out the 'White Room', so called because its walls bore a whitewash, as the most prominent one. The two entrances of the west shorter side of the 'White Room' are again matched by two niches in the inner face of the opposite east shorter side. The same arrangements appear in the case of a central-hall building south of the 'White Room' (No. 36) with the difference that the double entrance does not lead to the central hall from the west shorter hall side but through the west parts of the longer walls, again in a strictly symmetrical layout. All these structures yielded ordinary settlement rubbish, sufficiently demonstrating their profane character. Most of the buildings were of clay bricks, stone having been used very rarely for paving. Layers XIIA and XII contained 76 interments of babies, 25 of children and 19 of adults; this shows clearly the change as against layer XVII. The deceased were laid to rest on their right and left sides in simple pits, the children frequently in urns and the adults in clay-lined cists. Layer XII is the last one at Tepe Gawra to display any significant quantities of Ubaid-style painted pottery.

The individual find categories fall in with the evidence offered by other Chalcolithic sites. Artificial materials are represented by frit seals found first in layer XVII (von Wickede 1990, 293, *sub* No. 214) and then in layer XII (ibid. 304, *sub* Nos. 510 and 515). Bone supplied material for awls, spatulae and numerous whistles; a suspected mouthpiece of some blown instrument was found in layer XII. Clay, as usual, served first and foremost for building and for pottery making. Pure Halaf style of ornament characterized layer XX. In layers XIX–XVII Halaf pottery received an Ubaid-style complement which gradually prevailed in layers XVI, XVA and XV. Only Ubaid-style pottery is present in layer XIII–XII. Analyses using the neutron-activation method (NAA) revealed the fact that both Halaf- and Ubaid-style pottery was manufactured from the same clay source at Gawra (Davidson and McKerrel 1980, 161, 164). Transformation of the traditional potter's craft which left behind the exquisite but handmade pots of the earlier epochs occurred in layer XII. The pottery output increased substantially and local craftsmen introduced both the slow wheel (*tournette*) and sand tempering of the ceramic paste. A higher percentage of overfired pieces indicates experiments (or failures, or both) in the sphere of heating installations. Morphologically, this period saw multiplication of the local pottery types, including, for the first time, the distinctive Gawra period goblets with stamped decoration, as well as storage jars. Ancient Gawrans also fashioned female and animal statuettes, small wheels (three from layers XIX and XVIII), spindle whorls, tokens and the enigmatic mullers from clay, and clay received impressions of their seals. Less frequent products include the so-called hut symbols (one in layer XVI, another in layer XII), the ubiquitous clay balls or ovals usually identified as slingshot (particularly abundant in layer XII) and baked-clay pipes (layer XIII). The earliest Gawra statuettes depicted kneeling females holding their breasts in pure Halaf style (layers XIX, XVIII, XVII). Female images of layers XVII to XIII were accompanied by likenesses of animals (sheep, unidentified animal and a bird in layer XIII). Only animal representations were found in layer XII (gazelle?, dog, leopard). Metal finds were rare but the virtually omnipresent whetstones indicate that metal objects were hardly in short supply. Two copper fragments from layer XVII are followed by 1–5 pieces each from layers XIII and XII. The first gold of Tepe Gawra supplied material for sixteen beads arranged into a necklace deposited in a pot found in layer XII. Of work with organic matter, our only evidence consists of spindle whorls (textile production) and impressions of cords, ropes and other features of perishable matter on the reverse sides of sealings.

Stone found a manifold and versatile employment at Tepe Gawra. Among the materials for the production of chipped industry local flint and imported obsidian served for turning out mostly blades and scrapers; arrowheads are completely absent. Changes may again be registered in layers XIII–XII. The occurrence of new sorts of obsidian (XIII) is followed by an increase in quantity of implements and by the first occurrence of borers in layer XII. The lack of obsidian cores may point to the conclusion that, as was then usual, obsidian arrived at the site in the form of finished tools. Ground and polished stone items include celts, maceheads (from layer XVIII), weights(?), palettes, whetstones and stone vessels. Again, the quantitative peak of ground stone tools falls in layers XIII–XII. That period saw such innovations as miniature vases with incised ornaments, possibly with the function of cosmetic containers (XIII), grinding stones, first attested in layer XIII, as well as boat-shaped hammer-axes appearing in the same stage. Of the most usual stone ornaments, let us note the beads, occurring from layer XIX onwards in the typical colour triad of white–red–black (white paste, carnelian, obsidian, limestone, marble). Substantial multiplication of bead materials occurred in layers XIII–XII.

In addition to the above-mentioned stones, the Gawrans now boasted ornaments made of turquoise, amethyst, lapis lazuli, agate, quartz, jade, beryl, diorite, haematite, steatite, bone, ivory and shell. As against this, most of the tanged drop-shaped and incised pendants were

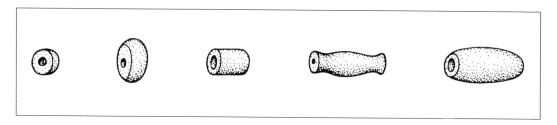

Figure 4.5 Neolithic beads of stone and obsidian from Tell Maghzaliya (after Yoffee and Clark 1993, 36, Fig. 2: 25: 1–30)

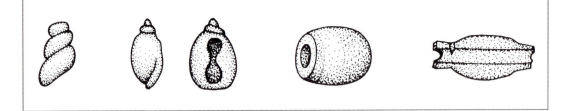

Figure 4.6 Neolithic beads of stone, obsidian and shell from Tell Maghzaliya (after Yoffee and Clark 1993, 36, Fig. 2: 25: 1–30)

manufactured – from layer XIX on – of white marble and, in lower quantities, of black steatite, quartz, haematite and amethyst. Obsidian pendants first turned up in layer XVI; black steatite reached the same popularity as white marble only in layer XII, of course, in other pendant types. Such pendants, likely to have been used as Halaf period seals, probably fell out of fashion by the time of layer XV.

A particular category of stone artifacts is represented by the seals, present from the very earliest times. One of the bodies thrown into the Halaf period well at the foothill area went down with his or her seal. The first depiction of an animal figure on a seal comes from layer XVIII (von Wickede 1990, Table 218) and for the following period the coexistence of geometric and naturalistic seals may be taken for granted. Again, the multiplication of seal impressions in layer XIII attests to the intensification of symbolized exchange activities carrying with it the distinctive style of the period. The overwhelmingly predominant mobile-container sealings may denote reciprocity (Charvát 1988a). The very first door sealing may date to layer XII (von Wickede 1990, 295, citing Table 259; on the site in general see Speiser 1935; Tobler 1950; Forest 1983a; Rothman 1990; von Wickede 1990, passim; Rothman 1997).

All in all, the slow changes taking place in Gawra XVII–XV, especially in the ritual sphere, and represented by such phenomena as the occurrence of animal statuettes together with female ones, changes in the burial rite (dead bodies on both sides instead of one predominating), the significance of the white–red–black colour triad and the introduction of the binary principle in the architecture of layer XV, paved the way taken by subsequent spiritual and material developments. A considerable 'leap forward', visible especially in the sphere of arts and crafts working with clay, metal and stone, took place in layers XIII–XII. The following principal characteristics of this change may be put forward: a) procurement of raw materials from a much wider geographical area than before; b) increase in the overall output of the crafts in question; and c) introduction of new tools and techniques for work with these materials. Such developments undoubtedly went hand in hand with increasing concern for public health (more sophisticated drainage by means of baked-clay pipelines). This new welfare must have resulted in re-assessments of the social situation. Some of the new materials improved the common everyday tasks (grinding stones); others such as the new exotic stones, flint borers, clearly for bead and pendant manufacture, or stamped goblets for ceremonial banqueting were, however, undoubtedly aimed at ostentatious public display. Nonetheless, such observations as the probable predominance of reciprocity of some non-institutionalized form of redistribution (sealing of mobile containers), egalitarian distribution of the newly acquired showy materials as well as traditional burial practices do show that the Gawra population group rose in social status as a corporate unit, and was likely to have conferred its markers on all its full members in order to distinguish them from members of other similar social bodies.

Figure 4.7 Summits and slopes of the Taurus mountain ranges. From landscapes of this kind the inhabitants of the Mesopotamian plain have obtained diverse varieties of stone, including obsidian, ever since the Middle Palaeolithic age. High quality wood as well as many kinds of metals became export commodities in later periods.

Tell Awayli

A tell 200 km north-west of Basra, a French excavation of 1976–1989 directed by J.-L. Huot and J.-D. Forest. C-14 dates: 5225–4570 cal. BC (level 1), 5350–4920 cal. BC (level 3), 4720–4380 cal. BC (final Ubaid), 5330–4915 cal. BC (final Ubaid, level 3), 5020–4435 cal. BC (final Ubaid, level 3) (Annex 726). The local settlement sequence comprises eight broadly conceived temporal phases. It starts with a culture designated by the excavators as Ubaid 0 or Awayli culture, datable to the Neolithic rather than the Neolithic/Chalcolithic transition period (C-14 date: 7430 +/–150 BP). The following series of layers has been assigned to the four classic phases of the Ubaid culture (Ubaid 1, 2, 3 and 4, from bottom to top). The last Ubaid layer is followed by a transitional Ubaid-Uruk settlement phase (a series of pottery kilns), by remains of Uruk culture structures and finally by a potters' establishment of the Late Uruk culture (hundreds of BRB, or bevelled-rim bowls). Palaeoecological evidence has been secured from layers dating to Ubaid 0–3 and Ubaid 4. In the earlier period the occurrence of six-row hulled barley (*H. vulgare*), einkorn wheat (*T. monococcum*) and flax (*Linum usitatissimum*, one seed), as well as date palm (*Phoenix dactylifera*, wood) have been recorded. Some features of the ancient landscape are revealed by the presence of poplar (*Populus euphratica*) and tamarisk (*Tamarix* sp.), as well as various water plants (*Cyperus rotundus* or the reed *Phragmites australis*). In the same period the group of animal remains shows a marked preponderance of cattle (45.5 per cent of all remains, slaughtered at a mature age) over pigs (36.7 per cent, two-thirds slaughtered below the age of 1 year) and ovicaprids (16.8 per cent). Very few remains belong to wild animals and no evidence for fishing is available; the latter fact, however, may be caused by incomplete preservation of material (see p. 182). These trends continue in the Ubaid 4 period when cattle remains make up 57.9 per cent of all animal bones, pig 36.9 per cent and ovicaprid 5.6 per cent. There is a slightly higher representation of wild (= hunted) animals and a marked presence of ichthyofauna, both of brackish and of sweet waters.

The architectural sequence starts with the lowermost Ubaid 0 strata (some 5 m of ruins). Intelligible ground plans include two types of structures. The local population probably lived in brick buildings of a three-nave plan with annexes consisting of series of long and narrow parallel rooms. Erected of elongated bricks ($55 \times 13 \times 6$ cm), they had brick-paved or simply trampled floors and their walls were (sometimes repeatedly) plastered with clay. The interior furnishings include hearths, brick blocks, the top parts of which bear fire stains, as well as brick platforms which might have contained provisions of grain in superstructures of reed matting, as has been argued for Tell Abada (Jasim 1989, 86). Such reed superstructures, as well as layers of reed matting resting on wooden floors borne by series of small cylindrical piles, have occasionally survived (Wilkinson and Matthews 1989, 260). The size of these buildings shows that the ancient architects could span intervals up to 5 m and they must thus have commanded good building timber (see above for the occurrence of poplar). The timber ceilings bore reed matting and insulation layers of clay, while bitumen was frequently used for the waterproofing of various structures. The other architectural type is represented by a series of walls perpendicular to one another and forming a grid pattern referred to by the excavators as 'pigeon-hole constructions'. Their bottoms were covered with reed matting and at least 80 square metres of them were laid bare in the lowermost strata. They seem to represent remains of granaries (Forest 1996, 47, Figs 43 and 44). In the Ubaid 1 strata this grid-pattern architecture is repeated. Of the Ubaid 2 phases only wall fragments, individual bricks and Hajji Muhammad-style pottery found in secondary deposits survive. The Ubaid 3 times saw the erection of a huge brick-built terrace at least 40 m long, subsequently deserted and covered with wind-blown sand. The end of the Ubaid sequence, belonging to Ubaid 4, witnessed again the emergence of a living quarter, represented probably by a central-hall building flanked by rows of smaller rooms and by 'pigeon-hole constructions' as well as by some kilns.

Small finds fall in with evidence from other Chalcolithic sites. Work with bitumen is well attested to throughout all Ubaid culture strata. It served both for the manufacture of objects (balls, spindle whorls, elongated pieces) and for waterproofing various structures. All along the Ubaid phase of the site it was procured from one single source which is not identical with the bituminous deposits of Hit. Clay was used, first and foremost, for the production of pottery. Creations of Ubaid 0 potters tend to be rather varied in the paste preparation, composition of colour for painting and in the firing time; they frequently display organic admixture or tempering. Tortoise jars are present from Ubaid 0 levels. By Ubaid 1 times the techniques of pottery production visibly improved and some items acquired the shiny, well-adhering black colour but the organic admixture was still present. This vanished only in the Ubaid 4 phase when the whole process of manufacture, painting and firing of pottery became standardized on a rather high professional level. The potters of this period introduced sand tempering and were able to fire their products at temperatures between 1,050 and 1,200 degrees centigrade. In addition to pottery-making the ancient inhabitants used the local clays for fashioning spindle whorls, loomweights, terracotta sickles, enigmatic cylindrical terracotta objects, perhaps net sinkers, boat models, mullers and small spheres. Terracotta seals turned up in the later Ubaid phases of the site. A pendant with the earliest known depiction of the 'master of animals' turned up in an Ubaid 3 context (von Wickede 1990, 149–150, 294, No. 227, Table 227). The Ubaid 4 settlement yielded seals with geometric patterns compatible with the 'international glyptic style' of the terminal Ubaid period (ibid. 218–220, 239–240, 303, Nos. 491–493, Tables 491–493). The well-known female statuettes of the Ubaid period also appear here (ibid. 242, n. 15).

No evidence for the manufacture or use of metal has been retrieved. Work with organic materials clearly involved textile manufacture (flax, spindle whorls, loomweights) and weaving reed mats. Stone products can be divided into chipped and ground industry and ornaments. Raw materials for chipped industry came from the most diverse sources and while a variety of techniques was applied to flint, obsidian cores were polished in order to increase the efficiency of stone use and then employed for the manufacture of blades and bladelets which were further treated by pressure flaking. Items of ground industry include hoes and grinding stones. The stones used as raw materials were carefully selected and the tools served for relatively long periods of time. A single example of an Ubaid 4 period bead seal may be connected with the 'international glyptic style' (von Wickede 1990, 218–220, 225–227, 303, No. 494, Table 494). On the site see Huot 1983, 1987, 1989, 1991a with ref., 1991b and 1996; Calvet 1987; Vallet 1990.

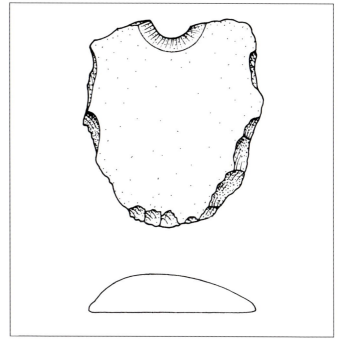

Figure 4.8 A Neolithic ground stone hoe. Hassuna culture, Yarimtepe I (after Munchaev and Merpert 1981, 125, Fig. 36)

Tell Madhhur

A site 140 km north-east of Baghdad, a British excavation of 1977–1981 directed by M. Roaf. C-14 date: 4550–4145 cal. BC (Ubaid – Annex 722). The site's occupation consisted of four Ubaid culture layers and a settlement phase of the Early Dynastic (ED) I–II period comprising a peculiar oval compound, the buildings of which were leaning on its enclosure, with Scarlet Ware and with burials equipped with bronze tools and weapons, carnelian and lapis lazuli beads and a shell-shaped cosmetic container, as well as (in one case) two equid bodies. The whole sequence was capped with an Islamic layer. Of the four Ubaid culture layers, stratum IV yielded a central-hall building with flanking alignments of smaller rooms and stratum III a round pisé construction. The most remarkable feature of the site is an unusually well-preserved and carefully excavated tripartite central-hall building in stratum II which will be considered in detail here as it offers exceptionally valuable information on the functioning of Chalcolithic structures of this type.

Plentiful palaeoecological evidence has clearly been obtained but I have not managed to find published results. The main crop seems to have been six-row hulled barley and the inhabitants presumably kept domestic animals. The building itself, the walls of which were preserved at some

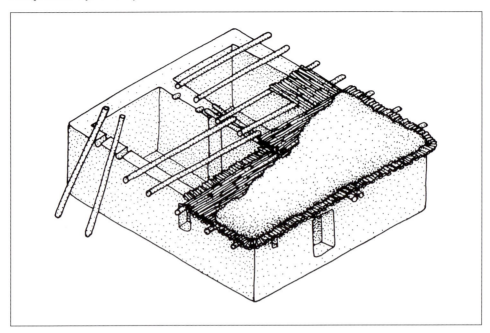

Figure 4.9 Reconstruction of a Neolithic house. Hassuna culture, the site of Hajji Firuz (after Voigt 1997, 459)

spots to a height of *c*.2 m and which might have originally reached 3.5 m in height, was built of unbaked bricks laid directly on the subsoil surface and had simple trampled floors. The ceilings which once probably covered all the house rooms, including the central hall, were constructed of timber baulks bearing reed matting and covered by insulating layers of clay. In this case it seems likely that the roof was accessible by means of a staircase in the south-west parts of the house (a plan in Roaf 1989, 93, Fig. 1, rooms 4 and 5) and that a number of finds remained there, at the very least the large quantity of clay spheroid objects usually identified as slingshot (of which some 4,000 items, weighing together *c*.196 kg, were found in the house). The interior of the structure contained three hearths, likely to represent the foci of domestic activities. One of these was in the west part of the central hall and the other two were situated in rooms 13 (north-east part) and 17 (south-east part). Together with the spatial distribution of a number of various finds (see p. 57) and with the communication layouts, the existence of the latter two hearths strongly suggests that room series 11–13–14 (north-east part) and 6–17–16 (south-east part) constituted two kitchen suites at the farthest end of the house (from the entrance). The west end of the central hall contained a hearth with a number of accompanying finds implying domestic activities, but such features were entirely absent from the hall's east end which, in its turn, yielded fragments of red-painted plaster. Door sockets, implying more solid door construction, turned up in the west half of the building, in the entrance vestibule 9 and in room 3, facing the vestibule across the central hall. The presence of a solid gate in the entrance vestibule presents no surprise but the question of room 3 is more complex. I do not exclude the possibility of a granary.

The house yielded the usual categories of small finds. Bone was used to make awls and spatulae. Clay offered material for the manufacture of pottery, spindle whorls, mullers, unbaked clay vessels, tokens, clay hearths and the above-mentioned slingshot. No evidence for the production or use of metal is reported. Work with organic matter is represented for the spheres of textile production (spindle whorls) and weaving of reed mats. Stone was employed for chipped and ground tools. Of the ground items, hoes, perforated spheres, hammers, palettes, grindstones, pestles and pounders have been recorded. Most chipped items assumed the form of blade sections, probably from sickles. Chert, flint and obsidian served as raw materials and floor finds consisted of 56 per cent chert/flint items and 35 per cent obsidian ones.

I believe that the most fascinating aspect of Tell Madhhur is constituted by the possibility of reconstruction of the internal activities at the local Ubaid culture house, however hypothetical this may seem. The 'kitchen suites' 11–13–14 and 6–17–16 obviously included rooms in which the necessary pottery was stacked, or pantries (Nos. 6 and 11, Roaf 1989, 121, Figs 13 and 14). Both of them contained common kitchenware pots and larger vessels, presumably storage jars. In addition to the numerous pottery finds the domestic functions of both suites are borne out by higher frequencies or sole instances of such finds as unbaked clay vessels, hearth accessories, spindle whorls, mullers and bone spatulae (Roaf 1989, 125, Fig. 15) and grinding stones (ibid. 129, Fig. 17). The character of these two room groupings is apparently shared by the west end of the central hall, where most of the above-mentioned find categories, except a few clay tokens which turn up only here, cluster around a hearth. I think that their absence from the east end of the central hall, with very few finds but with fragments of red-painted plaster, is meaningful and that an assumption of other than everyday subsistence activities for this area seems legitimate. A different function may be ascribed to rooms 9 and 10 (north-west part of the house) and 3 (south-west part, facing the former two rooms across the hall). As the entrance vestibule, room 9 had hardly any private functions but the absence or lower frequency of average finds from rooms 3 and 10 may carry some significance. Both rooms contained larger quantities of seeds (Roaf 1989, 133, Fig. 19). Unlike the animal bones that litter the floors of all house rooms, seed remains are not found in the 'kitchen suites' but turn up in addition to the two above-mentioned rooms, in the entrance vestibule 9 and in the staircase rooms 4–5. In the latter case, we cannot help imagining the family carrying the harvested crops to the roof to be dried there (and to be protected from birds, as the slingshot concentration shows) and back to the storage rooms 3 and 10. If this interpretation is correct, the house once had at least three 'feux', or kitchen foci, a 'holy area' (eastern half of the central hall) and two storage spaces, not counting the entrance vestibule. Such a differentiation finds an illuminating, though very remote, parallel in medieval Sicily, the rural houses of which similarly consisted of 'circulation zones', where food was cooked and eaten and most of the everyday domestic tasks performed, and of 'quiet zones', serving both for storage of the more precious possessions of the family and for sleeping (F. Piponnier, in Pesez 1984, 584–614, esp. pp. 604–605; B. Maccari-Poisson, ibid. pp. 447–450). In this vision the Tell Madhhur house would have sheltered two fully developed production-consumption units with their activity areas and quiet zones (rooms 10 and 11–13–14 in the north wing and 3 cum 6–17–16 in the south wing). The hall would have housed a third production-consumption unit deprived of its quiet zone (sleeping and storage) but carrying out special or ritual(?) functions (red-painted plaster, clay counters). Together with the communication spaces, including the entrance vestibule 9, staircase room 4–5 and the roof area, this interpretation could account for the functions of all rooms of the Madhhur house (Roaf 1989 with ref.).

INTERPRETATION

Economy

The economy of the Chalcolithic period, dominated by the Halaf (see Breniquet 1996; Copeland and Hours 1987; Watkins and Campbell 1987; and von Wickede 1986, 10, Fig. 1 for its diffusion sphere) and Ubaid cultures (Henrickson and Thuesen 1989) has been aptly described as the

Figure 4.10 On the outskirts of the modern city of Beirut, the estuary of the Nahr el-Kelb river into the Mediterranean sea has been opened up to modern traffic. In ancient times this was the spot at which many rulers of historical Mesopotamia terminated their military campaigns, 'washing their weapons in the sea' as a gesture of their victory over the waves of the abode of waters. Prehistoric Mesopotamians nonetheless maintained contact with the Mediterranean littoral regions from the Neolithic onwards.

outcome of the 'second Neolithic revolution' (Sherratt 1980b, 1983; see also Moore 1983). After the Neolithic phase of the 'broad-spectrum economy' in which intensive agriculture constituted no more than one of the possible subsistence strategies applied when and where the individual communities deemed it worthwhile, the Chalcolithic period saw systematic exploitation of all the Neolithic inventions and discoveries and their integration into a set of coherent economic approaches to the environment, exploiting with increasing efficiency and sophistication the whole range of natural resources available in the territories of individual human communities, ultimately enlarging the volume of production to such an extent that regular exchange among various human groups became practicable, even over very long distances. These profound changes worked together with a factor of which the consequences for civilized human life can hardly be overestimated – sedentarization of human settlement, the origins of which are, with a fair degree of probability, to be sought in this period, as I shall argue below.

The range of cereal cultigens, current in the Chalcolithic age, became more or less stabilized and constant. In its most complete sample groups it consisted of emmer (*Triticum dicoccum*), einkorn (*T. monococcum*) and bread wheat (*T. aestivum* and its various sub-forms), the majority barleys of the six-row (*Hordeum vulgare*) and two-row varieties (*H. distichum*), both hulled and naked, as well as lentils, vetch and vetchling (Hole and Flannery 1967, 184; Hole, Flannery and Neely 1969, 354ff.; Helbaek 1972, 45; Hijara *et al.* 1980, 154; Breniquet 1990, 80–81; 1996, 59–60, 75). A similar proportion of cultigens characterizes palaeoecological finds from contemporary sites of Mesopotamia (vicinity of Ur and Eridu: Wright and Pollock 1986,

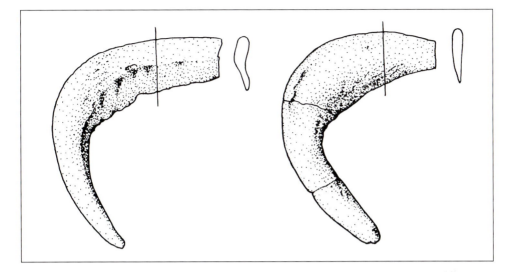

Figure 4.11 Chalcolithic sickles of burnt clay. Ubaid to Uruk age (fifth–fourth millennium BC), from Uruk (after Kohlmeyer and Hauser 1994)

319f.; Yarimtepe II: Munchaev and Merpert 1981, 290, Table 4 and 297), Iran (Tepe Farukhabad: Wright *et al.* 1981, 181, see also Neely, Wright *et al.* 1994, 167–172; Tepe Yahya V: Tosi 1976) and Syria (Hammam et-Turkman: van Loon 1985, 40; 1988, 582). Imprints of cereal grains of comparable composition on Ubaid culture pottery from Ur are accompanied by those of flax seeds, implying by their sizes artificial irrigation (Helbaek 1960, 192, 195; Oates and Oates 1976, 109, 117). Channels conveying water to the fields probably constituted an integral component of Chalcolithic cultural landscapes. In southern Mesopotamia, Wright and Pollock (1986, 319) estimate their maximum lengths at 5 km and actual examples have been excavated on very rare occasions (Tell Abu Husaini: Invernizzi 1980, 41). However, large-scale employment of irrigation must have launched Chalcolithic peasants into the vicious circle resulting from conflict with the eternal adversary of irrigation agriculture, salinization of arable soil (in general see Gibson 1974, but see van Zeist and Bottema 1999, 30–31). Indeed, palaeoecological evidence from contemporary Iran has been interpreted in this sense (Tepe Sabz: Hole, Flannery and Neely 1969, 364, see also Wright *et al.* 1981, 232). Needless to say, this danger was absent from the submontane zone above the 200-mm isohyet where agriculture without irrigation presented no special problems (see in general Weiss 1983, 39–41; Tell Abu Husaini: Tusa 1984, 275). In parts of Mesopotamia the practice of intensive agriculture might have led to substantial population, or rather settlement growth, parallel to developments occurring under similar conditions in contemporary south-western Iran (Deh Luran: Hole, Flannery and Neely 1969, 369–371) or Palestine (Moore 1983, esp. p. 100). Nevertheless, irrigation agriculture is likely to have led to extensive rather than intensive growth of cereal-growing, as under normal conditions one half of irrigated arable must lie fallow to divert the salinization threat (Gibson 1974); the discovery of this agricultural risk and provision of the means to cope with it must also lie in a period close to the first large-scale employment of irrigation agriculture. At any rate, the efforts needed in intensive cerealiculture, especially for channel building and maintenance, would have worked as an adverse factor against the traditional mobility of human groups.

Some figures that enable closer assessment of Chalcolithic agriculture have been published. Six hectares of irrigated fields, of which one half lies fallow, would, producing a harvest of *c.*1,500 kilos of grain (intense irrigation can push this up to 3,000 kilos), support a family of six. Using the plough will bring this figure up to 1.5 hectares per person. Rain-fed agriculture will bring forth about 630 kilos of wheat and 410 kilos of barley per hectare; the use of irrigation will increase these figures to 1,100 and 1,150 kg respectively (Lupton 1996, 109, nn. 32 and 33).

As to the dislocation of arable, a concentration of Ubaid period chipped-hoe finds in the north-west quarter of the city of Uruk could represent the location of fields vis-à-vis the contemporary settlement core, lying more to the south (Eichmann 1991, 178–179 and Table 237a on pp. 274–275). The matter, however, is far from clear.

A feature that constitutes a strong argument for Chalcolithic sedentarization is without any doubt the first evidence for horticulture coming from this period (Zohary and Hopf 1988, 212–213). Doubts have been cast on the Palestinian evidence (Liphschitz *et al.* 1991) but the Ubaid culture peasants of south-east Mesopotamia undoubtedly planted the first date-palm orchards (Wright and Pollock 1986, 319; see Tell Awayli, pp. 53–54). The fifth pre-Christian millennium is now believed to have witnessed the first cultivation of vines (Fagan 1991, 16).

In comparison with the preceding period the collection of wild plant food seems to have decreased in importance. From this period on such fruit as almonds and pistachio nuts reached only sites situated closer to submontane and montane zones (Tepe Sabz: Helbaek 1972, 45; Tepe Yahya: Tosi 1976). In Mesopotamia the Halaf and Ubaid culture communities probably lived in semi-arid steppes, woodland steppes and foothill zones (Watkins and Campbell 1987, 453–454) and seem to have relied primarily on self-produced food. The question of how far this exclusion from the exploitation of reserves of montane zones resulted from the occupation of spacious and well-drained valley bottoms of the mountain ranges by resident populations, as was the case in Iran (Smith-Young 1983), remains to be answered by future research.

In the sphere of animal husbandry (Clutton-Brock 1980; Meadow 1992; Ovadia 1992; Breniquet 1996, 61–62) the range of domestic animals did not expand but changes, apparently significant from the socio-economic viewpoint, took place. Animals domesticated by man included sheep, goat, cattle, pig and dog (for a summary of the Ubaid period evidence see Pollock 1999, 83, Table 4.1). Chalcolithic sheep tend to prevail numerically over goats (Hole, Flannery and Neely 1969, 265, 369–371) and evidence for long-distance sheep transfers may imply sheep-and-goat nomadic pastoralism (Tell Turlu: Breniquet 1990, 92; 1996, 66 – contact between herds pastured in the Taurus and Zagros). Two further points merit our attention. The first of these is the increasing significance of pigs as an indicator of differences in lifestyle (see in general Flannery 1983; Meadow 1992, 263–264). This change occurred in the course of the Halaf culture period and may be followed both in northern sites such as Arpachiyah (increasing representation of pigs from Hijara's layer XI or X, Hijara *et al.* 1980, 152) or Yarimtepe II (Munchaev and Merpert 1981, 301–302) and in southern ones (Tell Awayli, see pp. 53–54), as well as outside Mesopotamia (Tell Sabi Abyad, Syria: see the references in Breniquet 1990, 84 and 1996, 61, accompanied by a decrease in cattle numbers). This is important because pigs do not tolerate the nomadic way of life (Flannery 1983, 183) and their proliferation on archaeological sites probably indicates sedentarization. The slaughter age of the pigs, frequently below 1 year (Yarimtepe II, Tell Awayli, Tell Arpachiyah) implies that pigs constituted a meat source. The other phenomenon peculiar to Chalcolithic cultures is the marked presence of cattle on some sites, especially those of lowland character such as Eridu (Flannery and Wright 1966; Meadow 1971, 141f.), Tell Awayli (see pp. 53–54) and Ras al-Amiya by Nippur (Flannery and Cornwall 1969; Stronach 1982, 39). The same feature has been observed in the north (e.g. Tell Abu Husaini: Tusa 1984, 275) and of exceptional interest is the fact that at Arpachiyah, I. Hijara has registered an increase in cattle bones from his layer VII, but in an area outside the fortified enclosure this was accompanied by a decreasing proportion of sheep and goats. This fact, and the palaeozoological observation that most Chalcolithic cattle had reached a mature age before slaughter converge to indicate that these animals were perceived as more permanent sources of food. In view of subsequent developments, especially of the first occurrence of ploughs and carts in the immediately following Uruk culture script, the idea that the increasing proportion of cattle among Chalcolithic animal remains reflects the more urgently felt need for an alternative energy source, especially for traction (and carrying) power, as well as for the cattle's contribution to the ancient diet in the form of milk and milk products, comes to mind quite naturally. Indeed, plough marks have been registered on the KS-102 site in Iranian Khuzestan dating to the Susa A, or Ubaid 4, period (Wright, Miller and Redding 1980, 275). An alternative explanation would envisage the exploitation of cattle for long-distance transport as beasts of burden (Ovadia 1992, 26–27). The fact that Chalcolithic cultures display a visibly greater amount of interconnection and mutual contact than the preceding periods is undeniable. The growing importance of cattle seems to have been confined to Mesopotamian plains as the neighbouring communities of present-day Iran (Deh Luran plain: Flannery and Cornwall 1969, 436) indicate far less spectacular rises. Much as in the cereal-growing sphere, Chalcolithic animal husbandry indicates the development of specialization, professionalization and increasing labour inputs. One of the buildings excavated at Tell Abada (Jasim 1989, 80, Fig. 2 – layer II building I, discussion on pp. 83–85) very strongly suggests – by its situation at the settlement edge, by an alignment of shallow rectangular brick basins 70–80 cm high and containing reeds, straw and grain (a manger?), by a bitumen-lined basin (for watering?) and by a layer of black organic character covering its courtyard – an interpretation in terms of a communal sheepfold or cattle pen. Results of a surface survey in northern Iraq (Oates 1980, 308) suggest animal-husbandry activities specialized on a regional level. This idea may be supported by palynological data from north-west Syria (van Zeist and Woldring 1980, esp. p. 120), indicating that the first human interferences with the local floral, starting around 4000 BC, imply assarting activities accompanied by specialized horticulture as well as cattle-keeping. It should be pointed out that the exercise of agriculture and larger-scale animal husbandry within one and the

Figure 4.12 A Chalcolithic painted bowl. Halaf culture (sixth–fifth millennium BC), the site of Tell Brak (after von Wickede 1986, 20, Fig. 18)

Figure 4.13 A Chalcolithic painted bowl. Halaf culture, the site of Tell Halaf (after von Wickede 1986, 21, Fig. 21)

same agricultural area is by no means excluded and belonged to the salient features of pre-industrial Near Eastern communities as far back as the pre-Islamic era at the very latest (see Macdonald 1992, esp. pp. 9–10). The trends of professionalization and intensification of particular subsistence activities must thus have also led towards a more complex community organization, seeking to harmonize activities of the various subsistence groups in a manner that would favour the least harmful way of coexistence possible.

The sphere of animal husbandry, remaining within the traditional range of domestic animals, thus seems to reflect two important trends. One of these, sedentarization of human communities, is indicated by the increasing proportion of pig remains in palaeozoological evidence. The other, probably expressing a trend of more general character, shows an attempt to procure additional energy inputs, especially in the form of animals as suppliers of traction (and/or carrying?) power and of major dietary contributions. Animal-husbandry activities show a growing measure of professionalization.

An interesting sidelight on Chalcolithic specialization of subsistence activities dependent on geographical factors may be seen in evidence for hunting, fishing and food collection. These activities clearly occupied an important position in riverine or lacustrine landscapes that abounded in wildlife resources. Such Sumerian sites as Ras al-Amiya (Flannery and Cornwall 1969, 437; Stronach 1982, 39), Eridu (Flannery and Wright 1966, 61) or Ubaid culture Tell Uqair (Lloyd and Safar 1943, 149), as well as the Jebel Hamrin site of Tell Abada (Pollock 1999, 82 and 83, Table 4.1) all show evidence for hunting gazelle, onager and wild boar and for collection of freshwater molluscs (for southern Mesopotamia in general see Wright and Pollock 1986, 319f.). A most welcome addition to our information on this sphere of Chalcolithic economy is represented by the results of the excavations at Shams ed-Din Tannira, a Halaf culture site in northern Syria (Uerpmann 1982). Animal bones found at this site fell into the following groups: unidentified cases (19.33 per cent), domestic (34.43 per cent) and wild species (43.92 per cent). The domestic animal sample consists of roughly equal amounts of ovicaprid and cattle bones with admixtures of dog and goat remains. Most of the wild animal remnants belong to onager (53.20 per cent), the rest being made up of a rather varied array of such game as wild boar, buffalo, various kinds of deer, gazelle, fox, wild cat and birds (stork) and a single river shell. The inhabitants of this site, who must have been specialized hunters keeping domestic animals (or acquiring them from nomadic groups?) as a supplementary food source, probably frequented humid reed-covered areas, riverside woods but also steppes or half-desert. At another site of similar character, Khirbet esh-Shenef in the Balikh-river valley (Weiss 1991, 690–691), remains of domestic animals consisted of a majority of goats accompanied by somewhat fewer pigs and cattle but some 36 per cent of the overall count belonged to hunted species such as onager and, less so, gazelle. Another site of similar character has been at least hinted at (Weiss 1991, 690, n. 23). On the other hand, plain dwellers did hunt gazelle and sometimes even onager or fish but the prominence of this activity fell much below that of the riverine sites. The cases in point are Arpachiyah (Hijara *et al.* 1980, 152f.), Yarimtepe II (Munchaev and Merpert 1981, 304), Tell Abu Husaini (Tusa 1984, 276), the Deh Luran plain sites (Hole and Flannery 1967, 184; Hole, Flannery and Neely 1969, 265) and Tepe Yahya (Tosi 1976, 174). The last two cases also display a marked avoidance of wildfowl and aquatic foods, even if these had been consumed previously in the Deh Luran plain sites. On the other hand, hunting might have acquired some social prominence in the non-riverine communities. We owe to Henry T. Wright (Wright *et al.* 1981, 66) the observation that at contemporary Tepe Farukhabad in the Deh Luran plain, more prominent architectures tended to attract gazelle remains as well as conical beakers, presumably indicating more elaborate table manners and therefore increased status of inhabitants of such structures.

Average housing was accompanied by remains of equids, sheep and goats. A similar proposition, seeing in hunting activities a non-economic pursuit (for symbolic or training purposes?), has been advanced by Pierre Ducos (see Breniquet 1996, 62). Origins of the symbolical dimension of the Assyrian royal hunt (Wiggermann 1996, 219–220) may perhaps be sought in this remote age.

Thus it follows that the major trends of specialization and professionalization did not bypass the sphere of exploitation of wildlife resources. Inhabitants of whole sites specialized in hunting activities but even in cases where hunting represented only a component of the whole range of subsistence activities the most abundant and most easily accessible sources were usually exploited. In riverine/lacustrine areas the hunters targeted the resources of the watercourses themselves and the game of the adjacent ecological niches. In plain or submontane sites the traditional collective hunting techniques retained their importance, contributing perhaps even to incipient social differentiation, possibly in relation to personal skill and

Figure 4.14 A Chalcolithic painted bowl. Halaf culture, the site of Tell Arpachiyah (after von Wickede 1986, 20, Fig. 17)

Figure 4.15 A Chalcolithic painted bowl. Halaf culture, the site of Tepe Gawra (after von Wickede 1986, 20, Fig. 19)

achievement (or in consequence of the organizational duties of community leaders?).

By way of a conclusion of this brief sketch of Chalcolithic agriculture let us summarize the main points again. In comparison with the creative Neolithic the Chalcolithic performance lacks originality. Its strength, however, rests on two pillars: diffusion of Neolithic discoveries and inventions throughout the whole *oikoumene* and increasing professionalization and specialization, resulting in an inevitable economic intensification. Most of the cereal cultigens and domestic animals, as well as such sophisticated procedures as field irrigation, now circulated widely among Chalcolithic communities. Settlement sedentarization certainly occurred (horticulture, pig-keeping) but we are hard put to decide which came first, sedentarization or intensification. Sedentarization of human communities places an extraordinary strain on their environment, the carrying capacity of which is stretched to the utmost, while its maintenance requires special measures in order to support the human group in question permanently, without any chance at restitution of pristine natural conditions. On the other hand, intensive sedentary agriculture brings in considerably higher energy returns, estimated at about five times as much as shifting agriculture, with comparable working times (Peoples and Bailey 1988, 161, Box 82). Here it may be significant that the earliest evidence for sedentary communities comes from the southern Sumerian sites which must have enjoyed abundant and untouched resources, living in an environment with unusually strong faculties of recovery after human interference (pigs and orchards at Tell Awayli from Ubaid 0; on sedentarism in naturally rich landscapes: Bruce Dickson 1990, 186, 188). In the north, sedentarization seems to have lasted longer and involved special measures for harnessing more energy. The increase in pig quantity at Arpachiyah happened only after some time had elapsed since its foundation, and growth of the representation of cattle, a potential food and energy source, took place later still. At Yarimtepe II the local inhabitants slaughtered and ate a substantial amount of young cattle regardless of the disadvantages which their contemporaries elsewhere did not fail to perceive. Once achieved, sedentarization offers the best conditions for the full exploitation of the economic potential of the respective ecological niches and for the application of subsistence strategies most appropriate for the procurement of an optimum amount of comestibles without incurring irreparable damage to the natural recovery faculties of the environment. This, at least, seems to have happened in the Chalcolithic with its systematic tapping of whatever natural resources were available by means of increasing expertise and professionalization. Present evidence implies that the origins of large-scale agricultural specialization and the emergence of groups of peasants, cattle-herders and hunters from the initial indistinct mass of mixed-agriculturalists-cum-herders-cum-food-gatherers are to be sought in the Chalcolithic. What was happening at Neolithic Umm Dabaghiyah within one single community took place in the entire sphere of Chalcolithic Halaf culture.

In the sphere of processing natural resources the Chalcolithic period witnessed the introduction or initial diffusion of fundamentally new technologies in most production branches that may be investigated archaeologically. These changes, although sometimes applied on small scale only, opened the way for the seemingly enormous technological 'leap' of the following Uruk culture period.

Among the artificial materials, faience now moved in to occupy a position of ever-growing importance. Faience pendants and seals, mostly green (see the green head of a Tell Hassuna statuette from the Neolithic, p. 7) and blue, turned up at both Arpachiyah and Gawra, at the Ur Ubaid culture cemetery and at Eridu XI and VII (Moorey 1985, 142). Mesopotamian craft specialists had known about and applied glazing of various materials since at least Ubaid 3 times (ibid. 137–138). Although bitumen served human groups from at least the seventh pre-Christian millennium, Chalcolithic craftsmen and craftswomen reached a considerable degree of sophistication in its treatment, including refinement (Marschner and Wright 1978, 169–170; Connan and Ourisson 1993). Only bone remained untouched by the new inventions, supplying, as ever, a material for the production of awls, spatulae and occasional whistles (Tepe Gawra). Chalcolithic masters reached an unparalleled degree of perfection in working with clay, from which they made the most exquisitely decorated pottery of the entire prehistoric Near East, embodying one of the peak achievements of the potter's craft in human history. Halaf culture pottery was fashioned by hand but very carefully treated and painted with colours rich in kalium and iron (illite clays), poor in calcite and very finely levigated (Figures 4.16–4.19). Original patterns used red and black colours; slips and whitewash appeared in Late Halaf times so that true polychromy emerged only at Arpachiyah TT 6 (von Wickede 1986, 8–9). Also, some Late Halaf Arpachiyah patterns show clear antecedents in the Hajji Muhammad (= Ubaid 2) culture of the south (ibid. 32). Ornamentation of Halaf pottery possesses the same character and shows the same chronological developments throughout the whole Halaf culture diffusion sphere (von Wickede 1986, 27–30, see also Campbell 1986). The main principle of Halaf pottery decorative patterns, distinct from both the preceding Hassuna and Samarra cultures and from the (partly) later Ubaid culture, has been defined as bilaterality or axial symmetry (von Wickede 1986, 30). In general, however, Halaf and Hajji Muhammad-style painted pottery seem to constitute two responses to the initial impulse likely to have emanated from the Samarra culture style (von Wickede 1986, 31–32). The Halaf pots were fired at a temperature not much higher than 950 degrees centigrade (ibid. 8) and the

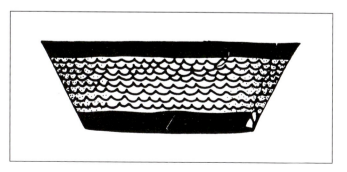

Figure 4.16 A Chalcolithic painted bowl. Halaf culture, the site of Tell Arpachiyah (after von Wickede 1986, 21, Fig. 22)

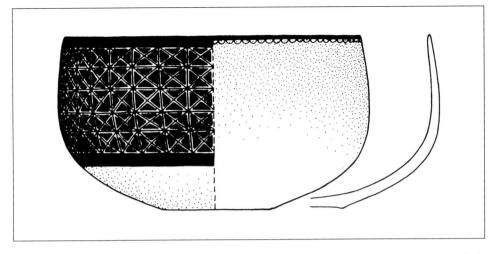

Figure 4.17 A Chalcolithic painted bowl. Halaf culture, the site of Tell Arpachiyah (after von Wickede 1986, 23, Fig. 31)

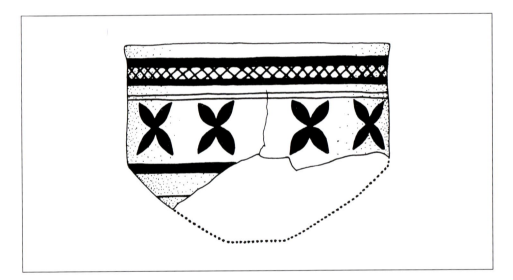

Figure 4.18 A Chalcolithic painted bowl. Halaf culture, the site of Chagar Bazar (after von Wickede 1986, 22, Fig. 29)

potters used technically advanced two-compartment vertical-updraught kilns of which the first safely identified examples may date to this period of time (Alizadeh 1985), though an earlier dating is not excluded (Yarimtepe I, see p. 19). Similar characteristics and a matching cultural homogeneity have been asserted at least for some regional groupings of Ubaid culture pottery (Wright and Pollock 1986, 324f.; on Ubaid pottery see also Wilkinson *et al.* 1996, esp. pp. 29–40). Ubaid culture potters gradually acquired a higher degree of professional skill so that by Ubaid 4 times they were able to fire their products at temperatures between 1,050 and 1,200 degrees centigrade (Tell Awayli, see p. 54). A. von Wickede (1986, 30) has observed that the main principle underlying Ubaid culture ornamentation is different from that of the Halaf sphere and has defined it as 'Gleitspiegelung' (roughly 'mirror image'). Ubaid culture potters were the first to turn out their products en masse. Of the 4 m thick sherd deposit that may be termed the 'Great sherd dump' at Ur, the lowermost 2.5 m represent an accumulation of Ubaid culture fragments (Woolley 1955, 28). The technical perfection of Ubaid culture potters enabled them to supply some clay products which could replace those parts of the contemporary tool kit that were presumably more difficult to procure or which simply did

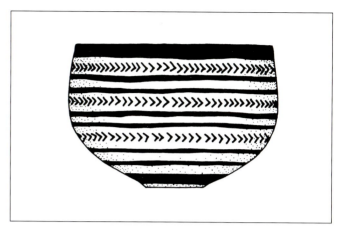

Figure 4.19 A Chalcolithic painted bowl. Halaf culture, the site of Chagar Bazar (after von Wickede 1986, 22, Fig. 30)

the same service at a tolerable quality of the result. This pertains first and foremost to clay sickles (Figures 4.11, 4.20), current from Ubaid 2 to Uruk times (Wright and Pollock 1986, 317) and quite definitely used to work with (Moorey 1982b, 19) and to the mullers or 'bent nails', probably employed for crushing softer materials. Both tool types occur throughout all settlements in southern Mesopotamia (Wright and Pollock 1986, 321). Relationships between Halaf and Ubaid culture pottery are difficult to assess. The C-14 dates indicate that both cultures must have lived together at least for some time, as those of Halaf culture sites cluster in the interval 5500–4000 BC (Watkins and Campbell 1987, 461, Fig. 1), the Ubaid datings falling between 4500 and 3500 BC (ibid. 462, Fig. 2). The respective communities must thus have run into each other and some information relevant to this aspect has been supplied by modern neutron-activation analyses (NAA) of Halaf and Ubaid period pottery (Davidson and McKerrel 1976, 1980). At Arpachiyah, for instance, Ubaid culture pottery was made of different clay than the Halaf products (Davidson and McKerrel 1980, 157) but at Tepe Gawra one single clay source served indiscriminately during the Halaf and Ubaid culture periods (ibid. 161). The extinction of Ubaid period Tell Arpachiyah as a supplier of fine tableware is indicated by the fact that no imports from Arpachiyah have been identified at Ubaid period Tepe Gawra, though some Arpachiyah vessels reached Tepe Gawra in Halaf times (ibid. 164). At least one Halaf sherd from the site of Kharabeh Shattani approximates in its composition those of Arpachiyah (Campbell 1986, 57–62, esp. p. 61, No. KS-20). Ubaid-style pottery thus constitutes a phenomenon differing from Halaf-style pottery culturally, not technologically, let alone ethnically; it was different because its manufacturers and users wished it so. Finally, it should be noted that the Ubaid-style pottery ornamentation as well as the growing technological sophistication of pottery production expanded beyond the frontiers of Mesopotamia (for Hammam et-Turkman in Syria see van Loon 1985, 42; Akkermans 1988, 128–129).

Progress may be registered in the sphere of metallurgy as well, though Mesopotamian products of this time can hardly rival the splendid achievements of contemporary Iranian coppersmiths (Moorey 1982a, 83–85). The somewhat sceptical assessments of the 1980s (Moorey 1982a, 1985), pointing to the paucity of the available evidence, nevertheless conceded to Chalcolithic metallurgists at least the continuous use of lead (Moorey 1985, 122) and the introduction of gold (the Ubaid culture cemetery of Ur: ibid. 76). Recent analyses do not deny the scarcity of

Figure 4.20 These Ubaid culture sickles of baked clay, found on the surface of a southern Mesopotamian archaeological site, have fused together because of the excessive heat of the potter's kiln in which they were fired. The fusing shows that the firing temperature must have reached about 1,000 degrees. This, in turn, points to the high level of Ubaid age pyrotechnology and know-how applied by Ubaid age potters.

information, but point to the fact that arsenic bronze of copper, which was to dominate Mesopotamian metallurgy for at least a millennium to come, first appeared in the upper Euphrates area in the Ubaid period (Müller-Karpe 1991, 110). The same author sees in the high technological level of Uruk period metallurgy and especially toreutics a strong argument for a long production tradition likely to reach back into the period under discussion (Müller-Karpe 1990a, 161). The fact that some sophistication of the Ubaid period metallurgical production may be expected follows from the observation that for the first time stonecutters of the period successfully attacked materials of Mohs's hardness scale 4–7; this is most likely to have happened with the aid of metal tools (see p. 70). Last but not least, we owe to M. Müller-Karpe (1990b, 192) the ingenious suggestion that the enigmatic clay models of Ubaid culture metal tools (Moorey 1982b, 19; 1985, 23) could be master versions for the production of models for lost-wax casting. As to gold, it appeared in the other areas of the Fertile Crescent roughly at the same time (Palestine, for instance: Wolff 1991, 498–499 for the Nahal Kana cave) and the Mesopotamians were thus not late in the employment of new natural resources. This must reflect a deliberate search for information as south-east Mesopotamia, where the Ubaid gold comes from, is hardly a place where findspots of such exotic materials would have been common knowledge.

Progress in work with organic materials may be measured only with difficulty given the perishable nature of the evidence. In addition to the ubiquitous and traditional reed matting we have at least some hints at developments in this sphere. The Deh Luran plain sites demonstrate that this period saw the introduction of coiled basketry replacing the earlier plaited work (Hole,

Flannery and Neely 1969, 220; in Anatolia the sequence is reversed). Making of finer cords is attested to by imprints in Halaf culture sealings from Arpachiyah (Charvát 1994, 10) and Tepe Gawra (von Wickede 1990, 99, 288, No. 80, Table 80). If the excavators of Tell Awayli identify the loomweights from their site correctly, this is the first moment in history when the weaving loom, representing a fairly sophisticated machine, appears on the archaeological horizon. Weaving activities might have acquired an important symbolic meaning (Ippolitoni-Strika 1996; on the symbolic meaning of human clothing see Shupak 1992). Only occasionally do minor art monuments allow us to catch a glimpse of contemporary dress fashions, such as a statuette from Awayli showing a skirt held on to the body by straps worn across the shoulders and crossed between the breasts and on the back (Forest 1996, 80, Pl. 24, lower register).

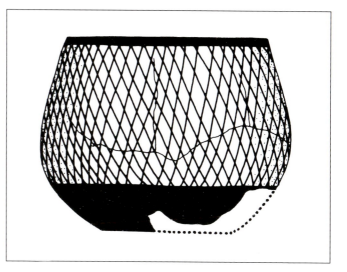

Figure 4.21 A Chalcolithic painted cup. Halaf culture, the site of Chagar Bazar (after von Wickede 1986, 23, Fig. 32)

Let us finally glance at developments in stone working. The best recently published sample is probably that of the Syrian site of Shams ed-Din Tannira (Azoury and Bergman 1980). Of its 4,207 chipped industry items most are cores or half-products and retouched tools make up no more than 18 per cent of the whole assemblage. Chert served as the most frequent material, obsidian making up 11 per cent of the total. The tool types

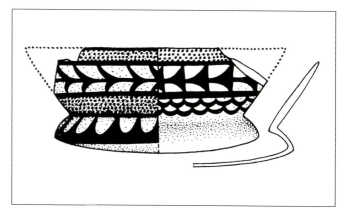

Figure 4.22 A Chalcolithic painted jar. Halaf culture, the site of Tell Arpachiyah (after von Wickede 1986, 23, Fig. 37)

present include scrapers, borers, burins, truncations, denticulates, notches, sickle elements and retouched blades. Chert blades were separated by percussion, obsidian ones perhaps by pressure flaking. Absence of obsidian cores and raw obsidian indicates that implements made of this material arrived at the site as finished products processed elsewhere. Nevertheless, the abundance and variability of chipped industry from this site, where the hunters undoubtedly required a tool kit different from that of peasants or shepherds, is somewhat exceptional. The general trend, manifested especially in lowland sites, points in the direction of impoverishment both of the quantity of tool types and of the quality of stone working (a case in point being the Deh Luran sites: Hole, Flannery and Neely 1969, 74–81, 356). Technological process is nonetheless perceptible. First and foremost, the degree of specialization and professionalization in stone working is illuminated

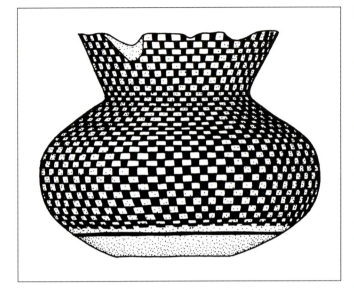

Figure 4.23 A Chalcolithic painted jar. Halaf culture, the site of Tell Arpachiyah (after von Wickede 1986, 24, Fig. 42)

Figure 4.24 A Chalcolithic painted jar. Halaf culture, the site of Tell Arpachiyah (after von Wickede 1986, 25, Fig. 48)

by hoard finds of raw materials (Tell Abu Husaini, Ubaid culture: Tusa 1984, 275). Second, some of the specialized procedures of chipped industry production, most frequent in the mining or primary-treatment sites, now ceased to be a monopoly of the highland dwellers and were mastered also by specialists working in the plains. This is the case of pressure flaking on obsidian (Tell Awayli; in general see Inizan 1985). Third, Ubaid period stonecutters evolved for the first time tools sophisticated enough to cope with materials of degrees 4–7 of Mohs's hardness scale; until then the threshold of Mohs 3 had not been crossed (Heimpel, Gorelick and Gwinnett 1988, graph on p. 202; see also Larsen 1991, 60–61, esp. Table 12, p. 61). Incidentally, this fact sheds light on Ubaid period metallurgy as well. Some of the more exotic stone types worked in those times not only bear out the professional skill of master craftsmen and craftswomen but even indicate at least some segments of the supply-line network that once interlinked the Chalcolithic communities. In addition to the well-known lapis lazuli, most likely brought over from Badakhshan, finds of turquoise probably indicate contacts with eastern Iran or central Asia (Ismail and Tosi 1976). Results of specialized analyses suggest that obsidian travelled to Arpachiyah and Eridu from several sources, most probably in eastern Anatolia (Renfrew 1964, 76).

As a conclusion to this section it may now be pointed out that nearly all branches of Chalcolithic craft activities leaving archaeologically retrievable evidence show the amount of attention focused by then on the processing of natural resources, on the development of technology and on specialized know-how. Though not all the innovations and inventions of the period were put to full use immediately, they certainly laid the foundations for the seemingly revolutionary changes of the subsequent period. The specialists of Mesopotamian cultures who learned both by making their own

Figure 4.25 The best Mediterranean ports, like Byblos which may be seen here, facilitated the diffusion of material and immaterial Mesopotamian products over a vast area of the Mediterranean, including the Balkans from which the first bearers of Neolithic cultures – ultimately also of Mesopotamian inspiration – advanced as far as central and north-western Europe.

discoveries and by borrowing from their highland neighbours were now in possession of a store of experience and knowledge which justified great expectations for the future.

Sketchy and incomplete as the evidence for changes in the sphere of transport and communication may be, it does offer a few hints. A trend which I have already mentioned involved the decrease in quantity of imported obsidian, perhaps reflecting more permanent lowland settlement and severing of more or less direct contacts with montane zones (see pp. 34–35 and, for the Deh Luran plain sites, Hole, Flannery and Neely 1969, 74 and 356–357). The plain dwellers either learned the stone-trimming technology themselves, laying great stress on economical handling of the imported obsidian (Tell Awayli) or compensated for the loss of the volcanic glass by procurement of a host of materials which sometimes arrived as finished tools and must thus have been produced elsewhere (e.g. the Ubaid culture site of Tell el-Saadiya: Kozlowski and Bielinski 1984, 106, or contemporary Tepe Farukhabad: Wright *et al.* 1981, passim, for instance 273). Far from having vanished altogether, imported obsidian, much like other stones brought in for the same purpose, took over the role of a status marker both in adornment and in interior furnishings (stone vessels), as is exemplified by the situation at Tepe Gawra XIII–XII. Other stones diagnostic as geographical indicators are the east Iranian turquoise and Baluchi lapis lazuli (see pp. 7, 23 and 51). Extremely limited information on the concrete modalities of overland contacts is available. The essentially uniform stylistic character of both Halaf and Ubaid culture pottery, for instance, does suggest that far-flung contacts, especially along the courses of both twin rivers, must have been fairly frequent. Whether ancient navigators used boats such as those exemplified by models from Eridu (Figure 4.26) or Tell Awayli or some other device such as keleks – rafts borne by a series of

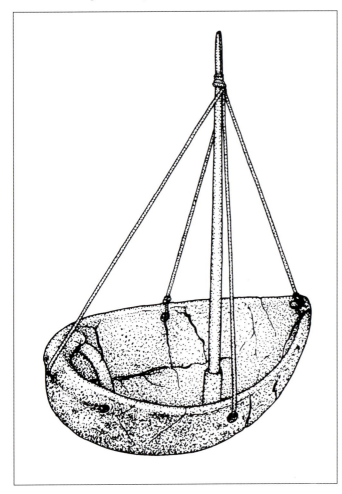

Figure 4.26 A Chalcolithic model of a seagoing ship. Late Ubaid culture, the site of Eridu, cemetery (= layers VII–VI) (after Safar, Mustafa and Lloyd 1981, 227)

inflated animal skins – (on this most recently see Tardieu 1990, 71–102) will be decided by future investigations. Such traffic must have continued far into the Gulf area, as Ubaid culture pottery has been collected from sites on its southern shores reaching a considerable distance into the south-east region (see Potts 1990; Rice 1994; Carter *et al.* 1999, esp. pp. 52–57). Data gathered by NAA analysis of such imports bear out a non-identity among Mesopotamian and Persian Gulf Ubaid-style pottery (Roaf and Galbraith 1994) and this points rather to the exposure of Gulf potters to Ubaid-style models than to direct importation of Mesopotamian pottery. On dry land the increasing representation of cattle remains on Ubaid sites, especially in the southeast, and the signs for waggons and sledges in the script of the immediately following Uruk culture make us suspect the introduction of animal-drawn wheeled transport or the use of cattle as beasts of burden during this time. In short, specialization and professionalization prevailed even in the sphere of Chalcolithic transport and communications. That exchange contacts may span considerable distances even in the conditions of clan societies is amply demonstrated by ethnographic parallels (e.g. Eggert 1991, esp. pp. 22–25).

Exchange of goods is also represented by finds of sealings on clay from a number of sites. The sealings, mostly impressions of different seals but invariably found together at a single findspot, may reflect packing and sealing of the conveyed goods outside the collection station and convergence of the sealed commodities on the 'address point', where the subsequent unsealing of the packages and dumping of mobile containers took place. Only very rarely can we catch a glimpse of the treatment of the goods conveyed at the 'address point' but we have absolutely no information as to whether the senders of the originally despatched goods received something in compensation for their deliveries (as would be normal practice in pre-industrial societies characterized by reciprocity exchange; see, for instance, Morris 1986) or whether the goods amassed at the 'address point' were purely and simply consumed in an act of non-institutionalized redistribution. The Halaf culture Arpachiyah supplied fine pottery not only to Tepe Gawra (Davidson and McKerrel 1980, 161f.), but possibly also to Kharabeh Shattani (Campbell 1986, 57–62 and esp. p. 61, No. KS-20). More and more sites have been yielding Halaf period sealings

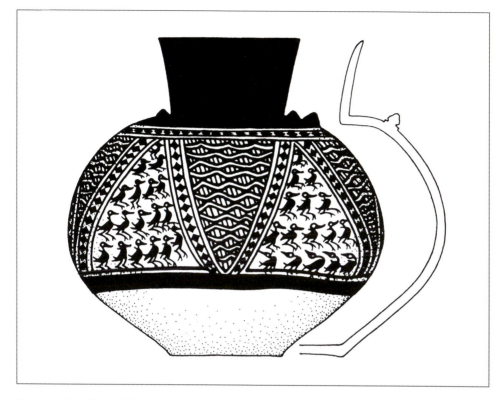

Figure 4.27 A Chalcolithic painted jar. Final phase of the Halaf culture, the site of Tepe Gawra (after Breniquet 1996, 156, Pl. 4: 2)

(see the container sealings of Tell Sabi Abyad: Akkermans 1993 and 1996 and Akkermans and Duistermaat 1997) and the question of how far the circulation of painted pottery and sealed goods were related to each other is gaining importance. The practice of reciprocity is generally compatible with such activities in pre-industrial societies (see Morris 1986) but the whole question is in need of further elucidation (see Charvát 1988a and 1992a and, for the material evidence, von Wickede 1990, 93–238).

All in all, the Chalcolithic economy seems to have been a success, as is borne out, inter alia, by physical-anthropological examination of contemporary human remains where available (Ubaid period cemeteries at Arpachiyah: Mallowan and Linford 1969; Eridu: Vértesalji 1984, 24f.). Though the average age at death oscillated between 20 and 40 years, as is usual in pre-industrial societies, these people had good nutrition and diet. The preponderance of strong young men at Arpachiyah and of adult (20–40-years-old) women at Eridu may reflect differences in the manner of use of these cemetery sites.

In the economic sphere, Chalcolithic communities undoubtedly set forth on a journey towards civilization and statehood. They applied the whole range of Neolithic discoveries and inventions to secure abundant supplies, sometimes at the cost of considerable energy expenditure. Sedentarization, first occurring in the south where the environment offered plentiful food sources, spread northwards where the local communities gradually adopted the new settlement system. Wholesale application of traditional inventions and deliberate efforts at maximization of the energy output (more cattle) must have brought in economic returns considerably surpassing

Figure 4.28 A Chalcolithic painted bowl. Early Ubaid culture (fifth millennium BC), the site of Eridu, layer VIII (after Safar, Mustafa and Lloyd 1981, 156 and 179, Fig. 82: 3)

those of traditional subsistence modes. Of course, this process was necessitated by population growth as a consequence of sedentarization (see p. 76). The amount of attention focused on more efficient exploitation of natural resources is particularly visible in the sphere of arts and crafts where successful innovations and improvements invaded nearly all production branches documentable by archaeology. Finally, the affluent Chalcolithic communities managed to create and maintain a network of regular contacts, sometimes over considerable distances, which served for the cultivation of all-purpose links with human groups far and wide. This exchange, probably assuming the garb of reciprocity or non-institutionalized redistribution (for institutionalized redistribution we will have to wait until the next, Uruk culture period) and providing also economic help in emergency cases, constituted a social linkage of the diversified human communities and enabled the circulation of technological know-how, new ideas and spiritual constructs. There was hardly any aspect of the economy of historical Sumer and Akkad which would not have been present, at least in an embryonic form, in the Chalcolithic age.

Society

Even if there were no unequivocal indications of sedentarization processes in the economic sphere, the massive stratigraphies of a number of sites 'cry out to heaven' to confirm the previous conclusions. By way of example let us review in passing the sixteen layers (themselves representing multiple stratigraphic sequences) of Arpachiyah, Eridu's and Gawra's twenty layers, or the tens of stratigraphic units at Tell

Awayli. Of course this pertains only to major centres around which subsidiary settlements took root, blossomed and withered as time passed by. A case in point is Eridu where the permanent 'temple' centre was at first accompanied by a Hajji Muhammad culture settlement under the Ubaid cemetery (parallel to Temple XVII–XIV). After its extinction a new settlement thrived in the vicinity in Ubaid 3 times ('Hut Sounding', parallel to Temple XII–VI). That even important sites with impressive architecture could have been deserted is shown by the fate of the Ubaid 3 terrace at Tell Awayli. Repeated observations of small size, short duration, minimalized energy expenditure and thinner refuse and especially ashy strata on Halaf culture sites (Hole 1987b, 561; Watkins and Campbell 1987, 453–454; see also Baird, Campbell and Watkins 1995) indicate the changing character of climate (hot and dry, see Moore 1983, 93 and Fig. 2 on p. 105) but concern mainly minor sites proliferating around major centres. A similar conclusion has been formulated recently for the Balikh valley sites of Syria (Weiss 1991, 690–691 – Khirbet esh-Shenef as against Tell Sabi Abyad; see also Akkermans and Le Miere 1992, 21), and processes of this kind, especially the burgeoning of minor sites, have been documented around Tepe Yahya (Damerow, Englund and Lamberg-Karlovsky 1989, viii). The absence of ashy layers applies to Halaf culture sites but not to the south-east Ubaid settlements (Wright and Pollock 1986, 319f.). How far this incipient lowland sedentarization, which was likely to have inhibited the movement of minor settlements that clustered around the centres and to have thus disrupted the traditional transhumance patterns,

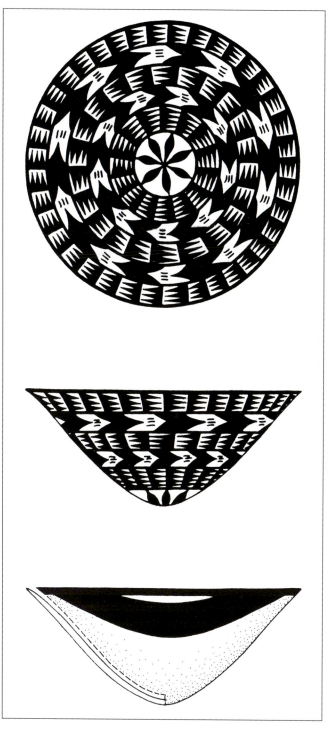

Figure 4.29 A Chalcolithic painted bowl. Early Ubaid culture, the site of Eridu, layer VIII (after Safar, Mustafa and Lloyd 1981, 156 and 179, Fig. 82: 1)

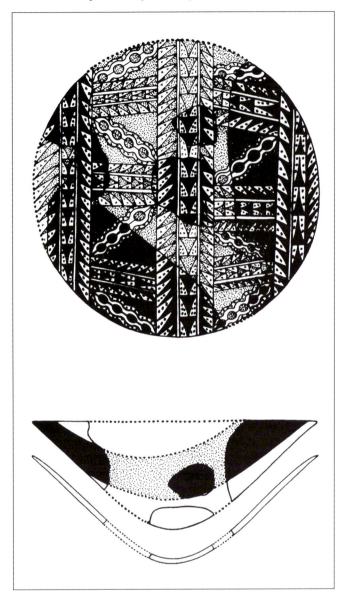

Figure 4.30 A Chalcolithic painted bowl. Early Ubaid culture, the site of Eridu, layer VIII (after Safar, Mustafa and Lloyd 1981, 156 and 179, Fig. 82: 2)

was influenced by the fact that the well-watered and larger valley bottoms, at least in the Zagros ranges, were by then inhabited by sedentary populations, remains an open question (Smith-Young 1983). As has already been noted, a parallel situation has been observed in early India (Fairservis 1991, esp. pp. 110–111), where the original unity of site pairs in the mountains and plains, likely to have been linked by transhumance, ultimately broke up and separate mountain and plain communities emerged.

Sedentarization leads to marked population growth (Maisels 1990, 121–130; Vencl 1991, 225 with ref.) and, in fact, the contemporary rise of population density in late Neolithic Palestine (Moore 1983, 100) has been explained with reference to economic intensification. Sedentarization of major centres might have resulted in more economic specialization of the short-term settlements. Such situations and series of 'service villages' are not unknown even in fully historic Sumer where such a cluster could exist around Nippur in Ur III times (Owen 1981, 46). Though Chalcolithic settlement excavations indicating a low degree of subsistence-gaining differentiation such as Tell Uqair (Lloyd and Safar 1943, 149f.), Ras al-'Amiya (Stronach 1982, 37–38) or Ubaid culture Yarimtepe III (Merpert and Munchaev 1982; Yoffee and Clark 1993, 225–240) do exist, other evidence tends to bear out the above-mentioned suggestion concerning spatial segregation of specialized activities. The Tell Abada 'communal sheepfold' (Jasim 1989, esp. pp. 83–85), suggestive of a village facility for feeding and watering cattle and thus of at least an elementary degree of economic specialization, has already been mentioned. The descriptions of site series implying regional specialization in animal husbandry (Oates 1980, 308) or of sites like Shams ed-Din Tannira in Syria with emphasis on a particular economic activity such as hunting (Azoury and Bergman 1980; on the site in general see Azoury *et al.* 1980–1982) have already been given. Another aspect is represented by those Chalcolithic sites which offer evidence

Figure 4.31 Foundations of the vernacular architecture of Mesopotamia were laid in the Neolithic age. Ever since that time the walls of local houses have been built of clay or stone with ceilings of timber. Reed matting, lying on these, was, in its turn, covered by well-trampled layers of clay which sometimes received a protective layer of bitumen.

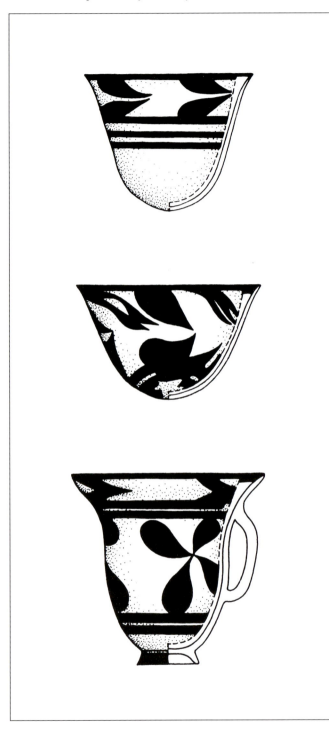

Figure 4.32 Chalcolithic painted cups. Late Ubaid culture (fifth–fourth millennium BC), the site of Eridu, cemetery (= layers VII–VI) (after Safar, Mustafa and Lloyd 1981, 160 and 166, Fig. 78: 10, 12, 15)

for craft activities carried out on a large scale such as pottery production documented by the Ubaid culture component of the 'Great Sherd Dump' at Ur (Woolley 1955, 28) or confined to a particular sector of the site which may even be physically enclosed. Developments exemplified at Tepe Gawra XVI, XVA and XV by the clear bipolarity of the residential and production-cum-storage quarters (e.g. Forest 1983a, Pls 6–8) are paralleled at the Jebel Hamrin sites of Tell Hassan (Fiorina 1984, 278, 285, Halaf and Ubaid cultures), Tell Songor B (Fujii 1981, 182–183, pottery kilns enclosed by a contemporary ditch), Tell Abada (Jasim 1989, 87, Fig. 10, layer I, square L 10, a group of kilns enclosed by a wall) and, finally, at Shams ed-Din Tannira itself (ar-Radi and Seeden 1980). An amplification of the argument for professional specialization may be seen in the boat-shaped hammer-axes, turning up at Tepe Gawra from layer XIII onwards and present in the contemporary Dum Gar Parchinah and Hakalan cemeteries of Iran (Vanden Berghe 1987, 118). Hammer-axes have been singled out as the oldest truly specialized weapons (Vencl 1979, 663–666, 692) and their presence may indicate social recognition of the warrior status ('caste'), distinguished by a particular professional symbol executed in imperishable material.

Differentiation and segmentation of Chalcolithic populations, visible in the archaeological record, thus pertain first and foremost to the professional sphere. Traces of social distinctions recoverable through settlement archaeology are less prominent. The Farukhabad evidence (Wright *et al.* 1981, 65–66), where minor architecture attracted equid and ovicaprid remains and more substantial struc-

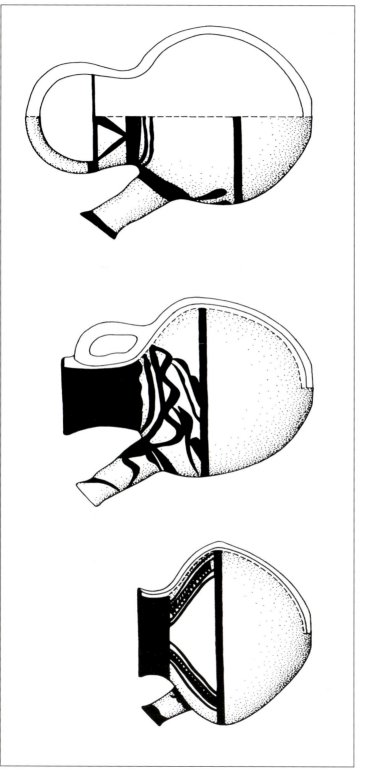

Figure 4.33 A Chalcolithic spouted bottle and spouted painted jugs, one with a stirrup handle. Late Ubaid culture, the site of Eridu, cemetery (= layers VII–VI) (after Safar, Mustafa and Lloyd 1981, 160 and 169, Fig. 79: 4, 5 and 7)

Figure 4.34 Modern houses with domed roofs of clay, like these photographed in Harran in south-east Turkey, may reflect the external appearance of the Neolithic and Chalcolithic round houses, especially of the Halaf culture tholoi.

tures gazelle bones and conical cups, while indigenous natural resouces such as flint and bitumen were omnipresent, has already been cited. Even this case, however, may reveal professional qualifications as gazelle hunting undoubtedly required careful organization and therefore some management skills. The higher frequency of tableware such as cups enhances the role of ostentatious commensality, perhaps with social undertones (a privilege/obligation of the incumbents of more substantial houses to entertain guests; see Milano 1994). Again, much later textual data give interesting comparative evidence including such gestures as raising the cup as a sign of allegiance to one's lord and liege or partaking of food and drink as a part of treaty rituals (Old Babylonia: Charpin 1990, 81, n. 51). In south-east Mesopotamia the perforated stone discs occur only in urban sites (Wright and Pollock 1986, 321). This could translate a social distinction, the more so as both authors also allude to the fact that the increased frequency of fine beakers and miniature vases on Ubaid culture cemeteries of this region and at Eridu Temple VI may point to socially relevant situations (ibid. 324).

Be that as it may, no socially relevant distinctions are offered by settlement-site layouts. These tend to be dominated by two types of structures: three-naved houses with annexes consisting of long and narrow rooms which might have evolved into buildings displaying a central longitudinal hall flanked on both longer sides by linear alignments of subsidiary chambers (referred to from now on as central-hall buildings) and by the well-known round houses or tholoi (Figure 4.34) (Breniquet 1996, 80–87). Well-documented excavations have established beyond any reasonable doubt that at least a number of the latter structures sheltered normal settlement activities (Yarimtepe II, see p. 45; Shams ed-Din Tannira: ar-Radi and Seeden 1980, 115 – Area A) or functioned as granaries (Akkermans 1987, 14–15). New excavations have proved that such constructions were known to Ubaid culture populations as well. In addition to the above-mentioned

Tell Madhhur III, there is another example from Khanijdal East (Wilkinson and Matthews 1989, 264–265; Wilkinson *et al.* 1996, esp. p. 44). Constructionally they may represent a response to the hot and dry climate and to the scarcity of usable wood within the steppe and pied-mont zones. Some of the tholoi rested on stone foundations and later they were provided with rectangular anterooms, also built on stone basements (Arpachiyah TT 10–7). In these cases builders of new tholoi constantly erected complete buildings, including new rubble foundations, which must have involved a considerable expenditure of energy. Facilities for communal use, the tradition of which continues from the Neolithic, include pipelines employing terracotta pipes and laid down either for draining the sites or for conveying water to them (in addition to Tepe Gawra XIII, Tell Abada: Jasim 1989, 86–88; Tell Abu Husaini: Invernizzi 1980, 41; on Near Eastern canalization in general: Hemker 1993). The Neolithic fortification tradition (Tell es-Sawwan) materialized at Arpachiyah (Hijara VII–VI) and at the Anatolian site of Degirmentepe (Mellink 1988, 112). As a Chalcolithic innovation, the building of well-prepared, paved roads leading to the foci of Halaf settlement is discernible: the Arpachiyah example may soon be accompanied by other finds of this kind (Kharabeh Shattani: Baird 1995, 13–14).

In conclusion to the social dimension of settlement evidence it may be pointed out that while a substantial amount of data confirms Chalcolithic professional specialization, unequivocal evidence on social stratification is missing save for a trend towards ostentatious commensality which may have become a vehicle for the expression of social pretensions on behalf of some community members. The degree of coherence and solidarity of Chalcolithic communities must have remained rather high. In fact, precisely such a social ordering is supposed to suit the economic character of early Mesopotamian agrarian communities (Gibson 1974).

This assessment is fully corroborated by other types of the archaeological record. Analyses of major contemporary cemeteries like those of Eridu and Ur (Pariselle 1985, esp. p. 10; Wright and Pollock 1986, esp. p. 328) and even of newly identified sites like Dum Gar Parchinah and Hakalan of Luristan (Vanden Berghe 1987, esp. pp. 92ff.) have outlined a basically egalitarian social structure (on Halaf mortuary practices see Akkermans 1989b). A major factor reflected by the funerary sphere seems to be the age, as at Eridu (Vértesalji 1984, 27) and at Gawra XVIII–XVI (Akkermans 1989a, 356), where children received grave goods different from those of adults. The Eridu children went to their graves accompanied by whole animal bodies but their fathers and mothers were given joints of fish and animal meat. At Gawra, children wore beads for the grave and adults had pottery. Reflection of age of the deceased in burial customs is believed to indicate essentially egalitarian societies without inheritance of social status (Wright 1978, esp. p. 213). Nevertheless, Lewis Binford, on whose results the above cited conclusion rests, goes on to say that burial of children together with adults does imply ranking and subgroup affiliation. The Eridu and Luristan cemeteries that display this feature may thus show a certain degree of manipulation of mortuary evidence as they clearly depart from the current practice of burying children under house floors (as at Gawra: Akkermans 1989a, esp. pp. 356–363, or the Hamrin sites, see p. 91). Here we may note the conclusion that the existence of cemeteries implies sedentarism (Bruce Dickson 1990, 195–196) and that in some instances they may play the role of a vehicle of expression of corporate rights to the territory on which the particular community burying their dead there resides (Charvát 1990, 459 with ref., 461–462; Talalay 1991, esp. pp. 48–49). The social image sought by the manipulation of the mortuary sphere at the Eridu and Luristan cemeteries stands out clearly in comparison with the Gawra sequence as perceived from the viewpoint of social history. As has been noted above, the innovations of Gawra XIII–XII include a visible expansion of the geographical range of natural resources tapped (new obsidian types, introduction of lapis lazuli), growth of the overall volume of manufactured goods and introduction of new techniques (flint borers from layer XII). While some of these developments facilitated the daily toil (grindstones), others, perhaps the majority, had clearly no other

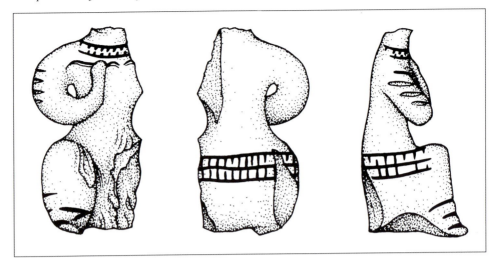

Figure 4.35 A Chalcolithic female statuette. Halaf culture, the site of Yarimtepe III (after Yoffee and Clark 1993, 202, Fig. 9: 38: 2)

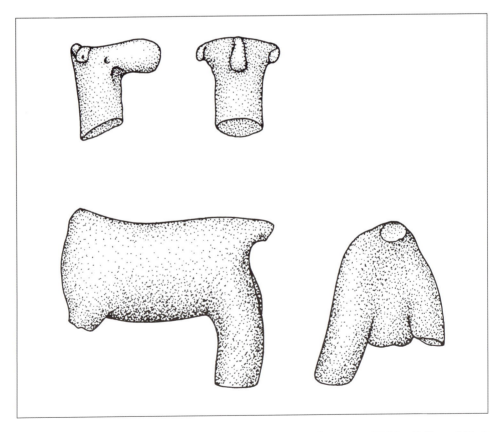

Figure 4.36 Chalcolithic animal figurines. Halaf culture, the site of Yarimtepe III (after Yoffee and Clark 1993, 204, Fig. 9: 42: 2–3)

purpose but ostentatious display (beads, pendants, stamped goblets). The new precious materials were apparently diffused throughout the site without attachment to particular contexts, structures or persons and the conclusion that they were accessible to all community members thus seems legitimate. Indeed, the introduction of flint borers in layer XII might have followed the increased demand for bored pendants; in such a case the motivation for this undoubtedly practical improvement must have emanated not from economic considerations but from the symbolic and representation sphere. This assumption of an essentially egalitarian comprehension of social groupings finds corroborative support not only in the mortuary sphere but also in the probably reciprocal character of socially engineered exchange practices (on the sealings, see Charvát 1988a). As far as social distinctions were operative in the Chalcolithic, they probably pertained to whole human groups which might have assumed different positions vis-à-vis one another in a system built on ranking complete (kin?) aggregates. The Gawra evidence shows us one of the component communities of Chalcolithic Mesopotamia, essentially egalitarian in their internal structure. On the other hand, the Eridu and Luristan cemeteries translate into archae-

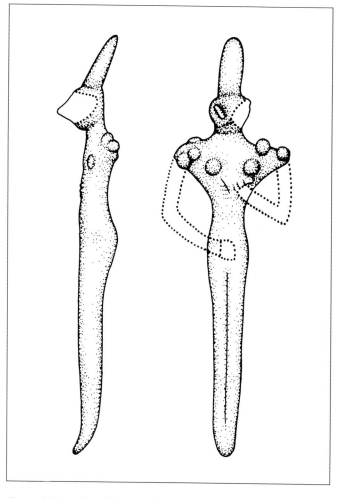

Figure 4.37 A Chalcolithic female statuette. Late Ubaid culture, the site of Tell Awayli, phase Ubaid 4 (after Forest 1996, 106, Fig. 80)

ological terms the aspirations of supralocal groupings of such communities, expressing ranking and subgroup affiliation of their component groups together with corporate rights to their territories.

The cemetery evidence thus points to the existence of essentially egalitarian communities forming supralocal units within which the individual component groups may have assumed various hierarchical positions and in which the corporate rights over the territories occupied by them were vested. These supralocal associations clearly varied in size, as is shown especially by the comparison with some adjacent cemetery sites. Though the grave goods of the deceased buried at Susa, Iran (Hole 1983) differed in no substantial manner from those of other burial sites, the sheer size of the site (some 2,000 interments) surpasses anything known from contemporary Mesopotamian cemeteries. The particular supralocal groupings within which the individual communities occupied positions defined by a preconceived hierarchy (on various types of such bodies including ramages and/or conical clans see Maisels 1987, 336–337; Thomas 1987, 408) could thus build 'catchment areas' of greatly varying extent.

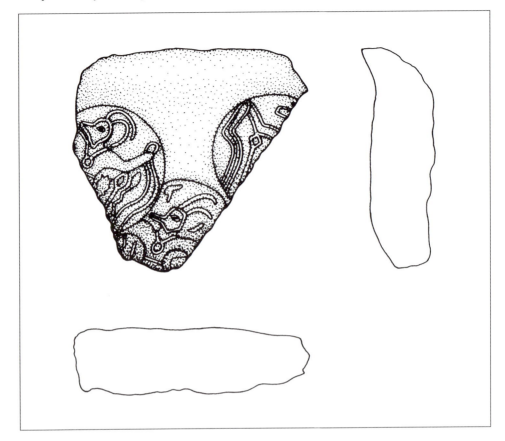

Figure 4.38 This Chalcolithic sealing from the west Iranian site of Susa (fourth millennium BC) shows well the essential characteristics of contemporary élites. Dressed up in a ceremonial robe and mask, a major personage of Chalcolithic Susa performs what may have been a rite triggering off the fertility of nature. This is likely to be symbolized by the streams flowing from his hands and by the creatures of the earth crowding around him. Impression of a shoulder of a jar, the mouth of which was closed by textile, on the reverse. Susa phase B (after a drawing by Petr Charvát, *Amiet*, No. 220, 1972, pp. 36, 37, 41, 80, 82, Pl. 2 and 49, SB 2050)

Another aspect of Chalcolithic society comes to the fore in the sphere of ostentatious commensality and use of the exquisite Halaf culture pottery. High-quality ornate tableware may be deployed in an effort to achieve a more prominent social position by means of a consumption ritual (Brumfiel 1987; on Mesopotamian commensality see Milano 1994). Something of this kind may be indicated by the neutron-activation analysis (NAA) of contemporary Iranian pottery (Berman 1989). In its earliest stage the painted wares were made in a uniform fashion, unlike the kitchenwares which show a most irregular and heterogeneous production base (ibid. 267, Phase 12). In the following Susa A period, the original unity of painted-ware production broke down and a number of workshops clearly participated in this enterprise (ibid. 268). Archaeological evidence may thus screen the gradual spread of a social privilege of fine tableware, once confined to one single centre, towards a number of agencies aspiring to the same social position. An ethnographic observation that may be relevant in this connection provides a parallel in the diffusion of pottery, in the decoration of which opinions concerning the structure of the universe are encoded, from ceremonial centres by persons of higher standing to commoners, so that the world order is 'ritually confirmed' (Pauketat and Emerson 1991, esp. p. 935). In decisions concerning the significance of the diffusion of the uniformly decorated Halaf and Ubaid culture pottery, we should bear in mind the universality of both pottery diffusion spheres; the ornate tablewares constitute phenomena of general order, links and integrative elements tying together communities of diverse economic background. In this vision the consumption ritual accedes to the position of highest importance for the bearers of both cultures, to the position of a distinctive sign which differentiated them from other humans, making them 'the community'. The significance of ritual, perceived by the ancients as a vital activity setting all components of the visible (and invisible) world in their proper stations and courses, is unquestionable in the earliest phase of Chinese (Kravtsova 1991, 33; Wechsler 1985, 17, 28; Overmyer *et al.* 1995) and Indian state building (Fairservis 1991, esp. pp. 112f.).

The evidence considered up to now thus seems to reveal a three-tiered hierarchy of Chalcolithic society. At the basic level, individual communities adhere to egalitarian rules. At an intermediate level, supralocal groupings proceed to define the positions of basic level communities within an ordered system, thereby determining their context of relationships, and constitute the agencies in which corporate rights to communal territories are vested (cemeteries). At the highest level, the entire population is held together by a uniform consumption ritual or rituals involving ostentatious commensality and the employment of exquisitely decorated tableware.

The unity of essential principles underlying the organization of Ubaid culture communities can be seen most convincingly in the standard plans of central-hall buildings (on which see Forest 1983b). A particularly fine example of these structures, the builders of which might even have known and applied the Pythagorean principle (Forest 1991), has been excavated at the Syrian site of Hammam et-Turkman (van Loon 1983, 2–3; 1985, 40; 1988, 582f.). The essentially identical character of their architectural forms and of the accompanying finds throughout the Ubaid culture sphere indicates their role as a basic component of the Ubaid social tissue. We may not err much if we see in them material incarnations of the individual households (in the sense of the Greek *oikiai*) integrated by adherence to commonly acknowledged principles into more extensive social bodies. Jean-Daniel Forest (1983b, 26) has suggested the interpretation of such structures in terms of sexual bipolarity, seeing in the central hall a common meeting room and hinting at the possibility of 'male' and 'female' house halves. Elaborating on this hypothesis he attempted an integration of clay tokens found at Tell Abada as records of dowry transactions into an explanatory scheme taking into account matrimonial strategies (Forest 1989). It will be observed that I am basing my interpretation on the unusually well-preserved and meticulously excavated house of Tell Madhhur II. I try to see in the suites of subsidiary chambers flanking the central hall (at least) two fully fledged settlement units consisting of 'activity zones' (cooking and partaking of food, common everyday tasks) and 'quiet zones' (storage and sleeping). In fact, should we rely on the information offered by the much later *šumma alu* house omens, both hearths situated at the northern ends of their respective suites would actually belong to women, as the north side of the house always belongs to its mistress (Guinan 1996, 64). The central hall functions as an incomplete unit, having only the 'activity zone', but an area of non-average activities at its farther end where the plaster is painted red and where clay tokens have turned up. What particular human groups once constituted the flesh and blood of these dry and lifeless mental constructs is most difficult to say though, for instance, an image of two nuclear families in the wings and a mother, father or an elderly relative exempted from subsistence activities but charged with ritual functions in the hall may come to mind quite naturally. In the house omens, the southern side of a house belongs to its master (Guinan 1996,

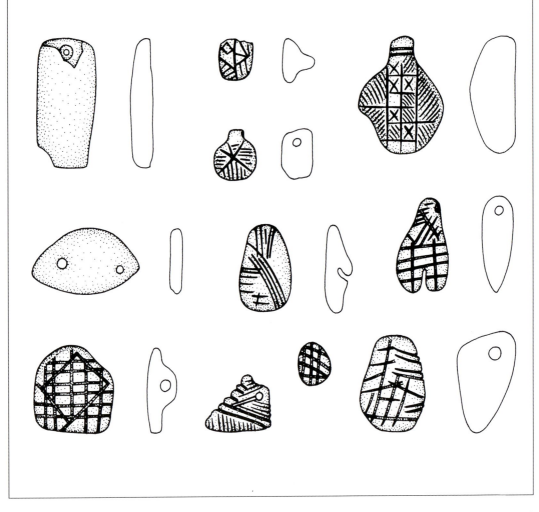

Figure 4.39 Pendant seals of stone of the Chalcolithic age. Halaf culture, the site of Yarimtepe II (after Munchaev and Merpert 1981, 213, Fig. 71)

64). Such a situation need not have been entirely fortuitous or exceptional, as artistic decoration of the interiors of such houses frequently embellished the central halls. Nevertheless, the high degree of interpenetration of the sacred and the profane in the interiors of these structures, the rooms of which probably once saw the gathering, processing and consumption of food, the daily menial tasks, storage of the fruits of the families' labours, births of their children, weddings and obsequies of their members as well as expressions of eternal values by means of colour symbolism and of the more earthly concerns by commodity substitutes of clay, gives eloquent testimony to the low degree of Ubaid social differentiation.

The character of relationships within the supralocal social groupings of which the individual household and site communities constituted component entities is elucidated by the evidence of socially engineered exchange activities. For the first time, Chalcolithic sites have yielded numerous finds of sealings, the reverse faces of which bear, in an overwhelming majority, impressions of mobile containers (Breniquet 1996, 106–115). I have argued above that this evidence is best interpreted as involving reciprocity measures in which the individual commodities would have been sealed by the despatching agencies (outside their findspot), travelled in a centripetal fashion to their respective 'collection points' and been unpacked there (with discarding of sealings) while other goods, material or immaterial, would have gone back to the original despatching agencies (Charvát 1988a and 1992a). A case which could prove this is Arpachiyah which clearly exported fine Halaf culture pottery, at least to Tepe Gawra (Davidson and McKerrel 1980, 161, 164) and perhaps to Kharabeh Shattani (Campbell 1986, 61) and received sealed goods which were unpacked there. The best historical parallels shedding light on similar early exchange systems come from Palestine. N. Avigad (1990) refers to a series of Phoenician 'city seals' of the fourth pre-Christian century each bearing an inscription consisting of the designation of payment type (a tithe), name of the despatcher city, initials of the royal name (i.e. even the 'address') and the date. Here is an example of the various despatching agencies to which I have alluded above, which supplied their goods to one single centre, identified here by initials of the royal name. The opposite case, when a great quantity of seals used at different spots mark goods sent to one single centre, giving their 'address', is exemplified by the Palestinian Iron Age 'lmlk' seals of which several hundred impressions have been found and which singled out deliveries to the royal administration (see, for instance, Mommsen, Perlman and Yellin 1984 with the important observation that all jars so marked were made of clay from one single source; Hestrin and Dayagi-Mendels 1979; Kelm and Mazar 1989, 43–44; Keel 1990, 417). The interpretation in terms of reciprocity seems to find support in the Ubaid culture data. Ubaid period sealings have turned up at more sites than Halaf period ones (von Wickede 1990, 126–217, and see also the newly published Khirbet Derak finds, dating to the Halaf–Ubaid transition age, but with parallels as late as Gawra XIII–XII: Breniquet 1990, 165–168, Vol. II, Pl. 56–65; 1996, 27, 40–47, 107–109) and their remarkable stylistic unity over a considerable territory (ibid. 239–252, now as far as Palestine: Keel-Leu 1989, esp. pp. 11–20, Nos. 7–24 as compared with von Wickede 1990, Tables 197–539) bears out the considerable frequency of contacts throughout the entire Fertile Crescent area, as well as the homogeneity of the social milieu in which the goods were circulating. If, then, gifts of a certain level require a corresponding reaction (Morris 1986), this suggests a chain of reciprocal obligations as the most likely explanation for the evidence that we have from Ubaid culture sealing practices. It would be interesting to speculate on the Halaf (seals everywhere but sealings only at Arpachiyah, Gawra, Tell Sabi Abyad: Akkermans 1993 and 1996; Akkermans and Duistermaat 1997; Duistermaat and Schneider 1998 and, most recently, Tell Kerkh, *cf. infra*) and Ubaid culture exchange practices (more frequent sealings) as mirroring categories of 'unifying exchange' (all partners make up a uniform whole) versus 'dividing exchange' (partners retain their positions: Duff-Cooper 1991, 181). The issue of such a debate will depend on the results of future excavations which may supply further data, especially on Halaf culture sealings. If these are found elsewhere than at the central sites of Arpachiyah, Gawra and Tell Sabi Abyad (for the last site see also Akkermans and Le Miere 1992, 15, Fig. 17: 9), then the interpretation should take this into account. In fact, this seems to be happening with new finds from the Syrian site of Tell el-Kerkh (Tsuneki *et al.* 1997, 31–32, 33, Fig. 24: 6; Tsuneki *et al.* 1998, 23–24, 25, Fig. 17: 12–13, and 26). Up to now, no clearcut answer can be given while new excavations such as Khirbet Derak (Breniquet 1990, passim, esp. pp. 46–59, 165–168, Vol. II, Pl. 56–65) have brought forth only Ubaid-style sealings. Of course, we cannot exclude that some redistribution took place but, to cut a long story short, I suggest that we classify Chalcolithic exchange activities, or at least those visible archaeologically, in terms of reciprocity. In fact, such mutual exchanges may well have constituted the blood flowing through the veins of the individual supralocal groupings by which these social bodies came to life. It could even be

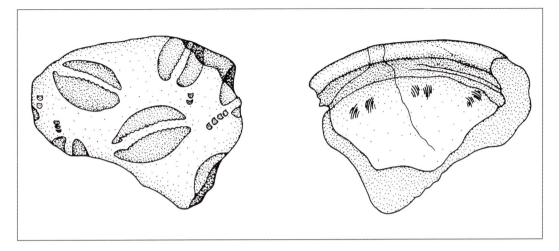

Figure 4.40 A necklace of cowrie shells, from the Mediterranean or the Red Sea, was used among groups of small beads for this Chalcolithic sealing of a jar with a lid. A rare find shows us many facets of the Chalcolithic age: use of purely personal ornaments, believed to have 'imbibed' a part of the personality of the bearer, to produce a sign of appropriation of goods; type and character of personal jewellery of the Halaf period; and evidence for long-distance contact with maritime regions. Incipient Halaf culture, the site of Tell Sabi Abyad, layer 6 (after Duistermaat 1994, 38 and Pl. 22).

imagined that if such groupings really claimed corporate rights over their territories, as seems to be implied by the cemetery evidence, then mutual gift-giving could express adherence to a particular alliance and enable the member communities to discharge their right to that part of the communal tenure which belonged to them by common consent. The Mesopotamian seals of this period usually assumed the form of pendants worn on the body and their use thus hints at the emergence of the idea of personal property from conferring the mark of a master or mistress of a certain object on it by means of a design that, having been long carried on his or her body, has become permeated with the invisible part of the bearer's personality (Figure 4.40). The exchange of such goods would then fall within the Maussian categories of giving gifts conferring parts of the donors' personalities on the receivers (Duff-Cooper 1991, esp. pp. 179–181, and Charvát 1992a; sealings and historical administration: Fiandra 1981a). A proposition has been advanced recently to the effect that propagation of a distinctive pottery style in societies up to the chiefdom level may indicate the diffusion of a language and ethnicity and that the same conclusion applies to the spread of the 'status kit' of such cultures (Ehret 1988, esp. pp. 571–572, see also Pinçon and Ngoïe-Ngalla 1990, but, for argument to the contrary, Vansina 1995). If the Chalcolithic seals belonged to the 'status kit' of the Halaf and Ubaid cultures, then it may be possible to view their spheres as those of ethnic and even linguistic unity. This, however, might have applied only to the network of communities leaving their traces in the archaeological record while the gaps between them could have been settled by human groups of the most diverse origins.

In conclusion to this section, then, Chalcolithic society may be characterized as follows:

a) The basic component of the social tissue was constituted by individual households in the broad sense of the term, incarnated most probably in the central-hall buildings which were each likely to have sheltered under their roofs several nuclear families (2–3?) and which represented typical residential units of individual sites. At least some masters of these houses disposed of their own seals.

b) These individual cells (households or whole sites) were affiliated together within wider social groupings in terms of which the component communities occupied positions determined by their internal structural principles, possibly with some ranking. Corporate rights to the territories settled by these community clusters seem to have been vested in the supralocal groupings which claimed them by the establishment of central cemeteries.

c) Considerable professional differentiation existed within human society. The archaeological record outlines such groups as peasants, shepherds, hunters, warriors and specialists in work with bitumen, clay, metal and stone, and possibly also personnel with cultic obligations.

d) In spite of these professional differences intra-group solidarity must have been high as, for instance, exotic materials procured by the efforts of all community members were apparently shared by a large majority, if not by all citizens (Gawra XIII–XII). Such materials served as group-status markers.

e) The principle of the underlying unity of all the diverse constituent groups of Chalcolithic cultures seems to have been embodied in a spiritual construct expressed by means of ostentatious commensality and employment of fine tableware.

f) The sense of both particular (regional) and general corporate identity of the Chalcolithic 'communities' was reinforced by the circulation of material-culture items bearing signs of their despatchers and presumably owners (seal impressions) throughout the contemporary *oikoumene*. Such commodities probably constituted reciprocal gifts, exchanged on the principle of conveying parts of the donors' personalities to the recipients in the sense suggested by M. Mauss (see more recently Toren 1988, 708; Carrier 1990, esp. pp. 693–694; Duff-Cooper 1991, esp. pp. 179–181).

Figure 4.41 These Ubaid culture beakers represent the simpler products of the potter's craft, presumably available to wide circles of Chalcolithic consumers.

Metaphysics

A factor that may help us in assessing changes in the spiritual and mental sphere of the Chalcolithic world is the way deceased community members were provided for on their way to the land of no return (see Akkermans 1989b; Hole 1989; Breniquet 1996, 96–106). While the initial practice of laying a certain segment of the population, both children and adults, to rest in the settlements (in addition to the above cited works, see the situation at Degirmentepe: Esin 1985, 254) persisted, this sphere underwent changes which must reflect transformations of the notions of life and death. First and foremost, even those interments deposited quite traditionally under house floors were now treated in a much more varied fashion. The single settlement site of Yarimtepe II has offered evidence for inhumation of whole bodies, of body parts (skulls) and for cremation (Munchaev and Merpert 1981, 207–208). What caused this extraordinary diversity? Investigating the case further, we cannot fail to notice the spatial limitation of cremation burials to the proximity of tholos LXVII, before the building of which a shallow pit excavated at its site received a broken painted pot, three trapezoidal microliths of obsidian and ashes from a pyre, strongly implying a fire ritual (ibid. 178). At Yarimtepe II, several categories of objects have clearly undergone such an 'ordeal by fire'. In addition to painted pottery and chipped stone items, stone vessels and stone pendants have been retrieved from such contexts (ibid. 209f.). Of course, such deposits sharply contrast with the general scarcity of ash strata on Halaf culture sites (Hole 1987ab, 561; Watkins and Campbell 1987, 453–454). Moreover, a two-compartment pottery kiln of considerable sophistication, rebuilt at least once and undoubtedly a device for qualified pyrotechnical work, existed south of this tholos (Munchaev and Merpert 1981, 180–181). Such a close spatial relation between high-level pyrotechnology and fire ritual applied both to artifacts and to human (but also animal, see p. 45) bodies seems to imply that the element of fire, the properties of which were undoubtedly perfectly known, played the role of a 'transformer', in terms of both technology and ritual transfer of both inanimate and (originally) animate objects across the cultic border (that between life and death for humans and animals: an animal cremation at Yarimtepe, Munchaev and Merpert 1981, 209). Fire, possibly as an element of the universe, may thus have played a major ritual role, perhaps that of a purifying agent in a broad sense (in general see, for instance, Vinogradova and Tolstaya 1990). As to the burial of incomplete bodies and especially heads, this finds a parallel in the new finds from Arpachiyah (Hijara *et al.* 1980, 132–133; Hole 1989, 156–157) and in the corresponding burials of headless bodies at the Halaf site of Tell Azzo I (Hole 1989, 160). A clue to the understanding of this macabre rite may be offered by the Arpachiyah case in which one of the heads reposed in an attractive painted pot (von Wickede 1986, 22, Fig. 26). Figural scenes on painted pottery from funerary contexts have been described for the third pre-Christian millennium (Bachelot 1991). This phenomenon may thus display both significance and longevity and, in view of the rather infrequent figural scenes, which certainly did not undergo the geometrical stylization usual for contemporary ornament (notice how awkward their treatment usually is), it may relate some story connected with the individual in question or with his or her death. The whole problem may connect with an observation by Lewis Binford (as cited in Wright 1978, 212) that the particular circumstances of death exercise an influence on the funerary ritual. At any rate, Halaf culture burial customs do apparently reflect a range of both general and particular factors of human life undocumented before, though it may well be asked to what extent these new features represent the treatment of deceased community members which had before occurred outside the settlements, the sole difference being the fact that in the Halaf culture period such activities concerned the dead buried within settlements and were thus able to be documented by archaeological excavations.

Other changes came along in the Ubaid culture period. The most visible of these concerns the gradual transfer of a number of deceased community members to regular cemeteries outside the settlements, which left children as the only ones to receive the traditional burial under house floors. The latter custom is evidenced at Yarimtepe III (Bader, Merpert and Munchaev 1981, 59ff.; Yoffee and Clark 1993, 225–240, esp. p. 235), Tell Abada II (Jasim 1989, 79–80), Tell Abu Husaini (Invernizzi 1980, 41ff.; Tusa 1984, 269–270), Tell Hassan (Fiorina 1984, 285f.), as well as at Tell el-Saadiya (Roaf and Postgate 1981, 187; Kozlowski and Bielinski 1984, 104f.). A contemporary innovation consisted of the extensive funerary sites of Ur (Woolley 1955, esp. pp. 20–28; Forest 1983a, 111–115) and Eridu (see pp. 48–49 and Vértesalji 1984) or the Luristan sites of Dum Gar Parchinah and Hakalan (Vanden Berghe 1987). The later phase of the Ubaid culture cemetery at Ur (Woolley's Ubaid II) displays a feature significant for the oncoming periods of time, namely the crouching position of the body with flexed legs and hands before the face, as against the earlier manner, attested to at Eridu and the Luristan sites, of the strictly supine position of the deceased (Woolley 1955, 21f.). Though the cemeteries do show a certain amount of regional peculiarity (Wright and Pollock 1986, 327–328 – beads and a few figurines at Eridu, figurines and a few beads at Ur), their students unanimously declare that the degree of internal variation is too low to warrant any safer historical conclusions. Nevertheless, the presence of children does indicate that ranking and subgroup affiliation may be expected in the collectives which left behind these cemeteries (see Wright 1978, 213) and the conclusion that these extensive sites, likely to entomb deceased members of a number of localized communities, display manipulation of the burial evidence in accordance with a preconceived system setting all member communities into stations appointed for them, absent from the individual communities which still adhered to egalitarian principles internally, seems to be legitimate. It has been observed that the earliest instances of ranking usually concern the mutual relations of whole social bodies, not individuals (e.g. Maisels 1987, esp. pp. 336ff., an example from ancient China; archaeologically see Wright 1978, 213; in the sphere of craft specialization see Saiko and Yankovskaya 1988, esp. pp. 17–18; in general see Lévi-Strauss 1974, 37–91, esp. pp. 72 and 88–89). It has already been noted that establishment of such extensive cemeteries may express corporate rights of the group concerned over its respective territory. Here we will do well to realize that a permanent vindication of a landscape segment must have resulted in changes in the apperception of the world.

In the case of these extensive cemeteries we begin to perceive their role in ancient public life and at least some of the activities that took place there. The ubiquitous clay statuettes (Oates 1978, 121–122), previously known only from settlement evidence, now turn up either as grave goods (Ur) or among the graves but below the cemetery surface (Eridu). The interpretation of such evidence put forward for Mediterranean sites (Talalay 1991; Hamilton *et al.* 1996), and proposing comprehension in terms of ancestor worship, may very well apply here as well since ancestor cults would have undoubtedly constituted a useful device through which the rapidly spreading kin aggregates, living over extensive territories in which considerable distances separated the farthest members, could operate to maintain group coherence. In early Anatolia, mother goddesses presided over cemeteries (van Loon 1991b, 265–266, n. 5) and there may thus be a connection with the predominantly female sex of our statuettes.

In addition to changes in the funerary sphere some other intellectual operations may now be documented with a varying degree of probability. Analysis of ground plans of the Ubaid culture central-hall buildings has recently induced Jean-Daniel Forest (1991) to suggest that the architects of such houses might have known and applied Pythagoras' theorem. This age must also have seen the birth of at least the graphic versions of some of the signs of earliest Uruk culture writing systems. This does not concern only the classical bucranium example. The SAL sign, depiction of a female pudenda, was certainly understood in this sense in the Halaf culture period, as is shown by an anthropomorphic vase from Yarimtepe II (Munchaev and Merpert

1981, 252, Fig. 98). The vase with figural scenes from Hijara's Arpachiyah excavations (von Wickede 1986, 22, Fig. 26) depicts, among others, two female figures flanking a rectangular object with plaits along its rim. This may very well show a weaving scene and the plaited object is thus likely to constitute a predecessor of various signs for mats or rugs, attested to in the Uruk IV script (Szarzyńska 1988a, 228, Table I: T-31 to T-34). The same goes for images of combs on Halaf culture pottery (von Wickede 1986, 21, Figs 20, 21; 16, Fig. 7, 4th line from top, 7th column from left) which may re-appear in the form of earliest cuneiform signs (Szarzyńska 1988a, 228, Table I: T-6 to T-9). Traces of another early spiritual construct came to light at Arpachiyah. Sir Max Mallowan (Mallowan and Rose 1935, 107ff.) noticed that until his layer TT 7, pottery painting was exclusively bichrome. The characteristic white–red–black colour triad pre-vailed only in TT 6 when relationships to the Hajji Muhammad culture patterns first appeared (von Wickede 1986, 31–32). In spite of its modernity, the white–red–black colour triad deter-mined the TT 6 fashion to such an extent that in addition to painted pottery, it is reflected by the mineral pigments brought to the site (Mallowan and Rose 1935, 100 – blocks of black, red and yellow clay with yellow substituting white), by materials for the palettes used for crushing the pigments (ibid., white, pink and grey stone) and by the abundant beads. In the latest case a com-plete necklace found in this layer (ibid. 97, A 909 on Pl. XIa) proves this beyond doubt by its composition of obsidian and white cowrie beads, the latter provided with interior red-paste inlays visible through the cut-away front parts of the shells. Moreover, inhabitants of prehistoric Tepe Gawra subscribed to the same colour triad from layer XIX onwards, taking over even some of the pottery decoration influenced by the south (von Wickede 1986, 32 – via Arpachiyah?). This distinctive colour pattern, though introduced in the Chalcolithic, did not percolate through the entire Ubaid culture sphere, as traditional two-colour schemes seem to prevail in the Luristan cemetery sites (Vanden Berghe 1987, 113–114, 116, 121). Its full potential was nonetheless unfolded in the colours of geometrical compositions of mosaic cones adorning the monumental architectures of Uruk in the following, Uruk culture phase. Much as in the use of pottery bear-ing figural scenes for funerary purposes, the 'message' of the white–red–black triad seems to have addressed both prehistoric and the earliest historic populations of Mesopotamia and I assume that however it may have been comprehended in the past, it probably expressed the essential unity, or at least compatibility, of the underlying spiritual constructs of the times in which it was publicly displayed (for a recent example of a religious statement conveyed by means of the same colour triad see Duff-Cooper 1991, 188). The fact that in other civilizations the earliest universally acknowledged spiritual activities pertaining to the welfare of the entire community are fre-quently articulated in rituals believed to constitute the essential moving factor behind all the natural and human activities, releasing the benign forces and keeping the world in harmonious relationships (Kravtsova 1991, esp. pp. 33–34, Overmyer *et al.* 1995), may indicate similar functions for our colour triad. A substantial component of such rituals is music and here we have a harmony of colours. Again, major social transitions tend to be expressed by changes in publicly displayed colours (T'ang China: Wechsler 1985, 6–7). I believe that we may be right in characterizing this development as a construction of a rational and coherent set of attitudes to the world expressed – undoubtedly among other means and ways – by the white–red–black colour triad, the significance of which was so profound that it continued to address the best brains of Mesopotamia for centuries after the extinction of the cultural system in which it had first been used. Symbolically, however, the set of attitudes to the world in question, or rather its visual rep-resentation, in Arpachiyah TT 6 sprang from two sources, the southern and the northern (see p. 65 on decorative patterns on pottery). For the first ascertainable time in history, representatives of communities distant from one another put their minds together to create something which would survive all of them and address the generations to come, and in this endeavour they succeeded. We may well be witnessing the process that left in the cultural tradition of ancient Mesopotamia the belief that Eridu (as a representative of the south?) constituted the source of all wisdom and the seat of the god of knowledge.

Thus the first intelligible universal religion seems to have been born. The colour triad would make good sense in ancient Egyptian religion, where it would affirm the progress from earthly existence (red) through death (black) to eternal life (white, Wilkinson 1994, 106–107, 109). It is, of course, a fact that if and when people distinguish more colours in their languages, they customarily recognize white, red and black colours (Wardhaugh 1992, 232). Remarkably, however, the colour triad black–white–red came to the fore in medieval alchemy, where it marked out progression from common everyday matter (black) via its transformation by the alchemical art (white) to the original archetypal substance which transforms all matters in the world (red). Such an interpretation of the colours may reach back to Greek antiquity (Roberts 1994, esp. pp. 54–56). This phenomenon may have

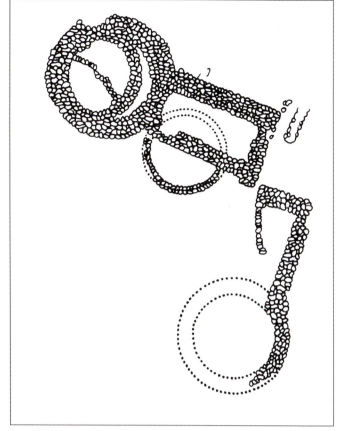

Figure 4.42 A series of Chalcolithic round buildings (tholoi) on stone foundations. Halaf culture, the site of Tell Arpachiyah, layers TT 10 to TT 7 (after Breniquet 1996, 185, Pl. 33a)

been accompanied by the first distinction between 'sacred' and 'profane' space retrievable from the archaeological record. Here I resort to categories put forward by Mircea Eliade (a bibliography of his writings on this subject is found in Bruce Dickson 1990, 224). The first case where we can find them highly relevant concerns the sudden change at Arpachiyah TT 10 where the round structures, or tholoi, are first built on stone foundations (Figure 4.42) and subsequently renewed throughout every successive layer as far as TT 7 followed by the remarkable TT 6 structure to which cultic aspects can hardly be denied. The introduction of stone foundations followed after the sequence of six stratigraphic layers (Hijara VI–XI), of which the two immediately preceding TT 10 (Hijara VII–VI) contained ordinary tholos architecture of clay, of purely profane character on other sites such as Yarimtepe II. It is nonetheless remarkable that as early as Hijara VI the ruins of the disused buildings were levelled to provide foundations for the succeeding structures, a procedure hardly belonging to ordinary settlement practices. The unprecedented change in TT 10, the extraordinary energy expenditure involved in the procurement of stone for each successive tholos generation and the non-average functions of the TT 6 settlement all converge, as I believe, to indicate that we are dealing with an archaeological sequence translating into material terms the transition between 'the profane' and 'the sacred'.

Apart from the profane items, the TT 6 house contained material features which strongly suggest its cultic function. The pair of limestone statuettes depicting a woman and a man, finds of a human finger bone and of stone models of such relics as well as the highly stylized stone shapes unearthed together in this layer (Mallowan and Rose 1935, 99–100, A 920 on Fig. 52: 3), add weight to the observation of the first occurrence of the white–red–black colour triad at the site to indicate the universal, sacred-cum-profane character of this edifice in which spiritual supremacy seems to have been vested in evidence for a general 'transformation' of the uncultivated environment by means of both ritual procedures and conversion of a number of natural resources into usable, and hence 'tamed', 'civilized' or 'humanized' items (production of material goods at TT 6 Arpachiyah: Mallowan and Rose 1935, 100–122, 130–135, 172). This gradual emergence of more distinct cultic features of the archaeological evidence seems to continue into the Ubaid culture period.

A similar transition from 'profane' to 'sacred' buildings may be suspected at Tepe Gawra where, after a purely secular development within strata XX–XV, a single stone-based central-hall building occupies the whole site in layer XIV. Again, as at Arpachiyah, the form replicates common buildings, but the extraordinary energy expenditure involved in the procurement of stone for the foundations, unparalleled at the site both before and after this moment, does point to a special, perhaps cultic, significance for this structure. The Ubaid period central-hall buildings frequently display a peculiar artistic finish in their largest rooms, usually in terms of wall paintings (Tepe Gawra XVI, Eridu VI, Tell Madhhur) and non-average activities were clearly taking place in the central hall of the Madhhur house (counters). A particularly fine example of a high-level layout of the central hall, provided, in addition to mural paintings in the familiar white–red–black polychromy, with hearths on terracotta plaques of geometrical shapes, has been studied recently at Degirmentepe (Esin 1983 and 1985; Mellink 1988). The elaborate hearths may point to the sphere of fertility and male procreation symbolism, frequently connected with fireplaces (Van der Toorn 1991, 45–46). In the light of this evidence, showing the comprehensive character of the apperception of the world in terms of closely interlocking sets of 'sacred' and 'profane' elements, so clearly expressed in domestic architecture, statements about Ubaid period 'temples' are to be assessed with caution (Anon. 1972, 149; Jahresbericht 1977, 640; and Heinrich 1982, 32–33, Figs 71 and 74). Purposefully cultic structures may be present in the Chalcolithic period in the form of huge brick platforms such as those of Eridu, Tell Awayli, or, on a really magnificent scale, Susa. Unfortunately, too little is known about them to warrant safe conclusions. The Susa evidence (Pollock 1989, esp. pp. 283–286) indicates that such edifices had both residential and funerary functions but that they were repaired with far less attention than the Eridu or Gawra 'temples' and the Awayli example shows that even sites with such huge structures could be entirely deserted. In periods when residential and cultic functions of buildings had not yet become clearly differentiated the ultimate decision must depend, for lack of any better criterion, on the presence or absence of ordinary settlement refuse, as was originally proposed by M. Hoffmann (1974; see Gibbon 1984, 156–161, esp. pp. 160–161). Here it is significant that even the most accomplished 'temples' of Eridu and Gawra did display settlement rubbish accumulations within their walls, a clear sign of their profane functions. My impression is that the Chalcolithic eye perceived the material and spiritual components of the world as so closely intertwined that no activities which would disregard any single one of these spheres of life were conceivable.

It is assumed that with sedentarization, the vision of the universe changes from a sequence or series of disparate worlds, which may or may not exist in relation to one another, to the idea of one single space disposed in concentric segments (A. Leroi-Gourhan, in Taine-Cheikh 1991, 113–114). In such conditions the geographical diffusion sphere of a given society may be manipulated to comply with sets of features deemed to be fundamental to the structure of a given society (e.g. Miller 1980). In a recent paper (Charvát 1994) I suggested that the fact that Halaf culture seals are present throughout the entire diffusion sphere of this culture, while Halaf culture sealings are found only at Arpachiyah and Gawra, may be interpreted in terms of the role of both sites as (successive?) centres and focal points of the whole Halaf culture *oikoumene*. At that time I was aware neither of the new mass find of sealings at Tell Sabi Abyad, for information on which I am obliged to Peter Akkermans (1993 and 1996; Akkermans and Duistermaat 1997), nor of the new finds from Tell Kerkh (Tsuneki *et al.* 1997 and 1998). The existence of such 'catchment areas' of the pristine élites who either collected sealed contributions or, alternatively, presided over socially acknowledged procedures requiring sealing of symbol sets, implies that the Halaf culture population groups could have seen their world as possessing at least a centre and a periphery, an observation which would comply with the above-mentioned proposition. The question how far this argument applies to the Ubaid culture with its system of (more or less) generalized exchange of goods awaits an answer. Whether any single centre of the Ubaid culture world existed must thus remain a question for future research, though in the following Uruk culture the centrality of Uruk is proved beyond any reasonable doubt by its heavy concentration of ceremonial buildings. Let us close this review by mentioning briefly the possibility that the introduction of seals and sealing into contemporary public life, likely to incarnate a stability of relationships between animate subjects and inanimate objects, heralds the appearance of signs of private property on the horizon of archaeological visibility.

CONCLUSIONS

Though the Chalcolithic period lasted probably for something like two millennia, which is not too long in the history of the human race, the conditions in which our ancestors lived at its end were quite different from those prevalent at its beginning. A factor for which archaeological evidence implies the most substantial role in the transformation of human life is sedentarization. Monocausal explanations are always suspicious and sedentarization can hardly be seen as a single major event 'that started it all'. Nevertheless, the occupation of permanent residential areas by human groups appears to have triggered a series of changes and transformations which were of substantial importance for human social and spiritual life.

Let us first try to assess the new, and hence in early human vision undoubtedly undesirable and wrong features that sedentarization brought for the men and women of yore. By releasing an irreversible trend of population growth, sedentarization must have resulted in economic intensification if all the new mouths were to be fed. Furthermore, this necessity of catering for the needs of more humans than before must have led to systematic and profound assessments of the economic potential of landscapes inhabited by human groups and to environmental exploitation far more intense than before. In the social sphere, people had to comply with situations of relative overpopulation. All of a sudden, whole landscapes clad themselves in settlements and, while in the Neolithic you were delighted to live with neighbours you saw only every six months or so, in the Chalcolithic you had them permanently 'on the other side of the hill'. Finally, sedentarization had to be brought into accord with the vision of the world, and human minds were flooded by the invasion of new facts, impressions and emotions to such an extent that, afraid lest the essential classificatory schemes melt away altogether in the maze of new experiences, they proceeded to catch the first glimpses of the essential unity in diversity, making now operative the universal principle or set of principles on which the world was built.

How did Chalcolithic populations react to this challenge? In the economic sphere the following general observations may be put forward:

a) Full use of the existing economic know-how.
b) Expansion of the range of natural resources tapped.
c) Overall increase of the output of the arts and crafts.
d) Introduction of new technologies and work procedures.

Thus apparently maximizing their economic output, Chalcolithic communities found no difficulty in parting with a section of their produce in the form of first centralized(?) and then generalized commodity exchange, probably along the principles of reciprocity.

The same trend of unity in diversity may be perceived in the social dimension of Chalcolithic life. Chalcolithic populations included numerous craft specialists, peasants, shepherds, hunters, warriors and masters in work with clay, metal and stone as well as, with a degree of probability, cultic personnel (perhaps at least part-time – elderly community members?); the 'three castes' or 'three estates' are, in fact, already in existence. These differences, however, were still firmly enveloped by, and embedded within, the matrix of essential social equality. This was expressed by the following features:

a) On the basic social level by the households, represented in the archaeological record by the central-hall buildings, offering under their roofs shelter to several (2–3?) nuclear families and constituting the stage for comprehensive human activities covering all aspects of relations between human beings and their visible and invisible environment.
b) On the regional level by groupings consisting of such households (or groups thereof), possibly kin aggregates. These were distinguished by the following characteristics:
   1 They acted as foci of pristine social stratification, setting their component communities, egalitarian in their character, to positions within a preconceived system appointed according to a commonly acknowledged social (hierarchical?) order.
   2 Relations within this system (and later on, among systems, when such groupings multiplied in the Ubaid culture period) were maintained by means of various systems of exchange of commodities bearing visible symbols of the donors (sealings), probably in terms of reciprocity.
   3 At least some of these groupings could have given articulation to their corporate rights over the territory in which they resided by the establishment of extensive cemeteries.
c) Finally, on the highest, 'humankind' level all such systems constituted 'the community' by commonly shared spiritual constructs expressed in ostentatious commensality and employment of exquisite tableware.

Chalcolithic men and women conquered their environment both by material and by spiritual means. The basic unity shining through superficial diversity is clearly perceptible in the Chalcolithic approach to the things of the mind. People were by then certainly aware of the variation in individual talents, abilities and destinies and gave such notions a clear expression in the multiplicity of roles played by human beings both before and after their death, as is reflected by the variation in burial customs. Nevertheless, spiritual unification left its traces not only on the level of the everyday 'consumer' magic (human and animal figurines in settlement refuse layers), but in the form of what was probably the first recognizable ritual (human figurines in cemeteries = ancestor cults?) and, above all, in the search for the basic constitutive principle of the universe. Though the stage on which spiritual life played its role was still constituted by the common, everyday spaces, areas and landscapes of human experience, the Chalcolithic witnessed the articulation of such a constitutive principle in terms of the first systematic application of the white–red–black colour triad at Arpachiyah TT 6, taken over by the sages of Tepe Gawra and ultimately by the creators of the Uruk culture where these colours enhanced the cultic message of monumental buildings by dominating the mural decoration adorning their walls. The individual aspects of this principle could have assumed various external forms. One of these might have been the duality, clearly present at Tepe Gawra XVI–XIII in architecture (twin entrances of central-hall buildings and then of 'temples'), burial customs (deposition of bodies on both sides) and ritual (renewed occurrence of animal statuettes together with female ones, duplicated at Yarimtepe III: Merpert and Munchaev 1982, 148). This implies that the world could have been perceived as ordered on a (sexual?) binary principle. This period of time is likely to have witnessed the emergence of not only humankind's first religion, but also private property.

It is thus in the Chalcolithic that the first predecessors of all the constitutive principles of civilized human life must be sought. In terms of Mesopotamia, the statement that all the essential forms of major features of the Uruk civilization were present at least in the preceding Ubaid culture may not be too far from the truth. From the viewpoint of human history, the Mesopotamian Chalcolithic, together with the local Mesolithic, ranks among the crucial and formative periods of a society that was to contribute major innovations on which the civilized world draws to this day.

Chapter Five

The Uruk culture

A civilization is born

Uruk

An extensive site 60 km west-north-west from Nasiriyah, a cornerstone of Mesopotamian archae-
ology, the almost century-long excavation of which by various German teams (1912–1913 under
J. Jordan and C. Preusser; 1928–1939 under J. Jordan, A. Nöldecke, E. Heinrich and H. J.
Lenzen; 1953–1967 under H. J. Lenzen; 1967–1977 under H. J. Schmidt; 1980–1990 under R.
M. Boehmer) has, in itself, entered history. This complex site has received extensive coverage in
the series of the 'Vorläufige Berichte über die von der Deutschen Forschungsgemeinschaft im
Uruk-Warka unternommenen Ausgrabungen' (abbreviated here as UVB), but the questions and

Figure 5.1 Pottery vessels of the Uruk culture

problems of its interpretation will provide grist to the mills of generations of
future archaeologists, historians and
Assyriologists. Major recent reviews of
the matter under consideration may
be found in Lenzen 1974,
Strommenger 1980a, Heinrich 1982,
Schmandt-Besserat 1988a, Boehmer
1991, and a register of find reports in
Finkbeiner 1993. The Berlin team has
most laudably initiated publication of
the series of 'Ausgrabungen in Uruk-
Warka-Endberichte', abbreviated here
as AUWE, which is of cardinal importance (among others, Becker and
Heinz 1993; Eichmann 1989;
Finkbeiner 1991; Kohlmeyer and
Hauser 1994; Limper 1988). A deep
sounding at the site within the
precinct of the goddess Inanna, bear-

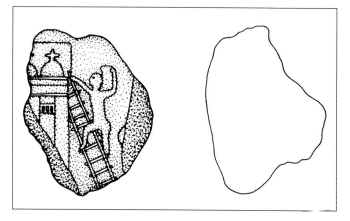

Figure 5.2 This Late Uruk sealing shows a man ascending a ladder in order to empty a sack of grain into one of the huge domed granaries of the period, likely to have inspired the proto-cuneiform sign MAH. Late Uruk period (*c*.3500–3200 BC), Susa (after a drawing by Petr Charvát, *Amiet*, No. 663, 1972, p. 103, Pl. 16, SB 2027)

ing the name of Eanna, has exposed a 'Chalcolithic' stratigraphy of eighteen layers (Schmandt-Besserat 1988a, Table 3 on p. 38). C-14 date: level XVIII – 5300–4575 cal. BC = Ubaid 4 (Annex 734). Of these, the lowermost three (XVIII–XVI) belong to the Ubaid culture, layers XVI–X to the Proto-Uruk and Early Uruk period (the last Ubaid pottery registered in layer XII), layers IX–VI to Middle Uruk and layers V–IV to the Middle and Late Uruk period, con- stituting the focus of my interest here. In terms of architectural structures, two plans of central-hall 'temples' of Ubaid IV or early Uruk have come to light under the Uruk period 'Steingebäude' (Heinrich 1982, 32–33, Figs 71 and 74, see also Finkbeiner 1991, 191–192). Summarized data only are available for the occurrence of various artifacts within these strata. The Ubaid culture displays, in addition to the ubiquitous pottery, sickles of baked clay in limited quantities; no metal finds of any consequence have turned up but stone vessels and rare obsid- ian tools are known. From layer XVII the material culture shows an essential continuity of all its constitutive features until layer VI. The last Ubaid pottery appeared in layer XII and layers XI and X have been assigned to the Early Uruk period. Among clay finds, the occurrence of baked sick- les is interrupted in layers XIVc and XIVb but from layer XIVa on they represent a constant feature of the find groups. Clay tokens exist from layer XVII up. The first mosaic cones have been registered in layer XIIa and from that time they continue, albeit in limited quantities. First metal tools also appear in layer XI. The strata of this time are characterized by an increase in the quantities of imported stone. Unworked items appear in layer XV and continue until the end of layer XIVa. Missing from layer XIII, they are limited to alabaster only from layer XII. Chipped industry consists of flint (from layer XIIb onwards), although most of the pieces are represented by unretouched items, and quantities of imported obsidian grow to make this material a normal component of the site assemblage. Layers XII–IX saw the limited occurrence of 'Steinwerfel' (stone weights?) as well as a temporary absence of stone vessels which had continued from the previous period. Finally, the fully fledged Uruk material culture (Sürenhagen 1986a, 9–10) gradually sets in after layer X. Bevelled-rim bowls (Figure 5.3) occur en masse from layer IX onwards (Sürenhagen 1986a, 8) as well as 'Blumentöpfe' (Strommenger 1980a, 482) and the technique of using a string to cut freshly formed vessels off the cone of the raw material

Figure 5.3 A bevelled-rim bowl, one of the most ubiquitous but also most enigmatic products of the Late Uruk age

positioned on the wheel is known since layer VIII (Sürenhagen 1986a, 8). Baked sickles go out of use after layer IX, appearing in secondary contexts in layers VIb2–VIa. Clay tokens disappear for a while in layers VIII/1–VII, becoming frequent in subsequent strata. Mosaic cones rise to a frequency peak in layers VIc2–VIb2, whereupon they disappear. Copper tools, a constant component of the find groups, terminate in layer VI. Flint tools vanish in layer VIb2 and their production is illuminated by rare finds of flint nuclei, present among finds from layers VIII–VIc1. Obsidian tools get rarer in layers VIc2–VIa, disappearing afterwards. Layer VIa is also the last instance when both raw alabaster lumps and stone vessels, which re-appeared in layer IX, are registered among the finds.

Cylinder seals are likely to have been invented and introduced in Uruk VII (Vértesalji 1988, 26; on Uruk cylinder seals recently see Rova 1994) and the invention of inventions, writing, could have appeared in Uruk VI (Vértesalji 1988, 26). The overall impression is one of a slow but steady growth of what had originally been a modest-sized rural centre into prosperity and social prominence. Early Uruk obviously launched the site into a reasonably affluent period at which imports of stone and metal constituted no particular luxury. The availability of chipped stone nevertheless did not lead to the abandonment of the age-old baked sickles which existed for a time together with stone tools. In some instances the community of this period deliberately chose to procure particular materials from afar (alabaster). A degree of social complexity seems to be signalled by the first occurrence of mosaic cones as a vehicle of embellishment of some architectural creations. The subsequent Middle Uruk period brought these trends to a further development but, surprisingly, seems to have extended the line of technological accomplishment into the area of such cheap materials as clay instead of more widespread expansion or social articulation. The emphasis appears to have been on communal, corporate behaviour patterns, as is indicated by the first appearance of cylinder seals and writing, both consequences of the emergence of a large-scale reciprocity-redistribution pattern of exchange activities (see pp. 146–150), by the end of this period. A remarkable feature of early Uruk is the absence of seals or sealings within these strata (von Wickede 1990, 212–214; a single jar sealing from layer XII: ibid. pp. 213–214, Table 482).

Things changed fundamentally when, in the period of layer VI, Uruk rose to the status of a supraregional centre (Nissen 1972). The grandeur of these early times was incarnated at first in two extraordinary structures. The 'Steinstifttempel', or stone-cone temple, was built in layer VI on a terrace sunk into a foundation trench, on what had probably been a standard central-hall plan with a T-shaped central hall. Its walls were cast in layers of concrete tempered with crushed brick ('Gips mit Ziegelsplitt') and oblong tiles with rounded perforated ends, perhaps for anchoring mural decoration, were set in horizontal rows in them. They carried mosaic ornamentation composed of pegs of red sandstone, alabaster and grey to black bituminous limestone. Its enclosure wall, whitewashed outside, bore a rich decoration of blue and green-yellow stone mosaics inside. The inner areas of this structure were covered by a layer containing Late Uruk pottery and tokens (Heinrich 1982, 45–46, 70–72, Figs 104, 106; Schmandt-Besserat 1988a, 13–14). A most difficult problem is represented by the huge 'Steingebäude', facing An's ziggurat but later than the inception of its building and belonging to the earlier segment of Late Uruk (Schmidt 1970, 71 – Uruk VI; see also Strommenger 1980a, 487; Heinrich 1982, 67–68). Before the establishment of this structure a foundation pit was sunk into the underlying Ubaid culture strata. The building rests on a layer of limestone boulders joined with mortar and laid on the bottom of the foundation pit and consists of a central chamber and two corridors forming an oblong plan, delimited by three massive sets of rectangular walls *c*.3.5 m high, built of limestone and mould-cast concrete blocks. Pits in the corners and in the centres of the shorter walls as well as paired cavities in the longer walls may have once held posts or other construction elements. The central cella contained a podium-like construction, the base of which was constituted by reed matting. This bore a layer of limestone pieces poured over with bitumen and a superimposed coating of fine lime mortar showing a layout of five small cavities disposed like a figure-of-five on dice. The surviving traces of internal furnishings included shallow conduits in the middle-oblong walls and tanks suggesting libation rites, implied also by the presence of vessels composed of parallel stone tubes cemented together and leading into a common container. In addition to these and to pottery fragments, the 'Steingebäude' contained only a roughly carved statuette of a prisoner with bound hands. The whole structure was buried under an enormous load of stones alternating with clay strata but has subsequently been opened at least once, poured over with mortar and backfilled (Schmidt 1970, 60–75; Strommenger 1980a, 487; Szarzyńska 1981; Schmandt-Besserat 1988a, 17). In addition to the ingenious interpretation of a 'gueule d'enfer', proposed by K. Szarzyńska (1981), this situation reminds me of Enuma elish I:6, where, at the beginning of the world, '*gipara la kissuru susa la she'u*'. The semantic field of the somewhat enigmatic 'giparu' includes a) residence of the enu/entu, b) part of a private house, c) pasture or meadow and d) taboo (*CAD* G 83–84). This evidence could become transparent if we assume that the word originally meant a reed mat spread on earth as a nuptial bed of the master and mistress of a house and, in a wider sense, a source of fertility, affluence and abundance of the house itself and of all those who lived in it. This original sememe could well develop into the directions of 'shrine, residence of cultically potent persons, privy chambers, taboo' and 'pasture, meadow, fertile plant-giving land'. The position of the matting below the figure-of-five ensign, which clearly represents the civilized human world (see p. 156), could well reproduce the likeness and function of some archetypal structure connected with fertility and infusing life into the human-dominated sphere of existence. The idea of the pontifical couple, EN and NIN, discharging universal fertility by the NA2 ceremony (Charvát 1997, 41–70, esp. pp. 57–58, and 84–85) seems to be of relevance here. Does the 'Steingebäude' mat represent the first giparu, 'tied together, plaited' (kissuru) at the beginning of the world and followed by the creation of humanity? However that may be, the 'Steingebäude' clearly represents the incarnation of an elaborate mythical concept. In connection with the extensive use of stone in these Uruk structures, references to Uruk and Eridu buildings erected of 'mountain stones' fetched by inhabitants of the mountain state of Aratta may be of relevance (J. Börker-Klähn, in Heinrich 1982, 52, n. 76).

In layer V, these two impressive architectures were followed by the 'Kalksteintempel', or Limestone Temple. It lies on a bed of trampled clay covered by layers of stone blocks. Though its state of preservation is lamentable, the temple does seem to represent an example of an architecture with a T-shaped central hall and to repeat thus the lesson learnt at the 'Steinstifttempel'. The dimensions of the 'Kalksteintempel' are respectable – it is 62 m long and 11.30 m wide – the flanking subsidiary chambers were accessed by doors both from outside the temple and from the central hall (in contrast with Ubaid culture central-hall buildings which regularly possess a single entrance only) and a staircase ramp at the end of one of the lateral wings once gave access to the roof of the building. The south-west shorter wall of its central hall bears two niches (Heinrich 1982, 46, 74, Fig. 114).

Within layer IV the chronology of individual buildings is complicated and has been re-arranged several times (see Eichmann 1989). Individual structures may, in consequence of this fact, be dated differently in the future. There is, first and foremost, evidence of re-orientations of the spiritual world resulting in ceremonial burial of disused cultic inventory. The 'Riemchengebäude', or building of strap-shaped bricks, is now being dated into layer IVc or IVb (Heinrich 1982, 72–73, Figs 106, 110 and 111; Limper 1988; Schmandt-Besserat 1988a, 14; Becker and Heinz 1993). A huge pit sunk for its foundations into the ruins of the north corner of the 'Steinstifttempel' received pavement with stones laid in bitumen. Upon this pavement was erected a structure consisting of an innermost rectangular chamber surrounded on all four sides by corridors with an extra room added on its south-east side. A fire kindled with wood of either a fruit (nut?) tree or a coniferous tree (Heinrich 1982, 73) and burning within the central chamber stained its north-west and north-east walls red. Objects recovered from this cella comprise vessels of pottery and stone, animal bones and small but stout pegs as well as obsidian blades and cores; they were poured over with bitumen. The richest array of objects, however, turned up in the four wings of the surrounding corridor, filled up to the height of 75 cm from the floor.

Among these finds the reports refer to storage jars, textile remains (some deposited in chests), animal bones (a ram skull with horn), copper vessels, wooden objects inlaid with coloured (black and white, for instance) mosaics including possibly furniture items (Becker and Heinz 1993, 18–23), stone (alabaster) vessels, vestiges of a more-than-life-size female(?) sculpture of 'artificial stone' (gypsum and sand, see Becker and Heinz 1993, 75, No. 940, and Wrede 1995 who identifies it as an image of a male ruler), personal ornaments (a golden earring, a copper mirror?), weapons

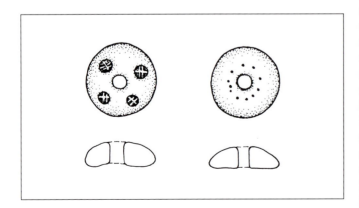

Figure 5.4 Ubaid or Uruk age spindle whorls from Uruk (after Kohlmeyer and Hauser 1994)

such as arrowheads, maces, knives and spears, parts of architectural decoration (terracotta pegs, gold foil, nails with gilt heads) and/or ceremonial objects (?, copper mounts of wooden rods at least 1.8 m long). Some of these treasures left their impressions in the wall plaster which must have been fresh at the time of deposition. The objects were covered with matting and all the intervening space filled in with ruins of the temple(?), save for the south-east room which was whitewashed, its floor covered with bitumen and matting and its interior filled in with clean earth. The 'Riemchengebäude''s external façade might have borne paintings displaying both geometric and figural motifs (Nunn 1985). The whole area was then covered by another layer of temple ruins with a few objects in secondary positions (tokens; see Lenzen 1958; Frankfort 1968, 14; Lenzen 1974, 127–128; Heinrich 1982, 72–73, Figs 106, 110, 111; Schmandt-Besserat 1988a, 14). It has been suggested that this structure may represent the ceremonial disposal of the cultic inventory no longer needed after the abandonment of the 'Steinstifttempel' (Schmandt-Besserat 1988a, 14).

The early phase of layer IV (IVd–IVb) witnessed the erection of an impressive series of brick temples. This is the time of introduction of the standardized 'Riemchen' brick, prevailing in the course of Uruk layers IV and III (Finkbeiner 1986, 47–48). The excavators of Uruk note that very few pottery items were found in any of the three stages of phase IV (Heinrich 1982, 72). First and foremost, let us refer to the 'Stiftmosaikgebäude' (Lenzen 1974, 116–119; Heinrich 1982, 46, 75–76, Figs 117, 119), an architectural group involving temples A (on the north–south terrace) and B, of a 'typical Sumerian tripartite' character (Frankfort 1968, 7). By the north–south terrace was a large courtyard with a spacious portico consisting of a double row of four massive pillars bearing cone-mosaic decoration. This portico could be entered from at least one door at one of the portico's ends between the pillar rows, as well as from the courtyard by means of a ramp bearing a double staircase (a reconstruction can be found in Mallowan 1965, 38, Ill. 25). The courtyard walls bore a cone-mosaic decoration in red, white and black; the round pillars displayed white and black colours, and the same kind of ornament (but in black only) embellished the façade of the stair ramp. In the same period Temple C, apparently with a transversal 'transept' close to one of its ends, followed by a suite of minor chambers between the 'transept' and the north-west façade, was built. This T-shaped arrangement, an elaboration on the architectural antecedents applied also in the case of Temple B, has been described by H. Frankfort as a 'combination of two tripartite temples set at right angles' (Frankfort 1968, 8). A number of hearths uncovered in the five layers of the temple's whitewashed floors did not yield any ash traces but the last floor layer bore burnt remains of a timber roof (Lenzen 1974, 123–129). Building E, referred to as a 'palace', was of a square plan with a large central courtyard enclosed by corridors opening onto it through a portico consisting of a double row of pillars. Its walls displayed no cone-mosaic decoration but were painted in a colour that today has a light orange hue (Lenzen 1974, 121–122, Pl. XVI on p. 113; Heinrich 1982, 77–78, Fig. 118; Schmandt-Besserat 1988a, 10, 16). Another impressive architectural creation consisted of the three structures F, G and H, displaying the now standardized plan of a T-shaped central hall flanked by suites of subsidiary chambers on three sides and disposed at right angles around a courtyard (Lenzen 1974, 119–121; Heinrich 1982, 46, 74–75, Fig. 116; Schmandt-Besserat 1988a, 10, 14–15). Room I by building H yielded a hoard of twenty-five clay tokens in a 'frying-pan shaped' hearth (ibid., a most interesting parallel to Tell Madhhur, see 56–57). Unfortunately, this group of structures has not been excavated in full and this pertains more or less to all structures of level IV. Though their plans clearly develop the Ubaid culture tradition of the central-hall buildings, including such mundane features as staircase ramps, frequently doubled now, differences are visible. In addition to the T-shaped ground plan of the central hall, the Uruk culture structures display quite different circulation patterns as they stood open to visitors streaming in through the numerous entrances piercing their walls (see, for instance, the Uruk temples B and C, in Parrot 1960, 66, Fig. 83A, B). This contrasts sharply with the Ubaid culture tradition when the norm was one single entrance through a vestibule (Forest 1983b, 7–8). The enormous difference in size strikes the eye but, on the other hand, it may be significant that the south-east shorter wall of the central hall of Uruk temple C displays two niches conforming with the binary tradition of Tepe Gawra XV–XII (see p. 50). The double niche is also borne by the shorter walls of the central halls of temples G, F and perhaps also H (Heinrich 1982, 75, Fig. 116). Among these three temples the earliest one seems to have been temple G, followed in due course by the other two structures.

All this huge construction was almost totally obliterated at the end of Uruk IVb with the sole exception of temple C, which remained in use (Heinrich 1982, 46–47, 50–51, 78–83, Figs 120 and 124; Schmandt-Besserat 1988a, 10). Building E, as well as temples B and F, had its walls pulled down to the height of 2–3 brick courses and the ruins were levelled with debris. New structures erected at that time included the 'Hallenbau' (hall building) and the 'Pfeilerhalle', or pillar hall, both decorated with cone mosaics. Contemporary architects must have prided themselves on such a magnificent creation as Temple D, the largest structure of Eanna, again on the standard plan of a T-shaped central hall flanked by alignments of subsidiary chambers, the external façades of which were visually articulated by alternating series of niches and engaged columns. This building had a much more complex circulation pattern than its predecessors. Of the two perfectly symmetrical staircases, the ramps of which survived in the plan (Parrot 1960, 66, Fig. 83C), one could be entered only from outside, and the other one only from inside. The northeast shorter wall of its central hall displayed, flanked by two multiple and two single recesses, one central niche, in contrast to the two apparent in a similar position in temple C of the earlier sublayer. Another building added at this stage was the bath, consisting of a numerous series of rooms, the floors and lower parts of walls of which (up to the height of 40 cm) were waterproofed with bitumen. Though round soakage pits were provided for the used water, frequent rebuilding documented in this complex indicates that the solidity of the construction was affected by the purpose to which the building was put. This period also saw the erection of the 'Red Temple', now believed to have played an administrative role. This building, situated on a terrace and rather imperfectly preserved, bore on its walls a coating of red paint. Among other finds, its vicinity yielded cone mosaics and fragments of a clay frieze with rosettes, rampant animals and bundles of reeds, as well as 120 inscribed tablets, found along one of its walls, and a number of broken jar sealings (Heinrich 1982, 83; Schmandt-Besserat 1988a,12; Englund 1994, esp. pp. 13–16). A most conspicuous component of the Uruk IVa architectural layout is the Great Courtyard, in reality another enormous pit, whose sides were revetted by masonry built of burnt and bitumen-coated bricks, making up two concentric squares of benches. The upper part of the retaining wall bore cone mosaics. The courtyard was provided with at least one staircase and with a cistern supplied by a vaulted conduit, but no other device for the evacuation of rain water from inside has been discovered. R. M. Boehmer (1991, 468) has suggested that it might well have served as a garden. The debris and levelling layers of the Great Courtyard yielded a quantity of inscribed tablets and sealings (Lenzen 1962, 7–8 and 1974, 127; Heinrich 1982, 47; Schmandt-Besserat 1988a, 15–16). The entire architectural group of Uruk IVa underwent total destruction, perhaps as a consequence of violent action, at the end of this period, and the following layer III manifests considerably different planning (see pp. 160–161; Lenzen 1962, 11; Lenzen 1964, 11; Finkbeiner 1986, 46; Schmandt-Besserat 1988a, 10–11).

The other religious centre of early Uruk, shrine of the sky god An, contains a series of structures the dates of which have caused a certain degree of controversy (Frankfort 1968, 13; Strommenger 1980b, 486; Schmandt-Besserat 1988a, 16–17). E. Heinrich (1982, 39, 61) insists on its dating in the Uruk period, corroborated by the fact that the foundation trench of the

'Steingebäude' was sunk into debris strata belonging probably to this structure (ibid. 67). An's ziggurat consists of a massive early core and a series of successive enlargements and rebuildings making up the total of fourteen phases of this structure, numbered from L or X (the early core) to the most recent A3 phase. From earliest times the building stood on a terrace of an irregular ground plan accessible by a ramp of which ten chronological phases have been identified (from L to B). Phase E ushered in a series of changes. First and foremost, the top part of the terrace walls bore from now on up to the

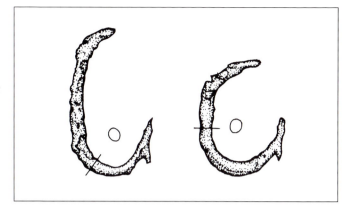

Figure 5.5 Late Uruk fishing hooks of copper from Habuba Kabira (after Strommenger 1980a, 53, Fig. 40)

B phase a frieze consisting of three strips of terracotta rings protruding from the masonry. Second, from this phase the terrace was accessible by a paired ramp and staircase, accompanied by a conduit for the disposal of rainwater. Finally, the first ground plan of very regular central-hall buildings with flanking wings of subsidiary chambers in the south-west part of the terrace has been documented in this phase. The door sill of this structure, coated with bitumen, bore a decoration of three wide copper belts. The road leaving the door for the ramp-cum-staircase was paved with flat slabs of limestone and a pair of bitumen-coated post-holes, likely to have accommodated erect shafts (symbols? standards?), came to light at both sides of the entrance. Layer D, immediately above E, contained a ground plan of a structure most similar to the E-phase temple. Phase C saw the transfer of building activities to the north-west part of the terrace. Here a small subsidiary terrace accommodated a rectangular building with two entrances in the centres of the east and west walls, built of palm trunks set in bitumen-coated post-holes. This structure was followed by another one of its kind and then by another subsidiary terrace (still within phase C), on which the contemporary architects outlined in red a plan of another regular central-hall building, subsequently erected on the spot. One of the floors of this phase bore, among other small finds, impressions of cylinder seals (Heinrich 1982, Fig. 85a–c). Finally, Phase B's popularity has been assured by the famous 'White Temple', built on a bitumen-coated pedestal again in the south-west part of the terrace. Its floors consisted of clay coatings of a brick layer resting on the bitumen surface; an exception is a pit left out in the east corner containing an offering of animal bones. The floors and walls bore a white gypsum coating. The other, north, west and east corner chambers of the building contained staircases, unfinished in the case of the north end. Both chambers in the midst of the north-east room suite might have been equipped with shelves of coniferous-tree wood anchored in the walls and displayed cavities for setting in pivot stones which imply more solid door construction. The north end of the central hall was occupied by a podium accessible by means of a small staircase and its middle part by an 'altar' with a fire-stained upper surface. In its central part, the terrace area outside the White Temple contained a huge fire-stained pit (2.2 × 2.7 m) and a massive loop hewn out of a stone boulder by the access ramp, as well as a system of shallow bitumen-coated conduits issuing from the terrace edges south-east and south-west of the temple, entering through its south-east and south-west doors and meeting in the midst of the central hall where the liquids collected in them flowed into a soakage pit. After the extinction of its functions the doors of the White Temple were immured and the whole area covered and infilled by large bricks, probably belonging to the A1 phase of the whole layout. This phase also yielded, among other finds, cylinder-seal impressions (Heinrich 1982, 35, 38–39, 61–66, Figs 78–80). It is not clear to which phase of the structure the gypsum tablets referred to by Robert Englund belong (1994, 18–19, Figs 8–9).

Stylistic analysis has led to the dating of some exquisite pieces of statuary found at Uruk to the time of the Uruk culture, though stratigraphic data are by no means decisive enough (see Becker and Heinz 1993). A sculpture of a female head, justly famous under the name of 'Lady of Uruk', was discovered in a pit sealed by a layer which yielded tablets of late Uruk III type (ibid. 77, No. 952). The lion-hunt stele turned up in the ruins of the Uruk-III temple but clearly in a secondary position. Finally, one of the male statuettes was deposited in a pot covered by a 'Blumentopf'. The lifespan of such pottery products has been estimated as Uruk IX–III/II (see Strommenger 1980b, 482 on the whole problem).

A more mundane but historically important source is represented by the settlement site WS 312, excavated in 1960–1961 some 4 km north-east of Eanna. Unlike the following time period, the earliest phase of this site, dating to the very end of the Uruk culture period (D) displayed no traces of professional specialization but exclusively average habitation structures. After desertion, its ruins were levelled to make room for the later structures (Vértesalji 1988), much as in the case of Eanna buildings. Late Uruk period habitation structures came to light in a test trench in squares O 11/12 (Finkbeiner 1991, 193), while a large area with traces of pyrotechnical activities was observed in the north-west quarter of the city (ibid. 194).

The overall settled area of Late Uruk period Uruk amounted to about 250 hectares, equalling thus the Greek polis of Athens around 500 BC (ibid.). On the site in general see also Boehmer 1997.

Finally, we must mention the extraordinary proliferation of rural settlement surrounding the Uruk culture centre. No less than approximately 100 sites of the Late Uruk period have been registered in its vicinity. In the northern part of this 'Greater Uruk', the rural sites turned up in clusters, avoiding, however, the closest proximity of the city (Nissen 1972), where the existence of fields may reasonably be expected (see Ball *et al.* 1989, 11–12). A similar phenomenon, albeit on a much more limited scale, has been registered for the Uruk period site of Tell Brak, Syria (Weiss 1983, 42).

Khafajeh – Sin 'temple'

A site some 35 km east of Baghdad excavated by a US mission directed by H. Frankfort within the Diyala Basin Project lasting from 1930 to 1938. Of all the sites elucidated by these excavations the Sin 'temple' at Khafajeh represents the earliest structure, established, as it seems, within the Uruk culture period. For this reason I have decided to include here the description of its four earliest phases, though they undoubtedly lasted until after the end of Uruk culture, Phase V with its solid-footed goblets being assignable to the end of Jemdet Nasr or to the very beginning of the ED period.

Throughout the first four phases of its existence, the Sin 'temple' retained its standardized plan, clearly relying on the Ubaid culture prototype of central-hall buildings, that of a longitudinal central hall flanked along its longer sides by suites of subsidiary rooms. The earliest structure was established on a settlement layer yielding such remains as red burnished and grey-black pottery wares, bevelled-rim bowls and mosaic cones, indicating a foundation date within the Uruk culture period. The earliest phase, Sin I, did not contain numerous finds but those retrieved mostly from subsidiary rooms (as was customary in the preceding, Ubaid culture period) clearly point to the habitational character of the structure: a storage jar and a group of utility pottery in room

Figure 5.6 Amulets and pendants worn in the Late Uruk age. Such trinkets, imbued with the personalities of their bearers, were frequently left in the temples, presumably as tokens of veneration of the local divinities and of the worshippers' loyalty to them.

Q 42:47 (Delougaz and Lloyd 1942, 14, Fig. 8), chipped flint tools with traces of bitumen hafting and a boat model, the position of which is ambiguous (ibid. 136). On the other hand, the two pendants in the shape of twin bird heads separated by vertical chequered bands of white and dark rhomboid fields (ibid. 12 and Fig. 6 on p. 13) certainly belong to non-average artifacts. Let us note that for the first time, a podium ('altar') is built on the north end of the central hall, establishing a tradition lasting until the final, X layer of the structure, almost half a millennium later. From Sin II, room Q 42:41 yielded two splendid cylinder seals bearing classical Uruk-style scenes with herds of animals and reed huts, provided with suspension loops of silver and, in one case, with the upper end displaying a belt of decoration consisting of triangular fields of mother-of-pearl and jasper. Sin III had two floors, the upper one being some 25 cm above the lower, again pointing to a profane character of the structure in which domestic rubbish was allowed to accumulate at such a rate (on élite and non-élite rubbish disposal see Gibbon 1984, 160–161). The finds concentrated in room Q 42:26 do nevertheless show some élite functions of this building. A bird-shaped pottery vessel and a stone vase with mother-of-pearl and jasper incrustations are accompanied here by a lunate ornament of gold and by a multitude of amulets in the shapes of most diverse animals, birds, reptiles or insects (Figure 5.6). However, a saw blade is also present among the finds of this phase (Delougaz and Lloyd 1942, 143). A small room abutting the enclosure wall of this phase contained a shelf with miniature vessels of pottery and stone. Finally, Sin IV is the first local case of a terrace building, the older structure having been torn down to a height of about 1 m and the inner space having been filled in by clay. In this manner the foundation for the fourth phase of the building was prepared. The court of Sin IV, Q 42:21, contained two large kilns rebuilt several times. As to finds, they now tend to turn up in the central hall rather than in the subsidiary rooms and are similar in character to those of Sin III. Again there are vessels and receptacles of pottery and stone, including a bull-shaped vase and a grey conical stone vessel with geometrical inlays. Ceremonial objects are represented by a fragment of a geometrical composition of stone, shells and beads set into clay, by the 'eye idols' and by a female statuette. Besides the amulets and pendants two categories of cylinder seals are present: long and thin ones of glazed steatite with geometrical patterns and smaller examples of limestone with summarily executed images of animals and a building (Delougaz and Lloyd 1942, 8–31; Hansen 1997a).

Grai Resh

A tell 4 miles east of Sinjar, an Anglo-Iraqi excavation of 1939 headed by S. Lloyd. Two soundings in the tell exposed, in one case, a stratigraphy of six layers (four Ubaid, IX–VI, and two of the Ubaid–Uruk transition, V–IV), and in the other a sequence of three phases belonging to the Uruk culture (layers III and II) and to the beginning of the ED period (layer I). C-14 dates: 3893 +/−88 BC (Hassan and Robinson 1987, 127); 3890–3635 cal. BC (Annex 712), 4135–3785 cal. BC (ibid.). The Uruk culture house of layer III was clearly bonded into a massive brickwork construction 5 m thick, possibly a town wall. The most interesting contribution of this operation, however, is another Uruk culture house in the overlying layer II, showing a standard central-hall layout. The builders of the house used large rectangular bricks and roofed their construction with timber baulks, reed matting and coatings of clay. The central hall received a whitewash and its shorter north wall was articulated by a pair of symmetrical niches starting at a height of 50 cm above the floor. Most of the unusually numerous finds were concentrated in the central hall and in the two rooms flanking it on the north side. The north-west room offered most instructive insights into the daily chores of the inhabitants. The housewife who worked here had at her disposal a series of pottery vessels standing on brick banks lining the north and west walls. Jars for the storage of provisions contained a mixture of wheat and barley (this one was sunk into the floor) as well as meat, attested by the presence of bones. The same room also contained chipped stone items of flint and obsidian such as two large points, two scrapers and a chert blade core, a small celt of polished stone and also a copper point. The north-east room was also provided with storage jars covered by the remains of the collapsed roof. A burial of an infant protected by two pottery vessels enclosing the body was concealed below the floor of one of the rooms.

The house contained an abundance of objects of which most lack exact data as to their find-spots, the only indication being that a majority of them turned up in the central hall and in the north-east room. In addition to animal bones which may represent domestic herds (bones and horns of sheep and goats, horns of water-buffalo) the inhabitants used eating implements of bone, sometimes highly polished. Clay served first and foremost for the production of classical Uruk culture pottery (the standard assemblage: D. Sürenhagen in Rothman 1990, 132f.). Moreover, there were two figurines of unidentifiable animals, a clay female statuette with a concave base, decorated spindle whorls, egg-shaped items usually interpreted as slingshot and pendants. An 'eye idol' is accompanied by a seal impression on clay with an image of a human figure, the closest parallel to which, I believe, comes from Tepe Gawra layer XII (von Wickede 1990, Table 267). Metal was freely available to the locals: in addition to the above-mentioned point they left a copper drill head lying on the site. As usual, stone finds turned up widely. Obsidian was used for the production of chipped industry (blades, simple flakes) and beads; most of it appears to have been fresh with very few weathered pieces. Chert served for the production of blades, in many cases for sickles (sometimes with traces of bitumen hafting) and flakes; there is a chert core. Ground stone items include a number of basalt querns and grinding stones, two hammer-axes bored through and a pear-shaped macehead of purple-coloured marble with veins as well as the above-mentioned celt. Some of the inhabitants of the house wore pendants of stone and one round seal. The volume of chipped industry, both of flint and of obsidian, was markedly lower than in the 'prehistoric' strata from layer V downwards (because of the accessibility of metal items?).

This is a small but highly significant excavation. First, it proves clearly that the Uruk culture 'temples' are by no means exclusively religious everywhere but that they could have sheltered common everyday activities, serving as habitation structures. Second, it contributes corroborative evidence for the distribution of 'activity zones' and 'quiet zones' within one architectural unit, as suggested for the Ubaid culture Tell Madhhur house. At Grai Resh the artifacts tend to cluster in the hall and the north-east and north-west rooms, very probably representing the ancient 'activity zones' where food was prepared, and probably also eaten, and specialized activities carried out. The south-east room, serving as vestibule, is a special case but the south-west room may be designated as a 'quiet zone', reserved perhaps for sleeping and storage (Lloyd 1940).

Tepe Gawra

This site of exceptional significance even for the preceding period now assumes a crucial role as a sample of indigenous development of the northern submontane zone in its layers XIA–VIIIA (on the assignation of these strata to the Uruk period see von Wickede 1990, 134–135; more specifically, to Early and Middle Uruk, parallel to Ninive 3, see Gut 1992, 32, and 1995).

Layer XII, in which painted Ubaid-style pottery occurs for the last time, is followed by layer XIA, which bears witness to a revolutionary change of layout. Even if the assumed 'bastions' in marginal settlement positions are discounted, the 'Round House', which dominates this settlement phase, strikes a definitely military or rather defensive note. It has yielded a fairly insignificant volume of ordinary settlement rubbish, showing it to be a settlement unit still undifferentiated as to sacred and profane functions. The fact that very few graves (if any – see Forest 1983a, 176, Pl. 12) turned up below its floors is interesting but difficult to explain. Was this a 'communal' building in the sense that it did not belong to any of the corporate kin groups(?) that interred some of their deceased members in their abodes? No peculiar features are displayed by the rest of the architectural layout save for the fact that the central hall of the rather regularly planned building in square J-K 5 bore a whitewash. Builders of this settlement used bricks extensively but stone only sparingly, reserving it for those architectural components most exposed to wear and tear. Their burial customs hardly differed from those of the preceding residents: children predominated in the subfloor interments, roughly equal numbers of them resting on their right and left sides, and grave goods seem to reflect age categories (beads for children, pottery and others for adults). As to peculiarities of material culture, the bone items which might have served as mouthpieces of musical instruments turn up regularly from this period on. All the remaining find categories continue from the preceding period. Sealings on clay also reflect age-old practices save for a single item from a door or chest (von Wickede 1990, 159–167; on sealings of this period at Gawra see also Rothman 1989 and 1994). The pottery of this period tends to be coarser and the slow wheel left its traces on fewer examples than before. Nevertheless, the 'impressed ware', mostly beakers with appliqué or stamped geometrical decoration, ranks now among the typical products (von Wickede 1990, 133). Clay statuettes of this period include images both of women and of animals (sheep).

The following layer XI is again dominated by a more or less homogeneous building layout among which two structures have drawn more attention. The first is the 'temple' on the eastern fringe of the settlement. Its plan alludes for the first time to those of similar structures of the subsequent layers IX and VIII, as does also a rectangular clay-and-cement plateau by its entrance, omitted on Forest's plan (Forest 1983a, Pl. 13 contra Tobler 1950, 14–15). The east faces of the short walls separating the 'nave' and the 'chancel' of the Layer XI 'temple' bear a coating of red paint; in contrast, a single niche 1 m wide, running through the vertical axis of the 'chancel' frontal wall and starting 30 cm above the floor is painted white. Room 2 by the 'chancel' has yielded a series of seal impressions including 'lock' (i.e. door) sealing or sealings. The 'temple' was surrounded by a kitchen, a pottery workshop and other domestic production facilities (Rothman 1990, 285f.). The other conspicuous building in square Q 5–6 also had some parts of its interior painted red and its room 61 was provided with a floor of reed matting. 'Lock' sealing or sealings appeared here again (Rothman 1990, 592f.). From this layer on, clay from one and the same source was used at Gawra until layer IX (ibid. 575ff.). Inhabitants of this phase site used stone for their thresholds and for street paving much more profusely than before. In the sphere of burial customs this period ushers in the richly equipped child interments. A grave from Locus 181 by the 'temple' plateau contained a body of a child with a rosette and repoussé-decorated disc of gold at his or her head, stone and golden beads at the wrists and stone tokens by the hands and knees (Tobler 1950, 90f., 116f.). Clay statuettes of this layer included animal images only (sheep, dog?) and the number of spindle whorls increased (eighty items found). This is the last layer in which stone vessels have been found in settlement contexts; from the next layer on they are present only in graves. Among the artisans active in this settlement the presence of woodworkers and weavers is suspected.

Layer XA shows an impoverished version of its predecessor and a shadow of its former glory. No 'lock' sealings are present (Rothman 1990, 287ff., 508ff., 593) and the only changes worth noting are the decrease in the quantity of spindle whorls ('to normal') and the presence of a stone imitation of an astragal bone. A symbolic function of this artifact is suggested both by the accumulation of sheep knuckle bones in the east 'temple' of layer VIIIA and by astragal-shaped tokens enclosed in clay bullae (Susa C: von Wickede 1990, 307, *sub* No. 628 and Table 628). This period of privation, however, was succeeded by times of plenty in the chronological phase of deposition of layer X. Settlement of this stage has all the appearance of a cluster of residences of well-established and affluent families of 'country gentry'. This is indicated first and foremost by finds of seal impressions indicating movement of goods in mobile containers across property boundaries; one single 'lock' sealing turned up in this phase (Rothman 1990, 595) although it is unfortunate that practically none of these finds were retrieved from secure contexts (von Wickede 1990, 167). Such evidence singles out first the central 'temple' and then a household south-west of the 'temple' (nine impressions of a single seal) as well as a settlement complex consisting of rooms 1043–1051. Another eloquent testimony of the welfare of the local group is supplied by a residence located in squares J-M 10–11, provided with all types of exquisite and average pottery, both for cooking and for food consumption, but lacking work tools and raw materials. Another manner of articulation of a non-average social situation appears in the form of the 'manor' situated in square M 5–6 with a central hall and a kiln. A deposit of three beakers had been sunk prior to the erection of the west corner of this structure. One of its rooms concealed below its floor tomb 107, enshrining the remains of an adult who received as funerary equipment six spheres of white stone. After extinction of the settlement functions of this complex, its hall was filled in with bricks to a height of about 1 m. This residence yielded no sealings whatsoever. As in the previous layer, the local settlers found no particular difficulty in transporting considerable quantities of stone for the paving of public space to the site. Of the extraordinary wealth displayed by prominent personages of the day samples have survived as grave goods. Jean-Daniel Forest's attempt to re-date to layer VIII some of the richest graves originally attributed to this layer (Forest 1983a, 42–43) does not seem to have found widespread acceptance (Moorey 1985, 76, on the electrum wolf's head as coming from layer X; Schmandt-Besserat 1988b, 3; Rothmann 1990, 348–349). Children predominate over adults as to the number of interments but even so, tombs of this period have yielded an incredible quantity of personal ornaments and other objects, especially in the case of the grave series 102, 107, 109, 110 and 114. The deceased wore such items as golden rosettes and hair pins, heavy bead necklaces with pendants, eye-shaped ornaments, bangles and sewn-on ornaments of gold, lapis lazuli, turquoise, carnelian and electrum. Some of the beads were also displayed sewn on clothing, as was the case of the deceased laid to rest in grave G 36–34, whose garment was decorated at the waist by a herringbone pattern of beads consisting of alternating black and white groups. Personal articles deposited in these graves included bone combs, golden tubes, a whetstone, spatulae and a lapis lazuli seal; weapons(?) were represented by a macehead. Other categories of burial equipment present in these graves are vessels of metal (electrum), pottery and stone, stone tokens (Schmandt-Besserat 1988b) and an obsidian core and blades. An artifact absolutely unique and likely to possess a symbolic value is the tiny wolf's head that accompanied the deceased of tomb 114. It is made of electrum with ears and jaw separately attached by copper and electrum pins and armed with golden-wire teeth; its interior contains a bitumen filling (Mallowan 1965, 79, Ill. 85). A peculiar procedure seems to have left the traces of blue and green pigment on the chest and blue pigment on the femurs of the body laid to rest in grave 110. Obsidian fashioned into the bowl and vase found by the hands of an adult in grave 102 was brought from central Anatolia (Rothman 1990, 348–349).

In the sphere of material culture, perceptible changes include the almost total disappearance of 'impressed ware' (von Wickede 1990, 134) and the curious scarcity of clay statuettes, of which a single example, depicting a human male, has been found. Nonetheless, the overall amount of pottery produced seems to have increased; the idea springs to mind that more exquisite materials for the articles of daily use, clearly freely available, were now preferred. The output of metal items might also have risen slightly. Elite individuals were obviously present at the site during the following phase IX as well, but some adjustments of the social situation clearly took place. The architectural layout is now dominated by a pair of impressive structures, the 'temple' and the complex of rooms east of it. The 'temple', the ground plan of which seems to have been more and more rigidly fixed throughout layers XI–VIII, is provided with a peculiar 'frying-pan-shaped' platform built of clay and cement in its central hall. Its top bears traces of fire and ashy deposits surround it. A similar platform occupies the west corner of room 904, obviously joined to the north-west façade of the 'temple'. The rooms of this structure have yielded a series of sealings including 'locks' from at least two doors; one seal left repeated imprints here both on jar stoppers and on doors (von Wickede 1990, 168–169; Rothman 1990, 595). The complex with massive walls and reinforced floor pavements east of the 'temple' may possibly be connected with the storage or processing of animal products (ibid. 382ff., 539ff.). These two most conspicuous structures are accompanied by minor buildings along the western edge of the hilltop, equipped with stone-lined conduits, a part of which housed a workshop turning out stone and bone beads, seals and bone furniture inlays (Rothman 1990, 382ff.). The main structural characteristics of the burial practices of the preceding period are retained: children still predominate over adults, the bodies are deposited on both sides and accompanied by luxury versions of personal ornaments and articles. Among minor changes, let us note the decreasing number of polished stone celts, illogical in light of the easy accessibility of stone used even in less pretentious buildings. Does some other material replace polished stone for these tools? Wheel-thrown vessels appear for the first time.

The next period VIII brought Tepe Gawra to the peak of prominence again, but also to an ultimate decline and the fall of this major pre- and protohistoric site into the state of a rural hamlet. In this text I am trying to remain faithful to the excavation report and retain E. Speiser's divisions of VIIIC, VIIIB and VIIIA. The VIIIC period ushered in an architectural layout consisting of four major structures or 'temples' (west 'temple', central 'temple', east and north 'temples'), a 'hammam' building and common utility housing filling in some of the intervening spaces. The west 'temple' shows evidence for several building phases; one of them saw the blocking of the main entrance while after the extinction of the building's function its users pulled the walls down to a height of 1 m and levelled the intervening spaces with debris to make room for a new building. The interior of the west 'temple' yielded traces of domestic and craft activities. The same observation relates to the central 'temple'; in neither of these structures were there found any seal impressions. On the contrary, the east 'temple', of the same plan as the west one and also likely to have served as a habitation structure (the central hall contained a podium but also a kiln – Forest 1983a, 102, contra Speiser 1935, 28), furnished us with a series of sealings from mobile containers (Rothman 1990, 384ff., 596), some of them identical with those of the north 'temple'. Of the latter structure we may note the 'frying-pan-shaped' podium in its central hall as well as two (*sic!*) niches in its south-west wall. The 'hammam', a building between the central and north 'temples', had its central hall paved with bricks; a number of its doorless walls enclosed bitumen-covered floors. This building contained settlement refuse including impressions of a number of seals of which one marked tags of both local and external clay (Rothman 1990, 575ff.; von Wickede 1990, 171). This major innovation, occurring on sealings from mobile containers, may imply travelling seals (that is, a seal normally marking goods at site A goes forth from that site and designates commodities at site B [C, D, E . . .], returning subsequently to its home base, see Charvát 1992a, 282) and thus also the collection of surplus from a second, lower level of suppliers. My reasoning runs approximately as follows: the centre is normally supplied by goods sealed at site A by the seal of Mr/Ms X. For some reason, this seal goes on to leave site A and move to site(s) B (C, D, E . . .) where it is impressed on tags of (a part of?) goods supplied to Mr/Ms X by Mr/Ms Y (Z, AA, BB, CC . . .). Both kinds of goods sealed by the seal of Mr/Ms X subsequently travel to the centre, conveying the tags bearing the seal impression but made of clay from (at least two) different sites. It goes without saying that such evidence suggests a rather advanced manner of surplus collection, certainly tending towards taxation. To come back to the 'hammam', M. Rothman (1990, 384ff.) suggests that such activities as slaughter of animals or sheep-shearing might have gone on there. No substantial changes occur in the funerary sphere: the deceased are again provided with a variety of personal ornaments and belongings of luxury materials such as gold or lapis lazuli. In the light of the above-mentioned evidence for the two-level surplus collection, the string of beads interspersed with a tiny golden hoof, a golden mini-shovel and a golden spiral on the wrist of the deceased buried in grave 111 offer interesting hints. Were some of the deliveries to the centre, for instance, supplied by nomadic herdsmen to whom the 'tax-collectors' travelled at an appointed time? In the sphere of the beads the essential dyad white–black with supplements of other colours remained in vogue, reminiscent of layer X. As to work with natural materials, there seems to have been a number of changes, though some of them may well derive from differences in evaluation of the excavation record by E. Speiser and A. Tobler. Aside from the ordinary bone artifacts (awls, spatulae), ivory, present in the form of beads at least from level XIII, now comes to the fore with the find of a broken and mended pin of this material from layer VIII (no more detailed data available: Speiser 1935, 116–117). The fact that this article of attire must have been worn for a considerable time accords well with the absence of ivory beads from this layer. The local pottery continues to be wheel-made and of good quality; clay statuettes are now fashioned only in the form of domestic animals (sheep, bulls) and clay horn and chariot models appear. A few artifacts of hammered, not cast, copper turned up, including a sickle fragment and metal bars. Nevertheless, their employment is attested by whetstones. Of organic materials, wood seems to have been worked on the site and the production of wickerwork, textiles and of cords or ropes are borne out by impressions in the sealings. Chipped industry is now much more prolific than in the previous layer. Local craftsmen and craftswomen used obsidian rather than flint for fashioning blades as well as scrapers and borers, but very few leaf-shaped arrowheads. The local inhabitants boasted necklaces composed of various materials, most of which were present in the preceding layer: obsidian, carnelian, agate, amethyst, lapis lazuli, turquoise and bone. Ivory beads have been dropped but new accessions include crystal, blue and white faience and chalcedony.

In contrast to all these changes, layer VIIIB represents a period of adjustments and alterations of the existing layout. A new building erected south of the central 'temple' had rectangular doorless rooms roofed over by timber constructions bearing reed matting and insulating clay layers. Its fillings contained a considerable quantity of slingshot. A communal feature of interest is a 24 m deep well with a water conduit of stones poured over with bitumen. Sealings, again on domestic and external clay and from mobile containers, were present only in the west 'temple'. Richly furnished graves again attest to the practice of ostentatious social display; a feature worth noting is the presence of green, red and blue pigment in grave 29. The material culture of this phase does not display any marked differences from the preceding layer VIIIC. The great epoch of the site closes with the last segment of this stratum, layer VIIIA. The nuclear buildings remain at the site but are considerably transformed, while the architecture becomes condensed, the intervening spaces being filled in by subsidiary housing. In addition to other annexes the west 'temple' now received what seems to be a bathroom with bitumen-covered floor and a pottery bowl in the corner. In the east 'temple' the floor of room 801 is covered by knuckle bones of sheep; what is their connection with a stone astragal of layer XA and with imitations of such bones enclosed in clay bullae and functioning as tokens, as exemplified by a Susa C find (von Wickede 1990, 307, *sub* No. 628 and Table 628)? After cessation of its functions the walls of this building were again demolished to a height of about 1 m and the ruins levelled by debris. The north 'temple' was also rebuilt and a courtyard by the central 'temple' received a pavement and a pottery bowl in a corner. In addition to these structures the new layout includes some other features of interest. At the north-east and south-west parts of the site where gates had once existed the inhabitants erected two round structures of bricks laid in mortar. The building with massive doorless rooms at the centre of the site, in the position of the preceding 'hammam', still flourished and contained now a kiln for firing pottery. A new building of four parallel aisles was built between the central and west 'temples' and another structure situated between the west 'temple' and the new 'hammam' boasts a vaulted hall over the length of 8.5 m and with a vault diameter of 3.25 m. A street running south-east of the west 'temple' is paved with sherds laid in lime mortar. Sealings of this layer on mobile containers display again both local and external clay as their carrier. A number of impressions of a single seal on local clay were found in the south, east, west and central 'temples'; sealings on external clay turn up in the east 'temple' and in the new 'hammam'. Again, rich graves point to ostentatious wealth display as an indicator of social status. In terms of the local material culture a rare find of a carving of a circumcised penis(?) in room 802 of the east 'temple' should be mentioned. This period witnessed two major innovations – the mass introduction of wheel-thrown pottery wares (Akkermans 1988, esp. pp. 128–129) and the first occurrence of tin bronze in ancient Mesopotamia (Moorey 1982b, 22).

In addition to the more conspicuous find categories the less prominent artifacts of common everyday use should not be forgotten. Among the artificially prepared materials faience is represented in the form of blue and green pendants and seals, especially in layers XII–XI, but blue and white faience is referred to in layer VIII. Of bone we have the usual points and spatulae, as well as a few ornaments (beads, seals) and the suspected mouthpieces of musical instruments (XIA–IX). In addition to building and making pottery and statuettes, clay was used to form spindle whorls, tokens, 'hut symbols' and what is usually identified as slingshot. Tepe Gawra displays a surprisingly underrepresented but, as it seems, also underdeveloped copper metallurgy. In contrast to expert work with precious materials the few copper items show hardly more sophisticated techniques than hammering, though the existence of metal bars and also of whetstones does bear out some degree of craft specialization in this sphere. Of course, artifacts of organic materials are only sampled by the archaeological record but such branches of production as basketry and mat weaving, cord- and rope-making or work with textiles and wood certainly went on at the site. Stone served for fashioning a variety of everyday-life needs. Chipped industry was complemented by a large number of items of ground stone including hammers, celts, axes, grinding stones, maceheads and boat-shaped hammer-axes. Moreover, tokens, weights, whetstones, palettes and stone vessels turn up throughout these strata of Tepe Gawra.

Developments of the economic aspect of life of the ancient Gawrans of this period may be subsumed under the headings of amplification and rationalization. Some resources may have become scarce in consequence of natural processes. The last ivory beads turn up in layer IX and only a worn-out and mended ivory pin represents this material in layer VIII. In consequence of the slow cooling of climate that began around 3000 BC (Moore 1983, esp. graph on p. 105, Fig. 2), vegetation may have retreated from its marginal zones and the elephants responded by taking refuge in more favourable spots. Amplification may certainly be seen in the work with stone, of which ever-increasing quantities were brought to the site, at least in some demonstrable cases from as far as central Anatolia, both for the production of chipped industry and for public-utility purposes such as paving. The complexity of the pottery supply of the site also grows and the vessels are observed to have been turned out in greater quantities, as well as more rationally: wheel-thrown pottery appears from layer IX on. In addition to these two trends, likely to be present throughout the entire period under discussion, there are other, short-term fluctuations. The increasing quantities of spindle whorls in layer XI may mean more textile production, but also, for instance, more spinning females, either wives (polygyny?) or slave-girls acquired in consequence of victorious wars (spinning workshops?). An overall increase in production is apparent in the affluent layer X: in addition to much stone and more pottery there is also more metal. The end of 'impressed ware' in layer X is probably to be viewed as a consequence of the shift from common to precious materials for public display. Metal vessels in graves of this period are likely to have been accompanied in such functions by stone items, the disappearance of which from settlement archaeological contexts after layer XI clearly indicates the increase in their value. Layer IX displays evidence for production of exquisite furniture, likely to have acted as a status marker. Finally, the symbolic role of animals, especially hooved, in layer VIII (hoof pendant in grave, sheep knuckles in the east 'temple' of VIIIA) introduces the question whether the wealth of the site at that period did not derive from animal husbandry. Let us note problems in the supply of traditionally available materials: the street of VIIIA, south-east of the west 'temple', was paved with mortar-laid sherds instead of stone, used for that purpose earlier. On the other hand, there are other branches of production which show no marked development at all, such as metallurgy, which continues up to the end of this period, with traditional, even conservative technologies. The crafts of pottery and stone-working that undergo the most conspicuous development at contemporary Tepe Gawra are those with the greatest potential for specialization (Sanders and Webster 1988, 541, Table 3) and represent thus a natural development in its own right. This gives us little reason to assume any more marked degree of intentional or engineered craft, or even industrial specialization, the more so as the economic focus changes from layer to layer, as we have seen.

Social developments visible at Tepe Gawra XIA–VIIIA may be roughly subsumed under the following headings:

a) Ascribed status. This category of major importance, characterizing the transition towards ranked and stratified societies (as reviewed in Creamer and Haas 1985, 739–740; see the tables on pp. 742–743 for the following discussion), appears first in layer XI, as the richly equipped child buried at Locus 181 could hardly have attained such an elevated status during his or her lifetime, and remains a constant feature of this whole period.

b) Redistribution alternating with reciprocity. If sealings of mobile containers point to reciprocity and those from doors to redistribution, as I argue elsewhere (Charvát 1988a and 1992a; see also pp. 87 and 176), then layers XI (with a single instance from layer X) and IX are characterized by redistribution while layers X and VIII, the richest and clearly most successful on the site, offer evidence for reciprocity. The services yielded by the centre in return for the material supplies may not necessarily have been material (cultic or military protection, for instance). The overall impression is one of a higher degree of group solidarity, evidenced by institutionalized redistribution, in less prosperous periods (XI and IX), alternating with individualized exploitation of available resources by only loosely cooperating collection agencies in times of abundance (X and VIII).

c) Commensality. This feature, interesting from the viewpoint of its earlier, Ubaid culture roots, seems to be incarnated by the 'impressed ware' table vessels, especially beakers, of layers XIA–X. Its development cannot be traced any further but seems to have affected the later strata as well in view of vessels of precious materials preserved in contemporary graves.

d) Ostentatious wealth display. It is needless to comment upon this in view of the rich grave goods, most of which represent ornaments or articles of attire, items of personal adornment or use, precious vessels and stone tokens, clearly objects intended to be visibly handled by persons or in personal use. The underlying principle of this could well be the legitimation of superior social status.

e) Two-level surplus collection. In layer VIIIC one single seal was used to impress articles marked with both local Gawran clay(?) and an external clay (von Wickede 1990, 171 and 297, *sub* No. 308). This seems to allow the assumption of a 'travelling seal' marking deliveries from both 'home' and 'abroad' (Charvát 1992a, 282).

The time has now come to summarize briefly the historical development of Tepe Gawra in the period XIA–VIIIA (on the site see also Rothman 1997). The 'Round House' phase of XIA was the last one in which the original social unity of the local community, articulated probably only along sex and age lines, likely to have represented achieved status and viewing itself as a single body distinct from other groupings of this kind, survived. In layer XI, this original unity gives way to the coexistence of several corporate groups in which ascribed status dominates from now on. The trend towards emphasis on status is, however, mitigated both by at least a rudimentary degree of institutionalized redistribution and by developed commensality. Reduction of the binary principle predominant in layers XV–XII, visible in architecture (a single niche in the central hall of layer XI 'temple') and in ritual (animal statuettes only) may imply an adoption of the principle of unity or 'oneness'. The new social order was so successful that it led to a most dynamic development in times of layer X when the relapse to reciprocity (= predominance of mobile-container sealings) went hand in hand with an exaggerated emphasis on ascribed status by means of ostentatious wealth display. Redistribution almost vanishes but commensality, employing now vessels of more precious materials, still exists. The volume of output and efficiency of some arts and crafts grow, but it is hard to decide whether this was a cause of social development or its consequence. The fact that no more permanent production plants emerged at Gawra and the overall heterogeneity of the production (developed clay- and stone-processing as against less sophisticated metallurgical technology) seem to point to the latter possibility.

Some of the new ritual features include the use of blue and green pigments in graves in contrast to the earlier layers (XII–XI), where they had been displayed by faience pendants, and ritualized demolition of old buildings pulled down and levelled with debris to make foundations for new structures. This insistence on the permanent occupation of the same spot may indicate that the corporate groups now perceived their existence as anchored also in time and that the individual laid to rest in tomb 107 under the eastern complex of this layer is likely to have been venerated as an ancestor. A contraction phase of this all-too-successful community is represented by layer IX when, in spite of the now permanent expression of ascribed status by means of ostentatious wealth display, the community reverted to institutionalized redistribution. A social attribute of the local élite group is now incarnated in the workshop turning out decorated furniture, perhaps representing a high prestige item. Technologically, this period saw the introduction of wheel-thrown pottery. The general impression is one of a high status group resorting to the introduction of socially controlled redistribution but insisting on their ostentatious life habits. Redistribution is done away with in the following layer VIII when the local population extends the sphere from which it collects the surplus to a two-level 'catchment area' from which goods marked both locally and in external sites by travelling seals converge on Tepe Gawra. One and the same resource appears to have been shared by several residences, as is witnessed by impressions of one seal at several 'temples'. Animal husbandry might have played a not unimportant role in the local life but the Gawra economy now shows some curious inconsistencies. The quantities of chipped industry increase but in the last segment of this stage a street is paved with pottery sherds instead of the stone normally used up to that time. Some indications of change in the ritual sphere such as differences in pigments used (green, red and blue in grave 29 of VIIIB, blue and white in faience pendants of this layer) complete the picture and suggest that this might have been a community different from its predecessors and perhaps less used to life in sedentary communities. The overall impression of Tepe Gawra XIA–VIIIA seems to be one of an originally egalitarian social grouping distinguishing itself only against outside bodies of its kind, which subsequently split up into several corporate groups asserting their status vis-à-vis one another but always finding ample resources to draw on without any higher degree of intra-communal conflict. These groups, developing various economic activities, thrived on the site for most of the period in question, alternating tapping of external resources with internal redistribution of the amassed goods if the need arose. Nevertheless, the original unity and equality was gone; differences in human nature and social position now became a force which made people go beyond the limits of everyday routine, procure exotic materials, invent, create and embellish the life of their community.

INTERPRETATION

Economy

The 'Uruk miracle' happened in an environment characterized by optimum climatic conditions of prevailingly hot and humid weather (Moore 1983; for the higher level of Uruk period groundwater at the site of Tell al-Hilwa see Wilkinson and Matthews 1989, 264; a recent general assessment is in Algaze 2001). A change likely to have had an impact on human settlement is represented by the rise in sea level, observable at the Arabo-Persian Gulf and dated currently to the fifth pre-Christian millennium (Dalongeville and Sanlaville 1987, esp. pp. 569–573). Such a change probably affected not only connections with the Gulf area, where the abundant evidence for contacts with the Mesopotamian mainland, available for the Ubaid culture period, ceases, but must also have influenced living conditions in the lower Mesopotamian plain, where the most exciting developments took place.

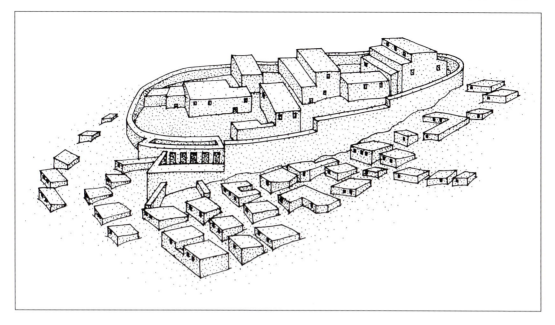

Figure 5.7 Reconstructed view of the Late Uruk fortified site at Hassek Höyük (after Behm-Blancke 1992, inside cover)

Uruk period agriculture differed in no substantial aspect from its Chalcolithic matrix (Hijara *et al.* 1980, 154), especially in the range of cultigens and clearly also in most of the practical approaches. First and foremost, this conclusion is based on palaeobotanical evidence. H. Helbaek (cited in Powell 1985, 15) even characterized a sample of seed imprints on pottery from Uruk, in which barley predominates slightly over emmer (74 imprints of emmer seeds against 85 of those of barley) as evidence for 'exceptionally favourable growth conditions free of any salinization traces'. More recent investigations attest to the presence of the traditional range of wheat and barley crops supplemented by lentils and linseed (?) (Tosi 1976, 173; Wright, Miller and Redding 1980, 275; Safar, Mustafa and Lloyd 1981, 317–318; Wright, Redding and Pollock 1989, 109; Pollock 1990a, 87f.). The presence of both summer- and winter-growing weeds in grain samples from Uruk period Abu Salabikh (Pollock 1990a, 87) indicates that at least on some sites the agricultural cycle now covered the whole year. Irrigation technology was probably currently used but there is no need to assume its application as a matter of course. Individual sites indicate that some cultivated plots were irrigated while others were not: witness the irrigated lentils but unirrigated flax at Tepe Shaffarabad (Wright, Miller and Redding 1980, 275). No irrigation was, of course, necessary in the piedmont areas (Weiss 1983, 39–41). The gradual preponderance of barley over wheat, contrasting with the initial state in which the wheat : barley ratio is estimated at 8 : 1 (Tosi 1976, 174) and of the progress of which the above presented Uruk evidence probably shows a middle stage, may well be due to salinization of arable land as suggested by H. T. Wright (*et al.* 1981, 181, 232, but see van Zeist and Bottema 1999, 30–31). Barley tolerates salinity better than wheat and is, in general, more reliable as a crop (Powell 1985, 12–13).

Of course, much more information on all aspects of agricultural work may now be culled from the first written texts though it has been observed that by and large such data are missing from the very earliest Uruk texts (Nissen 1985a, 358). Above the purely instrumental level, let us note, for instance, such hints as the sign *ZATU* No. 433, read RAD.gunu and depicting what appears to be a winding watercourse with cultivated soil in the meanders, quite in accordance with archaeological observations (Adams 1981, 62, Fig. 11). Here the settlements were never located in the innermost part of the meanders in which the graphics of the RAD.gunu sign permit the location of fields. Uruk period field plots were presumably disposed in large tracts of field strips running parallel to one another (Liverani 1996, 11–13). It is debatable how far this economic sphere may be illuminated by data from Proto-Elamite texts of later date, approximately equal to Mesopotamian Jemdet Nasr (Damerow, Englund and Lamberg-Karlovsky 1989, vi–viii). Most of these record various quantities of grain, interpreted as rations, disbursements to groups or individuals or harvests (ibid. 31–32, 62; on the problem of 'rations', some of which were returned, Charvát 1997, 54). The quantities concerned appear to be fairly limited, which is in marked contrast with data from the centres where very substantial amounts of grain could have been handled (for Susa and Uruk see Damerow, Englund and Lamberg-Karlovsky 1989, 63, n. 171). Some information is also offered by the figurative arts. D. Sürenhagen (1985, 230, Fig. 1) has published an impression of a cylinder seal found at Arslantepe VIA depicting a sleigh drawn by an animal and carrying a human figure under what appears to be a baldaquin. The scene is accompanied by other figures, two of which, standing behind the sleigh, carry fork- or pitchfork-like instruments. I see no reason why the short strokes below the sledge should not indicate either flints set into the sledge's lower planes or threshed grain, as is suggested by the instruments held by the assisting figures who may well be winnowing threshed grain. Remains of what might have been disused sledges or harrows (Latin 'tribulum') have been identified archaeologically (Adams 1975 and Eichmann 1991, 179, Tables 237b and 276: 9–13; on ethnographic record of such items see Cheetham 1982).

A word should also be said concerning the economic implications of the varied density of Uruk period occupation and especially the clustering of settlement around the major centres in the Nippur-Adab area for the Early and Middle Uruk and in the Uruk area for the Late Uruk (Adams 1981, 60–81, esp. pp. 70–71, Fig. 15). Robert Adams argues that agricultural innovations must be responsible for this phenomenon, which he sees as tremendous population growth, but he fails to produce evidence for them (ibid. 78–79). We have seen above that Uruk period agriculture has basically the same character as its Chalcolithic predecessor. Some time ago, I put forward a suggestion (Charvát 1988b, 102–104) that multiple settlement traces may rather be a feature of the archaeological record than of past reality as there is no means of knowing how many of the sites were occupied at a single time. If one and the same village were re-located six or seven times in the course of several generations of the existence of its inhabitants, as is not unlikely owing to the presumable exhaustion of arable soil, it will produce six or seven archaeological sites. The relevance of this factor, persistently overlooked by all those who base their conclusions on 'raw' surface survey data without the necessary source critique, has yet to be assessed, but some of us are aware of the problems concerned (McGuire Gibson on excavations of Hamoukar, cited in Algaze 2001, 227). In fact, a glance at Adams's (1981) Fig. 11 on his p. 62 makes it very unlikely that all the tiny hamlets, some of which are only 2 km apart, could have existed at one and the same time; and the balance of twenty Early–Middle Uruk sites against two Late Uruk ones speaks for itself. Moreover, the rather large quantities of grain handled at the centres, in contrast with the relatively small grain amounts mentioned in connection with the individual sites in Proto-Elamite texts, imply that the 'catchment areas' of the centres must have been fairly extensive. In view of the salinization problem (see p. 59) it would have been simpler to maintain the high level of yields by periodic relocations of village field systems, and by bringing fresh ground under the plough than to cultivate permanent agricultural bases, which would be labour-intensive, difficult to maintain and risky because of the precariousness of nature (salinization, flooding . . .). In fact, most of the Uruk period rural sites were subsequently deserted, as Nicholas Postgate (1986, 93f.) has brought to our notice, whereby their transitory character is at least hinted at. The key factor here is represented by the unchanged continuity of basic agricultural traits from the Chalcolithic period, as well as by a multiplicity of agricultural practices from large-scale field systems integrated with sophisticated irrigation networks via minor areas put under the plough occasionally, as time and opportunity permitted, to impromptu cultivation of pockets of land that might upon exceptionally favourable occasions offer a catch crop but otherwise lay waste and barren (conclusions based on signs). Population increase certainly occurred but it remains to be seen how much of it was caused by agricultural enterprise and how far it was a 'gravitation effect' of the status of the Uruk urban centre which must have required a quite extensive agricultural hinterland.

We would gladly welcome more information on Uruk culture gardening and orchardry. The lentils, grasspea and linseed(?) documented by the Shaffarabad (Wright, Redding and Pollock 1989, 109) and Hacinebi excavations (Stein *et al.* 1996, 248–257) may have been grown in gardens. Flax cultivation is attested to by a textile fragment of that material from fouth-millennium Eridu (Safar, Mustafa and Lloyd 1981, 318) and by an exceptionally high-quality iconographic source, a cylinder-seal carving (Matthews 1995, see also van Zeist and Bottema 1999, 32). The site of Eridu has yielded date stones (Safar, Mustafa and Lloyd 1981, 318). The texts are not very helpful either. Of course they do record a number of forms of enclosures with plants inside (*ZATU* Nos. 205–210, 445, 514 on pp. 211–212, 268, 284) but no precise details are available. The sign NAGA (= EREŠ$_2$, NISABA$_2$, UGA – *ZATU* No. 381, p. 250) indicates that lye plants (NAGA = *Šumerishes Lexicon* (hereafer *ŠL*) 165 = qiltu, *CAD* Q 252) or perhaps cardamom (NAGA = qaqullu, AHw II 901) may have been grown. Another case relevant in this aspect is the cultivation of onion (SUM = *ZATU* No. 496, p. 297, šumu = *ŠL* 164 = *Akkadisches Handwörterbuch* (hereafter *AHw*) III 1275, 'Lauch'). The systematic character of gardening activities is indicated by the fact that both of these plant products turn up in lists of regular deliveries ('tribute'). An idealized image of a perfectly organized and aligned garden has survived in Uruk period art (Strommenger 1967, Fig. 2 on p. 3; Becker and Heinz 1993, 58, No. 785). The site of Hacinebi has brought forth evidence for cultivation of almonds, figs, plums and pistachios (Stein *et al.* 1996, 248–257). A rather interesting issue is represented by the first documented instances of fermented alcoholic drinks in the Uruk culture. While the primacy of the Uruk brewers in supplying the first known beer in history (*ZATU* No. 286, p. 229) cannot be seriously questioned, the wine problem is slightly more complex. The sign GEŠTIN (*ZATU* No. 202, p. 210) clearly consists of the image of a tree trunk GIŠ and a container of pliable material DIN and is thus likely to refer to palm wine, prepared until now in many parts of the world by fermentation of palm juice oozing out of incisions in the trunk and gathered in a container. While this drink seems to have been the norm in Uruk culture Mesopotamia, its inhabitants also knew grape wine which, however, they imported from the montane regions to the west (Fagan 1991, 16 – palaeobotanical evidence from Godintepe; Tosi 1976, 174 – Proto-Elamite Tepe Yahya) and north (Hacinebi: Stein *et al.* 1996, 248–257; in general on fermented alcoholic drinks Sherratt 1995). All this evidence thus points not only to the frequency of such labour-intensive procedures but also to a great deal of knowledge of applied chemistry and related disciplines for practical use.

While organized agriculture clearly occupied an important position in Uruk culture society, the exploitation of uncultivated landscape (food-gathering) clearly retreats into a marginal position. Up to now, I have only come across the evidence from Tepe Yahya IV, of course only a parallel in this context (Tosi 1976). The local collection of wild grasses was supplemented by the consumption of pistachio nuts brought to the site from their natural biotope. Strangely enough, the fourth pre-Christian millennium saw a decrease in the utilization of the club rush (*Scirpus* spp.), turning up at large in prehistoric layers of the same site.

In sum, Uruk period agriculture in no way constitutes any qualitative departure from Chalcolithic practice, as far as can be seen at present. The relative wealth of information provided by the earliest texts fills in some gaps in the knowledge of particular and existential features of rural labour but no significant advance is discernible in comparison with the evidence offered by the Ubaid culture.

If it is difficult to measure the impact of the Uruk culture innovations on agriculture, animal husbandry certainly stands out far more vividly in the combined light of archaeological and written evidence (in general see Becker 1999). A good palaeozoological record is available from Henry T. Wright's excavations at the Farukhabad and Shaffarabad Tepes in the Deh Luran plain (Wright, Miller and Redding 1980, 276ff.; Wright et al. 1981, 181; Wright, Redding and Pollock 1989, 109–110) and from Susan Pollock's work at Uruk period Abu Salabikh (Pollock 1990a, 87ff.). The herds apparently consisted mainly of sheep and goats; cattle, not rare in the Ubaid and Early Uruk period (see Englund 1995a, Liverani and Heimpel 1995, esp. pp. 129–134), are less and less present, as are pigs (Englund 1995b). The Farukhabad sheep and goats might have been kept for food. The age-old tradition of agro-pastoral coexistence is shown by the fact that at least some of the Abu Salabikh grain samples might have passed through the intestinal tracts of animals and been used for fuel as a component of dried dung cakes. At Shaffarabad, adult cattle individuals seem to have been slaughtered in winter and juveniles (below one year of age) in summer. This would conform to the tradition of killing off weak and handicapped cattle in autumn or early winter (to spare fodder for the healthy) and unpromising young animals before the onset of transhumance to highland summer pastures to free the herd of possible obstacles hindering its movement. In a most interesting hypothesis, H. T. Wright (Wright, Redding and Pollock 1989) has attempted an interpretation of his team's Shaffarabad results as evidence for a famine year. In the local series of deposits in an Uruk culture deep pit, representing possibly a cycle of two summers with the intervening winter, the second summer is exceptional in the general numerical decrease of all livestock. The cattle values fell to 80 per cent in comparison with the preceding year but the pig values came to 60 per cent, sheep and goats to 26 per cent and hunted species such as birds and fish to less than 10 per cent of the original values. More older animals were also slaughtered in the second summer. If this interpretation is correct, then the observation that cattle and pigs probably represented the major asset of the local shepherds and that their decrease was kept under control is interesting. An innovation in terms of the range of domesticated animals is constituted by the first occurrence of domestic ass known to date (Boessneck, von den Driesch and Steger 1984, 166; in general see Clutton-Brock 1980, 40; the equids in E. Peltenburg's excavations at Jerablus-Tahtani: Weiss 1994, 106–107; Tell Rubeidhah in Jebel Hamrin: Henrickson 1994, 305; and Farukhabad: Neely, Wright *et al.* 1994, 214). The taming of this animal might not have occurred with an eye to the expansion of food production only; the early cultivators probably intended to procure a beast of burden to help both as a source of traction power and as a carrier of the now heavy loads involved in the redistribution of the manifold and abundant Uruk culture production (see p. 146). A similar goal might have been pursued by the attempts at domestication of steppe animals such as antelope and (or) gazelle. This is indicated by a sign depicting a head of such an animal with an ear of corn at its mouth, implying its feeding with grain (*ZATU* No. 72, p. 185). The Uruk culture texts shed light on contemporary animal husbandry (Green 1980). Herd lists show that their sizes ranked from 22 to 140 head of sheep with the average lying at 68 individuals. For goats the same figures reach from 10 to 50 with the average at 26. This is less than in the third-millennium Akkadian texts (200–500 heads) but approximately on the level of Ur III values. Some cattle and pigs are also mentioned. Both the denotation of animal texts with a bottle-like sign (Green 1980, 2–3) and the 1:1 ratio for males and females in sheep and goats (ibid. 11ff.) show that the primary purpose of herding was the products of living animals (wool, milk and dairy products) and not the procurement of edible meat. At Tepe Farukhabad the increasing numbers of spindle whorls in the Middle Uruk period may imply intensified weaving activities, perhaps in connection with export of textile (wool?) products to other sites (Wright *et al.* 1981, 271; Neely, Wright *et al.* 1994, 175). Both animals and animal products seem to have been given out as 'rations' (Green 1980, 7). The texts indicate that separate herds of male, female and young animals were kept (Englund 1988, 147–148 for sheep, goats and pigs). This shows that the records pertain to summer and early winter herds, since it would have been impossible to separate freshly born lambs from the ewes at the period when the former were yet unweaned, that is, from December to about May, at least in the case of sheep (see p. 33). Could these lists have been written out at the start of the summer transhumance, approximately in April or May, when the shepherds put together their animals to drive them to summer pastures, a time when the transhumance contracts were traditionally drawn up (Le Roy Ladurie 1975, 159, 166)? Another interpretative possibility is offered by the Egyptian practice of regular 'counting the cattle' every second year (see, for instance, Lorton 1979, esp. p. 375). The lists could well represent 'animal rolls' of beasts collected from owners who brought them up, for instance, to discharge their obligations towards the social centres. Various names of milk and milk products turn up in the sources (Englund 1991 and 1995a). Some features of Uruk culture animal husbandry may be documented both in the archaeological record and in written evidence. The fact that in Uruk IV times the product referred to as KISIM (?, *ZATU* No. 296, p. 232) is made only from goat milk while in Uruk III times both goat and sheep milk were used for its preparation may be connected with the decrease in the proportion of domestic cattle, observable in the palaeozoological evidence. The missing cattle milk might have been compensated for by sheep milk. Interesting spatial differences may be discerned in livestock-keeping practices. Wherever they came and settled down, bearers of the Uruk culture seem to have insisted on keeping sheep and goats even if the 'natives' were used to pig (Hacinebi: Stein *et al.* 1996, 257–260). Uruk IV texts offer the earliest evidence for the keeping of domestic fowl, most likely duck (*ZATU* No. 364, p. 246, a sign depicting a duck[?] having just laid an egg as a lexeme MUD = *aladu*, give birth, give life). If my hypothesis concerning the first writing tablets of organic materials bearing inlays of wax into which the signs were incised is correct (see p. 152), then the beginnings of bee-keeping may also reach as far back as the Uruk culture period (see also Volk 1999, 286–288). A question worth considering relates to the extent to which the idea of the great significance of animal husbandry, surpassing that of agriculture and presumed to have by its farther and farther centrifugal motion brought about the disintegration and end of cultural and social coherence of the Harappan civilization of the Indian subcontinent (Fairservis 1991, esp. pp. 111ff.), may be applicable to Mesopotamia. I hope to show below that the end of Uruk culture unity was brought about not by a systemic collapse but by a fragmentation and atomization process which disrupted the original structure of the Uruk culture sphere, transforming it into a cluster of tiny replicas of the pristine original.

Uruk culture animal husbandry may thus be seen as a sequence composed of three concentric circles. The innermost circle consisted of animals living close to human abodes such as dogs (amply documented by the signs such as ŠUBUR – *ZATU* No. 539, p. 290) or poultry. The middle circle would have featured sheep, goats, pigs and (less and less) cattle. Such animals, kept principally for their products (wool, milk and dairy products) but also eaten, lived off the open landscape but also in the fields and seem to have been congregated and driven out to summer pastures from which they returned in autumn. The surplus of the animal products was distributed (also) in the form of rations. Finally, the outer circle included animals which went far and wide loaded with provisions of all kinds to be delivered to related or friendly communities: these include beasts of burden such as the ass and other domesticates.

While Uruk period hunting is evoked in nearly every art history manual featuring the Uruk lion-hunt stele, this theme has received very little systematic attention with one notable exception, namely fishing (Englund 1984, inaccessible to me). Wherever this kind of evidence was sought in the archaeological sites, it was usually found (fish at Uruk period Abu Salabikh: Pollock 1990a, 87ff.). Ancient Mesopotamians might very well have availed themselves of the opportunity provided by mass fish migrations such as those of the Euphrates carp, which leave the rivers for backwaters in spring around April and come back with the main flood. This happens so regularly that a particular cereal received its name from the fish, perhaps because of the temporal connection of its sowing(?) with carp migration (še eštub: Powell 1984a, 59). Interesting evidence is supplied by contemporary Iranian sites. Inhabitants of Tepe Farukhabad in the Deh Luran plain supplemented their diet with fish, which greatly increased in quantity in Late Uruk times (Wright *et al.* 1981, 236, 260). The Tepe Shaffarabad site contained evidence for hunting gazelle (Wright, Miller and Redding 1980, 276–277) as well as wildfowl and fish (Wright, Redding and Pollock 1989, 109–110). Here the fact that in deposits of the second year the wildfowl and fish values fell to less than 10 per cent of the preceding year has been interpreted as evidence for famine. If this is so, then wildlife resources represented an energy input that could, in emergency cases, be dispensed with, unlike the cattle and pigs with numbers falling to 80 per cent and 60 per cent respectively, which obviously represented an 'iron reserve'. On the contrary, the evidence from Tepe Yahya (Tosi 1976, 174) highlights hunting of large mammals as the main feature with eggs, wildfowl and sweet-water fish playing distinctly minor roles. Water resources tapped included the sea coast, which produced marine molluscs, the shells of which frequently served as ornaments (Limper 1988, 24–28: *Turbinella pyrum L., Chicoreus ramosus L., Lambis truncata sebae Röding, Fasciolaria trapezinum L.*).

Some sites seem to give evidence in favour of 'hunting campaigns', organized as deliberate undertakings, either to procure food or possibly for sociopolitical or symbolic purposes. This is the case with the Habur-basin evidence for hunting gazelle from Tell Kuran and Umm Qseir (Weiss 1994, 104–105; Zeder 1994, esp. p. 116).

In its essence the sphere of Uruk period agricultural production continued the trends set forth by the preceding Halaf and Ubaid cultures. Some of its aspects were new or represented adaptations to accommodate new realities such as the marginalization of food-gathering or the domestication of new animal species. Revolutionary changes, however, were absent. Rather than introducing spectacular innovations, the architects of the Uruk culture community seem to have relied on regular and systematic exploitation of all the knowledge and technology available, supplemented by careful management of the resources, concerted effort of its component communities dovetailing by their activities into one another and diligent timing of the individual enterprise segments, and on corporate consumption of the redistributed fruit of human labours.

As to the processing of natural resources, it developed further in the Uruk period along the lines set in the preceding age. In some instances, Uruk culture artisans could boast truly magnificent achievements but by and large, the Uruk specialists built on foundations laid by their predecessors.

First let us glance at artificial materials. In Uruk times, these are represented by lime products in architecture and by faience creations. The introduction (?) of truly monumental architecture in Uruk VI entailed a considerable use of lime both for mortars (see pp. 101–102 on the 'Steingebäude') and for concrete. Though the tradition of such recipes goes back to the Mesolithic (Qermez Dere), the Uruk period saw as innovations both the employment of true concrete tempered with crushed baked brick for the erection of building walls (Uruk VI 'Steinstifttempel') and the introduction of a most peculiar manner of wall decoration. On the top of every layer of concrete poured into the walls of the 'Steinstifttempel' its builders inserted a horizontal row of oblong baked-clay tiles with rounded and pierced terminals protruding from the wall and fixed into their positions by the superimposed concrete layers. The protruding pierced ends of these tiles probably held some kind of lattice grid construction for holding in position blocks of plaster securing the series of small coloured-stone cones that made up the ornament of the wall surfaces (Huot and Maréchal 1985, esp. pp. 269ff. on lime plasterings or mortars used after the end of Ubaid culture). Ultimately, however, this technology, used, as far as known today, at Uruk, Larsa and Tell Awayli, was abandoned as the plaster could not hold the cone-decoration panels, which tore off and collapsed. It was gradually superseded by a cheaper version of the cone mosaic done entirely in clay. That the employment of lime products was not limited to cultic structures is indicated by a find of a 'basin of cement bricks' in the Uruk layers of the 'Great Sherd Dump' at Ur (Woolley 1955, 29). The other kind of chemically prepared product known from the Uruk culture period is faience, attested to primarily in the north (Tepe Gawra XIII–XI and VIII; see pp. 113–116 and Moorey 1985, 137–138, 142–143). The excavators of Uruk also refer to 'artificial stone' ('Gips und Sand'), used for fashioning the human sculpture found in the 'Riemchengebäude' (Heinrich 1982, 73).

Bitumen, extracted on sites naturally endowed with this material, was imported into lowland Mesopotamia (Deh Luran: Neely, Wright *et al.* 1994, 178).

Bone served as an ordinary and disposable material, employed because of its properties for the shaping of awls and spatulae, modest ornaments and other utility objects such as sickles made of split bone with stone blades held in position by bitumen and found at Habuba Kabira (Strommenger 1980a; see Figure 5.8). The rare ivory items were discussed above under Tepe Gawra; a few have turned up at Uruk (Limper 1988, p. 52, No. 9, W 16833/a–e).

The most mundane of materials, clay, yielded to human efforts in a variety of ways. First and foremost, potters turned out mass-produced wares which submerged all the culture's sites (in general see Sürenhagen 1974–1975; Vértesalji 1987, esp. pp. 490–492; D. Sürenhagen's conclusions as cited by Rothman 1990, 132f.). A good insight into the professional approaches of Uruk culture potters is offered by an extensive find group from the Habuba Kabira site on the Euphrates in present-day Syria (Sürenhagen 1974–1975; Strommenger 1980a, 57–60). The most significant technological innovation that took place in the Uruk period was without doubt the introduction of the fast potter's wheel on which the vessels were fully formed from a shapeless lump of clay with exploitation of the momentum of the centrifugal movement force. One such instrument was even found at the Ubaid and Uruk

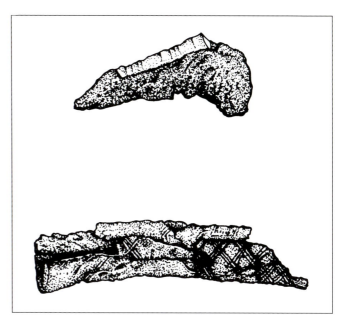

Figure 5.8 Late Uruk age tools. A knife with a flint blade set in bitumen (above) and a cutting tool made of flint blades set in a hollow bone bearing carved decorative patterns (below) from the site of Habuba Kabira (after Strommenger 1980a, 50, Fig. 35)

period 'Great Sherd Dump' of Ur (Woolley 1955, 28). This invention greatly enhanced the possibilities of mass production of pottery present ever since the Ubaid culture period, as is demonstrated by the same Ur site (Woolley 1955, 27–31). Fast-wheel products first appeared in Tepe Gawra IX, becoming frequent in layer VIII, and this trend seems to be reflected in the wider north Mesopotamian–Syrian area (Akkermans 1988, esp. pp. 128–129). However, the Uruk potters by no means limited themselves to a unilateral technological approach and applied many varied procedures at a time, including even hand-building in moulds, as is amply demonstrated by the 'leading fossil' of the culture, the bevelled-rim bowl (henceforth abbreviated as BRB). Discussions concerning this most ungainly creation of one of the first literary civilizations of the world have been ongoing for more than a decade, and the opinion of the Berlin team that the BRB served to measure out standardized rations has been challenged (see Balfet 1980; Le Brun 1980). I believe that taking into account K. Schmidt's (1982) and A. Millard's (1988) suggestion of viewing them as bread moulds, we may be able to assess the suggestion of J.-D. Forest (1987) who sees in them paraphernalia for a 'rituel de participation'. In fact, the idea that they were employed in confection of some kind of bread or pastry tallies very well with what we know about the role of commensality in the Ubaid and Uruk culture. Here attention may be drawn to the sign UKKIN, 'assembly' (*ZATU* No. 580, p. 302), symbolized clearly by a spouted pot implying ceremonial drinking as a distinguishing mark of a communal congregation. Another indication is supplied by the DUG:SILA$_3$ sign combination signifying the socially relevant act of alienation of immovable property in ancient kudurrus of an admittedly later date (Jemdet Nasr to ED I–II: Gelb, Steinkeller and Whiting 1991, 28–30). In this context the preparation of the most common baker's product which was to determine the Sumerian notion of eating, having been depicted at the mouth of a human head in the sign GU$_7$ (*ZATU* No. 235, p. 218) seems to have acquired a socially constitutive value. Indeed, the role of the product likely to have been baked in the BRB may be, with, of course, a great deal of licence, compared to the turkey eaten on Thanksgiving Day in the USA, Christmas pudding in Britain or the Christmas pastry of central Europe. Henry T. Wright's calculations indicate an enormous frequency of BRB utilization: one family might have discarded as many as 200 or even 280 of them annually (Wright, Miller and Redding 1980, 273–274). A degree of heterogeneity and irregularity of pottery production comes to the fore even in single sites, a case in point being the non-standardized finds of Jebel Aruda (van Driel and van Driel-Murray 1983, 25). Major centres of the Uruk culture seem to have been void of pottery workshops and, for that matter, of all art and craft establishments. This applies to Uruk where the installation cited by H.-J. Nissen as a production facility has been reinterpreted as a kitchen or cooking area (Barrelet 1974; Moorey 1982b, 17). It is also valid at Habuba Kabira South (Strommenger 1980a, 59). A growing amount of evidence indicates that such activities tended to retreat to minor sites in which, however, they may be represented rather profusely. This holds good for Uruk period Abu Salabikh (Pollock 1990a, 87; Pollock, Steele and Pope 1991, 61–62), Ahmad al-Hattu in Jebel Hamrin (Anon. 1979, 160; Sürenhagen 1979, 48–49; Sürenhagen 1983–1984) and for Tell Awayli (Huot *et al.* 1983, 18, 20; Forest and Calvet 1987, 153–154). The size of the clay-mining pits documented, for instance, at Ahmad al-Hattu is well exemplified by such a pit sampled by Henry T. Wright at Tepe Shaffarabad, which measured 10 × 4 m and was 4 m deep (Wright, Miller and Redding 1980, 268). No wonder that such huge cavities invited the settlers to dump rubbish in them. This fact carries some interest insofar as the location of pottery workshops is never a matter of purely technological considerations but reflects socio-cultural aspects as well (Nicklin 1979). The Uruk period witnessed transport of pottery vessels, even bulky storage jars, as is demonstrated by the find of a sealing from such a jar impressed into non-local clay at Tepe Shaffarabad (Wright, Redding and Pollock 1989, 110).

Uruk period craftsmen excelled in working with metal. The sources of their material are difficult to identify but eastern Anatolia, especially the area of the Euphrates and Tigris headwaters, comes into question here (Hassek Höyük: Mellink 1992, 135; Schmitt-Strecker, Begemann and Pernicka 1994; also Murgul, eastern Anatolia: Lutz, Pernicka and Wagner 1994), as does Iran where the only sources known to date to have been exploited in antiquity are located at Veshnoveh between Qom and Kashan (Moorey 1982a, 82–83). In addition to work with arsenic bronze, in which the arsenic might well have come from the ore and not from intentional admixtures (Müller-Karpe 1991, 110; Mellink 1992, 135; Riederer 1994), Uruk period coppersmiths experimented with various alloys to improve or condition the qualities of natural copper. A Late Uruk lion statuette contains 9 per cent lead, while an arrowhead from the 'Riemchengebäude', originally reported as a silver find, has been shown to be of copper containing over 25 per cent silver (Müller-Karpe 1991, 109–110). The first true tin bronze of Mesopotamia turned up at Tepe Gawra VIII (Moorey 1982b, 22). Here, as in work with artificial materials, the trial-and-error method seems to have been resorted to in order to seek plausible alternatives. Work with metal compounds requires knowledge of the properties of a variety of resources and indeed there is evidence to the effect that the Uruk period specialists expanded the traditional range of working materials. Gold of that time is chiefly known from Tepe Gawra (Moorey 1985, 76), the southern sites contributing but a trickle (necklace beads from Tello: Genouillac 1934, 44). This period also saw the introduction of iron (Jebel Aruda: Moorey 1985, 100; on Uruk-age hoard finds of copper chisels from the same site see Rouault and Masetti-Rouault 1993, 264, Fig. 115 and 435, No. 115) and the sudden diffusion of both silver and lead over contemporary Egypt, the Levant, Anatolia and Mesopotamia shows that in this case the source is likely to have been argentiferous ore accompanied by lead compounds, which occurs frequently (Moorey 1985, 114, 122–123; Kohlmeyer 1994). As a quite common everyday material, lead served for repairs and as admixture to alloys; a small bowl of lead turned up at the village site of Tell Rubeidhah (Henrickson 1994, 304; Kohlmeyer 1994). The frequency of Uruk-age silver finds is astonishing. As to the technologies applied, specialists agree that, on the one hand, Uruk period metallurgy made considerable progress in comparison with the preceding age with the introduction of such features as single and bivalve moulds, copper-smelting and finishing of products by hammering, use of sheet metal and copper wire (Heinrich 1982, 72) or the lost-wax casting technology (Moorey 1982b, 21–22 and 1985, 24–25; Müller-Karpe 1990a, 161 and 1990b, 173; Volk 1999, 286–288). On the other hand, they conclude that this production loses something of its glamour in comparison with other production sites of adjacent regions like, for instance, Chalcolithic Beersheba in Palestine (Moorey 1985, 24) or Iranian Susa (Moorey 1982a, 85–86; Tallon 1987). The latter site especially offers impressive evidence for an ancient and accomplished metallurgical tradition: as early as the Susa I stage (terminal Ubaid), tools were cast in single moulds and a compound with lead (up to 4.2 per cent) was known in the time of the Ubaid–Uruk transition. Coppersmiths of the Susa II/III period turned out a greater range of products, alloying copper both with arsenic and with lead (up to 5 per cent) and working also with pure lead, silver and gold. Up to now, no metallurgical workshops of Uruk period Mesopotamia are known but they supplied both major centres (Habuba Kabira: Strommenger 1980a, 51 and 56 for stone hammers for working out sheet metal?) and rural sites like Abu Salabikh (Pollock, Steele and Pope 1991, 61) or Grai Resh (see pp. 108–109). Even such outlying posts as Tepe Farukhabad in the Deh Luran plain were receiving metal tools, possibly in exchange for local products such as chipped stone, bitumen and perhaps woollen textiles (Wright *et al.* 1981, 274). Signs of the Uruk script depicting smelting furnaces (MIR, *ZATU* No. 362, p. 245) or possibly crucibles (UMUN$_2$, DIM$_6$, *ZATU* No. 582, p. 303) indicate that such activities might have gone on in the vicinity of great centres, but warn against too much emphasis on their absence, as installations of this kind may leave very few traces in the archaeological record if not working at a large scale. In the metallurgical sphere, Uruk period specialists markedly surpassed the documentable achievements of their Ubaid culture predecessors, though they attentively guarded their heritage. They introduced new materials and worked with new techniques, expanding the scope of their knowledge by bold experiments, some leading to errors but others representing distinct success.

As in other activity spheres, our idea of the Uruk period treatment of organic materials is somewhat distorted by the impact of information from written texts. Basketry products left their impressions in sealings (e.g. Wright, Miller and Redding 1980, 278) as well as on bitumen coatings; a fine example of such a basket which once contained pots with shells has been unearthed recently in one of the very rare Uruk period interments at Jemdet Nasr (Matthews 1990, 36, 38). A versatile material such as bitumen, which served a variety of purposes both in the building industry and in the domestic crafts, was usually extracted at its natural outcrops (Tepe Farukhabad: Wright *et al.* 1981, 270 – exported since Late Uruk), made into more or less standardized transportable pieces carried over to distribution centres (a hoard at Uruk period Abu Salabikh: Pollock, Steele and Pope 1991, 66) and ultimately supplied to the consumer sites such as Abu Salabikh itself (Pollock 1990a, 87) or Habuba Kabira (Strommenger 1980a, 63). Cord- and rope-making, which clearly flourished in the Uruk period, will have to be studied from imprints in sealings and from impressions in other materials (bitumen: Pollock, Steele and Pope 1991, 66). In view of the intensity of Uruk culture animal husbandry it comes as no surprise that leather-working should have risen to some degree of importance. Among its products, we have some idea of skins for the transport of liquid substances depicted by several token types (Schmandt-Besserat 1979, 39, Type XIII, No. 5; Schmandt-Besserat 1986, Tavola V). This craft also supplied plenty of articles of clothing (Szarzyńska 1988a, 222, No. T-2). For the first time we catch at least a glimpse of the varied and considerably developed industry of reed products, contributing first and foremost reed matting as building components, wrapping materials (impressions in bitumen: Pollock, Steele and Pope 1991, 66) and as interior furnishings (Szarzyńska 1988a, 223, Nos. T-31 to T-34), sometimes with decorative patterns. Uruk period herds must have constituted a virtually inexhaustible supply of hair which could be fashioned into textile products (see now Szarzyńska 1994). Both sheep wool (Szarzyńska 1988a, 223, No. T-29) and goat hair (ibid., No. T-28, as well as Neely, Wright *et al.* 1994, 175) were used. After shearing, animal hair was packed into large bales (Szarzyńska 1988a, 225, Nos. T-37, T-38) and taken in for treatment. This may provide another indication for Uruk period transhumance as the currency of wool bales 'conserved' in script signs shows that it must usually have arrived in this form at the registries. Sheep shearing is traditionally done in May or June, after the arrival of the herds at summer pastures (Le Roy Ladurie 1975, 159, 167). Wool was subsequently issued to weavers who made it into the final textile products (Szarzyńska 1988a, 223, Nos. T-28, T-29). The weaving shops (or at least a part thereof) might have belonged to EN (see pp. 135, 146; Szarzyńska 1988b, 10 on text W 21671) and the fact that the texts record hardly more than single garments (ibid.) may well indicate the low degree of specialization of the textile industry, normal in pre-industrial societies (Sanders and Webster 1988, 541, Table 3). Of course, cultivated flax was also used in textile production, as is borne out by the relevant signs (Szarzyńska 1988a, 223, Nos. T-5 to T-7; Szarzyńska 1994) and by a textile fragment, presumably of linen, found at fourth-millennium Eridu (see p. 49; another piece of linen? trapped by corrosion of a copper mirror? from Tello: Genouillac 1934, 48). Uruk culture communities employed a host of wooden articles. Those which may be documented in written sources are, first and foremost, various furniture items such as beds, the most ancient visible forms of which are attested both by the sign NA$_2$ (*ZATU* No. 379, p. 250) and by a token (Schmandt-Besserat 1979, 40, Type XV, No. 2 and

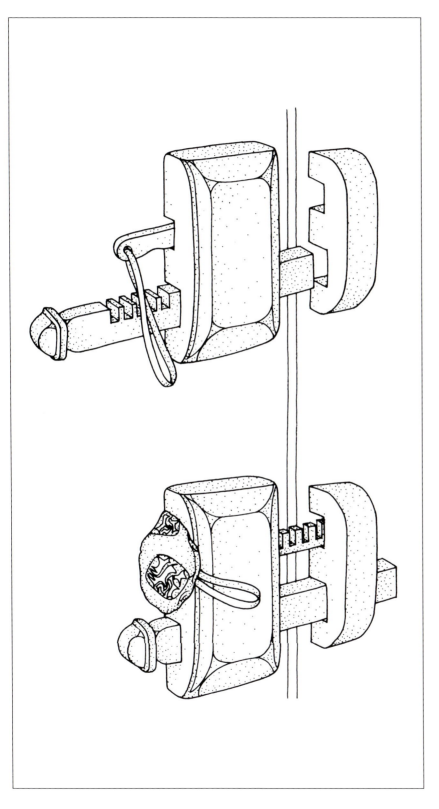

Figure 5.9 This Late Uruk lock is the first predecessor of a closing device that from the end of the fourth pre-Christian millennium became nearly universal and has turned up on all continents, lasting until the industrial age. Bearing out the high level of Uruk age craftsmanship in working with organic matters, it has been documented by sealings found at Arslantepe VIA (after Fiandra 1983, 499, Fig. 23).

p. 48 sub Type XV). The lack of good wood and the necessity to provide flexible and pliable constructions led to the combination of wooden frames with reed matting, clearly visible in both the above examples. Some exquisite furniture items, among others at least six benches decorated with chequer-pattern mosaics and covered by baldaquins, the poles of which bore bronze finials with horns, as well as remains of mosaic-covered standards of wood, survived in the 'Riemchengebäude' (Heinrich 1982, 72–73, Fig. 109; Becker and Heinz 1993, 18–23). The parallel existence of wooden furniture, especially beds, and sleeping mats, as well as the clearly élite position of the Tepe Gawra IX compound which comprises a workshop for exquisite furniture suggest a statutory value for more sophisticated furniture items which might have singled out socially prominent households. Another case of fine joiner's work worth mentioning here is the construction of the first peg locks, the functioning of which could be documented at the East Anatolian site of Arslantepe VI at the close of the fourth pre-Christian millennium (Ferioli and Fiandra 1983, 496–502, Figs 22–23 on pp. 498–499; Chighine, Ferioli and Fiandra 1985, Fig 5.9). Such locks, which from then on constitute an integral part of Mesopotamian material culture and are documented, for instance, by later omen texts (Leichty 1987; see also Charvát 1992b), now turn up not only in major centres but even in rural sites such as Tepe Farukhabad (Wright, Miller and Redding 1980, 278–281).

The considerable development of Uruk culture metallurgy in no way hindered the processing of stone, especially of everyday-use stone tools and objects of chipped and ground material, stone vessels, grinders, spindle whorls and various ornaments. Well-studied examples of Uruk culture chipped industry have come from the site of Tell al-Jir (Howe 1972: end-scrapers, micro-borers, bladelets, flakes and cores) but especially from the recent Abu Salabikh excavations (Pope 1989; Pollock 1990a, 87; Pollock, Steele and Pope 1991, 61). For the trimming of this industry, medium gray chert (abbreviated as MGC) from Khuzestan (Susa? Deh Luran plain?) and, to a lesser extent, fine mottled tan and gray chert (abbreviated as FMTGC), perhaps from the Khabur region in modern Syria, have been used. The stones arrived at the site as blade cores and were subsequently fashioned into harvesting tools (MGC) or various products, especially blades (FMTGC). A sample of what might have been the production areas of such industry came to light at the Farukhabad and Shaffarabad Tepes (Wright, Miller and Redding 1980, 276; Wright *et al.* 1981; Wright, Redding and Pollock 1989, 111; Neely, Wright *et al.* 1994, 175, 178). Most of the chipped items are, as usual, represented by sickle blades discarded, according to the ingenious interpretation of Henry T. Wright, especially at the end of winter (repairs) and summer (after harvest), much like the stone spindle whorls. Grinding stones and pebbles were discarded all year round. Even here, however, local craftsmen and craftswomen worked with cores and not with raw materials. An example of the changing pattern of stone supply is supplied by Tepe Farukhabad. While the coloured cherts gradually ceased to be imported in the Uruk period, the site started exporting chipped industry from one type of material in Middle Uruk with a climax in Late Uruk but with another interruption later on (Wright *et al.* 1981, 267, 273; Neely, Wright *et al.* 1994, 175, 178). This may reflect the abandonment of traditional supply patterns and the inclusion of the site into an aligned exchange system in which it was receiving raw materials from a determined source, working with them and sending them farther down the line as scheduled. The larger centres were in some instances provided with fairly mediocre products among which blades and scrapers may prevail. They received the material in cores (ibid.) which they themselves made into tools (Strommenger 1980a, 56). An export product of universal acceptance was constituted by the 'Canaanean blades' of striped hornstone, extracted and produced at the Late Uruk site of Hassek Höyük in eastern Anatolia (Behm-Blancke 1992). Chipped stone items may nonetheless accompany even such first-grade deposits as the Uruk 'Riemchengebäude' (Heinrich 1982, 72). An exceptional find includes a group of flints with sheen found together, possibly a trace of an ancient agricultural instrument, a sledge or a harrow (Adams 1975; Eichmann 1991, 179, Table 237b and 274–275). Raw stone constitutes good indications for the range of external contacts of the respective communities. While the Uruk population procured some low quality stone, especially for building purposes, locally from a limestone quarry some 50 km west of Uruk (Boehmer 1984), other stones came from south-west Iran, the Khabur region (see p. 128), eastern Anatolia (Nemrut Dag and Bingöl for the obsidian: Schneider 1991) and from a wider Iranian area (turquoise: Ismail and Tosi 1976, esp. p. 106). Not even here, however, was economy the sole concern of the buyers and users of the stone. A study by J. Asher-Greve and W. Stern (1983) indicated a general correlation between the colours of cylinder-seal stones and the scenes they bear. Most of these are made of softer stones like steatite, calcite and serpentine – no marked progress has been achieved beyond the technical capacities of the Ubaid culture stonecutters who were the first to treat stones harder than Mohs 3 – and displayed the classic colour triad of white–red–black. White colour correlates with fish and 'pseudo-fish' as well as with animal rows, red with pigtailed figures, animal rows, vessels and vessels on stands and black again with pigtailed figures. This may well reflect institutional manufacturing of seals, as suggested by the authors, but given the universal connotations of the white–red–black colour triad earlier and now, it is likely to reflect a particular view of the universe and may indicate an articulation of a certain world view, prevalent in the civilization centres of the period. I shall revert to this question later.

Far from having fallen into disuse, ground stone industry retained its importance, as is shown by such items as axes, grinding stones, loomweights and whetstones from Uruk (Becker and Heinz 1993, 113–121).

Stones used for decorative purposes at Uruk (alabaster, carnelian, faience, green marble, mother-of-pearl, lapis lazuli, etc.) have now been investigated and the results published (Limper 1988, esp. pp. 51–54).

Trying to sum up developments in the sphere of treatment of natural materials in the Uruk period, we may discern three major characteristics. One of these is the continuity of traditions of production. All Chalcolithic crafts survived into the period of the birth of literate civilization, and in this aspect economic life sustained no loss. The second major feature is, of course, innovation. Uruk period craftsmen and craftswomen embarked upon a course of systematic experiments, some of which succeeded while others failed. Attempts at building in concrete in the Uruk VI period were abandoned in favour of a more traditional material, clay. Of a number of experiments with metal alloys the smiths of the period invented the viable formula of tin bronze only at the close of the period and in one site only. On the other hand, the invention of the fast wheel for pottery making and the discovery of iron enriched human culture for millennia to come. Third and lastly, let us note the heterogeneity and unsystematic progress of economic development. In the sphere of artificial materials, experiments with lime and concrete were discontinued. Mass production of pottery on the technically sophisticated fast wheel was constantly accompanied by simpler technological procedures exemplified by the most rudimentary manner of making the BRB, which, however, must have carried a particular significance. The 'big leap' of metallurgy resulted in the confection of objects entirely redundant from a purely utilitarian point of view, mostly cultic paraphernalia. Finally, while the quality of stonework for practical purposes declined, the top creations of Uruk period stonemasons again consisted of objects destined either for administrative purposes (seals) or for public display (works of art). While a great deal of progress was obviously achieved during the Uruk culture period, we shall be hard put to discuss this solely in technological terms as these developments were clearly substantially influenced, if not initiated, by points of view beyond the frontiers of pure and simple know-how or economy.

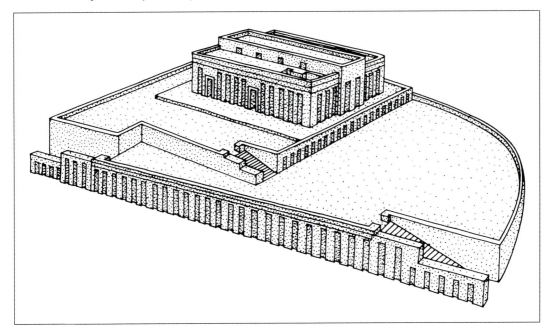

Figure 5.10 Reconstruction of a Late Uruk 'temple' on a terrace (after Forest 1996, 136, Fig. 98)

Rather similar developments may be registered in the important sphere of transport and communication. It follows from what has been said that a number of both animate subjects and inanimate objects were constantly travelling to and fro throughout the Uruk culture sphere, over both short and long distances. For the first documentable time in history, specialized production sites turned out a surplus of their commodities to be carried systematically into the centres and redistributed to other organs of the community. This may be proved, for instance, for Tepe Gawra VIII (sealings on external clay, see p. 112), for Tepe Shaffarabad to which storage jars sealed elsewhere were carried (Wright, Redding and Pollock 1989, 110) and, in fact, surmised for all sites where the seals and seal impressions do not match each other. In such cases the conclusion presents itself that local seals left their imprints in goods tags sent away from the site and unsealed elsewhere while goods sealed at other agencies arrived at the sites in question and were unsealed and consumed there. Redistribution of products made at the centre and exported to the periphery is assumed for Uruk period Susa (ibid. 106–107) and a particularly instructive lesson may be learnt at Tepe Farukhabad. In the Uruk period, this site exported chipped stone industry (Wright *et al.* 1981, 267), bitumen (ibid. 270) and possibly woollen textiles (ibid. 271), taking for recompensation metal tools (ibid. 274) and fish (ibid. 236, 260, see also Neely, Wright *et al.* 1994, esp. pp. 175–178). Of course, such connections were viable over very long distances, the major communications being represented by the 'routes that march', the two rivers of Mesopotamia. In fact, it seems that the Tigris was the more important of them in the Uruk period (Sürenhagen 1986a, 15; Lebeau 1990, 249–250). New research shows that the sea must not be excluded from such transactions: the easternmost location to which Uruk-type bevelled-rim bowls travelled is the Pakistani province of Makran (Besenval 1994, 521 – Miri Qalat phase IIIa, trench IX; on contacts with the East in general: Potts 1994). Such items as raw materials for chipped industry from south-west Iran or Khabur-region stones and Anatolian obsidian and metals(?) represent connections of this type. A good sample of materials spanning the whole range of external connections has turned up at Habuba Kabira: chert from Canaan, alabaster vessels from the Taurus and pottery from Anatolia, Palestine or Egypt (Sürenhagen 1986a, 19). Incidentally, research conducted in this direction may even revive the ancient question of contacts between Egypt and Mesopotamia, as Uruk-type terracotta cones for architectural decoration have turned up in the Nile delta (Tell el-Fara'in = Buto: Margueron 1991; von Beckerath 1995, 467, for the equation Buto II = Uruk Eanna VIII–VI; and Von der Way 1997). How far such sites as, for instance, the Sinaitic En Besor (Gophna *et al.* 1995) may represent the ways and means of such contacts remains to be seen. Contemporary Mesopotamians disposed of such transport facilities as sledges or wheeled vehicles, attested both in writing (*ZATU* Nos. 247 and 248, p. 220) and in the arts (e.g. Sürenhagen 1985, 231–232, Fig. 2). Alternatively, water transport activities brought to the rivers a number of barges of various types (*ZATU* Nos. 339 and 340, p. 241) and we may not err much in imagining a brisk kelek traffic enlivening the surfaces and banks of the great river (see pp. 71–72; Tardieu 1990, 71–102). The volume of goods travelling along the routes of Mesopotamia may be at least surmised from the fact that the domestication of the donkey, most probably as a beast of burden, took place in this period (see p. 120).

The economic activity sphere of Uruk culture thus appears in a particular light. While no qualitative progress beyond Chalcolithic agriculture may be discerned, and while the abundance in which the Uruk culture obviously lived may rather be ascribed to careful management and favourable natural conditions, the sphere of crafts and communications does display some development. Uruk period specialists boldly experimented with natural resources and repeatedly failed to find the proper solutions. This reveals two characteristics: the readiness and will to try alternative approaches and new solutions and the ability of the community's economic base to sustain loss of material and energy without marked disturbances. Indeed, the economic segment of Uruk culture society resembles a well-lubricated and smoothly running machine, choosing what is most appropriate for its inputs and maximizing output while all those who serve its needs clearly get the shares due to them. In fact, the overlapping and multiple activities of relocation of overhandled agricultural areas, incessant movement of livestock herds, prospecting for natural resources, experimentation with their treatment and conveyance of the fruits of everyone's labours to everyone else must have presented a fascinating sight for any external observer. The founding fathers of the Uruk culture must have 'run their homes precisely on schedule'. The ideal of the Uruk culture leadership seems to have been a society in which no one actually starved, as the best individuals racked their brains to procure for everyone what he or she needed and to release the potential of the natural resources in accordance with a preconceived vision of the external world in which non-economic aspects were not absent.

Society

An archaeological road most likely to take us in the right direction in investigations concerning Uruk culture society is without doubt history of the settlement patterns. Here a major issue is represented by the recurrent assertion of Uruk period urbanization, which is in need of some comment. The now prevalent opinion tends to see in cities of the ancient civilizations settlement agglomerates characterized by three basic features: a) presence of élite structures such as facilities for non-average residence, administration or cult; b) presence of crafts turning out objects interpretable as prestige goods; c) living off the surplus provided by the city's 'catchment area' (Trigger 1985, 348; on early urbanism see also Andreyev 1987). Let us start with a beautiful example of early urbanism offered by evidence from the early Egyptian capital of the fourth pre-Christian millennium, Hierakonpolis (Valbelle 1990, 262–264, plan on p. 263). In the earlier part of this period, the extensive settlement agglomeration with satellite complexes, outlying hamlets and craft centres could have housed some 5,000–10,000 inhabitants. The later part of the same period saw a process that may be termed 'implosion' of the settlement core. This process first assumed the form of clear spatial differentiation of the whole settled area into habitation, production, rubbish-disposal and cemetery areas. It then terminated in a substantial shrinking of the settled area and in the appearance of clearly discernible and circumscribed social foci denoted by monumental architecture (e.g. the Fort). This shows what urbanization is about: it appears only with the emergence of atypical, non-average settlement activities unequivocally documenting large-scale planning, locating various components of the inhabited area according to a set of pre-conceived and intelligible ideas and with clear presence of more complex structures of social life or of archaeological evidence thereof. Studies of similar phenomena in 'greater' Mesopotamia have only recently appeared (Vallet 1997).

The 'archaeological visibility' of urbanization involves the presence of two phenomena: a) deliberate manipulation of the spatial layout of individual settlement components such as residential areas, administrative and cultic precincts, production plants, cemeteries and the like; and b) a systematic and patterned manner of waste disposal. The centre of the period's social development, Uruk, has not been excavated in a manner that would permit an overall assessment of the whole municipal layout according to the categories enumerated above under a). This rules out urban-structure studies of a more general character such as those which have been carried out in the traditional capitals of ancient South American states (Wurster 1981). Neither are studies of waste-disposal patterns in major centres of the Uruk culture period overabundant, though at least at Uruk itself some regularity in the dumping of certain kinds of rubbish such as sealings and tablets may be suspected (Brandes 1979, 63–64). It has, in fact, been observed that the Uruk culture central sites invariably attracted extensive clusters of satellite settlements (Adams 1981, 60–81; Postgate 1986, esp. pp. 93–96; Lebeau 1990, 258–259). This conspicuous phenomenon, however, in no way constitutes a particularity of Uruk culture Mesopotamia, for it is present in contemporary Syria (the above cited example of Tell Brak: Weiss 1983, 42; Joan Oates in Algaze 2001, 223, with the author's answer on p. 227) as well as at fourth-millennium Tepe Yahya in south-east Iran (Damerow, Englund and Lamberg-Karlovsky 1989, viii). At Yahya, a survey of its catchment area even documented the subsequent settlement collapse so well-known from Uruk. Another instance of the same kind concerns the Iranian site of Godintepe VI–IV (Young 1986, 218–219). This does, in fact, point to the increasing importance of central sites but, in itself, does not suffice for an interpretation in terms of their urbanization (i.e. qualitative and permanent changes in their settlement structures), when proof that this was actually accompanied by such changes of the major centres is missing. The growth and decrease of satellite settlement clusters around important focal points tend to be linked rather straightforwardly with positive and negative changes of population density brought about either by economic factors or by growing power of the central sites. Some authors have even suggested large-scale and long-distance population transfers such as, for instance, between Susiana and Uruk (J. Alden in Chapter 6 of Hole 1987c). It need not be stressed that any application of such concepts would have to be argued much more exhaustively. The waxing and waning of satellite settlement zones around large centres, and even of whole settled landscapes, may have been caused by a variety of factors, including, of course, variances in the economic and social status of the centres (a good example being offered by such consequences of relocation of overland trade routes in medieval Tunisia: Bedford 1987, 147) but also, for instance, by religious zeal leading to the refusal of habitation on land polluted by heterodox practices (McIntosh and McIntosh 1983, esp. pp. 44f.). Much more detailed knowledge would be required before we could embark upon explanations of individual cases of such phenomena. On the other hand, cases of territories settled before Uruk culture times and after them and vacant in that historical period do show that large-scale population transfers took place. This applies to the Jebel Hamrin area (Moon 1986, 112) and possibly even larger areas of northern Mesopotamia including Tepe Gawra (Gut 1992, 32; 1995). We also possess indications of developments within Uruk culture settlement sites themselves.

Conscious manipulation of the spatial layout of habitation areas occurred in the form of the systematic removal of production facilities from major centres and their location in outlying but presumably not too distant areas. This has already been observed for Uruk and it applies also to Habuba Kabira which housed no specialized craft installations. The instances cited by Eva Strommenger (1980a, 56–63 – chipped industry, stone hammers?, production of chequer-boards[?]) all pertain either to domestic small-scale production, 'assembly plants' (production of sheet metal?) or individualized and atypical activities. Most eloquently, such mundane and every-day articles as pottery and grinding stones were brought to the site ready-made. This points to the incipient urbanism of Uruk culture but, at the same time, to the fact that economy was not the chief concern here. A similar conclusion may be put forward with respect to waste disposal. In Uruk period Habuba Kabira, considerable progress has been achieved but the situation was far from ideal. On the one hand, the streets were paved and provided with channels and conduits for the removal of liquid impurities and excess water; the latter case applied also to some houses (Strommenger 1980a, 44–45, 46, Fig. 28) and the paved streets were regularly cleaned (ibid. 36). On the other hand, rubbish was quite simply dumped in the minor lanes as well as in the street circling the city wall. This strips some of the glamour off the municipal fortifications, the more so as bastions of the city wall were used either as living quarters or for storage (Orthmann 1975, 141). Let us note that in the medieval cities of central Europe, the enclosed space offered by the fortifications was opened for such secular uses only after some 100–200 years of their existence. Rather more serious is the fact that the city apparently lacked any private or public sanitary instal-lations providing for the disposal of sewage (Strommenger 1980a, 45) and the only facility for the maintenance of public hygiene must have been represented by the Euphrates. Of course, the idea of removable latrines, known from Egypt (Dixon 1972, esp. pp. 647–648) may well apply here but even so, uncontrolled mass evacuation of their contents was surely enough to cause a public disaster (for urbanization and health of the local populations see, for instance, Boyd 1972). Periodical cleaning of streets and conduits for evacuation of liquid impurities and excess water is also known from Jebel Aruda (van Driel and van Driel-Murray 1983, 6) and from the Iranian site of Chogha Mish (Delougaz and Kantor 1973, 189).

It thus seems that at least basic progress was achieved in the Uruk culture period in the sphere of urbanization, although the tools enabling this were available to the local populations for mil-lennia before this moment, as is amply documented by instances like the Neolithic site of Tell es-Sawwan, which displays most of them. This conclusion is buttressed by the fact that, in addi-tion to the essential Uruk period site differentiation into élite centres and production facilities, a third type, introduced now, is a military installation, or, perhaps rather, a defensible settlement. The Uruk city wall is later but contemporary examples come from Chogha Mish (Delougaz and Kantor 1973, 190), Abu Salabikh (Pollock 1990a, 85; Pollock, Steele and Pope 1991, 63), Habuba Kabira (Strommenger 1980a, 33–36) with its 'perimeter' fortifications at Tell Bleibis (Finkbeiner 1995) and Tell Sheikh Hassan (Lupton 1996, 58–59), as well as from Grai Resh (see p. 108). An even greater surprise, however, has sprung from the discovery of true Uruk period cas-tles, perched atop rocky hills in zones bordering the Mesopotamian plains on the west and north. Two such structures have been documented so far, Godintepe V (Young 1986, esp. Fig. 1 on p. 214; 1997) in central western Iran and Hassek Höyük in Anatolia (Anon. 1987, 754; Mellink 1989, 115–116, plan on Fig. 5, p. 115; Behm-Blancke 1992). For the sake of completeness, let us refer here to transitory types such as the hilltop site of Tell Kannas above Habuba Kabira, which, in spite of the excavators' terminology ('temples') strongly resembles an élite residence with a series of representative buildings and provision stores (Heinrich 1982, 83–85, Fig. 129).

Settlement structure of the Uruk culture period thus points to a greater diversity of site types and to the first steps taken in the direction of true urbanization. It is now time to ask the question who lived in these pristine agglomerations.

In the social characterization of Uruk period communities the signs symbolizing them in written texts attain crucial importance. I readily admit that the procedure I am resorting to here – essentially iconic interpretation of the 'city' names – involves a number of uncertainties, and that it could lead us astray if there were no visual connection between the signs and their denotates, and if the signs represented attempts at, for instance, phonetic reproduction of the 'city' denominations. Nevertheless, I believe that the experiment is worth making as in the initial period of script development there must have been at least some connection between the visual form of the signs and their meaning. Individual interpretations may prove to be wrong but the general division of the 'city'-name group into several large and apparently coherent groups shows that such an approach is not entirely erroneous. As the members of the Berlin group admit themselves that the early texts cannot be read phonetically, it is tempting to try their visual interpretation, based on sign syntax in the sense of historical analysis of groups of signs into which other signs are written. In these cases the association seems safe and the information supplied by it relevant.

I found in the *ZATU* sign list references to 92 'cities' or territorialized communities. By far the largest proportion among these, 44 or 47.83 per cent, are derived from various anthropogenous structures, most probably buildings. Of these, fourteen are based on the AB/EŠ$_3$ sign = *ZATU* No. 7, p. 170 (Nos. 7, 8, 9, 10, 11, 34, 37, 389, 392, 550, 583, 584, 585 and 596), at least thirteen on the E$_2$ sign = *ZATU* No. 129, p. 196 (two instances under No. 31 and probably 53, Nos. 127, 129, 130, 131, 142, 230, 378, 381, 413 and 485), ten on the EZEN sign = *ZATU* No. 150, p. 201 (Nos. 44, 150, 151, 152, 153, 154, 155, 156, 157 and 326), four on the URU sign = *ZATU* No. 597, p. 306 (Nos. 598, 599, 600 and 601) and two on the IM sign = *ZATU* No. 264, p. 224 (ibid. and No. 396). Among these structures, AB/EŠ$_3$ will probably be readily recognized as a 'temple' building on an elevated terrace of which numerous instances were referred to in the pilot-site descriptions (for a particularly instructive reconstruction of the 'White Temple' as an example see Mallowan 1965, 39, Illus. 28–29). I see the E$_2$ sign as a frontal view of a façade of a rectangular building with buttresses, a door in its central part and an 'attic' represented by the flat roof construction (a different interpretation in Glassner 2000a, 200). This is suggested by the KA$_2$ sign showing such a structure with an emblem of crossed branches(?) above the entrance (*ZATU* No. 275, p. 226). The EZEN sign is obscure but its main feature is clearly its quintuple structure, confirmed by the EZEN:NUN variant for I:NUN, the sign I being written with five horizontal strokes (*ZATU* No. 259, p. 223). This fact brings it very close to the Mesopotamian notions of the earthly component of the universe, consisting of a centre, civilized in the proper sense of the word, and of four peripheral mythical regions (Glassner 1984, esp. pp. 29–30, and Wiggermann 1996, esp. pp. 208–209). As, however, this sign must have depicted very concrete and tangible realities, belonging to EN (*ZATU* No. 151, p. 201), supplying fish (ibid., No. 153, p. 202) or basketloads of some product (ibid., No. 154, p. 202), I suggest that it be best interpreted as a 'civilization centre', that is, an establishment or settlement laid out according to the Mesopotamian world view, a material incarnation of the ancient notion of the structure of the universe (see also the evidence in Glassner 2000a, 190). The same interpretation may apply to the IM sign, displaying the same structure specified by the identification of the most important quadrant, while URU seems to denote an enclosure or a walled area (in a plan or in a frontal view?) rather than an articulated structure. The fact that the communities in question, by far the most numerous in our sample, are symbolized by images of creations made by both human hands, most probably in the course of collective labour undertakings, and the human mind, carries a considerable significance. No symbols from uncultivated nature or reality, which might be expected to represent the essence of tribal or clan groups, are present here. These communities revealed their social affiliations by means of images of 'temples', houses, enclosures or even 'civilized' establishments, material incarnations of a particular spiritual construct. This brings out the more universal but perhaps also more artificial character of such communities in which kinship ties of a more elaborate nature, such as may be expected in a tribal society, hardly played roles crucial for identification. A major segment of the social landscape was obviously characterized by communities symbolically equated with man-made buildings and settlements, not with beasts, birds, insects, rivers, stars, winds and the like.

Sixteen community denominations (17.39 per cent of the total) may be classified as identifying themselves with various peculiar features of their environment. These are ŠIM:A (*ZATU* No. 1, p. 169), ALIM:MA:NUN (ibid., No. 26, p. 174; the graphic variants of the sign indicate that an animal depiction was actually intended), DINGIR:DU$_6$:DAB$_5$:BU (ibid., No. 31, p. 175 – an image of a vegetation-covered hill?), DINGIR:PA$_4$:SI (??, ibid.), DINGIR:SI (ibid. – ?? do both names refer to an abundance of the PA$_4$ plant??), U$_2$:UGA:MUŠEN:ZATU 647:IGI (ibid., No. 40, p. 178 – ?? after a bird on a tree?), BU:ŠA$_3$ (ibid., No. 56, p. 181 – perhaps 'inside the BU community', see p. 138), GI:UNUG (ibid., No. 204, p. 211 – connection with the yellow colour suggesting 'the marshes of Uruk', overgrown with yellow reeds), GI:ŠU$_X$/TAK$_4$ (ibid.), TU:TUR:MUŠEN (ibid., No. 376, p. 249 – connection with birds?), UR$_2$:RAD (ibid., No. 432, p. 264) and ŠIM:RAD (ibid. – possibly named after a watercourse), TIDNUM (written with the signs for bull and lion, ibid., No. 552, p. 294 – 'wild country', 'country of animals'?), U$_4$:ŠUR$_5$ (ibid., No. 566, p. 298 – 'a white site at the confluence of two watercourses'?), UR$_2$:U$_4$ (ibid. – tentative classification based on the UR$_2$:RAD name) and U$_4$-gunu:DAR (ibid., No. 569, p. 299 – 'Duck hill'?). These identifications are admittedly very tentative and we have to reckon with the possibility of alternative explanations including phonetic indicators. Nevertheless, the use of variants depicting other animal heads (but always animal heads: *ZATU* No. 26, p. 174), which shows variants of a donkey and lion for a stag, only makes sense if an overall notion of 'animal, quadruped' is intended) and the recurrent use of such images as animals, plants, landscape features and watercourses indicate, I believe, that this interpretation may be within the limits of possibility. The value of such names for social history is low and they are taken into consideration as a part of the toponymic context.

An extremely interesting category is represented by the twelve 'city' names (13.04 per cent of the total) derived from various professional designations. These are AK:SI:KI (*ZATU* No. 23, p. 173 'a place delivering mats, plaited products'?), AMA:ME (ibid., No. 28, p. 174. This sign is composed of signs GA$_2$/PISAN and AN. Given the semantic field of the GA$_2$/PISAN sign [ibid., Nos. 162–183, 185 and 189, pp. 203–208], a sense of 'enclosure or storage space' seems possible [also Glassner 2000a, 189–191]. The lexeme AMA = mother is then possible only if the AN sign refers to female animals about to give birth in a special corner of the enclosure in question. See also the two UD$_5$:AN in the inventory *ATU* 393:1. I suggest 'corral of ME/IŠIB'), AN:EZINU (*ZATU* No. 31, p. 175 – connection with matting, plaited work?), AN:AN:ŠU$_2$:E$_2$:SI (ibid., textile products?, see ibid., No. 534, p. 289), E$_2$:BAHAR$_2$:NUNUZ (ibid., No. 45, p. 179 – 'house of the kiln and stone beads'), BAPPIR (ibid., No. 50, p. 180 – 'brewery'), GAN$_2$:GI:BU (ibid., No. 56, p. 181 – 'fields and reed-grown areas of the BU community'?), AN:ŠUBUR:DU (ibid., No. 82, p. 187 – 'a city of those who walk with dogs or lead dogs'?, a parallel to what students of European medieval history know under the various toponyms of the 'caniductores', 'psáři', etc. type), GABURRA (ibid., No. 185, p. 207 – 'enclosure of the BUR vessels'?), GIR$_2$:SU (ibid., No. 218, p. 214 – 'a leather knife' – tannery?), E$_2$:IR (ibid., No. 267, p. 225 – 'house of the

IR pots'?), and PAD?/ŠUKUR? (ibid., No. 426, p. 262, given the semantic field of PAD = provisions, nourishment, *ŠL* 469). These names confirm the archaeological observations of the existence of a series of settlements specializing in the supply of certain goods or services to major centres. An insight into the activities of one such subsidiary industrial plant is offered by the sign UMUN$_2$/DIM$_6$ (*ZATU* No. 582, p. 303), showing most probably a crucible with a heated substance in it. The sememes supplied by *ŠL* No. 338, namely SIMUG = smith but also DE$_3$ = pour out, are self-explanatory in pointing to the metallurgical work based on melting some metal in a crucible. The DIM$_6$ workshop has a head (GAL:DIM$_6$), personnel? (ERIN:DIM$_6$) and registrar (SANGA:DIM$_6$, see Charvát 1996). The GAL:DIM$_6$ is connected with a particular territory (DIM$_6$:GAL:KI). In addition to DIM$_6$, there are also KU$_3$:DIM (silversmiths), directed by the GAL:KU$_3$:DIM$_6$ and connected with AB/EŠ$_3$. The relative coherence of this group and a correspondence with the archaeological record, which has supplied an example of a site producing, among others, both pottery and stone beads (Uruk period Abu Salabikh: Pollock, Steele and Pope 1991, 61; see our E$_2$:BAHAR$_2$:NUNUZ) shows that this interpretation may not be too far off the mark. On the other hand, the same situation warns us against the overestimation of data from written sources. Uruk period craft specialization did exist but the reality was obviously much more diversified than the textual data care to reveal, since they clearly register only those products of particular sites in which the registrars were primarily interested, which may have seemed typical or which covered as representative samples whole product classes turned out by the individual industrial establishments.

The last major intelligible type of iconically coherent 'city' name is represented by depictions of symbols, emblems, standards or portable(?) images which may, for the sake of brevity, be referred to as 'totems'. There are nine (9.78 per cent of the total) instances: ADAB (*ZATU* No. 19, p. 172, a new moon standard), possibly also the BU sign (a snake, a cobra?, ibid., No. 56, p. 181, for the analysis of which see p. 138; not included in the count here), GEŠTU (ibid., No. 203, p. 211. This is not designated as a 'city' but having an UKKIN, or assembly, it is likely to have been a community; a standard with a pair of horns), KALAM/UN (ibid., No. 282, p. 228, a standard with an oblong filled in by a grid pattern depicting a textile product?, not denoted as a city but meaning both 'country' and 'people', *ŠL* 312), KITI (ibid., No. 299, p. 232, a rectangular standard surmounted by the BU snake emblem), NAGA/EREŠ$_2$/NISABA/UGA (ibid., No. 381, p. 250, emblematic value clear from the denotations of the city Ereš and deity Nisaba), NIR (ibid., No. 414, p. 258, a standard with a pair of horns with protrusions, not denoted as 'city' but having an UKKIN and ŠAGAN, probably a delivery point for liquid commodities, see ibid., No. 506, p. 281), NUN/AGARGARA/ERIDU (ibid., No. 421, p. 260, again a divine and 'municipal' symbol), UB (ibid., No. 572, p. 300, symbol of a five-rayed star) as well as URI$_5$ (ibid., No. 596, p. 306, an AB/EŠ$_3$ shrine with a symbol of the moon god Nannar, see ibid., No. 388, p. 252). Here the signs identifying components of the Proto-Elamite corporate entity, perhaps depicting triangular textile(?) standards with embroidered(?) symbols, may be compared (Damerow, Englund and Lamberg-Karlovsky 1989, 16). This kind of symbol, which we tend to associate with tribal communities, was something that we would have expected in a more prominent position, but this is clearly not the case. In addition to that, some of these symbols clearly refer to local divinities which seem to be summarily identified with – or rather conceived in the form of a supernatural substance constituting the essence of – their shrines, human settlements adjacent to these and perhaps even the surrounding land. KALAM thus means both 'land' and 'people', NAGA/UGA/EREŠ$_2$/NISABA a plant, a city and a divinity, NUN/AGARGARA/ERIDU a divinity, a fish perhaps as a typical regional product and a city and the URI$_3$ semantic field constitutes the source of both the notion of the city of Ur (= URI$_3$+AB, read URI$_5$ by the authors of *ZATU*) and of the local divinity (URI$_3$+NA, read NANNA by the authors of *ZATU*). We know very little of these elusive communities some of which could well belong to the nomads. The GEŠTU community(?) had not only an assembly (UKKIN), but supplied milk (GA:GEŠTU) and imported stone beads (NUNUZ+3:GEŠTU). The NIR grouping also supplied some liquid commodity(?) and included a NIN. The extremely wide semantic fields of some of these signs, literally 'spanning the heaven and earth' and denoting almost everything from gods to fish, hardly allow any discernment of particular features of these human collectives. All we can say is that their members saw the world as a unified whole of which the god they worshipped, the shrine in which they performed the appropriate rites, their houses, the surrounding landscape and (at least some of) its produce were but individual and existential aspects of one essential unity (on this in Egypt see Bonnet 1999, esp. pp. 189–191). Pre-industrial societies, even nomadic ones, tend to identify themselves with the symbols of their divinities or of their socially constitutive acts, which thus acquire an enormous value, as they contain the quintessence of the community in question and are worth guarding at any price. Examples include the 'return of the gods into their temples' as a prerequisite of diplomatic negotiations between two African tribes of the fifth century AD (Skeat 1977, 166, ll. 19–23) or the extraordinary social value ascribed by the Maori tribes of New Zealand to their ancestor altars as embodiments of an appropriation ceremony of the lands which they claimed (Sahlins 1983). Something different is undoubtedly indicated by signs which probably depict symbols or standards in the form of animal heads: NAR/KA$_5$/LUL (*ZATU* No. 390, p. 252, a long-eared animal) and *ZATU* No. 672, p. 319, an animal with shorter round ears and a longer snout. Both cases concern clearly artificial symbols but the question whether they are standards or masks cannot be decided. A symbolic value may be assigned to the latter sign as it forms a ligature with the A-sign (*ZATU* No. 5, p. 169), and if this is a symbol of the community, as it seems (see A+EN, ibid., No. 2, p. 169; BU+A, ibid., No. 57, p. 182; NUN+A, ibid., No. 422, p. 261), we may be catching a glimpse of at least one 'tribal' community.

A small but highly interesting group of 'city' names is represented by instances composed of denominations of offices. Of the three (3.26 per cent of the total) cases, two are compounded with the NIMGIR sign (*ZATU* No. 56, p. 181: NIMGIR:BU:[ ], ibid., No. 399, p. 255: NIMGIR:SIG$_7$, both sememes are supposed to be a variant of one 'city' name but I do not see how that could be) and one with the NIN sign (ibid., No. 400, p. 256, NIN:U$_4$:[ ]). Such cases may represent either personal estates or 'service holdings' the usufruct of which was tied to the exercise of the office denoted by the sign.

The last group of eight (8.70 per cent of the total) 'city' names remains unintelligible to me. These are AN:NI (*ZATU* No. 31, p. 175), ARATTA (ibid., No. 35, p. 176), ASAR/SILIG (ibid., No. 36, p. 176), ERIM$_2$ (ibid., No. 144, p. 199), ŠURUPPAK/SUD$_3$ (ibid., No. 544, p. 291), [UB:PA:] RU (ibid., No. 435, p. 265), TILLA$_2$ (ibid., No. 553, p. 294) and TUM/IB$_2$ (ibid., No. 560, p. 296). The ŠURUPPAK/SUD$_3$ sememe confirms the identification of a divinity and a city.

Iconic analysis of the symbols used for 'city' names in the earliest Uruk texts has thus shown that nearly half of all the toponyms preserved in them (47.83 per cent) involve in one way or another signs depicting buildings, man-made structures or 'civilized' establishments as material correlates of spiritual constructs. We shall probably not err too much if we assign to these instances the interpretation of communities cemented together by the factor of common residence rather than by other links such as, for instance, kinship ties. A minor but still sizeable group of other settlements (13.04 per cent) refers to sites supplying various specialized products or services to the major centres, while another larger grouping (9.78 per cent) features emblems, symbols and standards as representations of the divine substances underlying all forms of local organic life rather than 'totems' of clan societies. As much as 17.39 per cent of 'city' names may have been chosen according to their environment while a tiny fraction of 3.26 per cent includes names of various offices. I am unable to explain 8.70 per cent of the 'city' names.

Unfortunately, the communities usually turn up in the texts as collective entities and particularities of their internal structure cannot be gleaned from them.

The inference that Uruk culture communities also laid claim to their uncultivated environment may be supported by the various sign combinations with the water denotator, sign A (*ZATU* Nos. 2–5, 57 and 422, pp. 169, 182 and 261). Watercourses were associated with signs like EN, BU and NUN/ERIDU while the sign *ZATU* 672, also featured in such a connection, clearly shows an animal head symbol, perhaps in an emblematic function. I do not understand the association with the signs ŠUBUR and U.

A case which may be to some extent exceptional and which may permit us to disclose a little more than the usual meagre data is represented by the community(?) symbolized by the sign BU/GID$_2$/SU$_{13}$ (*ZATU* No. 56, p. 181). It forms part of 'city' names NIMGIR:BU:[ ] ('the herald's BU'?), AN:DU$_6$:DA:BU(?), BU:ŠA$_3$ ('the inner BU'?) and GAN$_2$:GI:BU ('fields and reed-covered areas of BU'?). There is a connection with watercourses (BU+A, *ZATU* No. 57, p. 182) and with vegetation-overgrown hillocks (?, BU+DU$_6$, ibid., No. 59, p. 182). A value most probably emblematic is to be assigned to two crossed BU signs above the depiction of a bed (NA$_2$ = *ZATU* No. 379, p. 250 and No. 58, p. 182), denoting an entity provided with a registrar (SANGA). The DANNA sign (*ZATU* No. 68, p. 184) connects the BU emblem with the KASKAL sign, depicting probably two crossing roads. In the case of the KITI sign (ibid., No. 299, p. 232), the BU emblem is superimposed over a KALAM/UN standard and may thus refer to a symbol identifying a group of people settled in the open country. Another emblematic device my be represented by the double BU sign (ibid., No. 434, p. 265), while the gunu-form of BU (ibid., No. 487, p. 277) is difficult to interpret in any reasonable way.

A single community, likely to have been living dispersed over a larger territory, thus claimed its environment both uncultivated (A, DU$_6$) and cultivated or otherwise 'humanized' (GAN$_2$, GI, DANNA including the crossroads sign KASKAL). It developed some offices (NIMGIR) and included population groups of the open country (? – KITI with a KALAM sign). Its symbol is used to compose emblems of minor entities of which some might have constituted establishments yielding revenue to the Uruk centre (SANGA BU+BU+NA$_2$). The picture emerging is thus one of a corporate entity enjoying rights over both cultivated and uncultivated landscape, which it inhabits in a dispersed fashion, at least ranked but willing to share its resources with a major centre, the supremacy of which it apparently acknowledges.

May we dare to attempt a closer characterization of the socio-economic situation prevalent in these communities that made up the Uruk corporate entity? In fact, the only information that we possess must necessarily come from within the Uruk administration, and may thus help us to discern at least in outline the goings-on at both the centre and the periphery of the Uruk culture world. In the absence of safely documentable readings for the most ancient script, a way which may give us an insight seems to be connected with syntactic and semantic studies of sign associations in the cases of signs whose meanings, gleaned from later sources, converge with their graphemes to indicate structures and features of economic importance. Essentially, this is the procedure resorted to above – iconic analysis of signs unequivocally associated by being inscribed in each other.

First and foremost, there are signs probably related to facilities inherent to the Uruk administration and established by it, over which no other human grouping held sway. This interpretation rests on the assumption that the EN sign, by common consent intimately connected with the Uruk administration, fails to appear in them. Two types of such signs likely to denote economic structures may be culled from the texts: the LAGAB/GIRIM/NIGIN$_2$ signs (*ZATU* Nos. 127, 308–322, 370 and 488 on pp. 195, 235–237, 247 and 277) and the MAH signs (ibid., No. 341–349 on pp. 241–242). The MAH signs, which appear to depict a section through a high domed building with a feeding funnel at its top and an evacuation passage at its bottom, served, according to the signs inscribed in them, mostly for the storage of animal-husbandry products and of fish (Glassner 2000a, 187–188). A structure of this kind may have been excavated at Abu Salabikh (Pollock, Steele and Pope 1991, 65–66). A possible (genetic?) connection with the Ubaid culture round structures (see above, Tell Madhhur and Khanijdal East: Wilkinson and Matthews 1989, 264–265; Wilkinson, Monahan and Tucker 1996, 44) remains to be investigated. The other category of structures was earmarked by the inscribed signs in a less uniform fashion, serving again for the deposition of products (GA'AR, HI, KU$_6$, KUŠU$_2$, *ZATU* No. 766?) but also for goods connected with particular occasions or needs (BANŠUR), offices (ME/IŠIB, PA), sites (DU$_6$) or communities (NUN/ERIDU, NAGA/EREŠ$_2$). These data point to the incompleteness of specialization: while animal husbandry seems to have constituted a quasi-independent sector, only some of the fruits of other human labours were kept in facilities separated according to the kinds of goods deposited (mostly also animal products), while a quantity of commodities received treatment directed by such non-economic criteria as their cultic or institutional destination or, alternatively, their despatcher.

Another group of establishments is denoted by signs containing other signs, the latter including the designation of the EN office. Let me include here at least a brief outline of the basic purpose of the EN function as I observed it in the earliest cuneiform texts (in full: Charvát 1997). The EN constituted, together with his female counterpart NIN, the central pontifical couple, providing the land with fertility which they generated in the course of the NA2 ceremony. The fertility thus generated filled the entire building in which the act took place, together with its (presumably cultic) paraphernalia including statues (ALAN). Interested persons could partake of this fertility by performing the TAK4.ALAN rite, most probably 'touching the statue(s)'. The EN took the relevant symbols or statues around the country in order to make fertility accessible to all the people. How far this entitled him to the collection of reciprocal contributions which apparently constituted the base of his and the NIN's wealth in various commodities remains unknown, though a parallel to the great Makahiki festival of Oceania may not be entirely out of place. The existence of a clay token in the form of a bed, in clear connection with the NA2 sememe, accompanying presumably a delivery of some product, points to such a conclusion (Glassner 2000a, 95, Fig. 1b, centre). To revert to the sites with composite names, the fact that they were expressly assigned to EN implies that there were others of the same kind claimed by other holders and that the structures referred to in this manner represent a more general type of establishment which could have been founded by more communities of Uruk period Mesopotamia. The first instance of this kind concerns the EZEN sites (*ZATU* Nos. 44 and 150–157, pp. 201–202, see also No. 259, p. 223). Such establishments, which probably denote 'civilized' human settlements, may refer to structures newly founded on virgin soils such as, for instance, Habuba Kabira. Here the inscribed signs imply that these colonies specialized in supplying particular kinds of produce (KAB?, NIM, SU?) or that they were meant to tap the resources of particular regions or landscapes (RAD, U$_2$+A) or to supply certain offices (NIMGIR). Another type of such a structure concerns the GA$_2$ signs (*ZATU* Nos. 162–183, 189, 360 and 616, pp. 203–206, 208, 245 and 311; I have not managed to find the GA$_2$+ME/IŠIB sign referred to ibid., No. 358, p. 244). These structures, destined for all kinds of produce (GIŠ.tenu, HI, HI+SUHUR, KU$_6$, MAŠ, SUHUR, SUKUD, SUMAŠ, ŠE, ZAR), some offices (EN) and for deliveries of particular sites (NAGA/EREŠ$_2$), may have quite simply meant 'storehouses' or the like, as is indicated by the sign group SAL:PAP:GA$_2$+DUB:URI$_3$ (*ZATU* No. 166, p. 204), where the GA$_2$+DUB sign is associated with the URI$_3$ symbol of the Ur area. As a matter of fact, this evidence points to the conclusion that more settlements had their GA$_2$+DUB and that writing was not a sole prerogative of Uruk. A somewhat different specialization may be envisaged for still another type of such structure, symbolized by the signs *ZATU* Nos. 651–658 on pp. 316–317. These cases, in which a construction of flexible

Figure 5.11 Scenes carved on the Late Uruk alabaster vase from Uruk. The EN and NIN may be offering the 'first fruits' to the goddess of fertility here (after Schmandt-Besserat 1996, 320, Fig. 4).

material such as palm branches or reeds may be depicted, were reserved for the EN by an inscribed sign and sheltered plant products (GAR, MA = PEŠ$_3$?, ŠE, GA$_2$+ŠE). The last item on my list takes up the signs *ZATU* Nos. 737–748 on pp. 329–331. These rectangular structures with 'drive-in' entrances(?) were, approximately in equal proportions, associated with various products (DI?, GAR?, SAL?, SU, ŠE, ŠITA.gunu), offices and supplier sites (EN, NIMGIR, SAL?, UNUG).

We may thus guess a certain dichotomy of the economic sphere of the Uruk community. One production sector was in full and unquestionable command of the Uruk centre, perhaps in the manner of the demesne holdings of feudal domains; its produce went to the MAH and

LAGAB/GIRIM/NIGIN$_2$ facilities. Not surprisingly, animal husbandry, so prominent in the texts, played a major role here. The 'outer zone' of Uruk economy consisted of a series of structures, or perhaps rather collection points of types that were not an exclusive feature of the Uruk corporate entity and in which the Urukeans stored such quantities of surplus mobilized from other communities for themselves as may have been deemed justified by contemporary public consensus. While the Uruk corporate entity thus clearly vindicated its own environment both cultivated and uncultivated, much as seems to be the case in other communities, it had, in addition to this, the right to a certain share in the surplus of other communities which it raised by means of a network of collection points from which the deliveries might have been despatched to the centre. In fact, this does not sound too far from what we would expect of the Chalcolithic supraregional middle-level community associations represented by such archaeological features as the Eridu or Luristan cemeteries.

More light is shed on this aspect of surplus movements by signs inscribed in the vessel designation DUG (*ZATU* Nos. 88–124, pp. 189–194). Most cases fall under the general sememe of 'pot, container' but there are interesting exceptions. Combinations with sites denoting geographical entities (GEŠTU?, NAGA/EREŠ$_2$, KUR, LAM) may simply mean foreign pots but a DUG+GIŠ presents a problem (*ZATU* No. 100, p. 191 – a tree-juice product?) and DUG+KASKAL (ibid., No. 103, p. 191) would be better understood, in the light of DUG+BA, a ration pot (ibid., No. 93, p. 190) as 'journey provisions'. The DUG+BA points to the very interesting possibility of issuing 'rations' in containers of standard intakes which, as it seems, were hardly the BRB. This also implies the emergence of an at least pristine form of normalization of commodity units in circulation and, accordingly, the origins of both metrology and currency systemization. The sign NINDA$_2$+BA (*ZATU* No. 402, p. 256) introduces the possibility of coexistence of several ration systems. A hint that true trade may not have been entirely absent at this period is dropped by the sign ŠAM$_2$ (*ZATU* No. 510, p. 282).

In conclusion to this section we may point out that the archaeological record gives evidence of short-term minor settlements, major permanent centres in the case of which first steps towards urbanism occurred, and more narrowly specialized settlement types such as military installations ('castles'). In the texts, almost 50 per cent of the habitation sites are symbolized by signs depicting various man-made structures, which probably denoted communities in which the factor of common residence played a major social role. These establishments were accompanied by specialized production plants and by sites assigned to some of the major centre offices. Of the remaining minority, a part is represented by symbols which scan to express the divine substance underlying all forms of organic life current in the settlement in question and in its vicinity. Another part bears names that may be derived from various features of the environment. These individual communities claim both cultivated and uncultivated segments of their catchment areas and, displaying at least internal ranking, communicate with the centre(s) by means of part of their surplus which they assign to it (them). Their economic functioning is illuminated only by the Uruk example. The Uruk economy apparently consisted of an inner 'demesne' sector within which animal husbandry played a major role, accompanied by other production branches. This sector, comprising the EN-cum-NIN 'enterprises', might have been administered by the LUGAL(s). Uruk's 'outer zone' included a series of structures or rather collection points towards which the contributions of other communities converged, presumably for transport to the centre. No more than one of these agencies supplied predominantly field produce, while written records could have been made in these receptor sites and accompanied the goods into the centre(s). Comparison with the archaeological record brings out some probably significant differences. Details of craft production, prominent on some minor sites, are hardly ever mentioned in the texts. This indicates that such industrial plants were operated by the major centres themselves and that they also defined their obligations and disposed of their products. No property boundaries were crossed and there was thus obviously no need to register such deliveries, which were under direct control of the centres, in writing. The texts also maintain an absolute silence about the military sites, the existence of which is prominent in archaeology. That, of course, may be explained with reference to their entirely different position within the Uruk corporate entity and by the fact that military affairs, most probably handled by local commanders, did not fall within the essentially economic remit of the texts, which record, first and foremost, commodity circulation. Such facts then militate against excessive reliance either on the texts or on the archaeological record. Each of these source categories represents a part of the past inaccessible to the other category.

All in all, this socio-economic development of the Uruk culture seems to have gone on, by and large, along the same lines as that of the earliest Egyptian state, with gradual emergence and differentiation of its material base in the course of the first historical dynasty (Endesfelder 1991, esp. p. 148; for China and the chiefly ceremonial role of the king see Ching 1997).

Here I wish to add two notes of caution. First, archaeological evidence is structured by its own principles and on no account should it be expected to provide sensible answers to wrongly posed questions. The 'problem' of ethnicity of the Uruk culture, persistently re-appearing in specialized literature, belongs, as I urge, with the other decrepit and largely defunct relics of political archaeology. That archaeological material cannot identify ethnic communities, even well-defined ones, has been pointed out repeatedly; among the most recent studies treating this problem I wish to cite Esse 1992 and Vansina 1995 (esp. p. 195) and, for later Mesopotamia, Fleming 1989 (p. 176). The same kind of thought fossil is represented by the notion of irrigation systems functioning as a factor of social relevance and even stratification. Wittfogel's hydraulic theory was refuted shortly after its publication, by Sir Edmund Ronald Leach from the ethnographic angle and by Robert McCormick Adams from the point of view of Mesopotamian archaeology. It has repeatedly been observed since then that the excavation and maintenance of irrigation works may easily remain in the competence of local communities or institutions, and that no connection with accelerated social developments or interference of any higher social bodies are necessary (see Netherly 1984; Lansing 1987, esp. p. 338, and, most recently, Forest 1995).

Having defined at least the barest outlines of group social behaviour of the Uruk corporate entity, I now proceed to examine the social status of individual community members. This is an exceedingly difficult exercise since we have very few comprehensible data to go by. The remarkable professional differentiation, noticed up to now, as well as the complex character of functioning of the Uruk corporate entity must have placed great demands both on the smooth running of its component parts and on the coordination activities of the centre, and must thus have offered great incentives for the seizure of public power, which would have entailed command over huge masses of people and goods. No danger of such a kind materialized. Though the texts name a host of officials who must have played significant social roles, no traces of social differentiation are ascertainable in the archaeological record. All of the extraordinary achievements of the Uruk culture represent corporate undertakings destined for corporate use. The huge 'temples' hardly sheltered under their roofs common everyday activities of men, women and children though the manner of publication, focusing on the architectural features and less so on such key evidence for the employment of the buildings as occupation strata, hardly permits any decisive conclusions. Sculpture and probably also painting of the Uruk period depict memorable individual acts but these are typified and turned into visual formulae and lack any true individuality, while their heroes perform their feats – kill wild animals, defeat enemies or carry out cultic acts – as representatives of age groups rather than individuals ('Mann im Netzrock': Glassner 1993; in general see Stein 1999; on the extensive powers of pristine élite heads as exemplified by the duties of earliest Chinese kings see Ching 1997). Uruk period seals vanish from graves and become attached to institutions or to corporate and perhaps eternal entities (Damerow, Englund and Lamberg-Karlovsky 1989, 16; Charvát 1992a). To clinch the matter, there are no separate residential facilities for the élites, no external wealth markers destined for ostentatious display (with the exception of the possibly earlier Tepe Gawra, to be discussed below) and no singular funerary obsequies for élite individuals. We have seen that the roles of the first couple of the land, EN and NIN, were primarily ceremonial (Charvát 1997).

In spite of all this, traces of social development do exist and may be discerned, though this entails some effort. To take the texts first, they offer the term GURUŠ, known from the later texts to signify an able-bodied young (unmarried?) man, visualized, rather unexpectedly, by a sign depicting a sledge (*ZATU* No. 247, p. 220, see also Nagel and Strommenger 1994, esp. pp. 206–207). The sign for 'slave', IR$_3$ (*ZATU* No. 268, p. 225) turns up only from Uruk III times, but GAR3 may have had the same meaning (Charvát 1997, 50). The ordinary, full-privileged citizens, most probably adult married men and women, are likely to have been designated by the pair of terms LÚ (*ZATU* No. 332, p. 239; Charvát 1997, 71 76) and MÚRUB (*ZATU* No. 371, p. 286; Charvát 1997, 82–83). The LUGAL, present though not particularly prominent in the earliest texts, might have been 'speakers' of the age grade of adult men, though some cultic engagement on their behalf may be suspected (Charvát 1997, 77–81). In an absolutely perplexing manner, only one single kinship term, ŠEŠ(?), occurs in the earliest texts (*ZATU* No. 523, p. 286). Specialists refer to signs supposed to mean 'slave' and 'slave-girl' and related terms but the arguments are difficult to sustain (for a probably just critique of A. A. Vaiman's conclusions see Green 1980, 6, n. 17; in the meantime this notion has re-appeared in the Proto-Elamite sphere: Damerow, Englund and Lamberg-Karlovsky 1989, 56–57, 60). It thus seems safer to regard the non-élite population strata as a rather undifferentiated mass, most members of which are likely to wear the masks of the LÚ, GURUŠ, MÚRUB and SAL signs in the texts. The association of GURUŠ with the sledge may result from threshing grain by means of this device, likely to have been done by the younger and sturdier household heads. Alternatively, a symbolic function of a threshing sledge, especially in terms of provision of nourishment for the family, essentially the responsibility of the father, may be envisaged. On the other hand, archaeological evidence has yielded undeniable traces of practices involving the use of cosmetics and therefore presumably representing differences in social status within average population strata (toilet sets and a 'makeup container' from Tello: Genouillac 1934, 47; a palette from Habuba Kabira: Rouault and Masetti-Rouault 1993, p. 272, Fig. 140, p. 438). As to the functions of the élite, we have already hinted at the fact that these could most probably be subsumed under the following headings: a) protection of their communities both from the wrath of supernatural beings by the proper performance of the correct rituals and from external enemies both animal and human; and b) organization of the complex economic circulation of the Uruk corporate entity. This essentially accords with what we know, for instance, about the most ancient functions of the Chinese kings (Kravtsova 1991, 33; Ching 1997). Of all these activities, which would without doubt require far more detailed studies, those that stand out most clearly in our evidence are the operations documented by the texts, treated in more detail below, and the military activities, leaving massive and well-discernible evidence in the archaeological record.

The existence of fortified Uruk centres both in the plains (Abu Salabikh, Chogha Mish, Habuba Kabira, Grai Resh) and in the highlands (Godintepe V, Hassek Höyük) has already been mentioned (on Uruk-age colonization see also Algaze 1993a and 1993b). This evidence is accompanied by depictions of warfare in the arts such as the glyptics (Amiet 1987; 'Waffenkammer' – Brandes 1980) and by weapon finds both in the centre(s) such as those of the Uruk 'Riemchengebäude' (see p. 103) and at peripheral sites (Arslantepe-Malatya: Watkins 1983, 21). The Late Uruk period might have seen the invention and introduction of the double-curving, reflex bow (Collon 1983, esp. pp. 53–56). The LUGAL may be tentatively identified as fortress commanders and field officers of rank of the Uruk troops. If such interpretation of the military remains is confirmed by future finds, it may be of significance insofar as it fits the general evidence put forward by the dislocation of centrally commanded armies, usually stationed along the frontier of the area to be defended (for an interesting study of this kind see Willems 1984, esp. p. 222, Fig. 125). It is, of course, debatable how far Abu Salabikh may be considered a frontier position. Nevertheless, in view of the discontinuity of the Uruk culture sphere, which follows from the published site lists (Sürenhagen 1986a, 9–10; Schwartz 1988, 5–8; Sürenhagen in Rothman 1990, 132f.), the possibility is not to be excluded a priori. The initiation of such extensive building projects in connection with warfare may have been necessary as it has been observed that the impact of a civilization upon tribal societies may well result in the increase of cruelty of warfare and, in fact, in the introduction of genocidal practices (Blick 1988, esp. pp. 664–665). It follows from this that the Uruk élite may have functioned as an agency for central management of the whole cultural sphere of this civilization. The society itself, however, still retained a considerable measure of the egalitarian spirit. This is shown especially by evidence concerning the sign UKKIN, assembly (*ZATU* No. 580, p. 302; Glassner 2000a, 201; on contemporary assemblies see Selz 1998, esp. pp. 291–325, and Glassner 2000b, esp. pp. 43–47). Many of the component communities of the Uruk corporate entity apparently held their own assemblies and elected 'presidencies' (KINGAL, *ZATU* No. 294, p. 231). The UKKIN sign, an image of a spouted pot, alludes to the age-old practice of socially relevant commensality. A sidelight on this is provided by an Uruk culture grave from Jemdet Nasr (Matthews 1990, 36, 38–39; see Figure 5.12). For his or her journey to the nether world the deceased carried a complete meal: a

Figure 5.12 This Late Uruk grave from Jemdet Nasr (Matthews 1990, 36, 38–39, Fig. 12 on p. 39) attests to the significance of commensality in the period of emergence of the first statehood. For his or her journey into the nether world the deceased received a bitumen-coated basket, a stone bowl and a pot, all filled in with shells. At least one spouted vase and two, presumably, drinking cups completed the 'table service'.

bitumen-coated basket with pots filled with shells, as well as a drinking service consisting of at least one spouted vase and two cups. For later (OB) social dimension of commensality practices see Charpin 1990, 81 and Matthews 1990, n. 51. Of exceptional interest is the sign ŠAKIR(?) (*ZATU* No. 509, p. 282), likely to have denoted a vessel or a container and combining the UKKIN and DUB signs. If there indeed existed 'tablets of the assembly', the community may well have introduced some collective form of procedure or proceedings involving written records. Several possibilities are open: some of the texts could have recorded in a visible and hence controllable form the resolution(s) of the assembly; texts prepared before the occasion could have been approved or rejected by the assembly; written records of some transactions could have been checked by the assembly who may have had the right to demand a public account of running the community affairs; etc., etc. A parallel may be constituted by the later, Jemdet Nasr age NI+RU 'fund' which had a registrar (SANGA NI+RU, Charvát 1997, 16). Of course, nobody is perfect and there is probably no need to idealize the 'consensual democracy' of the Uruk culture period. Nevertheless, the facts that the UKKIN sign survived this epoch and that the KINGALs retained their positions and did not merge with the Uruk culture élite do show that the assembly managed to defend its position in public life.

As to the holding of outlying regions, the Uruk culture bearers left the existing structures in place and only superimposed the uppermost administrative layer (Lupton 1996, 57–58). Of course, the Sumerian overlords took care to insert their own agencies at vital points of the system, keeping them under their control. One such 'supervision point' has recently been excavated above the middle Euphrates ford at Hacinebi, Urfa province, south-east Turkey (Stein *et al.* 1996).

An attempt to discern the Uruk culture conceptualization of the social order may now be made, however theoretical and perhaps far-fetched it may sound. We have noted on several occasions the importance of the white–red–black colour triad for the Uruk culture. Now this triad seems to have influenced also the deliberate choice of materials and scenes of cylinder seals (Asher-Greve and Stern 1983). White correlates here with fish, pseudo-fish and animal rows, red with pigtailed figures, animal rows, vessels and vessels on stands, and black also with pigtailed figures. Let us now recall the decoration of the 'temple' of Tepe Gawra XI in which the front 'cella' wall with the single niche, clearly in the most important position, bore white paint while the short wall segments separating the 'cella' from the 'nave' displayed, turned into the 'nave' space, coatings of red paint. As noted above, white colour tends to be associated with divinity, purity and fertility while red carries the symbolism of life, energy and sex (Bruce Dickson 1990, 206). White may thus allude to the world of Uruk period gods, concerned principally with the fertility of all forms of the earth's organic life, and perhaps to the sphere of EN and NIN. The other two colours may stand for two 'estates' of the Uruk corporate entity, the élite (LUGAL, KINGAL – red) and the commoners (LÚ, MÚRUB, GURUŠ – black). Here, of course, the three-colour decoration of the court area of the Uruk–Eanna IVb structures (see p. 103), complemented by the black-and-white mosaic on the round pillars and black covering the façade of the staircase ramp, may be highly relevant. Were the individual areas 'assigned' by their colours to particular social groups? The lack of human depictions on white-colour seals may be symptomatic as early phases of religious systems tend to refuse images of the gods, referring to them by symbols only, as was undoubtedly the case in Mesopotamia (witness the symbolization of divinities in the script). On the other end of the social ladder, the later name by which the Sumerians referred to themselves, namely 'black-headed people' (sag-gig-ga, see Limet 1982, 259), might have originally belonged only to the lower echelon of the Uruk culture society and, by extension and the process of social ascent, might have later on referred to the people as a whole. Comparable cases close to the modern reader would include the German word 'Mann' (from the medieval designation 'vassal' to modern 'man, male') or Czech 'člověk' (from the medieval 'subject, serf' to modern 'human being'). That, however, is hardly more than a hypothesis.

The professionally differentiated Uruk culture society thus may have been socially articulated into two strata, the élite and the commoners. The role of the élite, comprising perhaps the brahmana (EN, NIN) and ksatriya (LUGAL, KINGAL) segments of the Indian caste system, was a harmonization of the divine and human world both in time and space and the protection of their communities from obnoxious influences both spiritual and temporal. The commoners (LÚ, MÚRUB, GURUŠ), conceivable in the vaisya roles, were to work faithfully and honestly, 'expected to do their duties'. The degree of cooperation and of group coherence remained high, consolidated by regularly held assemblies which continued the traditions of commensality of the preceding period. Any possible conflicts were turned against the outsiders to this system, who nevertheless posed a distinct threat to the Uruk community. A similar idea of Uruk culture social binarity has been developed by Mark Brandes (in his work on the Uruk 'Pfeilerhalle' mosaics, cited in Heinrich 1982, 51).

This social coherence of the Uruk culture sphere manifested itself most visibly in a conspicuous social phenomenon, the redistribution of surplus mobilized from the producers. Redistribution of goods produced in the centres of the Susiana plain and diffused over the countryside has been extensively studied and discussed (Wright and Johnson 1975, esp. pp. 279–281, 283; Johnson 1976; Wright, Redding and Pollock 1989, 106–107). I have argued elsewhere (Charvát 1988a and 1992a) that redistribution is to be inferred from the sealings of immovable storage spaces ('lock' sealings). Here something goes at first in and then, under somebody's control, out. Sealing of doors, for the first time practised more systematically in the Uruk culture sphere (Torcia Rigillo 1991), is virtually coterminous with the invention of the cylinder seal sometime in Uruk VII–VI. This is likely to represent an emblem of a collective entity (pp. 142–143; Charvát 1992a) and was probably introduced first in – or even by – the major centres of the period. In more recent excavations, redistribution is also attested by cases in which seals and sealings from a single site do not match one another. This has been documented at Habuba Kabira (Strommenger 1980b, 485), Tell Kannas (Finet 1975, 159) and Jebel Aruda (van Driel 1983, 34f.). More detailed information has been secured by Henry T. Wright and his team at Tepe Shaffarabad (Wright, Miller and Redding 1980, 278–281; Wright, Redding and Pollock 1989, 110–112). In addition to the proof that goods brought to the site had been sealed elsewhere (find of a pot sealing on non-autochthonous clay), evidence has been brought forward for impressions of the same seal on mobile containers and storeroom doors. I argue (Charvát 1992a, 282) that such a practice is compatible with employment of travelling seals in cases when all these impressions have been found on a single site. A seal that normally closes a storeroom door leaves its home base and goes forth to mark goods destined for its owner. Then it returns and carries on sealing the storeroom in which the goods, sealed with it outside and ultimately arriving on the site, are themselves deposited. This assumption of a surplus collection area consisting of two concentric zones alludes to the 'inner' and 'outer' sectors of the Uruk culture economy delineated above according to the texts. Both types of evidence may well point to one single historical phenomenon.

Any enquiry as to how much of the output of singular households could have been siphoned off for redistribution must remain a futile undertaking. Ethnographic data give us a bare outline: in pre-conquest Mexico, for instance, every household contributed about 10 per cent, possibly up to 16 per cent, of its total output. Of the overall quantity thus collected, the part going to the centre of the system is supposed to have amounted to about 29–46 per cent of the mobilized surplus while the rest was retained by the regional offices, through which the levy took contributions from individual households and the remainder was conveyed to the central office (Steponaitis 1984, esp. pp. 145–147).

Another facet of the redistribution processes is represented by the clay symbols of delivered commodities, the now famous tokens. Denise Schmandt-Besserat has worked extensively on these (the most recent works that have reached me are Schmandt-Besserat 1988a and b and 1991) and while the stretching of the token (= symbolic) system back into the Mesolithic would require a great deal more source criticism than that which has been presented up to now (on this see also Lieberman 1980, esp. pp. 353–354, and Glassner 2000a, 87–112), the significance of the Uruk period tokens as a recording device cannot be denied. To a certain extent, tokens reduplicate textual data and they might have possibly accompanied deliveries of goods playing specific roles. Why such commodities were not accompanied by written texts is not clear but several possibilities again present themselves. The accompanying texts might not have survived because their vehicles were of organic, and therefore perishable, matter (see p. 152). Alternatively, these deliveries might have reached the Uruk centre via another input than the GA$_2$+DUB, where the consignments seem to have been registered in writing. However that may be, a comparison of signs displayed by inscribed tokens and of some token shapes with textual data summarized above will perhaps bring out some interesting details. A few tokens bear the ŠE sign (Schmandt-Besserat 1979, 33, Type VI, No. 3d; 37, Type XI, *sub* No. 4) and the last of the signs, resembling a rake or a pitch, may also be connected with grain treatment (a winnowing instrument?). Such tokens, accompanying grain deliveries, may thus have been arriving at the centres via one of the 'outer zone' inputs employing the shelters denoted by signs *ZATU* Nos. 651–658 on pp. 316–317. The important thing is that two such tokens come from Uruk and one from Habuba Kabira. Redistribution systems involving these symbolic devices could thus be based on any of the major centres and the practices applied might have been identical. Another such case concerns a bedstead-shaped token interpreted by Denise Schmandt-Besserat (1979, 40, Type XV:2) as BANŠUR, elsewhere (ibid. 48, *sub* Type XV) as NA$_2$. The sign agrees neither with BANŠUR (*ZATU* No. 49, p. 180) nor with NA$_2$ (*ZATU* No. 379, p. 250) but it could be related to the sign *ZATU* No. 750, turning up in the tax lists, which would fit our context well. Some similar examples may be adduced from among the Uruk finds (Schmandt-Besserat 1988a). Here the signs borne by the tokens consist of names of geopolitical units, most probably communities like ADAB (ibid. 23 and 121, No. 553) or ŠENNUR (Schmandt-Besserat 1979, 100, Type 442 and 116, Type 539 = *ZATU* No. 522, p. 286), of designations of single craft activities like DIM$_6$, metal-smelting (Schmandt-Besserat 1988a, 23 = *ZATU* No. 582, p. 303) or DIN, a liquid container, wine? (perhaps ibid. 121, No. 554) and of titles of the Uruk hierarchy such as *ZATU* No. 749c, p. 331 (ibid. 119, No. 551), SUKKAL (?, ibid. 24) or even DIN:NIMGIR (ibid. 119, No. 552 = *ZATU* No. 349, p. 242, see also Glassner 2000a, 95, Fig. 1c). This comparison brings at least some points home. In addition to the community and office designations likely to have accompanied deliveries of goods in the function of tags identifying the despatcher, the signs DIM$_6$ and DIN suggest consignments dovetailing into the supply schemes illuminated by the texts. Written data pertain especially to disbursements of animal products, deliveries from particular locations and offices (or for them?) and only to a lesser extent supplies of grain. As against this, the tokens represent the grain supplies, which manifestly were not concentrated particularly in the GA$_2$+DUB receptor agency, and therefore were not likely to have been put down in writing, as well as the income from the metallurgical workshops and of gardening/orchardry establishments, which, as we have just noted, are missing from written texts. At least a part of the tokens thus represent recording systems supplementing writing and enabling registration of data concerning inputs of energy into the system by other receptors than those reserved for supplies recorded in the texts.

A problem of an even more complicated nature is represented by the so-called bullae, or clay envelopes, containing tokens (Schmandt-Besserat 1980; Amiet 1994; Glassner 2000a, 108–110). Probably of Middle Uruk date at the earliest (ibid. 364) and turning up with common everyday domestic necessities at Susa (Schmandt-Besserat 1986, 108), these display seal or cylinder seal impressions all over their surface (2–3 seals, 2 cylinder seals, one cylinder seal and one seal, three cylinder seals, or two cylinder seals and a seal), presumably to prevent unauthorized access to the contents. One of the Susa bullae contains tokens that may imitate sheep knuckle bones, and as one of the rooms of Tepe Gawra VIII contained a deposit of sheep knuckle bones and as a stone imitation of such a bone comes from Tepe Gawra XA (see p. 110), this may represent another manner of recording a particular type of contribution, at least in some cases perhaps of animal products.

Even written texts do occasionally hint at redistribution, mentioning, for instance, 'rations'(?, see 118, 141) of many vegetable, animal and other substances (Green 1980, 7). Surplus mobilization carried out by tax collectors, picking out their shares from the harvest or stationed at roadside posts to levy a toll on the passing goods, starts at this early period (Green 1984). On the other hand, there are reasons to believe that redistribution could accompany – or even constitute a component of – major social gatherings or religious events. This is indicated by imprints from seals 'quoting' the great Uruk vase which may have denoted commodity transfers occurring in connection with the ceremony depicted on that work of art (Brandes 1986, esp. p. 53) as well as by a cylinder seal from the Erlenmayer collection, bearing an inscription(?) containing the signs EZEN and MUŠ$_3$, which could also denote supplies taking place on such occasions (N.C.–H.N. 1991, 44, Fig. 5a on p. 45). Were such supplies brought in recompensation for the NA2 rite performed by EN and NIN?

In short, redistribution en masse constituted a dominant feature of the Uruk corporate entity, and indeed, goods are likely to have percolated along the land and water routes like life-giving

Figure 5.13 Brick masonry of the 'great residence' at Jemdet Nasr. Though the techniques of bricklaying became well-established around 3000 BC, the long horizontal join running between the bricks along the longitudinal axis of the building's wall must have posed a threat to the wall's stability and have ultimately led to its collapse. This shows how errors can occur at any historical time and place – a notion that perhaps brings our Mesopotamian predecessors closer to us, revealing their human failures.

blood in the arteries of a living organism. Outlying sites had their own catchment areas, on whose surplus they regularly drew, concentrating it and sending (a part of?) it down the line towards major centres. These received a great variety of supplies of most diverse goods from all directions and by all means, and it must have required considerable administrative skill to take care of all the commodities, to despatch them to their destinations, to watch over proper recompensation of their suppliers and to keep track of all the movements of the individual goods categories. Indeed, Uruk culture managers successfully passed the test for imperial administration.

Nevertheless, there is still something missing in this sketch of Uruk culture society. The statement that in most cases we can hardly descend deeper into the structure of component communities of the Uruk corporate entity holds true insofar as it pertains to the Uruk culture sphere proper. A notable exception that will instantly spring to the mind of anyone well acquainted with the subject concerns, of course, Tepe Gawra. This site does not fall within the sphere of Uruk material culture (Algaze 1986, esp. pp. 125–126, 131) and, by displaying a socio-cultural pattern completely different from the Uruk one, reminds us that we will do well to remember that as with a number of similar early systems, the Uruk culture settlement pattern was discontinuous and its density varied, leaving here and there pockets to accommodate human groups organized along completely different lines. Needless to say, in this aspect also, archaeological studies are likely to add some precision to the relations between Gawra and the Uruk culture sphere, as the Gawra assemblage had, in fact, preceded the Late Uruk expansion (Gut 1992, 32 and 1995). The reader has without doubt noticed that with Uruk culture society, a version of a primeval 'welfare state', the keyword was not display – that was reserved for the gods – but corporate undertaking and corporate consumption. Everyone worked according to his or her appointment and everyone received his or her remuneration accordingly. The gods commanded time, space and fertility, the cardinal categories of the Uruk world, and received the earth's most desirable goods – precious metals, stones and the like. People bowed to them and, at the very best, only discharged the mysterious life-giving force belonging to the realms of the guardians of heaven through the persons of EN and NIN. They nonetheless made the calculations and schedules, arranged things, administered, wrote out lists, vouchers and receipts, kept a vigilant eye on the enemy, sweated over the plough handles or cast fishermen's nets, grew almost deaf from incessant hammering on metal, and dared the devils of faraway mountains and gorges to bring home the desired goods. They all received what the gods measured out for them. Theirs was a world of community, a world to be shared out like the same kind of cake baked in the same manner by the same procedure thousands of kilometres apart. Tepe Gawra was different and, to our eyes, much more normal. After the last egalitarian period of XIA, the layers XI–IX were characterized by the emergence of ascribed social status, expressed by means of ostentatious display of wealth brought in (also) as the result of surplus collection in the form of reciprocity (sealing of mobile commodity containers). Intra-group solidarity was maintained by means of commensality and, in less successful periods (XI, possibly an initial period of the emergence of a new social order, and IX) by institutionalized redistribution (sealing of storage spaces) which, however, instantly vanished in times of plenty when each of the local social foci drew its wealth from its own source, falling back to (unilateral? negative?) reciprocity (layers X and VIII, sealing of mobile containers). In Uruk the most precious materials went to the shrines. In Gawra they bedecked the living incarnations of law and order, fashioned into ornaments and articles of personal attire. The system was carried a step farther in Tepe Gawra VIII. At that time, the solidarity of the local élite groupings must have been high as most of the residences obviously shared one and the same supply source (impressions of the same seal at several findspots). On the other hand, the surplus collection sphere of Gawra was extended and new resources were tapped, their contributions marked by travelling seals (sealings on non-local clay). In this case the evidence suggests a composite élite group capable of amassing a considerable quantity of surplus which it converts into visible legitimation of its superiority, maintaining its status successfully over a long period of time and even extending its 'catchment area' farther. Identification of the source from which the Gawra élite drew its wealth is, of course, pure guesswork but military, nomadic or merchant aristocracies represent some viable alternatives. In fact, not even a connection with the Uruk culture world is entirely excluded; the Gawra lords may have supplied rare commodities to the Uruk theocracy or, alternatively, might have offered military protection to caravans supplying the lowland centres, for instance.

The Uruk culture social sphere is somewhat peculiar. The development and diversification of settlement, including military installations and first steps towards urbanization, cannot be denied. On the other hand, the vast corporate entity headed by Uruk does display a most varied structure. Almost half of its component communities derived their names from man-made architectural creations and are thus likely to denote more complex social bodies than kin-based structures. The centres are accompanied by satellite sites sheltering production facilities and, to some extent, supplying individual offices within the Uruk culture administrative setup. Unfortunately, the level of these component groupings of the Uruk corporate entity is the last to which the texts permit us to descend in detailed analysis. These communities possibly claimed all their cultivated and uncultivated environment as property and contributed to the common cause by discharging (parts of?) their surplus into the supply-line network of the Uruk culture sphere. Uruk period economy, discernible only at the centre, relies on a variety of 'inner' establishments, probably founded and directed by the centre which disposes of their produce in the 'demesne' manner, comprising the EN-cum-NIN realms and administered possibly by LUGAL(s), as well as on a system of 'outer-zone' receptors of types not limited to the Uruk centre, by which energy is fed into its circulation system. Pronounced professional differentiation is still embedded in a relatively homogeneous social matrix. Hardly more is discernible than élites, whose task it is to harmonize the divine and human worlds and to ward off all evil menacing their communities, and suppliers of all kinds of goods, catering for the material needs of the system. Social distances are kept at a minimum by relatively important congregational activities, which probably developed out of the traditional commensality, and, above all, by the huge and complex redistribution machine, conveying goods registered in writing, symbolized by tokens free or enclosed in clay bullae, or merely sealed, to the centres where they are taken in charge, consumed, processed or sent farther while a stream of other commodities rushes back to reciprocate and to reward the original suppliers. Precious goods are systematically siphoned off to embellish the holy tabernacles. This huge and essentially egalitarian Leviathan, guarded by well-built and apparently well-garrisoned forts, may be watched from a distance by paramount chiefs who direct their communities in the traditional fashion. On this other side of the social frontier, wealth is not concealed in temples but proudly displayed to legitimize status. Careful redistribution counting how much to whom and for what gives way to contribution collection without any further questions asked. Power walks hand in hand with glory here and the relatively small holdings within sight of the dominant political configuration, so reminiscent of the native states of the British Raj, still dare to face it and to defy its challenge.

Metaphysics

As in other aspects, so too in this sphere the Uruk culture society approaches the threshold of a fundamental change. Indeed, spiritual matters may have undergone a most systematic transformation over this period of time. The first and most conspicuous feature of this situation pertains to the sphere of burial.

Figure 5.14 Large round kilns in one of the annexes of the Jemdet Nasr 'great residence'. When discovered, they were perfectly clean and without any trace of ashes. Were they maintained so scrupulously clean during the proto-historic age as well – or have they been used for some special purpose, such as, for instance, firing tablets?

To cut a long story short, an overwhelming majority of Uruk culture interments must be simply missing (Vértesalji 1987, 492). A few isolated graves occur throughout the land, from southern sites like Abu Salabikh (Pollock 1990a, 86) via the central region where such a grave turned up recently at Jemdet Nasr (Matthews 1990, 36, 38, 39, Fig. 12, Pl. Va) and Tell Rubeidheh in Jebel Hamrin (McAdam 1982) as far north as Erbil (Hirsch 1968–1969; Hirsch 1970, 148) or Tell al-Hilwa in the Mosul region (Wilkinson and Matthews 1989, 264). The thousands of dead bodies which must have been left behind by agglomerations of the size of Uruk or Habuba Kabira, however, have evaporated. Let us take notice of the excellent parallel which is offered by the Pre-dynastic capital of Upper Egypt, Hierakonpolis, where the overall count of the deceased laid to rest in the municipal cemeteries amounts to 1,804–8,047 graves (M. Hoffmann, cited in Hendrickx 1990, 646) and even this is considered a poor record since the estimate of the total goes up to some 22,000 individuals. This bears out most eloquently the anomalous situation of the Uruk culture but, at the same time, supplies interesting historical data. The manner of disposal of the dead bodies must have possessed a character leaving no discernible traces in the archaeological record. As a matter of fact, a number of ethnographic cultures actually display post-mortal treatment patterns which would present major obstacles to archaeological recognition. Some of the possibilities, such as throwing the ashes of the burnt corpses into the rivers or their exposure in the desert parts of the hinterland of major sites, are self-evident. Let us not forget that inhabitants of the slightly later Early Bronze Age towns along the Dead Sea coast buried the excarnated remains of their dead in collective ossuaries of considerable size (Rast 1987; Schaub and Rast 1989; Schaub 1997). In addition to this there is another important aspect. The

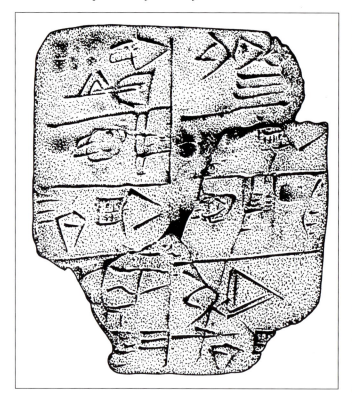

few surviving graves seem to belong to middle-status individuals but any funerary monuments of the creators and architects of the Uruk system, who must have enjoyed particular prestige in their days, are absent. All members of the Uruk corporate entity may thus have been entitled to one, single and uniform post-mortal treatment, regardless of whether they had been major political figures or mere swineherds. Nothing exemplifies better the truly revolutionary transformation of the Uruk culture attitude to the world than this radical departure from age-old veneration of the dead. This fact contrasts with the traditionality of Tepe Gawra, where the deposition of the dead, in accordance with the earlier custom (predominance of children) provided with fabulously rich grave goods and frequently in sophisticated funerary constructions, points in the direction of ancestral cults (Forest 1983a, see also Akkermans 1989a, esp. pp. 357–363).

Figure 5.15 A proto-cuneiform text from Uruk, likely to date to the Uruk III stage (after Damerow, Englund and Nissen 1988a, 75)

Of course, the major and capital innovation which Uruk culture Mesopotamia contributed to the cultural heritage of mankind is one of the first scripts of the world, thanks to which the Mesopotamian culture, so long buried under mute heaps of clay, has suddenly acquired the ability to address us in intelligible words. The Berlin team, headed by Professor Hans Nissen, has gained much merit by its systematic work on the most ancient texts, as have other scholars who have contributed to the theme (see Nissen 1985a, 1986a and 1986b; *ZATU*; Damerow, Englund and Nissen 1988a and 1988b; Damerow, Englund and Lamberg-Karlovsky 1989; Green 1991; Englund and Nissen 1993; Englund 1994; Englund and Matthews 1996; Veldhuis 1997; Glassner 2000a). Evidence for the use of this earliest script has come from the entire Uruk culture sphere (Strommenger 1980b; for Jebel Aruda see van Driel 1982), but it is not excluded that even the northern regions participated in the discovery (Tell Brak: Oates 1982, 191, Pl. XVc; Finkel 1985, 187–189). The surviving documents on clay seem to represent only a part of all the written evidence that once existed and has since perished. The earliest form of the sign denoting a tablet, DUB (*ZATU* No. 86, p. 188), consists of a rectangular handled frame filled in by a lattice pattern of intersecting oblique lines. The model for this sign must have been a tablet of some hard but probably organic material (wood or bone) bearing the crossed lines provided for better adherence of the soft writing surface, most probably a wax filling into which individual signs were incised. Such a tablet of wood has been found in the much later shipwreck of Ulu Burun, Turkey (fourteenth century BC: Payton 1991). That the tablets could also have been cut from bone is indicated by data concerning the most ancient annals of Egypt (Kaplony 1991, 198).

Why the Uruk culture intellectuals invented the script, or rather introduced it on a large scale, is not so difficult to guess. By its most complex and structured character the Uruk corporate entity constituted an elaboration of the principles of the earlier, more or less self-sufficient Chalcolithic communities, jealously preserving their rights and prerogatives, that surpassed them all and ascended to a qualitatively different social level. Tradition doubtless commanded an insistence on equality and fair shares for everybody, in relation to the particular position that the individual in question occupied in the community. Corporate consumption of the fruits of human labour; assignation of responsibilities and positions directed by regard for common benefit; decisions of important matters in the assembly; and finally, theoretically absolute equality even in death, such were the social principles inherited to a great part from the Chalcolithic ancestors. Nevertheless, the complex movement of a great quantity of commodity types required careful checking of this flow, the more so as the authorities guarded well the principle of 'differing contributions but equal remunerations'. If redistribution, socially anchored and institutionalized by means of systematic supervision of the storage facilities incarnated in the 'lock' sealings, was to work, if the managers were to make reliable calculations of the volume of goods to be consumed by the community and to be traded for other necessities, they simply had to know what was on hand. A good example of the problems with which the Uruk culture managers might have had to cope is the evidence from the Tepe Shaffarabad excavations (Wright, Redding and Pollock 1989, 112–113). The rubbish strata deposited there in the course of the second, perhaps famine year (ibid. 110) contain more mobile-container and 'lock' sealings. Facing a calamity, the local population opened more storerooms but also appealed for help to an external agency which reacted in due course, sending in contributions in sealed containers. Now the central office administrators would have been confronted with problems of this kind every now and then, their task being rendered even more complex by the fact that the economic base of Uruk culture was fairly extensive and far from concentrated in one single centre or site (see Charvát 1997). Moreover, the fact that the economic processes seem to have been run not by individuals but by offices or corporate groups (cylinder seals as emblems of agencies, Charvát 1992a) might have put information possessed by one individual but not by others in jeopardy. I believe that all these reasons converged in the emergence of a need for more complex recording devices of which several types were tested (sealings, tokens, envelopes, script) until the script was finally adopted. Its purpose was thus practical but at the same time it could also have fulfilled tasks of cultic character as a set of sacred signs by which ritual operations could be performed. Most ancient Egyptian hieroglyphs worked this way, representing both the 'divine word' in their essential character and a practical recording device in their existential form (Kaplony 1983, 150–151, 157). The patron deity of the earliest Egyptian scribes of the first half of the First Dynasty, Aker, was imagined in the form of a lion hunting game, its prey being likened to taxes and contributions recorded by the scribes (ibid. 158). This parable may help us to understand a little better the ideas connected with the earliest scripts of mankind. Needless to say, such parallels are to be used with caution since the earliest scripts may issue out of quite different sources. The Harappan script, for instance, records with all probability names and social affiliations of individuals (Fairservis 1991, 111–112). The considerable dimensions of the operational range of the Uruk culture script as well as its systematic character and stability in time all imply that scribal tradition must have been systematically cultivated, most probably as one of the prerogatives of the Uruk élite. This is borne out by the introduction of the lexical list tradition in this period. It may be added that the introduction of literacy exercises a benign influence on human capacities for more thorough reasoning and argumentation, for abstract thought and for viewing the past as unchanging and different from the present (Stevenson 1989, 159f.). In this aspect the Uruk culture intellectuals initiated a development that was to bear fruit for millennia to come.

Figure 5.16 A spindle whorl from Jemdet Nasr with a sign of proto-cuneiform writing, likely to denote a large unit of weight (Nissen, Damerow and Englund 1991, 64, EN-system E, probably N-10, N-11 or N-12). Having been set into a rotating motion in use, the whorl turned the sign around and thus presumably 'activated' its magical capacity with the aim of bringing abundance and plenty to the initiator of the action. Again, a perfect example of interpenetration of sacred and profane activities in proto-historic Mesopotamia.

Alternatively, however, the invention of script, or rather the introduction of a universally comprehensible set of visual symbols may be viewed in the perspective of a climax of the Uruk culture determination to manipulate the world. The Uruk élite designed and organized the structure and functioning of the visible section of the universe. They appointed all men and women to their posts, they assigned them remuneration for their labours, they saw to it that all received regularly the necessities of their lives. They even dared to manipulate the past and future by a radical change in burial customs. Would it be too presumptuous to think that in the script, their domination of the visible world infringed on the borders of the spiritual, introducing a device to manipulate even the invisible world to comply with their concepts?

Uruk culture tradition is the most ancient Mesopotamian one that allows us to catch at least a glimpse of the earliest pantheon of the land. Indeed, the complex hierarchy of the Uruk corporate entity presupposes a major role of religion: 'hierarchy implies divinity, the hierarchy itself may mirror the divinity' (Glass 1988, 67). Individual communities might have viewed themselves as one of the forms of manifestation of the existence of a particular local deity who, at the same time, represented the ultimate source and first cause of such phenomena as the local shrine, the adjacent settlement and probably also the surrounding landscape and its various forms of wildlife. The divinities were in most cases visualized in the form of symbols venerated in temples (on those of archaic Uruk see Szarzyńska 1992; on the symbols or emblems see Szarzyńska 1996), out of which the toponymy of the various anthropogeographical and geographical units ultimately evolved. In some instances, divine substances could be incarnated in very humble objects. The earliest occurrence of the divine name Enlil (Englund 1988, 131–132, n. 9) makes this god, in fact, EN:KID, the sign KID assuming the form of an oblong filled in with a checkerboard motif. The lexeme KID, however, may also denote a reed mat (ibid. 170, n. 43) and this reminds us instantly of the matting on which the central pedestal of the Uruk VI 'Steingebäude' rests (see pp. 101–102). Here, however, the key role is undoubtedly played by the checkerboard pattern, employed in numerical systems to construct artificially high numbers (ibid. 131–132, n. 9), which may point in the direction of the sememe 'everything, everybody, all things and beings' – indeed, a fitting audience over which Enlil could have exercised his EN-ship (see also Glassner 2000a, 200). The production of checkerboards is one of the few traces of professional activity recorded at Habuba Kabira (Strommenger 1980a, 57–58) which might have thus acknowl- edged the supremacy of Enlil. Of course, checkerboard patterns turn up at large in the decoration of Halaf period pottery (see figs on pp. 61–70) and they might thus represent another component of the Chalcolithic spiritual world which, like the white–red–black colour triad, survived into the age of the first civilization. Other divinities might have played roles of considerable importance in the social sphere. Inanna was (also) conceptualized as 'nu-gig', 'the lofty, unapproachable one', transferring her possession of the land and the kingly office to earthlings (Zgoll 1997). This seems to be very close to the role played by the Sumerian NIN, especially in the later periods (Charvát 1997, esp. pp. 85–89). In fact, a close connection between the worlds of spiritual powers and of actual social reality is sometimes interpreted in a manner opposite to what has been asserted by many until recently – cosmology is not supposed to reflect economy but vice versa, economy is developed to meet the needs of cult and ritual (Howe 1991, esp. p. 448 – Bali). The Uruk culture with its essentially Chalcolithic economy differing only by extension of its appli- cation and by its experimentation, with its considerable role of religion as a socially constructive factor elaborating upon mental achievements of the preceding age and with its strong egalitarian bias manipulating the lives and even the deaths of its bearers (and, with their post-mortal treat- ment, even the past and future), offers extremely interesting prospects for such an interpretation.

The multilateral, versatile and symbolic character of Uruk culture thinking is well-illuminated by contemporary numerical systems. Modern research has shown that several numeration sys- tems, using the same signs, existed together, being applied to counting various commodities, much as in some ethnographic cultures (Schmandt-Besserat 1984, esp. pp. 48–51; Damerow and Englund 1985, viii; Damerow, Englund and Lamberg-Karlovsky 1989, passim; Friberg 1999). The abstract notion of a number had not emerged yet and mathematical values were clearly per- ceived as correlates of particular categories of counted (or measured) objects and values.

Hardly more than hints at the apperception and explanation of the Uruk culture world may be submitted here. The characterization of the contemporary communities has already brought out the extraordinary variability of Uruk culture thought in which one and the same symbol may have stood, according to context, for anything from god to fish. For Uruk culture thinkers the reality had always a particular and concrete incarnation; they would surely have been at a loss to understand the Nominalist dictum popularized by Umberto Eco 'stat rosa pristina nomine, nomina nuda tenemus'. There were no nude names in Uruk times. A reed symbol was the god Enki, the town of Eridu or a type of fish but it was never emptied of its concrete contents. Ancient Egyptian evidence shows that this phenomenon was fairly frequent but that we would be hard put to distinguish between the divine presence in some object of the material world and this object's belonging to the manifestations of the immaterial substance of the divinity (Bonnet 1999). In such conditions, abstract thought presents certain problems. The identity of graphemes for periods of the day and directions of the wind, probably equivalent with the cardinal points (Englund 1988, 165–166, Uruk Plant List) reveals the Uruk culture vision of the basically unified spatiotemporal structure of the world in which cardinal points correlate with particular

Figure 5.17 This fragment of a protective bitumen coating bears a good impression of a reed mat, presumably from a ceiling construction.

time segments (and what else?). This complex vision of the world once enjoyed widespread popularity and to elucidate it, it suffices to borrow a few examples from various European languages. 'Deutsche Morgenlandische Gesellschaft' includes the word 'Morgenland', in literal translation both 'southern land' and 'morning land'. In Polish, 'pólnoc' means both 'midnight' and 'north' and 'poludnie' both 'noon' and 'south'. Essential unity of understanding of a geographical area and its human population is exposed by the grapheme KALAM/UN (*ZATU* No. 282, p. 228), still not differentiated into the sememes KALAM (= land) and UN (= people) (see Limet 1982, esp. pp. 259–260). Of course, this multiplicity, fluidity and, should some prefer the expression, evasiveness of the manner of expression of facts of real life must have entailed the definition and application of certain basic principles by means of which the essentials of the organization and functioning of the world could have been articulated. One such principle is undoubtedly the fivefold division of the world into its civilized centre and the 'oneirique' four outer districts (Glassner 1984, esp. pp. 29–30; Wiggermann 1996, esp. pp. 208–209), already present in the Uruk culture period (EZEN = *ZATU* No. 150, p. 201). This cosmological structure is universal in early cultures of the Old World, appearing in India (Dubuisson 1985, esp. p. 118) and China (Hisashi 1990). The Indian example, in which the centre and each of the four quarters are individually correlated with a particular season of the year, divinity, religious notion and a material substance, evokes particularly well the kind of ideas that may have circulated in this connection in ancient Mesopotamia. Its local incarnation may nevertheless have been somewhat different, as no more than two non-Sumerian names – Dilmun and Aratta, too conspicuously placed not to wake the suspicion of having been chosen as the two poles of the world – actually turn up in the earliest Mesopotamian texts (Nissen 1985b, esp. pp. 228–230). In later times, such a conceptualization of the world is perceptible in Mesopotamia itself: in

Sennacherib's times, the east was entrusted to a guardian in the form of a bison-man, the west (or, alternatively, the north) to that in the form of a scorpion man, the south to one in the form of a fish-man and an alternative figure symbolic of the west might have been the vulture (Huxley 2000). Another universal principle of this kind may have been constituted by the white–red–black colour triad which might have been operated to express a number of individual cases of which the tripartite social division of the community of gods and two ranks of humans, as delineated above, might have been one. In fact, the colour triad does appear in Uruk texts (*ZATU* No. 391, p. 253). Of course, a third example of application of such a principle may be seen in the funerary practices of the period. If all humans received the same post-mortal treatment, regardless of their actual achievements and of the communities' claims to their territories, human bondage must have been seen as following out of one single general principle, relating to everyone. Incidentally, this might well have been the most revolutionary of the Uruk culture spiritual achievements. It is pointless to repeat here the frequent statement as to how well-suited religion is for the role of a social welding agent bringing about the emergence of new societies. Examples from medieval India (Durga and Reddy 1992) point out to what extent the seemingly impossible, namely a synthesis of hunter-gatherer and highly sophisticated intellectual social milieux, can actually be achieved.

Of particular ritual usages, let us note the first hoard find of personal ornaments, especially necklace components, which was to become popular in subsequent periods, at Jebel Aruda (van Driel and van Driel-Murray 1983, 23–24). Leaving such intimately personal possessions as

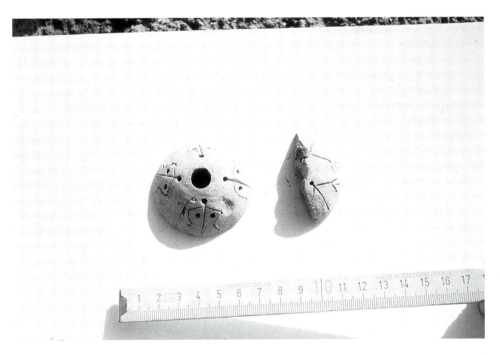

Figure 5.18 These two spindle whorls from Jemdet Nasr are decorated with simplified images of a circle of women (complete example) and men (broken example). With the spindles in action, the images rotated and the women and men 'danced'. In view of the fact that ancient Mesopotamian dances had a magical character and were supposed to produce fertility and well-being (Kilmer 1995, 2610–2611), the mere fact of setting these spindles into motion could have brought about the desired magical activity and effects. No better testimony on the close intertwining of sacred and profane activities in ancient Mesopotamia can be found.

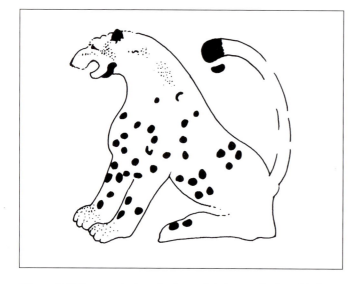

Figure 5.19 Fresco painting of a leopard dating to the Late Uruk age from Tell Uqair (after Spycket 1988, 292, Fig. 3)

necklace beads in a shrine may well have constituted a component of another 'rituel de participation', albeit very different from that involving the BRB. Some material culture items do bear out a non-negligible function of dance (a pin with a head in the form of two nude female dancers from Tello: Genouillac 1934, 46, Pl. 10:2–5, a; on dance in general Delavaud-Roux 1993, Kilmer 1995, esp. pp. 2608–2612; on Uruk age musical instruments Eichmann 1995, esp. p. 111). The fact that in the 'Curse of Agade', Inanna assigns dancing as a distinguishing feature to young women (Cooper 1983, 52–53, lines 29–33 and p. 238) could indicate the existence of age grades or age groups as early as this period, but the matter needs further consideration.

The NIN is referred to as a seasoned performer of harp music and this exercise thus seems to have had its place in fertility rites (Charvát 1997, 85). A peculiar feature seems to be the rarity of anthropomorphic clay figurines (Spycket 1992, 16), though animal depictions, especially those of the most frequent and useful domesticates such as sheep (in considerable quantities, reproducing even whole herds with shepherds and watchdogs), turn up widely at some sites (Uruk period Tello: Genouillac 1934, 37–38).

May I be excused for closing these remarks with a renewed note of caution repeated from the epilogue of the preceding section. Attempts at ethnic or linguistic classification of the Uruk culture and the persistent Sumerian problem re-emerge over and over again. Archaeological material alone cannot give evidence of ethnic affiliations save for very particular cases in which abundant and comprehensible non-archaeological evidence is available (for a good recent treatment of the problem see an example of the virtually invisible Jewish culture in Rome of Late Antiquity: Rutgers 1992; see also Esse 1992, Fleming 1989, 176 and Vansina 1995, 195). As I hope to have demonstrated, textual data may refer to a number of communities of most diverse ethnic backgrounds. Who laid down the actual foundations on which the Uruk culture was built, and what language this population group spoke, is most difficult to decide, and it is questionable how far it is relevant to truly historically oriented research. Their contribution to human history is capital and unquestionable. Whoever they may have been, their labours will always be with us, as long as humans have cultures.

CONCLUSIONS

This review of the Uruk culture developments, crucial in terms of the birth of one of the most brilliant civilizations of the ancient world, attempts a somewhat less traditional view. In all spheres of society the principle of universality and equality comes to the fore and struggles with the particular and concrete manifestations of the visible world in order to make way for human advance. In the spiritual sphere, the torrents, twists and turns of mythopoeic thinking in symbols embedded in reality are surmounted, if not straightened out, by applications of universal principles and rules. The world, perceived as unity in diversity, is accordingly organized into a social whole. The natural variability of communities, in most cases linked principally by the factor of co-residence and accompanied by industrial sites and service holdings interspersed by groupings that see themselves as manifestations of divine will, communities divided among élites and commoners, is constantly levelled. The material standard of living is equalized by means of redistribution, external threats are eliminated by garrisons posted to ward off any attack. Everyone is close to everyone else, people meet in assemblies to discuss and decide matters of common interest with at least some of the resolutions put down in writing. All receive the same treatment, both in life and in death. The world is an organized place where the economy thrives because all the discoveries and inventions of the previous ages are now put into practice and systematically exploited. Unity of purpose drives the best brains of the epoch to experiments both economic, some of which fail, and social and spiritual, some of which succeed. The flow of goods throughout the community is directed and scheduled. Vigilant eyes guard the assignation of 'suum cuique' – the most precious materials go to the gods concerned with the highest categories of the Uruk culture corporate entity, masters of time, space and fertility. All consumables are assigned to those who will ultimately also be consumed by the Great Unknown. Distribution of goods is subject to public control, in time gradually assuming a permanent form, as writing is adopted from among all the recording techniques put to test. The world is weighed, measured, disposed of and organized from cake-baking to manipulations of time and space.

To a considerable extent the Uruk culture heralds the advent of a new era. Building on the traditional principles of the corporate social entity as the highest ideal, architects of the Uruk culture applied them in dimensions surpassing all that had been known before. A grandiose success of this kind could nonetheless not have failed to create, in the matrix of traditionally oriented society, seeds of the new order, releasing human capabilities to such an extent that some tension must have been felt even then. The Uruk culture was no revolution. It represented the final stage of evolution of the traditional society, when the strength of age-old traditions in people's minds still prevented the new elements from prevailing over the ancient order. Some smaller communities approached the threshold of the new age individually, with the 'natural' social stratification involving the representation of acquired status by ostentatious display of wealth mobilized from the community in question. These groups, however, lacked the means to step into history by themselves. Nevertheless, elements of the new order were there, awaiting their future destiny.

Chapter Six

When kingship descended upon the earth

The Jemdet Nasr and Early Dynastic periods

Pilot sites

Uruk

After the total destruction of all IVa buildings and the obliteration of their remains (Finkbeiner 1986, 46), the architects of layer III resumed their task in the Eanna precinct, now the sole sacred area of Uruk, still using the ubiquitous Riemchen bricks, which remain frequent until layer I/7 when planoconvex bricks appear for the first time (ibid. 47–48). From the earliest IIIc layer the core of the cultic precinct was constituted by a terrace of which the most ancient (A) phase

Figure 6.1 Before the builders of proto-historic Mesopotamian structures used their clay bricks, they let them dry on reed mats. This brick from Jemdet Nasr preserves the impression of the mat on which it was laid to dry.

measured 18.3 × 23.5 m (Heinrich 1982, 55–57, 90–91, Fig. 142). On the south-west, south-east and north this terrace was enclosed by courtyard areas, some walls of which bore cone-mosaic decoration (ibid. Fig. 140) and perhaps also ornaments composed of terracotta sculptural plaques (ibid. Fig. 141 – 'Schilfringbündel'; on this see Glassner 2000a, 227, remarking that, in fact, this is an image of the goddess wrapped in a shawl). A notable feature of the following IIIb layer is represented by seven open chambers in the 'Opferstättenhof' south-east of the terrace, each of which contains a pair of long and narrow trough-like pits (*c.*5 × 0.8 m), partly revetted by bricks and heavily stained by heat. Such fire installations turn up frequently in the Uruk III layers all over the Eanna precinct. A building south of the terrace, nicknamed 'labyrinth', contains a niched hall No. 167, the plastering of which displays carved decoration in the form of a zone of spiraliform volutes, as well as painted patterns in black, white, red and yellow. The spiraliform decoration finds a parallel in the 'cella' of Building I of Arslantepe VIA (Sürenhagen 1985, 235–236). The IIIa phase saw the extension of the central terrace which now formed an L-shaped plan; a building situated in the internal corner of the L-form layout had very small chambers and cone mosaics. Another building, designated as M and situated north-west of the terrace, had its two rooms (Heinrich 1936, 2, Fig. 1) filled by the 'Sammelfund', a hoard of precious objects and materials, presumably disused temple inventory, comparable with the 'Riemchengebäude' deposit (see Limper 1988; Becker and Heinz 1993). The finds that turned up in the filling layers of the building included vessels of clay, metal and stone, sculpture (the famous 'Uruk vase'), both monumental and miniature, especially of various animals, as well as cylinder seals, several thousand diverse beads including examples carved from shell cores and bearing the distinctive spiral traces imitated in clay, mosaic and inlay components (Becker and Heinz 1993, 24–26) and various items of sheet metal, probably for plating objects of organic matter (gold, silver and copper; note the presence of silver wire, Heinrich 1936, 46). Materials of the 'Sammelfund' beads include most frequently various forms of limestone, carnelian, rock crystal and shell with a sprinkling of true beads, followed by gypsum stone and lapis lazuli and by trace quantities of such stones as quartz, calcite tuffo, amazonite, talc, chalcedony, agate, amethyst, diorite, aragonite and 'Brauneisenstein' (Heinrich 1936, 41–42, and Limper 1988, esp. pp. 57–59). The Jemdet Nasr period Eanna layout continued until layer I/7 when the first planoconvex bricks appeared. This layer is overlain by a heavy sheet of debris followed, in the I/6 layer, by a rebuilt version of the terrace which was now accompanied by fragmentary walls in the courtyard areas bearing cone-mosaic decoration (Heinrich 1982, 112, Figs 157–159; Finkbeiner 1986, 46–47). Layer I/5 ushered in the first nearly square terrace of dimensions amounting to 46 × 50 m and accompanied by a south-east court in which circular kilns replaced the earlier trough-shaped fire installations. Layer I/4, which more or less established the tradition of the ED Eanna, introduced a square-plan ziggurat with a façade of sharp vertical edges of 'saw-tooth' section, as well as two courtyard areas south-east and north-east of it.

The Jemdet Nasr and Early Dynastic periods saw a dramatic decrease of the numbers of rural settlements around Uruk (Nissen 1972). One such site some 4 km north-east of Eanna (WS 312) has been excavated (Vértesalji 1988) and yields interesting evidence on craft specialization and its stability in the 'catchment areas' of large centres. The settlement has four phases (D, the earliest, C, B and A) of which the first belongs to the final Uruk culture period. After levelling of the debris, the Phase C settlement was built in the early Jemdet Nasr period as a plant for manufacturing vessels and ornaments of stone and perhaps also for metallurgical work. Phase B retained the making of stone vessels, supplemented by then with pottery workshops and leather-working(?), while Phase A linked the stone-vessel production with turning out ornaments but possibly also with textile work, a dyeing industry and with the making of fishing nets (Vértesalji 1988, 23).

A limited amount of attention was received by the Uruk urban layout of the first half of the third pre-Christian millennium. The surface survey (Finkbeiner 1984 and 1986; Boehmer 1991; Finkbeiner 1991) shows that the municipal area, enclosed by an impressive city wall perhaps as early as ED I (Boehmer 1991, 468), was not completely settled; clusters may be observed in its south-west and north-west sectors, quite the contrary of the Akkad and Ur III periods when the north-east and west segments were occupied (Finkbeiner 1984, 88–89, Fig. A and Fig. B for the ED period). Some Uruk areas display evidence for specialized craft activities such as the manufacture of carnelian beads by means of flint implements north of the central shrines, dating perhaps to the ED period (von Müller 1963; Rau 1991, esp. pp. 65–67). Manufacturing sites for stone vessels seem to have been dispersed throughout the northern half of the city, only one of them having come to light in its south-west quarter (Eichmann 1991, 179–180, Table 238 and 276–278). One of the major architectural features of Early Dynastic Uruk, the 'Stampflehmgebäude' or hand-moulded clay building, was situated south-west of the Eanna terrace. It stands on the Eanna I/7 level and is covered by house ruins of the first pre-Christian millennium (Heinrich 1982, 112; Schmidt 1977, 105). This is a huge complex of 'tauf' walls displaying evidence of alterations after building (revetments, building up of floors). Among the finds such categories may be mentioned as numerous pottery sherds but also seal impressions, shell-inlay fragments with human figures, depicting also pots and landscape elements, terracotta plaques in the form of animal bodies and inscribed tablets dating from Uruk III to the Fara period including a fragment of a royal inscription of Lugalkiginnedudu. The excavators of Uruk now assign the building of the 'Stampflehmgebäude' to the very end of ED III, or to Lenzen 1964, 16–18 and 1965, 11–12; Schmidt 1977; Lugalzagesi (Anon. 1978, 641; Heinrich 1982, 112; Finkbeiner 1986, 44; Eichmann 1989, 61, 181; Boehmer 1991, 468; Boehmer 1997, esp. pp. 295–296).

Jemdet Nasr

A tell 19 km east of the town of Mashrua, excavated by a British–US mission in 1925–1926 (director S. Langdon) and 1928 (director Ch. L. Watelin) and by a subsequent British expedition of 1988–1989 (director R. J. Matthews). The two tells of the site lying close to each other – Mounds A and B – yield most ancient settlement evidence dating from Ubaid to Middle Uruk times on Mound A (pottery, baked sickles, a muller). The Late Uruk period saw a settlement transfer to Mound B accompanied by its substantial spatial growth and probably also internal structuration. A wall of 'Riemchen' bricks with a series of plastered floors accompanied by a quantity of BRB close to the south frontage of the Jemdet Nasr period residence may represent a predecessor of this major feature of the site on the north of the two hillocks, which were separated originally by a deep gully and were now covered by Mound B. In the same period, the south hillock displayed an architectural complex of thin walls with a number of fire installations and finds of numerous pottery and BRB. This area contained a unique Uruk culture interment of a crouched body accompanied by a complete meal of bivalve shells in a bitumen-coated basket and a stone bowl, and by a set of vessels used for serving food and drink. The most significant discoveries, however, pertain to the following period to which the site gave its name. At that time the most important component of the local settlement was constituted by a large-scale architectural complex, the interpretation of which has not yet been definitely settled upon. I propose here to refer to it as 'the residence'. This was set on a low platform, built of 'Riemchen' bricks and roofed over by timber ceilings bearing reed matting and clay coating layers. Baked bricks were used for the pavements of some of the rooms and baked-clay piping and bitumen were employed profusely throughout the building. Of minor constructions, a small brick platform supporting two jars and a podium approached by a flight of three steps are mentioned in Langdon's reports. The new excavations have not managed to identify with precision the features documented on the old plan (Moorey 1978, between pp. 148 and 149, Fig. S) but, by and large, have confirmed the old findings concerning the construction. Some parts of the building, or its closest proximity, contained kilns, both updraught installations with pierced floors and simpler domed constructions. A remarkable feature of these kilns seems to be the absence of larger amounts of production waste, ash or rubbish associated with them, which implies some regularity in waste-disposal patterns. The local inhabitants clearly dumped (at least some of) their refuse into the gully separating the north and south hillocks of Mound B. The residence has yielded a quantity of finds. The old excavators managed to secure some palaeobotanical evidence: grains of wheat (*Triticum turgidum* or *T. compactum, T. compactum*), barley (six-row, hulled) and a mixed seed sample of barley, 'an umbelliferous plant' and items 'very similar to those of certain species of *Panicum*' (i.e. millet; Moorey 1978, 152–153). Of clay, there were literally tons of pottery, both ordinary (dominated by coarse conical bowls with string-cut bases) and painted. The latter category turned up especially in the core areas of the residence and was rarer in the outlying buildings or industrial quarters (kilns). Clay was also used for implements such as shaft-hole axeheads or sickles, for typical ornaments ('shell-core' beads with spiral grooves on their surface along the longitudinal axis), for spindle whorls and for a single cylinder seal. The inscribed tablets from Jemdet Nasr have recently been republished (Englund, Grégoire and Matthews 1991); they bear impressions of seals stylistically close to those of Uruk III and Susa, and in at least six instances an imprint of a seal associating the city(?) names Ku'ara, Ur, Larsa, Uruk, Zabalam and Umma or Akšak. The tablet sealings find no matching items among seals found at the site itself. Moreover, a jar sealing of the eastern and northern 'Piedmont Jemdet Nasr' style has been found at Jemdet Nasr. The local metal implements include fishhooks, an adze blade, a spatula and a bowl. Work with organic materials is attested by impressions of cords in the sealings while traces of reed matting and spindle whorls for textile production supply other data. A bird-shaped shell pendant has come to light in the new excavations. Abundant finds of chipped stone industry were accompanied by heavier and ground stone

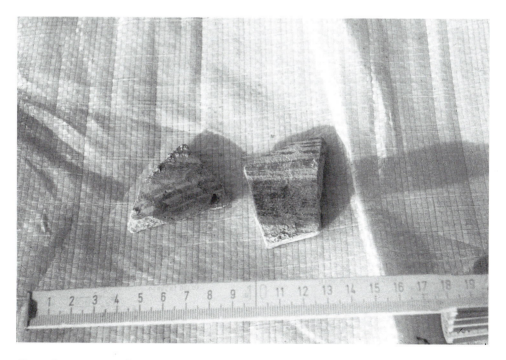

Figure 6.2 Fragments of painted pottery from Jemdet Nasr

items such as pierced or grooved 'maceheads' (bolas stones?), hoes and 'choppers'. No lapis lazuli finds occurred and only a few carnelian beads of poor workmanship could be retrieved, but stone cylinder and stamp seals turned up. In addition to the residence with its industrial and living(?) quarters, perched atop its terrace on the north hillock of Mound B, another, smaller 'Riemchen'-brick structure stood on the south hillock across the gully in which rubbish started now to accumulate. This small square building of at least four rooms displayed a series of plastered floors, relatively clean and resting on brick-paved bottoms. Rubbish was dumped around this structure which yielded finds of pottery (few painted items) and 'shell-core' beads. Another Jemdet Nasr culture building existed on Mound A, as is evidenced by a 'Riemchen' wall found there.

The whole layout changed in the following ED I period. The residence was clearly deserted and allowed to pass into oblivion though the front wall of its terrace received a revetment of planoconvex bricks. The most abundant settlement evidence for the very beginning of the period has come from the extensive and massive rubbish accumulation which now filled in the central gully. Its lower strata, starting in the preceding period, possess a clayey alluvial character while the middle, dark brown parts show clear instances of rubbish dumping with burnt spots. These are, in their turn, covered by a layer of big clay blocks with large sherds (a levelling layer representing remains of demolished architecture?). Abundant pottery finds date this dump to the earliest of the three segments of ED I. A large number of sealings on clay (180 so far), of which the published examples come both from doors and from mobile containers, show impressions of seals related to those which marked the Jemdet Nasr tablets. Among the other more conspicuous finds are clay human figurines (a bearded human head) and bone implements such as points and barbed hooks. The following, middle chronological segment of ED I saw the erection of a modest building of planoconvex bricks on the northern slope of the south hillock descending towards the now almost infilled central gully. This building with a series of floors and with settlement strata has yielded finds of pottery, bone (a point and a spatula) and stone (a bitumen-lodged basalt quern), as well as two sealings of mobile containers. A small vase with four carnelian beads hidden in the ruins of the north-east part of the residence is probably also of ED I date. At a later time, but still within the ED I period, the site functioned as a cemetery. A crouched body with pottery items was laid to rest in the ruins of the planoconvex brick building. Another, much more elaborate burial came to light in Mound A. A grave pit lined with bitumen-coated matting received a body provided with three stone bowls and a stamp seal bearing the image of three felines(?) by the wrist. The head rested on a quantity of beads of clay, shell, soft stone and carnelian, as well as on four marble amulets (two frog-shaped and two kidney-shaped) and a green-stone bead in the form of a shaft-hole axe. It is worthy of note that Mound A bears a construction of baked bricks enclosed by a wall with turrets, possibly of Parthian date.

On present evidence, the site's development from Ubaid to ED I times may be summarized as follows:

- Ubaid to middle Uruk: an average settlement site
- Late Uruk: a pyrotechnical production facility (a potters' quarter?)
- Jemdet Nasr: a residence, probably as a subsidiary production facility ('manorial farm') and a relay station, possibly destined for conveying goods from the periphery to the centre of the host social system and vice versa
- ED I: an address and consumption point for deliveries of sealed commodities bearing impressions of seals related to those which had marked tablets occurring in the preceding phase of the site.

On Jemdet Nasr see more recently Moorey 1978, 147–157; Matthews 1989, 1990 and 1997.

Abu Salabikh

A group of mounds 160 km south-east of Baghdad, a US excavation of 1963 and 1965 directed by V. Crawford and D. Hansen, a subsequent British mission of 1975–1989 directed by J. N. Postgate and another US expedition of 1988–1990 headed by S. Pollock. Settlement of the site (map in Postgate 1982, 58, Fig. 45) begins in the Uruk culture period in the west but mainly on the Uruk mound which by then housed a borough fortified by a city wall with several monumental structures and evidence for craft activities dealing with bitumen (for which Abu Salabikh might have served as a redistribution point), clay, metal, organic matter (textile) and stone. Some inhabitants of the site might have practised all-year agriculture as the local grain samples contain both summer and winter weeds, but animal remains (mostly sheep and goats, few cattle and pigs) may imply the presence of nomadic pastoralists (Pollock 1990a; Pollock, Steele and Pope 1991). The local settlement may represent a series of transitory episodes with a number of interruptions and gaps. Remains of the Jemdet Nasr period, limited so far to two refuse pits, indicate permanence of the dominant features of the local economic life with the exception of the transfer of the focus of overland trade in some commodities from Khuzestan to the Khabur region (materials for chipped stone industry: Pope 1989; Pollock 1990b). The binary settlement character known from the Uruk period re-emerges in ED I. At that time the west mound contained a habitation area consisting of several oval enclosures with rectangular buildings in their interior (Postgate 1980a, 98–100; Postgate 1981–1982, 256 and 1982, 59; Postgate and Moon 1982, 108ff.). Unlike the later structures of the site, these housing areas do not display any intramural burials (Matthews, Postgate and Luby 1987, 100). The building layout of the same period at the main mound differs strikingly, consisting of densely spaced, rectangular and thin-walled buildings. Only in late ED I or early ED II do the first graves appear; among these, grave 185 contained at least twelve bodies (three subadults of 5–18 years, nine adults of 18–40 years, among which three could be identified as women and four as men). Enamel hypoplasia, observed in the teeth of these people, indicates that they lived in conditions of nutritional stress (Matthews, Postgate and Luby 1987, 104–105).

In ED II, settlement on the main mound was enclosed by a city wall with gates (ibid. 107–109) while the oval residences in the west mound were apparently deserted. The ED III municipal quarter which came to light at the main mound can be studied in consequence of systematic efforts to understand the social context of a sizable rectangular building with a central court in which the US mission had excavated in the 1960s a unique collection of some 500 tablets written in Sumerian and including lexical texts and literary compositions, among the latter the Instructions of Šuruppak and the Kesh Temple Hymn, the UD.GAL.NUN texts and economic records (Biggs and Postgate 1978). Many scribes' names from the colophons of these texts are Semitic and some features of them point to the northern scribal sphere known as the 'Kiš tradition'. At least some hints as to the function of the building (a plan in Postgate 1982, 53, Fig. 40), enclosed by a quarter of spacious rectangular houses with central courtyards, are offered by the extensive rubbish accumulations south-east of it, though these are likely to have belonged to later structures, now completely eroded away. In addition to a complete skeleton of a donkey or onager, these strata have yielded, among others, clay figurines both human and animal, miniature bowls and jars, over a hundred 'counters' made of potsherds as well as more than 200 sealings in some of which the impression of a cylinder seal was overlaid by that of a stamp seal (Postgate 1980a, 91–92 and 1982, 50–54). Among these sealings those from doors prevail markedly over those from mobile containers (Matthews 1991, 4). Written texts which turned up in other contexts of ED III Abu Salabikh (Matthews, Postgate and Luby 1987, 100ff.) and indicating such features as the rationing of land, which might have belonged to a king or a 'house of the children' (é-tur-tur), point to a complex but not unusual social structure of the ancient community. The houses were invariably built around central square courtyards and included reception rooms which were kept relatively clean. Rubbish was either allowed to accumulate in the courtyards and kitchens or thrown out into the streets (ibid. 104, 107, 110, 115–118). Of the purely technical questions, let us note that the chipped industry, simplified to the extreme, supplied mainly blades, including those for sickles and micro-borers for bead production, thus throwing indirect light on the probable frequency of copper implements, though finds of the latter are scarce (Payne 1980).

A number of the ED III houses contained intramural burials, some of which might have been deposited – and, indeed, even robbed – in the lifetimes of the houses (Postgate 1980b). The bodies rested on their right or left sides with half-flexed knees and arms and with hands by the chest or before the face in simple pits, provided with personal possessions including ornaments, toilet sets and cosmetic shells, showy weapons and pottery sets (frequently a vertical-handle jar and a pedestalled bowl); stone and metal vessels are rare. As to the animal remains, two graves contained fish bones and one a skeleton of a quail-sized bird. Sheep and goat remains were more frequent than those of cattle and pigs. Among other personal items, grave 80 has yielded 140 conical bowls, a bottle and seven spouted jars. Some graves contained bones or skeletons of two or possibly up to four equids (grave 162: Postgate 1982, 55, Fig. 42; grave 234: Matthews, Postgate and Luby 1987, 97). In several instances, ritually(?) deposited objects were also found in the grave shafts. These consisted of ornaments, weapons, pottery and stone vessels but also copper tools such as a knife and a chisel in grave 80 (Postgate 1980b, 78). On the site see also Moon 1987 and Postgate 1997.

Fara

A tell 220 km south-east of Baghdad excavated by a German mission under R. Koldewey in 1902–1903 (results published in 1931 by E. Heinrich) and by a US expedition, directed by E. Schmidt, in 1931. Deep soundings indicate that the site's lowest occupation level dates from the Jemdet Nasr period and is followed by a sterile layer overlaid by five strata dating to the ED I period. These strata, containing ED II-period graves, bear, in their turn, buildings of the ED IIIa period, parts of which were eroded away. The local Jemdet Nasr layer, covering an original floor, yielded a quantity of settlement finds of bone (implements, fishhooks), clay (pottery, spindle whorls, net sinkers, baked-clay sickles), metal (implements such as two blades, rod-shaped items and an arrowhead) and stone (cylinder and stamp seals, chipped and ground stone industry including a blade set in bitumen and necklace beads in the total quantity of 184 items). The strata of the ED I period, when the site reached the greatest extent recorded in its history – 70 hectares – yielded traces of brick architecture of which at least some structures could be laid bare (building IIIa–c – Matthews 1991, 7). No texts and just a few sealings come from these buildings but it seems that this period witnessed centralized waste disposal in a rubbish pit at the north-east edge of the tell by the soundings Id/Ie (ibid. 1–7). This rubbish-disposal area produced hundreds of sealings among which those from doors predominate (88.17 per cent of the surviving and determinable 321) over those of mobile containers (8.72 per cent) and of other carriers. As to the more interesting small finds, clay net sinkers turn up in increasing quantities in late ED I and ED II (Martin 1988, 53) while the exact opposite is true for the spindle whorls, most frequent in the Jemdet Nasr to ED II strata and decreasing in quantity subsequently but existing until Ur III times. In the ED period some one-third of them were made of stone (ibid. 55). The toilet sets of the ladies and gentlemen of the Jemdet Nasr to ED I times included miniature single or multiple vessels of stone as well as the first cosmetic shells. They boasted necklaces of shell beads and even cheap clay imitations of the exquisite shell-core beads known from the Uruk 'Sammelfund' but also of carnelian, lapis lazuli and, in the Jemdet Nasr period, of turquoise, onyx, frit and perhaps blue rock crystal (Martin 1988, 57–62). According to the 'City League seal' of the Jemdet Nasr to ED I times (Moorey 1978, 154–155), Šuruppak allied herself most frequently with Larsa (7 occasions), Adab (5 occasions) and Ur (4 occasions; Martin 1988, 119–120). Burials turning up in the above-mentioned strata but belonging probably to the ED II period (Martin 1982, 149–152) assume most frequently the form of pits in which the bodies, accompanied by pottery, ornaments and personal belongings, rest wrapped in matting or lying in pottery coffins. Some of their shafts reach a depth of 3.5 m. In the ED IIIa period, when the overall extent of the site could have amounted to as much as 100 hectares (Martin 1988, 116), it was occupied by a group of residences of which a number displayed texts (840 in total) and some also sealings. Let us note the 'Tablet House' in trench XVh (its texts mention 9,660 don-keys and 1,200 men), a house in trench XVa–d (texts disposing of 250 acres = 100 hectares of arable), another house in trench IXa–c (lexical and literary texts only), another one in trench XVIIc–d (up to 6,580 working hands coming in from Ur, Adab, Nippur, Lagaš, Umma and Kiš in its texts); inscribed tablets were found in at least twenty-five locations (Matthews 1991, 11–12). The rectangular house, built around a square courtyard and exposed by trenches XIIIf–i (ibid. 8–11) yielded sealings of which 125 are now retrievable. Of these, seventy functionally determinable items demonstrate the preponderance of door sealings (75.72 per cent) over con-tainer (20 per cent) and other sealings. The northern third of the tell displayed evidence of circular sunk structures (axes of the mouths 3.82 x 3.7 m, total depth of 7.08 m) with layers of organic remains (wood, straw, date stones, bones) on their bottoms, interpreted as silos (Martin 1988, 42–47, 100). Two of these structures, built of planoconvex bricks and belonging probably to the ED III (a?) period, have been excavated, yielding finds of Akkadian(?), Ur III and Isin-Larsa periods including burials from their fillings. Let us be reminded here of the decrease in quantity of spindle whorls, some of which (*c.* one-third) are now made of stone. The miniature stone ves-sels of the preceding period are now replaced in the boudoirs of women and men of contemporary fashion by cosmetic shells, containing substances of red, orange, yellow, green and black colours. Necklaces display predominantly carnelian and lapis lazuli beads; the cheaper mate-rials of the preceding period have vanished but the variety of stones and types, a characteristic of the Jemdet Nasr strata, is absent. The texts indicate that in this period the site was ruled by an unknown lugal, and direct managing responsibilities devolved on officials titled GAR.ensi$_2$ and GAR.ensi$_2$-gal. These might have taken turns in office for limited periods of time, denoted by the term bala, which is also connected with names of other officials not recruited from among the GAR.ensi$_2$ or GAR.ensi$_2$-gal (Martin 1988, 119–120). The site existed in the Akkad/Ur III period when it acquired a city wall but was deserted after Ur III times (Martin 1982, 149–152, and 1988; Matthews 1991; Martin 1997).

Kiš

A group of tells of which the most conspicuous ones carry the names of Tell Uhaimir and Tell Ingharra, 14 km north-east of Hilla. French excavations of 1852 (F. Fresnel, J. Oppert) and 1912 (H. de Genouillac), followed by a British–US expedition headed successively by E. Mackay and L. Ch. Watelin under the direction of S. Langdon, in 1923–1933, and a Japanese undertaking of 1989 (H. Fujii). Both the head tells of Kiš, Uhaimir and Ingharra, display evidence of Ubaid settlement, followed, at Ingharra, by Uruk culture material and, on both mounds, by finds of Jemdet Nasr character including a stone plaque with a temple façade and two figures from a presently unknown context (Moorey 1978, 164). More consistent evidence for Early Dynastic settlement comes from the Ingharra excavations. Here the 'Y' sounding brought to light, above earlier layers that were difficult to excavate because of ground water, a series of superimposed strata of domestic architecture some 2 m thick ('Early Houses Stratum'). These consisted of layouts of more spacious rooms virtually free of intramural burials on the west and smaller and more densely packed chambers, frequently containing burials, on the east side of a narrow lane. These houses, subject to periodic flooding, had elaborate drainage systems, sometimes impregnated with bitumen, but repeated rebuildings give clear evidence of constructional problems caused by the excess of floodwater. No door sockets were recorded but one of the houses boasted panelling of wooden boards. Pottery found in these houses belongs to ED I–II (ibid. 99–103) and in the YW sounding their latest layers obviously contained inscribed tablets and Fara-style sealings, including seven cases of impression of a single seal (ibid. 115). Even sealings of ED I style, however, turn up at Ingharra (Moorey and Gurney 1978, 42, Nos. 3, 4 and 5, Fig. 1:3, 4, 5). In the case of burials recorded in these strata there seems to be no evidence that could shed light on the question whether they were sunk from the floor levels of these houses (being thus contemporary with the settlement) or whether they were sunk from above when the area was already deserted and covered by a sheet of later strata (being thus posterior to its date). Roger Moorey (1978, 104) believes in the latter possibility but at least one burial seems to have been excavated from a floor level of a standing house (Algaze 1983–1984, 139–141). The bodies, usually in a semi-flexed position, rested in some cases on brick platforms under brick vaults as well as in rectangular brick coffins; they might have been wrapped in matting and some of their equipment as well. A few of these burials contained remains of four-wheeled vehicles and traction animals (a team of four equids; one bovid; an equid and a bovid?) and some non-average equipment items such as rein-rings or copper saws, gouges, goads and other implements. Unlike the Ur interments, however, no retinue members(?) accompany the chief corpse into the nether world and there are no treasure chests, no cylinder seals and no perceptible differences in the range of objects interred in these and average graves. Upon burial the ordinary citizens received objects of artificial materials (faience beads), clay (pottery), metal (a single piece of gold, no silver, copper or arsenic bronze; also stands and vessel supports including a flagon of apparently the very first tin bronze of Mesopotamia: Müller-Karpe 1990a, 163, Fig. 2:4, 164 and 1991, 110, Fig. 4; Müller-Karpe, Pászthory and Pernicka 1993, 269), organic materials (shells as cosmetic articles, containers or materials for beads, food in the form of meat joints, evidenced by bones, and fish) and stone (vessels of calcite, two cylinder and two stamp seals, beads of carnelian, lapis lazuli, rock crystal, steatite, calcite and grey quartzite). These archaeological situations are overlaid by two 'Flood Strata' developed to a varying degree. The lower and more massive one contained, among others, freshwater mussels and skeletons of freshwater fish (Moorey 1978, 98–99). On top of the 'Flood Strata' sits another layer which has yielded habitation structures including a room with wood-lined floor and wall (ibid. 88), graves and ED II–III pottery finds. Some (or all?) of the graves excavated in the Early Houses Stratum could have been sunk from this level (ibid. 98). In its turn, this stratum then became a chronological marker followed by the erection of major architectures on the site in early ED IIIa. These include, first and foremost, the Ingharra ziggurats on a terrace with a buttressed and recessed revetment built of planoconvex bricks interspersed with strata of reed matting, plastered thickly with mud and then whitewashed with gypsum. Their façades also bore a plaster articulation (ibid. 85–89). The larger ziggurat was built over the preceding post-Flood stratum settlement (ibid. 88), as well as over one of the cart burials (ibid. 105). It may be noted that Zababa, the deity of Kiš, does not figure in the divinity lists from Fara, but a hymn addressed to him and to Kiš has been identified among the literary texts of ED IIIa Abu Salabikh (ibid. 19). South of the main Ingharra mounds the famous Kiš palace had by now been erected on Mound A (ibid. 55–61). It was built in three stages, first the north block, then a gate wing was added on the east and the south block followed as the last component (ibid. 55, Plan F between pp. 56 and 57). Some of its rooms might have served as workshops (ibid. 57) but the structure yielded disappointingly few small finds. Apart from pottery and stone vessels there is one cylinder seal of shell, a Fara-style tablet embedded in a brick platform (MSVO 1, 224, see Englund, Grégoire and Matthews 1991, 29, 79–80, Pl. 84) and two series of shell inlays. Of these, one with 'war and peace' themes comes from the gateway area while the other one, of more bucolic character, turned up in room 61 of the south block. Another conspicuous architectural complex excavated in area P north of Ingharra is referred to as the 'Planoconvex Building' (PCB – Moorey 1978, 34–44). This structure of a triangular plan, centred upon a square courtyard flanked by a series of rooms, had either plain or paved (sometimes bitumen-coated) floors, walls of planoconvex bricks repeatedly stuccoed white, and ceilings probably borne by timbers carrying layers of matting covered by thick mud plaster. Some of its parts were drained by bitumen-lined brick conduits covered by plates of micaceous schist. Its interior contained many bitumen-coated basins and wainscotted rooms with bitumen waterproofing and was provided with a well. Some circular features probably served as kilns and two of the rooms – XI and XII – might have originally housed a wine or oil press. Of the more remarkable finds, reference should be made to a cylinder seal, two sealings, a headless statue holding a cup and a plant and with an illegible inscription found in the well, a series of copper fragments strewn along a corridor floor and a series of inlay plaques, some of which still stick to a 'stucco' coating borne by wood, in the entrance area and elsewhere in the building. This was also the time when a ziggurat of planoconvex bricks was built at Uhaimir from where Pre-Sargonic texts are known.

Crisis struck ED IIIa Kiš with a truly dramatic impact at the end of this period. The PCB was abandoned altogether (Moorey 1978, 41–42), the palace destroyed and deserted (ibid. 64–65) and part of the larger ziggurat collapsed, leaving the distinctive 'Red stratum' as a debris layer (ibid. 96–98). Texts retrieved from this layer of red-stained material indicate the end of an administrative body of considerable sophistication, which handled large quantities of grain and numbers of people. Of the three sites, only the palace revived briefly with a rather simple 'squatter' settlement, frequently making use of its discarded components. The entire Ingharra area was then turned into an extensive burial site including cemetery A, sunk into the palace ruins, the graves of which yielded a multitude of objects throwing light on the craft level and social status of the population living here during the final part of ED III. Of artificial materials there is a faience shell-shaped vessel with a bull carved along one side as well as other fragments (Moorey 1978, 74). Ivory served as material for combs and for a unique stand in the form of four rampant bulls bearing some object in the sockets sunk into the backs of their necks. Clay products are most extensively represented by pottery, among which two types, very often occurring together, are prominent: the 'mother goddess-handled jars' and the 'fruit stands', the female symbolism of which could account for the general rarity of clay female statuettes in this time period (ibid. 67). The virtual absence of goblets (Mackay 1929, 150–151) is remarkable. The local inhabitants wore metal ornaments (silver headbands and roundels, copper pins), used metal weapons (axes, daggers) and tools including toilet sets, vessels (ibid. 175) and symbolic objects (a spindle with a whorl of copper – ibid. 168, Pl. lviii, Fig. 1). A dagger sheath of leather with an exquisite geometrical ornament (ibid. 137, Pl. lxii, Fig. 19) represents work in organic materials, which is attested also by the cosmetic shells (black and white pigments, some of them imitated by lapis lazuli amulets, ibid. 131–134) and by textile fragments sticking to diadems (ibid. 178–179). A stone bowl carved to represent a basket merits attention here (Moorey 1978, 211, *sub* 5 B). Among stone products, vessels visibly decrease in quantity (Mackay 1929, 134, 199) and the mass of finds is represented by beads (lapis lazuli, carnelian), amulets (lapis lazuli only: frogs, flies, beetles and imitation shells) and cylinder seals, usually of lapis lazuli, two of which come from children's

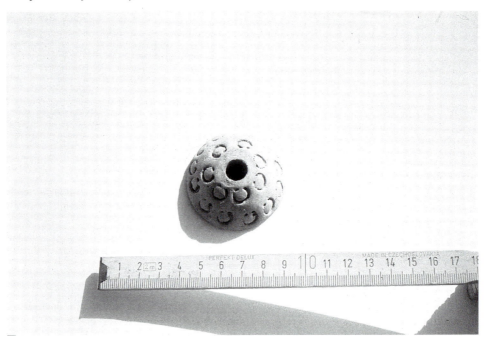

Figure 6.3 A spindle whorl from Jemdet Nasr. Such whorls, stuck on spindles, helped to maintain the thin rods on which the spinsters rolled the spinned thread, in rotating motion, thereby contributing to the quality and regularity of the thread spun. Spindles belonged to strictly personal articles and frequently bore designs attesting the convictions and desires of their possessors. This whorl bears a decoration of incomplete circles impressed with the hollow end of a metal(?) tube and thus attests the use of metal articles as well.

graves (Nos. 65 and 100: ibid. 190–191). The social structure of the community that left behind these graves has been characterized as fairly homogeneous and still essentially egalitarian, with age and sex as the main status determinants (Breniquet 1984). Burial equipment seems to be divided in accordance with the male–female binarity (Pollock 1991, 375, 380).

On the site see Moorey 1978; Algaze 1983–1984; Breniquet 1984; Hansen 1997b.

Ur

The present site of Tell Muqayyar, 25 km south-west of Nasiriyah. A British excavation of 1919 (H. R. Hall) followed by a British–US mission of 1920–1932 directed by Leonard (later Sir Leonard) Woolley. Though the existence of two walls with detached blocks of cone mosaics indicates public architecture of the Uruk–Jemdet Nasr period (Heinrich 1982, 113), it was the preceding Ubaid settlement of the site, at some spots interrupted by sterile strata, that established the local tradition of pottery-making. The huge waster-discard heap ('Great Sherd Dump'), probed by Woolley's Pit F, begins in Ubaid culture times, continues in the Uruk culture period with evidence of pottery kilns and even a find of a terracotta component of a potter's wheel, and terminates in the Jemdet Nasr epoch. Among other finds, its uppermost stratum yielded a cylinder seal of dark steatite and a steatite statuette of a boar, originally perhaps a piece of furniture inlay (Woolley 1930, 330–333; 1955, 27–31; Orthmann 1975, 162–163, Fig. 15b). This deposit is superimposed by three strata (H, G, F) of architecture employing rectangular bricks and with accompanying pottery finds dominated by solid-footed goblets. The last of these architectural phases is reduplicated in the next upper layer (E) by a virtually identical layout finished in planoconvex bricks and this building material remains in use for the next four strata (D–A). Phases H to A belong to ED I–ED IIIb (Woolley 1930, 330–333; Moorey 1978, 100–101; Gockel 1983, Table B.6, p. 52).

A source of extraordinary importance for the Jemdet Nasr and the earlier ED period is constituted by the 'Jemdet Nasr cemetery', unearthed in soundings W and X. The deceased were laid to rest in simple pits in strongly flexed positions. Their grave goods included items of clay, especially pottery (Jemdet Nasr polychrome ware in the earliest graves, pots, flagons, cups), metal, namely ornaments (silver earrings, copper or arsenic-bronze mirrors and spoons, pins), implements (fishing hooks) and vessels (copper bowls, lead tumblers and bowls) as well as items of stone, especially attire articles (carnelian and lapis lazuli beads) and the abundant stone bowls and cups of steatite/chlorite, brought from the Gulf area, and other stone receptacles such as lamps (Kolbus 1982 and 1983; Gockel 1983; Moorey 1985; Potts 1989, 140, 147). It seems that bowls of clay or stone constitute a stable component of funerary equipment; in the course of the period when the cemetery was in use stone vessels increased in frequency while the original lead tumblers with flagons and pots were being replaced with cups of stone and higher vessels of clay.

Another one of Woolley's soundings, Pit Z, laid bare a stratigraphy of settlement refuse strata interspersed by more or less continuous layers of organic rubbish containing seal impressions, referred to as 'Seal Impression Strata' and frequently abbreviated as SIS (Zettler 1989b). Eight of these extend over the period of ED I (SIS 8–4, roughly parallel to layer G of Pit F: Karg 1984–1985, 305), ED I–II (the enigmatic and apparently heavily disturbed SIS 3) and ED IIIa (SIS 1–2: Gockel 1983, 52, Table B.6). Occasionally, the SIS yielded finds of more than passing interest: SIS 8 was characterized by a preponderance of solid-footed goblets, unusual below and above this stratum (Moorey 1978, 101; Zettler 1989b, 372). SIS 4 contained four bull's legs from a large statue of sheet metal which could have been modelled over an organic core (Woolley 1930, 327). A sample of 51 Ur sealings dated to ED I and deposited now at the Philadelphia University Museum was examined by R. Zettler (1989a) and found to contain a majority of door sealings (30) with the rest being made up by container sealings and unidentified items (see also Zettler 1989b). This preponderance of door sealings, occurring here for the first time in early Mesopotamian history, has been noted by R. Matthews (1991, 4).

At a time when SIS 4 had already been deposited and a certain amount of waste had settled on its top the area started to be used as a cemetery, and that continued up to post-Akkadian times. This cemetery contained more than 2,500 graves and seems to be roughly contemporary with SIS 3, while at some spots its graves are overlaid by SIS 1–2, featuring sealings of kings of the First Dynasty of Ur (Mesannepadda). Most average graves entombed bodies wrapped in matting and laid down in flexed positions in simple pits, accompanied by equipment of clay (vessels), metal (tools, weapons and ornaments, the last ones also of gold) and stone (vessels and ornaments, typically of carnelian and lapis lazuli). Quite a number of them, however, had few or no grave goods. The most famous component of this cemetery, however, undoubtedly consists of sixteen presumably élite burials which Woolley called 'royal graves' (see most recently Reade 2001). The distinctive characteristics of such interments included tomb chambers of stone or mudbrick set at the bottom of deep pits and approached by ramps, as well as the fact that the principal burial is accompanied by bodies of men and women distinguished by peculiar equipment items and interpreted as persons in subordinate social roles (servants?). Woolley referred to cases when the actual tomb chambers were missing as 'death pits', interpreting the bodies accompanying the principal burials as human sacrificial victims (Moorey 1977). We owe to Hans J. Nissen (ibid. 29–30) the observation that these sixteen graves are likely to fall within a fairly narrow time interval. In them the deceased rested in the midst of incredibly rich grave goods consisting of all the precious materials available to the early Mesopotamians. Thanks to Susan Pollock (1991, 373f.) we may summarize here the sex-dependent key sets of personal articles from the Ur 'royal' graves. Gentlemen went down with weapons such as axes, daggers and knives, their appurtenances (whetstones), 'brims' or peculiar head ornaments consisting of several large beads of metal or stone linked together by a chainlet of gold or silver worn with beads across the forehead, as well as toilet sets. Ladies boasted first and foremost hair ribbons, as well as wreath-type hair- or hairdo ornaments, combs, bilunate earrings and 'choker' or 'dog-collar' type necklaces. The same author is to be credited with the important observation that some deceased were assigned both male and female attributes. Of the seven documented cases of this kind, one body has been identified as male and another one as female (Pollock 1991, 378). The male–female dichotomy is also reflected by iconography and materials of cylinder seals (Rathje 1977; Pollock 1991, 380).

As to the general characteristics of material culture of the Ur cemetery, this will always be an inexhaustible mine of information, so here I can hardly do more than point to the most conspicuous themes treated recently. Of the artificial materials, faience or glazed items do not turn up with any considerable frequency at Ur (Moorey 1985, 139). As against the earlier ED, ivory is visibly more plentiful here, suggesting easier access to this material by now (Moorey 1978, 73–74). The pottery chronology of the Ur cemetery has been refined by Pollock (1985, esp. Fig. 2 on pp. 136–137). The masters who supplied the metal items of the Ur graves had reached a considerable level of expertise. Gold was used not only for ornaments and showy weapons and armour but also for vessels and even for 'badges', status symbols such as the golden tools and implements. Pu-abi's grave contained a saw and adzes of gold (but some of them were merely gilt: La Niece 1995), and RT 580 yielded an adze, an awl and a chisel of gold as well as silver spindles with lapis lazuli whorls (possibly a woman's burial: Moorey 1985, 77, 114). Silver used for one of the Ur tumblers came from Anatolia (Yener *et al.* 1991, 561ff.). The Ur smiths used tin bronze for the production of metal vessels but arsenic bronze for arms and ornaments (Müller-Karpe 1990a, 162–164; 1991, 111; Müller-Karpe, Pászthory and Pernicka 1993, 269–270). They obviously mastered such procedures as annealing (Moorey 1985, 39) and soldering (ibid. 47, cf. Müller-Karpe, Pászthory and Pernicka 1993, 266–268). In the treatment of stone a change from Jemdet Nasr times is perceptible in the marked quantitative decrease of the steatite/chlorite vessels, of which just a few turn up in the ED IIIa graves (Potts 1989, 140) and in a low frequency of vessels carved out of harder igneous rocks or metamorphosed igneous rocks, likely to have been brought from inner Anatolia or Iran (as booty?) and to have carried a high measure of prestige (ibid. 141–143). The Ur steatite/chlorite vessels fall in with those of Nippur, Kiš and Khafajeh as to their physico-chemical characteristics, thus implying deliveries from one source (Kohl, Harbottle and Sayre 1979, 148). The men and women of fashion of ED IIIa Ur introduced the wearing of ornaments composed of etched carnelian beads (Moorey 1985, 141).

Architectural vestiges of this period have only come to light in the central ziggurat area (Heinrich 1982, 113–114, Fig. 162; Mallowan 1968, 37–39). Of the three ziggurat phases the first belongs to the Uruk–Jemdet Nasr period while the second, distinguished by planoconvex brickwork, comes from our period of time. In ED IIIa the ziggurat precinct was enclosed by a retaining wall 9 m thick with niches outside, built of planoconvex bricks upon a limestone footing outside. The north and east corners of the ziggurat precinct accommodated two architectural complexes, essentially of the central-hall type, accompanied by a series of parallel chambers, perhaps storerooms. The central hall of the east house was whitewashed and contained a pedestal with a step to facilitate access to it; finds from this room included remains of a figural frieze. The subsidiary chambers were filled in with thick ash deposits and contained various fire installations. Hearths in higher ashy strata imply that the rubbish accumulations come from the 'life period' of the house. The north room of the east suite of this house was also whitewashed and the paint corrected in red, but ashy strata filled in this chamber as well. The north house displayed similar characteristics with fire installations and ash deposits in the subsidiary rooms. A trough of kiln-bricks in the central hall contained pottery, matting, vertebral columns of fish and broken bones of small animals. A bitumen-lined conduit passing from the ziggurat court through the entrance into the central hall of the north house conveyed some liquid substance towards the inside of the house. The precinct also included other rooms, especially by its north-east side, as well as obviously free-air hearths.

On the site in general see Pollock 1997.

For the ED I texts of Ur (from the SIS) see Wright 1969, 40–42, 99–116. On local ED III texts see Alberti and Pomponio 1986; Bauer 1987; Jagersma 1990. The latter, from the end of ED III and the beginning of the Akkad period, shed light on the activities of a 'state pigsty', from which pigs were given out as offerings to deities by the king and consumed by the palace. This could be a distant predecessor of the Drehem establishment.

Sakheri Sughir

A surface site 6 km north-west of Ur, a US–Iraqi mission of 1966, headed by H. T. Wright and Gh. Wahida. This site is of interest as virtually the only rural settlement of the already historic third pre-Christian millennium on which more extensive information is available (early to middle ED I). The sounding of limited size laid bare a series of isolated architectural remains provided

Figure 6.4 A sealing on clay from Jemdet Nasr. Cylinder seals, with decorative patterns cut in the negative into their surface, were rolled over wet clay and the patterns thus impressed in the positive. The seal images and sometimes also inscriptions are a major source for Mesopotamian history, archaeology and iconography, but also for art history and studies of the Mesopotamian spirituality and mentality. Their reverse sides, revealing traces of the objects that were sealed, yield source data on Mesopotamian economy. For most of the prehistoric age, the seals left their imprints on mobile containers – pots, sacks, bales and the like – thus indicating reciprocal exchange. Only with the advent of the historic era do sealings from doors of storage spaces appear, heralding redistribution and, consequently, the emergence of the first systems of taxation. This impression shows, among others, the forepart of a scorpion image and a star, usually interpreted as a sign of divinity.

with such features as pits, floors, hearths and ovens. A shed with a long oven and rectangular hearth seems to have been replaced by an arrangement consisting of a more solid habitation house and another shed with an oven and a hearth in addition to a free-standing oven. The local population lived by agriculture, attested by the presence of hulled six-row barley and barley unidentifiable as to variety. One seed of the *Polygonum sp.* weed was associated with the barley. Other occupations documented archaeologically include animal husbandry with predominance of sheep and goats over cattle and pigs and a presence of dogs. Wildlife resource exploitation covered fishing and collecting freshwater mussels as well as hunting wild animals (an ass-size equid, wild boar, perhaps gazelle) and birds. Club rush served for mat-making and tamarisk and poplar wood as fuel. The local inhabitants used a variety of materials. Bone and shell served for bead-making, clay for the production of pottery, planoconvex bricks, drain pipes made on a potter's wheel, ring-shaped net sinkers and funnels. Of metal, a single lump of relatively pure copper was found on the site's surface. As for organic materials, the locals worked frequently with bitumen, which circulated on the site in the form of small cakes. They used it for the impregnation of mats, various architectural components and perhaps also for the construction of qufas, or simple boats. They also availed themselves freely of matting articles. Chipped stone articles, produced perhaps on the spot (at least flaking off blades from cores), include a majority of blades, first and foremost for sickles. Among ground stone artifacts, grinding slabs, fragments of stone bowls and two carnelian beads are present. The chipped stone industry used imported materials clearly in good supply; the other stones exploited include soft coarse limestones, perhaps of local origin, as well as harder translucent materials, perhaps marbles. The site obviously represents a simple, all-purpose rural settlement where the common daily chores were accomplished without any attempts at intensification or specialization (Wright 1969).

Tepe Gawra VI

In view of the considerable progress of technology and accumulation of know-how in the Early Dynastic period it may be interesting to review the sixth layer of Tepe Gawra, dating into the ED III–Akkad transition period (Speiser 1935; on the whole site: Rothman 1997). The settlement layout, consisting of rectangular brick-built structures on stone foundations, encloses on all sides a central free space accessible through two gates. Streets are paved with stone and provided with central conduits to evacuate liquid impurities. More precious finds such as beads, copper items and cylinder seals cluster in the east segment of the site. As to the individual find categories, bone turns up for the last time at Gawra but includes a fragment of an ivory comb. In terms of work with clay, the suppliers of Gawra VI excelled in making wheel-thrown and very well-fired pottery, in fact, of the best quality paralleled at Gawra only by second-millennium products. The quantity of spindle whorls decreases constantly from layer VIII but layer VI has yielded an unheard of quantity of clay reels bearing individual marks. Clay statuettes are again less numerous than in the preceding layers but in addition to the usual domestic animals (sheep, goats, bulls, dogs, horses), new types, introduced in layer VI, depict perhaps beasts of burden and possibly equids. No female figurines occur in this layer. The model chariots and carts, both two- and four-wheeled, must have been more popular now than ever, as the quantity of model wheels reaches its apogee in layer VI. The first clay model of a four-legged bed with upper surface of plaited work from this layer ushers in a clay creation enjoying wide popularity then and in the succeeding time periods. The abundance and complex character of metallurgical finds imply that Tepe Gawra VI housed an almost industrial-level plant supplying large quantities of metal, perhaps together with other products. There is, at first, the immense quantitative jump: as against 22 copper finds from layer VIII and 42 from layer VII, layer VI has yielded an incredible 334 items, followed by 43 pieces from layer V, 11 from layer IV and 7 from layer III. In addition to cold-working, casting of copper appears now for the first time, attested by a sandstone mould for making points, axes and chisels. Objects with shaft-holes occur almost exclusively in layer VI where they turned up in a hoard find of room 649, deposited in a pottery vessel with other copper products, beads and two cylinder seals. No earlier arrowheads and spear-points than those of Gawra VI have been excavated at the site. The twenty copper sickles from the same layer are preceded only by a single fragment from layer VIIIC. Another artifact type turning up widely in layer VI are copper needles; more than one hundred of these were found as against the eight examples from layer VIII. A fact that sheds a particularly clear light on the extent of the local metallurgical production is the occurrence of such common artifacts as awls, until now made up of the ubiquitous bone, in copper versions (14 from layer VI as against 2 from layer VIII). This layer has also yielded a unique pan of sheet copper. Of the non-utility artifacts, a series of ornaments and articles of attire should not be forgotten (hair pins, toggle pins as probable garment fasteners, bracelets, anklets, simple rings, toilet sets), as well as objects of possible cultic or ritual use (copper snakes – 2 in layer VII, 12 in layer VI, 3 in layer V) and half-finished items such as copper bars or unused copper wire. The local stonework shows some most interesting developments. First and foremost, there occurs a sharp decrease in the quantity of stone articles. Layer VIII has 132 flint and 152 obsidian blades; in layer VII this ratio is 82 : 78 but in layer VI it is 36 : 120 (in layer V 10 : 13, in layer IV 3 : 4, in layer III 1 : 8 and then the chipped industry ceases altogether). Another artifact type with a similar spatiotemporal distribution is represented by foliate arrowheads: 6 turn up in layer VIII, 74 in layer VII but 26 in layer VI, 3 in layer V and the last one in layer III. In contrast to layer VII, no cores, scrapers and borers occur in layer VI. A number of categories of ground stone items exist on the site: celts, maceheads, axes, hammers, grinding sets, whetstones, slingshot(?), weights (which may conform to the shekel standard), stone vessels and palettes. Quantifiable observations bear out the decrease of some of them, for instance, celts (41 in layer VIII, 29 in VI, 6 in IV) or maceheads (10 in layer VIII, 8 in VI, 3 in V, 1 in IV and III each). Significantly enough, there appears one sharp increase, namely that of whetstones (14 in layer VIII against 60 in layer VI), where a connection with the well-developed copper metallurgy seems almost inevitable. In comparison with earlier layers, personal ornaments put in a rather poor appearance. No more than one single string of beads, deposited in the room 649 hoard and consisting of carnelian, lapis lazuli and rock-crystal items, is complemented by two sculptured pendants showing a double ram protome and a crouching dog. The site has yielded a remarkable quantity of 21 cylinder seals, contrasting with 5 items in layer VII where this artifact occurs first, with 2 in layer V and 1 in layer III. No stamp seals are known from layer VI, the last ones having been retrieved from layer VII.

The state of affairs that has just been described leaves me in little doubt that at Tepe Gawra VI, the US mission has brought to light remains of a site that may well be called an industrial plant of the third pre-Christian millennium. The abundant and manifold evidence for coppersmithing activities point to the site's specialization in metallurgy and this is corroborated by a marked decrease in both quality and quantity of the chipped stone industry and by the fact that even some of the most common artifacts manufactured from time immemorial of other materials (awls of bone, sickles of stone and organic substances) exist in metal versions here. For those who are not yet convinced, there is the increasing number of whetstones which makes no sense without the matching metal implements. The source of the copper worked at Tepe Gawra VI, or at least the direction from which it came, may be inferred from the striking preponderance of obsidian blades among the chipped stone industry. Even more important, however, is the decrease in spindle-whorl numbers accompanied by higher quantities of clay reels and copper needles. This situation, quite unusual in average prehistoric communities, seems to suggest that the site's inhabitants paid no particular attention to spinning but that they worked with finished thread – perhaps even wove textile fabrics – and tailored garments. If valid, this conclusion would point to a considerable degree of local craft specialization since textile work is one of the branches of production least likely to develop into a specialized activity (for ethnological data from Mesoamerica see Sanders and Webster 1988, esp. Table 3 on p. 541). At any rate, Tepe Gawra VI must have been a production site well integrated into a regional exchange network, as is borne out by evidence for work with half-finished products likely to have been brought thither (copper, textile thread?), as well as by the higher representation of cylinder seals which might have marked the goods leaving for their consumer agencies. In looking for the centre which the Tepe Gawra VI craftsmen and craftswomen serviced, one feels inclined to think about the adjacent Nineveh where the splendid 'Sargon's head' of the immediately following period proclaims the significance of the site very close to the epoch under discussion here.

INTERPRETATION

Economy

Unlike the preceding Uruk period, the Jemdet Nasr to ED epoch (of course, longer in terms of absolute chronology than the Uruk culture phase) does display a series of perceptible changes, starting from the basic levels of all sectors of community life. Let us start with a description of what happened in the sphere of agricultural production.

The Jemdet Nasr period ushered in the appearance of at least two new cultigens: *Triticum compactum* or club wheat (Braidwood and Howe 1960, 104–105; Moorey 1978, 152; Ellison 1982, 173) and *Panicum* or millet (Braidwood and Howe 1960, 112; Moorey 1978, 153; Ellison 1982, 173). This looks strange, the more so as *T. compactum* does not grow too well in lowlands (Braidwood and Howe 1960, 105) and millet, the next appearance of which has been recorded as late as the seventh pre-Christian century, is a typical catch crop, requiring plenty of water and sunshine and not demanding in terms of manpower. This constitutes a visible departure from the traditional cultigen composition which must have been, by Jemdet Nasr times, sanctioned by usages dating back to hoary antiquity. Of course, the bulk of agricultural tradition must have survived, as is indicated, for instance, by Susan Pollock's findings at Jemdet Nasr period Abu Salabikh (*H. sativum*, *T. monococcum* and perhaps *dicoccum* – Pollock 1990b, 71). The local presence of both summer and winter weeds supplies sound evidence for the permanent character of agricultural practice in contemporary Sumer. Another relevant change is perceptible in the written sources. Not only do fields occur in them for the first time in Uruk III but they are classified in various ways (*ZATU* No. 128, p. 195; *ZATU* No. 356, p. 244 – MAŠ + GAN$_2$, perhaps as field quality). This may also imply more careful management of arable soil in response to unknown hardships.

The signs of change noted above are significant insofar as a major transformation obviously took place somewhere around 3000 BC (for a general review of Mesopotamian agriculture, including that time period, see Ellison 1982; Hruška 1990; caloric values of nourishment have been most conveniently tabulated in Newman *et al.* 1990, 107, Table 4.1). As a consequence of this transformation, bread wheats (*T. aestivum*) and six-row barleys are now supposed to have substantially decreased in quantity (Hijara *et al.* 1980, 154) and two-row barley is supposed to have been the cereal most frequently grown. This is assumed to have happened because barley tolerates aridity, soil salinity and crop diseases better than bread wheat, being generally more reliable (Ellison 1982, 174–175; Powell 1985, 17–18, but cf. van Zeist and Bottema 1999, 30–31). Palaeobotanical evidence confirms some of the changes in cultigen composition throughout the first half of the third pre-Christian millennium. Einkorn wheat (*T. monococcum*) now prevails over emmer (Helbaek 1972, 39) but six-row barley maintains its position both at the beginning (ED I Sakheri Sughir: Wright 1969, 90; Deh Luran: Neely, Wright *et al.* 1994, 178) and end of this period (Khafajeh-Temple Oval: Delougaz 1940, 154; ED III Ur: Ellison *et al.* 1978, 168–169; on barley imprints in ED pottery of Uruk and Ur: Helbaek 1960, 195, and Wright 1969, 90). At least some texts of archaic Ur refer to barley (Pomponio 1991). A change is nonetheless perceptible in comparison with Near Eastern montane zones in some of which bread-wheat cultivation continued well into the third millennium BC (Lechevallier 1976 for Korucutepe, Anatolia). While constant attention is being dedicated to these questions by specialists in philology who have published extensive overviews of the matter (Powell 1984a and 1985; Hruška 1987, 1988 and 1990), promising new insights have also come from the archaeological side. First and foremost, it has been suggested that on the non-salinized soil of the north, it may be possible to trace at least roughly the extent of ancient fields by mapping lower-density sherd scatters resulting possibly from the manuring of arable soil with settlement refuse containing broken pottery (Ball *et al.* 1989). In the case of major localities, fields are likely to have extended about 2 km from the site centres, in minor sites this distance amounts to 1 km (ibid. 15). Moreover, careful matching of archaeological and palaeobotanical evidence suggests the possibility of recognition of such post-harvest crop treatments as rationing. Elite sites tend to display grain samples with weeds (and chaff), likely to have been collected directly from the threshing floors (Ur: Ellison *et al.* 1978, 168, PG 208/TTE; a parallel at the acropolis of third-millennium Tell Leilan, Syria: Weiss 1991, 706). Subordinate sites, likely to have been living on rations, show relatively pure grain but also admixtures, probably a result of complementary activities like collecting wild seeds and fruit (Tell Leilan: Weiss 1991, 706). The first subterranean irrigation

Figure 6.5 This sealing on clay bears an image of a temple façade with a central doorway.

Figure 6.6 The reverse side of the preceding sealing shows clear impressions of a reed mat, probably from a bale of goods.

channels, the famous *qanát*, may date from this period (Deh Luran: Neely, Wright *et al.* 1994, 199–200). Let us add only as a marginal note that the range of ration quantities assumed for early Mesopotamia – 60 sila monthly for an adult man, 30–40 for an adult woman, 30 for a boy, 20–30 for a girl and 10 for a small child (e.g. Garelli 1969, 282–283) – may correspond to reality as some of the data match facts known from other spatiotemporal segments of the Near East (Achaemenid Persian texts from Egypt where one soldier received 1–2 litres of grain daily: Temerev 1980, 126; see also Hermansen 1991, 17; Miller 1991).

As to gardening and orchardry, most of the evidence for these production branches comes from written sources rather than archaeological data and, where evidence is found, it is frequently overshadowed by more conspicuous finds of remarkable artifacts. The texts supply abundant but mostly imprecise data: various enclosed areas clearly producing plant edibles and materials turn up in the contemporary sign list (*ZATU* Nos. 205–210, pp. 211–212, No. 445, p. 268, No. 496, p. 279 and No. 514, p. 284). The sign *ZATU* No. 446, p. 269, attested in the Uruk III period, even shows a combination of the sememes SAR and KU_6, denoting 'a type of fish'; keeping of fish in ponds may thus have appeared at this early period. The very scanty palaeobotanical evidence points to the cultivation of peas, chickpeas and apples (Ellison *et al.* 1978, 168–169, from ED III Ur graves) and, of course, date stones belong to rare but repeated finds (Ur: Ellison *et al.* 1978, 168, PG 296; Fara: Martin 1988, 43, from the silos) while flowers of date palms may have been copied in the form of ornaments of luxury materials from the 'royal tombs' of Ur (Miller 2000, 152–153). Seeds of lentils, flax and *Brasica* or *Sinapis* (cultivated for oil?) turned up at the Khafajeh Temple Oval, mostly in House D (Delougaz 1940, 154). Miguel Civil (1987) published textual evidence to the effect that more apples than figs were cultivated at the beginning of the third pre-Christian millennium while the exact opposite was true at its end. In Fara times, almost twice as many apples as figs entered the texts. In ED Lagaš the ensi$_2$ employed gardeners who specialized in singular products (apples, dates); at that time, apple and fig quantities were roughly balanced. In fact, apples have been identified in some exquisite ornaments from the 'royal tombs' of Ur (Miller 2000, 154). Figs definitely prevailed in Ur III times, though they occurred as early as the Ur 'royal tombs': residue of the pulp of the fruit was retrieved from a silver vessel in the form of an animal skin found in grave PG 337 (Reade 2001, 22, n. 120).

While our archaeological information on gardening and orchardry does not suffice for any more decisive conclusions, the sphere of animal husbandry does show transformations (in general see Becker 1999). The decrease in the quantity of cattle remains in palaeozoological finds continues and the situation soon reverts to 'normal' with a preponderance of sheep and goats. The last time when cattle remains occur in marked quantities is the Jemdet Nasr period (Uruk: Boessneck, von den Driesch and Steger 1984, 170); here the majority occurrence of old animals may imply their use either as a milk source or for traction or carrying power. Ovicaprid remains definitely predominate in ED times. This trend begins in the Jemdet Nasr period (Abu Salabikh: Pollock 1990b, 71; Tepe Farukhabad in the Deh Luran plain: Wright *et al.* 1981, 189) and is attested by the Early Dynastic assemblages of Uruk (Boessneck, von den Driesch and Steger 1984, 172 – young animals), Abu Salabikh (grave finds: Postgate 1980b, 74 – more ovicaprids than cattle or pigs), Sakheri Sughir by Ur (Wright 1969 and Meadow 1971, 142), al-Hiba/Lagaš (Mudar 1982) and the 'suburban' quarter of Tell Razuk, inhabited probably by a 'commoner' group (Boessneck 1987, 134; Gibson 1990a, 112), while the Round Building of this site shows a majority of hunted animals (equids, gazelle), followed by cattle and pig (ibid. 110–113), a fact likely to refer to differences in social status (for a general overview see Pollock 1999, 142, Table 5.4). A food offering(?) from an Ur private grave (Ellison *et al.* 1978, 169, PG 1054) of ED III associates ovicaprid(?) bones with dried apples and fish vertebra. This picture may nonetheless not be entirely representative as cattle were certainly kept at least in the big households, which even fed cultivated barley to plough oxen (archaic Ur: Pomponio 1991) and are definitely present in the pictorial record (the Al-Ubaid milking frieze: Gouin 1993; see Figure 6.7). Keeping of sheep, but also of cattle and dogs, is attested by the hoof and paw imprints in the court of the Khafajeh Temple Oval (Delougaz 1940, 81–82). In contrast, fired bricks show only imprints of children's feet and dog paws (ibid. 82, Fig. 72). Archaeological evidence for the employment of animal products is miserable, but goat hair might have served for cord- and rope-making (Matthews 1991, 4). The late ED III archive from Ur (Alberti and Pomponio 1986; Jagersma 1990) bears out larger-scale pig keeping. This finds archaeological confirmation at al-Hiba (Mudar 1982, 27–28), in the Diyala sites (Wright *et al.* 1981, 192), at Tell Razuk, especially in the Round Building (Boessneck 1987, 134ff.; Gibson 1990a, 111–112) and in contemporary finds from Syria (Tell Leilan: Weiss 1991, 703–707 – mostly pigs followed by sheep and goats). Benjamin Foster's observation (Foster 1982, 118) that until the Akkadian period, most of the Mesopotamian fats were procured from animal sources while vegetable fats gained popularity only after that time, replacing animal fats completely by Ur III times, is relevant to this section rather than to hunting activities. Archaeological evidence from Tepe Gawra VI (animal statuettes) suggests that the first appearance of domesticated equids may indeed be expected in this period (on the domestication of horse see most recently Anthony and Brown 1991, Horn 1995). Poultry-keeping is attested by eggshell finds (e.g. Shara Temple, Tell Agrab: Delougaz and Lloyd 1942, 256 – Room M 14:15). Interesting observations concerning socially determined differences in animal husbandry come from some Mesopotamian sites. At al-Hiba/Lagaš, for instance, Area A, Eannatum's temple, shows a predominance of ovicaprids (80 per cent) followed by pigs (8 per cent), cattle (7 per cent) and equids (1 per cent). No fish remains and just one bird bone occurred here (Mudar 1982, 31). Most of these animals may have been eaten (ibid. 25–28). On

Figure 6.7 An Early Dynastic (*c.*3000–2334 BC) depiction of milking cows and processing various milk products on a temple frieze. Early Dynastic III, the site of Tell al-Ubaid (after Gouin 1993, 136, Fig. 1)

the other hand, Area C, probably a residential quarter, also displays a preponderance of ovicaprids (68 per cent) but a much higher proportion of pigs (18 per cent), fewer cattle (4 per cent) and the presence of gazelle (2 per cent), fish and birds, absent in Area A, which indicates better accessibility of wildlife resources in these circles. The Area A sample may reflect remains resulting from deliberately managed food conveyance, while that of Area C may indicate meat procurement closer to the natural resources. Even more interesting information follows from comparison of the al-Hiba sample with that of (admittedly earlier) Sakheri Sughir (Mudar 1982, 33). Ovicaprids dominate at both but Sakheri Sughir has more cattle and fewer pigs. This is exactly the situation that would be expected at a rural site, which does not produce enough edible refuse to support a larger population of pigs, which find better conditions in more densely populated agglomerations, but where more cattle are needed for traction power (Mudar 1982, 28). A slightly different situation is offered by spatial analysis of animal remains found at another chronologically earlier site, Tell Razuk, where a Round Building, a surrounding circular corridor or lane and a quarter of 'suburban' houses have been excavated (Gibson 1990a). The Round Building is associated with a majority of equid and gazelle remains, wild and hunted according to the butchering marks (86 per cent of the total of animal remains; Gibson 1990a, 111), and with more cattle (71.7 per cent), ovicaprids (68.3 per cent) and pig (68.2 per cent) than the 'suburb'. In its turn, the latter is characterized by a preponderance of ovicaprid remains (more than 50 per cent in terms of 'suburb' remains) followed by pig (22.8 per cent) and cattle (5.3 per cent). The 'suburban' situation clearly approximates the ED norm while the Round Building inhabitants not only had access to many more cattle and pigs than the 'commoners', but also engaged intensively in hunting expeditions, the prey of which had to be procured with considerable energy expenditure and managerial skill (see pp. 62–63 and 122). This situation may imply that the Round Building population deliberately cultivated managerial and manly qualities, as would be expected from 'country gentry' for whom hunting would constitute a 'management school' and the best peace-time training for war. A further hint in this direction is offered by the distribution of skeletal parts of sheep and goats at Razuk, pointing to the conclusion that these animals were butchered else-where and only selected parts were consumed on the spot (Pollock 1999, 144–145, Table 5.10). The contrast with the later al-Hiba élite, which obviously consumed food allocated to them with-out any individual engagement in subsistence procurement, is striking.

This period is very likely to have seen the first truly nomadic communities, which emerged in response to full occupation of the fertile land tracts, adopting an alternative strategy focusing on the less endowed segments of the Mesopotamian environment. Unfortunately, little can be said of them given the present state of knowledge. Ethnological observations assess the yield of steppe fields at 80–200 kilos of grain per hectare (Kuz'mina 1997, 81). In contrast, one square kilometre of steppe landscape will suffice to support 6–7 bulls or horse yearly (ibid. 82). The daily performance of a team of yoked oxen is estimated at 12 miles (ibid. 84), making distances measurable in hundreds of kilometres passed during single summer campaigns a reasonable probability. Other pertinent insights may be found in Galaty and Johnson 1990.

The subsistence gathered by various food-production strategies still left room enough for the exploitation of uncultivated landscape. Remains of hunted animals have merited little attention up to now but they appear every now and then. A good series has emerged, for instance, from some Diyala sites such as the Abu Temple at Tell Asmar in its Archaic Shrine phase (ED I: Delougaz and Lloyd 1942, 165, 207, As 34:53 – an antler fragment, which could, of course, have been collected), Square Temple phase (ED II: ibid. 181 – room D 17:8 of Shrine I with bones of fish, small animals and birds) and Single Shrine, later sub-phase (ED III–Akkad: ibid. 202 – fish, bird and animal bones and ostrich eggshell fragments). Dogs accompanied their masters as far as the courtyard of the Khafajeh Temple Oval and were even allowed to tread on raw bricks drying before firing as building material of the same complex (Delougaz 1940, 81–82 – traces). One of the planoconvex bricks found in room M 14:16 of the Tell Agrab Shara Temple bears a hoof imprint of a gazelle or small antelope (Delougaz and Lloyd 1942, 257 – ED II). This sheds interesting light on the exposure from at least some of the production centres connected with large contemporary building projects to various forms of wildlife. Gazelle bones come from Area C at al-Hiba (Mudar 1982, 28–29, 32) and at Tell Razuk (Boessneck 1987, 134ff.; Gibson 1990a; see also p. 179), remains of hunted gazelle and equids characterize the kitchen refuse of the Round Building. Hunting of birds is very sparsely attested but it did exist. Bird remains indicate pro-curement of roughly duck- and dove-sized individuals at Sakheri Sughir (Wright 1969, 90) and a bird skeleton of the size of a sandgrouse or quail turned up in one of the Abu Salabikh graves (Postgate 1980b, 74). Inhabitants of the Area C residence at al-Hiba clearly hunted a number of aquatic birds (Mudar 1982, 30–31). Henry T. Wright (Wright *et al.* 1981, 260) has noted the rather enigmatic presence of large water birds with coloured plumage by the larger structures of Jemdet Nasr period Tepe Farukhabad (Deh Luran plain). Nor was even such an archaic food-pro-curement technology as gathering forgotten in ED times. It is attested to, without any doubt in a sample fashion, by the ubiquitous shell finds, likely to represent picked-up items and starting with the exquisite beads carved out of shell cores of the Uruk III 'Sammelfund' (see p. 161) and subsequently imitated in clay (e.g. Fara: Martin 1988, 61). Shells turn up at numerous ED archaeological sites, both as collected items (Tell Asmar, Abu Temple: Square Temple, ED II – Delougaz and Lloyd 1942, 210, As 33:692, 212, As 33:578; Abu Salabikh – Postgate 1980b, 75, grave 1; al-Hiba/Lagaš – Mudar 1982, 33–34) and, in secondary use, as cosmetic containers, first occurring in ED I but frequent only in ED II–III (Martin 1988, 59–60; Postgate 1980b, 76). Of course, one of the best documented manners of exploitation of wildlife resources is represented by fishing, attested from Jemdet Nasr times (Abu Salabikh: Pollock 1990b, 71). Some long-term trends in fish procurement have been noted by Henry T. Wright's team at Tepe Farukhabad (Wright *et al.* 1981, 236, 260). Fish consumption increased here markedly in Late Uruk times and reached its climax in the Jemdet Nasr period, declining subsequently. This may reflect adaptation to a warm and humid climatic micro-phase supposed to have occurred in Jemdet Nasr times (ibid. 188). After this age, written sources indicate that fishermen delivered not only fish but also wild boar, and continued to do so for most of the third millennium BC (Englund n.d., 11, 282, n. 568). The 'tax collectors' also seem to have been involved in transactions with fish (ibid. 347) while the term ŠU + HA = šuku$_6$ is first documented in the Fara texts where individuals so designated receive donkeys, barley and arable land (ibid. 349, 351). At any rate, contracts for apprenticeship in the fisherman's trade do turn up as late as the Late Babylonian period (Bongenaar and Jursa 1993, Sippar, Nabonidus year 7 – hunting of 'ušummu' = Rohrmaus, a rather unexpected early parallel of the 'Pied Piper of Hamelin'). The notion of 'fishermen' might thus have covered a slightly wider semantic field than that of the English expression, meaning 'hunter-fishermen', 'hunter-gatherers' or the like. The Fara term may then have been attached to members of food-gathering groups who settled down among the sedentary population, playing a specific role within its professional and social structure, perhaps in the manner illuminated by some written sources from medieval India (Durga and Reddy 1992, esp. pp. 159–165). It is only by way of randomly picked examples that we may refer to finds of ED fish remains or other evidence from Abu Salabikh (von den Driesch 1986, esp. Table 2 on p. 37), Fara (Martin 1988, 53–54 – terracotta net sinkers from late ED I and ED II), Sakheri Sughir by Ur (Wright 1969, 89–90 – hunting of carp, drum and catfish; also Meadow 1971, 142), Tell Agrab Shara Temple (Delougaz and Lloyd 1942, 266, Ag 36:378 – fish tail), Ur (Ellison *et al.* 1978, 169, from PG 1054 – a plate with dried apples, remains of fish and an ovicaprid; Heinrich 1982, 114 – fish bones from the central hall of the north house of the ziggurat precinct), Uruk (Lenzen 1940, 17 – an ED house in Square Oa XIV 3 with fish remains) and al-Hiba/Lagaš (Mudar 1982, 29–30, 32). The fish remains indicate fairly extensive hunting activities both in the rivers and along the sea coast, as well as regular deliveries of sea fish to inland sites (von den Driesch 1986, 37–38).

Let us note that at this period, people probably began to appreciate uncultivated landscape as an object *per se*, possibly even perceiving its aesthetic value. Particularly conspicuous vegetation features such as poplar (Neely, Wright *et al.* 1994, 214) or willow trees, for instance, inspired creations of the jeweller's craft, some of which have come to light in the 'royal graves' of Ur (Miller 2000, 149 for poplar and willow leaves on the diadem of Queen Pu-abi).

In concluding this review of Jemdet Nasr and Early Dynastic agriculture, we cannot fail to observe the change(s?) heralded by testing new crops in the Jemdet Nasr period (club wheat, millet) and resulting in ED in the retreat of bread wheat (*T. aestivum* s.l.). Nevertheless, the six-row barleys survived and this, together with the preponderance of einkorn over emmer (Helbaek 1972, 39), supposed to tolerate salinity even less than emmer, indicates that rather than a reaction to salinization (on this point see Powell 1985 and, most interestingly, the possibility of 'engineered disaster' suggested by Gibson 1974), this change could have resulted from occupation of fresh arable land, chosen perhaps with an eye to the best possible fields within the catchment areas of the individual sites. This assumption is buttressed by the fact that Jemdet Nasr is probably the very first period in Mesopotamian history in which we have evidence of both winter and summer weeds from a single site (Abu Salabikh: Pollock 1990b, 71) and where a full sedentarization of peasant groups may accordingly have occurred. Another argument in favour of this hypothesis is the optimization of settlement in the Jemdet Nasr period; at that time, a series of new habitation sites shows a marked discontinuity with the preceding Uruk period but, in most cases, develops with far fewer problems into ED (Postgate 1986). The desertion of Uruk culture rural sites and the establishment of Jemdet Nasr ones on virgin soil, as well as the survival of these into ED, is, I believe, mirrored by the palaeobotanical evidence outlined above. This process of optimization of the choice of settlement sites and their catchment areas is further attested by the well-developed gardening, orchardry and 'backyard' economy (keeping of poultry, fish in fishponds?, growing of apple trees), as well as by the return to 'normal' in keeping sheep and goats rather than cattle. The fact that pigs prevail only on some sites may, in the light of the rather sedentary character of pigs referred to above, point to a conclusion that the ubiquitous ovicaprid remains may have been left behind by groups of small-scale nomadic pastoralists co-existing with the sedentary populations. At any rate, these would have found plenty of vacant space in which they could insert their economy among the new rural sites and their catchment areas, deliberately chosen to yield the best possible harvests. Those nutritional components, which could be neither cultivated in the fields, gardens and orchards nor exchanged with the pastoralists, were procured by a set of wildlife exploitation strategies including hunting, food collection and fishing, perhaps exercised by specialized hunter-fisher population groups (the Marsh Arabs of yore?).

No knowledge of the ancient arts and crafts in working with natural materials was lost in the Jemdet Nasr to Early Dynastic times; indeed, the masters of this period elaborated upon the heritage of their predecessors, acquiring new experiences and accumulating more and more know-how (in general, see Moorey 1994). Among artificial materials, attention has been dedicated recently to the cosmetic pigments from the Ur 'royal cemetery', although such finds are much more widespread (Bimson 1980). Mineral substances, especially those containing copper, iron or manganese, were mixed with various other materials, including bone ash, to produce white, green, blue, yellow, red, purple and dark brown to black colours. A chemical analysis (Makovicky and Thuesen 1990, 53–58) of pigments used for the painting of 'Scarlet Ware' pottery from Tell Razuk has identified, among others, soot as the source of black colour. Faience finds of this period do not belong to a well-developed artifact category. In addition to a group of Proto-literate cylinder seals from the north-east periphery of Sumer, a few items turned up at Ur (Woolley 1930, 330, 333; Moorey 1978, 74 and 1985, 139–140, 142–144) and Uruk (Limper 1988, 39, type F 412). Interest in faience articles might have decreased with the common availability of such decorative materials as carnelian (at least since ED I, see pp. 164, 167, 174, Jemdet Nasr and Sakheri Sughir) or lapis lazuli (since ED III, see Moorey 1985, 144, and also Neely, Wright *et al.* 1994, 180–183 for the Deh Luran). Lime was burned at the Khafajeh Temple Oval's House D (Delougaz 1940, 133, 151 – a kiln). Bitumen might have been extracted at its natural outcrop sites such as, for instance, Tepe Farukhabad (Wright *et al.* 1981, 190, 270; Neely, Wright *et al.* 1994, 180–183). There it probably acquired the form of 'cakes', transported subsequently to consumers along the great rivers where it was put to further use (Abu Salabikh, Jemdet Nasr period: Pollock 1990b, 70; the same site in ED III: Postgate 1980ab, 75 – grave 1, and many other Mesopotamian finds). Bone continues to play the role of the cheapest material for common everyday objects (for instance, Jemdet Nasr: Matthews 1989, 242 and 1990, 36; Fara, Jemdet Nasr period: Martin 1988, 20), although industrial development leads to the diffusion of metal versions of such implements even to rural sites (Tepe Gawra VI, Deh Luran: Neely, Wright *et al.* 1994, 180–183). Seashells, circulating with particular intensity from Late Uruk times and in the Jemdet Nasr period (Wright *et al.* 1981, 274f.; Limper 1988, 24–28; Neely, Wright *et al.* 1994, 178), soon replace the miniature (cosmetic?) stone receptacles of ED I–II (see Potts 1989, 140–141), becoming the 'body shop' of ED III (e.g. Fara: Martin 1988, 59–60).

A workshop for the manufacture of shell articles of attire has been localized at al-Hiba/Lagaš (Killick and Black 1985, 222). As an exotic material, ivory tends to be rare at the beginning of ED (though it is present in the Uruk III 'Sammelfund': Limper 1988, 59, type 95c), growing more popular in ED III (Moorey 1978, 73–74). In view of the preceding rarity of this material, detectable especially at Tepe Gawra (see p. 112), the question of its origin does carry a certain amount of interest. Roger Moorey (1978, 74) has noted the foreign(?) origin of some ivory products of this period such as nude female statuettes. Taken into consideration with the influx of such extraneous materials as carnelian and, more specifically, etched carnelian beads (Moorey 1985, 141), or the Badakhshan lapis lazuli, this implies exchange of luxury materials, including ivory, brought in by the maritime route from the south-east (Indian subcontinent?, see Potts 1994 and 1995).

The most common material encountered in ancient Mesopotamian sites, clay, turns up in such quantities that any brief summary of recent developments seems an almost hopeless task. A number of studies of contemporary Sumerian pottery have been carried out and published recently (Pollock 1985 and 1990b; Martin 1988; Pongratz and Leisten 1988; Matthews 1989 and 1990; Sallaberger 1996 on textual sources), but it may be of interest to point to some historically relevant conclusions that may be outlined on the base of studies of clay artifacts. Only a passing reference need be made to building materials such as brick (Sauvage 1998) or various utility supplies such as drain pipes, although their presence even at rural sites such as Sakheri Sughir deserves attention. Clay statuettes, so frequent in earlier periods, occur in Jemdet Nasr and initial ED times in ordinary settlement refuse (Matthews 1990, 36 and Figs 11:1–3 and 5 on p. 37; Pollock 1990b, 71 – an animal statuette) but also in graves (ED I Khafajeh – a doll?, Moorey 1978, 68), becoming, at least in the case of their anthropomorphic component, a rarity in subsequent ED times (Moorey 1978, 67); animal depictions turn up more frequently (Tello: Genouillac 1934, 80). Another virtually omnipresent artifact type, the spindle whorl, does show a rather interesting distribution. Present on Jemdet Nasr culture sites (Abu Salabikh: Pollock 1990b, 71; Fara: Martin 1988, 55f.; Jemdet Nasr: Matthews 1989, 237), these survive in comparable numbers until ED II when their quantity decreases but maintains approximately the same level until Ur III times. Some one-third of ED spindle whorls from Fara are made of stone (Martin 1988, 55f.). This trend seems to be reflected over a wider geographical area: as noted above, Tepe Gawra VI displays an interesting dichotomy between decreasing numbers of spindle whorls but considerable quantitative growth of clay reels and copper needles, implying textile work with half-finished products on the site. Such a situation suggests a rather high degree of specialization of textile production which might have been concentrated close to the major ED centres. What seems to me to be really important is that as early as ED I, rural sites entirely without spindle whorls do exist (Sakheri Sughir), together with similar settlements which have them (Ahmad al-Hattu: Sürenhagen 1979, 44). Of clay ornaments, reference should be made to imitations of large beads or pendants cut from the spiraliform shell cores known from the Uruk III 'Sammelfund' (see p. 161), now considered a typical feature of the Jemdet Nasr culture (Matthews 1990, 25). As to pottery production, the Jemdet Nasr culture period obviously developed the trends of the preceding age, especially in terms of pottery production en masse in specialized rural sites. This is not only the case in Abu Salabikh (Pollock 1990b, 59–69) but also the message of the 'Great Sherd Dump' of Ur, beginning in the Ubaid culture period and ending in Jemdet Nasr times (Woolley 1930, 330–333 and 1955, 27–31). The output of such workshops is incredible: one single campaign at Jemdet Nasr yielded 48,217 pottery sherds weighing a total of 1,380 kg (Matthews 1989, 228). In the Jemdet Nasr and initial ED, pottery did connect with social status: one sector of the Ur 'Jemdet Nasr' cemetery (W) displayed a marked representation of pottery bowls matched by their stone counterparts in the other sector (X: Kolbus 1982, esp. p. 8, and 1983, 11–12). Material 'borrowings' do occur: a pottery type of sector W (JN 17/16)

Figure 6.8 A solid-footed goblet, one of the most distinctive pottery types of the earlier part of the Early Dynastic age

copies a sector X stone type (JN 27/28: Kolbus 1983, 12f.). The interesting chronological series of metal (lead) flagons followed by clay versions which subsequently disappear, occurring from the Jemdet Nasr to ED IIIb times (Kolbus 1983, 11–12), shows that clay was in no particular aspect considered inferior to metal but that it may have been gradually replaced in consequence of the accessibility of other, perhaps even precious materials exemplified by the Ur 'royal cemetery' (see Müller-Karpe 1990a and 1991; Müller-Karpe, Pászthory and Pernicka 1993). In contrast to the preceding periods, pottery production seems to be moving into the centres during the ED epoch. Phase III of the Khafajeh Nintu temple (ED I) has yielded a find representing apparently the turntable of a potter's wheel (Delougaz and Lloyd 1942, 101, but cf. Mayer-Opificius 1984, 147). Intra-urban pottery production obviously took place at al-Hiba/Lagaš (Killick and Black 1985, 222). The contemporary rural sites appear to have been well provided with professionally made pottery (Sakheri Sughir: Wright 1969, 61–74). In ED III, the role of a social status marker was probably taken over by metal (and stone?) vessels, and pottery served as an article of common everyday use, displaying nevertheless some specific semantic traits. The constant pottery component of the grave goods, represented by a set consisting of a jar with an upright ('goddess') handle and a pedestaled bowl both at Abu Salabikh (Postgate 1980b, 73) and at the A cemetery of Kiš (Mackay 1929, 146; Moorey 1978, 66–70) does seem to carry a message, especially in view of the clearly female symbolism of the pedestalled bowl or 'fruitstand' (Moorey 1978, 68; on another constantly recurring pottery group see Moorey 1980; on pottery forms and functions in ethnography see Henrickson and McDonald 1983). How far a 'Freudian' interpretation of such vessels may go, envisaging a possible symbolization of sexual binarity and perhaps the taking over of the role of clay female statuettes, next to nonexistent in the ED, by a distinct pottery type (see, for instance, Moon 1982, 61, Fig. 12:58 for a depiction of a female pudenda on a pedestalled bowl), remains to be investigated by further research. The same goes for the last vestiges of the mass consumption of pottery vessels exemplified by grave 80 of Abu Salabikh, containing, among other items, 140 conical bowls, a bottle and seven spouted vases (Postgate 1980b, 76). The general retreat of this usage has been confirmed by excavations of an ED I cemetery site at Kheit Qasim (Jebel Hamrin area) the later phase of which displays much more limited evidence for this custom than the earlier one (Forest 1983a, 140).

A considerable amount of attention has been dedicated to Early Dynastic metallurgy. In Jemdet Nasr times, both central and peripheral sites could boast a number of copper artifacts, as is exemplified by finds from Fara (Martin 1988, 20, 22 – a copper arrowhead), the Ur cemetery (Kolbus

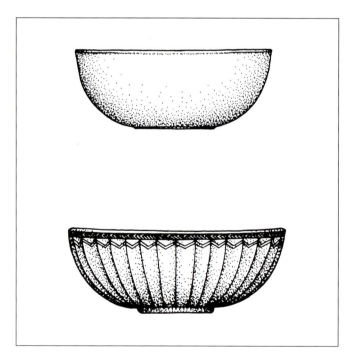

Figure 6.9 A copper/bronze bowl from the grave of King Meskalamdu at Ur (PG 755, 26th–25th century BC) (after Müller-Karpe, Pászthory and Pernicka 1993, Table 153: 850.851)

1983, 11–12 – copper vessels) and even from the faraway Tepe Farukhabad (Wright *et al.* 1981, 274). The situation at the last-named site (tools since Middle Uruk but slag first in ED) may again imply production of metal items in centralized facilities. The craftsmen of this period worked with arsenic bronze (Tallon 1987, cited in Pernicka 1992, 69 – Mesopotamian parallels to developments at Susa), although doubts have been expressed as to whether such an alloy had ever been intended (Müller-Karpe 1991, 110). Much in line with their Uruk culture predecessors, they also experimented with copper–lead alloys (Moorey 1985, 24, 26; Tallon 1987, cited in Pernicka 1992, 69; on the Uruk experiments see Müller-Karpe 1991, 109) and apparently introduced such highly complex innovations as the lost-wax casting technique, first attested in the Uruk 'Sammelfund' (Moorey 1985, 42f.). Artifacts previously reserved for élite centres appear now on minor sites as well. The only example of an Uruk culture copper mirror known to me found its way into the 'Riemchengebäude' deposit (see p. 102), but in the following Jemdet Nasr period even some of the deceased laid to rest in the rather modest Ur cemetery received such items for their journey into the nether world (Woolley 1955, 30).

The immediately following earlier segment of ED saw some changes. Most conspicuously, the quantity of metal finds decreases both in Mesopotamia (Moorey 1982b, 26–27 and 1985, 26–27) and at Susa (Tallon 1987, cited in Pernicka 1992, 70). Hoard finds of metal pieces such as that of the Tell Agrab Shara Temple (Delougaz and Lloyd 1942, 273, Ag 35:279) as well as the presence of half-finished items at such sites (ibid. 278, Ag 36:240–241 – unworked copper blades) indicate both the growing rarity of metal as a commodity and the transfer of metallurgical activities to major centres, rather like the pottery production commented upon earlier. The relativity of the quantitative decrease in metal objects is demonstrated by the presence of metal items at such peripheral sites as Kheit Qasim (Forest 1983a, 137) or Tell Ahmad al-Hattu (Sürenhagen 1981, 46–47) in Jebel Hamrin. The contemporary masters preserved the knowledge of the ancients (lost-wax casting: Moorey 1985, 42–46) and added further refinements. Innovations in toreutic techniques have been observed (Müller-Karpe 1990a, 162–163; Müller-Karpe, Pászthory and Pernicka 1993) and the first example of true tin bronze, a flagon from the Y cemetery of Kiš, dates to this period (Müller-Karpe 1990a, 163, Fig. 2:4, 164 and 1991, Fig. 4 on p. 110). The existence of east Anatolian mining sites from which tin, apparently missing from local contemporary artifacts, has been extracted since the early third millennium points to an assumption of extensive trade with this precious commodity which might have been exported far and wide (Vandiver *et al.* 1993). Coppersmiths of the period abandoned the attempts at lead–copper alloying (ED Tell Obeid: Moorey 1985, 26). The 'descent' of élite artifacts continues: the bronze mirrors, referred to above, now turn up not only at the Diyala sites (Moorey 1978, 112) but even at the distant Tell Ahmad al-Hattu (Sürenhagen 1981, 46, Fig. 14). The high degree of expertise in contemporary metalworking indicates that the rarefaction of metal is a consequence of archaeological processes of preservation and/or retrieval and in no way point to any impoverishment of this production sphere.

It may seem redundant to comment on ED III metallurgy but some points merit attention. There are sites, some of them not exactly peripheral, that display a scarcity of metal. That may not surprise us at the Tell Obeid cemetery (Wright 1969, 77–87; Moorey 1985, 26), but the rarity of metal vessels at Abu Salabikh is striking (Postgate 1980b, 73). On the other hand, major sites give evidence of a professional mastery unparalleled hitherto, when virtually all the techniques known until the present time, with the exception of steel-making, can be exemplified. This applies first and foremost to the Ur 'royal cemetery' (Moorey 1982b, 29 and 1985, 28–29, 39, 47; Müller-Karpe 1990a, 162–163; Müller-Karpe, Pászthory and Pernicka 1993; La Niece 1995). A similar quantitative increase in metal items occurs at Khafajeh (Moorey 1982b, 26), where even such average articles as fishhooks were now available in metal versions (Delougaz *et al.* 1967, 28). The location of metallurgical activities in major centres may have been the reason for the deposition of hoard finds including copper implements, such as that of Eannatum's oval temple at al-Hiba (Hansen 1973, 69, Figs 12, 13). Tin bronze probably constituted a common, if not universal, metal at Ur (Moorey 1985, 17). Michael Müller-Karpe (1990a, 164 and 1991, 111) has noted its use for the production of metal vessels as against tools and weapons made of arsenic bronze. The common occurrence of tin bronze finds a parallel at Susa (Tallon 1987, cited in Pernicka 1992, 70). The ores or ingots of raw copper/bronze could have been brought in from Oman (Moorey 1985, 11–12; Potts 1990, 90; Tallon 1987, cited in Pernicka 1992, 70) but iconographical evidence also indicates arrival of metal(?) vessels from western Iran and Anatolia (Müller-Karpe 1990a, 173–174). Work with gold finds most eloquent illustrations at Ur (Moorey 1985, 76–78), where the very first golden vessels from ancient Mesopotamia were found. That such lavish display of this precious material need not be limited to ED III, and that its absence from other contexts may again well be due to archaeologization problems, is indicated by inventories drawn up on the occasions of the official journeys of Akkadian kings, showing, at the very least, a wealth of luxury artifacts comparable to the Ur 'royal graves' (Foster 1980, esp. pp. 33ff.). Inhabitants of ED Mesopotamia did not lack artifacts of iron (Moorey 1985, 91–107) or silver (ibid. 107–121), apparently introduced in the second half of the fourth pre-Christian millennium to Egypt, the Levant, Anatolia and Mesopotamia, where it is accompanied by lead, rather commonly on both sides of 3000 BC, both in a pure state and in alloys (Moorey 1985, 122–123; Woolley 1955, 30–31 for the Ur 'Jemdet Nasr' cemetery). Mesopotamian silver, or at least a part thereof, came from Anatolia (Yener *et al.* 1991, 561–566). Though alloying of copper with lead was abandoned by ED III times (Moorey 1985, 123), the custom lived on in peripheral areas such as Luristan, even if the local smiths copied contemporary Mesopotamian implements (Vanden Berghe 1981, 24, 40, Fig. 3).

In their everyday life, population groups of the Early Dynastic period undoubtedly availed themselves of a number of articles made of organic material, but evidence for these survives only exceptionally. Traces of basketry products (Matthews 1991, 10; storage baskets at the Khafajeh Temple Oval: Delougaz 1940, 30f.) have sometimes been preserved by their bitumen coatings, as was the case at Kheit Qasim (Forest 1983a, 140). The dearth of evidence for the tanning and leather-working industry which must have supplied so many useful products is particularly deplorable (Crawford 1973, 236). Of personal articles, we should point to footwear, represented especially by luxury versions of sandals in precious metals from Abu Salabikh (Postgate 1980b, 73) and mentioned in the texts together with common leather shoes (an Akkadian example: Foster 1980, 33 – 2 golden and 120 leather sandals for a king and his retinue). Leather must have also served as a versatile material for containers and receptacles of every kind, exemplified by an exquisitely ornamented dagger sheath from the Kiš A cemetery (Mackay 1929, 137, Fig. 19 on Pl. lxii) or by the more down-to-earth bags or sacks which left their impressions on the reverse sides of sealings (an example from Fara: Matthews 1991, 5). Hides may have been used for sewing tents (an Akkadian text: Foster 1980, 33f.). One of the most ubiquitous materials of Mesopotamia, reed (Postgate 1980c) was employed in a variety of functions. In architecture, reed matting served both for floor insulation (e.g. Tell Asmar, Square Temple of ED II: Delougaz and Lloyd 1942, 179–180, room D 17:6; Tell Agrab, Shara Temple, same period: ibid. 258, room M 14:17) and in ceiling and roof constructions (Sakheri Sughir: Wright 1969, 59; Tell Ahmad al-Hattu: Sürenhagen 1980, 230). From among the movable reed articles certainly available at large in ED Mesopotamia, a fragment of what was probably a bitumen-coated round boat, or gufa, has been published from Sakheri Sughir (Wright 1969, 59). Abundant evidence for the use of reed matting as wrapping material has been yielded by the contemporary cemetery sites. Moreover, evidence for reed-matting bales or packages, made available up to now only in a sketchy manner

Figure 6.10 Impression of a cylinder seal on clay from Jemdet Nasr. This presumably shows a group of animals.

Figure 6.11 The reverse side of the preceding seal impression shows the folds and wrinkles of what was probably originally a leather bag containing a commodity to which access was controlled by means of the impressed seal.

(sealings from Tell Gubba: Ii 1988, 111, 126, Fig. 16; Fara: Matthews 1991, 5, 9–10, 13), must lie idle in immense quantities in museum and archaeological storerooms. The same probably goes for rope-making, of which serious studies have only just begun (Tell Gubba: Ii 1988, 113, No. 77, 129, Fig. 19; Matthews 1991, passim). Goat hair may have been used for the manufacture of cords and ropes (Matthews 1991, 4).

Equally lamentable is the archaeological record of the textile industry, so well attested by the texts. The ubiquitous spindle whorls (e.g. Fara: Martin 1988, 55f.) bear out domestic production and the now well-known movement of the craft into the centres is represented by such evidence as the find of a loom weight at the Tell Asmar Abu Temple in its ED II Square Temple phase (Delougaz and Lloyd 1942, 210, As 33:273). A higher degree of specialization of the textile crafts can be read from the Tepe Gawra VI materials where the number of spindle whorls decreases but an abundance of clay reels and copper needles indicates work with half-finished materials brought to the site from elsewhere (Nineveh?). Various textile items mentioned in the texts (by way of an example, Foster 1980: two baldaquins for a throne, a tent? of hides or woven fabric?) find very few archaeological materializations save for quite exceptional cases such as the headcloths(?), fragments of which have been trapped by corrosion products of silver and copper diadems worn by the deceased laid to rest at the Kiš A cemetery (Mackay 1929, 178–179). Remains of linen and woollen fabrics have been retrieved from the Ur cemetery (Crowfoot, Whiting and Tubb 1995, 114, PG 1). Results greatly enriching our knowledge of ED spinning and weaving are to be expected from studies of the reverse sides of clay sealings. It seems that weaving activities carried a great deal of symbolic value, representing an emblematic female activity and therefore deeply linked with female procreation, childbirth and propagation of the human species (see Breniquet and Mintsi 2000, esp. pp. 350–353).

Woodwork suffers, of course, from the same archaeological under-representation. Its use as a construction element in architecture, especially for various timber and beam structures such as ceilings or door-frames, the latter with their distinctive closing pegs which left their impressions in clay sealings, has already been referred to. Here it may be noted that the versatile and talented craftsmen and craftswomen of ED Mesopotamia resorted to wood as a carrying or core-construction component not only in architecture but also in the assembly of composite works of art of various materials, combining it with bitumen coatings to hold the surface elements of more exquisite materials. This procedure, exemplified by the famous pieces from the Ur 'royal graves' (the 'Standard', the 'Ram caught in a thicket') or from the Tell Obeid temple (e.g. Mallowan 1965, 38, Ill. 26, 51, Ill. 44) was known in ED I (Ur, SIS 4: Woolley 1930, 327). The extremely limited amount of evidence of contemporary furniture is particularly regrettable, as the Ur funerary examples indicate the level of luxury and sophistication to be expected from the interiors of contemporary élite residences, borne out by texts of the Akkadian period (Foster 1980, 33f.: thrones, baldaquins, stools, footstools, chairs, beds, tables). The social ascent of residents of certain Jemdet Nasr period sites may have resulted in the presence of sophisticated furniture items. The Ur 'Great Sherd Dump' of Ubaid to Jemdet Nasr times is topped by a layer which has yielded a Jemdet Nasr-style cylinder seal and a charming steatite figure of a boar bearing insets sunk into its sides, most probably an original furniture ornament (Woolley 1930, 333 and 1955, 31; Orthmann 1975, 162–163, Fig. 15b). Needless to say, joiners of the Early Dynastic period could supply whatever articles were desired, but the only surviving archaeological evidence points to the existence of wooden boxes and containers which left their impressions in the reverse sides of sealings on clay (Fara: Matthews 1991, 5, 9). Tamarisk and hawthorn wood made up a component of funerary furnishings of the Ur graves (Ellison *et al.* 1978, 172, PG I).

Specialists of Early Dynastic Mesopotamia were well acquainted with all kinds of work in stone. Chipped industry items turn up fairly constantly in the inventory of contemporary

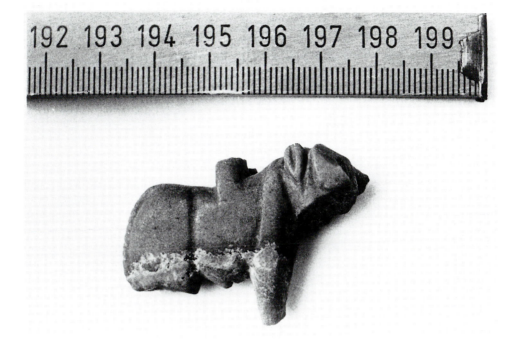

Figure 6.12 Statuette of a pink stone bull from Jemdet Nasr

archaeological sites (e.g. Fara: Martin 1988, 20–22). The earlier Uruk period distribution net-work, bringing to lower Mesopotamia supplies of raw materials, half-finished or finished implements from areas blessed with such natural resources such as the Deh Luran plain (Wright *et al.* 1981, 267f.) or eastern Anatolia (Behm-Blancke 1992), underwent some reconstruction at the beginning of the Jemdet Nasr period. The preceding medium to coarse gray chert of Khuzestan was thus gradually replaced by fine mottled tan and gray cherts, likely to have been supplied by sources in the Khabur region and typical of the Jemdet Nasr period chipped indus-try (Pollock 1990a, 87 and 1990b, 70). How far the 'Canaanean blades', still manufactured at Hassek Höyük (Behm-Blancke 1992, 170–173), were supplied to customers outside the upper Euphrates area is not known at present. Similar products were now manufactured in the lowland sites (Pollock 1990b, 70). The essence of ED chipped industry is constituted by the ubiquitous sickle blades hafted into wooden or bone handles by means of bitumen, occurring both at the beginning (Sürenhagen 1979, 44; Wright 1969, 56–58) and at the end of the period (Payne 1980, 112–113). Even this last-ditch stand of the chipped industry succumbed to the onslaught of the more and more common metal, as is shown by the twenty copper sickle fragments dis-carded at Tepe Gawra VI (see p. 175) or by the imports of copper into contemporary Deh Luran sites (Neely, Wright *et al.* 1994, 180–183). On-the-spot production in lowland sites can be doc-umented even for the initial ED period when stone seems to have been in good supply there (Wright 1969, 56, 58). Such mundane articles as sickle blades were, surprisingly, not limited to village sites (see p. 174 on Sakheri Sughir, Ahmad al-Hattu) but found their way even into major contemporary centres such as Fara (Martin 1988, 22), the Tell Agrab Shara Temple of ED II (Delougaz and Lloyd 1942, 269, Ag 36:292), the Khafajeh Temple Oval (Delougaz 1940, 30f.) or Kiš (Watelin 1929). The same goes for workshops turning out similar implements and exemplified by a site for manufacturing carnelian and rock-crystal beads by means of chipped stone blades and borers at ED(?) Uruk (von Müller 1963; Rau 1991, 65–67) or by a plant where shell was worked by means of serrated blades and micro-borers made of 'bullet cores' within al-Hiba/Lagaš (Killick and Black 1985, 222). Nevertheless, ED chipped industry production assumes the character of an extremely simplified craft, maintaining its position in well-defined and traditional work procedures such as bead-making (Larsen 1991, 91–100, esp. p. 99), but about to cede its role to other craft technologies, especially to metallurgy.

The coarser products of the ground stone industry such as various chopping tools or grinding slabs again characterize both village sites such as Sakheri Sughir (Wright 1969, 58) or Ahmad al-Hattu (Sürenhagen 1979, 44) and major centres, for instance, the Tell Agrab Shara Temple (Delougaz and Lloyd 1942, 258 – room M 14:17). Some one-third of the ED Fara spindle whorls were for the first time made of stone (Martin 1988, 55f.) and such items were also deposited in graves (Tell Owessat: Jakob-Rost, Wartke and Wesarg 1983, 127–128). The introduction of cutting discs into work with softer stones, supposed to have occurred in the Jemdet Nasr period (Moorey 1985, 51), has been questioned (Larsen 1991, 183–184) and refuted recently (Sax and Meeks 1994, esp. p. 165; Sax, Meeks and Collon 2000, esp. p. 159, Fig. 1) in favour of a hypothesis assuming work with files. P. Larsen has argued that rotating borers with chipped stone bits, working with powdered abrasive and evidenced by traces in Jemdet Nasr-style cylinder seals (Gwinnett and Gorelick 1987, 24), may be dated as far back as the Neolithic (Jarmo: Larsen 1991, 139). Nevertheless, the fact remains that the Jemdet Nasr period witnessed a further proportional increase in work with harder stones of Mohs 4–7, first occurring in the Ubaid culture period (Larsen 1991, 60–61, esp. Table 12, p. 61). Copper borers with emery as an abrasive and water or oil as a lubricating agent had to wait until *c.*2000 BC for their introduction (Gwinnett and Gorelick 1987; Larsen 1991, 134–138). Such specialized work could again be performed at the centres, as is shown by finds of unfinished cylinder seals at the Tell Asmar Square Temple of ED II (Delougaz and Lloyd 1942, 210, As 33:697) or at the Tell Agrab Shara Temple of the same age (ibid. 278, Ag 36:243).

Remarkable information is conveyed by studies of stone vessels (Casanova 1991). In the Jemdet Nasr and pristine ED times they constituted a fairly frequent component of the inventory of Mesopotamian archaeological sites. A number of them turned up at the Ur 'Jemdet Nasr' cemetery (Woolley 1955, 31; Kolbus 1982, esp. pp. 7–8 and 1983, esp. pp. 11–12) and the individual population groups might have distinguished one another by stone or pottery versions of one and the same vessel shape (pottery type JN 17/16 of group W = stone type JN 27/28 of group X; Kolbus 1983, 12). Another case in point concerns the Houses 12 layer at Khafajeh (Delougaz *et al.* 1967, 26) and even the rural cemetery of Tell Obeid (Martin 1982, 165) may be mentioned here. Far from being confined to cemetery contexts, however, stone bowls appear in settlements of Jemdet Nasr to ED I date (Fara: Martin 1988, 57–58; Sakheri Sughir: Wright 1969, 58) and even in rubbish-dumping areas (Abu Salabikh: Pollock 1990b, 70). Diffused as far as the periphery of Sumer, they played the role of grave goods at Tell Ahmad al-Hattu (Sürenhagen 1980, 230) and Kheit Qasim (Forest 1983a, 140). Stone-vessel types included miniature (cosmetic?) jars, as well as bowls and cups of greenish-grey steatite, most probably brought in from the Gulf area (Potts 1989, 140 and 1990, 66), and items of harder volcanic rocks or metamorphosed volcanic rocks, most likely originating in inner Iran or Anatolia (Potts 1989, 140). Much like the raw materials for chipped industry, these stone products were obviously freely available in Sumer at the end of the fourth and the beginning of the third pre-Christian millennium, having perhaps constituted an exchange commodity (Potts 1989, 147). This situation changed in ED II–III. First and foremost, the imported stone vessels became an item much rarer than before and some of their functions were taken over by other container types such as shells for cosmetic substances (Fara: Martin 1988, 59). Vessels of steatite/chlorite kept trickling in but they now bore exquisite carved decoration which probably rendered them a particularly esteemed item. Such vessels, manufactured in south-west Iran or central Arabia, were conveyed (also?) towards the Gulf island of Tarut (Potts 1990, 66–67), whence they set forth on their various journeys, taking them far and wide throughout the Near and Middle East (Kohl 1976 and 1978; Kohl, Harbottle and Sayre 1979; Potts 1989, 144 and 1990, 66–67, 77). Material analyses of these vessels (Kohl, Harbottle and Sayre 1979) identified three sites with vessel clusters of different origins, likely to have functioned as exchange centres (the islands of Tarut and Failaka and the city of Adab), as well as groups of sites probably supplied from single raw-material regions. One such network links Tarut, Failaka, Arabia, Adab and Mari (Kohl, Harbottle and Sayre 1979, 147), another one Ur, Nippur, Kiš and Khafajeh (ibid. 148) and a third one possibly Susa, Mari and Tepe Yahya (ibid.). The rarefaction of such stone objects, clearly discernible on contemporary sites such as Abu Salabikh (Postgate 1980ab, 73) or the Kiš A cemetery (Mackay 1929, 134) goes hand in hand with the rise in their prestige: in the Ur cemetery, they occurred three times, two instances of which concerned 'royal graves' (Potts 1989, 142–143). The same may be said of the volcanic rock vessels replaced by now by items of coloured or veined calcites (ibid. 147). Vessels of imported stones, freely available at first, gradually became rare and prized items, displayed only in élite circles.

Optimalization of the stone supply and concentration on particular, well-defined natural resources is also discernible in the sphere of stone ornaments worn as articles of attire, especially necklaces. Where present, Jemdet Nasr period necklace beads display a marked variety of materials and colours such as shell, carnelian, lapis lazuli, turquoise, onyx, frit and perhaps originally blue crystal (Fara: Martin 1988, 20–22, 61–62). Gradually, however, the foremost positions invariably go to carnelian and lapis lazuli (e.g. the 'Jemdet Nasr' cemetery of Ur: Woolley 1955, 32), even if they tend to be, at least in the ED I period, still accompanied by rock crystal and shell (Forest 1983a, 137) or even by green stone and gold (Tell Owessat: Jakob-Rost, Wartke and Wesarg 1983, 127–128). In the Khafajeh graves (Delougaz *et al.* 1967) the variety of stones is maintained, though carnelian and agate predominate from Proto-literate times until ED III. Lapis lazuli turns up first in ED II (Houses 6, ibid. 93–101; on dating see Karg 1984–1985, 306) and lasts until the end of the sequence, accompanied by frit. Even the rural population had access to exotic stones, as is shown by carnelian beads at Sakheri Sughir (Wright 1969, 58) or lapis lazuli in the Deh Luran (Neely, Wright *et al.* 1994, 180–183). This monopolization of the coloured-stone market is also paralleled at more distant sites such as Tepe Farukhabad in the Deh Luran plain (Wright *et al.* 1981, 273). The later part of the ED period is characterized by the virtual exclusivity of lapis lazuli and carnelian, as shown by the cemeteries of Ur, Abu Salabikh (Postgate 1980b, e.g. pp. 75–76) or Kiš A (Mackay 1929), as well as by a stray find from Uruk (Limper 1988, 30, type F 336; on the lapis lazuli trade: Casanova 1994). Ernest Mackay (1929, 183–184) noted the differing treatment of lapis lazuli (often only coarsely worked) and carnelian (treated with care), suggesting separate sources of both materials. An innovation of ED IIIa is represented by etched carnelian beads, surviving for the whole second half of the third and the beginning of the second millennium BC, perhaps imported from the Indus-valley regions (Moorey 1985, 141). The recent assessment of Uruk materials shows essentially the same picture (Limper 1988, esp. pp. 59–62). This choice of precious materials determined Mesopotamian taste for centuries to come. Upon his visit to paradise, Gilgameš saw trees with lapis lazuli leaves bearing fruit of carnelian (Dalley 1991, 10). Anyone who desires evidence for the imports of wholesale cargoes of foreign materials into ED Mesopotamia, very likely to have been brought in by specialized commercial agents commissioning them at large from their native suppliers, need only be reminded of the facts referred to above.

Undoubtedly, then, the sphere of processing of natural resources does indicate a great deal of sophistication and technical know-how, accompanied by considerable technological innovation. All this must have placed in the hands of Mesopotamian communities valuable tools for coping with the adversities of their environment.

Progress in the sphere of transport and communication may be measured only with difficulty (on contemporary international trade and exchange see Edens and Kohl 1993). Without any doubt, the twin rivers continued to function as first-grade circulation arteries carrying forth goods, people and ideas. The same was probably valid for a whole network of minor watercourses, both natural and artificial, which could have been used for transport by boats mentioned in the texts and, for the first time, possibly attested by archaeology (a gufa? fragment from Sakheri Sughir: Wright 1969, 59–60). The fairly numerous finds of both true examples and miniaturized three-dimensional versions of chariots, carts, waggons and sledges, clearly drawn by bovids and equids, point to the quality of the dry-land communication network and show that even heavy loads could move about fairly easily. Of course, all these devices should be perceived with an eye to the contemporary social context which determined their employment. That reciprocal exchange and redistribution procedures could have been realized over considerable distances seems to be rather clear (see pp. 71–73). Much ink has been spilled in debates concerning the character of Sumerian exchange, the possible existence of true commerce and the profit-oriented behaviour of Sumerian merchants (Powell 1977, 1978a and 1979; most recently Neumann 1992 with ref., and see also Charpin and Joannès 1992). Some of these studies brought out valuable evidence concerning the weight metrology of ancient Sumer which clearly begins in this period (Powell

Figure 6.13 The corner of a monumental brick building, rather a residence than a temple, from the earlier part of the Early Dynastic age at Jemdet Nasr. The photo shows both the extent to which even large-scale buildings fall prey to the action of time, and the amount of settlement refuse connected with such structures.

1979), as well as documentation for the hoarding of quantities of small silver fragments since ED II, which may imply the emergence of silver as a general purpose exchange equivalent in activities of this type (Powell 1978a, esp. pp. 228, 231, and 1996). The most recent research tends to view a commercial interpretation of such evidence with scepticism (Englund n.d. 21–26, 38f.), but cases in which goods in containers sealed with a personal seal leave their original storage facilities and proceed to distant sites in which their unsealing takes place do exist (Fiandra 1981b). Here the impression of a personal seal clearly functions as a signature or mark (of quality?) of some kind and though a variety of interpersonal relationships may be envisaged, I believe that they may well include true trade. At least the most general level of targets of exchange operations is marked out by heterochronous materials of which the sources may be identified. Enough has already been said of the Gulf (see Kohl, Harbottle and Sayre 1979; Potts 1989, esp. p. 144, and 1990, 85–92; and Glassner 1996 on Dilmun, Magan and Meluhha) but it should be added that the importance of exchange contacts with that area is suggested also by the comparison of Uruk and post-Uruk lexical texts in the latter of which the Dilmun tax collector is joined by the 'Tigris collector' who might have overseen the traffic both upstream and downstream (Green 1984). A Persian Gulf seal matrix of copper, bearing possibly signs of the Harappan script and fused with a copper pin by corrosion products, has been identified among finds from grave PG 489 of Ur (Reade 1995). It must also be noted that the 'black boats of Magan', seafaring craft built of reed bundles impregnated with bitumen, are now safely evidenced by a lucky find from the Arabian peninsula site of Ras al-Junayz (Cleuziou and Tosi 1994, see also Potts 1995, esp. pp. 567–568 – ships of carrying capacity up to 3 metric tons). Contacts with western Iran, virtually suspended around 3000–2400 BC (Gilbert 1983, esp. p. 112; Henrickson 1984, esp. pp. 104–106), were resumed in the final phase of the ED period, as is evidenced both by Mesopotamian-inspired artifacts in the highlands (Vanden Berghe 1981, 23–26, 40, Fig. 3) and by Iranian objects in Mesopotamia. Some of these such as a spouted vase from Tello (Müller-Karpe 1990a, 173) might have been traded but others such as the painted Susa-D pottery found at the Ibgal of Inanna at al-Hiba (Hansen 1973, 68–69, Figs 14–15; Henrickson 1984, 105, n. 17) may represent items acquired as booty, perhaps like the steatite/chlorite ED III pieces from the Gulf (Potts 1989, 147). The lack of archaeological evidence need not be conclusive as Elamites appear in cuneiform texts since the time of archaic Ur (Zadok 1994, esp. p. 37). Needless to say, the supplies of lapis lazuli continued (Casanova 1994, esp. pp. 141ff.). Similar contacts could have linked Mesopotamia with Anatolia, a supplier of metals (Lebeau 1990, 251–252; Yener *et al.* 1991, 561; Behm-Blancke 1992) but also of ready-made goods such as pottery or metal vessels (Müller-Karpe 1990a, 174; Müller-Karpe, Pászthory and Pernicka 1993, 285–287). This exchange obviously continued in spite of the thorough re-orientation of the (above all E) Anatolian material culture around 3000 BC (e.g. Winn 1981, esp. pp. 117f.). It need not be stressed that Anatolian goods are the most likely candidates for the interests of the 'Tigris tax collectors' (Green 1984). Goods brought from even farther included etched carnelian beads and ivory, for which an origin from the Indian subcontinent may be surmised (see p. 184).

As a conclusion to the economic character of the Jemdet Nasr to Early Dynastic periods, we may suggest the following major trends:

a) Continuous testing of possibilities of various economic specializations with an eye on intensive, not extensive production (appearance of new cultigens).
b) Selection of optimum economic strategies from a long-term viewpoint, exploiting the whole range of ecological niches accessible to the local population.

c)   Continuation of technological development and introduction of innovations (in metal-lurgy, for instance).

d)   Intensification by regional specialization, either within a single production branch (textile work at Tepe Gawra VI, for instance) or by entrusting whole sets of activities to specialized human groups such as nomadic pastoralists or 'fishermen', who exploit particular ecological niches of one and the same environment.

e)   Quantitative growth of the production volume of certain industries, resulting in the replace-ment of traditional items by the mass output of the new crafts, for example substitution of flint sickles or bone awls by their metal counterparts (Tepe Gawra VI).

It goes without saying that these transformations did leave pockets of traditional technologies unaffected. Whole interrelated clusters of manufacturing procedures such as the making of car-nelian beads at Uruk by means of chipped stone tools or the manufacture of seashell articles in the same way at al-Hiba (see p. 192) tended to stick to traditional approaches and materials (see also Larsen 1991, esp. p. 99). A certain social ascent of craft activities may be suggested in view of the fact that some of them were clearly carried out in the precincts of major contemporary centres.

Society

Starting this review of social change from the Jemdet Nasr to Early Dynastic periods, we must first consider the most significant observations published by Nicholas Postgate (1986; see also Lebeau 1990, 258–259 and Maisels 1990, 140–144; an archaeological review of this time period: Vértesalji and Kolbus 1985). Nicholas Postgate brings to our notice the fact that while there exists a series of discontinuities in the material culture (Postgate 1986, 91, Fig. 1) and in rural settle-ment (ibid. 93) between the Uruk and Jemdet Nasr periods, the transition between Jemdet Nasr and Early Dynastic is not exactly smooth, although the changes seem to have been of qual-itative rather than structural character (ibid. 92). The major agglomerations of the Uruk period seem to have survived into ED I while brand new rural settlement zones emerged in the Jemdet Nasr phase, serving the centres continuously through to ED (ibid. 93–96). This fact indicates the depth of changes occurring in Mesopotamian society in the Uruk/Jemdet Nasr transition period and provides an affirmative answer to the question whether the term 'Jemdet Nasr' has its own historical significance. However this period is referred to in specialized terminology, it is visibly different historically both from the preceding Uruk period and from the following, earlier seg-ment of the Early Dynastic period, as we shall presently see (in material culture, settlement patterns and ritual practices).

Let us first check Nicholas Postgate's observations against settlement changes registered by Uruk III period texts. We have noted the existence of the 'inner' or 'demesne' sector of the Uruk economy, the output of which might have been stored in structures referred to by the MAH (*ZATU* Nos. 341–349, pp. 241–242) and LAGAB/GIRIM/NIGIN$_2$ signs (ibid., Nos. 127 and 308–322, 370 and 488 on pp. 195, 235–237, 247 and 277). The 'outer zone' of the Uruk cor-porate entity economy also supplied establishments of types belonging to masters other than Uruk herself and denoted by the signs EZEN (*ZATU* No. 44 and 150–157, pp. 201–202, see also No. 259, p. 223), GA$_2$ (ibid., Nos. 162–183, 189, 360 and 616, pp. 203–206, 208, 245 and 311), and *ZATU* Nos. 651–658 on pp. 316–317 as well as *ZATU* Nos. 737–748 on pp. 329–331. Forms of these signs surviving into the Uruk III period show the changes concerned in a fairly instructive manner. Of the 'demesne sector' of the economy the MAH signs with the accompanying animal husbandry products all but vanish, showing the substantial diminution of the importance of this economic sector in post-Uruk times. As for the LAGAB/GIRIM/NIGIN$_2$ series, these structures lost the designations referring to particular products. Signs inscribed in them now give evidence for the departure points of the goods concerned, or their manner of delivery, rather than about the commodities stored (the ŠA and ŠITA containers, the NAGA community, the AMBAR environment characteristic[?] and the DUR$_2$ settlement unit). These data seem to indicate a shrinking of this component of the original Uruk economy as well as its simplification, in the sense that, rather than what was delivered, it mattered now whence and how the goods came. This may reflect a movement from the economically structured Uruk period corporate entity towards a cluster of more or less identical production units of the post-Uruk times, the relationships of which followed (also) non-economic principles. Such an interpretation seems to find support in the analysis of the other, 'outer-zone' signs as well. The EZEN signs behave quite like the LAGAB/GIRIM/NIGIN$_2$ series: far fewer products (only EZEN + SU, if this is a product at all) and only geographical entities (BAD$_2$, EZEN + U$_2$ + A). Major interest is carried by the fact that the 'casualty list' of Uruk III includes the EZEN + EN sign and that this type of establishment might thus even have left the activity sphere of EN altogether. Neither did the developments bypass the GA$_2$ signs though they remained connected with EN. The rising importance of the AB institution, so prominent in archaic Ur texts, results in the occurrence of the GA$_2$ + AB sign (*ZATU* No. 163, p. 203). In contrast to Uruk times, there is no 'lumber yard' (GA$_2$ + GIŠ$_2$.tenu, *ZATU* No. 168, p. 204) but a 'silver store' appears instead (*ZATU* No. 172, p. 205). Of much interest is the 'daily-delivery point' (GA$_2$ + U$_4$, *ZATU* No. 183, p. 206), indicating the new phenomenon of temporal regularity of deliveries; 'time was money' from the Jemdet Nasr period on. The other two sign groups show developments parallel to those referred to above: decrease in representation of particular goods and survival of attachment to persons, offices and institutions. In the case of *ZATU* Nos. 737–748 (pp. 329–331), newly formed signs show the usurpation of the structure originally belonging to EN (*ZATU* No. 740, p. 329) by AB (ibid., No. 738, p. 329), detachment of this establishment from UNUG (*ZATU* No. 748, p. 330) and again the combination with the U$_4$ sign (ibid., No. 747, p. 330), denoting the temporal dimension of the structure's utilization. The ensuing impression is one of a visible simplification, not to say impoverishment, of the economic organs of the one-time Uruk corporate entity. Of its original centre receptors, some nearly vanished, some left the Uruk sphere of influence and only in a limited number of cases did the management succeed in maintaining the relevant structures in a serviceable state. Moreover, the rich economic structuration and specialization of the Uruk culture period has virtually vanished and instead of 'who supplied what' the key information to be put on record now was either how the goods concerned were acquired or to whom they were addressed. This accords with the great proliferation of signs inscribed in the pot designation DUG (*ZATU* Nos. 88–124, pp. 189–194). Quite to the contrary of the storage-facility signs, the former multiply visibly in Uruk III times with the most conspicuous growth of signs denoting various goods (16 items as against 8 of the Uruk culture times). While storage space seems to have been undifferentiated, the variety of delivered goods was denoted on the container level, thus showing well the quantitative diminution of the commodity flow. It seems almost redundant to point out at the close of this section the fact that these observations, envisaging the chaining of more or less comparable production units which exchanged their output in a series of, by and large, equalized pottery containers differing only in their contents and perhaps according to non-economic principles, add flesh to the dry bones of the 'entente cordiale' represented by collective sealings attested, for the first time, in the Jemdet Nasr period (Moorey 1978, 154–155; Matthews 1993, 20, 33–50). The severing of external economic links and greater reliance on self-sufficiency is exemplified for this period at Tepe Farukhabad (Wright *et al.* 1981, 267–275; Neely, Wright *et al.* 1994, 178).

Unfortunately, with the sharp decrease in text quantities at the beginning of ED we have to shift our interpretations to the sphere of archaeological remains which, though representing a number of aspects of past reality that written sources cannot unveil, are nevertheless far more equivocal than the texts. For the earlier part of the ED period, three types of architectural layout stand out: spacious residences in enclosures (sometimes oval such as those observed on the west mound of Abu Salabikh and elsewhere); regular buildings on ordered plans, comprising most of those currently described as 'temples' and 'palaces'; and, finally, densely packed urban networks such as those of the Abu Salabikh Central Mound or of the 'Y' sounding at Kiš. In its turn, the later segment of ED displays only planned buildings ('temples' and 'palaces') and the dense urban quarters. It seems justifiable to me to base the interpretation of Early Dynastic social structures on these archaeological observations.

At first, let us focus on the spacious residences which may show curvilinear enclosures. Some of the best studied examples have come to light recently in the Jebel Hamrin campaigns, and sites such as Tell Gubba may provide priceless information. Phase VII of the circular enclosure at Tell Gubba, dating to ED I (Fujii 1981; Postgate 1981, 176ff.; Roaf 1997, 472–473) was originally centred on a circular podium 5 m in diameter and 3.5 m high, carrying a hearth in its topmost part and with a tunnel in the underlying masonry. This podium was at first enclosed by a double concentric wall. Sub-phase 2 saw, in addition to the sinking of a well (Fujii 1983–1984, 201), the erection of a third concentric wall and the excavation of a ditch which was levelled in the following sub-phase 3, when the structure received another concentric double-wall enclosure (Fujii 1983–1984, 201). The archaeological inventory of the site corresponds, by and large, to the situation in Early Dynastic Sumer. Variations to be noticed include a considerable quantity of grain finds, spindle whorls of stone just like at Fara (Fujii 1981, 146), a hoard find of copper implements (two axes, a chisel and a spear-point: ibid. 147), greater diversity of bead materials (steatite, crystal, quartz, shale, calcite, agate, carnelian, limestone, haematite, greenstone), absence of lapis lazuli but also of turquoise and occurrence of faience beads only in the earliest phase VII (ibid. 162). Phases VI, V and IV, also datable to ED I, represent renewed concentric layouts centred on the ruins of the earlier structures while phase III belongs to ED III to Akkadian times (Fujii 1983–1984, 200–201). An ancient tragedy has even preserved for historical research a sample of the site's population, buried in pit 14 in one of the corridors of the earliest phase. Among the eighteen bodies laid to rest here, three belonged to children under 6 years of age, seven to children of 6–12 years, two to individuals between 12 and 20 years, three to adult men, one to an adult woman, one to an elderly man and one to an adult man of undeterminable age (Ikeda, Wada and Ishida 1984–1985). The structure was embedded in a matrix of rather dense settlement, in apparent contrast to the preceding period in which the Jebel Hamrin – perhaps like other regions of northern Mesopotamia – seems to have been almost uninhabited (Moon 1986, 112–113). Similar structures have come to light in the same region at Tell Razuk (Gibson 1981, cited in Sürenhagen 1986b; Gibson 1984, 62 and 1990b; Roaf 1997) and in the upper strata of Tell Madhhur (Roaf 1982, 44–46; Roaf *et al.* 1984, 116–120, 160–162). Their excavators noted the absence of solid-footed goblets but, most significantly, found four tombs, of which the earliest one probably dates into final ED I, where the body was invariably accompanied by a pair of equids. The differentiated spatial distribution of animal remains at Razuk, showing a clear preponderance of hunted game in the Round Building (Gibson 1990a, esp. p. 113) probably implies that the privileges of hunting and very likely also meat-eating (perhaps as a 'sport of the noble' or as a peacetime exercise useful as war training) resided in the local élite. At Madhhur, the chariot(?) burial tradition persisted up to the Akkadian period (Roaf 1982, 45). Meanwhile, the Sumerian south has produced structures comparable to these findings, even if there is no exact and punctual correspondence. In addition to the curvilinear enclosures containing rectangular buildings at the western mound of Abu Salabikh, similar structures have been identified by recent excavations at al-Hiba/Lagaš (Matthews and Wilkinson 1991, 174–175) and at Nippur (Wilkinson and Matthews 1989, 260 – Area EA; on early Nippur see also Wilson 1986). I believe that these spacious structures, clearly possessing a settlement character, may be viewed as material incarnations of early social units which are now commonly denoted as *oikiai* (Henrickson 1982, 32; Maisels 1987, esp. p. 341, and 1990, esp. pp. 11, 166). The buildings of pristine ED, commonly referred to as 'temples' (useful summaries can be found in Mallowan 1968 and Heinrich 1982) may well have constituted, at least in some cases, focal points of such *oikiai* as the original find reports bear out their settlement character (for instance, Delougaz and Lloyd 1942). This follows from the fact that they have yielded finds of common everyday character, such as production waste, and that rubbish was frequently left to accumulate on the floors of such buildings, a feature unlikely in cultic precincts (see Hoffmann 1974 and Gibbon 1984, 160–161).

In characterizing these *oikiai* from the economic point of view, it is important to observe that at least in some instances they availed themselves of their own economic facilities, and had done so since the beginning of ED. In archaeological terms, I speak now of the movement of specialized craft activities from peripheral sites into the centres, as has been repeatedly pointed out in the foregoing discussion (work with seashells, clay, metal, perhaps textile and stone). This evidence antedates the testimony of written sources which bring this phenomenon to light only in ED III (see Charvát 1988b, 116, where I still thought that this process started at that time; the text published originally in Mesopotamia 8: Gelb, Steinkeller and Whiting 1991, 102, col. VI:6–VII:8). An especially eloquent example is constituted by the Khafajeh Temple Oval precinct in which the storage and production facilities occupied a structure distinctly designed for that purpose, the House D, a sort of a 'manor farm' (on the finds see Delougaz 1940, 53–55, 133, 151, 154). For this reason I find it difficult to follow the argument according to which House D was a residence of a socially important figure (Henrickson 1982). Some of these economic facilities might have arisen with employment of the know-how gathered in the preceding Uruk period. This may be argued for some branches of metallurgy where the technology transfer from major centres to mediocre sites exemplified by the mirror(?) of the 'Riemchengebäude' versus mirrors of the Ur 'Jemdet Nasr' cemetery and the ED I–II Diyala sites (Moorey 1978, 112) visibly takes place. An exceptionally clear case, however, concerns the borrowing and subsequent geographical diffusion of cylinder seals which, in addition to their continuous use in the appropriate social context, were now taken over as a purely decorative device for pottery ornamentation, and were used to impress bands of rouletted patterns into rims or shoulders of large storage jars. In spite of a very common assumption, I insist that pottery rouletting is different from sealing. Particularly instructive examples of pottery rouletted in this manner have come to light at Tell Gubba (Ii 1988), in Syria and the Levant (Mazzoni 1984; Weiss *et al.* 1990, 557–558), but only sporadically in the Gulf area (Potts 1990, 113). Transfer of the riches that had once been thought fit only for the holy tabernacles into more worldly spheres may be particularly well studied in the case of wealth hoarded from time to time in major centres of the respective periods. The earlier times are characterized by the preponderance of religiously inspired hoards. This seems to be the case of the Uruk 'Riemchengebäude' deposit but also of other instances where large numbers of what appear to represent articles of attire contributed by numerous worshippers(?) were left in cultic contexts, possibly in commemoration of collective rituals in which the believers participated en masse. The cases in point are the Uruk III 'Sammelfund' (Heinrich 1936, 4; Becker and Heinz 1993, 24–26; Limper 1988, 30–31, 58–59), the abundant beads and amulets discovered in Jemdet Nasr period Tell Brak, Syria (Moorey 1985, 143), finds at Khafajeh-Sin V (Delougaz and Lloyd 1942, 37–38, Fig. 32 on p. 37) and a similar situation at the Tell

Agrab Shara Temple of ED II (Delougaz and Lloyd 1942, 239), where a type of such 'personal record' may well be constituted by the two long copper nails and a poker-butted spear-head stuck into a hollow and wound around with a necklace in front of an 'altar' in room M 14:15 (ibid. 256). The Nineveh 'bead layer' presents a problem since it is dated into the late third millennium (Moorey 1985, 140). Nonetheless, it is the Tell Agrab Shara Temple itself which ushers in usages that were to become a hallmark of new ways and customs. Here begins the series of hoards that differ from the earlier collective offerings(?) in three substantial aspects. First, they are well circumscribed in the sense that care was usually taken to deposit all of them in a protective container – most frequently in a pottery vessel. Second, those responsible for their deposition usually concealed them in a manner enabling only a person knowing their exact location to retrieve them (immured in a wall, for instance). Third, these hoards contained a variety of objects the common denominator of which was usually their great preciousness and consequently high value which could, if need be, have been converted into whatever goods were desired (on such hoards see Boese 1978, 33, n. 124). The very first example to be cited here does, in fact, represent a hybrid between the two types, being composed of amulets and beads but deposited in a spouted pot and, as it seems, buried (later?) in Jemdet Nasr period ruins in Tell Uqair layer II (Lloyd and Safar 1943, 146ff.). In addition to a hoard of beads in a pot (Delougaz and Lloyd 1942, 253–254, Fig. 198 on p. 254), the ED II Shara Temple offers another mass find of silver containing even half-finished items (ibid. 250 and 273, room L 13:3, Ag 35:139–158). Such a treasure, so strongly reminiscent of the 'Hacksilber' finds of medieval Europe, presents a powerfully persuasive argument for the use of silver as a weighed-out exchange equivalent (Powell 1996, esp. p. 238). The introduction of these practices is confirmed by a find of a similar hoard in the Houses 6 layer at Khafajeh (Delougaz *et al.* 1967, 28, room P 43:25, Nos. Kh V 155 and Kh V 312–336), datable into ED II (Karg 1984–1985, 306). Finds of this character continue into later periods, both at the Khafajeh houses (Houses 2 of ED III, under the floor of S 41:1: Delougaz *et al.* 1967, 45) and, for instance, at Tell Asmar (a copper hoard at the ED IIIb palace: Delougaz *et al.* 1967, 184–185, room E 16:35, p. 241). A wider area where such practices may be expected is indicated by a find of a similar hoard at Susa (Schmandt-Besserat 1986, 94, 104), contrasting strongly with items deposited in pots earlier. An Uruk period 'hoard' from the Acropole I, for instance, consisted of a 'bulla', a spindle whorl, a flint blade, a shell and bored stone discs (ibid. 108). Here the transition from a record of essentially public ceremonies in which people left at the temples large quantities of a few object types towards testimony of private measures to protect wealth obviously gathered for secular purposes suggests itself as the most plausible explanation.

The *oikiai* thus appear to have disposed of their own economic facilities, which they developed with recourse to the know-how accumulated by preceding generations of craftsmen and craftswomen. These technologies were not only put to mundane uses but provided the means for gathering worldly possessions. Do we have any indications as to how the harvest of the manifold activities with which the *oikos* inhabitants busied themselves was divided? In this aspect we can only assess the circulation of those goods that either bore seal impressions on clay themselves or may have been stored in spaces to which access was controlled by means of sealing their entrances and other thoroughfares (doors, etc.). The sample of ED I seal impressions published from the new excavations at Jemdet Nasr (Matthews 1989, 240 and 1990, 34–35, Fig. 10 on p. 35) shows the continuation of the Uruk period mixture of container and door sealings, indicating mixed reciprocity and redistribution practices (see p. 146 ff.). A chain of reciprocal exchanges of small quantities of goods circulating among some of the contemporary communities is likely to have left behind evidence in the form of the so-called collective sealings, present at Jemdet Nasr (Moorey 1978, 154–155; Martin 1988, 119–120; Matthews 1993, esp. pp. 33–50). I have

Figure 6.14 The present state of the later Early Dynastic 'Abu temple' at Tell Asmar on the Diyala river

pointed above to the corroboration of this theory by written sources suggesting the disintegration of the unified and internally structured Uruk corporate entity, held together by a series of internal links defined by economic, social and cultic specialization, into a series of more or less homogeneous polities reproducing on a small scale their ancient Uruk model but essentially self-sustaining and exchanging, by way of recognition of mutual alliance ties, token quantities of basically the same kind of goods. Socially engineered exchange practices outside the sphere of Sumer such as those which left behind the Ninevite 4–5 series of sealings (e.g. Killick 1986, 232) remain to be investigated. How did this situation continue into the Early Dynastic? It seems that the north has now gone its own way. Though published data on the northern sealings are somewhat meagre (e.g. Roaf 1983, 74ff., but see also Pittman 1994), it seems certain that most of the 'sealings' turning up at that time represent, in fact, rouletted decoration on pottery. At Tell Gubba, for instance, two pottery stoppers and three clay appendages of bales bearing seal impressions make up a record that can hardly compare with the site's inventory of nine cylinder seals, five stamp seals and 128 motifs of rouletted ornament on massive jars (Ii 1988). In contrast, the south appears as traditional, indeed conservative. Early sealings from the Diyala sites (Frankfort 1955) still await their socio-historical assessment. At least some of the ED I sealings from Kiš (Moorey and Gurney 1978, 42, Nos. 3, 4 and 5) come from mobile containers. The traditional mixture of door and container sealings emerges from the study of materials from ED I Nippur (Hansen 1971; Zettler 1989a), though a feature of major importance should not be overlooked here. In two instances from Nippur IX B, the original cylinder-seal impression is countermarked by a stamp seal and one of these cases concerns a door sealing (Zettler 1989a, 3). This attests nothing less than a splitting of the seal-bearing authority, where the original seal requires a corroboration by another official within one and the same spatial unit, and indicates at least two levels of decision-making. The same type of evidence is offered by the ED I Ur sealings of which a sample in the Philadelphia University Museum, examined by R. Zettler (1989a, 6–8 and 1989b), consists of some 200 items of which thirty-five bear a countermark by a stamp seal or a stamp seal impression only. Twenty-six of the countermarked sealings once closed doors. For most of the ED I (–II?) period we may thus assume the situation which emerged in Uruk culture times. The higher social groupings probably collected surplus from the producers, who consented to the transaction, symbolizing their participation in such systems of socially engineered exchange by imposition of their seal impressions on that part of their output which they despatched towards the collection centres. After arrival at their destination points, the goods were stored in spaces to which access was controlled by (sometimes two hierarchical levels of) those entitled to bear seals. An analogy to such systems is represented by the Ur III bala system under which each province contributed to a common fund out of which projects of general utility were provided for (Englund n.d. 91; on the bala at Fara see Martin 1988, 119; on recent interpretations of early exchange practices see Pečírková 1989).

This situation underwent further changes in ED IIIa. Among the exceedingly numerous Fara sealings impressions from closed doors constitute the overwhelming majority (Martin 1988, 64–81, 225–277; Matthews 1991). Besides Fara, this situation is reported to prevail in the SIS strata of Ur and in the ash tip dumps at Abu Salabikh (Matthews 1991, 4). This statement conflicts with the above cited observations of R. Zettler (unless, of course, it pertains to SIS 1–2, the most recent ones, where such a situation could be legitimately expected) so some caution is necessary in the case of Ur. Nevertheless, the Fara record is so impressive that it constitutes an unequivocal argument for another historical change. The preponderance of storage-space sealings denotes the prevalence of redistribution in the context of a more clearly defined social hierarchy in which the one-time consent of the agency despatching the goods in question – most probably identical with their producers – vanishes as it loses its social relevance. The goods now travel straight from the production facilities to the storage spaces. Among the possible explanations for this situation we may ponder upon the subordinate position of the commodity despatchers who possibly lost their fully privileged status together with the right to express their social identity by leaving their personal mark on the part of their surplus destined for the socially coordinating centres. An alternative approach will see in this fact a testimony of a 'social contract', whereby the free producers would have surrendered their right to a personalization of their contributions in consequence of an agreement between them and the surplus-consumers, who might have recognized the full social status of the suppliers by other means (a written agreement? an oath in a temple?). The fact that it is the Fara period which ushered in greater reliance on sale contracts for fields, written on stone in a more consistent legal terminology and deposited in the temples (Gelb, Steinkeller and Whiting 1991, esp. pp. 13–26; also Glassner 1995 and Wilcke 1996) may point to the second possibility. (On this see also Charvát 1992a.) At any rate, the ED IIIa period brought a change in the social tradition, simplifying and facilitating the circulation of goods throughout the society and, as it seems, their convergence in the hands of the local élites. It is significant that the first inscriptions on cylinder seals, most probably denoting names of élite individuals, appear in this period (Fara: Martin 1988, 268–273, Nos. 362, 363, 365, 438, 441, 446, 448, 454, 495; on Mr. Anzusud see Matthews 1991, 10, Fig. 8:4; Khafajeh: Frankfort 1955, No. 258, Pl. 26, from L 43:7; Kiš: Mackay 1929, 191, Pl. xli:8), and that most of the impressions of such seals once closed doors. This is another indication of the trend from the mutuality of exchange practices, denoting all sorts of public allegiances in the past, towards the individualization and personalization of wealth-gathering, by whatever means it could be achieved. The model seems to have grown popular in the later ED period and groups of impressions from the same seals which turn up at that time even in private houses at Khafajeh (Delougaz *et al.* 1967, 39 – Houses 2, Kh III:329–335, Kh III 336–339; Frankfort 1955, 54 – room M 42:1, all of ED

III) or at Tell Asmar (Delougaz *et al.* 1967, 212, layer Vb of ED IIIb, As 32:1344) well merit an investigation of their reverse sides (for general assessments of these archaeological contexts see Henrickson 1981 and 1982). The same goes for the newly excavated Lagash sealings (Hansen 1987). At the same time, such practices could even have crossed Mesopotamian borders, as is shown by the contemporary Syrian site of Tell Leilan (Weiss and Calderone 1990; Weiss 1991, 703–707, esp. p. 706).

In addition to the arguments based on door sealings, another indication of redistribution is supplied by the evidence for ostentatious commensality, a tradition continuing from preceding times and likely to have had its bearing upon the occurrence of bevelled-rim bowls (see p. 124; on table manners in Mesopotamia: Ellison 1986; Milano 1994). The finds in question, dating from the pristine segment of ED, consist of large numbers – tens or even hundreds – of table vessels deposited in non-average contexts, either in public buildings or in graves. The cases in point include the famous 660 solid-footed goblets lying all over the floor of room D 17:26 (with a foot-path through its axis) of phase Archaic Shrine 3 of the Tell Asmar Abu Temple (ED I–II: Delougaz and Lloyd 1942, 166, Fig. 125), the earlier phase of the ED I Kheit Qasim cemetery (Forest 1983a, 136, up to forty goblets), the Khafajeh grave sequence in which the numbers of pottery items visibly increase in ED I–II (Delougaz *et al.* 1967, 69–114, Houses 11–4; on dating see Karg 1984–1985, 306) and grave 80 of Abu Salabikh (Postgate 1980b, 76 – 140 conical vessels). That communal partaking of food and drink could accompany occasions of wealth transfers, bordering on later exchange, commerce, purchase and sale activities, is also indicated by the occurrence of the sign group DUG.SILA$_3$ in the earliest land-sale(?) documents in a position implying the sememe of 'purchase', 'alienation', etc. (Gelb, Steinkeller and Whiting 1991, 28–30). The idea of a Sumerian 'potlatch economy' may well seem weird but in terms of pre-monetary society, various types of recompensations for different services could materialize in food

Figure 6.15 Two solid-footed goblets exemplifying pottery of the earlier part of the Early Dynastic age

transfers embodied in – or accompanied by – ceremonial banquets for all the participants in the transaction. That the social dimension of this custom died out by ED III times is borne out both by the absence of archaeological evidence (most significantly, already the later phase of the Kheit Qasim cemetery lacks the mass pottery deposits: Forest 1983a, 140) but also by the disappearance of the DUG.SILA$_3$ sign from the ancient kudurrus after the Fara period (Gelb, Steinkeller and Whiting 1991, 28–30). Needless to say, purchases of land were 'clinched' by a common meal even later (ibid. 243–244).

The *oikiai* of the pristine Early Dynastic period thus disposed of their own economic facilities, often employing technologies developed in the earlier centres and elaborated upon by inventions and innovations of the age, creating wealth not only for the gods but also for people. Social life of this period was dominated by élites, but these took care to preserve a balance of reciprocity and redistribution, recognizing thus the independent personal status of their suppliers, and publicly distributed a part of their wealth by the traditional ostentatious commensality, perhaps to gain popular support. In the later part of the period, the dominance of redistribution was accompanied by the decrease of social importance of the commensality practices and by individualization and personalization of the quest for wealth, now eagerly collected and anxiously protected in uncertain times. In ED I–II, public recognition depended on the number of those appreciating the help, generosity and prowess of the chiefs; in ED III the heaps of treasure in one's own chests constituted the most persuasive argument in questions of status. Can we proceed a little farther in our vision of these, up to now rather shadowy, social bodies?

In the assessment of Jemdet Nasr and Early Dynastic social contexts we dispose of a most welcome tool, the absence of which for the Uruk period is badly felt: the cemeteries. Analysis of their socially relevant dimensions leads to a number of significant conclusions. In this procedure I shall follow Lewis Binford (1971; a convenient summary and application in Near Eastern conditions: Wright 1978, 212–213) rather than Jean-Daniel Forest (1983a), who, though proceeding with remarkable determination and diligence, nevertheless focuses on situations of individual persons, failing to grasp the maxim proposed by Claude Lévi-Strauss (1974, 37–91, esp. pp. 72, 88–89) that primary social differentiation concerns whole kin groupings vis-à-vis one another, not individuals within any single grouping.

From the moment that they re-appear, cemeteries of the Jemdet Nasr and pristine Early Dynastic times bring forward evidence pointing to ranking and subgroup affiliation. The earliest phase of the Khafaje grave sequence (under Houses 12: Delougaz *et al.* 1967, 60–69; dating: Karg 1984–1985, 306) displays such features as common burial of adults and children, more or less universal grave equipment and even most peculiar gestures and object layouts likely to have carried a special significance. A stone bowl is 'handed in' by the deceased (graves 4, 5, 6, 27; graves 6 and 27 belong to children) or a pot covered by a stone vessel (graves 4, 20, 22, perhaps 25). It is highly significant that both adults and children underwent such treatment. In the subsequent ED I–II periods (Delougaz *et al.* 1967, 83–114, Houses 9–4; dating: Karg 1984–1985, 306) a similar role of a 'common denominator' is played by unworked natural stones and possibly also by built tombs, both of which (rather significantly) cease in ED III times (Delougaz *et al.* 1967, 114–133, Houses 3 and 2). Similar phenomena may be observed in the Ur 'Jemdet Nasr' cemetery, where the individual component groups are 'denoted', for instance, by stone bowls (sector X) as against clay bowls (sector W: Kolbus 1982, 8 and 1983, 11), while certain exotic products are represented in many graves, which implies free circulation of wealth throughout whole social segments (stone vessels from the Gulf: Potts 1989, 140, 141, 147) in the traditional manner. The lack of meaningful distinctions between male and female equipment in these graves (but see p. 207 on the position of the body in the grave) and the universality of peculiarities of burial customs pertaining even to children imply that the highest distinguishing criteria do not lie at the sex and age level but identify social bodies including men, women and children and describing themselves as different from other bodies of their kind existing in the same spatiotemporal context (Ur); these may well have been kinship groupings (on kinship terms in Sumerian see Sjöberg 1967; Götzelt 1995). A similar interpretation may hold for the two spatially distinct segments of the ED I Kheit Qasim cemetery, both apparently containing male and female burials (Forest 1983a, 138–139, Pl. 64, 65), as well as for spatially distinct groups at Ahmad al-Hattu of the same date (Sürenhagen 1980, 229–230). The recently published sample of Late Uruk to Ninevite V graves at Tell Mohamed Arab (Bolt 1992) is rather limited but most welcome as it fills the gap in our knowledge of the physical anthropology of the ancient Mesopotamians. The local population is characterized as living under approximately identical and physically demanding conditions with at least one individual of a fairly long life span (a woman more than 60 years old). This implies a low degree of social differentiation (ibid. 175–176). Kinship as an integrating factor of these groupings is also implied by the fact that, for the first time, Jemdet Nasr texts include the sign GIBIL (*ZATU* No. 214, p. 213; Glassner 2000a, 208–209) occurring, as St. Langdon notes (Langdon 1928, 10–11, No. 69), in contexts where the later sign NE + PAP conveys the meaning 'ancestor, grandfather', the root of the name Gilgameš. Ancestral cults played a not negligible role in later Sumerian history. Subsequently, kinship groupings enter the realm of history in ED III written texts. Though the terminology employed by the land-sale contracts of the Fara (= ED IIIa) period is extremely simplified (Gelb, Steinkeller and Whiting 1991, 227: lú, šeš, dumu), it is clear that consent of the whole relevant kinship grouping was required for the sale of land (ibid. 14, 17). How these groupings were internally structured is not clear, though the term im-ru, probably referring to a similar type of social body, does occur in this period (ibid. 214, in No. 14, the 'Chicago stone' of the Fara period – im-ru ENGUR; see also the seven im-ru of text TSŠ 245 in Edzard 1976, 173, numbering 539 'descendants'). M. Powell (1986, 11) sees in the Ur III im-ri-a extended families. Now while the existence of kinship groupings as such can hardly be doubted, it is debatable how far the property 'commune', visible in the ancient kudurrus in the light of consent of the seller's relatives with the alienation of arable land, reaches back in time. The argument of Gelb, Steinkeller and Whiting (1991, 25–26) that one buyer and one seller means private property of land may or may not hold as no land is actually held collectively (in the sense of cultivation and tilling) in prestate societies (on types of land tenure in such communities see most instructively Sahlins 1968, esp. pp. 74–95, as well as Sahlins 1972). Arable land is always assigned to individual families, or rather their heads, who arrange for its tilling, nourishing from its harvests all those who depend on them. Collectivity comes in when all the community land is periodically redistributed to its component families who receive allotments different from those previously held by them. This takes place in response both to soil exhaustion in the conditions of pristine agriculture and to the growth of the community, when new family heads receive their land not from their parents but from the community council which assigns vacant plots. The same instability prevails along the temporal axis. Family land is held by virtue of blood ties to the group in question and the acting family head bequeaths his or her social position to his or her successor, conferring right of access to such material provisions for the family as may be deemed appropriate by the matrix community, but not the means of production themselves (see, for instance, Maisels 1987, 333–334 and 1990). Individual sellers of land may thus be perfectly compatible with collective property, or rather collective distribution of land. In the question of the extension of these customs back in time, it pays to realize that social structures can react very swiftly to changing conditions of socioeconomic order and that societies in which new wealth becomes available may speedily adjust their kinship and inheritance rights in order to attract and retain as much of the earth's abundance as possible. The 'collective ownership of land' supplied great nineteenth-century theoreticians with historical arguments for attacks on private property, essentially politically inspired, but at present all such assumptions must be examined with the greatest possible caution. The role of kinship in societies in transition has been best illuminated by recent studies of early medieval France and Italy. The French social landscape of the eleventh century AD, characterized by new sources of wealth opened to the aristocracy by the appropriation of royal regional prerogatives, displays clear examples of systematic and deliberate creation of closely knit kinship groups pooling their property and trying to prevent its dispersal at all costs. One of the devices leading to this goal was the introduction of undivided property tenure by relatives (see Duby 1988, 83–116, esp. pp. 99–100). Another most meaningful example concerns the settlement concentration, or 'incastellamento', of ninth–twelfth-century central Italy (Toubert 1973, esp. pp. 711–714, 718, 721, 725–726, 728–729). When arable soil was being evacuated there and settlements transferred to barren rocky tops, the new settlers started drawing considerable profits from more systematic cultivation of larger areas of fertile fields than before. In order to achieve the tenure of land plots that were as big as possible, local cultivators not only formed more extensive kinship groupings which had not been present before, but introduced undivided property tenure as well, usually among brothers. It may be noticed *en passant* that while the peasants of Latium held their fields in undivided tenure, they reserved as private estates their gardens and other intensely worked land parcels. In view of this, the fact that in ancient Mesopotamia the collective rights to tilled land, visible in ancient kudurrus at first in ED IIIa, are preceded by archaeological evidence for the gathering and hoarding of private wealth reaching back to ED II (see 199–200), hardly needs comment. Kinship groupings of the ED III period have received illumination from a source of which much can be expected, namely physical anthropology. At Kiš of that time, males apparently displayed localized origin while females came from most diverse backgrounds (Rathbun 1975, cited in Strouhal 1979, 127). This indicates that matrimonial exchange probably assumed the generalized form, recently widespread in Europe and western Asia (Vestergaard 1991, esp. pp. 24–25; on Mesopotamian marriage see Stol 1995, esp. pp. 124–139), and that patrilocal residence, suggested for the Ur III period (Powell 1986, 11), may, in fact, be extended as far back in time as ED III. The most recent information here has been supplied by Ch. Maisels (1987, 347, Fig. 3 and 1990, 156–159, Fig. 6.1 on p. 157), who has noticed that members of one of the lineages recorded on the Maništusu obelisk received quantities of gifts in direct proportion to their genealogical proximity to the field owner. This principle of social status increasing in relation to proximity to the central figure (or group) of the kinship system in question constitutes an attribute of so-called ramages or conical clans, playing a considerable role in early statehood processes (Maisels 1987, 336–337; see also Thomas 1987, 408–409). It would be extremely interesting to know how far into antiquity this type of social body reaches but unfortunately that information cannot at present be recovered.

One of the organizational principles of the Jemdet Nasr and Early Dynastic *oikiai* thus appears to have been constituted by kinship, present from the very beginning of this period (on Sumerian kinship see Götzelt 1995). The 'sudden' emergence of this principle makes it likely that it had been present in Uruk times as well but that the sources at our disposal do not suffice for the establishment of its existence, save perhaps for the equivocal central-hall residences. In ED IIIa, the role of kinship ties acquired new significance as more wealth flowed into the community; the kinship groupings may have grown larger and introduced undivided property tenure. Contemporary Mesopotamian social bodies displayed patrilinear descent, patrilocal residence and generalized matrimonial exchange (the last two at least in some cases). The existence of ramages or conical clans cannot be documented before the Akkadian period.

Another apparently more universal classificatory aspect of Jemdet Nasr and Early Dynastic society was represented by sexual division. Traces of this survive in the earliest Sumerian texts, as is demonstrated by such signs as IR$_3$ (*ZATU* No. 268, p. 225), introduced in the Jemdet Nasr period and specified by a component sign denoting the male sex, or the MURUB$_2$ sign (*ZATU* No. 371, p. 248, Charvát 1997, 82–83), depicting apparently a figure in a long robe (or veil?) determined by an image of the female sex. We owe to Jean-Daniel Forest (1983a, 129) the identification of a sexual division in the positions of the deceased laid to rest in the Ur 'Jemdet Nasr' cemetery. Women were interred lying on their left sides and men on their right sides. A similar division may be assumed not only for the ED I Kheit Qasim cemetery (ibid., according to grave goods), but even for the Ur 'royal cemetery'. There, the ingenious observations of W. Rathje (1977; see also Pollock 1991, 380) pertaining to the distribution of seals with contest and conflict scenes, as well as those with banquet depictions and especially artifacts associated with bearers of these particular seal categories (Rathje 1977, Table I on p. 29), point to the conclusion that such seals may well accompany men (contest seals) and women (banquet seals). Unlike the record of kinship relations, visible rather through written sources than by means of archaeological evidence, masculinity and femininity figure rather prominently in the earlier part of ED III, especially at the Kiš and Ur cemeteries. The binary opposition shines through the grave goods which include, for instance, such exquisite and sophisticated outer signs of womanhood as the head ornaments of the Ur graves (Moorey 1977, 35; Pollock 1991, 373–376). This elaborate burial treatment of women may imply a connection with the ethnographically documented close relationships between female wedding and burial gear and rites in general (for Eurasia see, for instance, Bayburin and Levinton 1990). This emphasis on femininity is likely to reflect changes in the social position of women and perhaps also in matrimonial exchange (on this in general see Parkin 1990; Schlegel and Eloul 1988, as well as Wernisch 1994), but that remains a task for future research. What is clear, however, is that womanly status loses its exclusively biological value and assumes the character of a social category in the earlier part of ED III. This is indicated by luxury versions of objects likely to have denoted femininity such as spindles and spindle whorls found both at Ur (Woolley 1934, 53; Moorey 1985, 114 – grave 580, a silver spindle with lapis lazuli spindle whorls) and at Kiš (Mackay 1929, 168, Pl. lviii, Fig. 1 – a copper spindle with its whorl; for the symbolic character of such spinning apparatus, which symbolizes, in its exclusively female dimension, the female procreative force and the propagation of the human race, see Breniquet and Mintsi 2000, esp. pp. 350–353). A further development in this direction has been described by Susan Pollock (1991, 378ff.), who has brought it to our notice that seven of the Ur dead were given both masculine and feminine attributes, one of these being probably a man and another one a woman. Here the 'signs of womanhood' detach themselves completely from the sphere of biology, perhaps to provide alternative social categories after the collapse of the preceding stratification of whole kinship groupings under the impact of contemporary change, and above all, of the elevation of material wealth to the chief criterion of social success. In perfect accord with this, the Fara texts dissociate the supreme title NIN from its biological con-notations and, making the NIN ('queen') the transmitter of supreme social status, associate her title with toponyms even in divine names (Ningirsu, for instance: Charvát 1997, 85–89 and 91, cf. p. 213). Subsequent developments, however, must have cut short this trend as later third-mil-lennium texts, starting with the Uruinimgina records, display a resolutely masculine bias. The comparison of the Ur 'royal graves', with their excessive numbers of females, followed by a dis-tinct decrease in feminine status, with the situation in seventh–eighth-century Anglo-Saxon England, where women were congregated in élite households both for sexual and for servile pur-poses – since at a moment when inheritance in the male line constitutes the desired ideal, womanly status decreases but females are important for reproduction strategies (Hodges 1989, 40) – clearly opens up most attractive prospects for future comparative research.

Finally, another factor which may have had its bearing on the social constitution of the ancient Sumerian *oikiai* and which may again have been handed down by their Uruk period predecessors was the age of individuals. On the present extremely tenuous evidence, however, all statements in this direction must remain hypothetical. While the 'elders' occupied distinct places and enjoyed discernible dignities in the Pre-Sargonic age (Gelb 1984), the guruš population group, as far as can be seen, performed labour tasks in the same period (Englund 1988, 177–178, n. 48 and n.d. 126, n. 259). This binary composition apparently existed at Ebla in the form of a 'guruš-class' and a 'dam-class', possibly conceivable as young unmarried adults as against household masters and mistresses (Milano 1987, 550). How far into antiquity this system may be projected is unclear at the moment; the well-known Gilgameš-and-Agga instance has been recently interpreted as a literary topos (Katz 1987 and 1993). Its first visible trace has come from the ED II Tell Agrab Shara Temple, findspot of an inscription referring to an 'overseer of guruš' (ugula-guruš) (Delougaz and Lloyd 1942, 297, No. 10). Here a larger number of guruš, presumably out of their original social matrix, require a special official in charge of them, perhaps to perform (labour?) tasks agreed upon by common consent. That the employment of guruš labour gangs may not have accompanied Sumerian literate civilization from its inception is implied by the Egyptian parallels in which the first documented instances of 'Jungmannschäfte' come from the end of the first dynasty (Kaplony 1984, esp. p. 543). It need not be specially emphasized that the large numbers of people (men?) who streamed forth from all Sumer and Akkad and converged at ED IIIa Fara to discharge their labour obligations (see, for instance, Matthews 1991, 11, house in trenches XVIIc–d – up to 6,580 labour hands, or Edzard 1976, pp. 166, 183, 186 for the geographical range) could well belong to the guruš stratum. What makes this question so important is the fact that assigning collective tasks to various social groupings defined by age (on this see Treide and Treide 1984, 394, 402; Bernardi 1985; Spencer 1987) can greatly amplify the efficiency of the social mechanisms of pre-industrial communities, and contribute in a significant fashion to the emergence of higher-order social structures such as the early states. Social anthropologists have even described communities in which the distinction between young unmarried males, who perform the labour tasks, and the married seniors who hold key social posts due to their access to specialized knowledge, which is kept secret from all the uninitiated, constitutes one of the major social forces (Katz and Kemnitzer 1978, 600 on E. Terray's work on the Abron kingdom; Terray 1986; also Thomas 1987, 409).

Of the social factors affecting the life of Early Dynastic Sumerian *oikiai*, we thus catch a glimpse of sex and age. The sexual divisions exist probably from Uruk and clearly from Jemdet Nasr times on. They assumed a particular significance in ED IIIa when, bared of the protective 'upper layer' of the kinship groupings ranked among one another, in which sexual divisions played the role of an internal classificatory device, the manly and womanly statuses detached themselves from individual biological characteristics (at least in mortuary treatment) and assumed social dimensions (e.g. womanhood = direction of household production?). This trend was cut short by subsequent developments which took a decisive turn towards male domination and expressed status in graves by equipment far less obviously bound to the sex of the deceased. On the other hand, the age distinction, probably of significance insofar as the younger, guruš group had to perform labour tasks while the 'elder' stratum reserved for themselves the organizational and intellectual activities, seems to have been operative at least from ED II, attaining considerable importance in ED IIIa (Fara).

Returning to the traditional assessments of the ED Mesopotamian social scene, we may legitimately ask what became of the numerous 'temples' in which the preceding generations of cuneiformists believed so ardently. I am convinced that with such an amount of evidence of common everyday activities taking place within the precincts of, say, the Diyala sites, these structures can hardly be viewed exclusively as shrines and sanctuaries in which the colours, noises, odours and tastes of burgeoning community life were taboo. Temples, of course, did exist. In the 'collective sealings', for instance (Moorey 1978, 154–155; Martin 1988, 119–121), 'urban' communities are mostly symbolized by symbols of their gods, of whom it is most reasonable to suppose that they resided in their own temples. Relationships between the alliance represented by these 'city-league sealings' and the Kengir league, first attested in Fara times (Wilcke 1974, 202–232), which certainly did possess an economically real character (see p. 208, men as working hands? Of ki-en-gi: Edzard 1976, 188, No. WF 94; and Uruinimgina or his wife Šaša sending offerings to ki-en-gi: Marzahn 1991, No. 72 = DP 46, 51 and 203), will constitute a theme for future generations of scholars. I believe that an assumption of genetic links between the two may not be too far from the truth. Indeed, the 'symbolic' exchange of small quantities of (bottled?) goods may have been converted into a corvée obligation on behalf of the League partners by ED IIIa times. Moreover, taking into account the fact that the first dignitary of Early Dynastic Sumer to bear the en title, Enšakušanna of Uruk (Edzard 1974, 144; Pomponio 1994b), linked this rank expressly with the ki-en-gi entity, and recognizing the intimate connection between the en title and the city of Uruk, I feel tempted to postulate a unity of tradition between the Uruk culture corporate entity, the alliance represented by the Jemdet Nasr and Early Dynastic 'city sealings' and the Kengir league. But back to our problem: criteria for the recognition of temples – which, by ED times, may be imagined as ordinary *oikiai* with specialized religious functions – have to be found, since cultic and ritual practices need not necessarily have left discernible traces in the archaeological record. Sacerdotal specialization on behalf of wider social (even kin) groupings has been dwelt upon by E. Durkheim (see Wallwork 1984, passim, esp. notes on Phase 3, Clan confederations). One of the relevant criteria may be provided by careful observation and recording of rubbish disposal, as élite sites tend to differ in this aspect from ordinary settlements (Hoffmann 1974 and Gibbon 1984, 156–161, esp. pp. 160–161). Another factor in temple identification may perhaps be seen in the distribution of the (original) deposition sites of ancient kudurrus which clearly carried major social significance and may have been

Figure 6.16 The courts of Sumerian, Akkadian and Near Eastern temples of the third pre-Christian millennium frequently contained large jars of water at which worshippers could perform the necessary ablution rites.

judged best guarded by divine supervision (Gelb, Steinkeller and Whiting 1991, 27–67). Other criteria may be assessed on a case-by-case basis. Conspicuous features of the Khafajeh Temple Oval, for instance, are not only the enormous energy expenditure connected with sinking the huge foundation pit filled in with (ritually?) clean sand, but also the fact that, unlike the ordinary habitation houses of the period or even their ruins, the structure did not contain a single human grave (Delougaz 1940, 15–19, esp. p. 19). Moreover, the concentration of subsistence and production activities in House D implies that the rest of the complex served other purposes. Another rather curious situation concerns the Tell Agrab Shara Temple, the later phase of which displays a markedly denser building layout of rectangular courtyard units than its earlier phase within the same enclosure area (Delougaz and Lloyd 1942, Pl. 26 as against 27). Here the boundary of the whole precinct may have been fixed in some way and, of course, one of the ways in which this might have happened is the delimitation of a cultically sanctioned, 'sacred' limit. Still another possibility may be the verification of cultic connotations of buildings (or parts thereof), the interiors of which display coatings of coloured paints (a series of white-painted 'altars' on a white floor at the Tell Agrab Shara Temple: Heinrich 1982, 119).

With respect to socially relevant textual data, I shall add but a brief summary of my recent research here. The preponderance of the pontifical couple of EN and NIN seems to have received the first blow with the establishment of the Jemdet Nasr age 'city league' which intruded upon their spheres of activity. In the times of archaic Ur (ED I), the EN retained his sacerdotal function but the NIN, detached from him, conferred the highest social prestige on her new partner, the LUGAL, whose status rose considerably (because the Ur EN was a lady). From this time on, the LUGAL and NIN titles are probably to be understood as 'king' and 'queen'. The denominations linked with kinship groups, É, and with the individual household heads, LÚ, still reflected general harmony and a high degree of personal responsibility towards others as a social ideal, but the age group of adult married women, the MÚRUB, vanished from administrative texts and the designation survived in lexical lists only (Charvát 1997, 59–70, 78–83, 85–92). We thus perceive both a distinct division of spiritual and temporal power, and a bias towards the preponderance of masculinity.

This discussion of the social characteristics of the pristine (ED I–ED IIIa) period of Mesopotamian history may now be closed with a brief review of the main results. The chief configuration of the contemporary social landscape may be seen in groupings which left behind traces of distinctive settlement features employing particular architectural forms (rectangular and oval enclosures encircling residential, storage, production and cultic facilities) to which I apply the traditional term *oikiai*. The *oikiai* employed their own subsistence and manufacturing organs, some of which grew out of foundations built by the know-how of preceding generations by constant cultivation and development of the technological heritage. At first, the *oikos* inhabitants practised mixed reciprocity and redistribution (with recognition of personal identity of external suppliers who sent in goods marked by their own seals) and indulged in ostentatious commensality, through which contemporary élites may have sought popular support. At the end of this period, redistribution prevailed together with monopolization of the sources of wealth (supplied by now without any intervening sealing straight to the storerooms of the possessors), as well as by its gathering and careful hoarding. The existence of several principles of internal structuring of the *oikiai* may be surmised. The discernible kinship features include patrilinear descent and patrilocal residence (at least in some cases) in ED IIIa, generalized matrimonial exchange and the possible existence of conical clans (attested to only in the Akkadian period). The category of sexual divisions, likely to have been present as early as the Uruk culture period, became operative in the Jemdet Nasr phase but probably constituted an internal classificatory device of social groupings ranked into hierarchical systems vis-à-vis one another, as complete units. It is only with the extinction of this principle(?) in ED IIIa that masculinity and femininity rose to the status of socially constitutive forces, detached from the sphere of purely biological factors (Ur 'royal cemetery'). Subsequent developments nonetheless brought about a suppression of the feminine 'social gender' and the decrease in sexual attributivity of grave goods. At least from ED II, the age principle seems to have been operated by the architects of Sumerian society to divide the adult population into the guruš stratum, under labour obligations, and the 'elder' stratum, charged with organizing, administrative and intellectual tasks. Of course, transition between the two would have been effected very simply and naturally with the advancing age of every physical person. Some of the *oikiai* doubtlessly specialized in religious functions but criteria for their identification must be developed and verified by future research.

The first part of the earlier ED segment thus appears to have been an 'aristocratic age' of élites who systematically cultivated their prowess in all kinds of physical and mental exercise (hunting as an élite attribute at Tell Gubba) but had to seek public prestige constantly by ostentatious practices of commensality, wherein they certainly had to invest much of the goods they were entitled to receive, and the supply of which under their conveyors' seals they duly acknowledged. Only in ED IIIa did the individualization and personalization of the wealth sources, now attached directly to their consumers, lead to the predominance of redistribution and to the rise in social roles played by material abundance and riches, now carefully hoarded and protected. This prevalence of essentially economic principles may have gone hand in hand with changes in the social sphere: coherence of kinship groupings may have been reinforced (undivided tenure of arable land with obligatory consent of all kith and kin to its alienation), gender roles may have been expanded to accommodate decision-making functions in various economic sectors (external for men, internal for women? with subsequent suppression of the female role) and labour obligations may have been laid upon the younger segment of Sumerian society in order to maximize the energy output which contemporary élites were able to manipulate. If ever there was a decisive turn towards statehood in Mesopotamian history, I am inclined to date it to ED IIIa.

The situation described above underwent a thorough transformation in the later part of ED III (ED IIIb). Contemporary social structures seem to take a turn towards simplification and integration. The variety of regional groupings with diverse structures gives way to large and, as it appears, regionally roughly comparable social strata which I am very much tempted to call 'middle class', displaying a fairly high living standard and a marked degree of self-recognition, dominated by local élites not much different from their social matrix on the course of action of which they exercise considerable influence. Reference has already been made to the disappearance of settlement layouts composed of spacious building complexes with (sometimes oval) enclosures. From now on, the architectural aspect of Mesopotamian cities is dominated by temple and palace buildings (on the palaces see Matthews 1991, 13) and by dense urban networks, some of which may be enclosed by city walls (the Diyala region: Henrickson 1981 and 1982). In their turn, the municipal strata now become foci of goods redistribution (finds of sealings in Khafajeh, Houses 2: Delougaz *et al.* 1967, 39, Kh III:329–335, Kh III:336–339; Tell Asmar, house layer Vb – As 32:1344, ibid. 212) and they proudly display their wealth even on their way to the nether world, as is amply demonstrated by the rich grave goods of contemporary cemeteries at Kiš (Moorey 1978, 61–75), Abu Salabikh (Postgate 1980b) and Khafajeh (Delougaz *et al.* 1967, 114–133). What happens here, in fact, very much resembles developments in Greece of the sixth–fifth century BC, where aspirations to elevated social status resulted in a distinctive *abrosuné* lifestyle (Kurke 1992, esp. pp. 94–98). It would be most interesting to see if the Sumerian social homogenization is also expressed by the abandonment of the earlier cemetery structure, showing groups of graves denoting possibly kinship groupings, and by laying out large and unified burial fields in which all the dead are laid to rest in a single spatial unit, for instance, in regular

Figure 6.17 Even in their now ruined state, the spacious residences of the Near Eastern élites of the third pre-Christian millennium, frequently composed of a central hall and lateral suites consisting of smaller rooms, convey the impression of majesty and monumentality.

alignments. Such trends, well exemplified by the earlier site of Kheit Qasim, the later phase of which displays just this 'Reihengräberfeld' situation (Forest 1983a, 140–142, Pl. 74–75) in contrast to the earlier cluster-type layout, may be observed in the future by documentation of plans of more coherent and well-excavated cemetery sites. The ED IIIb élites invariably faced the political determination of the citizenry who did not hesitate to put forward their claims, sometimes in a bold and assertive manner.

How did this social upheaval come about? There are signs that at least some of its constituent features might have been present even before ED IIIb, the sole difference being only better visibility of historical trends either by means of more abundant textual documentation or through more plentiful archaeological evidence. A number of new traits, pointed to above, appeared at the key site of Fara, referred to in the Sumerian King List as the last of the antediluvian kingdoms (Martin 1988, esp. pp. 121ff.; see also Matthews 1991 and on the SKL: Steiner 1988 and Young 1988). The present evidence shows that the Šuruppak kingdom may actually represent a first attempt at a re-unification of Sumer undertaken by a group of *oikiai* (extended families? lineages? clans?) following the social trends outlined above: individualization and personalization of wealth sources and predominance of redistribution in public affairs, leading to an increasing concentration of material abundance and riches in the economic sphere; closer coherence of kinship groups, possibly with the intention of keeping together their possessions and perhaps of suppressing possible dispersal factors (lowering of feminine status after the time of the Ur 'royal cemetery' rich graves, which at any rate represent but a historical episode?), together with the imposition of labour obligations on a segment of the population of all Sumer (see in review Matthews 1991, 11) in the social sphere. In regional administration, the Šuruppak kingdom introduced the GAR-ensi$_2$ system whereby officials bearing this title directed individual sites and took orders from GAR-ensi₂-gal's who were distinguished by divine names (Martin 1988, 119–121). The system may thus have elaborated a religiously inspired network of exchanges, represented possibly by the Jemdet Nasr and archaic Ur 'collective sealings'. In its time, this kingdom must have constituted a formidable bastion of power. Prominent personages of the day certainly took no time in learning a number of important lessons here.

Textual data point to the almost total dominance of the LUGAL and NIN, true kings and queens. The NIN are now clearly persons conferring authority over something, which is reflected even in divine names: Ningirsu is not the 'lady of Girsu' but the 'person conferring authority over Girsu'. The EN, confined to the sphere of cult and ritual, are concerned with fertility and, interestingly enough, acquire an ambivalent gender, with at least some of their epithets feminine. The individual kinship groupings, the É (= *bitu*, 'house', 'home', 'kin'), now show a certain amount of social discord and competition for higher-status positions in society. The original denomination of individual household heads, the LÚ, now acquires a wider meaning of 'human being, individual of the human species' (Charvát 1997, 35–39, 67–68, 74–75, 80–81, 87–88).

For some reason, the Šuruppak kingdom did not survive very long. Nevertheless, the social situation following its fall developed in a direction so different from the preceding trends that the flood simile, used by the SKL, describes the state of affairs most fittingly, regardless of whether the foundations of the power of Šuruppak were actually undermined by a natural catastrophe or by some other fatal event.

Socio-political developments in the succeeding Early Dynastic segment may be roughly subsumed under a triadic sequence of notions pertaining to the character of direction forces prevalent in the community in question: charisma, power and divinity. These developments find their best illustration in the two successor kingdoms to the Šuruppak polity, namely Kiš and Ur. At Kiš, burials of persons equipped with wheeled vehicles, traction animals and non-average grave goods most likely belonging to charismatic leaders turned up in pre-ED III contexts (Moorey 1978, 103–115, in the Y sounding, see also Algaze 1983–1984, esp. pp. 137–154). This phase is followed by the erection of architectural monuments including those embodying the quest of charismatic leaders for public power, such as the Planoconvex Building and the Palace, probably sometime during ED IIIa (Moorey 1978, 34–61). At Kiš,

Figure 6.18 A Sumerian warrior of the Early Dynastic age on a mother-of-pearl inlay from Mari (after Spycket 1989, 417, Fig. 12)

this phase clearly ends in a violent destruction of these buildings; but this need not always be the case. The earlier residences on the West Mound of Abu Salabikh or those of Fara, for instance, seem to have been evacuated and simply abandoned to the elements. The only Kiš structure that proved its vitality for the subsequent period of time was the temple precinct containing both ziggurats and built also in ED IIIa (Moorey 1978, 88), which survived until another disaster in ED IIIb (ibid. 98). In this connection it is remarkable that while the Kiš deity, Zababa, is missing from the earlier Šuruppak records, it does turn up in contemporary Abu Salabikh texts (ibid. 19) and that one of the earliest inscriptions of Kiš rulers credits one Mr. Uhub ([?], Sollberger and Kupper 1971, 39, No. IA2; Steible and Behrens 1982, II:214–215; Cooper 1984, 92–93, Pl. Va; Pomponio 1994b, 10–11) with the somewhat unexpected title of ensi$_2$. Did the re-arrangement of the social structure at Kiš include a (deliberate?) rise in the status of a local deity (or even the introduction of an entirely new one?), provided with a new temple at the end of ED IIIa, as well as the taking over of the (incomplete) regional title of Šuruppak administrator by the local ruler? At any rate, the 'post-diluvial' Kiš-I dynasty sovereigns systematically developed (socially desirable?) sponsorship of religious institutions (see Sollberger and Kupper 1971, 39–41; Steible and Behrens 1982, II:213–222, and also Gelb, Steinkeller and Whiting 1991, 91–92, No. 26 on king Enna-Il; on texts linked with Urzaged of Kiš: Pomponio 1994a, 599; on a new source, a 'gazetteer of the Kish kingdom': Luciani 1999, 1–2). This trend may well have started with (En)Mebaragesi, listed in the Nippur Tummal inscription as builder of that temple, whose authentic text turned up in one of the Diyala region shrines(?), the Temple Oval, obviously the earliest of the oval sacred precincts(?) of ED III Mesopotamia (Delougaz 1940, 146–150, No. 2 of L 46:4; Steible and Behrens 1982, II:213). In view of the similarity of its oval outline to the enclosures of the earlier *oikiai* premises, and of the clear connection of the two remaining oval shrines (Aannepadda's Obeid structure and Enannatum's Ibgal at al-Hiba) with Sumerian royalty, it may legitimately be asked whether the oval ground plan does not constitute a sacred version of the earlier profane structures of its kind and whether the Khafajeh structure, visibly a major monument within an area dominated by the Kiš kings, was not established by (En)Mebaragesi himself who might thus have founded a tradition imitated subsequently by southern rulers. That buildings surrounded by oval enclosures did carry a cultic significance is indicated by the 'offering' of a model of such a structure, provided with domestic pottery, at Mari (Moorey 1978, 69; Mallowan 1965, 85, Ill. 92). At Ur, events apparently took much the same course. Whatever the roots of the social situation of personages buried in the foremost positions of its 'royal graves', the fact is that they enjoyed great respect among their fellow citizens and, in consequence of that, their charismatic nature can hardly be doubted. Nevertheless, charismatic or not, these leaders obviously took interest in building social structures that could keep them in power. This may be indicated by analysis of the 'production' or 'property marks' on objects from rich Ur graves (Woolley 1934, 64, 175, 309, 317, 553–554 and Pl. 190; for a more recent reproduction see Maddin, Wheeler and Muhly 1977, 40, Fig. 15). Such designs are hardly production marks as they occur on very different objects. The axe sign (Maddin, Wheeler and Muhly 1977, 40, Fig. 15) turns up on spear-heads (Woolley 1934, 64), copper (U.10081: Woolley 1934, 553, Pl. 190; U.7994, ibid. 526), electrum (U.10554, ibid. 317) and silver bowls (U 10864 = BM 121454, from PG 800: Reade 2001, 20, n. 102) and on a copper adze blade (BM 120732: ibid. 553–554, Pl. 190) but also on a stone bowl (U.8135, Woolley 1934, 64). Even more conspicuous is the case of the NU or ŠEŠ sign (Woolley 1934, 317), appearing on the blade of the famous golden dagger (Mallowan 1965, 101, Ill. 113), but also on the shoulders of an ordinary clay pot (Woolley 1934, 175, from PG 1374). Still less likely seems to be their interpretation as property marks, since objects bearing the same mark invariably turned up in several graves. The axe sign is borne by objects from PG 43 (Woolley 1934, 526, Pl. 190), 135 (ibid. 64), 755 (ibid. 317, Pl. 177; 553, Pl. 190), 789 (ibid. 64) and 800 (ibid. 317 and Reade 2001, 20, n. 102). The NU/ŠEŠ sign occurs on the dagger from PG 580 (Mallowan 1968, 42) and on a pot from PG 1374 (Woolley 1934, 175). These observations render unlikely the hypothesis that sees in such marks signatures of their manufacturers or users, but would not exclude their interpretation as an 'address', identifying, in this case, consumers of the marked objects from élite circles. Both the character of the axe sign and its occurrence on metal and stone items likely to possess a high military and social value may imply its role as a designator of goods to be used in the circles of the social élite, for instance by the retinues or entourages of Ur kings and queens. If this was so, then the power of charismatic figures at the head of the community could have been buttressed by the existence of very real social bodies to which the supplying of various specialized services, including law and order enforcement, could have been entrusted.

Nevertheless, the glamour of early Ur royalty faded fairly soon, as is indicated by archaeological evidence concerning the succeeding group of prominent personages of Ur, first and foremost its king Mesannepadda (Nissen 1966, 115, 143–146; Orthmann 1975, 232, Fig. 43f.; Sollberger and Kupper 1971, 41–42, No. IB4a). Refuse layers covering the 'royal graves' and containing impressions of Mesannepadda's seal bearing his royal Kiš title, as well as a hoard of precious objects discovered at Mari and including an inscribed bead referring to him (Orthmann 1970, 100–101; Sollberger and Kupper 1971, 42, No. IB4c; Moortgat and Moortgat-Correns 1974; Boese 1978; Steible and Behrens 1982, II:272–273; Renger 1984; Cooper 1986) show that his reign brought about another radical departure from earlier traditions and an orientation towards power based outside the maternal community, very likely in the direction of armed conquest. This policy might have been adopted even earlier: a new reading of the bead referring to him from Mari shows that the Kiš title might have been borne even by king Meskalamdu, Mesannepadda's father (Nagel and Strommenger 1995, 461). Even Mesannepadda's power, however, 'withered like grass cut in the morning' and his son and successor Aannepadda thought it most expedient to provide for his community by foundation of a temple of Ninkhursag, by an interesting coincidence also enclosed in an oval precinct (Delougaz 1938; Lloyd 1960, 29; Mallowan 1965, 16–17, Ill. 4; 38, Ill. 26; 51, Ill. 43; Nissen 1966, 136; Hrouda 1971, 34, 115, Fig. 40; Sollberger and Kupper 1971, 42–43; Steible and Behrens 1982, II:273–274). This deed of a descendant of a most powerful Sumerian ruler who instead of enjoying the prestige and glory of his father's conquests turns his mind to pious deeds must surely carry a meaning. A hint at the possible interpretation is offered by one of the later ED texts of Ur (Burrows 1935, Suppl. text 6:1, from SIS 1 or 2, p. 23), mentioning a 'bara$_2$ an-ne$_2$-pa$_3$-da'. Now if the bara$_2$ really represents a seat in the Kengir League assembly (Wilcke 1974, 228), it may refer here to Aannepadda's royal throne but, as I believe, could apply with equal ease to the throne-dais of the goddess Ninkhursag, residing in Aannepadda's temple. Perhaps the bara$_2$ notion expressed both royal and divine suzerainty embodied in an 'Eigenkirche', the Caesaro-papist idea of a divine tabernacle legitimizing a royal throne and vice versa. The charisma–power–divinity triad is by no means limited to the ED kingdoms of Kiš and Ur. At Lagaš, the charismatic leader and founder Urnanše (for he had apparently no other claim to the throne) is followed by Eannatum, a nearly perfect incarnation of the martial aspect of Early Dynastic leaders' policy, after whom Enannatum, building another oval temple (Hansen 1970 and 1973; Crawford 1974 and 1977; Biggs 1976; Mudar 1982), turned the ambitions of Lagaš rulers towards religion. After his time, running for public popularity seems to have taken on the form of sponsorship of perpetual institutions, as is demonstrated not only by the occurrence of Eannatum's and Enannatum's sealings found in Enannatum's Ibgal (Hansen 1973, 68, Fig. 19, 69f. and 1987), but also by such exquisite pieces as Entemena's silver vase (Sollberger and Kupper 1971, 69, No. IC7e; Steible and Behrens 1982, I:250–251; Müller-Karpe 1990a, 173; see Figure 6.19). The early history of Umma is slightly

Figure 6.19 A silver vase of Enmetena or Entemena, ensi of Lagash (*c.*25th–24th century BC) (after Müller-Karpe, Pászthory and Pernicka 1993, Table 106: 1280)

more nebulous, but it has been suggested recently that one of its early kings might have been identical with Agga, son of Gilgameš (Cooper 1981, 228, n. 25, and a bead inscription in Katz 1993, as cited by Böck 1996, 28; for the ED history of Umma see Nissen 1966, 122–123; Sollberger and Kupper 1971, 83–84; Steible and Behrens 1982, II:265–270). The city of Umma, constantly ordered around by its aggressive neighbour Lagaš, had to wait for its D-day until the united monarchy of Lugalzagesi, an embodiment of both the state-power component and the divine element. He is considered today – most pertinently, from the point of view expounded here – to have been the builder of the enormous 'Stampflehmgebäude' at Uruk (Boehmer 1991, 468), the spiritual or temporal character of which remains to be determined. Early Dynastic Uruk came to the fore with the reign of the energetic Enšakušanna (Pomponio 1994b). It thus seems that the emergence of most of the early state centres of Mesopotamia can be visualized as a drama in three acts: communal impact of the élite charisma, emanating out of individual and personal achievement, is followed by attempts to perpetuate it by socially engineered force, leading, in their turn, after strenuous efforts sometimes resulting in ruin and disaster befalling the community in question, to the decision to entrust the supreme power where it most appropriately belongs, to the realm of the immaterial.

What happened, in fact, with the demise of the old kin-based aristocracy and intensification of intra-community rivalry at the close of ED III was a sudden rush of wealth display both in the ordinary graves and at the places of worship, which seem to have assumed the role of an arena of vying for social superiority. This is likely to reflect an increase in competition for status, represented in two aspects. First and foremost, individual citizens might have displayed in the funerary equipment of their dead, richer and more diversified than before, ambitions and aspirations put forward by their social groupings, perhaps in the manner comparable to the 'Reihengräberzivilisation' of early medieval Europe, which is also characterized as an open, competitive and ranked society (Steuer 1989). The same social rivalry may be discerned in the sponsorship of public institutions which is well documented in archaic Greece in the eighth–sixth pre-Christian centuries as a vehicle for expression of social aspirations in an age when the power of traditional élites was crumbling (Morris 1986, esp. pp. 11–13). At any rate, all these changes point to the transformative character of the final ED III period when the old order gave way and only the basic constituents of the new structures were emerging out of the ensuing chaos.

Do we have any indications as to the position of the temples, terminal links of a prolonged communal development resulting in the transfer of the ultimate power to the celestial sphere, in the social life of Early Dynastic Sumer? First and foremost, let us notice that contemporary élites established temples as public institutions with the intention of serving all the needs of the respective communities. I proceed to illustrate this point in more detail. It is indicated, initially, by the landed property of the temples which, as far as can be seen, consisted either of 'public' lands, which the local rulers disposed of on grounds of their administrative powers (e.g. Enannatum I determining the 'šuku-^{d}nanše': Lambert 1956, 106; for Entemena see Sollberger and Kupper 1971, 66–67, No. IC7a, col. V–VI; Steible and Behrens 1982, I:213–214), or of gifts of privately held estates (Entemena gives away a part of the family heritage: Sollberger and Kupper 1971, 66, No. IC7a, col. V; Steible and Behrens 1982, I:213–214). Whatever the origin of the temple lands, the terms of their tenure changed profoundly upon their transfer to divine property. Unfortunately, in the investigation of transactions with temple land we can rely only on information involving the city rulers, with a silent hope that the other users of temple lands managed this property in more or less similar ways. Nonetheless, the affairs of city-state rulers are the only ones sufficiently illuminated by written sources, so that we have no other data to go by. With respect to the well-known tripartite division of temple land into ni$_2$-en-na, ni$_2$-šuku (allotments to temple personnel) and ni$_2$-uru$_4$-la$_2$ (land leased out to tenants), Benjamin Foster (1981,

240f.) suggests that the Lagaš ni$_2$-en-na belonged to the ensi$_2$ and his wife in pre-Uruinimgina times. Yvonne Rosengarten (1960a, 350f.; for a particular case see p. 55) denies this, identifying the type of land tenure of the ensi$_2$ and his wife as šuku. She goes on to observe that the ruling family did have private estates of a limited extent (ibid. 348; for an 'e$_2$-Lummaturak', likely to denote such a private estate of a person bearing the name of Eannatum's son, see Biggs 1976, 10:X:1–2). A similar point of view has been taken by Jean-Jacques Glassner (1993, 17–18). At any rate, the ruling family clearly did not dispose of the entire temple land, because if that were the case, the Uruinimgina reforms, aimed at a more regular and more appropriate distribution of arable land and the means of labour within the temple domains and their users, would not have made any sense and would not have happened at all. Tenure of temple lands by the ruling family thus shows that other citizens might also have held rights to their use, perhaps in a manner comparable to the Roman 'ager publicus'. It may be noted *en passant* that those who benefited most from Uruinimgina's reforms were by no means the most destitute among the citizens of Lagaš, but included a sizeable segment of craft specialists, officials and religious personnel (Foster 1981, 239f.). The same goes for the situation at Zabalam where king Lugalzagesi presided over the distribution of land allotments to a number of officials without trumpeting his intentions of a reform (Powell 1978b, 26–27). On the Nippur situation see Foster 1977, esp. p. 300; Maurice Lambert's 'Grand document juridique de Nippur' may, in fact, be from Isin and seems close to the Lugalzagesi texts, at least palaeographically (Wilcke 1996, 47–67, esp. p. 48). The right to allotments of temple land thus appears to have rested to a considerable extent in persons who were prevented from engaging in full-time agricultural activities by their professions and occupations. How far this was a consequence of purely practical considerations or of the fact that such persons could have enjoyed a special status (fully privileged citizens?), must be decided by future research. The Uruinimgina reform texts (Steible and Behrens 1982, I:278–322) go on to show that in addition to land, means of labour such as tools and traction animals were also available to the users of temple lands. Authentic documents point to the fact that these people also had a right to the usufruct of the temple fields (Rosengarten 1960a, 50 – a part of the harvest of a particular field 'sealed'[?] as property of ensi$_2$ while another part was stored apart; for 'rations' received by some personnel for only a part of the year = contributions from public funds in times of need see Lambert 1957, 128–129; Maekawa 1976, 43; Ellison 1981, 37). Economically, the temples thus appear to have constituted reserves of arable soil, to the use of which the citizenry (or at least a substantial segment thereof) had a right (šuku or uru$_4$-la$_2$), while the rulers presided over its assignment but were by no means the only ones to enjoy its possession or usufruct. Of course, the real state of things may have been infinitely more complex: the various possession rights and titles may have been sub-let, split, ceded and the like; various property operations of this time included, possibly, transactions close to the emphyteutic leases known from Late Antiquity or even loans of capital with interest (Powell 1977, 28; interest in early Mesopotamia: Hudson 2000; for a good review of Late Antique property modes of tenure: Rouche 1980, 101–104). It is my belief that the essential idea of temple lands as blocks of arable soil which could be used by entitled persons, administered by the temple personnel and distributed under supervision of the city-state rulers, may not be too far from the truth.

For the ED IIIb élites, the temples constituted an economically important 'reserve fund of power', by the skilful manipulation of which they could exercise a considerable influence over the welfare of the citizenry. The same trend may be discerned in the social sphere. The temples constituted separate organization units administered by the sanga officials (Rosengarten 1960a, 347) and foci around which social groupings of a particular kind crystallized, involving persons designated as 'elders' (Gelb 1984, 268ff. – elders of Suen of Ur and of Nanše and Siraran of Lagaš; Glassner 1993, 17–18). The coordinating and administrative roles of city-state rulers in the social life of the temples took on a similar garb as in the economic sphere. They exercised influence on the appointment of temple officials, if they did not nominate them straight off, deriving an extra income from the 'Begrüssungsgeschenke', or nomination gifts, of these dignitaries (mašdaria: Rosengarten 1960b, 71–85). In addition to this, they could in this way undoubtedly influence the composition of temple personnel or the management of their reserves in a manner which they deemed profitable. Of equal importance must have been the transfer of the guruš labour obligations from the Fara period *oikiai* to ED IIIb temples; contemporary rulers, directing this form of public energy expenditure as overall managers and protectors of the shrines, acquired by it a most powerful and efficient tool which, if handled properly, could help the communities in question for a long time in the future (on corvée-work modalities at Nippur see Foster 1977, esp. pp. 300–301). Here we perceive again the ED IIIb city-state rulers not as the richest citizens, who would have held extensive landed-property complexes and lived lives of leisure and luxury, but as managers and administrators who wielded considerable public power but whose strength and prestige was determined by the skill with which they fulfilled the tasks entrusted to them by their respective communities, rather than by noble blood, treasure chests or weaponry of followers. Of course, this role of administrators and overseers of public domains added further tasks to the burden of contemporary city-state heads. Their duties – occasionally illustrated in the sources – included decisions concerning questions of common interest such as, for instance, the codification of weights and measures (see Powell 1979, esp. pp. 79ff.), but, more pertinently, vigilance over public justice and blunting the impact of moments of crisis of various types by extraordinary measures such as the cancellation of debts (Entemena: Steible and Behrens 1982, I:267–270, esp. p. 269). It may be redundant to recall here such a typical component of the powers of Sumerian sovereigns as war command, since military operations not only find frequent descriptions in written sources, but the social prestige of warfare must have risen very high. That is demonstrated not only by the Ur cemetery, but also by subsequent texts from the Akkadian period, pointing to public ceremonies (exquisite tableware and furniture) and to warfare (weapons) as the main components of proceedings at the royal court, albeit in a symbolic manner (Foster 1980, 33ff.; for Ebla: Pomponio 1998). A transformation of tactical skills in the final ED III period brought about an increased deployment of archery (Miller, McEwen and Bergman 1986, esp. p. 189).

The temples thus functioned as an economic and social 'public reserve' of Early Dynastic Sumer. It now remains to establish how far and in what manner the spiritual and intellectual activities which took place in them contribute to the investigation of the social developments of the period in consideration. Up to that period, the foremost spiritual achievement of the early Sumerians – the script – served in the *oikiai* for the administration of temporal affairs and for the preservation of the ancient cultural heritage, as well as for the training of specialists in this art and the recording of deeds of permanent character. These were placed under the tutelage of the gods in the shrines (ancient kudurrus, see Gelb, Steinkeller and Whiting 1991; Glassner 1995 and 2000a). In itself, however, the script apparently possessed no particular intrinsic value and was handled rather summarily in earlier ED, as is indicated by the careless finish of the Diyala region inscriptions (Delougaz 1940, 146–150; Delougaz and Lloyd 1942, 290–297) or early Nippur dedication inscriptions (Goetze 1970). Things changed considerably in ED IIIb. Documents on permanent materials still occupied a major position among the inscribed monuments but the recording sphere grew beyond all measure, incorporating now and ever after all the complex redistribution transactions that had gone on at least since ED IIIa quite smoothly, absolutely without writing, evidenced by hardly more than the door sealings, in tens of thousands of carefully and elegantly written texts, a flood of which swept over the registry offices of the Lagaš authorities under the last rulers of the Urnanše dynasty (see, more recently, Marzahn 1991 and 1996). This

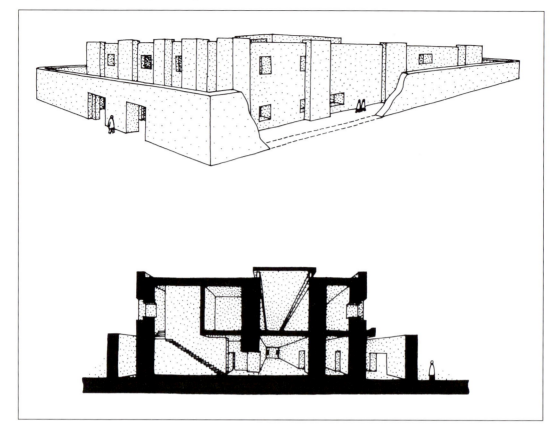

Figure 6.20 Reconstruction of an Early Dynastic Sumerian temple. The Bagara of Ningirsu at Lagash (after Margueron 1996, 37, Fig. 9)

proliferation of, and insistence on, written records for all the administrative goings-on, quite unexpected, illogical and ill-suited to the actual extent and complexity of the public tasks to be tackled, bears out eloquently the public character of the text-producing institutions which could be held responsible and accountable for their management of the public realm and henceforth felt induced to note down all their proceedings in writing. Such activities of the ancient scribes fill the hearts of present-day cuneiformists with delight but must have once represented a consider-able obstacle to the smooth and efficient running of Lagaš's affairs, and becoming ultimately, quite in the spirit of Professor Parkinson's laws, an end in themselves. It fills me with no wonder at all that when Lugalzagesi's troops marched through the Lagaš territories, all that the administra-tion of the realms of Nanše and Ningirsu could put up were the undoubtedly well-trimmed pens of their clerks, capable of releasing waterfalls of tears of righteous suffering, but hardly a match for spears, maces, bows, arrows and other military gear. On the other hand – and seriously – a substantial innovation was achieved with the appearance of the first literary texts ever written, which belong to this period (Civil and Biggs 1966; on Abu Salabikh see Postgate 1982; on early incantations see Cunningham 1997). The question why such compositions suddenly found their way to the domain of the written word certainly merits a deeper consideration. How far these texts – lexical materials, temple hymns, incantations, a father's advice to a son and proverbs – represent written samples of orally transmitted creations must be determined by future research (on relationships between oral and literary expression see, for instance, Hagège 1987, 75–99). Two reasons may be relevant here. First, textualization of a certain body of orally transmitted literature occurs at historical moments when such creations are in some way threatened, by a menace to the carrier society itself or to its social balance, or, alternatively, by the emergence of new versions thought for whatever reasons to depart from the canonical, and hence desirable, tradition. Both reasons may well apply to Early Dynastic Sumer. The ED IIIa period during which most of these texts turned up for the first time was certainly a turbulent period, seeing as it did the climax but also the subsequent decline and collapse of the traditional *oikos* system. An alternative solution may be found in the institutionalization of secular and public power, the representatives of which may have felt the urge to put forward binding and canonical versions of some of the spiritual constructs necessary for proper conduct of the relevant affairs. Signs pointing to the latter possibility may be perceived, I believe, in hints that these literary works constitute expressions of the mentalities of different social groups. This is very probably the case of the 'Instructions of Šuruppak' (most recently Alster 1991, 154), perhaps written as a 'Fürstenspiegel' for the offspring of élite social groups. Other bodies of professionals seeking legitimation of their social status by worship of divine representatives or embodiments of their own crafts or products (in the Fara divinity lists: Krebernik 1986, esp. pp. 165–166) may not have advanced as far as a consistent expression of their group mentality, but an alternative solution would place an initiative in this direction in the hands of temple élites who, trying to codify in writing their own visions of a civilized society (see also the courage to manipulate traditional textual material now receiving additions: Green 1984) and to handle these as vehicles for putting forward their own social pretensions, could have emerged as a group with a very distinct collective mentality (on this see pp. 153–154). Conscious of their indispensability to public administration, the implementation of the power of which they in fact enabled, but also to the citizenry, to which they provided the spiritual dimension of their existence, they might well have acted not only as assistants but even as partners and sometimes even superiors of the pretenders to secular power. All in all, even the intellectual sphere now underwent changes well in line with the overall historical trend. Elaborating on the earlier concepts of writing and its position in society, temple élites of ED IIIb, induced doubtless by their rulers with whose kith and kin they sometimes merged, wielded the script at once as an efficient tool for the control of a temple, and hence public(-property) management, and as a carrier of social recognition of the claims that the various professional groups and strata put forward. From a sacred-cum-profane recording and symbol-wielding device the script suddenly changes into a vehicle for political manipulation and a high-status tool which may be employed by the élites to control their followers (checking of temple records) but which can also voice the demands of those who feel they are being overmanipulated. Ultimately, the script became a corollary of real events both in a social crisis (Uruinimgina's reforms) and in a political disaster (lament over Lugalzagesi's raid on Lagaš, Steible and Behrens 1982, I:334–337). In the last words of the latter text, calling down divine sanction on the invader of the apparently helpless Lagaš, the quest for truly public power, apparent in the economic and social sphere of the temple activities, enters the intellectual realm as well.

The social characterisation of the Jemdet Nasr and Early Dynastic periods may now be closed with a brief review of the results. The Jemdet Nasr period witnessed the disintegration of the Uruk corporate entity into a cluster of small-scale replicas of it (or was this a re-emergence of its original components?), more or less self-contained but interlinked through a network of exchange activities through which limited quantities of goods in containers percolated, probably as a recognition of mutual obligations or rather of alliance ties among these communities. Of the structural principles on which such communities were built, only the existence of some kind of ranking and subgroup affiliation, as well as the sexual division, may be suspected. The earlier part of ED was dominated by *oikiai*, the relationship of which to the Jemdet Nasr period communities is to be elucidated by further research, directed by their élites, economically well developed and practising mixed reciprocity and redistribution with acknowledgment of the roles of the suppliers of exchanged commodities. Ostentatious commensality and the publicly proclaimed ideas of overall social harmony probably buttressed the political prestige of the élites and helped them to win public favour. Among the principles on which their internal structuring rested, we may guess at kinship (patrilineal descent, patrilocal residence?, generalized matrimonial exchange?), sex (sexual bipolarity in cemeteries; early textual signs of lowering of female status until ED IIIa, when a turn towards male domination is discernible) and age (labour obligations of the guruš, 'younger' stratum towards the elders?). In the political sphere, the position of EN, from now on confined to the religious sphere, was conferred by the NIN on the LUGAL. Long-term trends brought transformations in ED IIIa: the increasing status of material wealth, now anxiously amassed and carefully hoarded, was followed by the prevalence of redistribution with immediate subordination of the supplier agencies to the redistributors and weakening of the interpersonal character of producer–consumer relations. How far the adjustments of social order, including firmer coherence of kinship groups (consent of the entire kin in land alienation) and deeper hierarchical structuring in the sense of lowering of the status of some kin groups and persons (women), followed economic change remains to be assessed. These trends were apparently involved in the emergence of the Šuruppak polity, the first unified social body to cover all Sumer since the times of the Uruk corporate entity, in ED IIIa. This introduced a homogeneous system of regional administration and was clearly able to mobilize a fairly large amount of energy from the subordinate population (guruš corvée work); we may perhaps imagine it as an aristocratic kingdom under the sway of a few élite patriarchal lineages, acknowledging the supremacy of a single king. At that time, the LUGAL and NIN ruled over an increasingly competitive social scene in which the individual kinship groups, the É, tried to move as high as they could while the EN discharged their religious, cultic and fertility ritual duties. The end of the Šuruppak polity was followed by the 'translatio imperii' towards power bases in other regions built up by prominent personages with a very powerful charisma (Kiš and Ur graves) who attempted to stretch their social superiority over larger social segments but invariably failed, bringing to collapse the public functioning of the preceding social structures. Learning well the lesson of the decline and fall of their predecessors, sovereigns of the terminal ED invested in temples, intending to make them into spiritual and temporal 'reserve funds of power'. The last segment of the Early Dynastic period is characterized by the social predominance of the 'middle-class' citizenry who determined the course of public affairs together with the ruling élites; both these groups now compete with their claims to social prominence. The élites open the game with the establishment of temples as 'public reserves' of economic wealth, socio-political power and spiritual achievement; in this they perhaps imitate the deeds of sovereigns of the 'golden age' of Sumerian monarchy (Kiš and Ur). The citizenry accept but turn the rules to their own benefit, jealously guarding their own profits, public positions and intellectual prerogatives, and calling the élites to account if an infringement of the generally acknowledged rules is deemed to have occurred. Developments of this kind do, to a certain extent, remind the observer of what happened in Archaic and Classical Greece; there is almost the impression that civilization's first democracy was born in Sumer at the close of the Early Dynastic period.

Metaphysics

It has already been noted that the Jemdet Nasr period saw the re-emergence of archaeologically retrievable burials of human bodies (e.g. the Ur 'Jemdet Nasr' cemetery: Forest 1983a, 117–132;

Kolbus 1982 and 1983). The situation thus reverts to 'normal' in comparison with the preceding Uruk culture period. Let us start this review of spiritual developments over the period of key importance for the survival for one of the world's first civilizations with a glance at the burial evidence.

The extent of the surviving cemeteries implies, at first, the question as to what proportion of Jemdet Nasr to ED interments may be documentable by modern archaeological methods as against those unlikely to be retrieved at all (Pollock 1985, 129ff. and 1991, 372–373). Given the extent of the settled areas and especially urban agglomerations, the number of burials excavated appears ridiculously small; far more eloquent in this connection is the above cited Egyptian example of Proto-historic Hierakonpolis with thousands of graves unearthed and tens of thousands of graves postulated. This contradiction implies that we have to reckon with the existence of modes of burial that leave no discernible traces in the archaeological record. One of the cases which may explain such a situation in the Near East are the huge collective ossuaries containing remains of inhabitants of Early Bronze Age cities along the Dead Sea coast (Rast 1987; Schaub and Rast 1989; Schaub 1997). By way of an example, let us refer here to a most colourful but for our present tastes slightly gruesome review of burial practices current in a socially comparable stage of nascent South Indian statehood available in the classical works of Tamil Sangam literature from the beginning of the post-Christian era. These list disposal of the dead by cremation, exposure to the elements and pit-, tomb- or urn-burial (Casal and Casal 1956, 49–52, esp. p. 51; *Manimegalai* VI, 36–96). All this converges to indicate that the surviving cemeteries of the Jemdet Nasr to Early Dynastic age can hardly be considered an objective and unbiased historical source (to say nothing of their physical-anthropology value). They constitute no more than one component of a very specific context which clearly underwent deliberate manipulation, a fragment of evidence that we perceive today not because it supplies an accurate and exhaustive testimony of past human behaviour but because these procedures – and only these, of all that presumably existed – leave traces in the archaeological record (on a modern account of archaeological interpretation of the mortuary evidence see Bolt 1992, 1–5).

Let us then try to decode the message left by those burial practices accessible to us at present. Some of the sites excavated during the Jebel Hamrin campaign such as Ahmad al-Hattu (Sürenhagen 1980, 1981 and 1983–1984; Eickhhof 1993) or Kheit Qasim (Forest 1983a, 133–148 and 1996, 195–204) present clear evidence to the effect that ED I cemeteries functioned as a communication between the world of the living and of the dead, most probably in the form of ancestral cults, which are illustrated also by the introduction of the 'ancestor' sign at Jemdet Nasr (see p. 205). This is suggested both by finds of storage jars and drinking cups, sometimes together with animal bones, by some of the largest Kheit Qasim tombs (Forest 1983a, 136 and 1996, 198, Fig. 133; absent in the later ED I phase, ibid. 139–140) and by a peculiar type of building at Ahmad al-Hattu with a T-shaped ground plan, the easternmost part of which contained the burial while the central and western parts yielded ash deposits, bones and sherds (Sürenhagen 1981, 42). Such finds and structures seem to reflect the impact of ceremonies taking place by the tombs, perhaps in commemoration of the deceased or on some other occasion that brought the dead into contact with the living. These practices seem to have been present in the northern regions as well (Tell Mohamed Arab: Roaf 1983, 74, grave 54 V:23; on burials on the site in general see Bolt 1992), but again probably tended to single out socially prominent personalities, since other graves lacked such provisions (a girl's[?] grave with personal possessions only: Jakob-Rost, Wartke and Wesarg 1983, 127–128). Contemporary cemeteries in the south fail to exhibit such elaborate facilities for the cult of the dead but contain predominantly pottery grave goods of the same tableware character as that turning up by the northern tombs (spouted vases, solid-footed goblets and conical bowls – the Diyala region, for instance:

Delougaz *et al.* 1967, 77–114, Houses 10–4; on dating see Karg 1984–1985, 306), implying that the deceased could receive for their journey into the nether world vessels used in (or destined for?) a funerary feast. Nevertheless, it is probably significant that built brick tombs characterize this period even in the Diyala region (Delougaz *et al.* 1967, Houses 8 to 4, 88–114) as, together with remains of the funerary cults, they may imply that only persons of some social standing, in all probability household heads and their immediate dependants, were entitled to a more elaborate entombment and (or) to obsequies at the graveside.

The gate connecting the world of the living and of the dead clanged shut in ED IIIa. All the contemporary large cemeteries display the meaningful change: no more excessive quantities of tableware, no more individual built tombs (the tip of the élite always excepted, of course) and no more – or very little – evidence of graveside ceremonies. On the other hand, the large numbers of interments of ED IIIa show a wealth of grave goods unparalleled before but clearly intended to emphasize the individual status of every particular deceased individual. Personal ornaments, articles of individual use such as cosmetic containers or toilet sets and exquisite table vessels indicate the personal well-being of men, women and children buried at Khafajeh (Delougaz *et al.* 1967, 114–133, Houses 3–2; dating in Karg 1984–1985, 306), Kiš A (Mackay 1929, see also Moorey 1978, 61–75) and Abu Salabikh (Postgate 1980b). This accords with what I have suggested above concerning the superimposition of blood and kinship ties by the 'citizen' status, assumed in the course of individual life chiefly on account of personal achievement, during ED IIIb. Again, we should bear in mind that these 'citizens' represent but a fraction of the inhabitants of contemporary Sumerian cities (much as in Classical Athens?), a sample of a sample of the original population. All this notwithstanding, the change is apparent and systematic. A marginal note: this trend of rich personal equipment worn for the grave continues until the Akkadian period but there it tends to mark graves of truly 'middle class' individuals (Moorey 1984, 10). Nevertheless, its beginning is marked by a phenomenon of extraordinary significance which must be mentioned here at least briefly. I am, of course, referring to the now legendary 'royal graves' of Ur (Moorey 1977 and 1984; Pollock 1985 and 1991; Reade 2001, 15–26).

From the moment of their discovery, these fabulously rich interments served as vehicles for individual views and opinions rather than as targets of unbiased, strictly arguable and socially relevant interpretative procedures. Leonard (later Sir Leonard) Woolley,

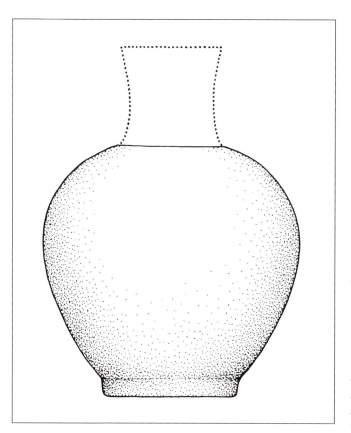

Figure 6.21 A copper/bronze jar from the grave of King Meskalamdu at Ur (after Müller-Karpe, Pászthory and Pernicka 1993, Table 153: 1281)

Figure 6.22 Excavation of the Early Dynastic building at Jemdet Nasr brought to light a contemporary burial, a good example of how the deceased were treated in the earlier part of the Early Dynastic age. The body was laid in the grave with contracted legs, arms bent in front of the body and hands in front of the face. The grave was equipped with a few pottery vessels, including three beakers, one of which rested in front of the deceased's face. This shows that the custom of putting a cup in front of the deceased's mouth, on which Leonard Woolley based his interpretation of the Ur interments as 'human sacrifices', was popular even before the Ur 'royal grave' interments.

who excavated this cardinal evidence with a degree of mastery unparalleled before and, in a number of cases, even afterwards, maintained that the multiple burials in some of the 'royal tombs' and 'death pits' represented the remains of human sacrifices. He based his interpretation on three observations: a) a find of a large copper cauldron, which he linked with goblets associated with bodies of the deceased, assuming death by poisoning, in PG 1237 (Woolley 1934, 36); b) the quantity of goblets found with the individual bodies (ibid.); and c) his own opinion that the transport of dead bodies would have left at least some traces in their equipment, for instance, the dislodging of their elaborate head-dresses (ibid.). The crucial and most significant fact of association between the dead bodies and the goblets is now known to have constituted a phenomenon frequent throughout most of the Early Dynastic period cemeteries (witness, for instance, both above cited sites of Ahmad al-Hattu and Kheit Qasim). This dispenses with the necessity of connecting the PG 1237 cauldron with any such rite, since most of the deceased would have been provided with drinking vessels anyway, and thus does away with points a) and b) above. Point c) is entirely subjective and irrelevant, as ethnography abounds in vivid, not to say macabre, descriptions of elaborate treatments of sometimes very long dead bodies, including dressing and bedecking with jewels. I call to witness only the abundantly documented ceremonial burials and re-burials of the saints of medieval Europe with constantly renewed sets of funerary paraphernalia or, for that matter, the Sunday afternoons of those Sicilian families of Palermo who, until recently, came to the catacombs below their cathedral to chat with their dead relatives, the bodies of which did not decompose owing to the favourable micro-climatic conditions of the crypt and catacombs, and occasionally to change the attire of their desiccated bodies. Although I regret that my point would almost fall in with the irreverent and sometimes purposefully denigrative fashion of the current day, I am afraid that Sir Leonard fell prey to his post-Victorian ideas of what was conceivable in a non-European civilization. To cut a long story short: as Sir Leonard himself notes (Woolley 1934, 35–36), the bones, quite decomposed, made all efforts to determine the manner of death hopeless. This statement is of cardinal importance because it shows that no exact and verifiable observations could have been made to shed light on the circumstances in which the persons buried in the Ur graves had died. That is a pity, but we have to insist that just as no firm conclusions are possible, so the interpretation of mass human sacrifice is equally unfounded and should be treated as no more than one of the possible explanations, not as a fact. On the other hand, Sir Leonard repeatedly refers to situations in which human bones were confused or even mixed with animal remains (Woolley 1934, 67–68, PG 789; 74, PG 800; 109, PG 1232). Of course, this could have happened in the course of deposition of the bodies in the soil, were it not for some fairly interesting observations hinting at the possibility of burials of disarticulated and hence long dead bodies. The bottom of the access shaft of PG 1050 bore a burial in a wooden coffin in an unanatomic position ('secondarily disturbed' – Woolley 1934, 95–96). Sir Leonard believes that the interference must have come about shortly before the closing of the shaft, as its upper layers were sealed by the ruins of a building and by intact layers of contemporary pottery. He puts forward an explanation according to which the robbers excavated a side tunnel which was not noticed in the excavation. Nevertheless, a clear case of a burial of excarnated remains of a human body wrapped in a mat was recorded in the corner of a shaft of PG 1850 (Woolley 1934, 200). And more: some human remains from third-millennium Mesopotamia, both preceding (Khafajeh: Delougaz *et al.* 1967, 73, grave 43, Houses 11 – Protoliterate) and following the Ur interments in time (Ur III, Ur: Moorey 1984, 6, subsuming such evidence from the cemetery) bear fire stains, likely to indicate preceding excarnation of the bodies. I proceed to suggest an alternative to Sir Leonard's idea of 'human sacrifices'. It goes without saying that the crucial question here pertains to the manner in which the people whose remains were retrieved from the 'royal graves' and 'death pits' died and to the events which passed between their death and burial. I see no obstacles to the proposition that the main burial might have been surrounded by corpses 'stored up for the occasion' and belonging to people who fervently wished to be laid to rest in the proximity of persons whose charismatic significance is likely to have been acknowledged by the whole community.

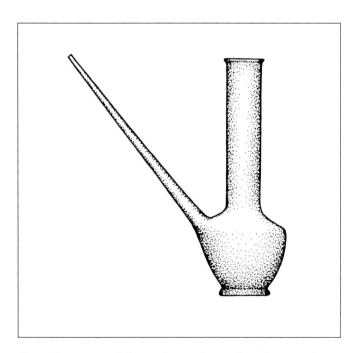

Figure 6.23 A spouted flagon of copper/bronze from the grave of King Meskalamdu at Ur (after Müller-Karpe, Pászthory and Pernicka 1993, Table 153: 10)

This leads us to the question who were, in fact, the chief personages occupying the central positions in the Ur graves. The direction in which the explanations put forward up to now have been moving – kings/queens or priests/priestesses – may not apply because, first and foremost, we should need to know how far they could be meaningful to ED IIIa society. I hope I have shown with sufficient clarity how dubious this is. The preceding ED I–II period is likely to have been dominated by kinship groupings in which individual sex and age constituted supplementary criteria for the attaining of social status, built on the principles of responsibility and social harmony. The end of ED (ED IIIb) saw, on the contrary, the superimposition (or suppression?) of such categories by a binary opposition between the economically, socially and spiritually active 'citizenry' and the managing and administrative élites. The Ur situation fits somewhere in between these two poles and is likely to receive illumination from what we know of the Šuruppak polity. There, the local élites who built the first unified political body of Early Dynastic Sumer took a series of easily discernible measures to render their economic, social and spiritual supremacy unquestionable. Probably amassing considerable quantities of wealth, they became undisputed masters of their sources of income, on which they drew for reserves to be redistributed. They probably manipulated social structures with the aim of increased coherence of kinship groups (consent of all relatives for the alienation of land), of inhibition of property dispersal(?), and of mobilization of socially available energy sources (the guruš labour obligations). Their LUGAL and NIN apparently maintained their kingdom with divine sanctions, based on worship of the same god in various Sumerian cities, and they even attempted to direct spiritual developments in contemporary communities, incorporating various local or even social-estate divinities into the official cults which the EN helped them to control. The society that they directed acquired a distinct virile, almost warrior ethos, with the individual kinship groupings (É) vying for higher status (Charvát 1997, 35–39, 67–68, 74–75, 80–81, 87–88). The Ur élites followed a similar trajectory but in simpler conditions. Instead of whole kin groupings, we seem to be dealing in their case with individuals of both sexes who enjoyed the 'ancestor' position, apparent in its pristine stage in the preceding ED cemeteries but grown beyond all measure and embellished by the lavish expenditure of precious materials made into articles of pure display and luxury. The generation of Ur leaders who chose such an extravagant burial rite were nevertheless successful enough to attract a number of their fellow citizens who chose their burial place close to these charismatic personages. Much as at Šuruppak, the latter managed to mobilize the socially available energy. While, however, the northern aristocrats handled it to achieve practical and concrete measures, the southerners concentrated on more theatrical and classificatory procedures. The Šuruppak leaders conscripted labour of living and able-bodied guruš; the Ur chiefs challenged the forces of the nether world at the head of a host of attendants of whom modern scholars have noticed that their composition shows signs of manipulation in the sense of a group of people resembling a great household, among whom a number were accorded the status of (married?) women. This is indicated by the preponderance of female head-dresses among the bodies lying in most of the rich graves (Moorey 1977, 35; Pollock 1991, 373f.). The classificatory nature of the Ur cemetery sexual distinctions follows from observations that the corpses of some men and women were given bisexual grave goods (Pollock 1991, 378) and that no children appeared in the 'death pits' (Moorey 1977, 35). Without texts, we know next to nothing about the secular government at the cemetery time or about the spiritual life in the local temple, though it is remarkable that Fara age texts do accord a 'bisexual' status to the EN (Charvát 1997, 67–68) and NIN (ibid. 87–88). Nevertheless, the subsequent predominance of the male sex in ED society invites a comparison with developments in seventh–eighth-century Anglo-Saxon England where, at a time when inheritance in the male line was the aim desired by contemporary superior strata, numerous females were assembled in élite households, both for sexual and servile purposes (Hodges 1989,

40); in similar contexts, females are significant in terms of reproduction strategies. In such a situation, we may summarize our observations by suggesting that the generation of charismatic personages of both sexes – terms like royalty or priestly personnel lack any verifiable social context for the time segment in question – buried in the Ur 'royal graves' undertook a complex social operation, the ultimate strategic perspective of which was, much as at Šuruppak, a radical transformation of the current social situation and the perpetuation of their own status. Elaborating on their prestige, based both on traditional (kinship?) values but also on personal achievement (Mr Meskalamdug, who died in his 30th year or so, might well have been a seasoned warrior), they proceeded to classify the rank and file of the Ur citizenry – or at least of their own households – into a gigantic *oikos* in which they assigned the central positions to themselves and which developed a considerable economic effort to encode its social structure in the externally visible signs of precious materials. Mobilizing the (supernatural?) powers of especially the female segment of the population, they took care to sanctify the ensuing social body by placing its postmortal, and hence eternal, model into the nether world. Some of the deceased lying at the Ur cemetery were supposed to subsist, at least for some time, on food they received (as 'viaticum'?) such as bowls with fish, sheep/goat joints and dried apples, or alternatively, apples and bread (Ellison *et al.* 1978, 169ff. and 1986, 158) and even fig juice in a silver vessel imitating a water skin (Reade 2001, 22, n. 120). The dead thus did continue their existence in the nether world and the whole Ur situation acquires features pointing in the direction of deification of the local élite, perceived as a constructing agent of the existing social order; 'hierarchy implies divinity, the hierarchy itself may mirror the divinity' (Glass 1988, 67). Parallels for such procedures do exist in ethnography (Sahlins 1983) as well as in historically described situations: Abu Bakr, an Almoravid chief of the eleventh post-Christian century, divided his followers into shepherds, students of the Koran and warriors (McDougall 1985, 15–17). Even such features as construction of descent groups by means of ancestral cults or encoding of a development programme of a particular social group in the layout of its cemetery are confirmed by the historical record (for ancient China see, for instance, Watson 1986, 280–281). In short, the Ur cemetery bears witness to the same process as the Šuruppak records: in both cases the communities attempted to build a more permanent and universal mode of administration of public affairs. Šuruppak leaned on

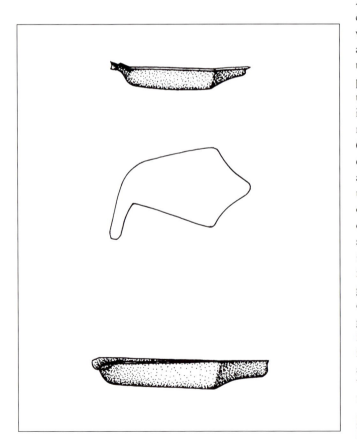

Figure 6.24 Two libation vessels(?) of gold and silver from the grave of King Meskalamdu at Ur (after Müller-Karpe, Pászthory and Pernicka 1993, Table 152: 85 and 92)

well-to-do kinship groups, Ur on charismatic leaders. Both failed, but they pointed in the right direction, Šuruppak (mainly) in the temporal and Ur (mainly) in the spiritual sense.

Turning now to another category of finds likely to have had a connection with contemporary collective mentality, we cannot fail to notice the decreasing numbers of clay figurines, both human and animal, after the Uruk culture (Spycket 1992, 16). Some of them turn up in ordinary settlement refuse (Jemdet Nasr period Abu Salabikh: Pollock 1990b, 71) while no more than two grave finds of human depictions are reported for the entire ED period (Khafajeh, Sin VI: Spycket 1992, 21; Ur: Moorey 1978, 67 – incipient Akkad period). Animal figurines do turn up more frequently (Tello, for instance: Genouillac 1934, 80–82). This fact may reflect the institutionalization of cultic practice, but it can also result from the bias of excavations towards the most conspicuous monuments, since the use of statuettes of all kinds is amply documented for subsequent periods of time in various ritual procedures of prophylactic or protective character (Faraone 1991, esp. pp. 176–180; or the increasing numbers of such figurines in later phases of Susa: Spycket 1992; figurines of the later third millennium of clay, bronze, wood and ivory: Wiggermann 1998, 47). Or did the ED sorcerers and witch doctors employ figurines made of organic materials?

Can we estimate developments in Sumerian thinking between the invention of writing and the conquests of Sargon of Akkad? Quite naturally, the preceding, comprehensive view of the universe in which the world was perceived as an essential unity held together by particular laws and rules, the visible parts of which 'masked' its basic structures, held on and affected the daily life of the Sumerian population to no small extent. One of the examples of the Sumerian perception of the entire world as a unified whole is constituted by the custom of giving animals such as cows names fully compatible with those of human beings, even including theophoric elements, amply documented in the Ur III evidence gathered by G. Farber (1982). Another rather interesting aspect of this traditional mode of thinking, perceiving even time as a component of the overall world structure that can be manipulated, if handled in an appropriate fashion, has been brought to our notice by Jerrold Cooper (1985, esp. pp. 99, 105). He has observed that all the historical narrative texts of the ED period are written on cones or cone-shaped objects such as pottery vessels, sunk since ED III into the upper parts of temple walls. Now we will do well to realize that sinking a wedge into a house wall constituted the core act of appropriation of that house (sale documents: Gelb, Steinkeller and Whiting 1991, 216–225). If a divinity symbolized his or her possession of a particular house/temple by sinking a (exquisite form of a) cone-shaped object in its wall, then the description of certain events written on that cone might have become hallowed by this act and the story might have acquired a canonical and presumably also eternal validity. This could have happened in the course of the action undertaken by Lummatur, son of Enannatum, in Inanna's Ibgal (Sollberger and Kupper 1971, 63, No. IC6b; Steible and Behrens 1982, 187). Such a procedure can represent a manipulation of the temporal sequence of events, attempting to sanctify a particular version of a given historical event 'frozen' in the script by placing it under the direct tutelage of a divinity. This 'in illo tempore' version of a peculiar story, regardless of whether taking place in the past, present or future, then constitutes a kind of a mythical 'biochronotope' which may interfere with actual events and influence them in a way desired by the author of the stratagem. Underlying this, of course, we may guess the principle of contradiction of mythical versus real time and their mutual influences so well known from historically later documentation; it need not be overemphasized that such an interpretation of the contemporary 'historical' texts would have a profound impact on assessments of the validity of information contained therein. That it may not be entirely erroneous is indicated by the persistently recurring divine sanctions against interference with these texts, clearly intended to be operative in the future. Nevertheless, signs of a perception of the world closer to our own vision do appear. First and foremost, this pertains to the very basic categories of individual physical position in space and time. It is significant that the geographical situation of fields, the alienation of which has been recorded in ancient kudurrus, as far as it is not indicated by their relative positions vis-à-vis other landed-property items, is defined by reference to the four cardinal points (Gelb, Steinkeller and Whiting 1991, 214). This indicates a rather coherent view of the geographical setting of Sumerian civilization, conceivable as a universal reference system and surpassing the heterogeneous apperception of space current in a number of vernacular cultures. In much the same manner, time units emerged, indicating the Sumerian inclination towards a homogenized and quantifiable attitude to the essentials of human existence in the world (see Englund 1988, 180–181, n. 52). Ultimately, however, the Sumerian philosophers of the period must be credited with substantial progress in abstract thinking. Unlike the Uruk culture period with its numeration systems depending on what kind of entities were counted, this epoch ushered in the basics of purely mathematical thought (Powell 1976a, 429–434, see also Powell 1984b), as well as the essentials of metrology, including the first consistent system of hollow measures (Fara period: Powell 1984b, 59–60), and the codification of weights (see p. 219; Powell 1979a, esp. pp. 79–83), as well as geometry (Høyrup 1997, esp. pp. 380–381). The penultimate case is particularly instructive in view of the lack of a general and universally accepted weight standard, instead of which individual Sumerian communities introduced a number of local values which, though not too far from one another, were nevertheless perceptibly different. A similar degree of increased exactitude in the expression of ideas emerges from what are commonly called 'ideograms' in writing. The specification of individual lexemes by semantic indicators that clarify their function in every particular context (that is, identifying the sememes in question), first systematically introduced in the Fara period (e.g. Krebernik 1986), supplies evidence for no less than the first instance of thinking in abstract notions. The development of the LÚ sememe towards 'human being, individual of the human species' (Charvát 1997, 74–75) points in the same direction. The significance of this step, which paved the way for the philosophers of future millennia, can hardly be overestimated; the ancient Sumerians proved by it that they did not belong to those fools who, in the words of St Anselm of Canterbury, 'do not know the difference between a horse and its colour'. Let us notice that this considerable transformation of the thought process is likely to have been substantially aided by the introduction and long-term usage of the script, as literacy frequently results in an increased capacity for more complex argument, derivation of consequences, abstract thought and even for the tendency to consider the past as immutable and different from the present (Stevenson 1989, 159ff.).

Developments in the sphere of script led, of course, to innovation in the uses to which it was put. Up to the beginning of ED IIIa the basic purposes for which script had always been used in Sumer – administrative and juridical recording and training of specialists in its employment – did not change (third-millennium administrative and legal texts: Steinkeller and Postgate 1992; Wilcke 1996). The lexical list tradition was developed to cover components of the world not included previously, but literary compositions then entered for the first time the realm of the written word: the Instructions of Šuruppak (Wilcke 1978; most recently Alster 1991, 154) and, among others, a series of what may be hymns to various temples including the Kiš shrine (Postgate 1982, 50 with ref.; see also Cunningham 1997 and Bauer, Englund and Krebernik 1998). Even in this aspect, which we today perceive as only loosely related to actual life, however, the spirit of codification and systematization of the Sumerian sages come to the fore. The collection of temple hymns, if it indeed constitutes anything of that sort, may well have been an essential 'tool kit' of a contemporary priest or magician, opening access to the main divinities of the period. The degree to which such evidence was manipulated is indicated by the observation already referred to, namely that the name of Zababa, the Kiš deity, is missing in the Fara lists but that the Abu Salabikh texts feature a hymn in his honour (Moorey 1978, 19). In their turn, the Instructions of Šuruppak might have served for the cultivation of desirable social relationships, especially with recourse to élite strata (for instance, clauses such as that pertaining to a peasant's son who built the addressee's irrigation ditch, Wilcke 1978, 208, l. 158, or that of the mode of procurement of slaves, ibid. 208, ll. 163–169). To a certain extent, they are thus reminiscent of the medieval 'Fürstenspiegeln', but have a wider impact as they seem to address a less limited audience. What, in fact, this Fara period literature was about is implied by analysis of the Fara divinity lists (Krebernik 1986). In addition to the main Sumerian gods, they include several hundred other names, among which they elevate to supernatural status various service personnel of the divine *oikiai* (Krebernik 1986, 165: divine cooks of Uruk, a divine cauldron and a divine overseer), including actual and real officials of the preceding, especially Uruk culture periods such as SANGA:DUB (*ZATU* No. 444, p. 268, and, in contrast, DUB ^dmes-sanga-unug in *WVDOG 43* t.1:VII:15, a Fara school text) as well as various natural substances (reeds: Krebernik 1986, 166) and human products including beeswax, incense, and metal and clay vessels (ibid.). Very much in line with Uruk culture reasoning, this somewhat weird array apparently represents an attempt at a systematic classification of both animate and inanimate notions which were considered of major importance and therefore presumably had a bearing on contemporary social equilibrium. A particular role seems to be played here by the natural substances, craft products and various specialized personnel, the elevation of which and whom to divine status clearly laid the foundations of recognized social status of people working with such materials or holding such offices. In this manner, the authors of the divinity lists played an active role in the stabilization of the existing social balance by placing the various crafts under the patronage of the gods and thus securing for them a safe and recognized, because divinized, social status. This was important insofar as the old lexical lists of the Uruk period were considered to be so sanctified by tradition that they continued to be copied word for word, even though the situation expressed in them was sometimes quite out of tune with present circumstances (Green 1984; for comparison of the roles played by the sanga officials in the profession lists and contemporary documents see Charvát 1996, 185–186). The fact that Fara period scribes held the ancient texts in such esteem but felt free to introduce new compilations bears out both the social urgency of this spiritual operation and the significance of the role played in deliberate articulation of the structure of ED IIIa communities by the written word. Elevation of the patronage of individual arts and crafts to the divine spheres is corroborated by further information. The role of the Zabalam deity, ^dNin-ildum, has been interpreted as that of a carpenter god (Powell 1976b, 102) and the office of the registrar of land deeds (sag-sug$_5$) rose to a deified status before Gudea's times (Lambert 1954, 207–208). In short, what the Šuruppak litterati undertook was an attempt at a systematic intellectual classification of the entire Sumerian anthropogeographical context, perhaps intended as a spiritual correlation to the temporal kingdom built by the rest of the Šuruppak élite.

New analyses of old finds can lead to meaningful insights. A new treatise on the lyres found in the Ur graves leads us to believe that there were originally five instruments, as heads of three bulls and two cows turned up. I assume that the iconography of the instruments' decoration refers to Nannar, the moon deity, in his functions of a) judge of the nether world, b) protector of the herds of livestock and c) donor of fertility (Borovskaya 1997, esp. pp. 7, 10; on identification of lyres see also Eichmann 1995, esp. p. 112).

Let us also take notice of the fact, relevant to my earlier conclusions concerning the significance of colours as indicators of change in the spiritual sphere, that transformations of the world views of the Jemdet Nasr to Early Dynastic periods did not bypass the colour range employed in contemporary art. How swift these changes may have been is indicated by the 'labyrinth' of Uruk-Eanna IIIb in which room 167 bore a plastering with carved spiraliform decoration painted

Figure 6.25 Fragment of a sculptured plaque of the later Early Dynastic age from Lagash, bearing the image of Anzud, the mythical lion-headed eagle

in black, white, red and yellow (Sürenhagen 1985, 235–236). Here the traditional trichromy reaching back to the Halaf period received a supplement of a fourth colour at the very centre of the contemporary Sumerian world. A similar example is provided by the Tell Brak Eye Temple, the interior walls of the nave of which bore rosettes whose heads displayed the white–red–black trichromy, but the 'altar' of which boasted a frieze consisting of a central white line flanked on both sides by decorated zones of blue and green–blue stone enclosed in linings of gold (Mallowan 1965, 46–47, Illus. 36–38). A colour repertory enriched in the same manner is displayed by the Jemdet Nasr culture pottery and by the Scarlet Ware of ED I–II (ibid. 24, Illus. 8–10, and 82, Illus. 89; see also Makovicky and Thuesen 1990). In contrast, the inventory of the ED IIIa Ur cemetery consistently repeats the white–red–blue or yellow/gold–red–blue colour triads (e.g. Mallowan 1965, 97, Illus. 107, 108). Cases of cylinder seals of blue lapis lazuli, denoting in all likelihood female graves, and those of white shell or calcite bearing contest scenes, accompanying deceased men (Rathje 1977; Pollock 1991, 380), may outline one of the contexts in which the colour symbolism was comprehended. How far these colour triads were influenced by the hues of the most fashionable materials of the day – gold, carnelian and lapis lazuli – or, vice versa, whether these minerals streamed in as a consequence of a preconceived symbolism elaborating on their colours as on the most desirable ones, must be decided by future research.

These notes on the development of spirituality of the Jemdet Nasr to Early Dynastic times may now be briefly summarized. The re-introduction of archaeologically discernible burial modes covers hardly more than a sample of the original population and contemporary burials represent thus a historical source in need of a critique to determine how far they were manipulated by the ancient communities, possibly as message carriers, and how far their fragmentary state reflects problems of archaeologization. One of the possible explanations may build on the tradition of claiming corporate rights to a territorial segment by establishing a cemetery on it (see pp. 81, 91), another points to the increasing importance of ancestor worship which certainly did play a role in the earlier segment of the period in question when the categories reflected by the burial evidence are likely to have been kinship and sex. The Ur cemetery seems to reflect an attempt to sanction a new social order invented and introduced by the local élite, while burial fields of the closing phase of ED show the replacement of categories of kinship and sex, significant in preceding times, with individual 'citizen' status, expressing roles assigned to the deceased by living members of their communities. Traditional everyday rituals involving clay statuettes seem to have receded sharply, or resorted to items of other materials. As far as the apperception of the world may be commented upon at all, the traditional holistic vision of the world as built on one (or several?) essential principles reflected by the multitudes of both its animate and inanimate denizens, including mankind, seen not as a dominating group but as a component of the universe, continued to hold sway. Nevertheless, major innovations in this sphere included attempts at a more exact and verifiable intellectual grasping and classification of various entities, including the first instances of mathematics, metrology and expression of abstract notions, but also the justification of the existing social order by systematization and even deification of its chief geographical and structural components. These transformations seem to underlie changes in the colour schemes chosen for the most socially prominent artifacts.

Chapter Seven

Conclusions

Ancient Mesopotamia constitutes one of the territories in which humankind reached the threshold of civilization very early. For this reason, conclusions based on this review of recent archaeological and historical research, as well as on relevant information published earlier, may be presumed to contain data useful not only for specialists in Mesopotamian civilizations but also for a wider segment of the academic community.

The first conclusion of a general order that strikes the eye is represented by a peculiar light thrown on the notion of progress. I believe that the evidence marshalled above shows convincingly that when human beings enter our field of historical vision, they possess all the capacities and faculties of modern men and women and even propose the same kinds of solutions to various problems of human existence as we do. Probably from the fiftieth century BC, but most certainly since the ninth pre-Christian millennium, humans have demonstrated their fully fledged capability of collecting empirical data relevant for their survival and sometimes for most sophisticated treatment of natural resources, of deriving from these data both theoretical and practical conclusions concerning (also) improvement of their living conditions and possibly even concerning the nature of the world, as well as putting these theoretical principles to practical use. Of course, all this is to be expected if we postulate the biological identity of the *Homo sapiens sapiens* species throughout its history. Mesolithic hunters and gatherers possessed the know-how required for such complex tasks as choosing particularly suitable food plants and cultivating them, which resulted ultimately in their genetic manipulation, including the creation of brand new cultigens without wild predecessors, or, for that matter, for the creation of entirely artificial materials such as the lime plasters of Qermez Dere. Not even major building projects or urbanistic concepts such as the rampart and tower of Early Neolithic Jericho, or the house terraces of the recently excavated seventh-millennium Jordanian village of Tell Basta (Gebel and Muheisen 1997), surpassed the competence of these early human communities. Progress thus appears less a motion of interlinked sets of material relationships independent of human will than a problem of deliberation and decision. Hunter-gatherer groups of the Mesolithic, living in the age of material affluence (see the data in Sahlins 1972), could transform nature, invent artificial materials or establish urban settlements just as we do – if they pleased. The chief historical question is thus not where they were pushed by blind forces of mechanically conceived material development but rather why they chose to do what they did, why they employed their intellect in just this way and not another. In their embryonic forms, all the inventions on which modern human civilization prides itself were present already in the Palaeolithic age. This points to the inevitable conclusion that as early as this period, extra-economic factors acquired for the development of the human race a significance at least as great as purely economic considerations. Instead of trying to find out how the Mesolithics could have developed further, we should ask why they chose to develop at all, living in an environment that was dangerously near to paradise on earth.

The first age of Mesopotamian civilization, reaching from the ninth approximately to the fifth pre-Christian millennium, may be termed the age of inspiration. There are reasons to imagine that the improvement of climatic conditions around 10,000 BC placed at humankind's disposal much more plentiful and varied subsistence resources than before; but material abundance alone hardly incites the human soul to apply itself to the transformation of natural resources in the manner ascertainable from contemporary archaeological record. The whole epoch is marked by a slowly but steadily advancing sequence of material incarnations of human ingenuity which ultimately changed the face of the earth. Deep-reaching knowledge of animal life, leading to deliberate and rational hunting practices and subsequently to domestication; preoccupation with plant life, resulting in the protection of, and care for, the most promising cultigens and, finally, in transformations of plant genetic structures to produce new species without wild ancestors – all these results would glorify any of the modern breeding stations and laboratories. These naked 'savages', endowed with a spirit of intellectual adventure worthy of any modern discoverer, handled nature with much more responsibility and understanding than modern industrial civilizations. Nevertheless, these inventions were still firmly embedded in the traditional lifestyle, involving spatial transfers of communities directed by a calendrical sequence built on the availability of energy sources determined by biological and chronological factors. Hunters, gatherers, shepherds and peasants of the Mesolithic and Neolithic made their discoveries 'on the way'. Theirs was the age of freedom: never did the contemporary communities allow any of their material creations to chain them to a particular site, landscape or specialized activity. Strange as it may seem to us, they expended much effort in such major building projects as the excavation of irrigation channels (Choga Mami, Samarra culture) or the erection of fortified sites with substantial buildings (Tell es-Sawwan, Samarra culture), subsequently leaving their works to decay and fall apart in the destructive elements of the Mesopotamian climate. Such projects did nonetheless represent a lesson well-learnt. The fame of such superhuman feats undoubtedly circulated far and wide. People must have talked them over around the campfires of their large winter congregation sites in the lowlands, where multitudes gathered to hunt game in the steppes, catch a winter crop, exchange experiences and perform the necessary rites before the whole community. In the following summers, when these large groups (dispersed? and) went to the higher-lying grounds that protected them from heat and offered fresh pastures to their animals, well-watered valley bottoms to their peasant-minded members and hitherto untapped wildlife resources for everyone, many of these experiences were undoubtedly tested and found useful. Thus the memory of them was not lost and generations of free-born and proud men and women challenged the forces of nature equipped with the experiences of their predecessors. This incessant traffic in the plains managed nevertheless to create a certain 'mental environment', common to all lowland communities among which ideas, experiences and manners of artistic expression (e.g. the seals) circulated at large, coalescing in the first cultural 'koine' of this part of the world.

I cannot say what brought about the transformation of this pattern in the late sixth and fifth millennium, in which the next epoch, reaching down to the early third pre-Christian millennium, which we may call the age of domination, began. The chief innovation of this time was sedentarization and all its consequences. The question of what came first, sedentarization or the overall intensification of human activities that made sedentarization possible, is a fascinating one and I sincerely hope that someone will one day provide an answer. In all spheres of human life we feel the tightened grip on nature. Peasants now round up the range of cultigens yielding nourishment to their communities and settle down to establish not only fields but even such labour-intensive cultures as gardens and orchards. Shepherds start keeping more cattle, for food but perhaps also as an energy source for traction and load-bearing. Specialists in all sorts of crafts attack the resources of nature, gather new experiences and apply new know-how. Sedentarization implies the necessity of transport: in this age, regular traffic on the twin rivers of Mesopotamia, most probably using rafts on inflated skins (*kelek* in Arabic), first becomes a reasonable probability. The sedentarization of major social centres now traps whole settlement zones, the inhabitants of which can no longer disperse and congregate at will, being bound by various means to their capitals which constitute the central points of the coordinate systems in which their activities now take place. Outlines of the social structure of local communities emerge: on grounds of the regular and canonical form of their central points (Ubaid culture central-hall buildings), these may have consisted of groupings of 2–3 nuclear families each with some evidence of age grading. On the other hand, the spheres of activity of contemporary cultures stretch far and wide: the Halaf culture occupied more or less the entire Fertile Crescent area, to which the Ubaid culture added the shores of the Arabo-Persian Gulf. This is the end of sometimes ragged and worn but blessed liberty: people now have to learn to work together, live together and even die together, this incarceration paying for the increase in living standards. Material seizing of the environment walked hand in hand with a better mental grip on things of the invisible world. The holding of private property now appears on the horizon of historical vision, both by individuals and by whole human communities, as is indicated by the establishment of the first extramural cemeteries, which probably anchored rights to territorial segments claimed by particular communities or rather community clusters. Socially engineered exchange of material goods, which probably constituted the cementing agent of political alliances, is now institutionalized for the first time in history, most probably in the form of reciprocity. In the Halaf culture, this concerned centripetal(?) movement of goods within the 'catchment areas' of major sites like Arpachiyah, Tepe Gawra, Tell Sabi Abyad or Tell Kerkh; Ubaid culture exchange practices probably assumed a generalized exchange pattern linking both the centres and their peripheries and the centres themselves. This is also the age when a more universal spiritual construct – presumably the first universal religion of Mesopotamia – which may have involved application of the dualistic principle and symbolization by means of the white–red–black colour triad, emerged in an atmosphere of creative fusion of northern and southern artistic elements at Tepe Gawra.

In this age, the loosely contiguous koine of the Neolithic age grew together in a number of steps. The Halaf culture probably operated a set of common beliefs and rituals revolving around ostentatious commensality (exquisite tableware). As in the original Thanksgiving Day ceremony, representatives of groups of most diverse economic, socio-political and spiritual background might have convened to articulate their intention to live together in peace, perhaps even more than that. In this perspective, the next step would have been represented by the Ubaid period 'Commonwealth'. This cluster of more or less compatible communities, displaying a number of common traits and features, exchanged both immaterial and material goods on a regular basis, which undoubtedly resulted in closer contacts among them, enhancing their temporal and spiritual capacities.

With the creation of the Uruk corporate entity, this essentially prehistoric development – prehistoric means here that the most important social component was not the individual but the community – came to its climax. Were I to choose a historical simile expressing the essence of Uruk culture, I would undoubtedly opt for the Chakravartin myth of India. According to this, the whole world shall one day be ruled by a just king who will subjugate it not by violence but by the sheer force of truth. His ensign shall be a wheel which reposes over aeons in the depths of the ocean but which upon the Chakravartin's ascension to the throne will begin a rotating motion, leave the ocean bottom and fly to his residence where it will lie still at his feet.

Nevertheless, as soon as the Chakravartin commits injustice and loses thereby his moral justification to universal rule, the wheel will fly back to the ocean where it will await the next just king. The Uruk corporate entity, short of introducing any major subsistence innovations, 'did the trick' by realistic analysis, rational administration, common consensus and intellectual attraction. It simply committed no mistakes and there was hardly any escape from the tyranny of its all-pervading success. The Uruk culture managers assessed the economic potential of all their component communities, determined the type of enterprise most suitable to every single one of them and arranged for the redistribution of results, maintaining a steady flow of goods throughout the entire community and buffering the impact of unexpected events. Tasks requiring specialized knowledge were carried out by the centres and the products released into the redistribution network. Some of them involved seeking alternative solutions by testing several hypotheses, the erroneous ones of which were subsequently abandoned (metalwork). The Uruk culture settlement network included large-scale settlement agglomerations which may be termed pristine urban centres and military bases, presumably with deterrent functions. All this went on in a predominantly egalitarian atmosphere without traces of social stratification other than the ability of the centre to mobilize manpower and with evidence for holding assemblies, presumably for the decision of common matters. This is important as it appears to be based on the essentially egalitarian Ubaid culture with public activities of whole corporate units forming wider associations, rather than on the more richly structured Halaf culture, covering a whole array of professional but also social groupings (chiefs, priests? – see the exclusive character of Tell Arpachiyah, for instance). One of the Chalcolithic regional groupings seems to have acquired such a social weight that its suzerainty was acknowledged throughout the contemporary civilized world. The Uruk élite must have buttressed their 'new deal' with a most efficient mental correlate of the prevailing situation since it obviously won the dedication of all citizens, in spite of the rather heavy-handed treatment of such issues as the spiritual links between local communities and their environment (disappearance of cemeteries).

Domination of the material world was accompanied by ordering of the spiritual realms and, first and foremost, by the act of triggering off the land's fertility by the NA2 ceremony performed by the pontifical couple, EN and NIN. The script, created deliberately by Uruk (or Ubaid culture?) sages, put at their disposal both an ordered series of symbols for things of the visible and invisible worlds which they could manipulate to their hearts' content and an efficient device for the tracing of movement of material goods throughout the complex circuits of the Uruk corporate entity. Thus they rose to the status of masters of the visible world, guardians and managers of its fertility and creators of a cosmic order. Nevertheless, they bowed low before their gods who represented the highest values of Uruk culture society, reserving for themselves all the most precious goods and justifying the mobilization of a considerable amount of manpower needed for all-community projects. The citizens who came to the shrines where they sometimes left their personal articles as tokens of faith even tolerated an absolute break in the treatment of their dead who now departed to the nether world in a manner radically different from those of the preceding periods. Far-reaching as these changes may seem to us, they nonetheless fell short of severing the deepest ties of the Uruk culture community with the traditional spiritual world of the local communities, and especially with the Ubaid culture universe. This is indicated both by the deliberate egalitarianism in which all members of the Uruk corporate entity were treated, essentially in the same manner both in life and in death, and by its vision of the world which still did not manage to shed the particular and concrete apperception of things oriented 'radially', according to the individual component entities of the visible world behind which the existence of other factors and forces, linked to their material manifestations by a set of complex interrelations, was presumed, rather than 'concentrically', with association of all phenomena of the same order into corporate spiritual constructs expressed both in a wealth of individual denominations and in abstract notions ordered into a mental system correlating with the assumed structure of the universe.

It is regrettable that we know only one community that may be compared in detail to the components of the Uruk corporate entity, namely Tepe Gawra, which may even pre-date the Leviathan of the south (see p. 109). At that site a normal social stratification process seems to have taken place with the local élite displaying their status in luxury personal articles and deriving their wealth from external sources which we are unable to specify. An interesting feature of the local economic situation seems to be the changing order of redistribution (present in layers XI and IX), perhaps a testimony to increasing group coherence in times of need, and reciprocal exchange practices, prevalent in the times when the material welfare of the Gawra élites reached the climactic points (layers X and VIII). Even this élite group, however, was able to hold on for centuries, constituting an early harbinger of the social stratification of individuals within a single community and contrasting with the basically egalitarian internal structure of other social bodies of Mesopotamian proto-history, which assumed hierarchical relationships only vis-à-vis one another in more extensive and ordered systems, apparently present in the Ubaid and especially Uruk culture periods. The character of other component communities of the Uruk corporate entity remains unknown.

All material things come to their end, the Uruk culture being no exception. Some violence was obviously involved, though the framework of the social structure of the immediately following Jemdet Nasr period clearly continued along Uruk lines. Climatic change, subsistence problems (salinization as a consequence of fallow violation?), loss of credibility of the system – whichever of these causes may have been instrumental, the wheel flew back into the ocean, the Round Table vanished. Nevertheless, Mesopotamian society lived in a sort of 'Uruk-less' Uruk heritage period until about the twenty-sixth pre-Christian century. Optimalization of the subsistence activities aimed at the most reliable and productive approaches, and coupled with maintenance and development of technological know-how, assured a tolerable living standard. Individual Sumerian communities of this age probably acquired a more or less self-sustained character but took care to maintain the connections that had once held together the Uruk corporate entity. How far their component *oikiai* may have represented descendants of the traditional Ubaid culture communities and how far we may assume in the pre-Uruk age the importance of the dominant features of the Early Dynastic social structures – kinship, sex and age – must be determined by future research. The Sumerian *oikiai*, maintaining the Uruk culture heritage including the script, soon witnessed dramatic changes.

The beginnings of the third period of Mesopotamian history, which may be termed the age of maintenance, lie in the twenty-sixth century BC. At that time, a group of charismatic *oikos* leaders attempted to introduce changes in the administration of public affairs. First attested at Šuruppak and archaeologically at some of the Diyala sites, such intentions were preceded by an increase in the importance of material wealth and by the monopolization and personalization of its sources as well as by systematic pooling of corporate property, attested by the predominance of redistribution. Other related features include a tightening of solidarity of kinship groups (obligatory collective consent in alienation of land), deeper stratification of the corporate groups by lowering the status of some of their members (women), perhaps in an attempt to prevent dispersal of group property by too extensive inheritance rights (disappearance of the sexual division in mortuary practices after this period of time), and imposition of labour obligation on certain population strata (guruš) for public utility projects. The Šuruppak polity apparently achieved the first unification of Sumer after Uruk culture times by means of regional administration based on a network of essentially religious interconnections. For the first time in world history, the throne (LUGAL and NIN) and the altar (EN) united to build a new world. In the spiritual sphere, these innovations were accompanied by attempts at a codification of the worlds of both inanimate and animate nature, and of sets of socially desirable relations by means of written texts placed under the tutelage of the gods and including earlier, Uruk culture material which obviously constituted a sacred textual canon to which supplements were added to bring it up to date. The earliest evidence for classification of groups of particular phenomena under abstract notions probably dates from this period. What happened at Šuruppak was perhaps not unlike the developments following the Warring States period in ancient Chinese history or in Ashoka's India, if his epithet 'destroyer of the kshatriyas' corresponds to reality. The Šuruppak polity vanished from history fairly soon; was its neck broken by the imposition of the labour obligation, judged to be an all too excessive burden, as may be evidenced by the initial stanzas of the Gilgameš epic? Nevertheless, successors set in immediately. Both kings of Kiš and kings of Ur claimed its heritage. At Ur, of which we know more, the élite tried to introduce a (new?) social classification represented externally by a considerable expenditure of energy (imported materials), trying to confer an eternal status on this model by placing it in the nether world with the help of particular layouts of segments of the municipal cemetery. This attempt at a new social order failed after a few generations of rulers. At Kiš too, the local sovereigns, who built a number of public structures including a (new?) temple in an attempt to embody their charisma in secular power, did not manage to convince their followers but may have contributed the idea of the erection of temples as 'reserve funds of power', detached from direct royal jurisdiction, perhaps in the sacralized form of the earlier *oikos* (the Khafajeh Temple Oval, see the curvilinear enclosures at ED I Abu Salabikh). This was to become a standard procedure of the rest of Early Dynastic times: relying on the temples which they had founded and endowed (albeit as public institutions), the élites used them as reserves of arable land and as sources of all sorts of material wealth, as social buttresses of their power and as means for the divine sanctification of their superior position. However, they now had to face the united citizenry among whom the old kinship, sex and age categories now ceded their social primacy to status achieved by personal performance. The temples thus gradually became public platforms on which the relationships among élites and citizens were determined according to the energy, skill and ingenuity of both parties. This provided an enormous boost to spiritual and especially literary creativity which now found its expression not only in the recording of all the temples' activities for public control but even in conveying corporate interests in social (Uruinimgina reforms) or political conflicts (lament over Lugalzagesi's raid on Lagaš). This age, terminated by the Akkadian conquests of the forties and thirties of the twenty-fourth pre-Christian century, saw the emergence of the principles of statehood, the embryonic forms of political democracy, but also of the foundations of modern thought, including mathematics, metrology and the first ethical categories, when such notions as freedom or justice but also guilt and sin found their way into human literary culture. One of the most creative periods of Mesopotamian history, this epoch enriched human civilization with achievements that affect the lives of humankind up to this very day.

Bibliography

Adams, R. McC. (1975) An ancient Uruk threshing-sledge or harrow? *Sumer* 31/1–2, 17–20.

—— (1981) *Heartland of Cities – Surveys of Ancient Settlement and Land Use on the Central Floodplain of the Euphrates*. Chicago and London: University of Chicago Press.

Adams, R. McC. and Wright, H. T. (1989) Concluding remarks, in Henrickson and Thuesen (1989), pp. 441–456.

AHw: W. von Soden (1965–1981) *Akkadisches Handworterbuch*. 3 vols. Wiesbaden: Verlag Otto Harrassowitz.

Akkermans, P. (1987) Tell Sabi Abyad: preliminary report on the 1986 excavations. *Akkadica* 52, 10–28.

—— (1988) An updated chronology for the northern Ubaid and Late Chalcolithic periods in Syria: new evidence from Tell Hammam et-Turkman. *Iraq* 50, 109–146.

—— (1989a) Tradition and social change in Northern Mesopotamia during the later 5th and 4th millennium B.C., in Henrickson and Thuesen (1989), pp. 339–368.

—— (1989b) Halaf mortuary practices: a survey, in *To the Euphrates and Beyond: Archaeological Studies in Honour of M. N. van Loon*. Rotterdam: Museum Boymans-van Wateringen, pp. 75–88.

—— (1993) written communication to the author dated 18 February 1993.

—— (ed.) (1996) *Tell Sabi Abyad – The Late Neolithic Settlement*. Report on the Excavations of the University of Amsterdam (1988) and the National Museum of Antiquities Leiden (1991–1993) in Syria. Istanbul: Nederlands Historisch-Archaeologisch Instituut.

Akkermans, P. and Duistermaat, K. (1997) Of storage and nomads – the sealings from Late Neolithic Sabi Abyad, Syria. *Paléorient* 22/2, 17–44.

Akkermans, P. and Le Miere, M. (1992) The 1988 excavations at Tell Sabi Abyad, a Later Neolithic village in Northern Syria. *American Journal of Archaeology* 96/1, 1–22.

Alberti, A. and Pomponio, F. (1986) *Pre-Sargonic and Sargonic Texts from Ur edited in UET 2 Supplement*. Studia Pohl, Series Major 13. Rome: Pontificio Istituto Biblico.

Algaze, G. (1983–1984) Private houses and graves at Ingharra, a reconsideration. *Mesopotamia* XVIII–XIX, 135–193.

—— (1986) Habuba on the Tigris: Archaic Nineveh reconsidered. *Journal of Near Eastern Studies* 45/2, 125–137.

—— (1993a) *The Uruk World System: The Dynamics of Expansion of Early Mesopotamian Civilization*. Chicago: University of Chicago Press. Review by R. Matthews, *Bibliotheca Orientalis* 51/5–6, 1994, 666–671.

—— (1993b) Expansionary dynamics of some early pristine states. *American Anthropologist* 95/2, 304–333.

—— (2001) Initial social complexity in southwestern Asia: the Mesopotamian advantage. *Current Anthropology* 42/2, April, 199–233.

Alizadeh, A. (1985) A protoliterate pottery kiln from Chogha Mish. *Iran* 23, 39–50.

Allan, W. (1972) Ecology, techniques and settlement patterns, in Ucko, Tringham and Dimbleby (1972), pp. 211–226.

Alram-Stern, E. (1996) *Die ägäische Frühzeit 1: Das Neolithikum in Griechenland (mit Ausnahme von Kreta und Zypern)*. Wien: Verlag der österreichischen Akademie der Wissenschaften.

Alster, B. (1991) The instructions of Urninurta and related compositions. *Orientalia* N.S. 60/3, 141–157.

Ambos, C. (1996) Prestige und Prestigegüter im beginnenden vorderasiatischen Neolithikum: Nemrik 9 and Qermez Dere, in J. Müller and R. Bernbeck (eds) *Prestige – Prestigegüter – Sozialstrukturen. Beispiele aus dem europäischen und vorderasiatischen Neolithikum*. Bonn: HOLOS, pp. 47–56.

Amiet, P. (1972) *Glyptique susienne, des origines à l'époque des Perses achéménides*. Paris: Geuthner.

—— (1987) Temple sur terasse ou forteresse? *Revue d'Assyriologie* 81, 99–104.

—— (1994) Sceaux et administration à Suse à l'époque d'Uruk, in Ferioli *et al.* (1994), pp. 87–96.

Andreyev, Yu. V. (1987) Ranniye formy urbanizatsii (Early forms of urbanization, in Russian). *Vestnik drevney istorii* 1/1987, 3–18.

Annex: Annexe: Liste des dates Radiocarbone (14000–5700 BP), in Aurenche *et al.* (1987), pp. 683–736.

Anon. (1972) Excavations in Iraq 1971–1972. *Iraq* 34, 139–150.

Anon. (1978) Jahresbericht des Deutschen Archäologischen Institut 1977. *Archäologischer Anzeiger* 1978/4, 602–649.

Anon. (1979) Excavations in Iraq 1977–1978. *Iraq* 41/2, 141–181.

Anon. (198/) Hassek Hüyük, in Jahresbericht 1986 des Deutschen Archäologischen Instituts. *Archäologischer Anzeiger* 1987/4, 723–787, pp. 753–754.

Anthony, D. W. and Brown, D. R. (1991) The origins of horseback riding. *Antiquity* 65/246, 22–38.

Ar-Radi, S. and Seeden, H. (1980) The American University of Beirut rescue excavations at Shams ed-Din Tannira, in Azoury *et al.* (1980–1982) – *Berytus* 28, 88–126.

Asher-Greve, J. and Stern, W. B. (1983) A new analytical method and its application to cylinder seals. *Iraq* 45, 157–162.

ATU: A. Falkenstein (1936) *Archaische Texte aus Uruk*. Berlin: Deutsche Forschungsgemeinschaft and Leipzig: Kommissionsverlag Otto Harrassowitz.

Aurenche, O., Evin, J. and Hours, F. (eds) (1987) *Chronologies du Proche Orient – Chronologies in the Near East. Relative Chronologies and Absolute Chronology, 16,000–4,000 B.P.* Maison de l'Orient Méditerranéen – Archaeological Series No. 3. BAR International Series 379 (i, ii).

Avigad, N. (1990) Two Hebrew 'Fiscal' Bullae. *Israel Exploration Journal* 40/4, 262–266.

Azoury, I. and Bergman, C. (1980) The Halafian lithic assemblage of Shams ed-Din Tannira, in Azoury *et al.* (1980–1982), pp. 127–143.

Azoury, I., Bergman, C., Gustavson-Gaube, C. E., al-Radi, S., Seeden, H. and Uerpmann, H.-P. (1980–1982) A stone age village on the Euphrates I–V. *Berytus* 28, 1980, 87–143; *Berytus* 29, 1981; *Berytus* 30, 1982, 3–96.

Bachelot, L. (1991) Image et pratique funéraire au IIIᵉᵐᵉ millénaire, in *XXXVIIIᵉᵐᵉ Rencontre Assyriologique Internationale*, Paris 8–10 juillet 1991. Résumés des communications, liste des participants, pp. 2–3.

Bader, N. O., Merpert, N. Ya. and Munchaev, R. M. (1981) Soviet expedition's surveys in the Sinjar valley. *Sumer* XXXVII/1–2, 55–63.

Baird, D. (1995) The stratigraphy and architecture, in Baird *et al.* (1995), pp. 6–31.

Baird, D., Campbell, S. and Watkins, T. (eds) (1995) *Excavations at Kharabeh Shattani*, vol. II. Edinburgh: University of Edinburgh, Department of Archaeology, Occasional Paper No. 18.

Balfet, H. (1980) A propos du métier d'argile: exemple de dialogue entre ethnologie et archéologie, in *L'archéologie de l'Iraq du début de l'époque néolithique 333 av. n. e.* Paris: Editions du CNRS, pp. 71–84.

Ball, W., Tucker, D., Wilkinson, T. and Black, J. (1989) The Tell al-Hawa project, archaeological investigations in the northern Jazira 1986–1987. *Iraq* 51, 1–66.

Bar-Yosef, O. (1997a) Ubeidiya, in Myers (1997), vol. 5, pp. 254–255.

—— (1997b) Carmel Caves, in Myers (1997), vol. 1, pp. 424–428.

Bar-Yosef, O. and Belfer-Cohen, A. (1992) From foraging to farming in the Mediterranean Levant, in A. B. Gebauer and T. P. Price (eds) *Transitions to Agriculture in Prehistory*. Madison, Wisconsin: Prehistory Press, pp. 21–48.

Bar-Yosef, O. and Khazanov, A. (eds) (1992) *Pastoralism in the Levant – Archaeological Materials in Anthropological Perspectives*. Madison, Wisconsin: Prehistory Press.

Barrelet, M.-Th. (1974) Dispositifs a feu et cuisson des aliments a Ur, Nippur, Uruk. *Paléorient* 2/2, pp. 243–300.

Bauer, J. (1987) Ortsnamen in den frühen Texten aus Ur. *Die Welt des Orients* 18, (pub. 1988), 5–6.

Bauer, J., Englund, R. K. and Krebernik, M. (1998) *Mesopotamien. Späturuk-Zeit und frühdynastische Zeit.* Annäherungen I. Orbis Biblicus et Orientalis 160/1. Freiburg and Göttingen: Universitätsverlag and Vandenhoeck und Ruprecht. Reviews by R. Matthews, *Bulletin of the School of Oriental and African Studies of the University of London* 62/3, 1999, 549–550, and G. Van Driel, *Bibliotheca Orientalis* 57/5–6, 2000, 493–509.

Bayburin, A. K. and Levinton, G. A. (1990) Pokhorony i svad'ba (Funerals and weddings, in Russian), in V. V. Ivanov and L. G. Nevskaya (eds) *Issledovaniya v oblasti balto-slavyanskoy dukhovnoy kul'tury – Pogrebal'nyi obryad.* Moscow: 'Nauka', pp. 64–99.

Becker, A. and Heinz, M. (1993) *Uruk – Kleinfunde I. Stein.* AUWE, vol. 6. Mainz am Rhein: Philipp von Zabern.

Becker, C. (1999) Der Beitrag archäolozoologischer Forschung zur Rekonstruktion landwirtschaftlicher Aktivitäten – ein kritischer Überblick, in Klengel and Renger (1999), pp. 43–58.

Bedford, I. (1987) Parasitism and equality: some reflections on pastoral nomadism and long-distance trade. *Mankind* 17/2 (Ch. Jayawardena papers), 140–152.

Behm-Blancke, M. R. (ed.) (1992) *Hassek Höyük – Naturwissenschaftliche Untersuchungen und lithische Industrie.* Tübingen: Ernst Wasmuth Verlag.

Berman, J. C. (1989) Ceramic production and its implications for the sociopolitical organization of the Susiana Plain during the Late 'Ubaid, in Henrickson and Thuesen (1989), pp. 257–280.

Bernardi, B. (1985) *Age Class Systems: Social Institutions and Polities based on Age* (transl. by D. A. Kertzer). Cambridge: Cambridge University Press.

Bernbeck, R. (1994) *Die Auflösung der häuslichen Produktionsweise – Das Beispiel Mesopotamiens.* BBVO, vol. 14. Berlin: Dietrich Reimer Verlag.

Besenval, R. (1994) *Le peuplement de l'ancienne Gédrosie, de la protohistoire à la période islamique: travaux archéologiques récents dans le Makran pakistanais.* Académie des Inscriptions et de Belles-Lettres, Comptes-rendus des séances de l'année 1994, avril–juin, Paris, pp. 513–535.

Biggs, R. D. (1976) *Inscriptions from Al-Hiba-Lagash: The First and Second Seasons.* Malibu: Undena Publications.

Biggs, R. D. and Postgate, J. N. (1978) Inscriptions from Abu Salabikh, 1975. *Iraq* 40, 101–117.

Bimson, M. (1980) Cosmetic pigments from the 'royal cemetery' at Ur. *Iraq* 42/1, 75–78.

Binford, L. (1971) Mortuary practices: their study and their potential, in J. A. Brown (ed.) *Approaches to the Social Dimensions of Mortuary Practices.* Memoirs of the Society for American Archaeology No. 25, pp. 6–29.

Blackham, M. (1996) Further investigations as to the relationship of Samarran and Ubaid ceramic assemblages. *Iraq* LVIII, 1–16.

Blazquez, J. M. (1981) Las pinturas helenisticas de Qusayr 'Amra (Jordania) y sus fuentes. *Archivo Español de Arqveologia* 54/143–144.

——(1983) La pintura helenistica de Qusayr Amra II. *Archivo Español de Arqveologia* 56/147–148, 169–212.

Blick, J. P. (1988) Genocidal warfare in tribal societies as a result of European-induced culture conflict. *Man* N.S. 23/4, 654–670.

Böck, B. (1996) review of Katz (1993), *Orientalistische Literaturzeitung* 91/1, pp. 27–31.

Boehm, C. (1993) Egalitarian behavior and reverse dominance hierarchy. *Current Anthropology* 34/3, 227–254.

Boehmer, R. M. (1984) Kalkstein für das urukzeitliche Uruk. *Baghdader Mitteilungen* 15, 141–147.

——(1991) Uruk 1980–1990: a progress report. *Antiquity* 65/248, 465–478.

——(1997) Uruk, in Myers (1997), vol. 5, pp. 294–298.

Boese, J. (1978) Mesanepada und der Schatz von Mari. *Zeitschrift für Assyriologie* 68/I, 6–33.

Boessneck, J. (1987) Tierknochenfunde vom Uch Tepe. *Acta Praehistorica et Archaeologica* 19, 131–163.

Boessneck, J., von den Driesch, A. and Steger, U. (1984) Tierknochenfunde der Ausgrabungen des Deutschen Archäologischen Instituts Baghdad in Uruk-Warka, Iraq. *Baghdader Mitteilungen* 15, 149–189.

Bökönyi, S. (1994) Domestication of animals from the beginnings of food production up to about 5000 years ago: an overview, in De Laet *et al.* (1994), pp. 389–397.

Bolt, D. G. (1992) *Burial in an Ancient Northern Mesopotamian Town: The Evidence from Tell Mohammed Arab*. Dissertation submitted in partial satisfaction of the requirements for the degree of Doctor of Philosophy in Near Eastern Studies in the Graduate division of the University of California at Berkeley. Ann Arbor: University of Michigan Press.

Bongenaar, A.C.V.M. and Jursa, M. (1993) Ein babylonischer Mäusefänger. *Wiener Zeitschrift für die Kunde des Morgenlandes* 83, 31–38.

Bonnet, H. (1999) *On Understanding Syncretism*. The original text of 1939 translated and actualized by J. Baines. *Orientalia* N.S. 68/3, 181–198.

Borovskaya, N. F. (1997) Liry iz 'tsarskikh grobnits' Ura kak pamyatniki shumerskoy kul'tury rannedinas-ticheskogo perioda (Lyres from the 'royal tombs' of Ur as monuments of Sumerian culture of the Early Dynastic age, in Russian). *Vestnik drevney istorii* 4(223), 1997, 3–13.

Bottema, S. (1993) The palaeoenvironment of prehistoric man in the Near East: some aspects of palyno-logical research, *Nichibunken Japan Review – Bulletin of the International Research Center for Japanese Studies* 4, 129–140.

Bottema, S. and Woldring, H. (1984) Late Quarternary vegetation and climate of SW Turkey. *Palaeohistoria* 26, 123–149.

Boyd, R. (1972) Urbanization, morbidity and mortality, in Ucko, Tringham and Dimbleby (1972), pp. 345–352.

Braidwood, R. J. and Howe, B. (1960) *Prehistoric Investigations in Iraqi Kurdistan*. The Oriental Institute of the University of Chicago, Studies in Ancient Oriental Civilizations No. 31. Chicago: University of Chicago Press.

Brandes, M. A. (1979) *Siegelabrollungen aus den archaischen Bauschichten in Uruk-Warka (FAOS 3)*. Wiesbaden: Franz Steiner Verlag.

——(1980) 'Waffenkammer', ein neues Siegelthema der Uruk-Zeit, in *Forschungen und Funde*, Festschrift B. Neusch. Innsbruck: University of Innsbruck, pp. 77–87.

——(1986) Commemorative seals? in M. Kelly-Bucellati, P. Matthiae and M. van Loon (eds) *Insight Through Images – Studies in Honor of Edith Porada*. Bibliotheca Mesopotamica No. 21. Malibu: Undena Publications, pp. 51–55.

Bray, W. (1976) From predation to production: the nature of agricultural evolution in Mexico and Peru, in G. Sieveking, I. Longworth and K. Wilson (eds) *Problems in Economic and Social Archaeology*. London: Duckworth, pp. 73–95.

Breniquet, C. (1984) Le cimetière A de Kish. Essai d'interprétation. *Iraq* 46/1, 19–28.

——(1990) *La disparition de la culture de Halaf, ou Les origines de la culture d'Obeid dans le nord de la Mésopotamie*. Université de Paris I: Panthéon/Sorbonne, UFR 03 – Histoire de l'Art et Archéologie. Thése pour le nouveau doctorat, Paris.

——(1991a) Tell es-Sawwan 1988–1989. Compte rendu des fouilles menées par la Délégation Archéologique Française en Iraq, *Orient-Expres* 1, 7–8.

——(1991b) Tell es-Sawwan – réalités et problemes. *Iraq* 53, 75–90.

——(1996) *La disparition de la culture de Halaf: les origines de la culture d'Obeid dans le Nord de la Mésopotamie*. Paris: Editions Recherche sur les Civilisations. Reviewed by O. Nieuwenhuyse, *Bibliotheca Orientalis* 55/3–4, 1998, 506–511.

Breniquet, C. and Mintsi, E. (2000) Peintre d'Amasis et la glyptique mésopotamienne pré- et protodynas-tique. *Revue des études anciennes* 102/3–4, 333–360.

Bruce Dickson, D. (1990) *The Dawn of Belief – Religion in the Upper Palaeolithic of Southwestern Europe*. Tucson: University of Arizona Press.

Brumfiel, E. (1987) Consumption and politics at Aztec Huexotla. *American Anthropologist* 89/3, 676–686.

Burrows, E. (1935) *Ur Excavation Texts II*. London: The British Museum.

CAD vol. G: A. L. Oppenheim *et al.* (eds) (1956) *Chicago Assyrian Dictionary*, vol. 5. Chicago: Oriental Institute of the University of Chicago and Glückstadt: J. J. Augustin Verlagsbuchhandlung.

Calvet, Y. (1987) L'apport de Tell el-'Oueilli a la chronologie d'Obeid, in Aurenche *et al.* (1987), pp. 465–472.

Campbell, S. (1986) The Halaf culture pottery from the 1983 season, in Saddam Husein Dam (1986), pp. 37–62.

Carrier, J. (1990) The symbolism of possession in commodity advertising. *Man* N.S. 25/4, 693–706.

Carter, R., Crawford, H., Mellalieu, S. and Barrett, D. (1999) The Kuwait–British archaeological expedition to As-Sabiyah: Report on the first season's work. *Iraq* 61, 43–58.

Casal, J.-M. and Casal, G. (1956) *Site urbain et sites funéraires des environs de Pondichéry: Virampatnam – Mouttrapaléon – Souttoukeny.* Paris: Presses Universitaires de France.

Casanova, M. (1991) *La vaisselle d'albâtre de Mésopotamie, d'Iran et d'Asie centrale aux IIIe et IIe millénaires avant J.C.* Mémoires de la Mission Archéologique Française en Asie Centrale 4. Paris: Centre de Recherches d'Archéologie Orientale, Université de Paris I, No. 9.

—— (1994) Lapis lazuli beads in Susa and Central Asia, a preliminary study, in A. Parpola and P. Koskikallio (eds) *South Asian Archaeology 1993*, vol. I. Helsinki: Suomalainen Tiedeakatemia, pp. 137–145.

Cauvin, J. (1978) *Les premiers villages en Syrie-Palestine du IXe au VIIe millénaire avant J. C.* Lyon: Maison de l'Orient.

—— (1994) *Naissance des divinités, Naissance de l'agriculture. La Révolution des symboles au Néolithique.* Paris: CNRS Editions.

Charpin, D. (1990) A contribution to the geography and history of the kingdom of Kahat, in S. Eichler, M. Wäfler and D. Warburton (eds) *Tall al-Hamidiya 2.* Freiburg, Switzerland: Universitätsverlag and Göttingen: Vandenhoeck and Ruprecht, pp. 67–85.

Charpin, D. and Joannès, F. (eds) (1992) *La circulation des biens, des personnes et des idées dans le Proche-Orient ancien.* Actes du 38e RAI, Paris 8–10 juillet 1991. Paris.

Charvát, P. (1976) The oldest royal dynasty of Ancient Mesopotamia. *Archív Orientální* 44, 346–352.

—— (1988a) Archaeology and social history: the Susa sealings, Ca. 4000–2340 B.C. *Paléorient* 14/1, 57–63.

—— (1988b) The origins of Sumerian states: a modest proposal, in P. Vavroušek and Vl. Souček (eds) *ŠULMU.* Papers on the ancient Near East presented at an international conference of socialist countries (Prague, 30 Sept.–3 Oct., 1986). Prague: Charles University, pp. 101–132.

—— (1990) Plus ultra: Kolonizace a její mechanismy v předindustriální společnosti (Plus ultra: colonization and its mechanisms in pre-industrial societies, in Czech with an English summary). *Památky archeologické* 81, 458–465.

—— (1992a) The token of the covenant: stamp seals of the ancient Near East. *Archív Orientální* 60, 279–284.

—— (1992b) Out of sight, out of mind: the limits of archaeological vision, in J. Prosecký (ed.) *Ex pede pontis – Papers presented on the occasion of the 70th anniversary of the foundation of the Oriental Institute, Prague.* Prague: The Oriental Institute, pp. 86–93.

—— (1994) The seals and their functions in the Halaf and Ubaid cultures (A case study of materials from Tell Arpachiyah and Nineveh 2–3), in R.- B. Wartke (ed.) *Handwerk und Technologie im Alten Orient – Ein Beitrag zur Geschichte der Technik im Altertum.* Internationale Tagung Berlin 12.–15. März 1991. Mainz: Verlag Philipp von Zabern, pp. 9–15.

—— (1996) On sealings and officials: Sumerian DUB and SANGA, c.3500–2500 B.C. in P. Zemánek (ed.) *Studies in Near Eastern Languages and Literatures. Memorial volume of Karel Petráček.* Prague: The Oriental Institute, Academy of Sciences of the Czech Republic, pp. 181–192.

—— (1997) *On People, Signs and States: Spotlights on Sumerian Society, c.3500–2500 BC.* Prague: The Oriental Institute, Academy of Sciences of the Czech Republic.

Cheetham, L. (1982) Threshing and winnowing – an ethnographic study. *Antiquity* 56/217, 127–130.

Chighine, M., Ferioli, P. and Fiandra, E. (1985) Controllo e sicurezza delle porte di Arslantepe – Confronto con sistemi moderni, in M. Liverani, A. Palmieri and R. Perroni (eds) *Studi di Paletnologia in onore di Salvatore M. Puglisi.* Roma: 'La Sapienza', 237–248.

Ching, J. (1997) Son of Heaven: sacral kingship in ancient China. *T'oung-pao* LXXXIII/1–3, 3–41.

Civil, M. (1987) Studies on Early Dynastic lexicography III. *Orientalia* N.S. 56, 233–244.

Civil, M. and Biggs, R. D. (1966) Notes sur des textes sumériens archaïques. *Revue d'Assyriologie* 60/1, 1–15.

Clark, G. (1967) *The Stone Age Hunters.* London: Thames and Hudson.

Cleuziou, S. and Tosi, M. (1994) Black boats of Magan: some thoughts on Bronze Age water transport in

Oman and beyond from the impressed bitumen slabs of Ras al-Junayz, in A. Parpola and P. Koskikallio (eds) *South Asian Archaeology 1993*, vol. II. Helsinki: Suomalainen Tiedeakatemia, pp. 745–761.

Clutton-Brock, J. (1980) The early history of domestic animals in western Asia. *Sumer* 36/1–2, 37–41.

Collon, D. (1983) Hunting and shooting. *Anatolian Studies* XXXIII (number celebrating the 75th birthday of R. D. Barnett,), 51–56.

Connan, J. and Ourisson, G. (1993) *De la géochimie pétrolière à l'étude des bitumes anciens: L'archéologie moléculaire*. Académie des Inscriptions et de Belles-Lettres, Comptes-rendus des séances de l'année 1993, novembre-décembre, fasc. IV, Paris: de Boccard, pp. 901–921.

Cooper, J. (1981) Gilgamesh and Agga: a review article. *Journal of Cuneiform Studies* 33/3–4, pp. 224–241.

—— (1983) *The Curse of Agade*. Baltimore, Md.: Johns Hopkins University Press.

—— (1984) Studies in Mesopotamian lapidary inscriptions III. *Iraq* 46, 87–93.

—— (1985) Medium and message: inscribed clay cones and vessels from presargonic Sumer. *Revue d'Assyriologie* 79/2, 97–114.

—— (1986) Studies in Mesopotamian lapidary inscriptions V. *Revue d'Assyriologie* 80, 73–74.

Copeland, L. and Hours, F. (1987) The Halafians, their predecessors and their contemporaries in northern Syria and the Levant – relative and absolute chronologies, in Aurenche *et al.* (1987), pp. 401–425.

Coursey, D. G. (1972) The civilization of the yam. *Archaeology and Physical Anthropology in Oceania* 7/3, 215–233.

Crawford, H. (1972) Stimuli towards urbanization in South Mesopotamia, in Ucko *et al.* (1972), pp. 761–762.

—— (1973) Mesopotamia's invisible exports in the 3rd millennium. *World Archaeology* 5/2, 231–242.

Crawford, V. (1974) Lagash. *Iraq* 36/1–2, 29–35.

—— (1977) Inscriptions from Lagash season four, 1975–1976. *Journal of Cuneiform Studies* 29/4, 189–222.

Creamer, W. and Haas, J. (1985) Tribe versus chiefdom in lower Central America. *American Antiquity* 50(4), 738–754.

Croft, P. (1995) The faunal assemblage, in Baird *et al.* (1995), pp. 165–172.

Crowfoot, E., Whiting, M. C. and Tubb, K. (1995) Textiles from excavations at Nimrud. *Iraq* LVII, 113–118.

Cunningham, G. (1997) *'Deliver me from Evil.' Mesopotamian Incantations 2500–1500* BC. Studia Pohl, Series Major 17. Roma: Editrice Pontificio. Reviewed by N. Veldhuis, *Bibliotheca Orientalis* 55/5–6, 1998, 850–852.

Curtis, J. (ed.) (1982) *Fifty Years of Mesopotamian Discovery*. London: British School of Archaeology in Iraq.

Dalley, St. (1991) Gilgamesh in the Arabian Nights. *Journal of the Royal Asiatic Society* 3rd Ser. I/1, 1–18.

Dalongeville, R. and Sanlaville, P. (1987) Confrontation des datations isotopiques avec les données géo-morphologiques et archéologiques à propos des variations relatives de niveau marin sur la rive arabe du Golfe Persique, in Aurenche *et al.* (1987), pp. 567–583.

Damerow, P. and Englund, R. (1985) *Die Zahlzeichensysteme der Archaischen Texte aus Uruk*. Max-Planck-Institut für Bildungsforschung, Forschungsbereich Entwicklung und Sozialisation, No. 5/ES, n.p., September 1985.

Damerow, P., Englund, R. and Lamberg-Karlovsky, C. C. (1989) *The Proto-Elamite Texts from Tepe Yahya*. Bulletin of the American Schools of Prehistoric Research No. 39. Cambridge, Mass.: Peabody Museum of Archaeology and Ethnology, Harvard University.

Damerow, P., Englund, R. and Nissen, H. (1988a) Die Entstehung der Schrift. *Spektrum der Wissenschaft* 2, February, 74–85.

—— (1988b) Die ersten Zahldarstellungen und die Entwicklung des Zahlbegriffs. *Spektrum der Wissenschaft* 3, March, 46–55.

Danti, M. D. (1997) Hassuna, in Myers (1997), vol. 2, pp. 483–484.

Danti, M. D. and Zettler, R. (1997) Eridu, in Myers (1997), vol. 2, pp. 258–260.

Davidson, T. E. and McKerrel, H. (1976) Pottery analysis and Halaf period trade in the Khabur headwaters region. *Iraq* 38/1, 45–56.

—— (1980) The neutron activation analysis of Halaf and Ubaid pottery from Tell Arpachiyah and Tepe Gawra. *Iraq* 42/2, 155–167.

De Contenson, H. (1971) review of P. Mortensen, *Tell Shimshara. Syria* 48, pp. 216–223.

De Laet, S. J., Dani, A. H., Lorenzo, J. L. and Nunoo, R. B. (eds) (1994) *History of Humanity I – Prehistory and the Beginnings of Civilization*. Paris, London and New York: UNESCO, Routledge.

Delavaud-Roux, M.H. (1993) *Les danses armées en Grèce antique*. Aix-en-Provence: Publications de l'Université de Provence.

Delougaz, P. (1938) A short investigation of the temple at Al-Ubaid. *Iraq* 5, 1–11.

—— (1940) *The Temple Oval at Khafajah*. Oriental Institute Publications No. 53. Chicago: University of Chicago Press.

Delougaz, P. *et al.* (1967) *Private Houses and Graves from the Diyala Region*. Oriental Institute Publications No. 88. Chicago: University of Chicago Press.

Delougaz, P. and Kantor, H. (1973) Chogha Mish. *Iran* 11, 189–191.

Delougaz, P. and Lloyd, S. (1942) *Pre-Sargonid Temples in the Diyala Region*. Oriental Institute Publications No. 58. Chicago: University of Chicago Press.

Dennel, R. (1980) Economic archaeology, in Sherratt (1980a), pp. 38–42.

Dixon, D. M. (1972) The disposal of certain personal household and town waste in ancient Egypt, in Ucko *et al.* (1972), pp. 647–650.

Dubuisson, D. (1985) Matériaux pour une typologie des structures trifonctionelles. *L'Homme* 93, XXV/1, 105–121.

Duby, G. (1988) *La société chevaleresque – Hommes et structures du Moyen Age*. n.p.: Flammarion.

Duff-Cooper, A. (1991) Balinese exchange: replication and reaffirmation of 'The One'. *Southeast Asian Studies* 29/2, 179–204.

Duistermaat, K. (1994) The clay sealings from Late Neolithic Tell Sabi Abyad. Doctoraalscriptie, Faculteit der Letteren, Universiteit van Leiden. Leiden. (My thanks go to the author for having kindly supplied me with a copy of her thesis.)

Duistermaat, K. and Schneider, G. (1998) Chemical analyses of sealing clays and the use of administrative artifacts at Late Neolithic Tell Sabi Abyad (Syria). *Paléorient* 24/1, 89–106.

Durga, P. S. K. and Reddy, Y. A. S. (1992) Kings, temples and legitimation of autochthonous communities: a case study of a South Indian temple. *Journal of the Economic and Social History of the Orient* 35/II, 145–166.

Edens, Ch. M. and Kohl, Ph. (1993) Trade and world systems in Early Bronze Age western Asia, in Ch. Scarre and F. Healy (eds) *Trade and Exchange in Prehistoric Europe*. Proceedings of a conference held at the University of Bristol, April 1992. Oxford: Oxbow Books – The Prehistoric Society – Société Préhistorique Française, pp. 17–34.

Edzard, D. O. (1974) Problème de la royauté dans la période présargonique, in *Le palais et la royauté (19ème Rencontre Assyriologique Internationale)*, Paris: Geuthner, pp. 141–149.

—— (1976) Fara und Abu Salabikh. Die 'Wirtschaftstexte'. *Zeitschrift für Assyriologie* 66, 156–195.

Eggert, M. K. H. (1991) Prestigegüter und Sozialstruktur in der Späthallstattzeit: eine kulturanthropologische Perspektive. *Saeculum* 42/1, 1–28.

Ehret, Ch. (1988) Language change and the material correlates of language and ethnic shift. *Antiquity* 62/236, 564–574.

Eichmann, R. (1989) *Uruk – die Stratigraphie. Grabungen 1912–1977 in den Bereichen 'Eanna' und 'Anu-Ziqqurat'*. AUWE, vol. 3. Mainz am Rhein: Philipp von Zabern.

—— (1991) 4. 5. Steingeräte, in Finkbeiner (1991), pp. 177–181.

—— (1995) Zithern vor den Lauten? in Finkbeiner *et al.* 1995, pp. 107–120.

Eickhoff, T. (1993) *Grab und Beigabe: Bestattungssitten der Nekropole von Tall Ahmad al- Hattū und anderen frühdynastischen Begräbnisstätten im südlichen Mesopotamien und in Luristān*. München-Wien: Profil Verlag. Reviewed by J.-D. Forest, *Bibliotheca Orientalis* 52/5–6, 1995, 787–793.

Ellison, R. *et al.* (1978) Some food offerings from Ur. *Journal of Archaeological Science* 5/2, 167–177.

—— (1981) Diet in Mesopotamia: the evidence of the barley ration texts (c. 3,000–1,400 B.C.). *Iraq* 43/1, 35–46.

—— (1982) The agriculture of Mesopotamia c. 3,000–600 B.C. *Tools and Tillage* 4/3, 173–184.

—— (1986) Table manners in Mesopotamia. *University College London – Institute of Archaeology Bulletin* 23, 151–159.

Endesfelder, E. (1991) review of W. Helck, *Untersuchungen zur Thinitenzeit*, Wiesbaden: Harrassowitz (1987). *Orientalistische Literaturzeitung* 86/2, 145–150.

Englund, R. (n.d.) *see* Englund (1990).

—— (1984) Die Fischerei im archaischen Uruk. Unveröffentlichte Magisterarbeit an der Universität München.

—— (1988) Administrative timekeeping in Ancient Mesopotamia. *Journal of the Economic and Social History of the Orient* 31, 121–185.

—— (1990) *Organisation und Verwaltung der Ur-III–Fischerei*. Berlin: Dietrich Reimer (the original doctoral dissertation cited as Englund n.d.).

—— (1991) Archaic dairy metrology. *Iraq* 53, 101–104.

—— (1994) *Archaic Administrative Texts from Uruk – The Early Campaigns*. ATU, vol. 5. Berlin: Verlag Gebrüder Mann.

—— (1995a) Late Uruk Period cattle and dairy products: evidence from the proto-cuneiform sources. *Bulletin on Sumerian Agriculture* 8, 33–48.

—— (1995b) Late Uruk pigs and other herded animals, in Finkbeiner *et al.* (1995), pp. 121–133.

Englund, R., Grégoire, J. P. and Matthews, R. J. (1991) *The Proto-cuneiform Texts from Jemdet Nasr I: Copies, Transliterations and Glossary*. MSVO 1. Berlin: Gebrüder Mann Verlag.

Englund, R. and Matthews, R. J. (1996) Proto-cuneiform Texts from Diverse Collections. MSVO 4. Berlin: Verlag Gebrüder Mann. Review by P. Steinkeller, *Bulletin of the School of Oriental and African Studies, University of London*, 62/1, 1999, 115–117.

Englund, R. and Nissen, H.-J. (1993) *Die lexikalische Listen der archaischen Texte aus Uruk*. Berlin: Verlag Gebrüder Mann. Review by N. Veldhuis, *Bibliotheca Orientalis* 52/3–4, 1995, 434–440.

Esin, U. (1983) Zur Datierung der vorgeschichtlichen Schichten von Degirmentepe bei Malatya in der östlichen Türkei, in R. M. Boehmer and H. Hauptmann (eds) *Beiträge zur Altertumskunde Kleinasiens – Festschrift für Kurt Bittel*. Mainz am Rhein: Philipp von Zabern, pp. 175–190.

—— (1985) Some small finds from the Chalcolithic occupation at Degirmentepe (Malatya) in eastern Turkey, in M. Liverani, A. Palmieri and R. Peroni (eds) *Studi di Paletnologie in onore di Salvatore M. Puglisi*. Roma: 'La Sapienza', pp. 253–263.

Esse, D. L. (1992) The collared pithos at Megiddo: ceramic distribution and ethnicity. *Journal of Near Eastern Studies* 51/2, 81–103.

Fagan, B. (1991) The civilizing influence of wine. *Archaeology* 44/5, 14–16, 87.

Fairservis, W. A., Jr. (1991) G. L. Possehl's and M. H. Raval's 'Harappan Civilization and Rajdi'. *Journal of the American Oriental Society* 111/1, 108–114.

Faraone, Ch. A. (1991) Binding and burying the forces of evil: the defensive use of 'voodoo dolls' in Ancient Greece. *Classical Antiquity* 10/2, 165–220.

Farber, G. (1982) Rinder mit Namen, in *Zikir Šumim (Festschrift zum 70. Geburtstag von Fritz R. Kraus)*. Leiden: E. J. Brill, pp. 34–36.

Feffer, L.-Ch. and Périn, P. (1987) *Les Francs 2: A l'origine de la France*. Paris: Armand Colin.

Felten, F. G. (1993) Neolithisierungsmodelle, oder: Der Umgang mit dem Neuen in der Urgeschichtswissenschaft. *Archäologische Informationen* 16/2, pp. 201–233.

Ferchland, A. and Wartke, R.-B. (1990) *Staatliche Museen zu Berlin – Handwerk und Technologie im Alten Orient*. Sonderausstellung des Vorderasiatischen Museums vom 29.11.1990–30.4.1991. Begleittext. Berlin: Staatliche Museen Preussischer Kulturbesitz.

Ferioli, P. and Fiandra, E. (1983) Clay sealings from Arslantepe VI A. administration and bureaucracy. *Origini* XII/2, 455–509.

Ferioli, P., Fiandra, E., Fissore, G. G. and Frangipane, M. (1994) *Archives Before Writing*. Proceedings of the International Colloquium, Oriolo Romano, 23–25 October 1991. Torino: Scriptorium and Ministero per i beni culturali e ambientali, Ufficio centrale per i beni archivistici.

Fiandra, E. (1981a) The connections between clay sealings and tablets in administration, in H. Härtel (ed.) *South Asian Archaeology 1979*. Papers from the 15th International Conference of the Association of South Asian Archaeologists in Western Europe held in the Museen für Indische Kunst der Staatlichen Museen Preussischer Kulturbesitz Berlin. Berlin: Dietrich Reimer Verlag, pp. 29–43.

—— (1981b) Attivita a Kish di un mercante di Lagash in epoca presargonica. *Oriens Antiquus* 3, 165–174.

—— (1983) Clay sealings from Arslantepe VI A: administration and bureaucracy. *Origini* XII/2, 455–509.

Finet, A. (1975) Les temples sumériens du Tell Kannas. *Syria* 52, 157–174.

Finkbeiner, U. (1984) Uruk-Warka XXXVI – Survey des Stadtgebietes von Uruk, Vorläufiger Bericht über die 2. Kampagne 1983. *Baghdader Mitteilungen* 15, 87–112.

—— (1986) Uruk-Warka. Evidence of the Gamdat Nasr Period, in Finkbeiner and Röllig 1986, pp. 33–56.

—— (ed.) (1991) *Uruk-Kampagne 35–37, 1982–1984, Die archäologische Oberflächenuntersuchung (survey).* AUWE, vol. 4. Mainz am Rhein: Philipp von Zabern.

—— (1993) *Uruk. Analytisches Register zu den Grabungsberichten. Kampagnen 1912/13 bis 1976/77 (unter Mitarbeit M. R. Behm-Blancke).* Berlin: Verlag Gebrüder Mann.

—— (1995) Tell Bleibis. Eine Burg der Urukzeit am mittleren Eufrat, in Finkbeiner *et al.* (1995), pp. 139–144.

Finkbeiner, U., Dittmann, R. and Hauptmann, H. (eds) (1995) *Beiträge zur Kulturgeschichte Vorderasiens. Festschrift für Rainer Michael Boehmer.* Mainz am Rhein: Philipp von Zabern.

Finkbeiner, U. and Röllig, W. (eds) (1986) *Gamdat Nasr – Period or Regional Style?* Papers given at a symposium held in Tübingen, November 1983. Wiesbaden: Dr. Ludwig Reichert Verlag.

Finkel, I. (1985) Inscriptions from Tell Brak, 1984. *Iraq* 47, 187–201.

Fiorina, P. (1984) Excavation at Tell Hassan, Preliminary Report. *Sumer* 40/1–2, 277–289.

Flannery, K. (1983) Early pig domestication in the Fertile Crescent: a retrospective look, in Young *et al.* (1983), pp. 163–188.

Flannery, K. and Cornwall, I. (1969) The fauna from Ras al-Amiya, Iraq: a comparison with the Deh Luran sequence, in Hole *et al.* (1969), pp. 435–438.

Flannery, K. and Wheeler, J. (1967) Animal bones from Tell es-Sawwan III (Samarra). *Sumer* 23/1–2, 179–182.

Flannery. K. and Wright, H. T. (1966) Faunal remains from the 'hut sounding' at Eridu, Iraq. *Sumer* 22/1–2, 61–64.

Fleming, D. (1989) Eggshell ware pottery in Achaemenid Mesopotamia. *Iraq* 51, 165–185.

Forest, J.-D. (1983a) *Les pratiques funéraires en Mésopotamie du cinquième millénaire au début du troisième, étude de cas.* Paris: Editions Recherche sur les Civilisations.

—— (1983b) Aux origines de l'architecture obeidienne: les plans de type Samarra. *Akkadica* 34, 1–47.

—— (1987) Les bevelled rim bowls: Nouvelle tentative d'interprétation. *Akkadica* 53, 1–24.

—— (1989) Les 'jetons' non-urukiens et l'échange des femmes, in Henrickson and Thuesen (1989), pp. 199–226.

—— (1991) 'Régularités métriques' de l'architecture obeidienne. *Orient-Express* 1, 18.

—— (1995) Le rôle de l'irrigation dans la dynamique évolutive en Mésopotamie. *Archéo-Nil, Bulletin de la société pour l'étude des cultures prépharaoniques de la vallée du Nil 5*, mai, 67–77.

—— (1996) *Mésopotamie – L'apparition de l'état, VIIe–IIIe millénaires.* Paris: Paris–Méditerranée.

Forest, J.-D. and Calvet, Y. (1987) Tall al-'Uwaili. *Archiv für Orientforschung* 34, 148–155.

Foster, B. R. (1977) review of A. Westenholz, *Old Sumerian and Old Akkadian texts, chiefly of administrative contents, from Nippur. Journal of Near Eastern Studies* 36/4, 299–302.

—— (1980) Notes on Sargonic royal progress. *The Journal of the Ancient Near Eastern Society of Columbia University* 12, 29–42.

—— (1981) A new look at the Sumerian temple state. *Journal of the Economic and Social History of the Orient* 24/3, pp. 225–241.

—— (1982) *Umma in the Sargonic Period.* Hamden, Conn.: Archon Books.

Frangipane, M. (1996) *La nascita dello Stato nel Vicino Oriente – Dai lignaggi alla burocrazia nella Grande Mesopotamia.* Roma-Barri: Editori Laterza.

Frankfort, H. (1955) *Stratified Cylinder Seals from the Diyala Region.* Oriental Institute Publications No. 72. Chicago: Chicago University Press.

—— (1968) *The Last Predynastic Period in Babylonia.* Cambridge Ancient History Fasc. 65 (vol. I, ch. 12). Cambridge: Cambridge University Press.

Freeman, L. (1980) The development of human culture, in Sherratt (1980a), pp. 79–86.

Friberg, J. (1999) Counting and accounting in the proto-literate Middle East: examples from two new volumes of proto-cuneiform texts. *Journal of Cuneiform Studies* 51, 107–138.

Fujii, H. (ed.) (1981) *Preliminary Report of Excavations at Gubba and Songor.* Hamrin Report 6. Baghdad: State Organization of Antiquities and Heritage and Tokyo: Kokushikan University Institute for Cultural Studies of Ancient Iraq.

——(1983–1984) The Japanese excavations in Hamrin. *Archiv für Orientforschung* 29–30, 199–206.

Galaty, J. G. and Johnson, D. L. (eds) (1990) *The World of Pastoralism – Herding Systems in Comparative Perspective.* New York: The Guilford Press and London: Belhaven Press.

Garelli, P. (1969) *Le Proche-Orient Asiatique, des origines aux invasions des peuples de la mer. Nouvelle Clio.* Paris: Presses universitaires de France.

Gebel, H.-G. (1984) *Das Akeramische Neolithikum Vorderasiens – Subsistenzformen und Siedlungsweisen.* Beihefte zum *Tübinger Atlas des Vorderen Orients* B 52. Wiesbaden: Dr. Ludwig Reichert Verlag.

Gebel, H.-G. and Muheisen, M. (1997) Basta, in Myers (1997), vol. 1, pp. 279–280.

Gelb, I. J. (1984) Šibut kušurra'im, 'witnesses of the indemnity'. *Journal of Near Eastern Studies* 43/4, pp. 263–276.

Gelb, I. J., Steinkeller, P. and Whiting, R., Jr. (1991) *Earliest Land Tenure Systems in the Near East: Ancient Kudurrus.* Oriental Institute Publications No. 104. Chicago: Oriental Institute of the University of Chicago.

Genouillac, H. de (1934) *Fouilles de Telloh I: Epoques Présargoniques.* Paris: Geuthner.

Gibbon, G. (1984) *Anthropological Archaeology.* New York: Columbia University Press.

Gibson, McG. (1974) Violation of fallow and engineered disaster in Mesopotamian civilization, in Th. E. Downing and McG. Gibson (eds) *Irrigation's Impact on Society.* Anthropological papers of the University of Arizona No. 25. Tucson: University of Arizona Press, pp. 7–20.

——(ed.) (1981) *Uch Tepe I. Tell Razuk, Tell Ahmed al-Mughir, Tell Ajamat.* Hamrin Report 10. Chicago: Oriental Institute of the University of Chicago and Copenhagen: University of Copenhagen – Carsten Niebuhr Institute.

——(1984) Chicago–Copenhagen excavations at Uch Tepe 1978–1979. *Sumer* 40/1–2, 62–63.

——(1990a) Chapter VII: differential distribution of faunal material at Razuk, in Gibson (1990b), pp. 109–120.

——(ed.) (1990b) *Uch Tepe II – Technical Reports.* Chicago: Oriental Institute of the University of Chicago and Copenhagen: University of Copenhagen – Carsten Niebuhr Institute.

Gilbert, A. S. (1983) On the origins of specialized nomadic pastoralism in western Iran. *World Archaeology* 15/1, 105–119.

Glass, P. (1988) Trobriand symbolic geography. *Man* 23/1, 56–76.

Glassner, J.-J. (1984) La division quinaire de la terre. *Akkadica* 40, 17–34.

—— (1993) Le roi prêtre en Mésopotamie, au milieu du 3e millénaire – mythe ou réalité? in *L'ancien Proche-Orient et les Indes – Parallélismes interculturels religieux.* Colloque franco-finlandais les 10 et 11 novembre 1990 à l'Institut finlandais, Paris. Studia Orientalia 70, Helsinki: Finnish Oriental Society, pp. 9–20.

——(1995) La gestion de la terre en Mésopotamie selon le témoignage des kudurrus anciens. *Bibliotheca Orientalis* 52/1–2, 5–24.

——(1996) Dilmun, Magan and Meluhha: some observations on language, toponymy, anthroponymy and theonymy, in J. Reade (ed.) *The Indian Ocean in Antiquity*, London and New York: Kegan Paul International, in association with the British Museum, London, pp. 235–248.

——(2000a) Ecrire à Sumer – L'invention du cunéiforme. n.p.: Editions du Seuil.

——(2000b) Les petits Etats mésopotamiens à la fin du 4e et au cours du 3e millénaire, in M. H. Hansen (ed.) *A Comparative Study of Thirty City-State Cultures.* Historisk-filosofiske Skrifter 21, Det kongelige Danske Videnskabernes Selskab. The Royal Danish Academy of Sciences and Letters. Copenhagen: C. A. Reitzels Forlag, pp. 35–53.

Gockel, W. (1983) Ur und al-'Ubaid. *Akkadica* 32, 32–52.

Goetze, A. (1970) Early dynastic dedication inscriptions from Nippur. *Journal of Cuneiform Studies* 23/2, pp. 39–56.

Gophna, R. *et al.* (1995) *Excavations at 'En Besor.* Tel Aviv University: Ramot Publishing House.

Götzelt, T. (1995) Zur sumerischen und akkadischen Verwandschaftsterminologie, in Finkbeiner *et al.* (1995), pp. 177–182.

Gouin, Ph. (1993) Bovins et laitage en Mésopotamie méridionale au 3eme millénaire. *Iraq* 55, 135–145.

Green, M. W. (1980) Animal husbandry at Uruk in the Archaic Period. *Journal of Near Eastern Studies* 39/1, 1–35.

——(1984) Early Sumerian tax collectors. *Journal of Cuneiform Studies* 36/1, 93–95.

——(1991) Early cuneiform, in W. M. Senner (ed.), *The Origins of Writing*. Lincoln and London: University of Nebraska Press, pp. 43–57.

Guinan, A. (1996) Social constructions and private designs: the house omens *Šumma alu*, in Veenhof (1996), pp. 61–68.

Gut, R. (1992) Das prähistorische Ninive – Zur relativen Chronologie der frühen Perioden Nordmesopotamiens, in *XXXIXᵉ Rencontre Assyriologique Internationale: Assyrien im Wandel der Zeiten*. Heidelberg, 6.–10. Juli 1992. Résumés – Coopération Internationale, pp. 31–32.

——(1995) Unbeabsichtigte Ergebnisse, in Finkbeiner *et al.* (1995), pp. 183–186.

Gwinnett, A. J. and Gorelick, L. (1987) The change from stone drills to copper drills in Mesopotamia: an experimental perspective. *Expedition* 29/3, 15–24.

Hagège, Cl. (1987) *Der dialogische Mensch – Sprache-Weltbild-Gesellschaft*. Reinbek bei Hamburg: Rowohlt Taschenbuch Verlag.

Hall, H. R. (1930) *A Season's Work at Ur, al-'Ubaid, Abu Shahrain (Eridu) and Elsewhere*. London: Methuen.

Hamilton, N., Marcus, J., Bailey, D., Haaland, G., Haaland, R. and Ucko, P. J. (1996) Can we interpret figurines? *Cambridge Archaeological Journal* 6/2, pp. 281–307.

Hansen, D. P. (1970) Al Hiba 1968–1969. *Artibus Asiae* 32/4, pp. 243–250.

——(1971) Some Early Dynastic I sealings from Nippur, in *Studies presented to George M. A. Hanfman*. Mainz, pp. 47–54.

——(1973) Al-Hiba 1970–1971: a preliminary report. *Artibus Asiae* 35, 62–78.

——(1987) The fantastic world of Sumerian art: seal impressions from Ancient Lagash, in A. Farkas, P. Harper and E. Harrison (eds) *Monsters and Demons in the Ancient and Medieval World*. Papers presented in honour of Edith Porada. Mainz am Rhein: Philipp von Zabern, pp. 53–64.

——(1997a) Khafajeh, in Myers (1997), vol. 3, pp. 288–290.

——(1997b) Kish, in Myers (1997), vol. 3, pp. 298–300.

Harlan, J. (1994) Plant domestication – an overview, in De Laet *et al.* (1994), pp. 377–388.

Harris, D. (ed.) (1996) *The Origins and Spread of Agriculture and Pastoralism in Eurasia*. London: University College of London Press.

Harris, D., Gosden, Ch. and Charles, M. P. (1996) Jeitun: recent excavations at an early Neolithic site in S Turkmenistan. *Proceedings of the Prehistoric Society* 62, 423–442.

Hassan, F. A. and Robinson, S. W. (1987) High-precision radiocarbon chronometry of ancient Egypt and comparisons with Nubia, Palestine and Mesopotamia. *Antiquity* 61/231, 119–135.

Hayden, B. (1990) Nimrods, piscators, pluckers, and planters: the emergence of food production. *Journal of Anthropological Archaeology* 9, 31–69.

Heimpel, W., Gorelick, L. and Gwinnett, A. J. (1988) Philological and archaeological evidence for the use of emery in the Bronze Age Near East. *Journal of Cuneiform Studies* 40/2, 195–210.

Heinrich, E. (1936) *Kleinfunde aus dem archaischen Tempelschichten in Uruk*. Berlin: Deutsche Forschungsgemeinschaft and Leipzig: Kommissionsverlag Otto Harrassowitz.

——(1982) *Die Tempel und Heiligtümer im alten Mesopotamien*. Berlin: Walter de Gruyter.

Helbaek, H. (1960) Ecological effects of irrigation in ancient Mesopotamia. *Iraq* 22, 186–196.

——(1972) Samarran irrigation agriculture at Choga Mami in Iraq. *Iraq* 34, 35–48.

Hemker, Ch. (1993) *Altorientalische Kanalisation: Untersuchungen zu Be- und Entwässerunsanlagen im mesopotamisch-syrisch-anatolischen Raum 1–2*. Münster: Agenda Verlag.

Hendrickx, S. (1990) review of B. Adams, *The Fort Cemetery at Hierakonpolis*, London & N.Y. (1987). *Bibliotheca Orientalis* 47/5–6, 643–646.

Henrickson, E. (1981) Non-religious residential settlement patterning in the Late Early Dynastic of the Diyala region. *Mesopotamia* 16, 43–140.

—— (1982) Functional analysis of elite residences in the Late Early Dynastic of the Diyala region: House D and the walled quarter at Khafajah and the 'palaces' at Tell Asmar. *Mesopotamia* 17, 5–33.

Henrickson, E. and McDonald, M. (1983) Ceramic form and function: an ethnographic search and an archaeological application. *American Anthropologist* 85/3, 630–643.

Henrickson, E. and Thuesen, I. (1989) *Upon this Foundation – the 'Ubaid Reconsidered*. Proceedings from the 'Ubaid symposium, Elsinore, 30 May–1 June 1988. Copenhagen: The Carsten Niebuhr Institute of Ancient Near Eastern Studies, University of Copenhagen, and Museum Tusculanum Press.

Henrickson, R. C. (1984) Šimaški and central western Iran: the archaeological evidence. *Zeitschrift für Assyriologie* 74/I, 98–122.

—— (1994) review of Killick (1988). *Journal of Near Eastern Studies* 53/4, 304–306.

Hermansen, B. D. (1991) Ancient Egypt in Barry Kemp's perspective. *Acta Orientalia* (Copenhagen) 52, 7–34.

Hestrin, R. and Dayagi-Mendels, M. (1979) *Inscribed Seals. First Temple Period, Hebrew, Ammonite, Moabite, Phoenician and Aramaic. From the Collections of the Israel Museum and the Israel Department of Antiquities and Museums*. Jerusalem.

Hijara, I. *et al.* (1980) Arpachiyah 1976. *Iraq* 42/2, 131–154.

Hirsch, H. (1968–1969) Ausgrabungen in Arbela. *Archiv für Orientforschung* 22, 134.

—— (1970) Ausgrabungen in Arbela. *Archiv für Orientforschung* 23, 147–148.

Hisashi, T. (1990) The Western Chou Dynasty and the vermillion bows and arrows: on the characteristics of the possessor (king) of the 'Four Quarters'. *Tohogaku* (Eastern Studies) 80, July, The Institute of Eastern Culture, Tokyo, p. 4.

Hodder, I. (1987) Contextual archaeology: an interpretation of Catal Hüyük and a discussion of the origins of agriculture. *University College London – Institute of Archaeology Golden Jubilee Bulletin* 24, 43–56.

Hodges, R. (1989) *The Anglo-Saxon Achievement – Archaeology and the Beginnings of English Society*. London: Duckworth.

Hoffmann, M. (1974) Social context of trash disposal in an Early Dynastic Egyptian town. *American Antiquity* 39, 1974/1, 35–50.

Hole, F. (1983) Symbols of religion and social organization at Susa, in Young *et al.* (1983), pp. 315–331.

—— (1987a) Chronologies in the Iranian Neolithic, in Aurenche *et al.* (1987), 353–379.

—— (1987b) Issues in Near Eastern archaeology, in Aurenche *et al.* (1987), pp. 559–563.

—— (ed.) (1987c) *The Archaeology of Western Iran: Settlement and Society from Prehistory to the Islamic Conquest*. Washington DC: Smithsonian Institution Press.

—— (1989) Patterns of burial in the 5th millennium, in Henrickson and Thuesen (1989), pp. 149–180.

Hole, F. and Flannery, K. (1967) The prehistory of southwestern Iran: a preliminary report. *Proceedings of the Prehistoric Society* 33, 147–206.

Hole, F., Flannery, K. and Neely, J. (1969) *Prehistory and Human Ecology of the Deh Luran Plain*. Memoirs of the Museum of Anthropology, University of Michigan No. 1. Ann Arbor, Michigan.

Hopf, M. (1988) Plant cultivation in the Old World: its beginning and diffusion, in Processes of Neolithization in the Mediterranean and Europe. Symposium held at the 12th International Congress of Anthropological and Ethnological Sciences, Zagreb, Yugoslavia, 24–31 July 1988. *Berytus* 36, 27–34.

Horn, N. (1995) *Das Pferd im Alten Orient: das Streitwagenpferd der Frühzeit in seiner Umwelt, im Training und im Vergleich zum neuzeitlichen Distanz-, Reit- und Fahrpferd*. Hildesheim, Zürich and New York: Olms Presse.

Howe, B. (1972) Flint cache found at site no. 213, Tell al-Jir, in McG. Gibson *The City and Area of Kish*. Miami: Field Research Projects, pp. 209–210.

—— (1991) Rice, ideology and the legitimation of hierarchy in Bali. *Man* 26/3, 445–467.

Høyrup, J. (1997) Geometry in the Near and Middle East, in H. Selin (ed.) *Encyclopaedia of the History of Science, Technology and Medicine in Non-Western Cultures*. Dordrecht, Boston and London: Kluwer Academic Publishers, pp. 380–383.

Hrouda, B. (1971) *Handbuch der Archäologie: Vorderasien I (Mesopotamien, Babylonien, Iran und Anatolien)*. München: C. H. Beck.

Hruška, B. (1986) K počátkům zemědělství na Předním Východě (On the origins of agriculture in the Near East, in Czech with a German summary). *Československý časopis historický* 34/2, pp. 209–227.

—— (1987) Efektivnost tradičního obilnářství starého Předního Východu (Efficiency of the traditional cerealiculture of the ancient Near East, in Czech with a German summary). *Československý časopis historický* 35/2, pp. 241–251.

—— (1988) Die Bewässerungsanlagen in den altsumerischen Königsinschriften von Lagaš. *Bulletin on Sumerian Agriculture* 4, 61–72.

—— (1990) *Tradiční zemědělství starověké Mezopotámie – Der traditionelle Ackerbau im alten Mesopotamien.* Praha: Orientální ústav ČSAV.

—— (1995) Herden für Götter und Könige. Schafe und Ziegen in der altsumerischen Zeit. *Altorientalische Forschungen* 22/1, 73–83.

Hudson, M. (2000) How interest rates were set, 2500 BC – 1000 AD. *Journal of the Economic and Social History of the Orient* 43/2, 132–161.

Huot, J.-L. (ed.) (1983) *Larsa et 'Oueili – Travaux de 1978–1981.* Paris: Editions Recherche sur les Civilisations.

—— (1987) *Larsa – 10e campagne, 1983, et 'Oueili – 4e campagne, Rapport préliminaire.* Paris: Editions Recherche sur les Civilisations.

—— (1989) 'Ubaidian villages of lower Mesopotamia – permanence and evolution from 'Ubaid 0 to 'Ubaid 4 as seen from Tell el-'Oueilli, in Henrickson and Thuesen 1989, pp. 19–42.

—— (1991a) Les travaux français a Tell el-'Oueilli et Larsa. Un bilan provisoire. *Akkadica* 73, 1–32.

—— (1991b) *'Oueili, Travaux de 1985.* Paris: Editions Recherche sur les Civilisations.

—— (ed.) (1996) *'Oueili – Travaux de 1987 et 1989.* Paris: Editions Recherche sur les Civilisations.

Huot, J.-L. *et al.* (1983) Tell el-'Oueilli: The works of 1978 and 1981. *Sumer* 39/1–2, 18–67.

Huot, J.-L. and Maréchal, C. (1985) L'emploi du gypse en Mésopotamie du sud à l'époque d'Uruk, in *De l'Indus aux Balkans, Recueil Jean Deshayes.* Paris: Editions Recherche sur les Civilisations, pp. 261–275.

Hurcombe, L. M. (1992) *Use Wear Analysis and Obsidian: Theory, Experiments and Results.* Sheffield: J. R. Collis Publications and Department of Archaeology and Prehistory, University of Sheffield.

Huxley, M. (2000) The gates and guardians in Sennacherib's addition to the Temple of Assur. *Iraq* 62, 109–138.

Ii, H. (1988) Seals and seal impressions from Tell Gubba (in Japanese with an English summary). *Al-Rafidan* 9, Kokushikan University, Tokyo, pp. 97–134.

Ikeda, J., Wada, Y. and Ishida, H. (1984–1985) Human skeletal remains of the Jamdat Nasr period from Tell Gubba, Iraq. *Al-Rafidan* 5–6, Kokushikan University, Tokyo, pp. 215–234.

Inizan, M.-L. (1985) Le débitage par pression au Moyen-Orient. Premières observations, in *De l'Indus aux Balkans, Recueil Jean Deshayes.* Paris: Editions Recherche sur les Civilisations, pp. 43–54.

Invernizzi, A. (1980) Excavations in the Yelkhi area (Hamrin Project, Iraq). *Mesopotamia* 15, 19–49.

Ippolitoni-Strika, F. (1996) Halafian art, religion, society: the funerary bowl from Arpachiyah – the fringed square as a 'sacred rug'. *Mesopotamia* XXXI, 5–31.

Ismail, B. K. and Tosi, M. (1976) A turquoise neck-stone of king Ninurta-apal-Ekur. *Sumer* 32/1–2, 105–112.

Jagersma, B. (1990) review of Alberti and Pomponio (1986). *Bibliotheca Orientalis* 47/5–6, 671–674.

Jahresbericht (1977) Jahresbericht 1977 des Deutschen Archäologischen Instituts. *Archäologischer Anzeiger* 1978/4, 602–649.

Jakob-Rost, L., Wartke, R.-B. and Wesarg, B. (1983) Tell Owessat. *Sumer* 39/1–2, 103–136.

Jasim, S. A. (1989) Structure and function in an 'Ubaid village, in Henrickson and Thuesen 1989, pp. 79–90.

Jawad, A. J. (1974) The Eridu material and its implications. *Sumer* 30/1–2, 11–46.

Johnson, G. A. (1976) Uruk villages on the Susiana Plain. *Iran* 14, 171–172.

Kaplony, P. (1983) Der Schreiber, das Gotteswort und die Papyruspflanze. *Zeitschrift für Aegyptische Sprache und Altertumskunde* 110, 143–173.

—— (1984) Ein 'Senior der Jungmannschaft' der Frühzeit und seine Opferliste (Sp 53), in *Studien zur Sprache und Religion Aegyptens (Festschrift Wohlfart Westendorf).* Göttingen: Vandenhoeck und Ruprecht, pp. 521–546.

—— (1991) *König Niuserre und die Annalen.* Mitteilungen des Deutschen Archäologischen Instituts (Abteilung Kairo) 47 (Festschrift Werner Kaiser), pp. 195–204.

Karg, N. (1984–1985) review of W. Gockel, *Die Stratigraphie und Chronologie der Ausgrabungen des Diyala-Gebietes und der Stadt Ur in der Zeit von Uruk/Eanna IV bis zur Dynastie von Akkad,* Rom 1982. *Acta Praehistorica et Archaeologica* 16/17, 304–306.

Katz, D. (1987) Gilgamesh and Akka: was Uruk ruled by two assemblies? *Revue d'Assyriologie* 81, 105–114.

—— (1993) *Gilgamesh and Akka.* Groningen: Styx.

Katz, N. and Kemnitzer, D. (1978) Social anthropology and some trends in contemporary Marxist thought. *American Anthropologist* 80/3, 597–604.

Keel, O. (1990) Früheisenzeitliche Glyptik in Palästina/Israel, in O. Keel, M. Shuval and Ch. Uehlinger, *Studien zu den Stempelsiegeln aus Palästina/Israel III: Die Frühe Eisenzeit, Ein Workshop.* Freiburg, Switzerland: Universitätsverlag and Göttingen: Vandenhoeck und Ruprecht, pp. 331–421.

Keel-Leu, H. (1989) Die frühesten Stempelsiegel Palästinas. Von den Anfängen bis zum Ende des 3. Jahrtausends, in O. Keel, H. Keel-Leu and S. Schroer, *Studien zu den Stempelsiegeln aus Palästina/Israel II.* Freiburg, Switzerland: Universitätsverlag and Göttingen: Vandenhoeck und Ruprecht, 1–38.

Kelm, G. L. and Mazar, A. (1989) Excavating in Samson Country. *Biblical Archaeology Review* 15/1, 36–49.

Keswani, P. S. (1994) The social context of animal husbandry in early agricultural societies: ethnographic insights and an archaeological example from Cyprus. *Journal of Anthropological Archaeology* 13/3, 255–277.

Killick, R. (1986) The Eski Mosul region, in Finkbeiner and Röllig (1986), pp. 229–244.

—— (ed.) (1988) *Tell Rubeidhah: An Uruk Village in the Jebel Hamrin.* Warminster: Aris and Phillips.

Killick, R. and Black, J. (1985) Excavations in Iraq, 1983–1984. *Iraq* 47, pp. 215–239.

Kilmer, A. D. (1995) Music and dance in ancient western Asia, in Sasson *et al.* (1995), pp. 2601–2613.

King, T. F. (1978) Don't that beat the band? Nonegalitarian political organization in prehistoric central California, in Ch. L. Redman *et al.* (eds) *Social Archaeology – Beyond Subsistence and Dating.* New York, San Francisco and London: Academic Press, pp. 225–248.

Kiple, K. (1996) The history of disease, in R. Porter (ed.) *The Cambridge Illustrated History of Medicine,* Cambridge, New York and Melbourne: Cambridge University Press, pp. 16–51.

Kirkbride, D. (1982) Umm Dabaghiyah, in J. Curtis (ed.) *Fifty Years of Mesopotamian Discovery.* London: The British School of Archaeology in Iraq, pp. 11–21.

Klengel, H. and Renger, J. (eds) (1999) *Landwirtschaft im Alten Orient – Ausgewählte Vorträge der XLI.* Rencontre Assyriologique Internationale, Berlin 4–8 July 1994. BBVO, vol. 18. Berlin: Dietrich Reimer Verlag.

Kohl, P. (1976) 'Steatite' carvings of the early 3rd millennium B.C. *American Journal of Archaeology* 80/1, 73–75.

—— (1978) The balance of trade in southwest Asia in the 3rd millennium B.C. *Current Anthropology* 19/3, 463–492.

Kohl, P., Harbottle, G. and Sayre, E. (1979) Physical and chemical analyses of soft stone vessels from southwest Asia. *Archaeometry* 21/2, 131–159.

Köhler-Rollefson, I. (1992) A model for the development of nomadic pastoralism on the transjordanian plateau, in O. Bar-Yosef and A. Khazanov (eds) *Pastoralism in the Levant – Archaeological Materials in Anthropological Perspectives.* Madison, Wisconsin: Prehistory Press, pp. 11–18.

Kohlmeyer, K. (1994) Zur frühen Geschichte von Blei und Silber, in Wartke (1994), pp. 41–48.

Kohlmeyer, K. and Hauser, St. (1994) *Uruk – Kleinfunde IV: Die Kleinfunde aus Ton.* AUWE, vol. 13. Mainz am Rhein: Philipp von Zabern.

Kolbus, S. (1982) Unter dem Schutt aus einem der ersten Handelskontore von Ur: wohin datiert der sog. Gemdet Nasr-Friedhof? *Akkadica* 30, 1–11.

—— (1983) Zur Chronologie des sog. Gamdat Nasr-Friedhofs in Ur. *Iraq* 45/1, 7–17.

Kosso, P. (1991) Method in archaeology: middle-range theory as hermeneutics. *American Antiquity* 56(4), 621–627.

Kozlowski, J. K. and Śliwa, J. (1977) *Archeologia wschodniej czesci basenu Morza Srodziemnego* (Archaeology of the Eastern Part of the Mediterranean Basin, in Polish). Kraków: Uniwersytet Jagiellonski.

Kozlowski, S. K. and Bielinski, P. (1984) Tell el Saadiya – a preliminary report on the first season of excavations, 1979. *Sumer* 40/1–2, 103–106.

Kozlowski, S. K. and Kempisty, A. (1990) Architecture of the pre-pottery Neolithic settlement in Nemrik, Iraq. *World Archaeology* 21/3, 348–362.

Kravtsova, M. E. (1991) Ot magii – k etike. Predstavleniya o verkhovnoy vlastyi i yeyo nositele v drevnem i rannesrednevekovom Kitaye (From magic to the ethics. Ideas of the supreme rule and its bearer in ancient and early medieval China, in Russian). *Vostok* 1991/3, 32–41.

Krebernik, M. (1986) Die Götterlisten aus Fara. *Zeitschrift für Assyriologie* 76/II, 161–204.

Kurke, L. (1992) The politics of abrosuné in archaic Greece. *Classical Antiquity* (California) 11/1, 91–120.

Kuz'mina, E. E. (1997) Ekologiya stepey Evrazii i problema proiskhozhdeniya nomadisma II: Vozniknoveniye kochevogo skotovodstva (Ecology of the Eurasian steppes and the problem of origins of nomadism II: emergence of nomadic cattle-keeping, in Russian). *Vestnik drevney istorii* 221/2, 81–95.

Lambert, M. (1954) Epigraphie présargonique IX. *Revue d'Assyriologie* 48, pp. 207–210.

—— (1956) review of E. Sollberger, *Corpus des Inscriptions 'Royales' Présargoniques de Lagaš*, Geneve 1956. *Revue d'Assyriologie* 50, 105–106.

—— (1957) Le quartier Lagash. *Rivista degli Studi Orientali* 32/I, Festschrift G. Furlani, pp. 123–143.

Langdon, St. (1928) *The Herbert Weld Collection of the Ashmolean Museum -Pictographic Inscriptions from Jemdet Nasr.* Oxford Editions of Cuneiform Studies, vol. VII. London etc.: Oxford University Press.

La Niece, S. (1995) Depletion gilding from third millennium BC Ur. *Iraq* LVII, 41–47.

Lansing, J. St. (1987) Balinese 'water temples' and the management of irrigation. *American Anthropologist* 89/2, 326–341.

Larsen, P. (1991) Technologische Aspekte zur Entwicklung der Rollsiegelproduktion von ihren Anfängen bis zur Zeit der ersten Dynastie von Babylon. Magisterarbeit, eingereicht am Fachbereich Altertumswissenschaften der Freien Universität Berlin.

Lebeau, M. (1990) Esquisse d'une histoire de la Haute Mésopotamie au début de l'Age du Bronze. *Zeitschrift für Assyriologie* 80/II, pp. 241–296.

Le Brun, A. (1980) Les écuelles grossières: état de la question, in *L'archéologie de l'Iraq du début de l'époque néolithique a 333 av. n. e.* Paris: Editions du CNRS, pp. 59–70.

Lechevallier, M. (1976) review of M. van Loon, *Korucutepe, Final Report*, Chicago and London 1973. *Revue d'Assyriologie* 70/1, 93.

Leichty, E. (1987) Omens from doorknobs. *Journal of Cuneiform Studies* 39/2, 190–196.

Le Mythe (1988) Le Mythe et ses métamorphoses. *L'homme* 106–107, 28(2–3), the entire number.

Lenzen, H. (1940) Die Grabungsergebnisse, in *11. Uruk Vorläufiger Bericht.* Berlin: Preussische Akademie der Wissenschaften, philosophisch-historische Klasse, pp. 6–31.

—— (1958) Mosaiktempel und Riemchengebäude in Md-Na XV 4–XVI 2, in *14. Uruk Vorläufiger Bericht,* Berlin: Abhandlungen der Deutschen Orient-Gesellschaft, pp. 21–35.

—— (1962) Die hocharchaischen Schichten von E-anna, in *18. Uruk Vorläufiger Bericht,* Berlin: Deutscher Archäologischer Institut, Abteilung Baghdad, pp. 7–11.

—— (1964) Uruk IV, in *20. Uruk Vorläufiger Bericht,* Berlin: Deutscher Archäologischer Institut, Abteilung Baghdad, pp. 8–10.

—— (1965) Uruk III, in *21. Uruk Vorläufiger Bericht,* Berlin: Deutscher Archäologischer Institut, Abteilung Baghdad, pp. 11–12.

—— (1967) Anu-Zikurrat, in *23. Uruk Vorläufiger Bericht,* Berlin: Deutscher Archäologischer Institut, Abteilung Baghdad, pp. 10–21.

—— (1974) Die Architektur in Eanna in der Uruk IV periode. *Iraq* 36/1–2, 111–128.

Le Roy Ladurie, E. (1975) Montaillou, village occitan de 1294 a 1324. n.p.: Gallimard.

Lévi-Strauss, C. (1974) *Anthropologie structurale.* Paris: Plon.

Levy, T. E. (1992) Transhumance, subsistence and social evolution in the northern Negev Desert, in O. Bar-Yosef and A. Khazanov (eds) *Pastoralism in the Levant – Archaeological Materials in Anthropological Perspectives.* Madison, Wisconsin: Prehistory Press, 65–82.

Lieberman, S. J. (1980) Of clay pebbles, hollow clay balls and writing: a Sumerian view. *American Journal of Archaeology* 84, 339–358.

Limet, H. (1982) 'Peuple' et 'humanité' chez les Sumériens, in *Zikir Šumim* (Festschrift zum 70. Geburtstag von F. R. Kraus). Leiden: E. J. Brill, pp. 258–267.

Limper, C. (1988) *Uruk – Perlen, Ketten, Anhänger. Grabungen 1912–1985.* AUWE, vol. 2. Mainz am Rhein: Philipp von Zabern.

Liphschitz, N., Gophna, R., Hartman, M. and Biger, G. (1991) The beginning of olive (Olea Europaea) cultivation in the Old World: a reassessment. *Journal of Archaeological Science* 18/4, 441–454.

Liverani, M. (1996) Reconstructing the rural landscape of the Ancient Near East, *Journal of the Economic and Social History of the Orient* 39/1, 1–41.

Liverani, M. and Heimpel, W. (1995) Observations on livestock management in Babylonia. *Acta Sumerologica* (Japan) 17, 127–144.

Lloyd, S. (1940) Iraq Government soundings at Sinjar. *Iraq* 7, 13–21.

—— (1960) Ur, al-Ubaid, Eridu . . . *Iraq* 22, pp. 23–31.

Lloyd, S. and Safar, F. (1943) Tell Uqair – excavations by the Iraq Government Directorate of Antiquities in 1940 and 1941. *Journal of Near Eastern Studies* 2, 131–158.

—— (1945) Tell Hassuna – excavations by the Iraq Government Directorate General of Antiquities in 1943 and 1944. *Journal of Near Eastern Studies* 4/4, pp. 255–289.

Lorton, D. (1979) review of W. Helck, *Wirtschaftsgeschichte des alten Aegypten. Journal of the American Oriental Society* 99/2, 374–376.

Luciani, M. (1999) Zur Lage Terqas in schriftlichen Quellen. *Zeitschrift für Assyriologie* 89/I, 1–23.

Lupton, A. (1996) *Stability and Change – Socio-Political Development in Northern Mesopotamia and Southeastern Anatolia, 4000–2700 BC.* BAR International Series 627. n.p.: Tempvs reparatum.

Lutz, J., Pernicka, E. and Wagner, G. A. (1994) Chalkolithische Kupferverhüttung in Murgul, Ostanatolien, in Wartke (1994), pp. 59–66.

McAdam, E. (1982) Tell Rubeidhah – a short note on the pottery. *Sumer* 38/1–2, 163–164.

—— (1995) The Proto-Hassuna pottery, in Baird *et al.* (1995), pp. 32–54.

McCall, J.C. (1995) Rethinking ancestors in Africa. *Africa* 65/2, pp. 256–270.

Macdonald, M. C. A. (1992) The seasons and transhumance in the Safaitic inscriptions. *Journal of the Royal Asiatic Society* Series 3, 2/1, 1–11.

McDougall, E. A. (1985) The view from Audaghost: war, trade and social change in the southwestern Sahara from the 8th to the 15th century. *Journal of African History* 26/I, 1–31.

McIntosh, R. J. and McIntosh, S. K. (1983) Forgotten tells of Mali. *Expedition* 25/2, 35–46.

Mackay, E. (1929) *A Sumerian Palace and the 'A' Cemetery at Kish, Mesopotamia.* Chicago: Field Museum of Natural History.

Macneish, R. S. (1972) The evolution of community patterns in the Tehuacán valley of Mexico and speculations about the cultural process, in Ucko *et al.* (1972), pp. 67–93.

McNett, Ch. W., Jr. (1979) The cross-cultural method in archaeology, in M. Schiffer (ed.) *Advances in Archaeological Method and Theory 2.* New York etc.: Academic Press, pp. 39–76.

Maddin, R., Wheeler, T. S. and Muhly, J. (1977) Tin in the Ancient Near East. *Expedition* 19/2, 35–48.

Maekawa, K. (1976) The erín-people in Lagash of Ur III times. *Revue d'Assyriologie* 70, 9–44.

Maisels, Ch. K. (1987) Models of social evolution: trajectories from the Neolithic to the state. *Man* 22/2, 331–359.

—— (1990) *The Emergence of Civilization – From Hunting and Gathering to Agriculture, Cities and the State in the Near East.* London and New York: Routledge.

—— (1993) *The Near East: Archaeology in the 'Cradle of Civilization'.* London and New York: Routledge.

Makovicky, E. and Thuesen, I. (1990) Paint and paste studies on selected pottery sherds from Tell Razuk, Iraq, in McG. Gibson (ed.) *Uch Tepe II – Technical Reports.* Chicago: The Oriental Institute of the University of Chicago and Copenhagen: University of Copenhagen – Carsten Niebuhr Institute, pp. 19–64.

Mallowan, M. E. L. (1965) *Early Mesopotamia and Iran.* London: Thames and Hudson.

—— (1968) *The Early Dynastic Period in Mesopotamia.* Cambridge Ancient History Fasc. 62. Cambridge: Cambridge University Press.

Mallowan, M. E. L. and Linford, H. (1969) Rediscovered skulls from Arpachiyah. *Iraq* 31, 49–58.

Mallowan, M. E. L. and Rose, J. C. (1935) Excavations at Tall Arpachiyah 1933. *Iraq* 2, 1–178.

Margueron, J.-Cl. (1991) Information: de l'Uruk dans le delta du Nil? *Orient-Express* 1, 10.

——(1996) La maison orientale, in Veenhof (1996), pp. 17–38.

Marschner, R. F. and Wright, H. T. (1978) Asphalts from Middle Eastern archaeological sites, in G. F. Carter (ed.) *Advances in Chemistry Series No. 171: Archaeological Chemistry II*. n.p.: American Chemical Society, pp. 150–171.

Martin, H. (1982) The Early Dynastic cemetery at Al-Ubaid, a re-evaluation. *Iraq* 44/2, 145–185.

——(1988) *Fara: A Reconstruction of the Ancient Mesopotamian City of Shuruppak*. Birmingham, UK: Chris Martin and Associates.

——(1997) Fara, in Myers (1997), vol. 2, pp. 301–303.

Martin, H. P., Moon, J. and Postgate, J. N. (1985) *Graves 1–99. Abu Salabikh Excavations,* vol. 2. London: British School of Archaeology in Iraq.

Marx, E. (1978) The ecology and politics of nomadic pastoralists in the Middle East, in W. Weissleder (ed.) *The Nomadic Alternative – Modes and Models of Interaction in the African-Asian Deserts and Steppes*. The Hague and Paris: Mouton Publishers, pp. 41–74.

Marzahn, J. (1991) *Altsumerische Verwaltungstexte aus Girsu/Lagaš*. Berlin: Akademie-Verlag. Reviewed by G. Selz, *Orientalistische Literaturzeitung* 88/3, 1993, pp. 270–273.

——(1996) *Altsumerische Verwaltungstexte und ein Brief aus Girsu/Lagaš*. Mainz am Rhein: Philipp von Zabern.

Matthews, R. J. (1989) Excavations at Jemdet Nasr, 1988. *Iraq* 51, pp. 225–248.

——(1990) Excavations at Jemdet Nasr, 1989. *Iraq* 52, pp. 25–39.

——(1991) Fragments of officialdom from Fara. *Iraq* 53, 1–16.

——(1993) *Cities, Seals and Writing: Archaic Seal Impressions from Jemdet Nasr and Ur*. MSVO, vol. 2. Berlin: Gebrüder Mann Verlag.

——(1995) Offerings to the gods: seal impressions on archaic tablets, in Finkbeiner *et al.* (1995), pp. 389–394.

——(1997) Jemdet Nasr, in Myers (1997), vol. 3, pp. 211–213.

Matthews, R. J., Postgate, J. N. and Luby, E. J. (1987) Excavations at Abu Salabikh, 1985–1986. *Iraq* 49, 91–119.

Matthews, R. J. and Wilkinson, T. (1991) Excavations in Iraq 1989–1990. *Iraq* 53, 169–182.

Mayer-Opificius, R. (1984) review of B. Hrouda: *Isin – Išan Bahriyat II*, München 1981. *Zeitschrift für Assyriologie* 74/I, 143–148.

Mazzoni, S. (1984) Seal-impressions on jars from Ebla in EB I AB. *Akkadica* 37, 18–45.

Meadow, R. (1971) The emergence of civilization, in H. Shapiro (ed.) *Man, Culture and Society*. London, Oxford and New York: Oxford University Press, pp. 112–167.

——(1992) Inconclusive remarks on pastoralism, nomadism, and other animal-related matters, in O. Bar-Yosef and A. Khazanov (eds) *Pastoralism in the Levant – Archaeological Materials in Anthropological Perspectives*. Madison, Wisconsin: Prehistory Press, pp. 261–269.

Mellink, M. (1988) Archaeology in Anatolia. *American Journal of Archaeology* 92/1, 101–131.

——(1989) Archaeology in Anatolia. *American Journal of Archaeology* 93/1, 105–133.

——(1992) Archaeology in Anatolia. *American Journal of Archaeology* 96/1, 119–150.

Merpert, N. Ya. and Munchaev, R. M. (1982) Poseleniye ubeydskoy kul'tury Yarim-Tepe III v severnoy Mesopotamii (in Russian with an English summary: Yarimtepe III settlement of the Ubaid culture in northern Mesopotamia). *Sovetskaya Arkheologiya* 4/1982, 133–149.

Milano, L. (1987) Food rations at Ebla, in *Mari, Annales de Recherches Interdisciplinaires 5*. Paris: Editions Recherche sur les Civilisations, pp. 519–551.

——(ed.) (1994) *Drinking in Ancient Societies: History and Culture of Drinks in the Ancient Near East*. Papers of a symposium held in Rome, 17–19 May 1990. Padova: Sargon.

Millard, A. R. (1988) The bevelled-rim bowls: their purpose and significance. *Iraq* 50, 49–58.

Miller, D. (1980) Settlement and diversity in the Solomon Islands. *Man* N.S. 15, 451–466.

Miller, J. C. (1982) The significance of drought, disease and famine in the agriculturally marginal zones of west-central Africa. *Journal of African History* 23/1, 17–61.

Miller, N. F. (1996) Seed eaters of the Ancient Near East: human or herbivore?, *Current Anthropology* 37/3, 521–528.

—— (2000) Plant forms in jewellery from the royal cemetery at Ur. *Iraq* 62, 149–155.

Miller, R. L. (1991) Counting calories in Egyptian ration texts. *Journal of the Economic and Social History of the Orient* 34/III, pp. 257–269.

Miller, R., McEwen, E. and Bergman, C. (1986) Experimental approaches to ancient Near Eastern archery. *World Archaeology* 18/2, 178–195.

Molleson, T. and Jones, K. (1991) Dental evidence for dietary change at Abu Hureyra. *Journal of Archaeological Science* 18/5, 525–539.

Mommsen, H., Perlman, I. and Yellin, J. (1984) The Provenience of the lmlk jars. *Israel Exploration Journal* 34/2–3, 89–113.

Monteil, K. (1995) L'état des recherches en archéologie sous-marine au Levant I–II. Mémoire de maîtrise sous la direction de Jean-Louis Huot. UFR 3, Université de Paris I – Sorbonne.

Moon, J. (1982) The distribution of upright-handled jars and stemmed dishes in the Early Dynastic period. *Iraq* 44/1, 39–69.

—— (1986) The Lower Diyala and the Hamrin Basin: ceramic relations during the early third millennium, in Finkbeiner and Röllig (1986), pp. 112–120.

—— (1987) *Catalogue of Early Dynastic Pottery. Abu Salabikh Excavations*, vol. 3. London: British School of Archaeology in Iraq.

Moore, A. M. T. (1983) The first farmers in the Levant, in Young *et al.* (1983), pp. 91–112.

Moorey, P. R. S. (1977) What do we know about the people buried in the Royal Cemetery? *Expedition*, Fall, 24–40.

—— (1978) *Kish Excavations 1923–1933.* Oxford: Clarendon Press.

—— (1980) Abu Salabikh, Kish, Mari and Ebla: mid-third millennium archaeological interconnections. *American Journal of Archaeology* 84, 447–448.

—— (1982a) Archaeology and Pre-Achaemenid metalworking in Iran: a fifteen year retrospective. *Iran* 20, 81–102.

—— (1982b) The archaeological evidence for metallurgy and related technologies in Mesopotamia, c. 5,500–2,100 B.C. *Iraq* 44/1, 13–38.

—— (1984) Where did they bury the kings of the IIIrd dynasty of Ur? *Iraq* 46, 1–18.

—— (1985) *Materials and Manufacture in Ancient Mesopotamia: The Evidence of Archaeology and Art.* Oxford: BAR – International Series 237.

—— (1994) *Ancient Mesopotamian Materials and Industries.* Oxford: Clarendon Press. Reviewed by T. Potts, *American Journal of Archaeology* 100/1, 1996, 176–177.

Moorey, P. R. S. and Gurney, O. (1978) Ancient Near Eastern cylinder seals acquired by the Ashmolean Museum, Oxford, 1963–1973. *Iraq* 40, 41–60.

Moortgat, A. and Moortgat-Correns, U. (1974) Archäologische Bemerkungen zu einem Schatzfund im vor-sargonischen Palast in Mari. *Iraq* 36/1–2, 155–167.

Morris, I. (1986) Gift and commodity in archaic Greece. *Man* 21/1, 1–17.

Mortensen, P. (1972) Seasonal camps and early villages in the Zagros, in Ucko *et al.* (1972), pp. 293–297.

—— (1973) A sequence of Samarran flint and obsidian tools from Choga Mami. *Iraq* 35, 37–55.

—— (1983) Patterns of interaction between seasonal settlements and early villages in Mesopotamia, in Young *et al.* (1983), pp. 207–230.

Mudar, K. (1982) Early Dynastic III animal utilization in Lagash: a report on the fauna of Tell al-Hiba. *Journal of Near Eastern Studies* 41/1, 23–34.

Müller-Karpe, M. (1990a) Metallgefässe des dritten Jahrtausends in Mesopotamien. *Archäologisches Korrespondenzblatt* 20/2, 161–176.

—— (1990b) Der Guss in der verlorenen Sandform in Mesopotamien. *Mitteilungen der Deutschen Orient-Gesellschaft* 122, 173–192.

—— (1991) Aspects of early metallurgy in Mesopotamia. *Archaeometry* 90. Basel, Boston and Berlin: Borkhauser Verlag, pp. 105–116.

Müller-Karpe, M., Pászthory, E. and Pernicka, E. (1993) *Metallgefässe in Iraq I (Von den Anfängen bis zur Akkad-Zeit)*. PBF, Part II, vol. 14. Stuttgart: Franz Steiner Verlag.

Munchaev, R. M. (1997) Yarimtepe II: K izucheniyu arkhitektury severnoy Mesopotamii V tysiachiletiya do nashey ery (Yarimtepe II: On studies of the architecture of N Mesopotamia of the fifth millennium BC, in Russian). *Rossiyskaya Arkheologiya* 1997/3, 5–19.

Munchaev, R. M. and Merpert, N. Ya. (1981) Rannezemledel'cheskiye poseleniya severnoy Mesopotamii – Earliest agricultural settlements of northern Mesopotamia (in Russian with extensive English summary). Moskva: 'Nauka'.

Myers, E. M. (ed.) (1997) *The Oxford Encyclopaedia of Archaeology in the Near East*, vols 1–5. New York and Oxford: Oxford University Press.

Nagel, W. and Strommenger, E. (1994) Der frühsumerische Kultschlitten – ein Vorläufer des Wagens? in P. Calmeyer, K. Hecker, L. Jakob-Rost and C. Walker (eds) *Beiträge zur Altorientalischen Archäologie und Altertumskunde*. Festschrift für Barthel Hrouda zum 65. Geburtstag. Wiesbaden: Harrassowitz, pp. 201–209.

—— (1995) Sechzig Jahre Forschung zur früdynastischen Bildkunst und ein neues Denkmal des Urdynastikums, in Finkbeiner *et al.* (1995), pp. 455–468.

N. C.-H.[ans] N.[issen] (1991) Die archaischen Siegel der Erlenmayer-Sammlung, in H. Nissen, P. Damerow and R. K. Englund (eds) *Frühe Schrift und techniken der Wirtschaftsverwaltung im alten Vorderen Orient*. Bad Salzdethfurth: Verlag Franzbecker und Max-Planck-Institut für Bildungsforschung, pp. 44–45.

Neely, J. A., Wright, H. T. *et al.* (1994) *Early Settlement and Irrigation on the Deh Luran Plain – Village and Early State Societies in SW Iran*. Ann Arbor: University of Michigan, Museum of Anthropology, Technical Report 26.

Negev, A. (ed.) (1990) *The Archaeological Encyclopaedia of the Holy Land*. Third edition. New York etc.: Prentice-Hall.

Netherly, P. J. (1984) The management of late Andaean irrigation systems on the northern coast of Peru. *American Antiquity* 49/2, 227–254.

Neumann, H. (1992) Nochmals zu Kaufmann in neusumerischer Zeit: Die Geschäfte des Ur-Dun und anderer Kaufleute aus Nippur, in *La circulation des biens, des personnes et des idées dans le Proche-Orient ancien. XXXVIIIeme Rencontre Assyriologique Internationale*. Paris: Editions Recherche sur les Civilisations, pp. 83–94.

Newman, L. F. *et al.* (1990) Agricultural intensification, urbanization, and hierarchy, in L. F. Newman (ed.) *Hunger in History – Food Shortage, Poverty, and Deprivation*. Oxford and Cambridge, Mass.: Blackwell, pp. 101–125.

Nicklin, K. (1979) The location of pottery manufacture. *Man* N.S. 14, 436–458.

Nissen, H. J. (1966) *Zur Datierung der Königsgräber von Ur*. BAM 3. Bonn: Rudolf Habelt Verlag.

——(1972) The city wall of Uruk, in Ucko *et al.* (1972), pp. 793–798.

——(1985a) The emergence of writing in the Ancient Near East. *Interdisciplinary Science Reviews* 10/4, 349–361.

——(1985b) Ortsnamen in den archaischen Texten aus Uruk. *Orientalia* N.S. 54, 226–233.

——(1986a) The archaic texts from Uruk. *World Archaeology* 17/3, 317–334.

——(1986b) The development of writing and of glyptic art, in Finkbeiner and Röllig (1986), pp. 318–331.

Nissen, H. J., Damerow, P. and Englund, R. (1991) *Frühe Schrift und Techniken der Wirtschaftsverwaltung im alten Vorderen Orient*. Bad Salzdetfurth: Verlag Franzbecker und Max-Planck-Institut für Bildungsforschung.

Noy, T. and Brimer, B. (1987) Flashback one million years: reconstructing Ubeidiya's ancient landscape. *The Israel Museum Journal*, Spring, 95–96.

Nunn, A. (1985) Die Wandmalereifragmente aus Uruk-Warka. *Baghdader Mitteilungen* 16, 7–16.

Oates, D. (1982) Excavations at Tell Brak, 1978–1981. *Iraq* 44/2, 187–204.

Oates, D. and Oates, J. (1976) Early irrigation agriculture in Mesopotamia, in G. Sieveking, I. Longworth and K. Wilson (eds) *Problems in Economic and Social Archaeology*. London: Duckworth, pp. 109–135.

Oates, J. (1969) Choga Mami, 1967–1968): a preliminary report. *Iraq* 31, 115–152.

—— (1972) Prehistoric settlement patterns in Mesopotamia, in Ucko *et al.* (1972), pp. 299–310.

—— (1978) Religion and ritual in 6th millennium Mesopotamia. *World Archaeology* 10/2, 117–124.

—— (1980) Land use and population in prehistoric Mesopotamia, in *L'archéologie de l'Iraq du début de l'époque néolithique à 333 av. n. è.* Paris: Editions du CNRS, pp. 303–314.

—— (1982) Choga Mami, in J. Curtis (ed.) *Fifty Years of Mesopotamian Discovery.* London: British School of Archaeology in Iraq, pp. 22–29.

Orthmann, W. (1970) review of A. Parrot, *Mission Archéologique de Mari IV: 'Le trésor d'Ur'. Archiv für Orientforschung* 23, 97–101.

—— (1975) *Das Alte Orient.* Propyläen-Kunstgeschichte vol. 14. Berlin: Propyläen-Verlag.

Ovadia, E. (1992) The domestication of the ass and pack transport by animals. A case of technological change, in O. Bar-Yosef and A. Khazanov (eds) *Pastoralism in the Levant – Archaeological Materials in Anthropological Perspectives.* Madison, Wisconsin: Prehistory Press, 19–28.

Overmyer, D. L., Keightley, D. N., Shaughnessy, E. L., Cook, C. A. and Harper, D. (1995) Chinese religions – the state of the field I early religious traditions: the Neolithic period through the Han Dynasty (ca. 4000 BCE to 220 CE). *The Journal of Asian Studies* 54/1, 124–160.

Owen, D. (1981) Of birds, eggs and turtles. *Zeitschrift für Assyriologie* 71/I, 29–50.

Pappu, R. S. and Shinde, V. S. (1990) Site catchment analysis of the Deccan Chalcolithic in the central Tapi basin. *Bulletin of the Deccan College Post-Graduate and Research Institute* 49 (Sankalia Memorial Volume), Pune, pp. 317–331.

Pariselle, Chr. (1985) Le cimetière d'Eridu: Essai d'interprétation. *Akkadica* 44, 1–13.

Parkin, R. (1990) Ladders and circles: affinal alliance and the problem of hierarchy. *Man* N.S. 25(3), 472–488.

Parrot, A. (1960) *Sumer.* London: Thames and Hudson.

Pauketat, T. R. and Emerson, T. E. (1991) The ideology of authority and the power of the pot. *American Anthropologist* 93/4, 919–941.

Payne, J. C. (1980) An ED III flint industry from Abu Salabikh. *Iraq* 42, 105–119.

Payton, R. (1991) The Ulu Burun writing-board set. *Anatolian Studies* 41, 99–106.

Pečírková, J. (1989) Hospodářské dějiny starověku v buržoazní historiografii a ekonomický model nejstarších států Předního Východu (Ancient economic history in bourgeois historiography and the economic model of the earliest states of the Near East, in Czech with English and Russian summaries). *Československý časopis historický* 37/6, 863–876.

Peoples, J. and Bailey, G. (1988) *Humanity - An Introduction to Cultural Anthropology.* St. Paul, New York, Los Angeles and San Francisco: West Publishing Company.

Pernicka, E. (1992) review of Tallon 1987. *Journal of Near Eastern Studies* 51/1, 67–71.

Pesez, J.-M. (ed.) (1984) *Brucato – Histoire et archéologie d'un habitat médiéval en Sicile I–II.* Palais Farnèse, Rome: Ecole française de Rome.

Pfaffenberger, B. (1988) Fetishised objects and humanized nature: towards an anthropology of technology. *Man* N.S. 23/2, pp. 236–252.

Pinçon, B. and Ngoïe-Ngalla, D. (1990) L'unité culturelle kongo à la fin du XIXème siècle. L'apport des études céramologiques. *Cahiers d'études africaines* 30(2), 118, 157–178.

Pittman, H. (1994) *The Glazed Steatite Glyptic Style: The Structure and Function of an Image System in the Administration of Protoliterate Mesopotamia.* Berlin: Dietrich Reimer Verlag.

Pollock, S. (1985) Chronology of the royal cemetery of Ur. *Iraq* 47, 129–158.

—— (1989) Power politics in the Susa A period, in Henrickson and Thuesen (1989), pp. 281–292.

—— (1990a) Archaeological investigations on the Uruk mound, Abu Salabikh, Iraq. *Iraq* 52, 1990, 85–93.

—— (1990b) Political economy as viewed from the garbage dump: Jemdet Nasr occupation at the Uruk mound, Abu Salabikh. *Paléorient* 16/1, 57–75.

—— (1991) Women in a men's world: images of Sumerian women, in J. Gero and M. Conkey (eds) *Engendering Archaeology – Women and Prehistory.* Oxford: Basil Blackwell, pp. 366–387.

—— (1997) Ur, in Myers (1997), vol. 5, pp. 288–291.

—— (1999) *Ancient Mesopotamia – The Eden that Never Was.* Cambridge, New York and Melbourne: Cambridge University Press.

Pollock, S., Steele, C. and Pope, M. (1991) Investigations on the Uruk mound, Abu Salabikh, 1990. *Iraq* 53, 59–68.

Pomponio, F. (1991) Antiche sementi. *Rivista degli Studi Orientali* LXV/3–4, 161–163.

—— (1994a) review of Steinkeller and Postgate 1992. *Bibliotheca Orientalis* 51/5–6, 598–600.

—— (1994b) Re di Uruk, 're di Kiš'. *Rivista degli Studi Orientali* 68/1–2, 1–13.

—— (1998) The transfer of decorative objects and the reading of the sign DU in the Ebla documentation. *Journal of Near Eastern Studies* 57/1, 29–39.

Pongratz-Leisten, B. (1988) Keramik der frühdynastischen Zeit aus den Grabungen in Uruk-Warka. *Baghdader Mitteilungen* 19, 177–319.

Pope, M. (1989) 'Rock around Iraq': the Uruk lithic industry at Abu Salabikh. Dissertation Research Prospectus. State University of New York at Binghamton, Anthropology Department. 10 October 1989. Manuscript on file, SUNY, Binghamton. (I cite this work with the kind permission of the author.)

Postgate, J. N. (1980a) Excavations at Abu Salabikh 1978–1979. *Iraq* 42/2, 87–104.

—— (1980b) Early Dynastic burial customs at Abu Salabikh. *Sumer* 36/1–2, 65–82.

—— (1980c) Palm-trees, reeds, and rushes in Iraq ancient and modern, in *L'archéologie de l'Iraq du début de l'époque néolithique à 333 av. è.* Paris: Editions du CNRS, pp. 99–109.

—— (ed.) (1981) Excavations in Iraq 1979–1980. *Iraq* 43/2, 167–198.

—— (1981–1982) Abu Salabikh 1981. *Archiv für Orientforschung* 28, pp. 255–257.

—— (1982) Abu Salabikh, in J. Curtis (ed.) *Fifty Years of Mesopotamian Discovery.* London: British School of Archaeology in Iraq, pp. 48–61.

—— (1986) The transition from Uruk to Early Dynastic: continuities and discontinuities in the record of settlement, in Finkbeiner and Röllig (1986), pp. 90–106.

—— (1994) *Early Mesopotamia: Society and Economy at the Dawn of History.* London and New York: Routledge.

—— (1997) Abu Salabikh, in Myers (1997), vol. I, pp. 9–10.

Postgate, J. N. and Moon, J. A. (1982) Excavations at Abu Salabikh, 1981. *Iraq* 44/2, 103–136.

Potts, D. T. (1989) Foreign stone vessels of the late third millennium B.C. from southern Mesopotamia: their origins and mechanisms of exchange. *Iraq* 51, 123–164.

—— (1990) *The Arabian Gulf in Antiquity I–II.* Oxford: Clarendon Press.

—— (1994) *Mesopotamia and the East: An Archaeological and Historical Study of Foreign Relations c. 3400–2000 BC.* Oxford: Institute of Archaeology. Review by M. Liverani, *Orientalia* N.S. 66/1, 1997, 106–108, and by K. Abdi, *Journal of Near Eastern Studies* 59/4, 2000, 277–284.

—— (1995) Watercraft of the Lower Sea, in Finkbeiner *et al.* (1995), pp. 559–571.

Powell, M. A., Jr. (1976a) The antecedents of Old Babylonian place notation and the early history of Babylonian mathematics. *Historia Mathematica* 3, 417–439.

—— (1976b) Evidence for local cults at Presargonic Zabala. *Orientalia* N.S. 45/1–2, 100–104.

—— (1977) Sumerian merchants and the problem of profit. *Iraq* 39, pp. 23–29.

—— (1978a) A contribution to the history of money in Mesopotamia prior to the invention of coinage, in B. Hruška and G. Komoróczy (eds) *Festschrift Lubor Matouš II* (publ. 1981). Budapest: Eötvös Loránd University of Budapest, pp. 211–243.

—— (1978b) Texts from the time of Lugalzagesi – problems and perspectives in their interpretation. *Hebrew Union College Annual* 49 (publ. 1979), 1–58.

—— (1979) Ancient Mesopotamian weight metrology: methods, problems, and perspectives, in M. A. Powell, Jr. and R. H. Sack (eds) *Studies in Honor of Tom B. Jones. Altes Orient und Altes Testament* 203. Neukirchen-Vluyn: Butzon & Bercker Kevelaer Neukirchener Verlag, pp. 71–109.

—— (1984a) Sumerian cereal crops. *Bulletin on Sumerian Agriculture* I, 46–72.

—— (1984b) Late Babylonian surface mensuration – a contribution to the history of Babylonian agriculture and arithmetic. *Archiv für Orientforschung* 31, 32–66.

—— (1985) Salt, seed, and yields in Sumerian agriculture. A critique of the theory of progressive salinization. *Zeitschrift für Assyriologie* 75/I, 7–38.

—— (1986) Economy of the extended family according to Sumerian sources. *Oikumene* 5, 9–14.

—— (1996) Money in Mesopotamia. *Journal of the Economic and Social History of the Orient* 39/3, pp. 224–242.

Racine, L. (1986) Les formes élémentaires de la reciprocité. *L'Homme* 99, 26(3), 97–118.

Rashid, S. A. (1996) Kapitel I. Die Musik der Keilschriftkulturen, in A. Riethmüller and F. Zaminer (eds) *Die Musik des Altertums*, Neues Handbuch der Musikwissenschaft vol. I. Laaber: Laaber Verlag, 1–30.

Rast, W. E. (1987) Bronze Age cities along the Dead Sea. *Archaeology* 40/1, 43–49.

Rathbun, T. A. (1975) *A Study of the Physical Characteristics of the Ancient Inhabitants of Kish, Iraq.* Miami. (I cite this work according to a review by E. Strouhal in *Archív Orientální* 47, 1979, 127–128.)

Rathje, W. (1977) New tricks for old seals: a progress report, in McG. Gibson and R. D. Biggs (eds) *Seals and Sealing in the Ancient Near East.* Malibu: Undena Publications, pp. 25–32.

Rau, P. (1991) 2. 2. 3. Werkstoffe und Produktionsrückstände im Stadtgebiet von Uruk-Warka, in Finkbeiner (1991), pp. 57–67.

Reade, J. (1995) Magan and Meluhha merchants at Ur? in Finkbeiner *et al.* (1995), pp. 597–599.

—— (2001) Assyrian king lists, the royal tombs of Ur, and indus origins. *Journal of Near Eastern Studies* 60/1, 1–29.

Renfrew, C. (1964) The characterization of obsidian and its application to the Mediterranean region. *Proceedings of the Prehistoric Society* 30, 111–133. Reprinted in C. Renfrew (1979) *Problems in European Prehistory.* Edinburgh: Edinburgh University Press, pp. 66–86.

Renger, J. (1984) Zur Inschrift Mesannepadda 1. *Revue d'Assyriologie* 78, 175.

Reynolds, V. and Kellett, J. (eds) (1991) *Mating and Marriage.* Oxford, New York and Tokyo: Oxford University Press.

Rice, M. (1994) *The Archaeology of the Arabian Gulf.* London and New York: Routledge.

Riederer, J. (1994) Die frühen Kupferlegierungen im Vorderen Orient, in Wartke (1994), pp. 85–94.

Roaf, M. (1982) The Hamrin sites, in J. Curtis (ed.) *Fifty Years of Mesopotamian Discovery.* London: British School of Archaeology in Iraq, pp. 40–47.

—— (1983) A report on the work of the British archaeological expedition in the Eski Mosul dam salvage project from November 1982 to June 1983. *Sumer* 39/1–2, 68–94.

—— (1984) Excavations at Tell Madhhur – the results of the third season. *Sumer* 40/1–2, 144–148.

—— (1989) Ubaid social organization and social activities as seen from Tell Madhhur, in Henrickson and Thuesen (1989), pp. 91–148.

—— (1997) Hamrin Dam salvage project, in Myers (1997), vol. 2, pp. 471–474.

Roaf, M. *et al.* (1984) Tell Madhhur: a summary report on excavations. *Sumer* 43/1–2, 108–167.

Roaf, M. and Galbraith, J. (1994) Pottery and p-values: 'Seafaring merchants of Ur?' re-examined. *Antiquity* 68(261), 770–783.

Roaf, M. and Postgate, J. N. (eds) (1981) Excavations in Iraq, 1979–1980. *Iraq* 43/2, 167–198.

Roberts, G. (1994) *The Mirror of Alchemy – Alchemical Ideas and Images in Manuscripts and Books from Antiquity to the Seventeenth Century.* Toronto and Buffalo: University of Toronto Press.

Röhrer-Ertl, O. (1996) Über Habitationsgrenzen der Population von Tell es-Sultan/Jericho im Mesolithikum und Präkeramischen Neolithikum anhand paläoökologischer Einzelbefunde. *Ethnographisch-Archäologische Zeitschrift* 37/4, 503–515.

Rosengarten, Y. (1960a) *Le concept sumérien de consommation dans la vie économique et religieuse.* Paris: de Boccard.

—— (1960b) *Le régime des offrandes.* Paris: de Boccard.

Rothman, M. S. (1989) written communication to the author, not dated but received 14 March 1989 and accompanied by 12 pp. of computer printout concerning Tepe Gawra sealings of layers XI/XA to VIII. (My thanks to M. Rothman for the prompt delivery of these materials.)

—— (1990) Centralization, administration and function at fourth-millennium B.C. Tepe Gawra, Northern Iraq. A dissertation in anthropology, University of Pennsylvania, 1988. Ann Arbor: University of Michigan, Dissertation Information Service.

—— (1994) Sealing use and changes in administrative oversight and structure at Tepe Gawra during the fourth millennium BC, in Ferioli *et al.* (1994), pp. 97–124.

—— (1997) Tepe Gawra, in Myers (1997), vol. 5, pp. 183–196.

Rouault, O. and Masetti-Rouault, M. G. (eds) (1993) *L'Eufrate e il tempo – La civiltà del medio Eufrate e della Gezira siriana.* Milano: Electa.

Rouche, M. (1980) Les survivances antiques dans trois cartulaires du Sud-Ouest de la France aux Xe et XIe siècles. *Cahiers de la Civilisation Médiévale* 23/2, 93–108.

Rova, E. (1994) *Ricerche sui sigilli a cilindro vicino-orientali del periodo di Uruk/Jemdet Nasr.* Orientis Antiqui Collectio XX. Roma: Istituto per l'Oriente C. A. Nallino.

Ruf, F. (1993) Die ältesten Formen der zubereiteten Nahrung in der Geschichte unserer Ernährung: Brei, Mus und Suppe. Inaugural-Dissertation zur Erlangung des Doktorgrades beim Fachbereich Ernährungs- und Haushaltswissenschaften der Justus-Liebig-Universität Giessen. Velbert-Neviges: BeRing Verlag.

Rutgers, L. V. (1992) Archaeological evidence for the interaction of Jews and non-Jews in Late Antiquity. *American Journal of Archaeology* 96/1, 101–118.

Saddam Husein Dam Salvage Archaeology Project, Edinburgh University Archaeology Department (1986) *Excavations at Kharabeh Shattani* vol. 1. Edinburgh University, Department of Archaeology, Occasional Paper No. 14.

Safar, F., Mustafa, M. A. and Lloyd, S. (1981) *Eridu.* Republic of Iraq Ministry of Culture and Information, State Organization of Antiquities and Heritage, Baghdad.

Sahlins, M. D. (1968) *Tribesmen.* Englewood Cliffs, NJ: Prentice-Hall.

—— (1972) *Stone Age Economics.* London: Tavistock.

—— (1983) Other times, other customs: the anthropology of history. *American Anthropologist* 85/3, 517–544.

Saiko, E. V. and Yankovskaya, N. B. (1988) Remeslennyi typ organizatsii truda na Blizhnem Vostoke v IV–II tysiatchiletii do nashey ery (The craft type of labour organization in the Near East in the 4th–2nd millennium BC, in Russian). *Vestnik drevney istorii* 3(186), 3–18.

Sallaberger, W. (1996) *Der babylonische Töpfer und seine Gefässe nach Urkunden altsumerischer bis albaby-lonischer Zeit sowie lexikalischen und literarischen Zeugnissen.* Mesopotamian History and Environment, Series II, vol. 3. Neuchâtel: Recherches et Publications. Review by T. Potts, *Bibliotheca Orientalis* LV/3–4, 1998, 448–449 and by W. Heimpel, *Journal of Near Eastern Studies* 60/2, 2001, 140–141.

Sanders, W. T. and Webster, D. (1988) The Mesoamerican urban tradition. *American Anthropologist* 90/3, 521–546.

Sasson, J., Baines, J., Beckman, G. and Rubinson, K. S. (eds) (1995) *Civilizations of the Ancient Near East,* vols I–III. New York: Charles Scribner's Sons and Macmillan Library Reference USA, Simon and Schuster Macmillan.

Sauvage, M. (1998) *La brique et sa mise en oeuvre en Mésopotamie: Des origines l'époque achéménide.* Paris: Editions Recherche sur les Civilisations. Review by G. Wright, *Bibliotheca Orientalis* 57/5–6, 2000, 695–696.

Sax, M. and Meeks, N. D. (1994) The introduction of wheel cutting as a technique for engraving cylinder seals: its distinction from filing. *Iraq* 56, 153–166.

Sax, M., Meeks, N. D. and Collon, D. (2000) The early development of the lapidary engraving wheel in Mesopotamia. *Iraq* 62, 157–176.

Schaub, R. T. (1997) Bab ed-Dhra', in Myers (1997), vol. 1, pp. 248–251.

Schaub, R. T. and Rast, W.E. (1989) *Bab edh-Dhra': Excavations in the Cemetery Directed by Paul W. Lapp (1965–1967).* Reports of the Expedition to the Dead Sea Plain, Jordan, vol. I. Winona Lake, Ind.: Eisenbrauns. Cited from a review by K. N. Schoville, *Journal of the American Oriental Society* 112/3, 1992, 491–492.

Schirmer, W. (1990) Some aspects of building at the 'aceramic neolithic' settlement of Çayönü Tepesi. *World Archaeology* 21/3, 363–387.

Schlegel, A. and Eloul, R. (1988) Marriage transactions: labor, property, status. *American Anthropologist* 90/2, pp. 291–309.

Schmandt-Besserat, D. (1979) An archaic recording system in the Uruk–Jemdet Nasr period. *American Journal of Archaeology* 83/1, 19–48.

—— (1980) The envelopes that bear the first writing. *Technology and Culture* 21/3, 357–385.

—— (1984) Before numerals. *Visible Language* 18/1, 48–60.

—— (1986) Tokens at Susa. *Oriens Antiquus* 25/1–2, 93–125.

—— (1988a) Tokens at Uruk. *Baghdader Mitteilungen* 19, 3–173.

—— (1988b) Tokens as funerary offerings. *Vicino Oriente* 7, 3–9.

—— (1991) Clay tokens as forerunner of writing: the linguistic significance, in E. Feldbusch, R. Pogarell and C. Weiss (eds) *Neue Fragen der Linguistik. Akten des 25. Linguistischen Kolloquiums, Paderborn Bd. 1: Bestand und Entwicklung.* Tübingen: Max Niemeyer Verlag, pp. 485–499.

—— (1992) *Before Writing I–II.* Austin: University of Texas Press.

—— (1996) Art, writing and narrative in Mesopotamia, in *Civilisations du Proche-Orient Série I, Archéologie et environnement*, vol. 3, Paris (H. Gasche and B. Hrouda (eds) *Collectanea Orientalia – Histoire, arts de l'espace et industrie de la terre – Etudes offertes en hommage à Agnès Spycket*), pp. 315–321.

—— (1998a) A stone metaphor of creation. *Near Eastern Archaeology* 61/2, 109–117.

—— (1998b) Ain Ghazzal 'monumental' figures. *Bulletin of the American Schools of Oriental Research* 310, 1–17.

Schmidt, J. (1970) Uruk-Warka, Zusammenfassender Bericht über die 27. Kampagne 1969. *Baghdader Mitteilungen* 5, 51–96.

—— (1977) Uruk-Warka. *Sumer* 33/1, 105–118.

Schmidt, K. (1982) Zur Verwendung der mesopotamischen 'Glockentöpfe'. *Archäologisches Korrespondenzblatt* 12, 317–319.

Schmitt-Strecker, S., Begemann, F. and Pernicka, E. (1994) Untersuchungen zur Metallurgie der Späten Uruk- und Frühen Bronzezeit am oberen Euphrat – Resumé, in Wartke (1994), pp. 97–98.

Schneider, G. (1991) Herkunftsbestimmung von Obsidianartefakten aus Uruk-Warka mittels Röntgenfluoreszenzanalyse, in *XXXVIIIème Rencontre Assyriologique Internationale*, Paris 8–10 juillet 1991. Résumés des communications, liste des participants, p. 20.

Schwartz, G. M. (1988) Excavations at Karatut Mevkii and perspectives on the Uruk/Jemdet Nasr expansion. *Akkadica* 56, 1–41.

Selz, G. (1998) Über Mesopotamische Herrschaftskonzepte – Zu den Ursprüngen mesopotamischer Herrscherideologie im 3. Jahrtausend, in M. Dietrich, O. Loretz and Th. Balke (eds) *dubsar anta-men*, Studien zur Altorientalistik, Festschrift für Willem H. Ph. Römer, Münster: Ugarit-Verlag, pp. 281–344.

Sherratt, A. (ed.) (1980a) *The Cambridge Encyclopaedia of Archaeology.* Cambridge, London, New York, New Rochelle, Melbourne and Sydney: Cambridge University Press.

—— (1980b) The beginnings of agriculture in the Near East and Europe, in Sherratt (1980a), pp. 102–111.

—— (1980c) Water, soil and seasonality in early cereal cultivation. *World Archaeology* 11/3, 313–330.

—— (1983) The secondary exploitation of animals in the Old World. *World Archaeology* 15/1, 90–104.

—— (1995) Alcohol and its alternatives – symbol and substance in pre-industrial cultures, in J. Goodman, P. Lovejoy and A. Sherratt (eds), *Consuming Habits – Drugs in History and Anthropology.* London and New York: Routledge.

Shupak, N. (1992) A new source for the study of the judiciary and law of Ancient Egypt: 'The tale of the eloquent peasant'. *Journal of Near Eastern Studies* 51/1, 1–18.

Sjöberg, A. (1967) *Zu einigen Verwandtschaftsbeziehungen im Sumerischen.* Heidelberger Studien zum alten Orient (Adam Falkenstein zum 17. September 1966). Wiesbaden: Harrassowitz, pp. 201–233.

Skeat, T. C. (1977) A letter from the king of the Blemmyes to the king of the Noubades. *Journal of Egyptian Archaeology* 63, 159–170.

ŠL: A. Deimel (1925–1934) *Šumerisches Lexikon.* 5 vols. Roma: Pontificio Instituto Biblico.

Smith, P. and Young, T. C., Jr. (1983) The force of numbers: population pressure in the central western Zagros 12,000–4,500 B.C., in Young *et al.* (1983), pp. 141–162.

Solecki, R. L. and Solecki, R. S. (1983) Late Pleistocene–Early Holocene cultural traditions in the Zagros and the Levant, in Young *et al.* (1983), pp. 123–137.

Solecki, R. S. (1954) Shanidar cave: a palaeolithic site in northern Iraq. *Annual Report of the Smithsonian Institution 1954*, pp. 389–425.

—— (1997) Shanidar cave, in Myers (1997), vol. 5, pp. 15–16.

Sollberger, E. and Kupper, J.-R. (1971) *Inscriptions royales sumériennes et akkadiennes.* Paris: Les éditions du cerf.

Speiser, E. A. (1935) *Excavations at Tepe Gawra I*. Philadelphia: University of Pennsylvania Press.

Spencer, P. (1987) review of Bernardi 1985. *Man* 22/1, 189–190.

Spycket, A. (1988) Malerei, in D. O. Edzard *et al.* (eds) *Reallexikon der Assyriologie und Vorderasiatischen Archäologie*, vol. 7, 3/4 *Lieferung, Luhuzattija-Maltai*. Berlin and New York: Walter de Gruyter, pp. 287–300.

—— (1989) Mari, B. Archäologisch, in D. O. Edzard *et al.* (eds) *Reallexikon der Assyriologie und Vorderasiatischen Archäologie*, vol. 7, 5/6 *Lieferung, Maltai – Masse und Gewichte*. Berlin and New York: Walter de Gruyter, pp. 390–418.

—— (1992) *Les Figurines de Suse I – Les figurines humaines, IVᵉ–IIᵉ millénaires av. J. C. Mémoires de la Délégation Archéologique en Iran 52: Mission de Susiane – Ville Royale de Suse VI*. Paris: Gabalda.

Steible, H. and Behrens, H. (1982) *Die altsumerische Bau- und Weihinschriften I–II* (FAOS 5). Wiesbaden: Franz Steiner Verlag.

Stein, G. (1999) *Rethinking World Systems. Diasporas, Colonies, and Interactions in Uruk Mesopotamia*. Tucson: University of Arizona Press.

Stein, G., Bernbeck, R., Coursey, Ch., McMahon, A., Miller, N., Misir, A., Nicola, J., Pittman, H., Pollock, S. and Wright, H. (1996) Uruk colonies and Anatolian communities. An interim report on the 1992–1993 excavations at Hacınebı, Turkey. *American Journal of Archaeology* 100/2, 205–260.

Steiner, G. (1988) Der 'reale' Kern in den 'legendären' Zahlen von Regierungsjahren der ältesten Herrscher Mesopotamiens. *Acta Sumerologica* (Japan) 10, 129–152.

Steinkeller, P. and Postgate, J. N. (1992) *Third-Millennium Legal and Administrative Texts in the Iraq Museum, Baghdad*. Winona Lake, Ind.: Eisenbrauns.

Steponaitis, V. P. (1984) Some further remarks on catchments, nonproducers, and tribute flow in the Valley of Mexico. *American Anthropologist* 86/1, 143–148.

Steuer, H. (1989) Archaeology and history: proposals on the social structure of the Merovingian Kingdom, in Kl. Randsborg (ed.) *The Birth of Europe – Archaeology and Social Development in the First Millennium A.D.* Roma: L'erma di Bretschneider, pp. 100–122.

Stevenson, J. (1989) *The Beginnings of Literacy in Ireland*. Proceedings of the Royal Irish Academy section C – Archaeology, Celtic studies, History, Linguistics, Literature vol. 89C, no. 6. Dublin: Royal Irish Academy.

Stol, M. (1995) Women in Mesopotamia. *Journal of the Economic and Social History of the Orient* 38/2, 123–144.

Strommenger, E. (1967) Zu einem frühsumerischen Stelenfragment aus Uruk. *Archäologischer Anzeiger* 82/1, 1–7.

—— (1980a) *Habuba Kabira – Eine Stadt vor 5000 Jahren*. Mainz am Rhein: Philipp von Zabern.

—— (1980b) The chronological division of the archaic levels of Uruk-Eanna VI to III/II: past and present. *American Journal of Archaeology* 84/4, 479–487.

Stronach, D. (1982) Ras al-'Amiya, in Curtis (1982), pp. 37–39.

Strouhal, E. (1979) review of Rathbun 1975. *Archív Orientální* 47, 127–128.

Sürenhagen, D. (1974–1975) Untersuchungen zur Keramikproduktion innerhalb der Spät-Urukzeitlichen Siedlung Habuba Kabira-Süd. *Acta Praehistorica et Archaeologica* 5/6, 43–164.

—— (1979) Ahmad al-Hattu 1978. *Mitteilungen der Deutschen Orient-Gesellschaft* 111, 35–50.

—— (1980) Die Frühdynastisch-I–zeitliche Nekropole von Tall Ahmad al-Hattu. Ausgrabungen der Deutschen Orient-Gesellschaft im Hamrin-Becken. *Paléorient* 6, 229–232.

—— (1981) Ahmad al-Hattu 1979/80. Vorläufiger Bericht über die von der Deutschen Orient-Gesellschaft aus Mitteln des Kulturhilfefonds des Auswärtigen Amtes der Bundesrepublik Deutschland und des iraqischen Antikendienstes in Tall Ahmad al-Hattu (Iraq) unternommenen Ausgrabungen. *Mitteilungen der Deutschen Orient-Gesellschaft* 113, 35–51.

—— (1983–1984) Die Frühdynastisch-I–zeitliche Nekropole von Tall Ahmad al-Hattu (Iraq). *Archiv für Orientforschung* 29–30, 193–195.

—— (1985) Einige kulturelle Kontakte zwischen Arslantepe VIA und den frühsumerisch-hochprotoe-lamischen Stadtkulturen, in M. Liverani, A. Palmieri and R. Peroni (eds) *Studi di Paletnologia in onore di Salvatore M. Puglisi*. Roma: 'La Sapienza', pp. 229–236.

—— (1986a) The dry-farming belt: the Uruk period and subsequent developments, in H. Weiss (ed.) *The Origins of Cities in Dry-Farming Syria and Mesopotamia in the 3rd Millennium B.C.* Guilford, Conn.: Four Quarters, pp. 7–43.

—— (1986b) review of Gibson 1981. *Zeitschrift für Assyriologie* 76/II, 314–318.

Szarzyńska, K. (1981) Some remarks on the so-called 'Steingebäude' in archaic Uruk-Warka. *Akkadica* 23, 45–49.

—— (1988a) Records of garments and cloths in archaic Uruk/Warka. *Altorientalische Forschungen* 15/2, 220–230.

—— (1988b) Records of garments and cloths in archaic Uruk-Warka: addenda to the 1988 article in *Altorientalische Forschungen.* (Unpublished MS in possession of the author to whom I owe a debt of gratitude for access to it.)

—— (1992) Names of temples in the archaic texts from Uruk. *Acta Sumerologica* (Japan) 14, pp. 269–287.

—— (1994) Archaic Sumerian signs for garments and cloths. *Rocznik Orientalistyczny* XLVIII/2, 9–22.

—— (1996) Archaic Sumerian standards. *Journal of Cuneiform Studies* 48, 1–16.

Taine-Cheikh, C. (1991) Le vent et le devant: De l'orientation chez les maures. *Journal asiatique* 279, 93–136.

Talalay, L. E. (1991) Body imagery of the ancient Aegean. *Archaeology* 44/4, 46–49.

Tallon, F. (1987) *Métallurgie susienne I: De la fondation de Suse au XVIIIᵉ siècle av. J. C. 1–2.* Musée du Louvre, Département des Antiquités Orientales. Paris: Editions de la Réunion des Musées Nationaux.

Tardieu, M. (1990) *Les paysages reliques – Routes et haltes syriennes d'Isidore à Simplicius.* Louvain and Paris: Peeters.

Tattersall, I. and Schwartz, J. H. (2000) *Extinct Humans.* Boulder, Col.: Westview Press.

Temerev, A. K. (1980) Sistema snabzheniya v akhemenidskikh garnizonakh (The supply system of Achaemenid garrisons, in Russian). *Vestnik drevney istorii* 1/1980, 124–131.

Terray, E. (1986) L'Etat, le hasard et la nécessité. *L'homme* 97–98, 26/1–2, 213–224.

Thomas, J. (1987) Relations of production and social change in the Neolithic of northwestern Europe. *Man* N.S. 22/3, 405–430.

Tobler, A. J. (1950) *Excavations at Tepe Gawra II.* Philadelphia: University of Pennsylvania Press and London: Geoffrey Cumberlege, Oxford University Press.

Torcia Rigillo, M. (1991) Sealing systems on Uruk doors. *Baghdader Mitteilungen* 22, 175–222.

Toren, Ch. (1988) Making the present, revealing the past: the mutability and continuity of tradition as a process. *Man* N.S. 23/4, 696–717.

Tosi, M. (1976) Tepe Yahya project: palaeobotanical survey. *Iran* 14, 173–174.

Toubert, P. (1973) *Les structures du Latium médiéval I.* Rome: Ecole française de Rome.

Treide, D. and Treide, B. (1984) Das Konzept der militärischen Demokratie und einige Fragen der ethnographischen Forschung. *Ethnographisch-Archäologische Zeitschrift* 25/3, 380–407.

Trigger, B. (1985) The evolution of pre-industrial cities: a multilinear perspective, in *Mélanges offerts à Jean Vercoutter.* Paris: Editions Recherche sur les Civilisations, pp. 343–353.

Trinkaus, E. (1983) *The Shanidar Neanderthalers.* New York, London etc.: Academic Press.

Trinkaus, E. and Shipman, P. (1993) *The Neanderthals: Changing the Image of Mankind.* New York: Alfred Knopf.

Tsuneki, A., Hydar, J., Miyake, Y., Akahane, S., Nakamura, T., Arimura, M. and Sekine, S. (1997) First preliminary report on the excavations at Tell el-Kerkh (1997), NW Syria. *Bulletin of the Ancient Orient Museum, Tokyo* XVIII, 1–40.

Tsuneki, A., Hydar, J., Miyake, Y., Akahane, S., Arimura, M., Nishiyama, Sh., Sha'baan, H., Anezaki, T. and Yano, S. (1998) Second preliminary report of the excavations at Tell el-Kerkh (1998), northwestern Syria. *Bulletin of the Ancient Orient Museum, Tokyo* XIX, 1–40.

Tusa, S. (1984) Excavation at Tell Abu Husaini – preliminary report. *Sumer* 40/1–2, 262–276.

Ucko, P., Tringham, R. and Dimbleby, G. (eds) (1972) *Man, Settlement and Urbanism.* London: Duckworth.

Uerpmann, H.-P. (1982) Faunal remains from Shams ed-Din Tannira, a Halafian site in northern Syria. *Berytus* 30, 3–52.

Valbelle, D. (1990) L'Egypte pharaonique, in J.-L. Huot, J.-P. Thalman and D. Valbelle (eds) *Naissance des cités. Collection Origines.* Paris: Nathan, pp. 257–324. (My thanks for access to this publication go to Jiří Prosecký.)

Vallet, R. (1987) Luristan, Pusht-i-Kuh au Chalcolithique moyen (Les nécropoles de Parchinah et de Hakalan), in *Colloques internationaux de CNRS: Préhistoire de la Mésopotamie.* Paris: Editions du CNRS, pp. 91–126.

—— (1990) *Note d'information – Les habitations à salles hypostyles des débuts de l'époque d'Obeid.* Comptes-rendus de l'Académie des Inscriptions et Belles-Lettres. novembre-décembre 1990, Fasc. IV. Paris: de Boccard, pp. 867–874.

—— (1997) Habuba Kebira, ou La naissance de l'urbanisme. *Paléorient* 22/2, 45–76.

Vanden Berghe, L. (1987) *Luristan – Vorgeschichtliche Bronzekunst aus Iran,* Katalog der Ausstellung. München.

Van der Toorn, K. (1991) Funerary rituals and beatific afterlife in Ugaritic texts and in the Bible. *Bibliotheca Orientalis* 48/1–2, 40–66.

Vandiver, P. B., Kaylor, R., Feathers, J., Gottfried, M., Yener, K. A., Hornyak W. F. and Franklin, A. (1993) Thermoluminiscence dating of a crucible fragment from an early tin processing site in Turkey. *Archaeometry* 35/2, pp. 295–298.

Van Driel, G. (1982) Tablets from Jebel Aruda, in *Zikir Šumim* (Festschrift zum 70. Geburtstag von F. R. Kraus). Leiden: E. J. Brill, pp. 12–25.

—— (1983) Seals and sealings from Jebel Aruda 1974–1978. *Akkadica* 33, 34–62.

Van Driel, G. and van Driel-Murray, C. (1983) Jebel Aruda, the 1982 season of excavation, interim report. *Akkadica* 33, 1–26.

Van Loon, M. (1983) Hammam et-Turkman on the Balikh: first results of the University of Amsterdam's 1982 excavation. *Akkadica* 35, 1–11.

—— (1985) Découvertes au pays de Rebecca et de Rachel. *Archaeologia Préhistoire et Archéologie* 208, 38–47.

—— (1988) New evidence for north Syrian chronology from Hammam et-Turkman. *American Journal of Archaeology* 92, 582–587.

—— (1991a) review of J. V. Canby, E. Porada, B. S. Ridgway and T. Stech (eds) *Ancient Anatolia: Aspects of Change and Cultural Development. Essays in Honor of M. J. Mellink.* Madison: University of Wisconsin Press 1987. *Mnemosyne* 44/1–2, 300–304.

—— (1991b) review of L. Schneider (ed.) *Source: Notes in the History of Art* VII/3–4, Spring/Summer 1988. Special Issue: Phrygian Art and Archaeology. *Bibliotheca Orientalis* 48/1–2, 265–266.

Vansina, J. (1995) New linguistic evidence and 'the Bantu expansion'. *Journal of African History* 36, 173–195.

Van Zeist, W. and Bakker-Heeres, J. A. H. (1984) Archaeobotanical studies in the Levant 3: Late Palaeolithic Mureybit. *Palaeohistoria* 26, 171–199.

Van Zeist, W. and Bottema, S. (1999) Plant cultivation in Ancient Mesopotamia: the palynological and archaeological approach, in Klengel and Renger (1999), pp. 25–42.

Van Zeist, W. and de Roller, G. J. (1991/1992) The plant husbandry of aceramic Çayönü, SE Turkey. *Palaeohistoria* 33/34, 65–96.

Van Zeist, W. and Woldring, H. (1980) Holocene vegetation and climate of northwest Syria. *Palaeohistoria* 22, 111–126.

Veenhof, K. (ed.) (1996) *Houses and Households in Ancient Mesopotamia.* Papers read at the 40th Rencontre Assyriologique Internationale, Leiden, 5–8 July 1993. Istanbul: Nederlands Historisch-Archaeologisch Instituut.

Veldhuis, N. (1997) Elementary education at Nippur: the lists of trees and wooden objects. Proefschrift ter verkrijging van het doctoraat in de Letteren aan de Rijksuniversiteit Groningen. Groningen.

Vencl, Sl. (1979) Počátky zbraní – The origins of weapons (in Czech with an English summary). *Archeologické rozhledy* 31, 640–694.

—— (1991) Interprétation des blessures causées par les armes au Mésolithique. *L'Anthropologie* 95/1, 219–228.

Vértesalji, P. P. (1984) Zur chronologischen und sozial- sowie religionsgeschichtlichen Bedeutung des Eridu-Friedhofs. *Baghdader Mitteilungen* 15, 9–33.

—— (1987) The chronology of the Chalcolithic in Mesopotamia, in Aurenche *et al.* (1987), pp. 483–523.

—— (1988) Das Ende der Uruk-Zeit im Lichte der Grabungsergebnisse der sogenannten 'archaischen' Siedlung bei Uruk-Warka. *Acta Praehistorica et Archaeologica* 20, 9–26.

Vértesalji, P. P. and Kolbus, S. (1985) Review of protodynastic development in Babylonia. *Mesopotamia* 20, 53–109.

Vestergaard, T. A. (1991) Marriage exchange and social structure in Old Norse mythology, in R. Samson (ed.) *Social Approaches to Viking Studies.* Glasgow: Cruithne Press, pp. 21–34.

Vinogradova, L. N. and Tolstaya, S. M. (1990) Motiv 'unichtozheniya – provodov nechistoy sily' v vostochnoslavyanskom kupal'skom obryade (The motif of 'destruction – seeing off evil powers' in the East Slavic bathing ceremony, in Russian), in V. V. Ivanov and L. G. Nevskaya (eds) *Issledovaniya v oblasti bal'to-slavyanskoy dukhovnoy kul'tury – Pogrebal'nyi obryad.* Moskva: 'Nauka', pp. 99–118.

Voigt, M. M. (1997) Hajji Firuz, in Myers (1997), vol. 2, pp. 458–460.

Volk, K. (1999) Imkerei im alten Mesopotamien, in Klengel and Renger (1999), pp. 279–290.

Von Beckerath, J. (1995) review of Th. van der Way *Untersuchungen zur Spätvor- und Frühgeschichte Unterägyptens,* Heidelberg 1993. *Orientalia* N.S. 64/4, 465–467.

Von den Driesch, A. (1986) Fischknochen aus Abu Salabikh/Iraq. *Iraq* 48, 31–38.

Von der Way, Th. (1997) *Tell el-Fara'în. Buto I. Ergebnisse zum frühen Kontext Kampagnen der Jahre 1983–1989.* Mainz am Rhein: Philipp von Zabern. Reviewed by T. A. H. Wilkinson, *Bibliotheca orientalis* 55/5–6, 1998, 764–768.

Von Müller, A. (1963) Feuersteingerät und Perlenfabrikation – Auswertungsmöglichkeiten eines Oberflächenfundplatzes in Uruk-Warka. *Berliner Jahrbuch für Vorgeschichte* 3, pp. 187–195.

Von Wickede, A. (1986) Die Ornamentik der Tell Halaf-Keramik – Ein Beitrag zu ihrer Typologie. *Acta Praehistorica et Archaeologica* 18, 7–32.

—— (1990) *Prähistorische Stempelglyptik in Vorderasien.* München: Profil Verlag.

—— (1991) Chalcolithic sealings from Arpachiyah in the collection of the Institute of Archaeology, London, in *University College London, Institute of Archaeology Bulletin* 28, 153–196.

Wallwork, E. (1984) Religion and social structure in 'the division of labor'. *American Anthropologist* 86/1, 43–64.

Wardhaugh, R. (1992) *An Introduction to Sociolinguistics.* Second edition. Oxford and Cambridge, Mass.: Blackwell.

Wartke, R.-B. (ed.) (1994) *Handwerk und Technologie im Alten Orient – Ein Beitrag zur Geschichte der Technik im Altertum.* Internationale Tagung Berlin 12.–15. März 1991. Mainz am Rhein: Philipp von Zabern.

Watelin, L. (1929) Notes sur l'industrie lithique de Kish. *L'Anthropologie* 39, 65–76.

Watkins, T. (1983) Cultural parallels in the metalwork of Sumer and northern Mesopotamia in the 3rd millennium B.C. *Iraq* 45/1, 18–23.

—— (1990) The origins of house and home? *World Archaeology* 21/3, 336–347.

—— (1992) Pushing back the frontiers of Mesopotamian prehistory. *Biblical Archaeologist* 55/4, 176–181.

—— (1996) The origins of the household in North Mesopotamia, in Veenhof (1996), pp. 79–88.

Watkins, T. and Campbell, St. (1987) The chronology of the Halaf culture, in Aurenche *et al.* (1987), pp. 427–464.

Watson, J. L. (1986) Anthropological overview: the development of Chinese descent groups, in P. B. Ebrey and J. L. Watson (eds) *Kinship Organization in Late Imperial China 1000–1940.* Berkeley etc.: University of California Press, pp. 274–292.

Watson, P. J. (1997) Jarmo, in Myers (1997), vol. 3, pp. 208–209.

Wechsler, H. J. (1985) *Offerings of Jade and Silk.* New Haven and London: Yale University Press.

Weiss, H. (1983) Excavations at Tell Leilan and the origins of North Mesopotamian cities in the 3rd millennium B.C. *Paléorient* 9/2, 39–52.

—— (1991) Archaeology in Syria. *American Journal of Archaeology* 95/4, 683–740.

—— (1994) Archaeology in Syria. *American Journal of Archaeology* 98/1, 101–158.

Weiss, H., Akkermans, P., Stein, G. J., Parayre, D. and Whiting, R. (1990) 1985 excavations at Tell Leilan, Syria. *American Journal of Archaeology* 94/4, 529–582.

Weiss, H. and Calderone, L. (1990) Third-millennium urbanization and state formation at Tell Leilan. The 91st General Meeting of the Archaeological Institute of America. *American Journal of Archaeology* 94/2, 306.

Weniger, G.-Ch. (1991) Überlegungen zur Mobilität jägerischer Gruppen im Jungpaläolithikum. *Saeculum* 42/1, 82–103.

Wernisch, R. (1994) Die Frau in der Gesellschaft Mesopotamiens im 3. und 2. Jahrtausend v. Chr. Ihr Vermögen und ihre wirtschaftliche Aktivitäten, in E. Specht (ed.) *Frauenreichtum. Die Frau als Wirtschaftsfaktor im Altertum*. Wien: Wiener Frauenverlag, pp. 21–44.

Whalen, M. E. (1983) Reconstructing Early Formative village organization in Oaxaca, Mexico. *American Antiquity* 48/1, 17–43.

Wiggermann, F. (1996) Scenes from the shadow side, in M. E. Vogelzang and H. L. J. Vanstiphout (eds) *Mesopotamian Poetic Language: Sumerian and Akkadian*. Cuneiform monographs 6, Proceedings of the Groningen group for the study of Mesopotamian literature vol. 2. Groningen: Styx publications, pp. 207–230.

—— (1998) Nackte Göttin (Naked Goddess) A. Philologisch, in D. O. Edzard *et al.* (eds) *Reallexikon der Assyriologie und Vorderasiatischen Archäologie 9/1–2, Nab-Nanše*. Berlin and New York: Walter de Gruyter, pp. 46–53.

Wilcke, Cl. (1974) Zum Königtum in der Ur III-Zeit, in *Le palais et la royauté* (19eme Rencontre Assyriologique Internationale). Paris: Geuthner, pp. 177–232.

—— (1978) Philologische Bemerkungen zum Rat des Šuruppag. *Zeitschrift für Assyriologie* 68/II, 196–232.

—— (1996) Neue Rechtsurkunden der Altsumerischen Zeit. *Zeitschrift für Assyriologie* 86/I, 1–67.

Wilkinson, R. H. (1994) *Symbol and Magic in Egyptian Art*. London: Thames and Hudson.

Wilkinson, T. J., Monahan, B. H. and Tucker, D. J. (1996) Khanijdal East: a small Ubaid site in northern Iraq, *Iraq* LVIII, 17–50.

Wilkinson, T. J. and Matthews, R. J. (eds) (1989) Excavations in Iraq 1987–1988. *Iraq* 51, 249–265.

Willems, W. J. H. (1984) Romans and Batavians: a regional study in the Dutch Eastern River Area II. *Berichten van de Rijksdienst voor het Oudheidkundig Bodemonderzoek* 34, 39–331.

Wilson, K. L. (1986) Nippur: the definition of a Mesopotamian Gamdat Nasr assemblage, in Finkbeiner and Röllig (1986), pp. 57–89.

Winn, S. M. M. (1981) Burial evidence and the Kurgan culture in East Anatolia c. 3,000 B.C.: an interpretation. *Journal of Indo-European Studies* 9/1–2, 113–118.

Wolff, S. R. (1991) Archaeology in Israel. *American Journal of Archaeology* 95/3, 489–538.

Woolley, L. (later Sir) (1930) Excavations at Ur. *The Antiquaries Journal* 10, 315–343.

—— (1934) *Ur Excavations II: The Royal Cemetery*. London: The British Museum.

—— (1955) *Ur Excavations IV: The Early Periods*. Philadelphia: The Trustees of the British Museum and the University Museum Philadelphia.

Wrede, N. (1995) Relief einer Göttin oder Herrscherstatue? in Finkbeiner *et al.* (1995), pp. 677–689.

Wright, G. A. (1978) Social differentiation in the Early Natufian, in Ch. L. Redman *et al.* (eds) *Social Archaeology – Beyond Subsistence and Dating*. New York, San Francisco and London: Academic Press, pp. 201–223.

Wright, H. T. (1969) *The Administration of Rural Production in an Early Mesopotamian Town*. Ann Arbor: University of Michigan Press.

Wright, H. T. *et al.* (1981) *An Early Town on the Deh Luran Plain (Excavations at Tepe Farukhabad)*. Ann Arbor: University of Michigan Press.

Wright, H. T. and Johnson, G. A. (1975) Population, exchange and early state formation in southwestern Iran. *American Anthropologist* 77, 267–289.

Wright, H. T., Miller, N. and Redding, R. (1980) Time and process in an Uruk rural centre, in *L'archéologie de l'Iraq du début de l'époque néolithique à 333 av. n. è.* Colloques internationaux du CNRS 580. Paris: Editions du CNRS, pp. 265–284.

Wright, H. T. and Pollock, S. (1986) Regional socio-economic organization in southern Mesopotamia: the middle and later fifth millennium, in *Colloques internationaux du CNRS: Préhistoire de la Mésopotamie –* 17–18–19 décembre 1984. Paris: Editions du CNRS, pp. 317–329.

Wright, H. T., Redding, R. W. and Pollock, S. (1989) Monitoring interannual variability: an example from the period of early state development in southwestern Iran, in P. Halstead and J. O'Shea (eds) *Bad Year Economics – Cultural Responses to Risk and Uncertainty.* Cambridge: Cambridge University Press, pp. 106–113.

Wurster, W. W. (1981) Cuzco und Tenochtitlan, in H. Müller-Karpe (ed.) *Allgemeine und Vergleichende Archäologie als Forschungsgegenstand.* München: C. H. Beck, pp. 21–72.

WVDOG 43: A. Deimel (1923) *Die Inschriften von Fara II: Schultexte aus Fara.* Leipzig: J. C. Hinrich'sche Buchhandlung.

Yener, K. A. *et al.* (1991) Stable lead isotope studies of central Taurus ore sources and related artifacts from eastern Mediterranean Chalcolithic and Bronze Age sites. *Journal of Archaeological Science* 18/5, 541–577.

Yoffee, N. and Clark, J. J. (eds) (1993) *Early Stages in the Evolution of Mesopotamian Civilization – Soviet Excavations in Northern Iraq.* Tucson and London: University of Arizona Press.

Young, D. W. (1988) A mathematical approach to certain dynastic spans in the Sumerian king list. *Journal of Near Eastern Studies* 47, 123–129.

Young, T. C., Jr. (1986) Godin Tepe Period VI/V and central western Iran at the end of the fourth millennium, in Finkbeiner and Röllig (1986), pp. 212–228.

—— (1997) Godin Tepe, in Myers (1997), vol. 2, pp. 416–417.

Young, T. C., Smith, P. E. L. and Mortensen, P. (eds) (1983) *The Hilly Flanks and Beyond: Essays on the Prehistory of Southwestern Asia presented to Robert J. Braidwood November 15, 1982.* Studies in Ancient Oriental Civilization No. 36. Chicago: Oriental Institute of the University of Chicago.

Zadok, R. (1994) Elamites and other peoples from Iran and the Persian Gulf region in early Mesopotamian sources. *Iran* XXXII, 31–52.

ZATU: M. W. Green, H.-G. Nissen *et al.* (1987) *Zeichenliste der archaischen Texte aus Uruk.* Berlin: Gebrüder Mann Verlag.

Zeder, M. (1994) After the revolution: post-Neolithic subsistence in N Mesopotamia. *American Anthropologist* 96(1), 97–126.

Zettler, R. (1989a) Clay sealings from the Early Dynastic I levels (levels XI–IX) of the Inanna Temple at Nippur: a preliminary analysis. Text copy of a lecture held at the Baltimore Archaeological Meetings, January 1989. (I owe a debt of gratitute for access to this text to Professor A. D. Kilmer.)

—— (1989b) Pottery profiles reconstructed from jar sealings in the lower seal impression strata (SIS 8–4) at Ur. New evidence for dating, in A. Leonard, Jr. and B. B. Williams (eds) *Essays in Ancient Civilizations Presented to Helene J. Kantor.* Studies in Ancient Oriental Civilization No. 47. Chicago: Oriental Institute of the University of Chicago, pp. 369–387.

Zgoll, A. (1997) Inanna als nugig. *Zeitschrift für Assyriologie* 87/II, 181–195.

Zohary, D. and Hopf, M. (1988) *Domestication of Plants in the Old World. The Origin and Spread of Cultivated Plants in Western Asia, Europe and the Nile.* Oxford: Clarendon Press. (The second edition of this work was published in 1994.)

Index

Aannepada 214–215
Abrosuné (in Greek Antiquity) 211
Abstract notions 230, 233
Abu Hurayra 27
Abu Salabikh 120, 122, 124–126, 128, 133,
    136, 139, 143–144, 151, 165, 168, 176,
    179, 181–183–184, 186–188, 192–193,
    198–199, 202–203, 211, 214, 220, 224,
    229, 231, 239
Adab 147, 167, 193
Adams, Robert McC. 142
Africa 137
Agate 51, 113, 161, 193, 198
Age 35, 81, 115, 158, 170, 205, 207–208,
    210–211, 218, 222, 227, 236, 238–239
'Ager publicus' (Roman state land), 218
Agga 208, 217
Ahmad al-Hattu (Tell) 124, 184, 187–188,
    191–192, 205, 223, 225
Ain Ghazzal 37
Akkad period 120, 162, 167, 173, 174, 179,
    181, 188, 190, 198, 219, 224, 239
Aker 153
Akšak 163
ALAN (= Sumerian for 'statue') 139
Alchemy 93
Al-Hiba 179–182, 184, 186, 188, 192,
    195–196, 199, 203, 214
Alabaster 16, 23, 30, 99–102, 129, 131, 140
Ali Koš 26, 31
Al-Ubaid 179–180, 187, 190, 192, 214
Amazonite 161
Amethyst 51–52, 113, 161
An 101, 104; precinct of at Uruk 104–106
Anatolia 70, 91, 111, 114, 125, 128–131, 172,
    177, 187–188, 191–192, 195
Anglo-Saxon England 227–228
Anselm of Canterbury, St. 230

Antimony 17; Neolithic 17
Antiquity, Greek 93, 211, 217, 222
Antiquity, Roman 218
Antiquity, Roman Late 158, 218
Anzusud (personal name) 202
Arabia 193
Aragonite 161
Aratta 102, 156
Arms 103, 111, 143–144, 166, 169, 172, 175,
    186, 198, 200, 213–215, 219
Arsenic 68, 125, 171–172, 187–188
Arslantepe 127–128, 143, 161
'Artificial stone' 102, 123
Assembly 124, 136–137, 144–146, 150, 159
Assur 32
Athlit 36
Australopithecus 3

Badakhshan 70, 184
Bagara (a shrine at Lagaš) 220
Baghdad 21, 22, 55, 106, 165, 166
Bala (Sumerian = term of office) 167, 202
Balikh river 62, 75
Basalt 108, 164
Basra 53
Beads 161; *see also* Pendants
Beer 119, 135
Beersheba 125
Beirut 58
Bernbeck, Reinhard 36
Berlin 134, 152
Beryl 51
Bevelled-rim bowls (BRB) 99–100, 106, 124,
    129–130, 141, 158, 162, 203
Binarity 5, 23, 50, 52, 78, 97, 102, 104, 108,
    112, 115, 140–141, 150, 170, 186, 196,
    207–208, 227
Binford, Lewis 90, 204

Bingöl 129
Birds 7, 28, 51, 62, 107, 120, 135, 163, 166, 174, 179–181, 232
Bitumen 65, 77, 125, 130, 183; Chalcolithic 44, 47, 54, 61, 65, 80; Early Dynastic 164, 168–169, 173–174, 183, 188, 190–191; Jemdet Nasr 107, 144, 156, 166; Mesolithic 6, 7; Neolithic 17, 22, 23, 24, 29; Uruk 101–105, 107, 111–113, 123, 125–126, 130, 162, 165
'Blumentöpfe' (Uruk-age pottery) 99, 106
Bone 65, 196; Chalcolithic 43–44, 45, 47, 50–51, 56–57, 65; Early Dynastic 164, 174–175, 183, 196; Jemdet Nasr 166; Mesolithic 6, 7; Neolithic 14, 16, 17, 20, 23, 29; Uruk 108, 109, 111–113, 123
Bone, human 11, 18, 27, 42–43, 48, 94, 226
Brahmana caste of India 146
Brandes, Mark 146
'Brauneisenstein' 161
Bread 228
Bronze 68, 125, 129; Chalcolithic 68; Early Dynastic 168, 172, 187–188, 229; Jemdet Nasr 171; Uruk 113, 125, 128–129
'Bullae' of clay 110, 113, 147–148, 150, 200
Burials 96–97, 151–152, 157, 167, 186, 214, 222–229, 233; Akkadian 224; Akkadian and post-Akkadian 226; Chalcolithic 42–43, 45, 49–50, 52, 90, 97; Early Dynastic 55, 164–167, 184, 186, 192, 198, 203, 210, 213–214, 222–229, 233; Jemdet Nasr 144–145, 222–223, 233; Mesolithic 6; Neolithic 17, 18, 20, 23, 35; of animals 20, 45, 90; Palaeolithic 1, 4, 5; Uruk 108, 109–113, 115–116, 126, 151–152, 154, 157, 162; *see also* Graveside offerings
Bus Mordeh 26
Byblos 71

Calcite 65, 129, 161, 168, 193, 198, 233
Caloric intakes of food 176
Canaan 131
'Canaanean blades' 128, 191
Carnelian 18, 20, 23, 39, 46, 47, 55, 111, 113, 129, 161–162, 164, 167–169, 171–172, 175, 183–184, 192–193, 196, 198
Catal Hüyük 10, 27, 37, 40
Çayönü Tepesi 18, 19, 32
Cemeteries 11, 33, 35–36, 81, 83, 88–89, 91, 96, 132, 222–229, 233, 236–237, 239; Chalcolithic 42, 44, 46, 48–49, 65, 67, 72, 75, 78–79, 81, 83, 89–91, 96; Early

Dynastic 169–170, 171–172, 186–188, 190, 193, 203–205, 207, 211, 222–229, 233, 239; Jemdet Nasr 171, 186–188, 192–193, 199, 204–205, 207, 222–223, 233; Neolithic 16, 22, 35; *see also* Graveside offerings
Cereals 4, 6, 8, 9, 13, 15, 17, 18, 21, 23, 25–26, 31, 32, 42, 45, 48, 49, 53, 55, 57–59, 64, 108, 117, 122, 163, 174, 176–177, 179, 182, 234
Ceremonies *see* Magic, Religion, Ritual
Chagar Bazar 66–67, 69
Chalcedony 18, 113, 161
Chemchemal 7, 13
Chiefdom 88, 150
Children 4, 6, 17, 18, 20, 35–36, 45, 48–50, 81, 91, 108, 109–111, 115, 169, 198, 204–205, 224, 227
China 85, 91, 142–143, 156, 228, 239
Chlorite 43, 171–172, 193
Choga Mami 21, 26, 29, 31, 32, 34, 37, 42, 235
Chogha Mish 133, 143
'City-league' seals (= 'collective sealings") 163, 167, 197, 200, 208–210, 213
Clay 7, 10, 13, 15, 16, 17, 19, 20, 21, 23, 24, 29–30, 44, 45, 47, 50, 52, 54, 56–57, 65, 67–68, 77, 92, 94, 99, 101–102, 104–108, 110, 112–113, 123, 163–165, 166, 168–169, 171–175, 177, 184, 186, 189–190, 199, 214, 229
Climate: Chalcolithic 75, 81; Jemdet Nasr 182; Mesolithic 6, 8, 235; Neolithic 28, 40; Palaeolithic 1, 2, 4; Uruk 116
Colours 5, 41, 92–94, 145; black 5, 43, 51–52, 54, 65, 92–94, 96, 101–103, 111–112, 129, 145, 155, 157, 161, 167, 169, 183, 233, 236; blue 18, 65, 101, 111, 113, 116, 167, 183, 193, 233; brown 183; dark 107; green 17, 18, 65, 111, 113, 116, 129, 164, 167, 183; green-blue 233; green-yellow 101; grey 18, 43, 49, 92, 101, 108, 168; grey-green 18; grey-yellow 18; orange 103, 167; pink 43, 48, 92; purple 183; red 5, 6, 7, 10, 11, 13, 15, 17, 18, 20, 38, 43, 50–52, 56–57, 65, 85, 92–94, 96, 101, 103–105, 106, 110, 113, 116, 129, 145, 155, 157, 161, 167, 169, 173, 183, 233, 236; white 5, 10, 18, 39, 43, 46, 47, 48–52, 65, 92–94, 96, 101–103, 105, 107–108, 109–113, 116, 129, 135, 145, 155, 157, 161, 168–169, 172–173, 210, 233, 236;

yellow 18, 43, 92–93, 135, 161, 167, 183, 233

Commensality 80–81, 84–85, 89, 96, 115, 124, 144–145, 149–150, 203–204, 210–211, 222; Chalcolithic 63, 80–81, 84–85, 89, 96; Neolithic 36; Uruk 110, 115, 124, 144, 149–150

Concrete 101, 122–123, 129

Copper 68, 125, 183, 207

Copper Chalcolithic 43–44, 45, 51, 68; Early Dynastic 166, 168–169, 174–176, 183, 186, 188, 190–192, 198, 207, 214, 224–226; Jemdet Nasr 161, 163, 166, 170–171, 186–187; Mesolithic 6, 7; Neolithic 17, 20, 23, 30; Uruk 49, 100, 102–103, 105, 108, 111–112, 114, 125–126, 187; *see also* Malachite

Cosmetics 126, 143, 166–167, 169, 172, 175, 181–183, 187, 192–193, 224

Crystal *see* Rock crystal

Cultivation of plants: Chalcolithic 59–60; Early Dynastic 176–179, 183; Jemdet Nasr 176, 195; Mesolithic 8–9; Neolithic 13, 15, 25–27, 31–35; Uruk 117–119, 131

'Curse on Agade' 158

Cylinder seals 100–101, 105–108, 118–119, 129, 145, 148, 153, 161, 163–164, 168–170, 172–176, 183, 189–190, 192, 199, 201–202, 207, 233

Dance *see* Music and dance

Dead Sea coast 151, 223

Debts, cancellation of 219

Degirmentepe 81, 90, 94

Deh Luran plain 26–28, 31–34, 59, 61, 63, 68–69, 71, 120, 122–123, 125, 128, 178–179, 181, 183, 191, 193

Deutsche Morgenlandische Gesellschaft 156

Dilmun 156, 195

Diorite 51, 161

Diyala river 106, 179, 181, 187, 199, 201, 208, 214, 219, 238

Domestic cattle 15, 17, 18, 21, 23, 27, 31–35, 42, 45, 46, 53–54, 60–64, 72, 76, 120, 122, 165–166, 168, 174, 179–181, 183, 194, 236

Domestic cattle, names of 229

Domestic dog 2, 13, 15, 18, 21, 23, 45, 47, 48, 50–51, 60, 62, 121, 135, 158, 174, 175, 179, 181

Domestic donkey 45, 120, 131, 135, 165, 167, 182

Domestic equids 55, 63, 78, 120, 166, 168, 179, 194, 198

Domestic goat 8, 13, 15, 16, 17, 18, 21, 23, 27, 42, 44, 45, 46, 53–54, 60–63, 78, 108, 120, 165–166, 174, 179–183, 190, 228

Domestic pig 13, 15, 18, 21, 27, 33, 42, 45, 53–54, 60, 62–64, 120, 122, 165–166, 173–174, 179–180, 183

Domestic poultry 121, 179, 183

Domestic sheep 8, 15, 17, 18, 21, 23, 27, 33, 42, 44, 45, 46, 51, 53–54, 60–63, 78, 102, 108, 110, 113, 120, 126, 148, 158, 165–166, 174, 175, 179–183, 228

Domestic water-buffalo 108

Domestication: animals 9, 25, 27–28, 120, 235; Neolithic 13, 15, 17, 25–28; plants 9, 25–27, 235

Drainage: Chalcolithic 51–52, 81; Early Dynastic 168, 173–174, 184; Jemdet Nasr 162; Neolithic 17; pipes 51–52, 81, 174, 184; Uruk 101, 104–105, 111, 113, 133

Dum Gar Parchinah 78, 81, 91

Eanna, precinct of Inanna at Uruk 99–104, 106

Eannatum 215, 218

Ebla 208

Eco, Umberto 155

Egypt 93, 121, 125, 131, 133, 137, 142, 151–153, 155, 178, 188, 208, 223

'Eigenkirche' 215

Elam 118–119, 136, 143, 195; *see also* Susa

Electrum 111, 214

Eliade, Mircea 93

Emblems 136–138, 154, 207

Emery 192

Emphyteutic leases of income 218

EN (Sumerian pontifical function) 101, 138, 139–141, 143, 145–146, 148–150, 155, 197, 209–210, 213, 222, 227, 237–238

En Besor 131

Enannatum 214–215, 217, 229

Enki 155

Enlil 155

(En)Mebaragesi 214

Enna-Il 214

ensí (incl. GAR.ensí) 167, 179, 212–214, 218

Enšakušanna 209, 217

Entemena/Enmetena 215–216, 217

Entourage, 'royal' 214–215

'Enuma elish' (Babylonian creation epic) 101

Erbil 151

Ereš 136
Eridu 46, 58, 60, 62, 65, 70–76, 78–79, 81,
    83, 91, 93–94, 102, 119, 126, 141,
    155
Ethnicity 142, 158
Exchange 72, 86–88, 96, 112, 125–126,
    129–131, 200, 209, 236; Chalcolithic 52,
    58, 61, 70–72, 86–88, 96; Early Dynastic
    192–194, 200, 202, 209, 221; Jemdet Nasr
    165, 221; Mesolithic 7; Neolithic 15, 17,
    18, 22, 30, 31; Palaeolithic 1; Uruk 112,
    125–126, 129, 141
'Eye idols' 108

Faience 113, 116, 122–123, 129, 183;
    Chalcolithic 65; Early Dynastic 168–169,
    172, 183, 198; Uruk 113, 116, 122
Failaka 193
Fara 166, 182–184, 186, 188, 190–193, 198,
    202, 204–205, 207–209, 212, 214, 219,
    221, 230–231
Fertility 84, 94, 101, 139–140, 149, 157–158,
    190, 207, 213, 231
Fish 32, 42, 47, 49, 62–63, 120, 130,
    136–137, 139, 145, 155, 182–183;
    Chalcolithic 53–54, 62–63, 81; Early
    Dynastic 166, 168, 173–174, 178–182,
    187, 228; Jemdet Nasr 161, 163, 166;
    Neolithic 23, 28; Uruk 105, 120, 122, 129,
    130, 134, 136–137, 139
'Fishermen' *see* ŠU+HA
Fishponds (?) 178, 183
Food collection 1, 2, 4, 6, 7, 8, 13, 15, 18, 21,
    23, 25–28, 31–32, 60, 62, 119, 122, 157,
    177, 181–183
Forest, Jean-Daniel 110, 204
Fortifications: Akkad/Ur III period 167;
    Chalcolithic 42, 60, 81; Early Dynastic 162,
    165, 211; Neolithic 23, 24; Uruk 108, 109,
    117, 133, 143, 165
Foster, Benjamin 179
Four quarters of the world (= EZEN) 134,
    139, 156–157, 196–197
Frit 43, 47, 50, 167, 193
Furniture, ceremonial 111, 114, 128,
    169–170, 174, 190, 219

Game hunted 1, 2, 6, 7, 8, 13, 15, 18, 21, 23,
    27–28, 31, 42, 45, 46, 51, 62–63, 78, 80,
    174, 179–182, 198
GAR.ensí *see* Ensí
Gardens 49, 53, 60–61, 64, 104, 119, 147,

178–179, 183, 236; cardamom 119; lye
    plants 119; mustard (*Sinapis*) 178; onions
    119; turnip (*Brassica*) 178; *see also* Orchards,
    Vineyards
Gender 10, 35, 38, 85, 158, 172, 186,
    204–205, 207–208, 210–213, 222, 227,
    233, 238; *see also* EN, NIN
Gilgameš 193, 205, 208, 217, 239
Giparu (residence of EN) 101–102
Glassner, Jean-Jacques 218
Godintepe 119, 132–133, 143
Gold 51, 67–68, 102–103, 107, 110–112,
    125, 161, 168, 171–172, 188, 193, 214,
    228, 233
Grai Resh 108–109, 125, 133, 143
Grain 99, 108, 117–118, 120, 147, 165, 169,
    177, 181, 198
Graveside offerings 223–224
Greece, classical *see* Antiquity
Greenstone 193, 198
Gudea 231
Gulf, Arabo-Persian 15, 31, 72, 116, 171,
    192–193, 195, 199, 204, 236
Gypsum stone 161

Habuba Kabira 105, 123–126, 131, 133, 143,
    146–147, 151, 155
Habur river 122, 128–130, 165, 191
Hacinebi 119, 121, 145
'Hacksilber' 200; *see* Silver
Haematite 31, 51–52, 198
Hair styles 3, 17, 172, 225
Hajji Firuz 56
Hajji Muhammad culture 46, 54, 65, 75,
    92
Hakalan 78, 81, 91
Halaf culture 21, 23, 24, 33, 42, 44–45,
    49–52, 57, 60–67, 69–70, 72–75, 78,
    80–82, 84–88, 90–91, 93, 95, 122, 155,
    233, 236–237
Hammam et-Turkman 59, 67, 85
Hamoukar 118
Harran 80
Harrows see 'Tribulum'
Hassek Höyük 117, 125, 128, 133, 143
Hassuna culture 18, 19, 22, 23, 25, 32, 36,
    38–40, 45, 55–56, 65
Hierakonpolis 131–132, 151, 223
Hijara, Ismail 60, 92
Hit 54
Hoard finds 187–188, 195, 199–200
Hodder, Ian 10

Hoffmann, Michael 94
Homo erectus 3
Homo habilis 3
Homo sapiens 3, 234
Houses 77, 80, 94, 96–97, 148, 198, 211;
  Houses Chalcolithic 42–44, 45, 46–47,
  49–50, 54, 55–56, 93–94, 96–97; Early
  Dynastic 165–168, 170, 172–174, 178, 183,
  190, 194, 198–199, 210–211; Jemdet Nasr
  148, 160, 162; Mesolithic 7, 10–11;
  Neolithic 7, 13, 15, 17, 18, 19, 20, 21, 23,
  24, 35; Uruk 49, 108–110, 112–113, 134,
  137, 162
Human sacrifice (?) 171, 224–229
Hunting 1, 4, 6, 8, 15, 18, 21, 24, 27–28,
  32–35, 53–54, 62–63, 76, 80, 106, 122,
  180–181, 183

Ibgal (a shrine at Lagaš) 214–215, 229
im-ru(-a), a kinship grouping (extended
  family?) 205
Inanna 99, 153, 158, 195
India 31–34, 76, 85, 121, 146, 153, 156–157,
  182, 184, 193, 195, 223, 236–237, 239
Interest (in financial loans) 218
Iran 18, 23, 59–61, 67, 70, 78, 81, 83–84,
  91–92, 122, 125, 129–130, 132–133, 172,
  188, 192–193, 195
Iron 125, 129, 183; Iron Early Dynastic 183,
  188; Neolithic(?) 30; Uruk 125, 129
Irrigation 22, 142; Chalcolithic 59–60, 64;
  Early Dynastic 178, 231; Neolithic 21, 26;
  Uruk 117, 119
Isin 218
Isin-Larsa period 167
Ivory 7, 51, 112–114, 123, 169, 172, 174, 184,
  229

Jade 51
Jarmo/Qalaat Jarmo 13, 23, 30, 40, 192
Jasper 107
Jebel Aruda 124–125, 133, 146, 152, 157
Jebel Hamrin 60–62, 78, 120, 133, 151, 186,
  187, 198, 223
Jebel Sinjar 15, 31

Jemdet Nasr 126, 144–145, 151, 157, 160,
  162, 163, 170, 173, 183–184, 189, 191,
  194, 200, 223, 225
Jemdet Nasr period 165–167, 170, 176, 179,
  182–184, 186–187, 190–193, 196–197,
  199–200, 204, 206–7, 210, 213, 221–223,

229, 231, 233, 238
Jerablus Tahtani 120
Jericho 31, 234
Jewish culture 158
Jordan 27, 37

Karim Shahir 7, 9, 38
Kashan 125
Keleks *see* Ships and related craft
Kengir 209, 215
Kesh 165, 230
Khafajeh 106–108, 172, 178, 181, 183–184,
  186–188, 191–193, 199–200, 202–204,
  210–211, 214, 224, 226, 229, 239
Khanijdal 81, 139
Kharabeh Shattani 33, 67, 72, 81, 87
Kheit Qasim 186–188, 192, 203–205, 207,
  212, 223, 225
Khirbet Derak 87
Khirbet esh-Shenef 62, 75
Khirbet Garsour 36
Khuzestan 128, 165, 191
Kilns 20, 42, 44, 45, 46, 49, 66, 78, 107,
  110, 112, 135, 151, 161, 163, 169, 174; for
  pottery firing 19, 30, 45, 66, 78, 90, 113,
  163, 170
Kinship 96, 135–137, 205–206, 210–213, 222,
  233, 238–239; Chalcolithic 83, 96; Early
  Dynastic 205–206, 210–213, 222, 224, 227,
  233, 238–239; Jemdet Nasr 222, 233;
  Neolithic 35–37, 41; Palaeolithic 4, 5; Uruk
  109, 135–137; *see also* Ramages
Kiš 165, 167, 172, 186–188, 190–191, 193,
  198, 201–202, 206, 211, 213–215, 222,
  224, 230, 239
Korucutepe 177
Ksatriya caste of India 146
Ku'ara 163

Lagaš 167, 179, 184, 192, 203, 215–217,
  218–221, 232, 239
Lambert, Maurice 218
Landscape 137–138, 150, 182; Chalcolithic 45,
  53, 60, 62, 95; Early Dynastic 182;
  Mesolithic 7; Neolithic 13, 14, 21, 31, 40;
  Palaeolithic 2; Uruk 117, 137–138, 141, 150
Lapis lazuli 18(?), 51, 55, 70–71, 81, 111–113,
  129, 161, 164, 167–169, 171–172, 175,
  183–184, 193, 195, 198, 207, 233
Larsa 123, 163, 167
Late Babylonian period 182
Leach, Sir Edmund R. 142

Lead 125: Chalcolithic 43, 67; Early Dynastic
    186, 187–188; Jemdet Nasr 171, 186;
    Neolithic 14, 20, 30; Uruk 125
Leopard 158
Levant 125, 188, 199
Lévi-Strauss, Claude 12, 204
Life expectancy 73, 205
Lime 122–123, 129, 183; Early Dynastic 183;
    Mesolithic 9, 10, 11; Neolithic 16, 29; Uruk
    101, 113, 122–123, 129
Limestone 20, 43, 94, 101–102, 105, 108,
    129, 129, 172, 174, 198
Lion 135, 153
Locks 127–128
LUGAL (Sumerian administrative function)
    141, 143–146, 150, 167, 210, 213, 222,
    227, 238
Lugalkiginnedu 162
Lugalzagesi 162, 217–218, 220–221, 239
Lummatur 218, 229
Luristan 81, 83, 91–92, 141, 188

Maces of stone 48, 49, 51, 80, 102, 109, 111,
    164, 175
Mackay, Ernest 193
Magan 195
Magic 154, 157
Makran province, Pakistan 130
Makahiki festival of Oceania 139
Malachite 17, 20
Mandali 21
Manganese 183
Maništusu 206
Manure, manuring 177
Maori (New Zealand) 137
Marble 16, 20, 47, 52, 109, 129, 164, 174
Mari 193, 213–215
Mashrua (an Iraqi town) 162
Masks 137
Mašdaria gifts 219
Mathematics 155, 230, 233, 239; Early
    Dynastic 230, 233, 239; Neolithic 20; Uruk
    155
Matrimonial exchange 206–207, 210–211
Mauss, Marcel 88–89
Measures *see* Weights and measures
Meluhha 195
Mesannepada 171, 215
Meskalamdu(g) 186, 215, 224, 226, 228
Mesoamerica 176
Metrology 141, 194–195, 230, 233, 239
Mexico 146

Middle Ages, European 33, 57, 93, 135, 140,
    145, 155, 200, 206, 207, 212, 215, 217,
    225, 227
Middle Ages, Near Eastern 132, 228
Military matters *see* Arms, Fortifications,
    Warfare
Miri Qalat, Pakistan 130
Mirrors 102, 187, 199
Mohammad Jaffar 26
Mosaic cones: Jemdet Nasr 161, 170; Uruk
    99–101, 103–104, 106, 123, 131, 170
Mosaics 102, 108, 111, 128, 145, 161
Mosul 14, 16, 42, 49, 151
Mother-of-pearl 18, 107, 129
Mousterian 1
Mullers of clay 46, 48, 51, 54, 56–57, 67, 162
Murgul, east Anatolia 125
Music and dance 20, 43, 50, 92, 109, 113,
    157–158, 231

NA2, sign and ceremony 102, 139, 147–148,
    237
Nahal Kana 68
Nahr el-Kelb 58
Nanna(r) 136, 231
Nanše 217–218, 220
Nasiriyah 46, 98, 170
Neanderthal(s) 1, 3
Nemrik 7, 36
Nemrut Dag 129
NI+RU, 'fund' of the Jemdet Nasr age 145
ní-en-na (mode of land tenure) 217–218
ní-šuku (mode of land tenure) 217–218
ní-uru4-lá (mode of land tenure) 217–218
NIN (Sumerian pontifical function) 101, 137,
    139, 141, 143, 145–146, 148–150, 155,
    207, 210, 213, 222, 227, 237–238
Nineveh 176, 190, 200–201
Ningirsu 213, 220
Ninildum (a divine name) 231
Ninkhursag 215
Nippur 76, 167, 172, 193, 199, 201, 214,
    218–219
Nisaba 136
Nissen, Hans-Jörg 152, 171
Nomadism 4, 5, 9, 16, 26, 27, 32–36, 41, 60,
    75, 165, 181, 183, 235

Obsidian 1, 2, 6, 7, 9, 15, 17, 18, 20, 22, 23,
    30, 31, 34–35, 43–44, 46–48, 51–53,
    55–57, 69–71, 81, 92, 99–100, 102, 108,

111, 113, 129–130, 175
Oceania 139
Oikos, oikiai 85, 88, 96, 199–200, 209–212,
  219, 221–222, 228, 231, 238–239
Oil 169, 192
Oman 188
Onyx 167, 193
Orchards 49, 60, 119, 147, 178–179, 183, 236;
  almonds 119; apples 178–179, 182–183,
  228; dates 49, 53, 167, 178–179; figs 119,
  178–179, 228; palm wine 119, 147; plums
  119; pistachios 119; *see also* Gardens
Organic materials (leather, reeds, wood and the
  like) 77, 125–128, 135, 152, 155, 160, 228;
  Chalcolithic 43–44, 46, 47, 48, 51, 53–56,
  68; Early Dynastic 164, 167, 168–169,
  173–175, 179, 188–189, 191, 197,
  228–229; Jemdet Nasr 144–145, 156,
  160–163, 178, 189; JD to ED 189;
  Mesolithic 6; Neolithic 14, 15, 17, 19, 20,
  22, 23, 30, 31; Uruk 101–105, 108, 110,
  112–114, 125–128, 135, 140, 147, 152,
  155, 162, 165; *see also* Textiles
Ostrich 181

Paintings 90–94; Chalcolithic 43, 50, 90–94;
  Early Dynastic 173, 210; Neolithic 15, 19,
  34; Uruk 49, 103, 142, 158
Palaces 168–169, 198, 211–213
Palegawra 2, 7
Palermo, Sicily 225
Palestine 36, 59–60, 68, 76, 87, 125, 131
Parthian constructions 164
Pavements: Chalcolithic 43, 47, 50, 81; Early
  Dynastic 174; Jemdet Nasr 162; Neolithic
  24, 36, 41; Uruk 102, 110–111, 113–114,
  116
Pendants 6, 9, 11, 20, 21, 23, 30, 43, 44, 46,
  47, 48, 51–52, 54–55, 81, 83, 88, 91–92,
  107–113, 125, 135–137, 157, 161, 164,
  166–169, 172, 174–175, 184, 192–193,
  200, 215, 217
Persia, Achaemenid 178
Phoenicia 87
Pigtailed figures 129, 145
Plough 60–61, 118–119, 179
Polish language 156
Pollen 1, 2, 6, 8, 26, 27, 61
Postgate, Nicholas 118, 196
Potter's wheel 51, 99–100, 109, 111–114, 116,
  123–124, 129, 170, 174, 186
Prestige 11, 36, 115–116, 142–143, 149–150,

217, 219, 227; *see also* Stratification, social
Progress, notion of 234–235
Property, private 95, 97, 142, 205–206, 217,
  227, 236, 238
Pu-abi, 'queen' (NIN), 182
Pulses 9, 13, 14, 21, 31, 58, 117, 119, 178
Pythagorean theorem 85, 91

Qafzeh 3
Qermez Dere 9, 10, 36, 37, 122, 234
Qom 125
Quartz 20, 22, 45, 51–52, 161, 198
Quartzite 168
Qufa *see* Ships and related craft
Quseir Amra 27

Ramages (= conical clans) 206
Ras al-Amiya 60, 62, 76
Ras al-Junayz 195
Ras Shamra 40
Rations 118, 121, 124, 141, 148, 165, 177,
  218
Rawanduz 1, 6
Reciprocity 72, 74, 86–87, 96, 115–116,
  149–150, 173, 194, 204, 210, 222, 236,
  238; Chalcolithic 52, 72–74, 83, 87, 96;
  Early Dynastic 204, 210, 222; Jemdet Nasr
  200, 222; Neolithic 35; Palaeolithic 5; Uruk
  101, 115–116, 149–150
Redistribution 74, 115–116, 130, 141, 146,
  148–150, 153, 159, 173, 194, 202, 204,
  210–212, 222, 237–238; Chalcolithic 52,
  74, 87; Early Dynastic 202–204, 210–212,
  222, 237–238; Jemdet Nasr 200, 222; Uruk
  101, 112, 115–116, 122, 130, 141, 146,
  148–150, 153, 159, 237
'Reihengräberfelder' 212, 217
Religion 92–96, 137, 140, 145, 153–155, 157,
  173, 228, 231, 233, 236–237; *see also*
  Shrines
Retinue, 'royal' *see* Entourage, 'royal'
Ritual 84–85, 92–94, 97, 143, 158;
  Chalcolithic 52, 84–85, 90, 92–94, 97; Early
  Dynastic 229; Mesolithic 12; Neolithic 34;
  Uruk 102–103, 115, 143, 158; *see also* Magic
Roads 42–44, 81
Rome 158
Rock crystal 18, 113, 161, 167–168, 175,
  192–193, 198

Sakheri Sughir 173, 179–184, 186, 188,
  191–193

Salinization 21, 35, 59, 117–118, 176–177, 182

Samarra 22, 29, 35

Samarra culture 18, 21, 22, 23, 26, 29, 30, 32–33, 37–40, 65, 235

Sandstone 101

Sanga (Sumerian temple official, registrar) 218, 231

Sangam literature of Tamil India 223

'Scarlet Ware' pottery, ED I period 183, 233

'Schilfringbündel' (a ringed bundle of straw, likeness of the goddess Inanna) 161

Schist 169

Script 91–92, 100–101, 104, 106, 117, 126, 134–136, 138–139, 145, 147, 150–154, 156–157, 159, 162, 163, 165, 167, 168, 169, 173, 176, 182, 195, 196, 202–203, 205, 209, 214–215, 219–221, 229–230, 237, 239

Sculpture (monumental) 102, 106, 123, 129–140, 142, 148, 161, 167, 169–170, 171, 232; *see also* ALAN (Sumerian for 'statue')

Seals and sealings 72, 86–89, 96, 129, 142–143, 145–146, 148, 150, 173, 177, 195, 207, 210, 235; Chalcolithic 43–44, 45, 46, 47, 50–52, 54–55, 69, 72–73, 81, 84, 86–89, 95–96; Early Dynastic 162, 164–165, 166–169, 171, 188, 190, 195, 201–202, 207–211, 215, 219; Jemdet Nasr 163, 166, 173, 177, 178, 200, 208–209; JN to ED 167, 189; Neolithic 17, 20, 23, 24, 32, 36, 39, 235; Uruk 36, 99, 101, 104, 108–113, 115–116, 124, 126–127, 130, 142–143, 145–146, 148–150, 153; *see also* 'City-league seals', Cylinder seals

Sedentarization 5, 58, 60, 62, 64, 73–76, 81, 94–95, 182, 235–236

Sennacherib 157

Serpentinite 129

Sex 5, 11, 14, 23, 35–36, 39, 92, 113, 115, 170, 186, 206–208, 221–222, 227, 233, 238–239

Shale 198

Shams ed-Din Tannira 62, 69, 76, 78, 80

Shanidar 1, 3, 4, 6, 9

Shell 18, 46, 51–52, 55, 108, 161, 163–164, 166–169, 181–182, 184, 192–193, 199, 200, 233

Shell inlays 162, 169

Shells, marine 15, 31, 43, 88, 92, 122, 161, 163–164, 166, 183–184, 196

Shells, riverine 1, 2, 7, 13, 23, 28, 62, 126, 144–145, 162, 168, 174

Ships and related navigation craft 49, 71–72, 107, 131, 174, 188, 194–195, 236

Shrines 37, 46–47, 50, 75, 85–86, 93–94, 99, 101–107, 109–113, 132, 134, 136–137, 142, 149–150, 177, 198–200, 202–203, 208–211, 214–215, 217–220, 222, 227, 229–230, 233

Sicily 225

Sickles 47, 48, 54, 59, 67–68, 99–100, 108, 112, 123, 128, 162–163, 166, 175, 191

Silver 107, 125, 136, 161, 169, 171, 172, 179, 188, 190, 195, 197, 200, 207, 214, 228; *see also* 'Hacksilber' (hoard finds containing broken silver items)

Sin (Suen) 106–108, 218

Sinjar 108

Siraran 218

Slavery 143, 207, 231

Sledges for threshing grain *see* 'Tribulum'

Smelting of metals 68, 125, 136, 147

Solid-footed goblets (a pottery type of early ED date) 170–171, 185, 198, 203

Soot 183

Specialization 70–72, 76, 78, 81, 89, 96, 114, 126, 161, 187, 199; Chalcolithic 61, 63–65, 69–72, 76, 78, 81, 89, 96; Early Dynastic 162, 176, 184, 187, 192, 197, 199; Jemdet Nasr 161, 184, 187; Mesolithic 9; Neolithic 30; Uruk 106, 114, 126, 187, 197, 201

Stag 135

Standards *see* Emblems

Statuettes 91, 96–97, 158, 184, 233; Chalcolithic 43–44, 45, 46, 48–49, 51–52, 55, 69, 91, 94, 96–97; Early Dynastic 165, 169, 174, 179, 184, 186, 229, 233; Jemdet Nasr 108, 164, 184; Mesolithic 7, 11; Neolithic 13, 16, 17, 20, 21, 23, 29, 32, 34, 37, 41; Uruk 101, 106, 108, 109–113, 115, 158, 229

Steatite 51–52, 108, 129, 168, 171–172, 192–193, 198

Stone industry 199

Stone industry chipped 125, 130, 196; Chalcolithic 43–44, 45–46, 47, 51, 55–57, 60, 69–70, 90; Early Dynastic 166, 174–175, 190, 192, 196, 200; Jemdet Nasr 163, 165–166; Mesolithic 6, 7, 8; 14, 15, 16, 17, 18, 20, 21, 23, 24, 26, 30, 31, 38;

Palaeolithic 1, 2; Uruk 99–100, 107–109, 113–114, 116, 123, 125, 128, 130–131, 133

Stone industry ground 2, 6, 7, 8, 9; Chalcolithic 43–46, 47, 48, 51, 55–57, 81; Early Dynastic 174–175, 192, 200; Jemdet Nasr 163–164, 166; Mesolithic 2, 6, 7, 8, 9; Neolithic 14, 15, 16, 17, 19, 20, 22, 23, 30, 31, 39; Uruk 99, 108, 111, 114, 128–129, 133

Stone vessels: Chalcolithic 43, 45, 46, 48, 51, 90, 99; Early Dynastic 162, 164, 166, 168–169, 171, 175, 183, 186, 192, 204, 214; Jemdet Nasr 144–145, 161, 171, 204; Neolithic 16, 18, 20, 23; Uruk 99–100, 102, 107–108, 110–111, 114, 131, 135, 140, 162

Storage facilities 138–139, 196–197, 202

Stratification, social 78, 80–81, 83, 85, 88–89, 115–116, 143, 145–146, 159, 171, 181, 198, 202, 204, 211, 217, 221, 224, 237–238; *see also* Prestige

Sulaimaniyah 2

Sumerian King List (SKL) 212–213

Susa 36, 61, 83–84, 94, 99, 113, 118, 125, 128, 130, 147–148, 163, 187–188, 193, 195, 200, 229

Susiana 132, 146

Syria 23, 26, 27, 34, 36, 59, 67, 75, 85, 87–88, 124, 128, 132, 179, 199, 203

Syro-Cilicia 32, 36

Šaša, consort of Uruinimgina of Lagaš 209

ŠU+HA ('fishermen') 182, 196

Šuruppak 165, 167, 212–214, 221–222, 227–231, 238–239; *see also* Fara

'Šumma ālu' house omens 85

Talc 161

Tarut 193

Tell Abada 54, 61–62, 76, 78, 81, 85, 91

Tell Abu Husaini 59–60, 63, 70, 81, 91

Tell Afar 18, 45

Tell Agrab 181–182, 187–188, 191–192, 199–200, 208, 210

Tell al-Hilwa 116, 151

Tell al-Jir 126

Tell al-Kaum 23

Tell Arpachiyah 42, 60, 63–67, 69–70, 72–74, 81, 87, 90, 92–96, 236–237

Tell Asmar 181, 188, 190, 192, 200–201, 203, 211

Tell Awayli 21, 46, 49, 53, 60, 64, 69–71, 74–75, 83, 94, 123–124

Tell Azzo 90

Tell Basta 234

Tell Bleibis 133

Tell Brak 61, 106, 132, 152, 199, 233

Tell Buqras 23

Tell al-Fara´in (= Buto, Egypt) 131

Tell es-Saadiya 71, 91

Tell es-Sawwan 22, 30, 32, 36, 39, 41, 46, 133, 235

Tell Gubba 190, 198–199, 201, 211

Tell Halaf 62

Tell Hassan 78, 91

Tell Hassuna 16, 65

Tell Inghara 167–169

Tell Judeideh 40

Tell Kannas, 133, 146

Tell Kerkh 87, 95, 236

Tell Kuran 122

Tell Leilan 177, 179, 203

Tell Madhhur 55, 81, 94, 139, 198

Tell Maghzaliya 44, 46, 47, 52

Tell Mohammed Arab 205, 223

Tell Obeid *see* Al-Ubaid

Tell Owessat 192–193

Tell Razuk 179–181, 183, 198

Tell Rubeidheh 120, 125, 151

Tell Sabi Abyad 60, 73, 75, 87–88, 95, 236

Tell Sheikh Hassan 133

Tell Songor 32, 37, 78

Tell Turlu 60

Tell Uhaimir 167

Tell Uqair 62, 76, 158, 200

Tello 125–126, 143, 158, 184, 195, 229

Tepe Farukhabad 59, 63, 71, 78, 120, 122, 125–126, 128, 130, 179, 181–183, 187, 193, 197

Tepe Gawra 49, 64–65, 67, 69, 71–74, 78, 81, 83, 87, 89, 92, 94–97, 104, 108, 109, 123–124, 130, 133, 143, 145, 148–150, 152, 174, 179, 183–184, 190–191, 196, 236–237

Tepe Guran 28, 32, 33

Tepe Sabz 59–60

Tepe Shaffarabad 33, 119–120, 122, 124, 128, 130, 146, 153

Tepe Yahya 33, 59, 63, 75, 119, 122, 132, 193

Terraced buildings 130; Chalcolithic 47, 54, 75; Early Dynastic 164, 168; Jemdet Nasr 107, 130, 160–161; JN to ED 161; Uruk 105, 107, 130

Texts *see* Script

Textiles 69, 125–126, 130, 135–136, 184, 190, 196, 199, 207; Chalcolithic 44, 47, 51, 54–57, 69, 84, 92; Early Dynastic 166–167, 169, 174–176, 184, 190, 192, 196, 198–199, 200, 207; Jemdet Nasr 154, 157, 161, 163, 166, 170; Neolithic 16, 17, 20, 23, 29, 30; Uruk 49, 102, 108, 110–111, 113–114, 119, 121, 125–126, 128, 130, 135–136, 165

Tholoi (round buildings) 24, 42–43, 45, 49, 55, 80–81, 90, 93, 139, 179–180, 198

Time-reckoning 155–156, 197, 229

Tin 125, 129, 168, 172, 187–188

Toilet sets *see* Cosmetics

Tokens 44, 51, 56–57, 85, 94, 99–101, 103, 110–111, 113–114, 126, 146–147, 150, 153, 165

'Totems' 136–137

Trees 1, 2, 7, 13, 21, 26, 31, 42, 53, 60, 102, 105, 141, 174, 182, 190, 193

Transhumance 32–35, 40–41, 75–76, 120–121, 126

Trepanation of skulls 6

'Tribulum' (a sledge or a harrow for threshing grain) 118, 129, 143

Tuffo 161

Tummal 214

Turkey 152

Turquoise 17, 18, 20, 23, 31, 39, 51, 70–71, 111, 113, 167, 193, 198

Ubaid culture 21, 42, 44, 46, 47, 49–50, 53–55, 57, 59–61, 65–68, 70–72, 74–76, 78–79, 80, 83, 85, 87, 89–92, 94–95, 97, 99, 101–102, 104, 108, 115, 116, 122–126, 139, 162, 167, 170, 184, 190, 192, 236–238

Ubaidiya 3

UD.GAL.NUN texts 165

Uhub 214

Ulu Burun (Kaş, Turkey) 152

Umm Dabaghiyah 14, 26, 29, 30, 31–33, 36, 65

Umm Qseir 122

Umma 163, 167, 215, 217

Ur 58, 65, 67, 78, 81, 91, 124, 163, 167, 168, 170, 177–179, 182–184, 186–188, 190, 192–193, 195, 199, 201–202, 204–205, 207, 210–215, 218–219, 222–229, 231, 233, 239

Ur III period 76, 120, 162, 167, 179, 202, 205–206, 226

Urbanization 106, 118, 131–141, 150, 196, 198, 211, 237

Urnanše 215, 219

Uruinimgina/Urukagina 207, 209, 218, 220–221, 239

Uruk 92, 95, 98, 117, 123–125, 129, 132–133, 138, 140, 147, 149, 151–152, 154, 160, 163, 179, 182–183, 192–193, 195–196, 201, 209, 217, 221–222, 231, 236–237; An´s precinct 104–106; An´s precinct 'White temple' 105–106, 134; Eanna 160; Eanna bath building 104; Eanna building E ('palace') 103–104; Eanna Great Courtyard 104; Eanna Hallenbau 104; Eanna Kalksteintempel 102; Eanna Opferstättenhof 161; Eanna Pfeilerhalle 104, 146; Eanna Red temple 104; Eanna Riemchengebäude 102–103, 123, 125, 143, 161, 187, 199; Eanna Sammelfund 161, 167, 184, 187, 199; Eanna Steingebäude 99, 101–102, 105, 122, 155; Eanna Steinstifttempel 101–103, 122–123; Eanna Stiftmosaikgebäude 103; Eanna temple A 103; Eanna temple B 103–104; Eanna temple C 103–104; Eanna temple D 104; Eanna temple F 103–104; Eanna temple G 103–104; Eanna temple H 103–104; Stampflehmgebäude (SW of the Eanna terrace) 162, 217

Uruk culture 33, 53, 61, 92, 95–159, 162, 165, 167, 170, 187, 230–231, 236–239

Uruk period 30, 36, 49, 59, 67–68, 74, 92, 183, 191, 195–197, 200, 204, 231

Urzaged 214

Vaisya caste of India 146

Vaulting 113

Vehicles, wheeled 27, 61, 72, 112, 131, 168, 174, 194, 198, 213

Veshnoveh 125

Vineyards 60, 119

Warfare 143–144, 150, 213, 219

Waste disposal 132–133, 163–164, 166, 172, 199, 209

Wax 68, 121, 125, 187

Weights and measures 219, 230

Wells 36, 43, 49–50, 113, 169, 198

Wine *see* Vineyards

Wittfogel, Karl 142

Woolley, Sir Leonard 224–229

Yarimtepe 18, 19, 23, 25, 30, 32–34, 36, 37–38, 45, 49, 55, 59–60, 63–64, 66, 76, 80, 82, 86, 90–91, 93, 97

Zababa 168, 214, 230
Zabalam 163, 218, 231

Zarzian 1
Zawi Chemi Shanidar 6, 9
Zettler, Richard 202
Ziggurats 101, 105, 161, 168–169, 172–173, 214